T0181872

Lecture Notes in Computer Science 12883

More information about this subseries at http://www.springer.com/series/7409

Khalid Saeed · Jiří Dvorský (Eds.)

Computer Information Systems and Industrial Management

20th International Conference, CISIM 2021
Ełk, Poland, September 24–26, 2021
Proceedings

 Springer

Editors
Khalid Saeed
Bialystok University of Technology
Bialystok, Poland

Jiří Dvorský 🆔
VSB - Technical University of Ostrava
Ostrava, Czech Republic

ISSN 0302-9743   ISSN 1611-3349   (electronic)
Lecture Notes in Computer Science
ISBN 978-3-030-84339-7   ISBN 978-3-030-84340-3   (eBook)
https://doi.org/10.1007/978-3-030-84340-3

LNCS Sublibrary: SL3 – Information Systems and Applications, incl. Internet/Web, and HCI

This Springer imprint is published by the registered company Springer Nature Switzerland AG
The registered company address is: Gewerbestrasse 11, 6330 Cham, Switzerland

Preface

CISIM 2021 was the 20th conference in a series dedicated to computer information systems and industrial management applications. This year it was held during September 24–26, 2021, in Ełk, Poland, organized by the Faculty of Computer Science at the Bialystok University of Technology.

69 papers were submitted to CISIM 2021 by researchers and scientists from universities around the world. Each paper was assigned to three referees initially, and the decision of acceptance was taken after receiving two positive reviews. In case of conflicting decisions, another expert's review was sought for a number of papers. In total, about 220 reviews were collected from the referees for the submitted papers. Because of the strict restrictions of Springer's *Lecture Notes in Computer Science* series, the number of accepted papers was limited. Furthermore, a number of electronic discussions were held between the Program Committee (PC) chairs and members or external reviewers to make decisions on papers with conflicting reviews and to reach a consensus. After the discussions, the PC chairs decided to accept for publication in the proceedings about 55% of the submitted papers.

The main topics covered by the chapters in this book are biometrics, security systems, multimedia, classification and clustering with application, and industrial management. Besides these, the reader will find interesting papers on computer information systems as applied to wireless networks, computer graphics, and intelligent systems. This is in addition to the five interesting papers on Kansei engineering that were selected from the ten papers submitted to the Workshop on Biometrics and Kansei Engineering (ICBAKE).

We are grateful to the three esteemed speakers for their keynote addresses. The authors of the keynote talks were Alessandra De Benedictis (University of Naples Federico II, Italy), Witold Pedrycz (University of Alberta, Canada), and Roy Maxion (Carnegie Mellon University, USA). Also Anna Bartkowiak from Wrocław University, Poland, submitted a very interesting invited paper.

We would like to thank all the members of the PC and the external reviewers for their dedicated efforts in the paper selection process. We are indebted to Nobuyuki Nishiuchi and Makoto Fukumoto for their efforts in conducting the workshop of ICBAKE. Special thanks are extended to the members of the Organizing Committee, both international and local, and the Springer team for their great efforts to make the conference another success. We are also grateful to Andrei Voronkov, whose Easy-Chair system eased the submission and selection process.

We hope that the reader's expectations will be met and that the participants enjoyed their stay in the beautiful city of Ełk along with the conference.

September 2021

Khalid Saeed
Jiří Dvorský

Organization

Conference Patron

Marta Kosior-Kazberuk   Białystok University of Technology, Poland

General Chair

Khalid Saeed   Białystok University of Technology, Poland

Conference Co-chairs

Marek Krętowski	Białystok University of Technology, Poland
Rituparna Chaki	University of Calcutta, India
Katherinne Salas	Universidad de la Costa, Colombia

Advisory Committee

Nabendu Chaki	University of Calcutta, India
Agostino Cortesi	Ca' Foscari University of Venice, Italy
Nobuyuki Nishiuchi	Tokyo Metropolitan University, Japan
Young Im-Cho	Gachon University, South Korea
Sławomir Wierzchoń	Polish Academy of Sciences, Warsaw, Poland
Emiro De-La-Hoz-Franco	Universidad de la Costa, Colombia

International Organizing Committee

Zenon Sosnowski (Chair)	Białystok University of Technology, Poland
Pavel Moravec	VŠB – Technical University of Ostrava, Czech Republic
Jiří Dvorský	VŠB – Technical University of Ostrava, Czech Republic
Tito Jose Crissien Borrero	Universidad de la Costa, Colombia
Dionicio Neira	Universidad de la Costa, Colombia

Local Organizing Committee

Maciej Szymkowski (Chair)	Białystok University of Technology, Poland
Mirosław Omieljanowicz	Białystok University of Technology, Poland
Grzegorz Rubin	Łomża State University of Applied Sciences, Poland
Mariusz Rybnik	University of Białystok, Poland
Aleksander Sawicki	Białystok University of Technology, Poland
Marcin Adamski	Białystok University of Technology, Poland
Miguel Jimenes	Universidad de la Costa, Colombia
Kitti Koonsanit	Tokyo Metropolitan University, Japan

Program Committee

Chairs

Khalid Saeed	Białystok University of Technology, Poland
Jiří Dvorský	VŠB – Technical University of Ostrava, Czech Republic

Members

Anna Bartkowiak	Wrocław University, Poland
Daniela Borissova	Bulgarian Academy of Sciences, Bulgaria
Rahma Boucetta	University of Sfax, Tunisia
Nabendu Chaki	University of Calcutta, India
Rituparna Chaki	University of Calcutta, India
Young-Im Cho	Gachon University, South Korea
Agostino Cortesi	Ca' Foscari University of Venice, Italy
Pietro Ferrara	IBM T. J. Watson Research Center, USA
Makoto Fukumoto	Fukuoka Institute of Technology, Japan
Marina Gavrilova	University of Calgary, Canada
Raju Halder	Indian Institute of Technology Patna, India
Christopher G. Harris	University of Northern Colorado, USA
Władysław Homenda	Warsaw University of Technology, Poland
Valentina Janev	The Mihajlo Pupin Institute, Serbia
Marek Lampart	VŠB – Technical University of Ostrava, Czech Republic
Flaminia Luccio	Ca' Foscari University of Venice, Italy
Jan Martinovič	VŠB – Technical University of Ostrava, Czech Republic
Pavel Moravec	VŠB – Technical University of Ostrava, Czech Republic
Romuald Mosdorf	Białystok University of Technology, Poland
Nobuyuki Nishiuchi	Tokyo Metropolitan University, Japan
Tadeusz Nowicki	Military University of Technology, Poland
Andrzej Pacut	Warsaw University of Technology, Poland
Jerzy Pejaś	West Pomeranian University of Technology in Szczecin, Poland
Piotr Porwik	University of Silesia, Poland
S. P. Raja	Vel Tech Institute of Science and Technology, India
Kenneth Regan	University of New York at Buffalo, USA
Anirban Sarkar	National Institute of Technology Durgapor, India
Rafał Scherer	Częstochowa University of Technology, Poland
Ewa Skubalska-Rafajłowicz	Wrocław University of Technology, Poland
Kateřina Slaninová	VŠB – Technical University of Ostrava, Czech Republic
Zenon Sosnowski	Białystok University of Technology, Poland
Jarosław Stepaniuk	Białystok University of Technology, Poland
Marcin Szpyrka	AGH Kraków, Poland

Sławomir Wierzchoń	Polish Academy of Sciences, Warsaw, Poland
Michał Woźniak	Wrocław University of Technology, Poland
Sebastiaan J. van Zelst	Fraunhofer Institute for Applied Information Technology/RWTH Aachen University, Germany

Additional Reviewers

Marcin Adamski	Białystok University of Technology, Poland
Tapalina Bhattasali	St. Xavier's College, Kolkata, India
Janusz Bobulski	Częstochowa University of Technology, Poland
Robert Burduk	Wrocław University of Technology, Poland
Tomasz Grzes	Białystok University of Technology, Poland
Yuri Hamada	Aoyama Gakuin University, Japan
Yoshiko Hanada	Kansai University, Japan
Teruhisa Hochin	Kyoto Institute of Technology, Japan
Jun-Ichi Imai	Chiba Institute of Technology, Japan
Makio Ishihara	Fukuoka Institute of Technology, Japan
Wiktor Jakowluk	Białystok University of Technology, Poland
Miguel A. Jimenez-Barros	Universidad de la Costa, Colombia
Dariusz Kacprzak	Białystok University of Technology, Poland
Keiko Kasamatsu	Tokyo Metropolitan University, Japan
Romuald Kotowski	Polish-Japanese Academy of Information Technology, Poland
Małgorzata Krętowska	Białystok University of Technology, Poland
Saerom Lee	Kagawa University, Japan
Wojciech Mazurczyk	Warsaw University of Technology, Poland
Isao Nakanishi	Tottori University, Japan
Dionicio Neira Rodado	Universidad de la Costa, Colombia
Akihiro Ogino	Kyoto Sangyo University, Japan
Miroslaw Omieljanowicz	Białystok University of Technology, Poland
Satoshi Ono	Kagoshima University, Japan
Krzysztof Ostrowski	Białystok University of Technology, Poland
Dariusz Pierzchała	Military University of Technology, Poland
Wiesław Półjanowicz	University of Białystok, Poland
Magdalena Roszak	Poznan University of Medical Sciences, Poland
Grzegorz Rubin	Lomza State University, Poland
Jarosław Rudy	Wrocław University of Technology, Poland
Mariusz Rybnik	University of Białystok, Poland
Aleksander Sawicki	Białystok University of Technology, Poland
Soharab Hossain Shaikh	BML Munjal University, India
Maciej Szymkowski	Białystok University of Technology, Poland
Hiroshi Takenouchi	Fukuoka Institute of Technology, Japan
Jiří Tomčala	VŠB – Technical University of Ostrava, Czech Republic
Lukáš Vojáček	VŠB – Technical University of Ostrava, Czech Republic

Keynotes

Toward the Automation of Security Analysis, Design and Assessment in the Development Process

Alessandra De Benedictis

University of Naples Federico II, Naples, Italy
alessandra.debenedictis@unina.it

Abstract. Modern software development methodologies like DevOps or Agile are very popular and widely used, especially for the development of cloud services and applications, as they dramatically reduce the time-to market by means of continuous software delivery. Unfortunately, traditional DevOps processes do not include security design and risk management practices by default, and often take security into account only after the completion of the coding stage, with the risks that security flaws may be found too late and cause significant delays in the development process.

Recent SecDevOps methodologies aim at integrating security activities such as threat modeling, countermeasure selection, static and dynamic code analysis, security assessment and security testing into DevOps workflows. Since security operations typically require the engagement of (expensive) security teams and inevitably slow down the development process, automated security design and assessment techniques are needed to preserve DevOps productivity and reduce costs.

Despite the efforts that have been recently made to provide techniques and tools able to fully or partially automate security-related activities, security analysis and testing operations still heavily require the intervention of security experts, typically assisted by a plethora of tools whose adoption requires deep technological skills.

This talk aims to discuss possible strategies and techniques meant to reduce the complexity of security management in a development process, and to support developers from the early security analysis stages to post-development security testing by means of partly or fully-automated techniques for threat modeling, risk evaluation, countermeasure selection, static and dynamic assessment.

Experiments, Methods, Measurements, Instruments: A Few Details

Roy Maxion

Carnegie Mellon University, Pennsylvania, USA
maxion@cs.cmu.edu

Abstract. Much of computer science and computer security & privacy is based on the results of experiments. The dependability or reliability of these results turns on a number of details regarding the experimental methodology itself, how various experimental factors are measured, and the instruments with which those measurements are taken. This talk reviews a few details of experimentation that are overlooked at the risk of failure or, perhaps worse, propagating wrong results.

Logic Constructs with Information Granules: Data Analytics

Witold Pedrycz

University of Alberta, Edmonton, Canada
pedrycz@ee.ualberta.ca

Abstract. In data analytics, system modeling, and decision-making models, the aspects of interpretability and explainability are of paramount relevance, just to refer to explainable Artificial Intelligence (XAI). They are especially timely in light of the increasing complexity of systems one has to cope with. We advocate that there are two factors that immensely contribute to the realization of the above important features, namely, a suitable level of abstraction in describing the problem and a logic fabric (topology) of the resultant construct. It is advocated that their conceptualization and the consecutive realization can be conveniently carried out with the use of information granules (for example, fuzzy sets, sets, rough sets, and alike).

Concepts are building blocks forming the interpretable environment capturing the essence of data and key relationships existing there. The emergence of concepts is supported by a systematic and focused analysis of data. At the same time, their initialization is specified by stakeholders or/and the owners and users of data. We present a comprehensive discussion of information granules-directed design of concepts and their description by engaging an innovative mechanism of conditional (concept)- driven clustering. It is shown that the initial phase of the process is guided by the formulation of some generic (say, low profit) or some complex multidimensional concepts (say, poor quality of environment or high stability of network traffic) all of which are described by means of some information granules. In the sequel is explained by other variables through clustering focuses by the context. The description of concepts is delivered by a logic expression whose calibration is completed by a detailed learning of the associated logic neural network. The constructed network helps quantify contributions of individual information granules to the description of the underlying concept and facilitate a more qualitative characterization achieved with the aid of linguistic approximation. This form of approximation delivers a concise and interpretable abstract description through linguistic quantifiers. A detailed case study of systematic interpretability concerns functional rule-based models with the rules in the form "if x is A then y=f(x)". The layers at which interpretability is positioned are structured hierarchically by starting with the initial fuzzy set level (originating from the design of the rules), moving to information granules of finite support (where interval calculus is engaged) and finally ending up with symbols built at the higher level. The rules emerging at the level of symbols are further interpreted by engaging linguistic approximation. For high-dimensional problems, dimensionality reduction is realized with the aid of relational matrix factorization which transforms original fuzzy set-based encoded variables and results in a logic-oriented level of activation of individual rules.

Contents

Industrial Management and other Applications

Machine Learning and Artificial Neural Networks

Modelling and Optimization

Invited Paper

Importance of Variables in Gearbox Diagnostics Using Random Forests and Ensemble Credits

Anna M. Bartkowiak[1($\boxtimes$)] (ID) and Radoslaw Zimroz[2] (ID)

[1] Institute of Computer Science, University of Wroclaw,
Jolliot-Curie 15, 50-383 Wroclaw, Poland
aba@cs.uni.wroc.pl
[2] Machinery System Division, Wroclaw University of Science and Technology,
Na Grobli 15, 50-421 Wroclaw, Poland

Abstract. We consider a multivariate data matrix of size $n \times d = 2183 \times 15$, where $n = 2183$ is the number of time segments recorded from vibration signals of two gearboxes, and $d = 15$ is the number of variables (traits) characterizing these segments. To learn about the role played by each of the 15 variables in the gearbox diagnostics, we use the Random Forest (RF) methodology with its 'Variables Importance Plot' (VIP) algorithm, which yields a kind of ranking of the variables with regard of their importance in the performed diagnostics. This ranking is different in various runs of the RF. We propose to use at this stage an additional module performing a specific ensemble learning yielding credits scores for each variable. It shows clearly the *top* most important variables.

Keywords: Machine state diagnostics · Random Forests · Importance of variables · Credits scores

1 Introduction

In the paper we will analyse power spectra data obtained from vibrations emitted by two heavy duty machines, one of them in the healthy, the other in the not-healthy (faulty) state. These states will be labeled as 'yes' and 'no', or alternatively, as *class1* and *class2* appropriately. The data contain 2183 time segments derived from vibration signals recorded during the work of the two machines. The variables denote power spectra densities (called $pp1, \ldots, pp15$) obtained from Fourier analysis of the vibration segments notified for each gearbox, see more details in [1,16,24]. Our goal is to build a predictive function permitting to estimate – on the basis of the recorded variables solely, without any invasive examinations – the true state of the two machines: *class1* or *class2*.

The data were recorded as set of $n_1 = 951$ data vectors characterizing the vibration of the healthy gearbox; and a set of $n_2 = 1232$ data vectors characterizing vibration signal of the faulty gearbox [24]. These two sets will be labeled

© Springer Nature Switzerland AG 2021
K. Saeed and J. Dvorský (Eds.): CISIM 2021, LNCS 12883, pp. 3–13, 2021.
https://doi.org/10.1007/978-3-030-84340-3_1

shortly as *class1* and *class2*. The recorded data were put together into the size 2183×15 data matrix MM.

For the present analysis we have subdivided our data into the *train* and *test* subsets, whose composition is as follows:

- The `train` data set contains $n_1 = 1000$ data vectors, sampled from the entire data matrix: firstly $n = 500$ healthy and next 500 non-healthy (faulty) data vectors.
- The `test` data set contains the remainder of the MM data, that is $n_2 = 1183$ data vectors (451 healthy and 732 faulty).

In the following we will use for diagnostic purposes the Random Forest (RF) method [4–6,15]. Its goal is outlined in the seminal paper [5] titled 'Statistical Modelling: The Two Cultures'. It reads in page 1: "There are two goals in analyzing the data: *Prediction.* To be able to predict what the response are going to be in future input variables; *Information:* To extract some information about how nature is associating the response variables to the input variables." The idea is discussed in 30 pages.

The proposed RF algorithm is computationally very effective [8,10,12,13] and may be considered in various aspects like constructing random subspace or dynamic ensemble selection depending from the given problem [7,9,11]. The RF method works on an ensemble of binary decision trees, and as such it benefits from the Collective Intelligence Methodology and Ensemble Learning which has a long history [14,17–20].

The RF algorithm may also evaluate importance of variables in the given problem and depict this in so called Variables Importance Plot (VIP). What means the concept 'importance of variables'? Generally, one might expect here an index (score) indicating influence of the given variable on the performed diagnostics.

Genuer [10] expressed the view that there are two objectives when considering variables importance:

1. To find important variables highly related to the response variable for interpretation purposes; and
2. To find a small number of variables sufficient for a good prediction of the prediction variable.

The RFs have their ways to computing *importance* of the variables. Moreover, they may also rank the variables according their *importance*, and display this in a plot referred to by us as Variables Importance Plot (VIP).

Inspecting the VIPs for various runs of RF for our data, we stated that the ranking of the same variables obtained in the various runs is slightly different. We mused: Would it possible to establish some confidence scores for the rank of a variable appearing in the VIP? We got the idea that this can be done. Our proposal is to use for this an additional module based on Ensemble Learning where variables will compete to win some credit points. The number of credits won by each variable will constitute for that variable a confidence score for being 'important' in the assumed model.

Our proposal is to create an ensemble $\mathcal{E}$ composed of a number say n_e of differentiated VIPs. Let's call them e-VIPs. Each of them will provide for the considered variables a specific vector **s** of their importance values. Each of the e-VIPs will create its own vector **s**. Next we will aggregate the results in a specific way, where the variables compete to win some credit points.

Summarizing the won credit points one will obtain a kind of weight (confidence score) indicating for each variable how much is it important in the considered model.

This ends Sect. 1. Next Sect. 2 presents the methods which are: the principles of the Random Forest classification Algorithm, and our proposal for computing Credits Scores. Section 3 shows results of analysis of the gearbox data when using the Random Forests combined with our proposed method. Discussion and concluding remarks are in Sect. 4.

2   Methods: The Random Forest and Ensemble Credits

2.1   Random Forest as Composed from Binary Decision Trees

Random forests consist of larger number of randomly constructed trees, each voting for *class1* (yes) or *class2* (no). A bootstrap sample is used to construct each tree (see more in [3]). Two such trees are shown in Fig. 1.

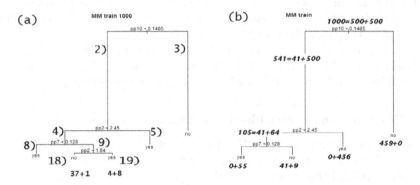

Fig. 1. Two Trees constructed from the train data set $n=1000$. Label 'no' means class2, 'yes' means class1. (a): Unpruned tree with 4 splitting rules. (b): Pruned tree with 3 splitting rules.

The essential terms for describing a tree (BDT) are: *node, branch, leaf.* A **node** is given as a point located on the axis of a variable. Its function is to split the actual data space into two non-overlapping parts (sub-spaces) which are relatively pure with respect to their content of data points of class *class1* or *class2*. After performing the split, two **branches** are drawn to the left and right of that node: they represent the two sub-spaces obtained by the last split. A sub-pace is eligible for further splits, if it contains more than an assumed *min-size* number of the data points included into its minority class (we used *min-size* = 10). If so, the procedure of search of a new splitting node begins for that branch anew; otherwise the branch is final and becomes a `leaf`.

The procedure works hierarchically downwards till all branches have become leafs. The final end of such a branch is then labelled 'no' or 'yes' depending on the majority class of data vectors, identified by that branch.

Looking at Fig. 1 one may see that the tree (a) depicted in the left graph needed for its final classification of the data only 4 nodes provided by variables *pp10, pp2, pp7* and once more *pp2*. The splits occurred in nodes provided by the inequalities: $pp10 < 0.1485$, $pp2 < 2.45$, $pp7 < 0.128$, $pp2 < 1.184$.

Branches 8), 18), 19), 5) and 3) appeared to be final (become 'leafs') and were labeled as 'yes', 'no', 'yes', 'yes', and 'no' correspondingly.

Sub-spaces 8), 5), and 3) are pure: they contain 55 'yes's, 436 'yes's and 459 'no's appropriately. Sub-spaces 18) and 19) are mixed: they contain $(37 + 1)$ and $(4 + 8)$ data points of class 'no' and 'yes' respectively; and as such they are not eligible for further splitting; for that reason they become leafs labeled 'no' and 'yes' appropriately.

The depicted tree (a) was subjected to further examination for finding 'weak' nodes of subdivision. This was done performing so called *cost-effective pruning*, where the tree (its depth) is subjected to a lasso-like penalty [12]. As result of this examination, the split at node 9) appeared to be non-relevant. The pruned tree is shown in Fig. 1, right graph (b).

Looking at Fig. 1 one may state that both trees yielded a minuscule rate of wrongly classified objects: namely $5 = (1 + 4)/1000$ and $9/1000$ miss-classified objects from the `train` data set containing 1000 objects.

The constructed tree may serve for classification of a (new) data vector **x**. Putting the vector down through the tree, one obtains in a simple way an indication of its class. It is just the label of the *leaf*, where the given **x** has landed.

2.2   The 'mtry' and 'variables Importance' Options of RFs

For a given train sample, the RF constructs B bootstrap samples (we used B=500), and next, using the principle of majority voting, it provides for each data point its final classification [4–6, 15].

The nodes of the working trees were obtained in a specific way: Namely, when building the trees, at each split only a number $mtry < d$ was given the chance to appear as classifiers. Default value $mtry$ is computed as square root of d, where d denotes the number of variables (in our data $d = 15$).

To obtain the value of *importance* of a variable, say, no j, the classification task by RF is run twice: in the usual mode, and next permuting values of that variable. Then one looks at the deterioration of the classification outcome (e.g., the criteria *Accuracy* or *Gini*) of both runs. For important variables that matter in the classification task, the <u>difference</u> in the outcome of both runs should be noticeable.

This task is performed for all d variables of the data. After properly scaling, the obtained differences constitute a new feature called *importance* possessed by each of the variables. Now the variables may be ranked according to the value of their *importance* and depicted in a VIP (Variables Importance Plot). In such a VIP the variables are displayed in the order of their ranking with respect of their *importance* value. The most important variable obtains rank=1, next one rank=2, etc. For example, considering $d=15$ variables labeled *pp1, pp2,* ......, *pp15*, the VIP may display their *importance* as the sequence *pml* or *pmr* expressing their labels or rank:

pml = [pp10,pp2,pp1,pp14,pp7,pp6,pp13,pp9,pp12,pp4,pp15,pp3,pp5];
pmr = [10,2,1,14,7,6,13,9,12,4,15,3,5].

The sequence *pml* shows the ordered variables as sequence of their labels (above this is the permutation [pp10, pp2, ...]). The sequence *pmr* shows their ranking (above this is the respective permutation [10, 2, ...]).

Say, we are interested to identify the *top four* most important variables. Both sequences *pml* and *pmr* say, that these are the variables *pp10,pp2,pp1,pp14*.

2.3 Our Proposal: Create an Ensemble of VIPs Providing Credit Scores

We have observed that the ranking of variables displayed in the VIP obtained from two runs of the RF with slightly - change of parameters in the assumed model, or a different sample from the same data - yields also (slightly) different ordering of the variables according to their *importance*. In particular, this happens, when using the *Accuracy* and *Gini* criteria of fit. E.g., this may be seen in Fig. 2.

Therefore our proposal to obtain a more stable information on the *importance* of individual variables one should perform the ranking and graphing of the VIPs not solely using one VIP, but TO CREATE AND CONSIDER AN ENSEMBLE OF THEM. We propose for this a procedure *Credits Scores* that may be outlined as follows:

Defining an ensemble $\mathcal{E}$ containing n_e individual e-VIPs. Define also an inter t, $1 <= t <= d$ meaning how many important variable we are interested in. Define also an integer table Scores of size $d \times n_e$.

Next, for each individual e-VIP perform the operations:

(i) Calculate the sequences *pml* and *pmr* introduced in Subsect. 2.2
(ii) Using the assumed t, convert the sequence *pmr* into a binary vector **s** ('score') composed from '0's and '1's according to the rule:

For j in [1:d], if pmr[j] > t then s[j] = 0, else s[j]= 1

(iii) Locate the values of the binary vector **s** in the table Scores as subsequent *column* of that table.

After completion of the above operations, the table Scores is filled with 0 and 1 values. To obtain the *Credits Scores* won by subsequent variables, calculate simply the sum of values of subsequent *rows* of the table Scores. This will yield the number of 'credits' won by subsequent d variables.

Details how this works are shown in Subsect. 2.3 presenting the results of our calculations for the gearbox data data MM.

3   Results of Calculations

All the calculations were obtained using free software developed in R [15,22]. Many indications how to use this software are included in the books [12,13].

Firstly (3.1) we show the results obtained by a Random Forest, being a forest composed from $B=500$ individual trees. We show here the VIPs obtained when using the parameters $mtry = 3, 5$.

Next (3.2) we show our experiments (results) with credit scores assignments to the 15 variables, leading to two reduced sets of the investigated 15 variables.

Finally (3.3), we show classification results when using all and two reduced subsets of variables ($top = 5$ and $top = 7$) yielded by Neural Networks.

3.1   Classification and VIPs Using RFs

The RFs were constructed from 500 trees evaluated on 500 bootstrap samples drawn out from the train data set. For a data vector $\mathbf{x}$, put down through all the 500 trees, we obtained 500 votes for class of the given $\mathbf{x}$. The final prediction of that $\mathbf{x}$ (its class category) was then obtained by the principle *maximum votes*. This was done for all the data vectors $\mathbf{x}$ belonging to the analyzed data set. The predictions are summarized as confusion matrices shown in Table 1. On may see there classification error rates obtained using $mtry = 3, 4, 5$ and 7 – both for the train and the test data sets.

Table 1. Confusion matrices yielded by Random Forests applied to the MM data, in dependence on the parameters $mtry = 3, 4, 5, 7$. Symbol †ErrRate means fraction of miss-classified objects (segments)

Data set		Train data set $n_1 = 1000$			Test data set $n_2 = 1183$		
MM		No	Yes	† ErrRate	No	Yes	† ErrRate
$mtry = 3$	No	500	0	0.0	732	0	0.0
	Yes	0	500		0	451	
$mtry = 4$	No	500	0	0.0	732	0	0.0
	Yes	0	500		0	451	
$mtry = 5$	No	500	0	0.0	728	0	0.0034
	Yes	0	500		4	451	
$mtry = 7$	No	500	0	0.0	727	0	0.0042
	Yes	0	500		5	451	

Generally, for the **train data** ($n_1 = 1000$) we obtained a perfect fit (0 errors) for all four values of $mtry$.

The results in the **test data** ($n_2 = 1183$) are variable. In one of the runs we obtained for $mtry = 3$ and $mtry = 4$ a perfect fit; while when using $mtry = 5$ and $mtry = 7$ we got 4 and 5 miss-classified data vectors, which means error rate 0.0034 and 0.0042 respectively. This constitutes equivalently an Accuracy 99.66%, and 99.58%, which is a also very good result.

Variables Importance Plots. Such plots, when using the parameters $mtry = 3, 5$ and the classification criteria *Accuracy* and *Gini*, are shown in Fig. 2. One may see in these plots that there are slight differences in the rankings of variables in dependence of the classification criteria and values of $mtry$.

3.2 Computing Credits Scores in an Ensemble Learning

We have used here our method *Credits Scoring* described in Subsect. 2.3.

To create the necessary ensemble $\mathcal{E}$ we used 3 independent **train** data sets containing $n = 1000$ data vectors. From each of these *train* data we obtained 8 VIPs by running the RFs when taking into account two factors: the *mtry* parameter (values 3, 4, 5, 7) and criterion of classification *Accuracy* and *Gini*. Jointly, we obtained 24 diversified VIPs ($24 = 3 \times 4 \times 2$) constituted an ensemble $\mathcal{E}$ containing n_e e-Vips. Next we have run our module *Credits scoring*.

Using the parameter $t = 4$ indicating search for top Four variables with the highest value of *importance*, we obtained the following list of variables with positive credits:

Variable:	pp1	pp2	pp6	pp7	pp10	pp14
Credits:	10	24	2	12	24	24

Analogous list for $t = 6$ reads:

Variable:	pp1	pp2	pp6	pp7	pp9	pp10	pp11	pp12	pp13	pp14
Credits:	12	24	14	24	5	24	3	12	2	24

These lists (these two statistics) may serve as a guide for choosing relevant variables. After analysis of the credits list we decided to retain for further analysis the following subsets of variables:
topFIVE = [1, 2, 7, 10, 14], and *topSEVEN* = [1, 2, 6, 7, 10, 12, 14].
The diagnostics of these two subsets of variables will be analyzed in next subsection using Neural Networks.

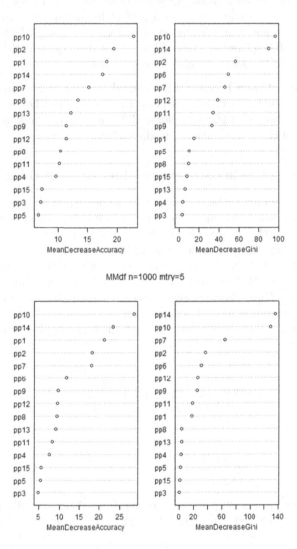

Fig. 2. Importance of variables for original (non-scaled) data MM memorized by R as the data frame MMdf. From top to bottom: Graphs obtained using parameters $mtry = 3$ and $mtry = 7$. Left: using accuracy criterion. Right: using Gini criterion.

3.3   Neural Networks Check the Top FIVE and Top SEVEN Variables

To see if really the *topFIVE* and the *topSEVEN* subsets of variables are important when making classification, we have performed the classification task using Neural Networks [21,22].

We have used for the calculations a popular neural network called multi-layer perceptron (MLP) with the architecture: 15-2-1 and 15-1-1 [21,22]. The classification was performed using the data MM firstly in its original form, next data using the data sets MM, MMS and MMR (MMS means data MM standardized to have zero means and unit variances; MMR means data MM standardized to range [0,1].

The classification task was performed firstly for for the data containing ALL 15 variables, and next using for the subsets topSEVEN and topFIVE found by our module Credits Scoring. In Table 2 we show the number of miss-classifications from the confusion matrices produced by various runs of the NN algorithm.

Table 2. Miss-classifications yielded by NN (MLP) when applied to data sets MM, MMS and MMR. H means nb. of neurons in the hidden layer of the applied network. Symbols 'tr' and 'te' stand for training and testing data subsets with n1=1000 and n2= 1183 data vectors appropriately. SEVEN=[1,2,6,7,10,14], FIVE=[1,2,7,10,14]

Data sets:→	MM		MMS		MMR		MM		MMS		MMR	
Hidden: →	H=2						H=1					
nb. of variables ↓	tr	te	tr	te	tr	te	tr	te	tr	te	tr	te
All 15	0	0	0	0	0	1	0	1	0	1	0	2
Top SEVEN	0	4	0	4	0	1	0	0	0	0	0	1
Top FIVE	0	3	0	0	0	1	0	1	0	2	0	1

The results from various runs look similar. The training set ($n1 = 1000$) could be in all runs classified perfectly (0 miss-classification). The test set ($n2 = 1183$), The data vectors were classified nearly perfectly, with - in average - one (precisely 1.3) data vector classified wrongly.

Thus we may conclude that the subsets *topFIVE* and *topSEVEN* possess the to perform alone the classification task of the analyzed gearbox data MM.

4 Summary and Concluding Remarks

We have investigated the Random Forests (RFs) in their aspects of establishing importance of variables in a two-class diagnostics problem met when considering vibration data emitted by a healthy and a faulty gearbox.

The RFs yielded also an index called *importance* that says says how important is the given variable in the considered diagnostics model. Ranking of the variables according to their *importance* may slightly vary in different runs of the RF. Our novel method, named by us *Credits Scoring*, computes a kind of confidence weights for the 'ranks' of variables. The method may be applied to find the best subset of the d variables appearing in the diagnostic model.

Our proposal is illustrated using the planetary gearbox data gathered by Bartelmus and Zimroz [1]. We found two subsets called by us *topFIVE* and *topSEVEN* which are as good for the diagnosis as all the $d = 15$ variables contained in the analyzed data. The efficacy of the found subsets was confirmed by Neural Networks.

It would be interesting to know how our *Credits Scoring* method works for other data sets, in particular with a larger number of variables. It is known that the RFs work even for $d=1000$ and $d=4682$ variables (see [5, 15]).

We intend to continue our analysis considering other data and possibly combined with other diagnostic methods. In particular, this might be a nonlinear hybrid approach performing all subset search by using multivariate linear regression and variables shrinkage operator Lasso (see [2]). Another important topic is to combine the considered diagnostic issues and developed algorithms with a thorough statistical analysis. In particular, tests of statistical significance may indicate that the obtained results are not spurious. How to do it, in other words how to design the fair experimental classifier evaluation (see [23]). All this needs intensive planning and simulations; the description of them, analysis and reporting is beyond this paper.

References

1. Bartelmus, W., Zimroz, R.: A new feature for monitoring the condition of gearboxes in non-stationary operating systems. Mech. Syst. Signal Process. **23**(5), 1528–1534 (2009)
2. Bartkowiak, A., Zimroz, R.: Dimensionality reduction via variables selection - linear and nonlinear approaches with application to vibration-based condition monitoring of planetary gearbox. Appl. Accoustics **77**, 169–177 (2014)
3. Breiman, L., Friedman, J., Stone, C.J., Olshen, R.A.: Classification and Regression Trees. Taylor & Francis (1984)
4. Breiman, L.: Random forests. Mach. Learn. **45**(1), 5–32 (2001)
5. Breiman, L.: Statistical modeling: the two cultures. Stat. Sci. **16**(3), 199–231 (2001)
6. Breiman, L., Cutler, A.: Random Forest Manual v. 4.0. Technical Report UC Berkeley (2003)
7. Burduk, R., Baczyńska, P.: Ensemble of classifiers with modification of confidence values. In: Saeed, K., Homenda, W. (eds.) CISIM 2016. LNCS, vol. 9842, pp. 473–480. Springer, Cham (2016). https://doi.org/10.1007/978-3-319-45378-1_42
8. Cerrada, M., et al.: Fault diagnosis in spur gears based on genetic algorithm and random forest. Mech. Syst. Signal Process. **70**, 87–103 (2016)
9. Dey, A., Shaikh, S.H., Saeed, K., Chaki, N.: Modified majority voting algorithm towards creating reference image for binarization. In: Kumar Kundu, M., Mohapatra, D.P., Konar, A., Chakraborty, A. (eds.) Advanced Computing, Networking and Informatics- Volume 1. SIST, vol. 27, pp. 221–227. Springer, Cham (2014). https://doi.org/10.1007/978-3-319-07353-8_26
10. Genuer, R., Poggi, J.M., Tuleau-Malot, Ch., Elsevier: Variable selection using random forests. Pattern Recogn. Lett. **31**(14), 2225–2236 (2010)
11. Heda, P., Rojek, I., Burduk, R.: Dynamic ensemble selection – application to classification of cutting tools. In: Saeed, K., Dvorský, J. (eds.) CISIM 2020. LNCS, vol. 12133, pp. 345–354. Springer, Cham (2020). https://doi.org/10.1007/978-3-030-47679-3_29

12. James, G., Witten, D., Hastie, T., Tibshirani, R.: An Introduction to Statistical Learning. STS, vol. 103. Springer, New York (2013). https://doi.org/10.1007/978-1-4614-7138-7
13. Kuhn, M., Johnson, K.: Applied Predictive Modeling. Springer, New York (2013). https://doi.org/10.1007/978-1-4614-6849-3
14. Li, Y., Wu, F.X., Ngom, A.: A review on machine learning principles for multi-view biological data integration. Briefings Bioinf. **19**(2), 325–340 (2018)
15. Liaw, A., Wiener, M.: Classification and regression by random forest. R News **2**(3), 18–22 (2002)
16. Lipinski, P., Brzychczy, E., Zimroz, R.: Decision tree-based classification for planetary gearboxes' condition monitoring with the use of vibration data in multidimensional symptom space. Sensors **20**, 1–17 (2020). https://doi.org/10.3390/s20215979
17. Maqsood, I., Abraham, A.: Weather analysis using ensemble of connectionist learning paradigms. Appl. Soft Comput. **7**, 995–1004 (2007)
18. Polikar, R.: Bootstrap inspired techniques in computational intelligence: ensemble of classifiers, incremental learning, data fusion and missing features. IEEE Signal Process. Mag. **24**(4), 59–72 (2007)
19. Polikar, R.: Ensemble based systems in decision making. IEEE Circ. Syst. Mag. **9**(3), 21–45 (2006)
20. Polikar, R.: Ensemble learning. Scholarpedia **4**(1), 2776 (2009)
21. Ripley, B.D.: Pattern Recognition and Neural Networks. Cambridge University Press, Great Britain (1996)
22. Ripley, B.D.: Package 'nnet'. Package for feed-forward neural networks with a single hidden layer, and for multinomial log-linear models, pp. 1–11. cran.r-project.org. 3 May 2021
23. Stapor, K., Ksieniewicz, P., Garcia, S., Wozniak, M.: How to design the fair experimental classifier evaluation. Appl. Soft Comput. J. **104**, 107219 (2021)
24. Zimroz, R., Bartkowiak, A.: Two simple multivariate procedures for monitoring planetary gearboxes in non-stationary operating conditions. Mech. Syst. Signal Process. **38**, 237–247 (2013)

Biometrics and Pattern Recognition Applications

Typing Pattern Analysis for Fake Profile Detection in Social Media

Tapalina Bhattasali[1]([✉]) and Khalid Saeed[2,3]

[1] St. Xavier's College (Autonomous), Kolkata, India
tapalina@sxccal.edu
[2] Bialystok University of Technology, Bialystok, Poland
k.saeed@pb.edu.pl
[3] Department of Electronics and Computation Sciences, Universidad de La Costa,
Barranquilla, Colombia

Abstract. Nowadays, interaction with fake profiles of a genuine user in social media is a common problem. General users may not easily identify profiles created by fake users. Although various research works are going on all over the world to detect fake profiles in social media, focus of this paper is to remove additional efforts in detection procedure. Behavioral biometrics like typing pattern of users can be considered to classify genuine profile and fake profile without disrupting normal activities of the users. In this paper, DEEP_ID model is designed to detect fake profiles in Facebook like social media considering typing patterns like keystroke, mouse-click, and touch stroke. Proposed model can silently detect the profiles created by fake users when they type or click in social media from desktop, laptop, or touch devices. DEEP_ID model can also identify whether genuine profiles have been hacked by fake users or not in the middle of the session. The objective of proposed work is to demonstrate the hypothesis that user recognition algorithms applied to raw data can perform better if requirement for feature extraction can be avoided, which in turn can remove the problem of inappropriate attribute selection. Proposed DEEP_ID model is based on multi-view deep neural network, where network layers can learn data representation for user recognition based on raw data of typing pattern without feature selection and extraction. Proposed DEEP_ID model has achieved better results compared to traditional machine learning classifiers. It provides strong evidence that the stated hypothesis is valid. Evaluation results indicate that Deep_ID model is highly accurate in profile detection and efficient enough to perform fast detection.

Keywords: Typing pattern · Keystroke · Mouse click · Touch stroke · Fake profile · Deep_ID · Social media

1 Introduction

Social media is a platform where each user has one or more profiles to share their updates, type and share various posts, can keep in contact with friends, meet new people who have the same interests, allows users to interact with each other through chat. Social

© Springer Nature Switzerland AG 2021
K. Saeed and J. Dvorský (Eds.): CISIM 2021, LNCS 12883, pp. 17–27, 2021.
https://doi.org/10.1007/978-3-030-84340-3_2

networking sites are growing rapidly and changing the way people keep in contact with each other. Users can easily expand their contacts as online social media brings people with the same interests together. Computing devices like desktop, laptop, tablet, smart phone are the interacting devices which are commonly used to access profiles in social media. However, online social networks are facing a lot of challenges like fake profiles, online impersonation, which in turn may give rise to various cybercrimes. Although one user may create multiple profiles in social media, fake users often create profiles of targeted victims either to retrieve any confidential information about the victim or misuse victim's identity to confuse others within the network or negatively affect victim's reputation. Malicious users often send friend request to the users from victim's friend list as if request comes from genuine user. Fake profiles are created to ask for financial assistance or any other facilities from the users in the social network. Sometimes genuine user's profile has been hacked in the middle of a session to misuse the profile.

With the rapid growth of social media usage, it becomes necessary to focus on providing better services for social network. One user may create multiple profiles or multiple users can create different profiles for a single identity in social network users. If fake identities in online platform cannot be identified in time, it may give rise to cybercrimes. Traditional or one-time authentication cannot work well in these scenarios. Research works from various aspects are going on all over the world to find out feasible solutions. To reduce any additional efforts and limitations of existing approaches, behavior biometric methods seem to provide better solution. It is better to identify fake profiles, while users use desktop, laptop, or touch devices to interact in social network. User's typing pattern tends to produce consistent results over time while being less disruptive to user's experience.

In traditional systems, once the user's identity is verified during login, the resources are available to that user until user exits or session terminates. Any user can also access system resource in the middle of valid session of other user as it considers identity verification for one time. This may lead to session hijacking, in which an attacker targets an open session, e.g., when people leave the social profile unattended for shorter or longer periods. For this type of scenarios, user's identity needs to be verified iteratively. This type of identity verification is not an alternative security solution for initial login; it provides an additional layer of security.

Keystroke dynamics and mouse dynamics are soft behavioral biometric traits, which are used to recognize genuine users and fake users during the interaction in social media through desktop and laptop. Touch dynamics is used when user access social media through touch devices (smart phone, tablets).In this paper, fake profile detection in social platform has been considered to secure social life of people. It can also help the social sites to manage huge number of profiles easily by differentiating the profiles used by genuine users from the profiles used by false identities.

Proposed work focuses on the following two directions – i) differentiation between fake profile and genuine profile in social media, ii) identification of genuine profile hijacking by intruders in the middle of a session. Here focus is on how accurately fake profiles can be detected and how fast and accurately social media profile hijacking can be detected. DEEP_ID procedure is proposed here to detect fake profile using multi-view deep learning method [1–2]. Several experiments have been conducted to demonstrate the effectiveness and superiority of the proposed model against various baseline methods. Several analyses and insights have been performed through the experiments. Main contributions of this paper are as follows:

- DEEP_ID model has been proposed, which is based on a multi-view multi-class neural network framework to recognize user based on keystroke, mouse-click and touch-stroke patterns.
- The design of the proposed model is based on simple category of deep learning neural network. This makes it easy to interpret and modify based on the scenarios.

The remaining sections are presented as follows. Section 2 gives idea about the background of DEEP_ID model. Section 3 briefly discusses about the related works. Section 4 presents proposed work to detect fake profile and profile hijacking. Section 5 narrates the analysis part and interprets the result. Finally, Sect. 6 concludes the paper.

2 Background

Deep learning or deep neural network [3] is a subset of machine learning algorithms, which is used to model high level abstractions in data. Recurrent Neural Network (RNN) and Convolutional Neural Networks (CNN) are the two major categories in deep neural network. RNN is frequently used to solve problems in natural language processing, whereas CNN is used in computer vision areas. Long Short Term Memory network (LSTM) is a type of RNN, which can learn long-term dependencies. RNN can only capture the relationship between recent typing information to use it for prediction. LSTM is more effective in typing pattern analysis. However, it is a complex structure that may cause high overhead. Gated Recurrent Unit (GRU) can produce similar or better result in typing pattern analysis compared to LSTM. As it uses less parameter, the structure of GRU is simple. GRU is considered here as each unit in the network can easily remember specific patterns in input stream for a long time. Any important patterns can be overwritten by update gate. If one view or one specific type of pattern is selected, then single view single tasking deep learning model can be designed with GRU. In that case, GRU can take normalized typing dataset as input and produces final output vector to recognize user. In DEEP_ID model, single view single class framework is extended to multi-view multi-class framework to consider keystroke, mouse-click and touch-stroke patterns.

3 Related Works

Many researchers have investigated topics related to keystroke, mouse-click and touch-stroke analysis for user recognition, but there are limitations too. According to Zhong and Deng [4], keystroke dynamics can be combined with other biometric modalities, like fingerprint scan or face recognition to provide more authentic solution. In [5], ant colony optimization is used for feature subset classification and Euclidean distance is used for classification to provide 83% recognition rate is 83% with 0.15% FAR (False Acceptance Rate) and 2% FRR (False Rejection Rate). Liu and Deng found number of clusters using Elbow and K-means clustering method [6]. Feature extraction has been done using PCA [7]. They introduced gradient based method long short-term memory (LSTM) to truncate the gradient,so that it does not produce errors [8–10]. In that paper, fuzzy ARTMAP technique used for recognizing binary input vector,radial basis function networks (RBFN) used for activation,learning vector quantization (LVQ) used to classify the patterns based on inter-key time. Obaidat and Sadoun found that sum-of-products (SOP), Baye's algorithm, backpropagation with sigmoid activation function, hybrid sum-of-products (HSOP) produce average results [11].

In recent years, more research works on continuous authentication have been emerged for mobile users. There are many research efforts focusing on studying touch-screen gestures [12] to offer better security services for mobile users. However, most of the security models have to be installed on the mobile devices,so that models can perform binary classifications to detect unauthorized users. There are research works on mobile user identification based on web browsing information [13–14]. Abramson and Gore try to identify users' web browsing behaviors by analyzing cookies information.

Another major problem faced during this type of research is that the researchers prepared their own dataset using different techniques and the evaluation criteria are not uniform. Therefore, comparison among the algorithms from the literature becomes a difficult task. To address this issue, benchmark datasets on keystroke, mouse-click and touch stroke are publicly available to provide standard platforms for experiments [15–17].

From the literature survey, it can be seen that designing generic user identification model, which can be deployed on web and local devices are still neglected. The focus of this paper is to design generic DEEP_ID model, which can classify users only based on user's interaction patterns on the interface.

4   Proposed Work: DEEP_ID

DEEP_ID is based on a simple multi-view and multi-class generic authentication framework, which is based on GRU structure. It includes the following major steps (Fig. 1) to continuously authenticate users in social media based on multiple views associated with keystroke, mouse-click and touch-stroke for multiple tasks in the users' profiles.

Step1: Data Collection
Step 2: Multi-View Dataset Generation from keystroke, mouse-click and touch-stroke
Step 3: Multi-View Multi-Class (MVMC) Learning
Step 4: Evaluation

DEEP-ID model is also capable to detect genuine profile hijacking in the middle of log-in session.

In step 1, raw typing data were collected from 50 volunteers, who were using social media profiles. Profiles of five volunteers are considered as genuine. For each genuine profile, nine fake profiles were created to detect typing pattern of fake users in real-time against one genuine identity. It was continued for 6 weeks.

MVMC Learning

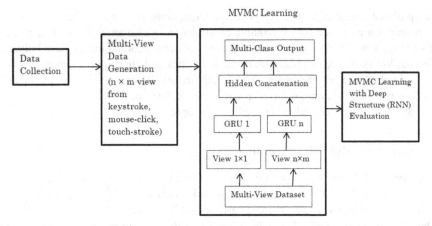

Fig. 1. DEEP-ID model

In step 2, multi-view dataset was prepared from the collected information for user recognition.

In step 3, multi-view data was modeled through a deep learning structure to perform multi-view multiclass learning.

In step 4, performance of the proposed MVMC learning with deep structure is evaluated in comparison with traditional machine learning algorithms random forest and support vector machine.

4.1 Data Collection

Data has been collected for two cases. Data Collection process involves 50 volunteers, who are experienced enough to use Facebook like social media from any devices like desktops, laptops, smart phones, tablets, who have good Internet connection, who are active users in social media by typing or uploading story, clicking stickers, doing chat, scrolling posts, using touch gestures frequently during their log-in sessions. Case 1 is considered to collect data from 50 volunteers, and divide them into 5 groups. In each group 9 users create 9 fake profiles against one genuine user and their typing patterns are considered for classification purpose. Case 2 is considered where five volunteers' profiles are considered as genuine and data are collected when other volunteers enter into the genuine profiles during their log-in session.

4.2 Data Processing

Users used social media profile either from desktop, laptop, smart-phone or tablet. Keystroke and mouse-click patterns are considered for desktops and laptops, whereas touch-gestures are considered for smart-phones and tablets. Collected data are processed to generate n × m multi-view dataset. Here n represents view and m represents modality (keystroke, mouse-click, touch-stroke). In the data collection process, missing data are inevitable. That is why, keystroke views are created from the temporal feature of n-graph [18–19]. It represents the time difference between keydown of first character and key-up of last character until space is encountered, divided by no. of characters. Average n-graphs are created for all possible combination of characters from the keyboard [20–23]. Continuous [24] movement of cursor has been recorded until mouse button is released. Views are created based on duration of click and change of position of cursor in x and y direction with respect to time (dx/dt, dy/dt). Touch stroke views are created based on v-stroke, z-stroke, s-stroke, p-stroke, w-stroke, t-stroke [25].

Outliers in the processed data have been discarded.

4.3 Multi-view Multi-class Learning

In this paper, different views of three different modalities have been considered. Each view contains different number of samples and different number of features. Fusion method can also be used to combine datasets of different views. However, it is difficult to build single-view dataset due to the different number of features in each view of each session. To avoid information loss multiple views are considered separately instead of concatenation. Multi-view multi-class learning [3] can help to improve the performance for profile recognition. It can be easily determined that which view can mostly contribute to the identity detection process.

At first, the dataset is separated into multiple views. Bidirectional Recurrent Neural Network along with GRU (GRU-BRNN) is used here to build the hidden layers for each view. Softmax function is used to perform multiple classifications in the output layer. Finally, performance of each view can be evaluated. Last layer information from each GRU-BRNN model is concatenated. This concatenated layer contains all information for accurate authentication. Use of GRU in DEEP_ID model removes the problem of heterogeneity in the time-series of each view and improves the performance of prediction.

5 Analysis

5.1 Fake Profile Detection

The number of session usage for each user is different. To analyze the performance of the proposed DEEP_ID model on detecting fake profile, four performance metrics are considered here (Fig. 2).

$$\text{Recall} = \text{True Positive(TP)} \big/ (\text{True Positive(TP)} + \text{False Negative(FN)}) \qquad (1)$$

$$\text{Precision} = \text{True Negative(TN)} \big/ (\text{False Positive(FP)} + \text{True Negative(TN)}) \qquad (2)$$

$$\text{F1} = (2 * \text{Precision} * \text{Recall}) \big/ (\text{Precision} + \text{Recall}) \qquad (3)$$

$$\text{Accuracy} = (\text{TP} + \text{TN}) \big/ (\text{TP} + \text{TN} + \text{FP} + \text{FN}) \qquad (4)$$

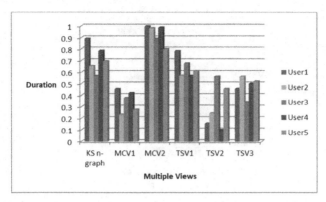

Fig. 2. Multi-view multi-class learning (Keystroke n-graph, Mouse click view 1, view 2, Touch Stroke view 1, view 2, view 3)

Performance of proposed DEEP_ID model is compared with the state-of-the-art machine learning algorithms (Figs. 3 and 4).

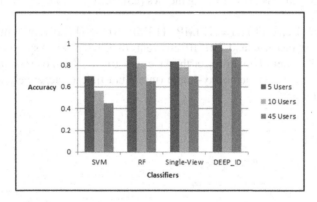

Fig. 3. Comparative analysis of DEEP_ID model accuracy

Support Vector Machine (SVM) and Random Forest algorithms are commonly used for multi-class identification. SVM is widely used in authorization and identification works. Linear SVM determines the best hyperplane by maximizing the margin between multiple classes. Random Forest (RF) builds many decision trees during training and combines their outputs for the final prediction using ensemble approach.

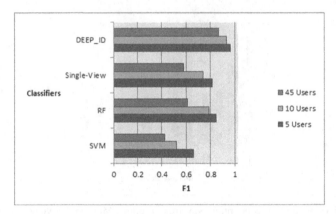

Fig. 4. Comparative analysis of F1 of DEEP_ID model

5.2 Social Media Profile Hijacking

Traditional metrics used for authentication are not feasible to detect profile hijacking in the middle of log-in session. Following metrics [25] are considered here to detect profile hijacking.

Time to True Reject (TTR) = |TFIMP −TRIMP|, where TFIMP represents timestamp of first activity of fake user and TRIMP represents timestamp, when system truly rejects that intruder. If system fails to reject the fake user truly, TTR moves to infinity. TTR should be less than a vulnerability-frame (minimum time to negatively affect social media profile) (Fig. 5).

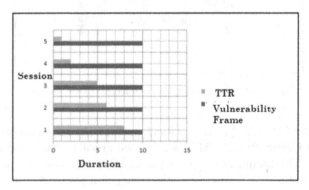

Fig. 5. Time to detect genuine profile hijacking

Validity = t/T, where t is the duration when genuine user is active in social media platform and T is the log-in session of that user in social media (Fig. 6).

Probability Time to True Reject (PTTR) – If system takes longer time than vulnerability frame, then PTTR is less than1, which is tolerable. If system always fails to reject intruders within vulnerability frame, then PTTR equals to 0.

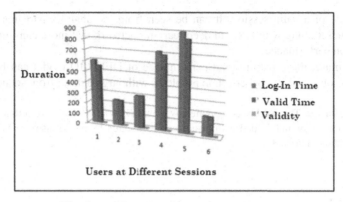

Fig. 6. Validity of genuine users in social media

Validity-Acceptability Characteristic Curve (VACC) - Curve of validity versus PTTR (Fig. 7) gives rise to Validity-Acceptability Characteristic Curve (VACC). Like ROC, area under VACC is used to measure the overall performance of profile hijacking detection procedure.

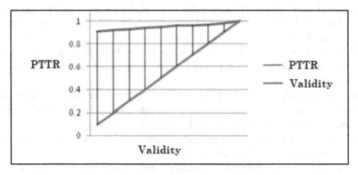

Fig. 7. PTTR vs. Validity in VAAC

6 Conclusions

In this paper, DEEP_ID model is proposed to detect fake profiles on social media. It does not need data preprocessing or manual feature selection and extraction compared to most of the ML classifiers from the literature. Multi-view multi-class learning makes it capable to classify all the features separately and do the fusion to take final decision. Proposed model can detect fake profiles on social media with utmost accuracy. It can also quickly identify profile hijacking within a session. If all the TTR values are within vulnerability frames, risks of cyber-crimes in social media can be reduced.

In summary, it can be said that DEEP_ID model can work effectively to detect fake profiles in social media. It also detects genuine profile hijacking attempt of the intruders in the middle of a valid session. It can be seen from the analysis part that multiple views of dataset along with GRU in deep learning network that more can improve the identification performance.

In the future, the capability and performance of DEEP_ID model can be further extended to solve real-life cyber-crime problems with large dataset from social media.

Acknowledgement. This work was supported by grant WZ/WI-IIT/4/2020 from Bialystok University of Technology and funded with resources for research by the Ministry of Science and Higher Education in Poland.

References

1. Hinton, G.E., Osindero, S., Teh, Y.W.: A fast learning algorithm for deep belief nets. Neural Comput. **18**(7), 1527–1554 (2006)
2. Cruz, M.A.D.S., Goldschmidt, R.R.: Deep neural networks applied to user recognition based on keystroke dynamics: learning from raw data. In: Proceedings of the XV Brazilian Symposium on Information Systems. Article No.: 35, pp. 1–8 (2019)
3. Sun, L., Wang, Y., Cao, B., Yu, P.S., Srisa-an, W., Leow, A.D.: Sequential keystroke behavioral biometrics for mobile user identification via multi-view deep learning. In: Altun, Y., Das, K., Mielikäinen, T., Malerba, D., Stefanowski, J., Read, J., Žitnik, M., Ceci, M., Džeroski, S. (eds.) ECML PKDD 2017. LNCS (LNAI), vol. 10536, pp. 228–240. Springer, Cham (2017). https://doi.org/10.1007/978-3-319-71273-4_19
4. Zhong, Y., Deng, Y.: A survey on keystroke dynamics biometrics: approaches, advances, and evaluations. In: Recent Advances in User Authentication Using Keystroke Dynamics Biometrics, pp. 1–22 (2015)
5. Baynath, P., Soyjaudah, K.M S., Khan, M.H-M.: Implementation of a secure keystroke dynamics using ant colony optimization. In: Proceedings of International Conference on Communications, Computer Science and Information Technology (2016)
6. Liu, F., Deng, Y.: Determine the number of unknown targets in open world based on elbow method. IEEE Trans. Fuzzy Syst. **29**(5), 986–995 (2021)
7. Lever, J., Krzywinski, M., Altman, N.: Points of Significance: principal component analysis. Nat. Methods **14**(7), 641–642 (2017)
8. Sherstinsky, A.: Fundamentals of recurrent neural network (RNN) and long short-term memory (LSTM) network. Physica D **404**, 132306 (2020)
9. Hochreiter, S., Schmidhuber, J.: Long short-term memory. Neural Comput. **9**(8), 1735–1780 (1997)
10. Du, Y., Wang, W., Wang, L.: Hierarchical recurrent neural network for skeleton based action recognition. In: Proceedings of IEEE Conference on Computer Vision and Pattern Recognition (CVPR), pp. 1110–1118 (2015)
11. Obaidat, M.S., Sadoun, B.: Verification of computer users using keystroke dynamics. IEEE Trans. Syst. Man Cybern. B Cybern. **27**(2), 261–269 (1997)
12. Zhao, X., Feng, T., Shi, W.: Continuous mobile authentication using a novel graphic touch gesture feature. In: Proceedings of IEEE Sixth International Conference on Biometrics: Theory, Applications and Systems (BTAS), pp. 1–6 (2013)
13. Abramson, M., Gore, S.: Associative patterns of web browsing behavior. In: AAAIFall Symposium Series (2013)

14. Zhang, H., Yan, Z., Yang, J., Tapia, E.M., Crandall, D.J.: Mfingerprint: privacy-preserving user modeling with multimodal mobile device footprints. In: Proceedings of International Conference on Social Computing, Behavioral-Cultural Modeling, and Prediction, pp. 195–203. Springer, Cham (2014). https://doi.org/10.1007/978-3-319-05579-4_24

15. Ahmed, A.A., Traore, I.: Biometric recognition based on free-text keystroke dynamics. IEEE Trans, Cybern. **44**(4), 458–472 (2014)

16. Killourhy, K.S., Maxion, R.A.: Comparing anomaly-detection algorithms for keystroke dynamics. In: Proceedings of IEEE/IFIP International Conference Dependable Systems & Networks, pp. 125–134 (2009)

17. Killourhy, K.S., Kevin, S., Maxion, R.A., Roy, A.: Free vs. transcribed text for keystroke-dynamics evaluations. In: Proceedings of Workshop: Learning from Authoritative Security Experiment Results, pp. 1–8 (2012)

18. Bhattasali, T., Saeed, K.: Two factor remote authentication in healthcare. In: Proceedings of IEEE International Conference on Advances in Computing, Communications and Informatics, pp. 380–381 (2014)

19. Bhattasali, T., Saeed, K., Chaki, N., Chaki, R.: Bio-authentication for layered remote health monitor framework. J. Med. Inform. Technol. **23**, 131–140 (2014)

20. Maxion, R., Killourhy, K.: Keystroke biometrics with number-pad input. In: Proceedings of IEEE International Conference on Dependable Systems & Networks, pp. 201–210 (2010)

21. Xu, H., Zhou, Y., Lyu, M.R.: Towards continuous and passive authentication via touch biometrics: an experimental study on smartphones. In: Proceedings of Symposium on Usable Privacy and Security, pp. 187–198 (2014)

22. Feng, T., et al.: Continuous mobile authentication using touchscreen gestures. In: Proceedings of IEEE International Conference on Biometrics: Theory, Applications and Systems, pp. 451–456 (2013)

23. Frank, M., Biedert, R., Ma, E., Martinovic, I., Song, D.: Touchalytics: on the applicability of touchscreen input as a behavioral biometric for continuous authentication. In: IEEE Transactions on Information Forensics and Security, vol. 8, pp. 136–148 (2013)

24. Bhattasali, T., Panasiuk, P., Saeed, K., Chaki, N., Chaki, R.: Modular logic of authentication using dynamic keystroke pattern analysis". In: Proceedings of ICNAAM, vol. 1738, p. 180012. AIP Publishing, American Institute of Physics (2016)

25. Bhattasali, T., Chaki, N., Saeed, K., Chaki, R.: U-stroke pattern modeling for end user identity verification through ubiquitous input device. In: Saeed, K., Homenda, W. (eds.) CISIM 2015. LNCS, vol. 9339, pp. 219–230. Springer, Cham (2015). https://doi.org/10.1007/978-3-319-24369-6_18

Determination of the Most Relevant Features to Improve the Performance of RF Classifier in Human Activity Recognition

Geovanna Jiménez-Gómez[1], Daniela Navarro-Escorcia[1], Dionicio Neira-Rodado[1(✉)], and Ian Cleland[2]

[1] Universidad de la Costa, Calle 58 No. 55-66, Barranquilla, Colombia
{gjimenez14,dnavarro13,dneira1}@cuc.edu.co
[2] Ulster University, Shore Road, Newtownabbey, County Antrim BT37 0QB, Northern Ireland, UK
i.cleland@ulster.ac.uk

Abstract. The impact that neurodegenerative diseases have in our society, have made human activity recognition (HAR) arise as a relevant field of study. The quality of life of people with such conditions, can be significantly improved with the outcomes of the projects within this area. The application of machine learning techniques on data from low level sensors such as accelerometers is the base of HAR. To improve the performance of these classifiers, it is necessary to carry out an adequate training process. To improve the training process, an analysis of the different features used in literature to tackle these problems was performed on datasets constructed with students performing 18 different activities of daily living. The outcome of the process shows that an adequate selection of features improves the performance of Random Forest from 94.6% to 97.2%. It was also found that 78 features explain 80% of the variability.

Keywords: HAR · Machine learning · Feature selection · RF classifier

1 Introduction

Dementia is a syndrome in which memory, thinking, behavior and the ability to carry out daily activities are impaired [1]. According to Prince et al. [2], IHME describes the health status of people with mild dementia, as memory impairment, particularly for recent events. These people also find it difficult to concentrate, think flexibly, plan, and make decisions, making dementia one of the major causes of disability and dependency among older people worldwide. All these conditions associated with dementia can be overwhelming, not only for the people who suffer from it, but also for their caregivers and families. Therefore, it is considered that dementia has a an impact in four dimensions, which are the physical, psychological, social, and economic [1].

Nevertheless, the cost of dementia, which is estimated to be around $2 trillion by 2030 [2], might be meaningfully reduced improving clinical management. This can be achieved, implementing improvements in care and support for these people and their

© Springer Nature Switzerland AG 2021
K. Saeed and J. Dvorský (Eds.): CISIM 2021, LNCS 12883, pp. 28–42, 2021.
https://doi.org/10.1007/978-3-030-84340-3_3

carers, which can also reduce the probability of future admissions [3]. In this sense, smart environments arise as prominent research field [4] to deploy reminding solutions, based on assistive technologies. Through the implementation of these systems, not only more independence and autonomy for elders, who live alone, might be achieved, but also an enhancement their quality of life might be possible as well. As a result, the cost for society and public health systems could be reduced [5, 6], alleviating the burden faced because of this disease.

The key component of these smart environments is human activity recognition (HAR) [7, 8]. HAR applications to smart environments or assisted living systems (ALS), may vary from monitoring of long-term chronic conditions to promoting physical activity [7]. HAR uses computational methods to automatically recognize and interpret human activity. Nevertheless this is still a very complex task [7, 9], making it necessary to find ways to improve the ability to recognize the different activities, either by developing new classification algorithms or by determining the most relevant features in the process. One of the ways used to gather the data to be analyze with the classifiers, is the use of body-worn accelerometers. The data obtained through these sensors, make it possible the recognition of activities or actions through the interpretation of human body motion or gestures. Once data have been preprocessed the use of adequate features is relevant, in order to minimize classification errors and reduce computation time [10, 11], making it vital the determination of the features that most affect the performance of the selected classifier.

The remainder of the paper is structured as follows. Section 2 provides a review of the literature in features for HAR. Following this, Sect. 3 describes the used methodology and the study case. Section 4 contains the analysis of the results obtained with the implementation of the proposed methodology to the study case. Finally, Sect. 5 shows some conclusions derived from the present study.

2 Literature Review

In many areas such as pervasive computing, ambient assistive living and connected health, HAR has become a fundamental element [12]. In this sense, it is important to point out that the management and prevention of chronic diseases is possible due to HAR. HAR makes this possible through the surveillance of daily activities of elderly residents [9], frequently supported on wearable sensors, such as the accelerometer. Accelerometers have become very popular in this field, due to the easiness for real-time implementation, their low cost and the fact of not being location dependent [13, 14]; making them suitable for monitoring activities such as sitting, running, standing, ascending stairs, and walking [12].

According to Pires et al. [15], feature extraction is considered to be the most important stage in HAR process. Therefore, it is necessary to determine the best features according to each application. Features can be split into statistical and structural ones (or time-based features) [17, 18]. Statistical features include mean, median, and range among others, and correspond to descriptive statistical analysis within the time window of sensor data. On the other hand, structural features (or time-based features), such as entropy and energy, are extracted from time-based relationships or sequence of data obtained by the sensor.

As it was mentioned before, improving the outcome of HAR depends, in a relevant manner, on the selection of the most adequate features. The selection and calculation of features can be made with either the support of experts or in automated way with the use of deep learning [14]. Nevertheless, expert-driven features extraction methods depend on the knowledge of the experts and applicability of the feature vectors in the problem domains [8]. Additionally this kind of features cannot represent in many occasions the outgoing characteristics of complex activities and involve time-consuming feature selection techniques to select the optimal features [16]. Considering this difficulty, deep learning has gained a lot of focus due to its ability to learn features from data [15]. In this sense, convolutional neural networks (CNN) are used by many researchers for feature extraction through the transformation of motion signals into images. This process is intended to extract the best features for the triaxial accelerometers and improve the performance of classifiers. Nevertheless, researchers have found that the performance obtained in the classifiers when automatically generating features via CNN is similar to the performance obtained with hand-crafted features [17].

In the literature related to HAR and wearable sensors, different features were found that could improve the performance of the classifier. In [18] several features in the context of activity recognition, were used. Many of these features were time-domain features, due to their low computational cost and high discriminatory ability, what makes them suitable for real-time applications [18]. Considering that the purpose of this work is to determine the most relevant features in HAR when using accelerometer data, it is important to use the outcomes of previous studies. For example, according to Tian et al. [19], wavelet energy spectrum features can increase the discrimination between different activities and improve the activity recognition accuracy. Other features used in [19] include autoregressive (AR) coefficients. Finally, in [20] hand-crafted features were used, such as zero-crossings. Other relevant features were used in [18], including roll angle, pitch angle, median crossings, Pearson correlation among others. Considering that this study is based on the study of Neira et al. [8], the features of this previous work can be found on Table 2 and the new features including the findings of the literature review can be found on Table 3. Considering that the performance obtained in the classifiers when automatically generating features via CNN is similar to the performance obtained with hand-crafted features [17], all the features used in the study are hand crafted and no comparison was made between these features and automatically generated features.

3 Methodology

The dataset used in this study was collected by students enrolled in the Pervasive Computing module at Ulster University using a wearable triaxial accelerometer, placed on the dominant wrist [21]. The acceleration data across x, y, and z axis were gathered. The students were each assigned to an AR scenario and perform three activities within the scenario. Then, they had to collect, process, and classify data as part of the module assessment. In total, there were 6 scenarios and 18 activities recorded amongst the cohort (Table 1).

Data was collected with sample rate of 51.2 Hz. Then data were windowed, considering time windowing, as is a common approach with accelerometers where sensor data is sampled at a sustained rate. A non-overlapping window size of 4 s was considered appropriate [22] as it has been observed that energetic activities such as walking, jogging, and running can be optimally detected between 1 and 3.25 s, while more complex activities may require longer time windows.

R® (4.0.2 version) was used for data cleaning, creation of time windows, calculation of variables, division of data into test and training sets, and creation of aggregated files. The classifier models and their performance measures were obtained with Weka® (3.8.3 version).

Table 1. Scenarios and activities performed.

No.	Scenario	Activities	Number of files
1	Self-care	Hair grooming, washing hands, brushing teeth	24 (72 files)
2	Exercise (cardio)	Walking, jogging, stepping-up	23 (69 files)
3	House cleaning	Ironing clothes, washing windows, washing dishes	25 (75 files)
4	Exercise (weights)	Arm curls, dead lift, lateral arm raise	21 (63 files)
5	Sport	Bounce ball, catch ball, pass ball	25 (75 files)
6	Food preparation	Mixing food, chopping vegetables, sieving flour	23 (69 files)
Total			141 (423 files)

3.1 Feature Extraction

A compilation of standard time and energy domain features were extracted from the windowed data to obtain relevant information and to represent the characteristics of various activity signals. The features included the mean, natural logarithm, exponential, maximum, minimum, standard deviation, variance, root mean square (RMS), signal magnitude area (SMA), range, and median for the x, y, z axis and signal magnitude vector (SMV), and the cross correlation for each axis, as it has been suggested that these features are suitable for activity recognition [9, 21]. In order to improve the performance of the classifiers, additional features were selected after a review of the literature related to HAR and portable acceleration sensors. From [18] the features were selected Pearson's correlation coefficient, percentiles, inter-quartile range, skewness, kurtosis, pitch angle, coefficients of variation, roll angle and median crossings. From [19] the features were chosen acceleration variance, AR coefficients, wave-let energy spectrum and finally, from [20] was selected zero-crossing. Also, three features that could improve the performance of the classifiers, were added. The sum of all these features totaled more than 190 variables. These are shown in Table 3.

Table 2. Extracted features in the previous study.

Feature number	Feature name	Feature description
1–3	Mean acceleration	Mean acceleration in x, y, and z, in the time window
4	Mean SMV	Mean SMV in the time window. SMV was calculated with the relation: $$SMV_i = \sqrt[2]{(acc_x^2 + acc_y^2 + acc_z^2)}$$ Where acc_x, acc_y, acc_z, denote the acceleration in each axis of the i-th observation
5–7	Mean logarithm	Mean logarithm in x, y and z in the time window
8–10	Mean exponential	Mean value of the exponential function powered at the value of the acceleration in each axis. This was also calculated in the corresponding time window
11–13	Mean exponential squared	Mean value of the exponential function powered at the squared value of the acceleration in each axis. This was also calculated in the corresponding time window
14–16	Mean squared acceleration	Mean of the squared values of the acceleration in x, y and z, in the time window
17–20	Trapezoidal rule	Trapezoidal rule of acceleration in each axis, and SMV, in the time window
21–24	Minimum	Minimum value of the acceleration in each axis, and SMV in each time window
25–28	Maximum	Maximum value of the acceleration in each axis, and SMV in each time window
29–32	Range	Range of the values of acceleration in each axis and SMV in the time window
33–36	Standard deviation	Standard deviation of the values of SMV and acceleration in the three axes, in the time window
37–40	Root mean square (RMS)	Root mean square of the values of SMV, and acceleration in each axis, in the time window. RMS is calculated according to the relation: $$RMS_x = \sqrt[2]{mean(acc_x^2)}$$

(continued)

Table 2. (*continued*)

Feature number	Feature name	Feature description
41	Signal magnitude area (*SMA*)	Signal magnitude area in the time window. It is calculated with the equation: $$SMA = \sum_{i=1}^{n}(|acc_{xi}| + |acc_{yi}| + |acc_{zi}|)$$ where, $|acc_{xi}|$ corresponds to the absolute value of the i-th observation of the acceleration across x-axis in the time window
42–44	Mean square	Mean of the square values of individual observations in the time window
45–48	Entropy	Fast Fourier transform of *SMV*, and across x, y, and z-axis, in the time window
49–51	Median	Median of the acceleration values across x, y, and z-axis in the time window

The notation for Table 3 is as follows:
$n \rightarrow$ Number of observations in the time window.
$\sigma \rightarrow$ Standard deviation of the acceleration in the time window across each axis.
$s_i \rightarrow$ Acceleration value in each timestamp in each axis.
$\mu_s \rightarrow$ The mean value of acceleration in the time window on each axis.

Table 3. Added features.

Feature number	Feature name	Feature description
52–54	Pearson's correlation coefficient	Correlation between each pair of axes (x,y), (x,z) and (z,y), in the time window. For example, correlation between x-axis and y-axis can be calculated as follows: $\frac{cov(x,y)}{\sigma_x \sigma_y}$
55–69	Percentiles	The values of the variable below which 10%, 25%, 50%, 75% and 90% of the acceleration data lie on the x axes, y, and z, in the time window
70–72	Interquartile range	Difference between the third and first quartiles of the acceleration data on each axis $(x, y$ and $z)$, in the time window $percentile75 - percentile25$

(continued)

Table 3. (*continued*)

Feature number	Feature name	Feature description
73–75	Skewness	Asymmetry measurements in the 3 axes, in the time window $\frac{1}{n\sigma_s^3}\sum_{i=1}^{n}(s_i - \mu_s)^3$
76–78	Kurtosis	Measures the degree of data concentration around the mean acceleration at x, y, and z, in the time window $\frac{1}{n\sigma_s^4}\sum_{i=1}^{n}(s_i - \mu_s)^4$
79	Pitch angle	Average pitch angle between the three axes, in the time window. The pitch angle for each timestamp is calculated with the following formula: $arctan\left(\frac{x_i}{\sqrt{y_i^2+z_i^2}}\right)$
80–82	Coefficients of variation	Relation between the mean and the variability of the acceleration in x, y and z, in the time window $\frac{\sigma_s}{\mu_s}$
83	Roll angle	Average roll angle between the y axes and z, in the time window. The roll angle for each timestamp is calculated with the following formula: $arctan\left(\frac{y_i}{\sqrt{x_i^2+z_i^2}}\right)$
84–86	Median crossings	Total number of times the x, y, and z-axis observations cross the median, in the time window
87–89	Acceleration variance	Variability of the acceleration data in x, y, and z with respect to their mean, in the time window
90–92	Zero-crossing	Total number of times the x, y, and z-axis observations cross the value 0, in the time window
93–95	Peak intensity	The number of signal peaks in each axis, in the time window

(*continued*)

Table 3. (*continued*)

Feature number	Feature name	Feature description
96–98	Average of peaks	Average of peaks in each axis, in the time window
99–101	Average of valleys	Average of valleys in each axis, in the time window
102–173	Autocorrelation	The autocorrelation between the observation at the current timestamp and the observations at previous timestamps, in the time window. In this case, the calculation was based on the 24 previous timestamps
174–185	AR coefficients	ARIMA autoregressive coefficients in each axis, in the time window
186–188	Power spectral density	The calculation is based on the evaluation Fast Fourier Transform, in the time window
189–191	Wavelet energy spectrum	The wavelet energy spectrum is computed by applying the Morlet wavelet. P-values to test the null hypothesis that a period (within lowerPeriod and upperPeriod) is irrelevant at a certain time are calculated if desired; this is accomplished with the help of a simulation algorithm. The function to achieve this was *analyze.wavelet* from the package *WaveletComp* from $R^{®}$ (4.0.2 version)
192–194	Inter-axis cross-correlation	Cross-correlation between each pair of axes (x,y), (x,z) and (y,z), in the time window. For example, the inter-axis cross-correlation between x-axis and y-axis can be calculated as follows: $$\frac{\sum_{i=1}^{n}(x_i-\mu_x)(y_i-\mu_y)}{\sqrt{\sum_{i=1}^{n}(x_i-\mu_x)^2\sum_{i=1}^{n}(y_i-\mu_y)^2}}$$
195	Squared signal magnitude area (SMA^2)	Squared signal magnitude area in the time window

3.2 Process Stages

The procedure developed in the current work is described below:

Stage 1: Preprocessing

The data obtained from the triaxial accelerometers, were cleaned, and grouped in time windows of 4 s using the $R^{\circledR}$ software (version 4.0.2). No filtering was used in the process.

Stage 2: Features calculations

To calculate the features added in the present study, a literature review related to HAR was performed, extracting some features that contributed to the performance of classifiers in other studies. Subsequently, these features were calculated.

Stage 3: Data split

Once the dataset was pre-processed, it was divided to obtain two sets. A set containing 80% of the observations, which was used for the training process, the creation of the classifier model and the evaluation using the 10-fold cross-validation. And the other set containing 20% of the observations was used to test and evaluate the classifier performance. The training and test sets were created 10 times and the RF classifier performance was obtained. Random Forest (RF), was used in this work, considering that it is one of the best classifiers in HAR due to the f-measure it yields [8].

Stage 4: Analysis of results.

This analysis will be performed once the approach is applied to the study case data. It should be noted that F-measure is used to evaluate the precision of the RF classifier.

4   Analysis of Results

A ranking of the features was generated according to the contribution they make to variability to determine the most relevant. The most relevant features and least relevant are shown in the Table 4 and in the Table 5, respectively.

It should be noted that mean value of the squared exponential function was among the most relevant features despite exponential function is a measure that is not related to this type of process.

Table 4. Most relevant features

| Pearson's correlation coefficient |
| Inter-axis cross-correlation |
| Pitch angle |
| Roll angle |
| Wavelet energy spectrum |
| Entropy |
| Autocorrelation |
| Peak intensity |
| Zero-crossing |
| Mean squared exponential |
| Median crossings |

Table 5. Least relevant features

| Mean logarithm |
| Skewness |
| AR coefficients |
| Kurtosis |
| Mean exponential |
| Percentiles |
| Root mean square (RMS) |
| Mean acceleration |
| Trapezoidal rule |
| Average of peaks |
| Average of valleys |
| Signal magnitude area (SMA) |
| Mean SMV |
| Standard deviation |
| Median |
| Maximum |
| Interquartile range |
| Range |
| Minimum |
| Mean squared acceleration |
| Squared signal magnitude area (SMA^2) |
| Acceleration variance |
| Power spectral density |
| Coefficients of variation |

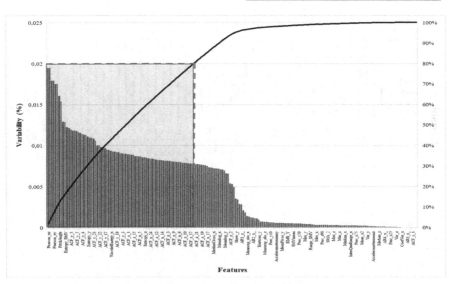

Fig. 1. Pareto chart of the contribution of the features to variability.

The diagram above represents those features that contribute 80% of the variability (shaded area) and those that only contribute the remaining 20%. 80% of the variability is represented by 78 features.

Although, the most relevant features are only 11 as shown in Table 4, actually the calculations of these features in different axes are those that add up to the "78 most relevant features". For example, in the case of *Pearson's correlation coefficient*, three features are included in itself, since the calculations of this coefficient between the x and z axes (*Pearson_xz*), between the x and y axes (*Pearson_xy*), and between the z and y axes (*Pearson_zy*) they were relevant.

The next 2 figures are breakdown of Fig. 1, which allow us to know the number of features that explain a certain percentage of the variability (Figs. 2 and 3).

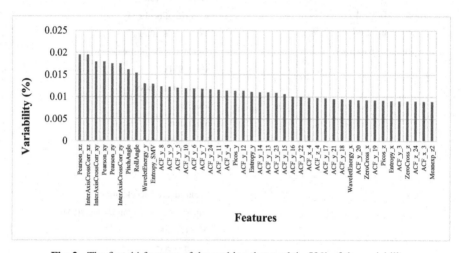

Fig. 2. The first 44 features of the ranking that explain 52% of the variability.

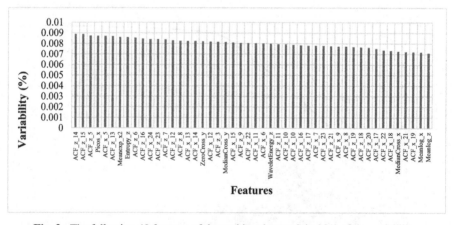

Fig. 3. The following 48 features of the ranking that explain 38% of the variability.

The values of the 10 repetitions of the F-measure of the RF of the present study were recorded, as well as the values of the previous study. These values are presented in the Table 6 and in the Table 7. Normality tests were executed with the 10 values obtained in each study. This is important to guarantee the validity of the t-test. On Tables 8 and 9 it can be observed the mean and standard deviation of the F-measure values of the RF classifier of the present study and of the previous study, and p-value for Shapiro-Wilk normality test. The test was made considering a significance level of 0.05.

As can be seen, the p-value yielded for Shapiro-Wilk test applied to the values of the F-measure of the RF classifier of the present study is less than 0.05, which means that the hypothesis that the data follow a normal distribution must be rejected. A histogram was prepared in which the presence of an outlier was appreciated. For this reason, a Grubbs test was carried out, which allows us to detect whether the highest or lowest value in a data set is an outlier. In this case, it was sought to check whether the lowest data (0.9517) from Table 6 was an outlier. The test was performed, and it yielded a p-value of 2.411e-5, which is less than the established level of significance, then the null hypothesis that the lowest value is not an outlier is rejected and it can be said that the

Table 6. F-measure value of the RF in each repetition of the present study.

Repetition	F-measure
1	0.9517
2	0.9760
3	0.9727
4	0.9737
5	0.9750
6	0.9721
7	0.9734
8	0.9757
9	0.9704
10	0.9760

Table 7. F-measure value of the RF in each repetition of the previous study.

Repetition	F-measure
1	0.9435
2	0.9447
3	0.9409
4	0.9444
5	0.9473
6	0.9461
7	0.9515
8	0.9444
9	0.9447
10	0.9510

Table 8. Mean and standard deviation of the F-measure values of the RF of the present study, and p-value for Shapiro-Wilk test.

Mean	0.9717
Standard deviation	0.0073
p-value	5.45e-5

Table 9. Mean and standard deviation of the F-measure values of the RF of the previous study, and p-value for Shapiro-Wilk test.

Mean	0.9459
Standard deviation	0.0033
p-value	0.2325

lowest value (0.9517) is an outlier. The Shapiro-Wilk normality test was repeated for the 9 remaining F-measure values of Table 6 study after removing the outlier and it yielded a p-value of 0.4269, higher than the level of significance, therefore it cannot be rejected null hypothesis and the data set is considered to follow a normal distribution.

After verifying normality assumption was checked, Student's t test was used to compare the means of the two samples (present and previous study). The test was performed and yielded a p-value of 5.516e-13 which is less than the significance level of 0.05, concluding that the values of the F-measure of each study differ in their mean.

5 Conclusions

Considering that the objective of this study was to improve the performance of the RF classifier by determining the most relevant features after conducting a review of the literature that included studies related to HAR, it can be said that an adequate selection of features can improve the performance of the classifier. In this case, a 2.6% improvement was achieved in its performance. This difference was found to be statistically significant after performing the t-test. It was also found that 80% of the variability is explained by only 78 features, while the rest of the features (117) explain only 20% of the variability. In this sense, it is important to point out that the fact of using such amount of features in the process causes and increase in the training process of the classifier, that is completely compensated with the increase in the f-measure in such an important application. This additional computational effort is required only during training process. In addition, it is important to highlight that mean exponential squared was among the most relevant features, even though the exponential function is a measure that is not related to this type of process.

It is important to note that the relevance of a feature is not the same in the different axes, for example, the *median crossings* feature was found within the most relevant when it was calculated along the y-axis, however, this feature was also found among the least relevant when it was calculated along the x and z axes.

On the other hand, it is also worth mentioning that of the total of the features that explain 80% of the variability, 79.49% of them are statistical features and represent 63.37% of the variability, while 20.51% of them are structural (time-based) and explain 16.75%. In this sense, it can be affirmed that the structural features were able to complement the statistics.

For future research, it will be important to check the combinations of models so that a hierarchy could help in the determination of the different classes. In this sense, it would be interesting to consider the combination of random forest with a CNN, similar to what was done by [22] where a hybrid hierarchical classification algorithm (HHC) is presented combining deep learning and threshold-based methods to improve accuracy and rapid computation classifying 15 complex activities. A hierarchical strategy could also be carried out by combining a clustering algorithm and the RF classifier.

It is also necessary to point out that for future research it would be interesting to use additional classification algorithms, to verify is the selected features for Random Forest, affect in a similar way other algorithms such as neural networks, SVM, random subspace and other. In this sense, the comparison against random subspace would be important considering that both classifier (Random forest and random subspace), considering that both of them rely on randomly created feature subspaces to increase the diversity of the ensemble [23]. Finally, it is important in feature research to do additional experimentation verifying how the effectiveness of the classifier in recognizing particular activities is affected for different selection of features.

References

1. Dementia: https://www.who.int/news-room/fact-sheets/detail/dementia. Accessed 15 May 2021
2. Prince, M., Wimo, A., Guerchet, M., Ali, G.-C., Wu, Y.-T., Prina, M.: World Alzheimer Report 2015, The Global Impact of Dementia: An Analysis of Prevalence, Incidence, Cost and Trends, p. 87
3. Prince, M., Comas-Herrera, A., Knapp, M., Guerchet, M., Karagiannidou, M.: World Alzheimer Report 2016 Improving Healthcare for People Living with Dementia Coverage, Quallty and Costs Now and in the Future
4. De-La-Hoz-Franco, E., Ariza-Colpas, P., Quero, J.M., Espinilla, M.: Sensor-based datasets for human activity recognition - a systematic review of literature. IEEE Access **6**, 59192–59210 (2018). https://doi.org/10.1109/ACCESS.2018.2873502
5. Aparisi, F., Carlos, J., Díaz, G.: Aumento de la potencia del gráfico de control multivariante T 2 de Hotelling utilizando señales adicionales de falta de control (2001)
6. Noor, M.H.M., Salcic, Z., Wang, K.I.K.: Adaptive sliding window segmentation for physical activity recognition using a single tri-axial accelerometer. Perv. Mob. Comput. **38**, 41–59 (2017). https://doi.org/10.1016/j.pmcj.2016.09.009
7. Cerasuolo, J.O., et al.: Population-based stroke and dementia incidence trends: age and sex variations. Alzheimers Dement. **13**(10), 1081–1088 (2017). https://doi.org/10.1016/j.jalz. 2017.02.010
8. Neira-Rodado, D., Nugent, C., Cleland, I., Velasquez, J., Viloria, A.: Evaluating the impact of a two-stage multivariate data cleansing approach to improve to the performance of machine learning classifiers: a case study in human activity recognition. Sensors **20**(7), 2020 (1858). https://doi.org/10.3390/s20071858
9. Ni, Q., García Hernando, A., de la Cruz, I.: The elderly's independent living in smart homes: a characterization of activities and sensing infrastructure survey to facilitate services development. Sensors **15**(5), 11312–11362 (2015). https://doi.org/10.3390/s150511312
10. Mukhopadhyay, S.C.: Wearable sensors for human activity monitoring: a review. IEEE Sens. J. **15**(3), 1321–1330 (2015). https://doi.org/10.1109/JSEN.2014.2370945
11. Chen, L., Hoey, J., Chris, N., Cook, D., Yu, Z.: Sensor-based activity recognition. IEEE Trans. **42**(6), 790–808 (2012)
12. Kleinberger, T., Becker, M., Ras, E., Holzinger, A., Müller, P.: Ambient intelligence in assisted living: enable elderly people to handle future interfaces. In: Stephanidis, Constantine (ed.) UAHCI 2007. LNCS, vol. 4555, pp. 103–112. Springer, Heidelberg (2007). https://doi.org/ 10.1007/978-3-540-73281-5_11
13. Chen, Y., Xue, Y.: A deep learning approach to human activity recognition based on single accelerometer. In: Proceedings of the 2015 IEEE International Conference on Systems, Man, and Cybernetics, SMC 2015, pp. 1488–1492 (2016). https://doi.org/10.1109/SMC.2015.263
14. Qi, W., Su, H., Yang, C., Ferrigno, G., De Momi, E., Aliverti, A.: A fast and robust deep convolutional neural networks for complex human activity recognition using smartphone. Sensors (Switzerland) **19**(17), 3731 (2019). https://doi.org/10.3390/s19173731

15. Domingos, P.: A few useful things to know about machine learning. Commun. ACM **55**(10), 78–87 (2012). https://doi.org/10.1145/2347736.2347755

16. Pires, I., et al.: From data acquisition to data fusion: a comprehensive review and a roadmap for the identification of activities of daily living using mobile devices. Sensors **16**(2), 184 (2016). https://doi.org/10.3390/s16020184

17. Veeriah, V., Zhuang, N., Qi, G.-J.: Differential recurrent neural networks for action recognition (2015)

18. Janidarmian, M., Roshan Fekr, A., Radecka, K., Zilic, Z.: A comprehensive analysis on wearable acceleration sensors in human activity recognition. Sensors **17**(3), 529 (2017). https://doi.org/10.3390/s17030529

19. Tian, Y., Zhang, J., Wang, J., Geng, Y., Wang, X.: Robust human activity recognition using single accelerometer via wavelet energy spectrum features and ensemble feature selection. Syst. Sci. Contr. Eng. **8**(1), 83–96 (2020). https://doi.org/10.1080/21642583.2020.1723142

20. Li, F., Shirahama, K., Nisar, M.A., Köping, L., Grzegorzek, M.: Comparison of feature learning methods for human activity recognition using wearable sensors. Sensors **18**(3), 679 (2018). https://doi.org/10.3390/s18020679

21. Irvine, N.: The Impact of Dataset Quality on the Performance of Data-Driven Approaches for Human Activity Recognition, pp. 1–8

22. Cornacchia, M., Ozcan, K., Zheng, Y., Velipasalar, S.: A survey on activity detection and classification using wearable sensors. IEEE Sens. J. **17**(2), 386–403 (2017). https://doi.org/10.1109/JSEN.2016.2628346

23. Koziarski, M., Krawczyk, B., Woźniak, M.: The deterministic subspace method for constructing classifier ensembles. Pattern Anal. Appl. **20**(4), 981–990 (2017). https://doi.org/10.1007/s10044-017-0655-2

Augmentation of Gait Cycles Using LSTM-MDN Networks in Person Identification System

Aleksander Sawicki[(⊠)] [iD]

Faculty of Computer Science, Bialystok University of Technology, Bialystok, Poland
a.sawicki@pb.edu.pl

Abstract. This paper presents a novel data augmentation method to improve a walk-based person identification system. The proposed algorithm is based on trainable deep learning models, that are able to model the gait cycle of individual participants and generate perturbed augmented signals. In this study generative model involving two layers of Long Short-Term Memory (LSTM) and Mixture Density Network (MDN) was implemented.

The proposed approach was evaluated on a publicly available human gait database collected with 30 participants and captured with IMU sensors. The impact of using the proposed algorithm was compared with the case without data augmentation (baseline) and the case of augmentation with the classical state-of-the-art method. The use of an LSTM-MDN model in the augmentation process has promising results increasing f-score from 0.94 to 0.96. Whereas, use classical state-of-the-art augmentation method did not affect the person identification metrics.

Keywords: Biometrics · Augmentation · Deep Learning

1 Introduction

Recently deep learning methods have gained great popularity in the area of gait-based person identification system. Deep networks with special emphasis on convolutional networks (CNNs) show excellent performance in classification problems when numerous training datasets are available. However, it is challenging to apply this type of models when only a small number of sample sets is available [1].

Data augmentation can be a successful solution to data scarcity where further data acquisition is too time consuming, financially expensive or impossible [2]. Although, it should be noted that while data augmentation by applying affine transformations (scaling, rotation, etc.) is a standard process in the field of image recognition, motion augmentation in general tends to be more challenging.

In this paper the results of augmentation methods for gait cycles captured by wearable sensors (accelerometer) and used for person identification are presented. Human gait signals can be successfully used as an additional criterion in the access granting applications. The advantage of this type of biometric system is that the theft of a device

© Springer Nature Switzerland AG 2021
K. Saeed and J. Dvorský (Eds.): CISIM 2021, LNCS 12883, pp. 43–54, 2021.
https://doi.org/10.1007/978-3-030-84340-3_4

equipped with motion sensors does not allow a criminal to obtain authorisation. In contrast, the loss of media in many other cases (e.g. RFID cards), may be related to granting unwanted access to third persons.

In the actual data augmentation process, the generative LSTM-MDN model was used. The network architecture consisted of two Long-Short Term Memory (LSTM) layers and an output Mixture density network (MDN) layer. Neural networks of this type have previously been used to model handwriting sequences [3]. The impact of augmentation using a generative model was compared with the results of the classical method [4]. Experiments were undertaken using a publicly available data corpus [5], which contains IMU signals recorded during the gait of 30 participants.

The paper is organised as follows. Section 2 discusses selected state-of-the-art literature in field of IMU signal augmentation and LSTM-MDN generative model application. The methodology is described in Sect. 3 which includes descriptions of: data corpus, augmentation methods and classifier architecture. The results of person identification are presented in Sect. 4. The Sect. 5 contains conclusions and gives a future work outlook.

2 State-of-the-Art

This section provides an overview of the state-of-the-art researches related to the study, which is divided into two groups as follows.

2.1 IMU Data Augmentation

At the beginning it should be emphasised that the IMU data augmentation methods presented in this section are mostly concerned with Human Activity Recognition (HAR) issues and lesser extent with biometric applications.

In [1] a series of basic methods of transforming accelerometer signals for use in monitoring Parkinson Disease (PD) progression were presented. The authors proposed the use of methods changing the magnitude of the signal: jittering, scaling, rotation, permutation, magnitude warping; and changing the signal phase: warping and cropping. A general purpose IMU data augmentation method was presented in [6]. The algorithms included methods of magnitude modification (i.e. noise, permutation, scaling, rotation), and advanced methods of signal editing in time domain. The authors developed methods such as data stretching (slightly changes the sampling rate) and random sampling (interpolates parts of the data frame by partially perturbing the time of data occurrence). In [4], a three-step data augmentation was used to process gait cycles. The method described consisted of transformations such as noise addition, magnitude scaling and simulating sampling irregularities.

The methods described in the literature [2, 4, 6] are closely related. The algorithms have constant values of the parameters that modify the input data. Furthermore, each of the described methods affects both the amplitudes and phases of the IMU signals. With the application of HAR, the recorded signals are not repeatable, while those recorded during gait can be segmented into single cycles. In the case of [4], in which human walk analysis was performed, the signal augmentation 'modifier' setups remain constant for each research participant. In the present case the use of information of known gait cycles could potentially have a positive impact on the data augmentation process.

It should be noted that descriptions of the use of generative machine learning models in the field of data augmentation are reported in the state-of-the-art literature. An example generative adversarial network (GAN) type models have been successfully applied to graph data augmentation in [7]. However, architectures of this type require a significant number of learning samples which in practice makes it impossible to use them for smaller human gait collections.

Meanwhile, in [8], the authors used LSTM autoencoders to augment motion capture data (represented as kinect skeleton animations). The paper proposed a novel LSTM autoencoder model linked to a dedicated classifier in the form of a recurrent network. A great value of the work was the definition of a unique cost function, which was determined from the combination of the cost of generation model and the classifier. However, the presented approach obstructs the possibility of an independent learning process for the architecture sub models. The selection of the classifier hyperparameters obliged recalculation of the augmentation model weights.

On the other hand, very promising results of sequence generation using LSTM-MDN models have been achieved by independent authors in the papers [3, 9]. In the original work, above mentioned network architecture was applied in the problem of varied handwriting generation. In the second one, the architecture was used for the generation of accelerometer signals in the HAR problem. The promising results of previous studies were the motivation for conducting the author's research in the field of behavioural biometrics.

2.2 LSTM-MDN Data Generation

In [3], concept of a model consisting of two layers LSMT and MDN for handwriting sequence generation is presented. The model was trained using a publicly available dataset and used to create an artificial handwriting samples. The input data of the network were matrices of dimension $N \times 3$, where N is the length of the sequence. The second dimension stored information about displacements relative to the previous point (delta X, delta Y), and information about the "touch" of the sketchbook. This publication includes a very good mathematical description of the network architecture.

On the other hand, in [9], an architecture consisting of an LSTM network and a output MDN layer was used to model IMU signals. The aim of the study was to develop a model that generates data and a neural network capable of distinguishing between real and synthetic data. The sequences used in the study were related to Human Activity Recognition issues. The study used a network architecture with three LSTM layers, two fully-connected intermediate layers and a output MDN layer. The authors pointed out that using only the LSMT layers would not generate new data due to the deterministic nature of the network ("the model will generate the same sequence again at every-time" [9]). The authors ultimately highlighted the difficulty in being able to clearly measure the quality of the generated data.

Both network architectures [3, 9], consisted of a similar number of LSTM network layers and a final MDN layer. In the latter, additional fully connected layers were included. The publication [7] seems to present the results of preliminary research, with the difficulty of clearly evaluating the performance of this type of architecture.

In the presented work, a modified architecture of the LSTM-MDN network, which was initially designed for handwriting generation [3], is proposed for modelling and generating of gait. At the same time, a classical augmentation method [4] was implemented to provide a baseline and enable their comparison.

3 Methodology

This section presents: the characteristics of the used dataset, with particular emphasis on the gait cycles waveform; details of applied data augmentation methods; description of the classifier applied in person identification task. Mentioned points are discussed in detail in the following sections.

3.1 Dataset

The research study used a publicly available human gait database described in detail in [5]. The data corpus was created with 30 participants and inertial motion sensors were used for motion acquisition. Individual motion tracking sessions were conducted using the commercially available MTw Awinda product from the renowned company Xsens. The device consists of 6 battery-powered IMUs located respectively on torso, right wrist, right and left thigh and right and left shin. In original form the database contains recordings recorded on 9 types of different surfaces (e.g. concrete, grass). The paper presents the results of a preliminary study using only signals collected on one type of Flat Even (FE) surface.

The acceleration, angular velocity, and magnetic field strength signals were acquired at 100 Hz, and subjected to a low-pass filter with a cutoff frequency of 6 Hz. The quantities measured by the IMU such as acceleration are registered in the local coordinate system associated with the sensor orientation. It is challenging to have the sensors attached at a specific orientation and location on each participant's body [10]. The software developed by Xsens allowed to transform the measured quantities from coordinates related to the orientation of the sensors to an artificially created coordinate system of the person, which eliminated the previously mentioned disadvantage.

The data corpus provided block recordings in which the participant performed a varying number of gait cycles rather than individual segmented steps. Therefore, in order to conduct a proper study, gait cycles were segmented using the algorithm described in detail in our previous work [11].

Figure 1 presents an example of the gait cycles of two research participants. Each of the subplots (A, B, C) presents signals recorded by the following accelerometer axes. According to the literature [12], the beginning of the gait cycle is assumed to be the moment when the limb on which the sensor is located hits the ground. In Fig. 1(A), at time $t = 0$ s, a characteristic low-value acceleration measurement can be observed. On the other hand, a peak in the signal value with a much smaller scale at time t = 0.2 s (20 samples) is connected with hitting the ground with the second limb (to which the sensor is not attached). Due to the cyclic nature of the gait, a slow decrease to a near

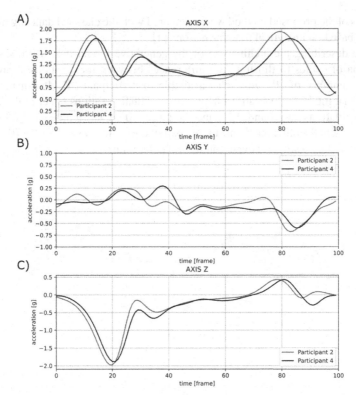

Fig. 1. Gait cycle comparison between two study participants. X axis signals of accelerometer A), Y axis signals of accelerometer B), Z axis signals of accelerometer C)

value (about 0.5 g) can be observed at the end of the gait in Fig. 1(A), from which the next gait cycle will start.

Comparing the signals recorded for the two subjects (Fig. 1), it can be seen that they have both similar shapes and very similar magnitude values (in all seniors axes). There-fore, the data augmentation process in this case must be remarkably well chosen, and should result in a multiplication of the learning set while maintaining the characteristic features of the signals.

Finally, it should be noted that each participant performed 6 trials on the Flat Even ground type, and for data segmentation the accelerometer signal located on the right shin was used. Single gait cycles had an approximate length of 1 s and were clipped to a constant length of 100 signal samples for classification purposes. Thus, the input data of the classifier were fragments of gait of constant dimension 100 × 3, where the second dimension was related to the presence of three axes of the sensor. The assumed length of gait cycles is equal to that presented in [4].

3.2 Gait Cycle Augmentation

During the present work the possibility of using the data augmentation method based on Mixture Density Network [3] in the field of gait cycle augmentation was examined.

The results of the proposed method were compared with the classical data augmentation algorithm based on analytical transformations [4].

Before describing the architecture of the generative model it is worth showing a comparison of cycles to illustrate the differences between them. Figure 2 presents a graphical summary of all gait cycles available to participant "1". It can be seen in the figure that the largest variations between individual iterations occur at the moment of large oscillations, at around 0.2 s and 0.8 s (i.e. 20 signal samples and 80 samples respectively). On the other hand, the middle part of the cycle 0.4 s–0.7 s (40–70 samples) is characterised by a similar course for all of the iterations.

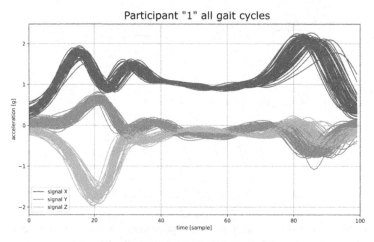

Fig. 2. Gait cycles of Participant "1"

In this study, a two-part generative model consisting of LSTM and MDN layers was used for data augmentation. The model consisted of two LSTM layers, containing 16 and 8 hidden units and one MDN output. The first layer returns all hidden states of the units (argument `return_sequences= True` in the keras package), while the second cell returns only the last unit hidden state. The final MDN layer provides four outputs describing Gaussian distributions (π, μ, σ). The first recursive segment of the model is closely related to the LSTM encoder. It results that the learning of the MDN layer was not performed directly on the input data, but on features in the latent space (which models the temporal features of the signal). Figure 3 presents the proposed model architecture.

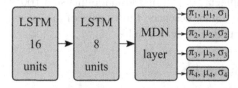

Fig. 3. Structure of the LSTM-MDN generative model

The model contained a total of 2322 trainable parameters. Its learning was performed using the Adam optimiser over a period of 4000 epochs. Changing the network weights was performed using dedicated cost functions [3]. Furthermore, the network itself did not strictly model the output signal but the parameters (μ, σ, π) of modelled normal distributions. The generation of augmented motion trajectories was done by prediction of the learned generative model, using the original signal waveforms.

Important from the point of view of network learning is the matter of the ratio between the number of training data and the number of trainable network parameters. For the first of the validations the data sizes of participant '1' were 64 learning cycles and 13 test cycles. The training data in the raw form was a matrix of dimension $64 \times 100 \times 3$. In the first step, the sequences were concatenated to form a matrix of dimension 6400×3. The sliding window technique of 60 samples was then applied, which resulted in the creation of subsets: X of dimension $6297 \times 60 \times 3$, and y of dimension 6297×3. The subset X stores information about historical samples (t_{-30}, t_{-29},...t_{-1}), and the set y stores values of signals at time t. In the presented approach the size of the training set significantly exceeds the number of model parameters.

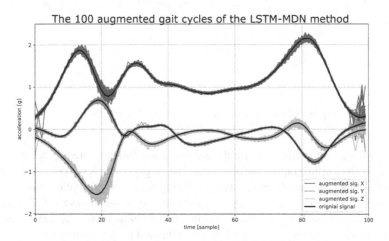

Fig. 4. 100 gait cycles generated by LSTM-MDN model

To illustrate the method in Fig. 4, one original gait cycle and 100 augmented cycles are plotted. In the attached illustration, significant variations in oscillations can be observed in the initial period of about 0.2 s (20 frames) as well as in the end of the gait cycle of 0.8 s–1 s (80–100 frames). That periods coincides with the periods of greatest variability in Fig. 2. In contrast, the middle sections of the gait cycle (which looks similar for each gait cycle - Fig. 2.) generated (augmented) gait cycles, practically follow the original waveforms.

The three-step data augmentation described in [4] was used as a reference as to the method of data augmentation using a generative model. The algorithm involved performing the following transformations:

– addition of Gaussian noise with constant sigma factor $\sigma = 0.01$;

- scaling of the magnitude of the original cycle by a random value S (uniform distribution) from the range 0.7–1.1;
- addition of disturbances simulating sampling irregularities. For this purpose, for every two measurement points, 10 artificial sub-measurements were introduced using interpolation. Finally, one value was selected at random from each of the 10 newly created quantities.

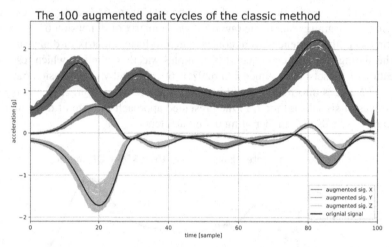

Fig. 5. 100 gait cycles generated by the classical algorithm

To illustrate the method, one original gait cycle and 100 generated cycles are plotted in Fig. 5. Analysing the graph it can be noticed that the generated X signals have relatively large deviations from the original waveform during the entire gait cycle. This is a direct result of the presence of the S factor (scaling the signal in the range 0.7–1.1). The high variability of the X signal also occurs in a rather characteristic typical period from 0.4 s–0.7 s (40–70 samples). The LSTM-MDN method proposed in this paper in these passages seems to reflect the signal characteristics more closely.

Finally, it should be noted that the generation of 100 gait cycles was used only for the purpose of generating Figs. 3 and 4 illustrations. For identification purposes, 10 new cycles were generated for the LSTM-MDN method and 3 artificial gait cycles for the classical algorithm [4].

3.3   Architecture of the Classifier

Considering the positive results obtained in previous work [11], we have again applied a classifier in the form of a deep LSTM network. The model consisted of two LSTM cells with a number of hidden neurons equal to 32. The measurement values of the accelerometer located on the right shin were applied to the input of the network. Data had a constant dimension B × 100 × 3, which resulted from the size of each validation (B), the length of the signals (100 samples), and the use of three sensor channels. The network was trained using a learning rate of 0.0025 for 300 epochs. The learning process used the ADAM algorithm and the categorical cross-entropy cost function. Details of the applied learning parameters are detailed in [11].

Model evaluation was performed using 6-fold cross-validation in a leave-one-trial-out configuration. Which means that to measure the performance of identifying a person on the n-th gait trial, the data collected on the remaining trials were use. To ensure the reliability of the experimental results, the classification process was repeated 90 times for each validation. The number of iterations resulted from a balance between the time limitation and the number of available graphics.

Experiments were performed using an open-source implementation of mixture density network – "keras-mdn", using the Python language and the TensorFlow package. The experiments were conducted using Eager mode, with calculations performed simultaneously using three NVIDIA 2080TI GPU accelerators.

4   Identification Results

The results of the conducted experiments allowed comparing the results of person identification performance in the case: without data augmentation (baseline); with the classical augmentation method [4]; with the proposed LSTM-MDN augmentation.

The identification performance was evaluated using 6-fold cross-validation in a leave-one-trial-out configuration. For statistical testing, each validation was repeated 90 times [13]. The f-score measure (Eq. 1) was used to evaluate classification quality.

$$Precision = \frac{TP}{TP + FP}, \ Recall = \frac{TP}{TP + FN}, \ f\text{-}score = 2 \cdot \frac{Precision - Recall}{Precision + Recall} \tag{1}$$

where:

TP – true predicted as positive (true positive);

TN – false predicted as negative (true negative);

FP – false predicted as positive (false positive);

FN – true predicted as negative (false negative).

Person identification results expressed by the f-score parameter are presented in Table 1. In individual cells, mean values were placed along with standard deviations determined from 90 replicates.

It can be observed from Table 1, that the identification results with the two tested data augmentation methods are not drastically different from the identification on the original non-augmented dataset (baseline method). The largest observable difference in the f-score parameter was 0.04 and occurred for validation 5. For the baseline method, the f-score was equal to 0.93 ± 0.11, while for the proposed LSTM-MDN method, the score increased to 0.97 ± 0.02.

The application of the analytical method [4], in some of the validation trials not only did not improve the identification results, but even had a negative impact by lowering the final result. In the case of validation 1 the application of the above mentioned algorithm resulted in a decrease of the f-score parameter from 0.94 ± 0.02 to 0.93 ± 0.02. Finally, the mean achieved identification score was only slightly different from the mean

Table 1. Summary results table reporting the f-score for the average of 6-fold Cross-Validation repeated 90 times

#Validation	f-score1a		
	No augmentation (baseline)	Classic augmentation	LSTM-MDN based augmentation
1	0.93 ± 0.04	0.92 ± 0.05	0.95 ± 0.04
2	0.94 ± 0.02	0.93 ± 0.02	0.95 ± 0.01
3	0.94 ± 0.09	0.96 ± 0.02	0.96 ± 0.07
4	0.96 ± 0.03	0.95 ± 0.04	0.96 ± 0.05
5	0.93 ± 0.11	0.95 ± 0.03	0.97 ± 0.02
6	0.96 ± 0.04	0.96 ± 0.05	0.97 ± 0.02
Mean	0.94 ± 0.07	0.94 ± 0.04	0.96 ± 0.04

identification score of the case without data augmentation (0.94 ± 0.04 and 0.94 ± 0.07 respectively).

On the other hand, using the LSTM-MDN method slightly decreased the person identification score only for validation 4 (change from 0.96 ± 0.03 to 0.96 ± 0.05), while improved performance for the other cases. The mean f-score increased from 0.94 ± 0.07 to 0.96 ± 0.04 relative to the baseline case.

Using the paired sample T-Test the statistical difference between the results obtained without (baseline) and with classical [4] augmentation was tested. The obtained p-value was 0.35809704, indicating that the results are not statistically different.

In contrast, using the same test, the statistical difference between the identification results without data augmentation (baseline) and with data augmentation using the LSTM-MDN method was examined. The obtained p-value was $1.88942521 \cdot 10^{-6}$ and means that the results obtained for the two presented approaches are statistically different.

5   Conclusions and Future Work

The proposed data augmentation method based on the LSTM-MDN network model allowed to slightly improve the results of the gait-based person identification system. For the used dataset corpus the mean f-score parameter increased from 0.94 ± 0.07 to 0.96 ± 0.04 (Table 1). The conducted t-test confirmed the statistical difference of the results.

It should be noted that the use of one of the classical methods [4] of gait augmentation only slightly affected the mean score of the person identification - changing the f-score from 0.94 ± 0.07 to 0.94 ± 0.04 (Table 1). For some of the cross-validations, the use of this type of augmentation even affected the final result negatively. A statistical test showed no difference in the results of the classical augmentation method [4] and baseline results.

The process of gait cycle augmentation is a challenging issue due to the fact that gait signals belonging to other subjects are relatively similar in both shape and magnitude (Fig. 1). The data augmentation algorithm in this case should lead to an enlargement of the training set while preserving the characteristic features of the signals. At the same time it should introduce changes to the data that are probable and may occur in the test sets. The classical method of gait cycle augmentation [4] used in this paper has fixed parameters that distort the signals. Such simple data augmentation can lead to the generation of gait patterns of participant A, which will be very similar to the gait cycles of participant B. Ultimately, such a phenomenon may lead to a situation where the data augmentation process will not increase the person identification score.

The classical method of augmentation [4] has permanently set parameters of signal distortion. The information available in the database regarding the gait cycles of individual participants is not considered and does not affect the augmentation process. Proposed LSTM-MDN-based method, originally used in another field, allowed us to omit the limitation of immutability of the augmentation procedure. The process of deformation of the gait cycles of participant "A" will depend on the other gait cycles belonging to this person.

The use of an LSTM-MDN type architecture in the augmentation process has led to promising initial results. Planned further work includes verification of the performance of the proposed method using the author's human gait database.

Acknowledgment. The work was also supported by grants from Bialystok University of Technology and funded with Resources for Research by the Ministry of Science and Higher Education, Poland, under Grant WI/WI/1/2019.

References

1. Um, T.T., Pfister, F.M.J., Pichler, D., et al.: Data augmentation of wearable sensor data for Parkinson's disease monitoring using convolutional neural networks. In: Proceedings of the 19th ACM International Conference on Multimodal Interaction, Glasgow, UK, 13–17 November (2017)
2. Eyobu, O.S., Han, D.: Feature representation and data augmentation for human classification based on wearable IMU sensor data using a Deep LSTM Neural Network. Sensors **18**, 2892 (2018)
3. Graves, A.: Generating sequences with recurrent neural networks. arXiv:1308.0850v5 [cs.NE] (2014)
4. Delgado-Escaño, R., Castro, F.M., Cózar, J.R., Marín-Jiménez, M.J., et al.: An end-to-end multi-task and fusion CNN for inertial-based gait recognition. IEEE Access **7**, 1897–1908 (2019)
5. Luo, Y., Coppola, S., Dixon, P., et al.: A database of human gait performance on irregular and uneven surfaces collected by wearable sensors. Sci. Data **7**, 219 (2020)
6. Kim, M., Jeong, C.Y.: Label-preserving data augmentation for mobile sensor data. Multidimension. Syst. Sig. Process. **32**(1), 115–129 (2020). https://doi.org/10.1007/s11045-020-00731-2
7. Antoniou, A., Storkey, A., Harrison, E.: Data augmentation generative adversarial networks. arXiv:1711.04340 (2017)

8. Juanhui, T., Hong, L., Fanyang, M., et al.: Spatial-temporal data augmentation based on LSTM autoencoder network for skeleton-based human action recognition, pp. 3478–3482 (2018)

9. Alzantot, M., Chakraborty, S., Srivastava, M.: SenseGen: a deep learning architecture for synthetic sensor data generation. In: 2017 IEEE International Conference on Pervasive Computing and Communications Workshops (PerCom Workshops), pp. 188–193 (2017)

10. Ngo, T.T., Makihara, Y., Nagahara, H., et al.: Similar gait action recognition using an inertial sensor. Pattern Recogn. **48**, 1289–1301 (2015)

11. Sawicki, A., Saeed, K.: Application of LSTM networks for human gait-based identification. In: Zamojski, W., Mazurkiewicz, J., Sugier, J., Walkowiak, T., Kacprzyk, J. (eds.) DepCoS-RELCOMEX 2021. AISC, vol. 1389, pp. 402–412. Springer, Cham (2021). https://doi.org/10.1007/978-3-030-76773-0_39

12. Hoang, T., Choi, D., Nguyen, T.: On the instability of sensor orientation in gait verification on mobile phone. In: Proceedings of the 12th International Conference on Security and Cryptography, vol. 4 (2015)

13. Demsar, J.: Statistical comparisons of classifiers over multiple data sets. J. Mach. Learn. Res. **7**, 1–30 (2006)

Raspberry Pi-Based Device for Finger Veins Collection and the Image Processing-Based Method for Minutiae Extraction

Maciej Szymkowski[✉]

Faculty of Computer Science, Bialystok University of Technology, Bialystok, Poland
m.szymkowski@pb.edu.pl

Abstract. Biometrics is one of the most important ways to secure users' data. It gained popularity due to effectiveness and ease of usage. It was proven that diversified solutions based on measurable traits can guarantee higher security levels than traditional authentication-based (logins and passwords). The most popular are fingerprint and iris (especially in mobile devices). In this work we would like to present our own algorithm connected with finger veins features extraction. At the beginning all details of the device for samples collection are given. In the further part significant information related to finger veins extraction are described in the details. Image processing methods were used to show that even with traditional, well-known algorithms it is possible to obtain precise information about human veins. The final step in our algorithm is connected with feature vector generation. In this work we do not present a classification stage as it is out of its scope.

Keywords: Biometrics · Human veins · Image processing methods · k-means · Feature vector · Segmentation

1 Introduction

In 2017 German hacker claimed that he created a fake retina of German Chancellor – Angela Merkel. It could be a breakthrough that would undermine vein-based biometrics traits. He provided some general details connected with the way in which fake samples were created as well as what was the idea of breaking the algorithm placed within retina-based security system. However, the most significant tackle stages were not described. In fact, different researchers tried to repeat his results but without any valuable effects. It is why veins-based biometrics are still recognized as an efficient and accurate method for human identity recognition. There are still no real evidences that it is possible to recreate a retina or vascular pattern. Diversified analysis and surveys show that it is clearly impossible for two people (even twins) to have exactly the same pattern of veins-based measurable traits (e.g., retina, hand veins, finger veins).

In this work, we are dealing with a problem of human identity recognition based on finger veins. This trait was selected due to its huge distinguishability and acquisition process easiness. Even a simple device based on infrared light emitting diodes (IR-LEDs) is enough to get precise finger veins images. The solution architects and

© Springer Nature Switzerland AG 2021
K. Saeed and J. Dvorský (Eds.): CISIM 2021, LNCS 12883, pp. 55–65, 2021.
https://doi.org/10.1007/978-3-030-84340-3_5

software developers who are working under security procedures have to keep in mind that biometrics-based systems should be easy to use as well as effective and accurate. On the basis of the previously proposed system [1], the new one was worked-out. In comparison to the recent idea, changes are as follows: completely new device (based on Raspberry Pi) for data acquisition, new procedure for image processing and the novel concept for feature vector generation.

In this work, we describe the full worked-out algorithm for feature extraction and descriptive vector creation. At the beginning procedure for image preprocessing is given. It is how little distortions (gathered during image acquisition) are removed as well as veins are better visualized. After the first stage, the image is segmented with simple binarization techniques. By this step we divide the sample into background and foreground (consisting of veins). In the penultimate stage, all veins are thinned (to remove unnecessary information). Finally, minutiae are extracted, and feature vectors are constructed on their basis.

This work is organized as follows: in the first section the authors analyze the current state of the art with particular emphasis on the latest approaches both from software and hardware sides (especially published in years 2018–2021). In the second chapter, the novel approach is presented and all stages with significant details are described. Third section presents all performed experiments, especially different image processing methods used in the process of algorithm design. Finally, the conclusions and future work are given.

2 Related Works

In the literature, the problem of human identity recognition based on finger veins is not well described. Most of the approaches based on veins are using retina or hand veins for identity recognition. It is puzzling because, on the basis of our observations, finger veins are much easier to collect than previously mentioned two measurable traits. In this subchapter we would like to present different ideas connected with finger veins extraction and identity recognition.

The first interesting work was presented in [2]. In the experimental phase the Authors used three publicly available datasets that are: SDUMLA-HMT, MMCBNU6000 and HKPU. In their approach we can observe two main stages: image preprocessing and identity recognition. In the work it was said that the first stage is based on image processing methods whilst Convolutional Neural Network (CNN) was used for data classification. The Authors claimed that their approach reached around 90% of correct identity recognition.

Another approach based on deep neural networks was proposed in [3]. In this case the Authors used only one well-known database – SDUMLA-FV. What is interesting is that in their approach image preprocessing stage is not considered. The only operation proposed is to convert image to grayscale and then to the form of the one dimensional vector. In the next part ResNet-50 was used for classification (identity recognition). In the paper it was claimed that the algorithm reached around 99% of accuracy. In fact, it is hard to evaluate as it was done on the only one publicly available dataset. Moreover, the description of the data processing in the selected neural network was not described in the details.

Both device and image processing algorithm were developed in [4]. The proposed apparatus consists of three main modules: finger veins image acquisition device, image processing module and matching display module. What is interesting is that the whole algorithm was created with usage of FPGA technology. It means that the Authors not only prepared simple implementation with traditional programming language (as Python) but also, they tried to speed up all calculations. The major disadvantage of this work is that traditional algorithmic and hardware-based approaches were not compared. It can be really interesting to observe whether the speed up is significant or not. Without this information, it is really hard to properly evaluate the proposed work. The novelty is observable; however, the final results are not clear enough.

Another Artificial Intelligence-based approach was described in [5]. In this case the Authors proposed to reduce the time needed for human identity recognition based on finger veins by preparation of lightweight convolutional neural network model. In the paper it was claimed that such approach can also be used in embedded system and can be a part of a real biometrics-based security module. To gain high accuracy the Authors used center loss whilst dynamic regularization was proposed to avoid overfitting and reduce training time. In the experimental phase two publicly available datasets were used: MMCBNU6000 and FV-USM. The work is rather theoretical as the recognition results are not given in a clear way.

In the literature, we can also find diversified methods which main aim is identity recognition rather than feature extraction and descriptive vector creation. In [6] an algorithm based on sparse matching approach was described. The whole proposed process is really similar to the traditional image processing-based algorithm. On the other hand, in [7] the verification based on curvature in Radon space was proposed. The Authors of [8] used Local Line Binary pattern to deal with this problem. It shows that there are plenty of different approaches to automatic (or semi-automatic) human identity verification on the basis of finger veins pattern. However, one major point has to be claimed. Not in all of the cases the results are acceptable. It is mostly connected with the accuracy of the algorithms as well as the time needed for processing. It is why, next experiments are needed to obtain more precise results and to prepare less time-consuming method.

In the literature we can observe different approaches to analyze all recent algorithms connected with finger veins, their processing and their features extraction. Of course, in such papers also different classification methods are taken into consideration. The significant representative of survey papers on finger veins as biometrics trait is [9].

3   Proposed Approach

The proposed approach is related to two main areas. The first of them is preparation of the device for finger veins acquisition whilst the second one is related to feature extraction and descriptive vector generation. To be clear enough both parts will be described in two separate subsections.

It also has to be claimed that the main reason why such experiments were conducted was the fact that recently published papers are mostly concentrated on software only. There are not so many ideas in which novel hardware-based devices are proposed. The author created his own complex approach were both apparatus and algorithms are presented. The gathered results will also be used in the broader idea of multimodal biometrics system.

3.1 The Device for Finger Veins Samples Collection

The first step of the work was related to creation of the efficient and accurate device for finger veins acquisition. Such apparatus was constructed as a part of the multimodal biometrics system consisting of modules for fingerprint collection and for finger veins/geometry acquisition. The first component was based on a ready-to-use fingerprint scanner DigitalPersona U.Are.U® 4500. In the case of the second module, the Author proposed his own solution.

The device consists of three infrared diodes, that illuminate the finger from below, Raspberry Pi Camera – ArduCam OV5647 5 MP Night vision, and Raspberry Pi 4B as the central part responsible for data processing and classification. Similar device [10] is shown in Fig. 1 and Fig. 2. It has to be claimed that the proposed apparatus is an extension of the idea presented in the previous work [1]. The scheme of the device is presented in Fig. 3.

During the device design phase, the author compared results gathered with different cameras as: Raspberry Pi NoIR Camera HD v2 and Camera HD Night Vision H OV5647 with specialized IR modules. However, neither of them guaranteed more precise results than the one finally used in the device.

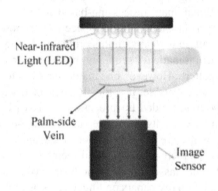

Fig. 1. The method connected with veins collection [10]

3.2 Image Processing for Finger Veins Feature Extraction

At the beginning it has to be claimed that the proposed approach was needed to properly obtain features from the finger veins. Our feature vector consists of information about minutiae that are traditionally used in the process of human fingerprint recognition (e.g., ridge endings and ridge bifurcations). To precisely obtain the data, we proposed an algorithm consisting of three main stages: image preprocessing, features extraction and descriptive vector creation. In this section all three steps are described in the details.

The first stage is related to image preprocessing. Its main aim was to remove additional distortions observable after image acquisition. Such elements can be connected with ambient light (for better veins visualization it was needed to reduce the impact of such light). To remove additional unnecessary information, we used a simple median filter (mask: 3 × 3, operation repeated 3 times). After this operation the sample was converted into grayscale on the basis of green channel. It was done, once again, to enhance the veins region. The green channel was selected on the basis of literature analysis [11, 12]. It was proven that it can guarantee much better enhancement than any other channel (especially for veins visualization). In the next steps we analyzed image histogram and its contrast. This stage can be divided into two substages. The first of them was related to histogram equalization and the following brightness correction (the image was dimmed for better veins visualization). The second substage consisted of histogram stretching and contrast modification. Such operations were needed to properly observe veins and to prepare sample for further segmentation. The initial image and the one obtained after preprocessing stage are shown in Fig. 4.

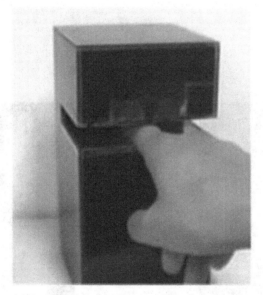

Fig. 2. Similar device for finger veins collection [10]

When image preprocessing was finished, the sample was sent to the next module. This part was responsible for finger veins extraction. In fact, one can conclude that its main aim was image segmentation – veins have to be separated from unnecessary background. The first operation made was edge detection. During the experimental phase of the work, multiple diversified methods related to this operation were tested (as Canny Edge Detector [13], Prewitt algorithm [14] and Laplacian method [15]). However, the best, most precise results were observed when bidirectional Sobel filter [16] was used. We assume that the most precise stands for the most clearly visible veins and the least visible additional, unnecessary objects. Moreover, Sobel algorithm was selected due to

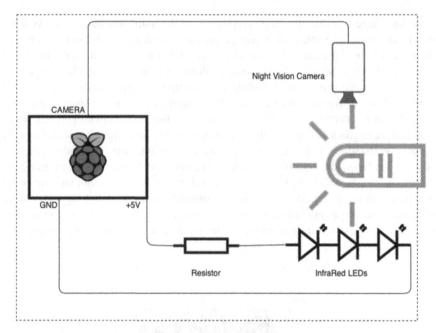

Fig. 3. Scheme of the device

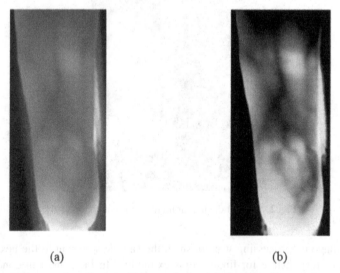

(a)   (b)

Fig. 4. Finger veins sample collected with the worked-out device (a) and image after preprocessing stage (b).

its efficiency. It was proven that even with the devices with low computing power, it can provide results relatively fast.

When all edges were pointed, the real segmentation algorithm has to be applied to our sample. In this case, once again, we analyzed diversified possibilities. Beginning with waterfall segmentation [17] and machine learning-based approaches like k-Means algorithm [18]. However, once again the most precise results were obtained with the simplest approach. In this case it was Otsu binarization method [19]. The term "the most precise" once again is related to the best separation of the veins from the background. For algorithms as waterfall or k-Means, the accuracy of this procedure was questionable – sometimes part of the veins was claimed as the background whilst in the other cases, part of the background was selected as the region of veins. It is why, Otsu binarization method was selected. Moreover, such approach was also not time-consuming.

The segmentation result was also enhanced by median filtering. This procedure was used to properly remove unnecessary artifacts observed after binarization. We assume that small distortions (as separate pixels) can be removed without any damage to the vascular pattern. In this case, the author once again tested different approaches – both median filtering and morphological operations were used to remove unnecessary elements. However, the second mentioned had influence on the veins pattern. It is why median filtering was selected for this aim – as the safer method that does not change the real pattern.

As the final stage of the feature extraction module, color inversion was done. It means that veins were marked in the black color, and the background in white. This operation was needed to properly prepare our sample for thinning. The samples obtained after the first module (image preprocessing) and the final result of the second module (feature extraction) are presented in Fig. 5.

In the last module of the solution, all operations connected with feature vector creation were realized. As the first one, image thinning was done. This algorithm was selected to prepare finger veins to feature extraction. During the experimental phase we tested different algorithms as Zhang [20], KMM [21], K3M [22] and morphological hit-or-miss operator [23]. On the basis of all observations, it has to be claimed that the K3M algorithm provided the best, most precise results. All edges were converted to one-pixel wide without loss of important information. All other methods were losing certain elements of the veins structure (e.g., certain portions of the veins). As the stop condition, we established coincidence – it means that no changes in the veins structure stopped the thinning process.

On the basis of thinned sample, feature extraction procedure was done. As it was stated before, minutiae-based approach was selected as the way to describe finger veins. In our algorithm we are looking for ridge bifurcations only. Other types were not selected as they can be really rare (as bridge) or really frequent (as ridge endings). Moreover, part of them can occur due to some minor artifacts related to the acquisition process. It is why only ridge bifurcations were selected in our algorithm. For minutiae extraction we used, well-known approach, the Crossing Number (CN) method. Moreover, to remove false minutiae, we calculated a distance between all extracted specific points. If the distance between pair of them was too small (on the basis of selected threshold in pixels), then one was removed. It allowed us to obtain only real minutiae. The result of the thinning process and minutiae detection was presented in Fig. 6.

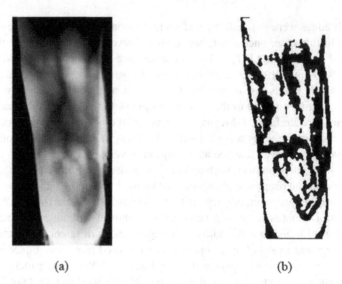

(a)   (b)

Fig. 5. Finger veins after preprocessing stage (a) and after features extraction module (b).

Finally, we generated a feature vector. It was based on a mathematical graph. Each minutiae was connected with the two closest. By this operation, we obtained a graph. Then all distances between connected minutiae were measured. Each of them was expressed as a percentage of the sample height. Percentage values were placed in the feature vector. In the case of this paper, we did not test the accuracy of classification on the basis of the proposed feature vector. The main reason is connected with the fact that the main goal of our experiments was to process images, extract veins and only propose a conceptual approach to feature vector generation.

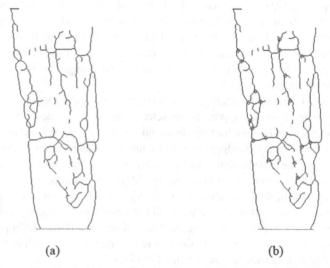

(a)   (b)

Fig. 6. Image after thinning (a), sample with all found minutiae marked by the circles (b).

4   Experiments

The experimental phase of the proposed approach was connected with two main aspects. The first of them was related to the device construction whilst the second one was based on selection of diversified algorithms for finger veins enhancement and extraction. At the beginning all experimental configurations of the device will be presented and described.

As the first stage of device construction, diversified evaluation boards were considered. In this part, Raspberry Pi [24], Nano Pi [25] and LattePanda [26] were selected. However, during analysis of each module, diversified advantages and disadvantage were observed. Connection between Raspberry Pi and cameras was really fast as well as preparation of the code for camera control was simple – Python and Linux scripts can be used for that aim. On the other side, sometimes Raspberry Pi can stop working even on the simplest operations (as opening the program). The second tested solution was Nano Pi. In this case, we observed that it is much smaller than Raspberry Pi (so it can reduce final device dimensions) and faster. The most important problem was to connect modules with Nano Pi. Of course, we can deal with this by specialized pins, but it is not as convenient as in Raspberry Pi. Moreover, preparation of the code was not as simple as in the previous case. The third analyzed module was LattePanda. This is a typical embedded system where also visual part is available. Despite the fact that it is based on Microsoft Windows 10, it was really hard to prepare a code for camera control as well as to connect the camera with this device (it was hard even with the Arduino part of the module). On the basis of these observations, we decided to use Raspberry Pi as it can guarantee high efficiency and provides multiple environments for code preparation. What is more, we can easily connect different modules to the embedded system.

During device construction, we also checked different cameras available for Raspberry Pi. These were: ArduCam OV5647 5Mpx Night vision, Raspberry Pi NoIR Camera HD v2 and Camera HD Night Vision H OV5647 with specialized IR modules. It was observed that the most precise results (where finger veins were clearly observable as well as not too many distortions were gathered during acquisition process) can be guaranteed by ArduCam. In the case of other cameras, the image was too much distorted as well as too dimmed. It is surprising because Raspberry Pi NoIR Camera and Camera Nigh Vision H OV5647 were claimed as the cameras that can be used under low light conditions. On the basis of all observations, ArduCam OV5647 was selected and placed as the significant system part.

Finally, in the experimental phase we also tested different image processing methods. On each stage, we tried different algorithms (e.g., not only Sobel operator but also Canny Edge detection and Prewitt method were checked during development process). Such approach allowed us to propose precise algorithm for finger veins extraction. We observed that the finally selected methods can guarantee accurate representation of finger veins. Moreover, we can simply gather information about minutiae observed in the finger veins pattern.

5   Conclusions and Future Work

The main goal of this work was to create an efficient and accurate device for finger veins collection as well as to design algorithm for finger vascular pattern extraction and descriptive vector creation. During development process diversified tools and circuits were checked. Moreover, different algorithms were used to extract finger veins. The software part was created with Python programming language. Such environment was selected due to its efficiency, huge amount of libraries availability and ease of usage. What is more, scripts created in this language can be easily deployed to different embedded systems (as Raspberry Pi). The obtained results have shown that the worked-out algorithm and device are efficient and accurate. The precision of the computer methods was evaluated on the basis of comparison between the original sample and final pattern of the veins. We can claim that the similarity between them is high.

Finger veins as a biometrics trait was selected due to its high efficiency and distinguishability. In the literature it was proven that accuracy level of the algorithms based on this trait is satisfactory. It allows to use them directly in a real security biometrics-based system.

The author current work is to prepare a classification algorithm based on worked-out processing method. Moreover, such approach will be a significant part of the designed multimodal system. In the nearest future, the author also would like to share his database with all interested researchers.

Acknowledgment. The author is thankful to Professor Khalid Saeed for his continuous support and all advice given during the algorithm construction as well as for verification of the proposed approach correctness.

This work was supported by grant W/WI-IIT/2/2019 from Białystok University of Technology and funded with resources for research by the Ministry of Science and Higher Education in Poland.

References

1. Szymkowski, M., Saeed, K.: Finger veins feature extraction algorithm based on image processing methods. In: Saeed, K., Homenda, W. (eds.) CISIM 2018. LNCS, vol. 11127, pp. 80–91. Springer, Cham (2018). https://doi.org/10.1007/978-3-319-99954-8_8
2. Zeng, J., et al.: Finger vein verification algorithm based on fully convolutional neural network and conditional random field. IEEE Access **8**, 65402–65419 (2020)
3. Madhusudhan, M., Udayarani, V., Hedge, C.: Finger vein based authentication using deep learning techniques. Int. J. Recent Technol. Eng. **8**(5), 5403–5408 (2020)
4. Yong, Y.: Research on technology of finger vein pattern recognition based on FPGA. J. Phys. Conf. Ser. **1453**, 1–5 (2020)
5. Zhao, D., Ma, H., Yang, Z., Li, J., Tian, W.: Finger vein recognition based on lightweight CNN combining center loss and dynamic regularization. Infrared Phys. Technol. **105**, 103221 (2020)
6. Hernández-García, R., et al.: Fast finger vein recognition based on sparse matching algorithm under a multicore platform for real-time individuals identification. Symmetry **11**(9), 1167 (2019)
7. Qin, H., He, X., Yao, X., Li, H.: Finger-vein verification based on the curvature in Radon space. Exp. Syst. Appl. **82**(1), 151–161 (2017)
8. Hernández-García, R., et al.: Massive finger-vein identification based on local line binary pattern under parallel and distributed systems. In: 2019 38th International Conference of the Chilean Computer Science Society (SCCC), pp. 1–7 (2019)

9. Sabbih, M., Al-Tamimi, H.: A survey on the vein biometric recognition systems: trends and challenges (2019). https://www.semanticscholar.org/paper/A-SURVEY-ON-THE-VEIN-BIOMETRIC-RECOGNITION-SYSTEMS%3A-Sabbih-Al-Tamimi/f2a1647f0b3104ff25d4c197286e9929216dc17c
10. Yang, J., Zhang, B.: Scattering removal for finger-vein image restoration. MDPI Sens. **12**(3), 3627–3640 (2012)
11. Lili, X., Luo, S.: A novel method for blood vessel detection from retinal images. BioMed. Eng. Online **9**(1), 14 (2010)
12. Siva Sundhara Raja, D., Vasuki, S.: Automatic detection of blood vessels in retinal images for diabetic retinopathy diagnosis. Comput. Math. Meth. Med. **2015**, 1–12 (2015)
13. Zhou, P., Ye, W., Wang, Q.: An improved Canny Algorithm for edge detection. J. Comput. Inf. Syst. **7**(5), 1516–1523 (2011)
14. Prewitt, J.M.S.: Object Enhancement and Extraction. Picture Processing and Psychopictorics. Academic Press (1970)
15. https://www.owlnet.rice.edu/~elec539/Projects97/morphjrks/laplacian.html. Accessed 12 Jan 2021
16. https://homepages.inf.ed.ac.uk/rbf/HIPR2/sobel.htm. Accessed 12 Jan 2021
17. Hanbury, A., Marcotegui, B.: Waterfall segmentation of complex scenes. In: Narayanan, P.J., Nayar, S.K., Shum, H.-Y. (eds.) Computer Vision – ACCV 2006. LNCS, vol. 3851, pp. 888–897. Springer, Heidelberg (2006). https://doi.org/10.1007/11612032_89
18. https://www.kdnuggets.com/2019/08/introduction-image-segmentation-k-means-clustering.html. Accessed 24 Jan 2021
19. Otsu, N.: A threshold selection method from gray-level histograms. IEEE Trans. Sys. Man. Cybern. **9**(1), 62–66 (1979)
20. Sudarma, M., Sutramiani, N.P.: The thinning Zhang-Suen application method in the image of balinese scripts on the Papyrus. Int. J. Comput. Appl. **91**(1), 9–13 (2014)
21. Saeed, K., Rybnik, M., Tabedzki, M.: Implementation and advanced results on the non-interrupted skeletonization algorithm. In: Skarbek, W. (ed.) CAIP 2001. LNCS, vol. 2124, pp. 601–609. Springer, Heidelberg (2001). https://doi.org/10.1007/3-540-44692-3_72
22. Tabędzki, M., Saeed, K., Szczepański, A.: A modified K3M thinning algorithm. Int. J. Appl. Math. Comput. Sci. **26**(2), 439–450 (2016)
23. https://homepages.inf.ed.ac.uk/rbf/HIPR2/thin.htm. Accessed 29 Jan 2021
24. https://www.raspberrypi.org. Accessed 11 Feb 2021
25. http://wiki.friendlyarm.com/wiki/index.php/NanoPi_NEO. Accessed 20 Feb 2021
26. https://www.lattepanda.com. Accessed 20 Feb 2021

Identification of Humans Using Hand Clapping Sounds

Cezary Wróbel and Sławomir K. Zieliński$^{(\boxtimes)}$ (ID)

Faculty of Computer Science, Białystok University of Technology, Białystok, Poland
s.zielinski@pb.edu.pl

Abstract. This paper demonstrates that hand clapping sounds could be employed as a useful biometric trait. The identity of 16 people was automatically recognized using their hand clapping sounds recorded with two mobile phones. To enhance the validity of the experiment, the audio recordings were made in six domestic environments (kitchen, living room, anteroom, and three bedrooms). The subjects were requested to clap their hands in three different hands configurations (A1, A3, and P1, using Repp's taxonomy [1]). The three identification methods were compared. They were all based on the same classification algorithm (support vector machines) but differed in the way the acoustic features (cepstral coefficients) were extracted. In the first method, for each individual clap recording, the cepstral coefficients were derived only from the time frame exhibiting the highest energy. In the second method, the cepstral coefficients were computed for all the time frames and subsequently aggregated by calculating their mean values and standard deviations. In the third method, all the coefficients were preserved (no aggregation performed). The last-mentioned method produced the best results, yielding 99% and 61% identification accuracy for room-dependent and room-independent test conditions, respectively. Out of the three hands configuration compared, the one in which the hands were aligned straight to each other (P1) was the most conducive in terms of the identification accuracy.

Keywords: Person identification · Audio feature extraction · Machine learning

1 Introduction

Person identification is nowadays frequently applied in security, surveillance, and authentication systems. Examples of popular biometric procedures include fingerprint recognition, facial recognition, iris scanning, and voice recognition. To enhance the reliability of the identification systems, researchers still pursue possibilities of merging various biometric traits, e.g., using audio-visual recordings (multi-modal fusion) [2].

In his pioneering work on hand clapping acoustics, Repp [1] provided early evidence that hand clapping sounds might be used for biometric purposes. This idea was taken further by Jylhä et al. [3], demonstrating that people could be identified with an accuracy level of 64% using hand clapping sounds. Considering potential benefits of using hand clapping sounds in biometric systems [4], it is surprising that this approach has not attained more widespread attention yet.

© Springer Nature Switzerland AG 2021
K. Saeed and J. Dvorský (Eds.): CISIM 2021, LNCS 12883, pp. 66–77, 2021.
https://doi.org/10.1007/978-3-030-84340-3_6

The purpose of this paper is to demonstrate that hand clapping sounds constitute a useful (and still unexplored) biometric trait. In the experiment undertaken in this study, the identity of 16 people was automatically recognized using their hand clapping sounds recorded with the two mobile phones. To enhance the validity of the experiment, the audio recordings were made in six domestic environments (kitchen, living room, anteroom, and three bedrooms). The participants were requested to clap their hands in three different hands configurations (A1, A3, and P1, using Repp's taxonomy [1]).

The three identification methods were compared. They were all based on the same classification algorithm (support vector machines) but differed in the way the acoustic features (cepstral coefficients) were extracted. According to the obtained results, the best-performing method provided almost 99% and 61% identification accuracy for room-dependent and room-independent test configurations, respectively, markedly outperforming the techniques proposed by Repp [1] and Jylhä et al. [3]. Out of the three hands configuration compared, the one in which the hands were aligned straight to each other was the most conducive in terms of the identification accuracy.

It is worth noting that the previous studies undertaken by Repp [1] and Jylhä et al. [3] were limited to a single acoustic environment, hence, restricting the methodology to a scenario whereby the algorithms were trained and tested using the recordings acquired in the same room (room-dependent testing). By contrast, six acoustical environments were included in this work, allowing the authors to test the proposed method both under room-dependent and room-independent conditions, enhancing the validity of the study. To the best of the authors' knowledge, this is the first work investigating the influence of hands configuration on the accuracy of the person identification, while also attempting to quantify the robustness of the method to changes in room acoustics.

2 Related Work

As already mentioned above, Repp [1] pioneered the research into hands clapping acoustics as early as in 1987. His experiments involved a panel of 22 participants. They were requested to individually clap their hands in a single acoustical environment (a sound-insulated booth). Although Repp's work is renowned for introducing a taxonomy of hand configurations, referred to as "clapping modes", the participants were not instructed as to the way they should clap, which could have introduced a confounding factor to the results. One of the main outcomes of his work was the observation that the average spectra of the hand clapping sounds bear distinctive individual character – a clap "signature." He developed an algorithm, based on spectral matching, capable of correct person identification in 91% of cases. This result, however, could be regarded as questionable (inflated) since the algorithm was likely to be trained and tested on the same data (no division between the train and test data was reported).

In 2006, Takai et al. [4] filed a patent application describing the method for "user identification" based on clapping sounds. In contrast to the previously discussed Repp's [1] method, which was solely based on spectral matching, their algorithm also exploited user-specific "rhythm" of clap sounds. No results were provided in the patent description, preventing a quantitative evaluation of the performance of their invention.

In 2012, Jylhä et al. [3] undertook a study building on Repp's [1] work. A group of 16 people took part in their experiment. They were instructed to clap freely with a constant tempo. Since the clapping style was not controlled, similarly to Repp's [1] work, the obtained results could have been confounded by the hand clap configurations. The audio recordings were made in a single acoustic environment, exhibiting a reverberation time of 0.5 s. To facilitate the automatic person identification, Jylhä et al. developed a spectral model-based method, which was tested in a more rigorous way compared to Repp's study. Half of the audio repository was used for the training procedure whereas the remaining recordings were exploited for the testing purposes. Their method reached the identification accuracy of 64%, a considerably lower value than that reported earlier by Repp [1].

Repp [1], Jylhä and Erkut [5], as well as Şimşekli et al. [6] demonstrated that certain hands configurations produce unique spectra of the clap sounds, e.g., due to palm-to-palm or palm-to-fingers resonances. They showed that such spectral patterns might be utilized by machine learning algorithms to automatically recognize hands configuration based on the audio recordings. However, the aforementioned authors did not investigate how variations in hands configuration might affect the performance of any algorithms intended for the automatic person identification using hand clapping sounds. Another limitation of the studies by Repp [1] and Jylhä et al. [3] alike is that their methods were both trained and tested using the recordings acquired in the same venue (room-dependent scenario), preventing the researchers to check how their methods would generalize when applied in an unknown acoustic environment.

To the best of the authors' knowledge, since 2012, no further work regarding the person identification using hand clapping sounds has been reported in the literature, which probably points out to potential difficulties faced by researchers in the deployment of such a method. For example, such a technique might be prone to variations in hands configurations, room acoustics, or recording equipment – the issues which have not been reported in the literature so far but, to an extent, are explored in this study.

3   Method

3.1   Acquisition of Clapping Sounds

A group of 16 people took part in the study. The participants were requested to individually produce sequences of 15 clap sounds with a rate of approximately two claps per second. Each sequence was produced by the participants in one of the three hands configurations. In the first configuration, referred to as clap type 1, the hands were kept parallel to each other. In the next two configurations, the hands were arranged at an angle of approximately 45°, with either palm-to-palm alignment (clap type 2) or palm-to-fingers alignment (clap type 3), as illustrated in Fig. 1. Although Repp [1] in his work distinguished eight different hands configurations, the above three types were included in the study due to their distinct timbral differences. They refer to clapping modes signified as P1, A1, and A3, respectively, using the original Repp's taxonomy [1].

The audio recordings were made in two different recording sessions. Of the group of 16 subjects, 7 participants (4 male and 3 female) took part in the first session. The recordings were made in two bedrooms and the anteroom, using Xiaomi Mi 9 Lite smartphone, giving in total 945 individual clap recordings (7 participants × 3 hands configuration types × 3 rooms × 15 claps). The remaining 9 subjects (5 male and 4 female) took part in the second session. To introduce a variation in the acoustical environment, the recordings were undertaken in three different venues, namely, in the living room, the kitchen, and the bedroom. A different smartphone was used (Xiaomi Redmi Note 4) to introduce a change in the recording equipment. Overall, 1215 individual clap sound recordings were made in the second session (9 participants × 3 hands configuration types × 3 rooms × 15 claps). In total, 2160 individual clap sound recordings were acquired in both recordings sessions.

While a sample rate in the first session was equal to 44.1 kHz, it was set to 16 kHz in the second session (the latter setting was introduced inadvertently, by selecting the default sample rate in the recording application). To equalize the sample rate between the sessions, all the recordings from the first session were down-sampled to 16 kHz. The differences between the recording sessions are outlined in Table 1.

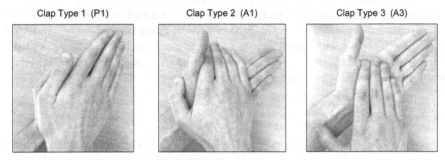

Clap Type 1 (P1)   Clap Type 2 (A1)   Clap Type 3 (A3)

Fig. 1. Hands configurations considered in the study. Symbols in brackets refer to Repp's taxonomy of hands configurations [1].

Table 1. Differences between the recording sessions.

Room ID	Session 1			Session 2		
	Room 1	Room 2	Room 3	Room 4	Room 5	Room 6
Recording venue	Bedroom A	Anteroom	Bedroom B	Living Room	Bedroom C	Kitchen
Volume	15 m³	11 m³	13 m³	30 m³	17 m³	9 m³
Number of participants	7 (4 male and 3 female)			9 (5 male and 4 female)		
Recording device	Smartphone, Xiaomi Mi 9 Lite			Smartphone, Xiaomi Redmi Note 4		
Sample rate	44.1 kHz (down-sampled to 16 kHz)			16 kHz		
Number of recordings	945 clap sounds			1215 clap sounds		

3.2 Segmentation and Signal Conditioning

The raw recordings, containing the sequences of clapping sounds, were segmented in such a way that each segment contained an individual clap sound. To this end, an amplitude envelope of the raw recordings was computed based on Hilbert transform. The beginning of each clap sound (start-time) was determined as a time index of a sample for which its amplitude envelope exceeded a threshold of 13% (a value determined heuristically) with respect to the maximum value of the envelope. To reduce the risk of incidentally cutting the initial sound "transients" during the segmentation procedure (e.g., due to noise or distortions), the beginning of each segment was set 10 ms earlier compared to the clap start-time determined by the above threshold criterion. The duration of each segment was set to 200 ms – a value deemed by the authors to be sufficient to accommodate both direct clap sounds and associated room reflections (duration of a clap sound in anechoic conditions is equal to approximately 5 ms [5]).

Time and frequency domain analysis of the segmented signals (omitted here due to space limitations), revealed that the recordings made by the mobile phones were affected by noise with prominent energy levels at low-frequencies, including subsonic signals. Therefore, all the recordings were high-pass filtered using the 12th-order Chebyshev Type I filter with a cut-off frequency of 200 Hz.

3.3 Feature Extraction

In this study, Mel-frequency cepstral coefficients (MFCCs) were selected as the acoustic features. MFCCs are known to be efficient descriptors of spectral envelopes [7]. Consequently, it was hypothesized that they could well account for peaks and dips in sound spectra caused by palm-to-palm or palm-to-fingers resonances. Pilot studies revealed that additional spectral features such as spectral flux or brightness [8], bring a negligibly small improvement to the performance of the model, hence, they were ignored.

MFCCs seem to be selected most commonly by researchers in the area of machine audition [7]. However, linear-frequency cepstral coefficients (LFCCs) could produce better classification results under circumstances whereby distinct spectral characteristics are distributed across higher frequencies [9]. Therefore, for comparative purposes, LFCCs were also included in the study.

For feature extraction purposes, a signal in each segment, representing an individual clap sound, was divided into m overlapping time frames. The length of each frame ranged from 128 to 1024 samples, depending on the strategy of feature extraction (see below). The overlap between the adjacent frames was set to 25% of a frame duration. A Hann window was applied to a signal in each frame. Subsequently, cepstral coefficients (MFCC and LFCC) were computed for signals in all consecutive time frames.

The three following strategies for cepstral coefficients extraction were considered. The first strategy, referred to as a Single-Frame (SF) extraction procedure, was inspired by the work of Şimşekli et al. [6] in the area of the automatic recognition of clapping hands configurations. In order to suppress the adverse influence of room reflections, for each clap sound, cepstral coefficients derived from only the maximum-energy time frame were retained (assuming that the maximum-energy time frame was the least affected by the reflections), while the coefficients extracted from the remaining time frames were omitted. In the second approach, signified as a Multi-Frame method with Aggregated Features (MF-AF), for each clap sound, the cepstral coefficients were "aggregated" across the time frames by calculating their mean values and standard deviations. In the third strategy, referred to as a Multi-Frame method with Concatenated Features (MF-CF), no aggregation was performed but the cepstral coefficients derived from all consecutive time frames were "concatenated."

The literature shows that in some applications delta features could enhance the performance of the classification algorithms [10]. Therefore, in addition to the original cepstral coefficients, their delta values were also included in the MF-AF and MF-CF methods (For the SF method the delta features were not estimated since they cannot be derived from a single frame). Similarly as before, for the MF-AF method, the delta features were aggregated over time, by calculating their means and standard deviations, whereas for the MF-CF method the delta features were concatenated.

In line with the studies of Jylhä and Erkut [5], for the SF method, the frame duration was set to 10 ms, being equivalent to 160 samples. The signal was zero-padded to 256 samples prior to undertaking a fast Fourier transform. For the remaining two methods, the frame length was "tuned" during the pilot tests. Separate simulations were undertaken using MFCC and LFCC coefficients, respectively. For the MF-AF method, the best results were obtained when the frame length was set to 1024 samples for MFCCs and 512 samples for LFCCs. In the case of the MF-CF method, for MFCCs and LFCCs the best results were achieved when the frame duration was adjusted to 512 and 256 samples, respectively. The above-quoted frame lengths refer to room-dependent test conditions (see the next section for the description of room-dependent and room-independent test methodologies). For the room-independent test scenario, the best results were obtained when the frame length was decreased to 128 samples for both the MF-AF and MF-CF methods. For the SF method, the frame length was kept intact.

The data (extracted features) were standardized prior to being fed to the input of the classification algorithm, described in more detail in the next section.

3.4 Machine Learning

In this study, the support vector machines (SVM) method was used as a single classification algorithm, due to its well-proven performance in the area of machine audition. Radial basis function (RBF) was selected, as yielding the best classification outcomes in the pilot tests.

As mentioned above, in contrast to the earlier studies [1, 3], six acoustical environments were considered in this work, allowing the authors to train and test the proposed method both under the room-dependent and room-independent conditions. In the former approach, the recordings from all the venues were included in the train and the test repositories, whereas in the latter strategy, the model was tested using the recordings acquired in the rooms which were not "seen" by the model during its training.

Under the room-dependent test scenario, 70% of data were allocated for training, whereas the remaining 30% of data were used for testing purposes. To validate the results statistically, the above data split was repeated randomly 10 times. For each repetition, the model was trained and tested separately, with the results reported below as mean values and associated standard deviations.

For the room-independent test conditions, nine data folds were considered, as illustrated in Table 2. The table shows how the audio recordings were divided between the train and test repositories, depending on the recording venue. For each data fold, a separate model was trained and tested, with the outcomes for all the models summarized with mean values and standard deviations.

Table 2. Data folds applied under the room-independent test conditions. See Table 1 for the description of the rooms.

Fold number	Recordings from the following rooms were used for training	Recordings from the following rooms were used for testing
1	2, 3, 5, 6	1, 4
2	2, 3, 4, 6	1, 5
3	2, 3, 4, 5	1, 6
4	1, 3, 5, 6	2, 4
5	1, 3, 4, 6	2, 5
6	1, 3, 4, 5	2, 6
7	1, 2, 5, 6	3, 4
8	1, 2, 4, 6	3, 5
9	1, 2, 4, 5	3, 6

The hyper-parameters of the classification algorithm were optimized with a grid-search technique performed using 10-fold cross-validation method. The following SVM hyper-parameter values were considered during the grid search procedure: $C \in \{0.1, 0.1, 1, 10, 100, 1000\}$ and $\gamma \in (1/n) \times \{0.01, 0.1, 1, 10, 100\}$, where n is the number of features used.

For the SF method, the number of features n was relatively small, being equal to only 40. In this case, the number of features was the same as the number of the cepstral coefficients extracted. For the MF-AF method, the number of features equaled 160. For the MF-CF method, the number of features n was much higher, ranging from 280 to 4040, depending on the frame length used during the feature extraction procedure. Due to a relatively large number of features, a feature selection procedure was applied to the last two methods (MF-AF and MF-CF). The employed procedure was based on the F-statistics derived from the analysis of variance (ANOVA). The number of selected features $n_s \in \{n, n/2, n/4\}$ was optimized during the same grid-search technique as before (along with the hyper-parameter values search).

The feature extraction technique and the SVM classification algorithm were implemented in the Python ecosystem using *NumPy* and *scikit-learn* libraries.

4 Results

4.1 Spectral Analysis

Examples of the average periodograms, estimated for selected five participants, are presented in Fig. 2. The periodograms are averaged across all the individual clap sounds recorded in room 1 and are presented separately for the three hands configurations. They are quantitatively similar to the average clap sound spectra obtained by Repp [1]. For example, for clap type 2, a prominent resonance below 1 kHz occurs, which could be attributed to a palm-to-palm resonance.

While some distinct spectral patterns could be identified for each clap type (e.g., the aforementioned resonance at low frequencies for clap type 2), potentially allowing for the automatic recognition of hands configuration such as in [5], it is difficult to establish any clear spectral differences between the participants. This observation indicates that the identification of humans based on their hand clapping sound spectra is not a trivial task.

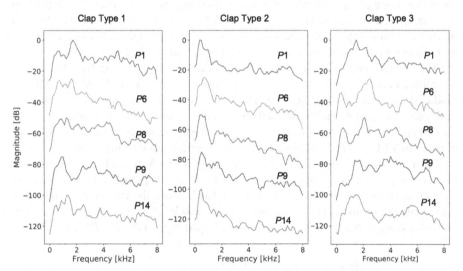

Fig. 2. Examples of average periodograms for three clap types recorded in room 1 for selected participants (*P*1, *P*6, *P*8, *P*9, and *P*14). For clarity each consecutive plot is offset by 25 dB.

4.2 Room-Dependent Versus Room-Independent Tests

The person identification results obtained for three hands configurations (clap types) under the room-dependent test conditions are presented in Fig. 3. The first method (SF) produced the worst results, with the mean identification accuracy levels ranging from 49% to 61%, regardless of the participants' hands arrangement during the recordings. Considerably better results were achieved using the second method (MF-AF), as it produced the mean accuracy values between 79% and 98%. The third method (MF-CF) exhibited the best performance, yielding the mean identification levels ranging from 97% to 99%.

While the SF and MF-CF methods produced similar results regardless of the type of the cepstral coefficients employed, incorporation of MFCCs instead of LFCCs yielded markedly better results for the MF-AF method. The differences were statistically significant at $p < 7 \times 10^{-10}$ level for all three clap types, according to a double-sided t-test. The benefit of using MFCCs instead of LFCCs was marginal for the MF-CF method. However, it proved to be statistically significant for clap types 1 and 2 ($p < 2.8 \times 10^{-3}$).

The obtained results depend on the participants' hands configuration. According to Fig. 3, the highest accuracy values were achieved for clap type 1 across all the methods. Even for the best performing method (MF-CF with MFCCs as features), the mean identification accuracy for clap type 1 was 0.9% greater than that for clap type 2. While the observed difference was small, it was statistically significant at $p < 1.4 \times 10^{-3}$ level.

Figure 4 illustrates the results obtained under the room-independent test conditions. The mean accuracy levels are considerably lower compared to those observed under the room-dependent test conditions, indicating that changes in room acoustics hinder the performance of the method. Nevertheless, the mean accuracy levels still exceed no information rate, which in this study equals 6.25% (an accuracy rate to be obtained by chance). Similarly to the results discussed above, all the methods tested under the room-independent conditions tended to produce the best results for clap type 1.

The MF-CF method outperformed all the other methods for clap type 1, yielding a maximum accuracy level of 61%. For clap types 2 and 3 both MF-AF and MF-CF produced similar results, ranging between 27% and 46%, with no statistically significant differences between them. The SF method proved to be the worst performing across the clap types. In contrast to the results discussed above, the incorporation of LFCCs, as opposed to MFCCs, appeared to produce better results across the methods.

Examples of confusion matrices are presented in Fig. 5. It can be seen that under the room-dependent test conditions the identity of all 16 participants was correctly recognized in almost all cases. On the other hand, under the room-independent test conditions, the performance of the model was considerably worse. In particular, the exemplified algorithm failed to correctly identify participants $P7$, $P8$, $P15$, and $P16$.

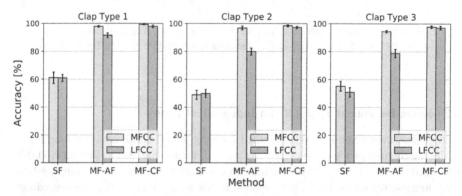

Fig. 3. Room-dependent person identification accuracy (mean values and standard deviations).

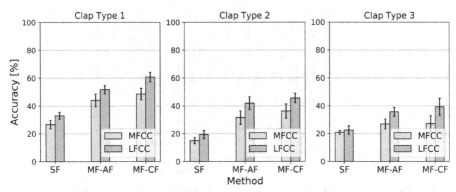

Fig. 4. Room-independent person identification accuracy (mean values and standard deviations).

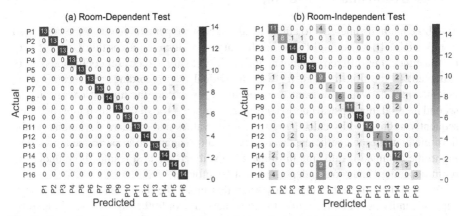

Fig. 5. Examples of confusion matrices for predicting the identity of 16 participants: (a) room-dependent test conditions, (b) room-independent test conditions.

4.3 Influence of the Number of Clap Sounds Used for Training

Figure 6 demonstrates an influence of the number of clap sounds used for training on the person identification accuracy. It can be seen that under the room-dependent conditions only a single clap sound used for training is sufficient to attain an identification accuracy exceeding 90%. If the total number of clap sounds available for training is increased to three or more, the accuracy of the model saturates at almost 99%.

An interesting phenomenon could be observed under the room-independent test conditions. The test accuracy value grows as the number of clap sounds used for training increases from 1 to 6, reaching a maximum level of approximately 60%. Further increase in the number of clap sounds causes a progressive deterioration of the model's performance. This effect is likely caused by the overfitting effect.

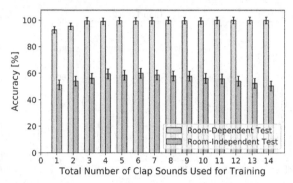

Fig. 6. Influence of the number of clap sounds used for training on the test identification accuracy (mean values and standard deviations).

5 Discussion and Conclusions

The three methods intended to automatically recognize person identity were compared in this study. They were all based on the same classification algorithm (support vector machines) but differed in the way the acoustic features (cepstral coefficients) were extracted. In the first method, for each individual clap recording, the cepstral coefficients were derived only from the time frame exhibiting the highest energy. In the second method, the cepstral coefficients were computed for all the time frames and subsequently aggregated by calculating their mean values and standard deviations. In the third method, all the coefficients were preserved (no aggregation performed). According to the obtained results, the third method exhibited the best results, both under the room-dependent and room-independent test conditions.

The results obtained in this study show that under the room-dependent conditions person identity could be recognized with an accuracy of 99%, based on hand clapping sounds. The technique proposed in this paper considerably outperformed the methods developed by Repp [1] and Jylhä et al. [3], who reported the identification accuracy levels of 91% and 64%, respectively. The above outcome indicates that hand clapping sound could be regarded as a useful biometric trait.

The reason for the exceptionally good performance of the proposed technique could be attributed to the fact that, in contrast to studies by Repp [1] and Jylhä et al. [3], in this work, participants' hands configurations were controlled, reducing the risk of confounding sound spectra by changes in hands arrangements. Out of the three hands configuration compared, the one in which the hands were aligned straight to each other was the most conducive in terms of the identification accuracy.

Testing the method under the room-independent conditions revealed that its performance is mediocre, reaching a maximum accuracy of 61%. This outcome indicates that the robustness of the method to changes in room acoustics still needs to be improved.

In contrast to a general trend in machine audition, favoring Mel-frequency cepstral coefficients as the acoustic features, this study shows that linear-frequency cepstral coefficients give better results when the method is tested under the room-independent conditions. This outcome could be explained by the work of Zhou et al. [9], who suggested that linear-frequency cepstral coefficients are better in estimating information at higher frequencies compared to their Mel-frequency constituents.

Future work regarding the automatic identification of humans based on their hand clapping sounds could involve the incorporation of deep learning techniques as well as including a broader range of acoustical conditions, to enhance the generalizability of the proposed method.

Acknowledgments. The work was supported by the grant from Białystok University of Technology (WZ/WI-IIT/4/2020) and funded with resources for research by the Ministry of Science and Higher Education in Poland.

References

1. Repp, B.H.: The sound of two hands clapping: an exploratory study. J. Acoust. Soc. Am. **81**(4), 1100–1109 (1987). https://doi.org/10.1121/1.394630
2. Choudhary, S.W., Naik, A.K.: Multimodal biometric authentication with secured templates – a review. In: Proceedings of the 3rd International Conference on Trends in Electronics and Informatics, Tirunelveli, India, pp. 1062–1069. IEEE (2019). https://doi.org/10.1109/ICOEI. 2019.8862563
3. Jylhä, A., Erkut, C., Şimşekli, U., Cemgil, A.T.: Sonic handprints: person identification with hand clapping sounds by a model-based method. In: Proceeding of the AES 45th International Conference, Helsinki, Finland, pp. 1–6. AES (2012)
4. Takai, M., Sako, Y., Terauchi, T.: User Identification Method, User Identification Device, Electronic Apparatus, and Electronic System. US Patent, US 2006/0067164 A1 (2006)
5. Jylhä, A., Erkut, C.: Inferring the hand configuration from hand clapping sounds. In: Proceedings of the 11th International Conference on Digital Audio Effects (DAFx-08), Espoo, Finland, pp. 1–4 (2008)
6. Şimşekli, U., Jylhä, A., Erkut, C., Cemgil, A.T.: Real-time recognition of percussive sounds by a model-based method. EURASIP J. Adv. Sig. Process. **2011**(1), 1–14 (2011)
7. Li, Q., et al.: MSP-MFCC: energy-efficient MFCC feature extraction method with mixed-signal processing architecture for wearable speech recognition applications. IEEE Access **8**, 48720–48730 (2020)
8. Peeters, G., Giordano, B., Susini, P., Misdariis, N., McAdams, S.: The timbre toolbox: extracting audio descriptors from musical signals. J. Acoust. Soc. Am. **130**, 2902–2916 (2011). https://doi.org/10.1121/1.3642604
9. Zhou, X., Garcia-Romero, D., Duraiswami, R., Espy-Wilson, C., Shamma, S.: Linear versus MEL frequency cepstral coefficients for speaker recognition. In: Proceedings of 2011 IEEE Workshop on Automatic Speech Recognition & Understanding, Waikoloa, HI, USA. IEEE (2012). https://doi.org/10.1109/ASRU.2011.6163888
10. Kim, Y., Roh, J., Cho, K., Cho, S.: How to aggregate acoustic delta features for deep speaker embeddings. In: Proceedings of 2020 International Conference on Information and Communication Technology Convergence (ICTC), Jeju, South Korea. IEEE (2020). https://doi.org/10.1109/ICTC49870.2020.9289205

Computer Information Systems and Security

Analyzing and Predicting Colombian Undergrads Performance on Saber-Pro Test: A Data Science Approach

Eugenia Arrieta Rodríguez[1]([✉])([iD]), Paula María Almonacid[2]([iD]),
Santiago Cortés[3], Rafael Deaguas[4], Nohora Diaz[5], and Maria Paula Aroca[6]

[1] Universidad del Sinú Cartagena Elias Bechara Zainum, Cartagena, Colombia
investigacionsistemas@unisinucartagena.edu.co
[2] Universidad EAFIT, Medellín, Colombia
fpalmona1@eafit.edu.co
[3] Universidad Antonio Narino, Bogotá, Colombia
santiago.cortes@uan.edu.co
[4] KNAUF, Bogotá, Colombia
Aguasr@knauf.com
[5] iFood, Bogotá, Colombia
nohora.diaz@ifood.com.co
[6] Data Science IU Bloomington, Bloomington, USA
http://www.unisinucartagena.edu.co,
https://www.eafit.edu.co/docentes-investigadores/Paginas/
paula-almonacid.aspx, https://www.uan.edu.co, http://www.knauf.com.co,
http://www.iFood.com.co, https://online-distance.ncsu.edu

Abstract. In this paper, we present an analytic tool solution for universities and the Colombian government, which allows them to identify the main factors that impact the performance of undergraduate students and also to predict the performance of the future cohorts of students. This solution consists of an interactive dashboard that visualizes two different types of analysis: in the first place, the descriptive statistics of variables related to the different entities implicated in the education process such as students, universities, and the state governments; and in the second place, the solution helps to visualize the results of different predictive models.

Keywords: Saber-Pro test · Spatial models · Machine learning

1 Introduction

[8] highlights that few governments have been able to simultaneously increase coverage and quality in education. Following evidence suggests that the rapid expansion of professional programs in Colombia deteriorated their quality [5].

Supported by ZettaNet Digital Transformation and Correlation One x.

© Springer Nature Switzerland AG 2021
K. Saeed and J. Dvorský (Eds.): CISIM 2021, LNCS 12883, pp. 81–99, 2021.
https://doi.org/10.1007/978-3-030-84340-3_7

This could be argumented, since the standard state exams, such as the Saber tests, allow an evaluation of the progress in the quality of education and permit documenting socioeconomic and spatial differentials [2, 3].

In Colombia, the Saber-Pro standardized test was developed to evaluate the quality of higher education. It assesses math, reading, citizenship, writing and English skills amongst undergraduates at every higher education institution. The scores of this test become publicly available each year, with the idea that institutions can identify vulnerable populations and adjust their education policies. But raw data alone is not enough for institutions to gain insights.

This problem is exacerbated for lower-income institutions that don't have the resources to hire teams to analyze these raw scores. Academic performance is a fundamental pillar for achieving the long-awaited educational quality. The Saber tests not only allow the evaluation of quality in education but also offer the possibility of adjusting educational policy in both public and private institutions.

Therefore, we built an interactive dashboard that allows universities and other institutions to easily explore which factors matter the most to student performance on the Saber-Pro. In addition, our application lets institutions visualize the results of predictive models to explore how changing some of these factors could affect scores in future exams. With our application, institutions will easily gain insights into which student populations would benefit from targeted interventions.

We also expect to contribute because we are linking the same students who took the standard state tests at the end of high school and undergraduate education.

Some studies mention the importance of reading comprehension and its impact on performance in the Saber Pro tests. The objective of this study was to correlate the total and reading comprehension scores in the Saber Pro tests (2011-I) versus the scores obtained in tests that evaluate working memory, verbal intelligence and general intelligence. This work shows that working and general intelligence can be used as estimators of performance in the Saber Pro tests. Another work in which the efficiency of education programs is evaluated shows the importance of environmental factors, suggesting that, although many educational institutions have a margin to improve their levels of efficiency, they could be restricted by the influence of environmental factors. Socioeconomic status of the students [7].

Moreover, we mention this work that applies the CRISP-DM data mining methodology for the construction of 3 analytical models to study the results obtained in the Saber-Pro tests of engineering students in Antioquia (Colombia). As a result of this work, it is indicated that the most relevant variables are: the number of dependents, teaching method, whether the home is permanent, the academic nature of the institution and economic facilities such as having a micro gas oven and a motorcycle [4].

Finally, mention is made of the work carried out in 2014 by researchers from the Universidad del Rosario, who propose a methodological model for the development of a scientific study within the School of Administration of the Universidad del Rosario that allows developing strategies for improvement in admission policies and pedagogical structuring of the Business Administration [6].

After a literature review and consultation with experts, Colombia seems to be the only country in the world where it is possible, making Colombia a leader in the area of education quality evaluation.

Additionally, the spatiality of the data is taking into account. According to [5] the fact of not considering it could lead to wrong conclusions of regression analysis, and specification problems emerge in the models when the spatial dependence is present in the data. By means of the SAR model, we explore the spatial dependence of the phenomena of study. After this brief introduction, we present the structure of the document: in the first place, we describe the different characteristics of the solution for each of the application panels. After that, we present the sources of information, then the process of data wrangling, finally, the architecture and the final thoughts and conclusions.

2 Materials and Methods

The steps followed to develop this research basically consisted of obtaining the necessary databases SaberPro and Saber11, as well as in the proper pre-processing of the data, the analysis of the relevant variables, and their modeling and prediction. For this, the standard analysis procedure was followed, dividing the database into a training part and a validation part and comparing the prediction precision metrics.

2.1 DataSet Construction

We explored three main public datasets, gathered from datos.gov.co [1]:

- Saber-Pro dataset: this is a student-level dataset of the higher education level students, with 986k+rows per year and 132 variables, which contain the student's test scores from 2016 to 2019, as well as a variety of variables related to socio-demographic.
- Saber11 dataset: this is a student-level dataset of high school education level students, with 91 variables containing student's test scores, as well as a variety of variables with socio-demographic, financial, academic and, geographic information for each student.
- Saber Pro Key database: this dataset contains observations that store key that allows us to merge the Saber 11 and Saber PRO databases for students that have taken both tests.
- Additional Data: we compile data regarding department-level and municipality-level sociodemographic and economic variables from the National Administrative Department of Colombia-DANE.

The process of data wrangling and cleaning could be summarized in the following steps: Dataset Appending, Dataset Merging, and Dataset cleaning (See Fig. 1).

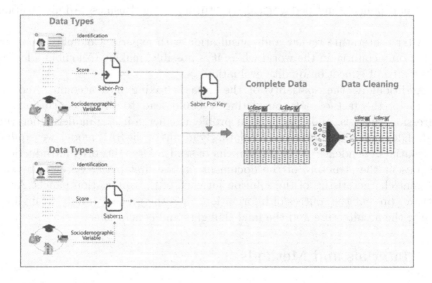

Fig. 1. Data wranglig and cleaning process

We decided to focus our solution on the Generic Test of Saber PRO. We found information available from 2006, and we decided to limit the analysis using data from 2016 to 2019. Four years of information are enough to see the trends and changes by analysis period (Show Table 1).

Table 1. Table captions should be placed above the tables.

Year	Rows	Columns
2016	242.629	99
2017	245.593	106
2018	237.112	106
2019	260.756	105

Additionally, we use the data that we called *Llave*, as is the data that can join the information of Saber 11 with Saber Pro. This Data contains information of the Student ID that presented the test from 2006 and has the following structure:

2.2   Dataset Appending

When we append the different years of information, we found some of the following processes fix:

Some years had the information in lowercase, not all. We decided to leave them in lowercase before appending the data. Some variables as the Student key, does not have the same name. We rename the ones necessary to have just one column for the Student Key. Because of the number of rows Saber 11, we decided to first merge the data with the key before appending it.

After Appending the four years of Saber PRO we got a dataset of 986.090 and 132 rows.

2.3   Dataset Merging

Using the data *Llave* was possible to merge Saber PRO and Saber 11 (Show Fig. 2). Having a final data of 1.045.290 rows as a same student can present different any of the two tests more than once. For example, this students gave the test more than 3 times:

```
EK201730077444    5
EK201830224318    4
EK201950226991    4
EK201630049777    4
EK201830102855    4
```

Fig. 2. Keys

If all the columns are included in the merge, it is obtained a dataset of 434 columns. That is why it was decided to continue with the exploratory data analysis adding just the variables considered important.

From the 1.045.290 rows related to Saber Pro, there are 414.701 of them with Saber 11. It means 40% of the data.

Some of the reasons why was not possible to obtain more information are:

- There was just possible to use the information from 2006. There could be students that present the Saber Pro exam from 2016 to 2019 and Saber 11 before 2006, that ones don't have the information available.
- Information from 2010 to 2012 in Saber 11 was not possible to merge with the data *Llave*. We contacted the owner of the data (ICFES) without getting any answer.

We will validate during future analysis that the data available is still enough to find some patterns that help us to suggest possible actions that the stakeholders interested in this project can do.

2.4 Dataset Cleaning

In this step, the data is cleaned before the analysis. The first thing we did was verify whether or not our variables contained null values.

Figure 3 below shows an example of academic variables with their number of null values for each of them. A large amount of missing values in some of them led us to removing most of the variables, since they were missing in over 80% of the test-takers. However, we made an effort to find other variables that approximated these. For example, we had a large number of missing values in *estu_prestigioinstitution*, *estu_instporcostomatricula* and *inst_porprestigio*. These are variables that measure the tuition level at the university and the university ranking. Thankfully we have a student-level variable that measures how much they pay for tuition, and that is correlated to the variables we had to remove. We followed a similar process for all variables in each of the variable categories.

estu_consecutivo_x	242629
mod_razona_cuantitat_punt	29
mod_lectura_critica_punt	29
mod_competen_ciudada_punt	29
mod_ingles_punt	105
mod_comuni_escrita_punt	11039
punt_global_x	242657
estu_nucleo_pregrado	0
inst_cod_institucion	28
inst_nombre_institucion	0
inst_caracter_academico	0
inst_origen	0
estu_razoninstituto	981752
estu_prestigioinstitucion	1017347
estu_instporprestigio	847988
estu_instporcostomatricula	847988
estu_instporunicaqueofrece	847988
estu_instporoportunidades	847988
estu_instporamigosestudiando	847988
estu_instporotrarazon	847988
estu_cole_termino	66832
cole_valor_pension	884439
cole_nombre_sede	687502
cole_calendario	687502
cole_genero	687502
cole_naturaleza	687502
cole_bilingue	687873
cole_jornada	687502
cole_caracter	687502

Fig. 3. Null values in academic variables

Additionally, we had to clean a large number of variables. For example, many of our categorical variables were duplicated because the values had accents, trailing spaces, numbers and other symbols. Misnamed and duplicate categories were identified and replaced by using string replacement operations. Show Fig. 4.

Finally, some of our categorical variables had large numbers of categories, so we created new variables where we renamed these into a smaller number of categories. For example, a variable identifying the undergrad major of the student with 58 categories, was re-grouped into a new "school" variable with 11 categories.

	estu_consecutivo_11	estu_consecutivo_PRO
0	SABER1120082416622	EK201210000523
1	SABER1120082072880	EK201210000528
2	SABER1120062195960	EK201210000532
3	SABER1120072075157	EK201210000533
4	SB11201020158376	EK201210000535

Fig. 4. Key Join

Even when the key has different structures per year, as it is seen in the registers 1 and 4, this data makes it possible to join the information available.

As the data *Llave* is available from 2006, We decided to use Saber 11 from 2006 to 2019. Each year has more than 400.000 rows and from 53 to 150 columns depending on the year. There are two different data sets per year, which is a total of 28 datasets for this period of analysis.

Finally, we handle missing values and exclude variables that did not aggregate value to our models and create new variables such as the age, the time Letter elapses between the year in which a high school student presented the Saber11 test and the year the student presented the Saber Pro test, and if the department where the student lives is the department where the student study or presented the test. It is essential to mention that we found a large proportion of missing values for the year 2016 in the Saber Pro data, therefore we decided to exclude from our sample of interest.

In this sense, we consolidated one database with the following clean and preprocessed CSV,

- Saber11
- Saber-Pro
- Basic Education Indicators
- State and city locations

3 Exploratory Data Analysis (EDA)

As we are dealing with a large amount of information about socioeconomic and academics aspects of Colombian undergraduate students (as well as their corresponding SABER, and SABER PRO, test results, and this for different years and from all Colombian regions), we distributed the different categories of variables between each of the members of the team. Each team member was responsible to break down the data into summarized CSV files according to its corresponding category; manipulate the data to create more subcategories from the existing columns; find the biggest players in the different subcategories. And find the main trends in the data. See Fig. 5.

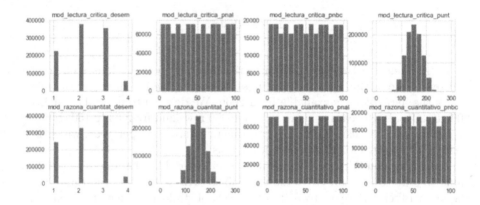

Fig. 5. Exploration features

4 Construction DashBoard

We propose an innovative application that allows different agents who participate in the education process to easily and quickly access various statistics related to students' performance, universities, academic programs, and departments (states). This information enables the analysis and prediction of variables of interest.

4.1 Architecture

Figure 6 presents the architecture of the proposed solution. Specifically, it shows the main elements used for the Front and Back-End, the application, and it's connections. Additionally, we named the technologies used hosted on AWS cloud.

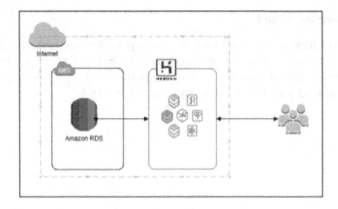

Fig. 6. The architecture of software

4.2 General Panel

In the initial panel, we find a suggestive and organized page that allows access to panel possibilities such as the panel related to the University, the panel related to geographic location, and a panel related to the models and predictions of results for the panel students. This panel also includes links to access to the GitHub and documentation of the Project. This application is open to the public to be complemented and improved in favor of developing the education sector in the country. See Fig. 7.

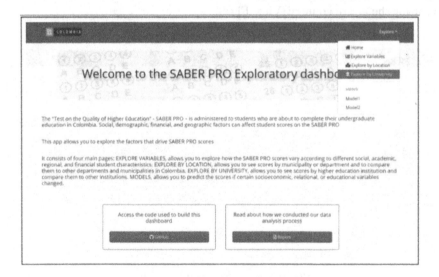

Fig. 7. General panel layout

4.3   University Panel

In the Universities panel, it is possible to compare student performance in the different competencies that are evaluated in the Saber Pro tests. Universities or academic programs can make such comparisons. All this is done through interactive graphics with interesting designs. View Fig. 8.

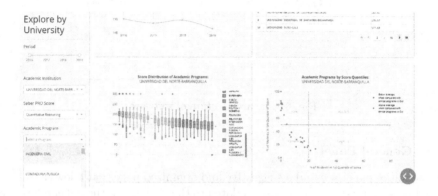

Fig. 8. University panel layout 1

These comparisons allow us to establish which universities and programs should include improvements in their academic processes. When identified, they could be the center for government aid and programs to improve the education sector for the entire country. View Fig. 9.

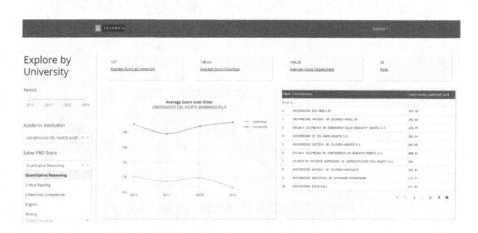

Fig. 9. University panel layout 2

4.4 Location Panel

Generating insights by location will allow that each state will be able to make their own decisions and to understand their context in order to improve their social and economic goals (Fig. 10).

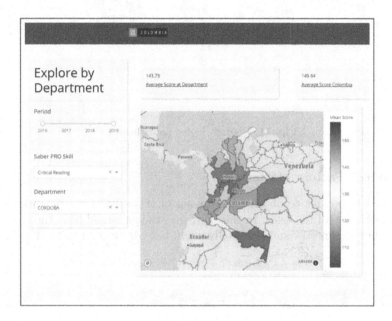

Fig. 10. Location panel layout

4.5 Predict Scores Panel

The objective of this panel is to provide students who aspire to take the Saber-Pro tests, the possibility of obtaining a prediction about their future test scores with precision which could vary in a range between 88.88% and 93.6%. For this, the student must complete the information required on the page, which has to do with the variables identified by the model as the main factors that determine student performance on the tests. Show Fig. 11.

Fig. 11. Predict Scores panel layout

4.6   Which Factors Matter

Students will be able to observe the impact of their characteristic variables on their score value of the tests. In this way, the student would have the chance to address her weaknesses and eventually could her education quality (Fig. 12).

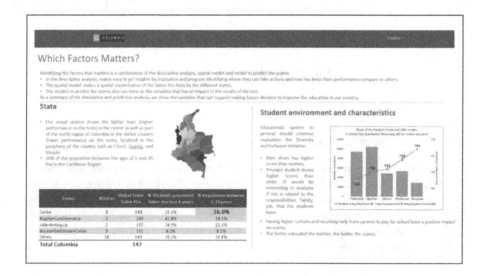

Fig. 12. Which factors matter panel layout, first part

5   Results

To attain the main factors that explain the undergrad's performance on the Saber-Pro tests, we employ different model approaches such as Linear Regression, Random Forest, XG Boosting, and spatial models.

We began exploring the most relevant variables that explain the student's academic performance with linear regression, a very simple approach for supervised learning. We found linear regression a useful tool for predicting our quantitative response variable, the test scores in the Saber-Pro tests, based on some important explaining variables. This model helped us as a tool for feature selection and as a first approximation to variable relationships. Our first objective is to identify evidence of an association between the students' test scores in the Saber-Pro and variables, in which the literature has not been conclusive, such as gender, the parent's education, the social strata, or the fee of tuition, which could be a proxy of the quality of the University.

According to our preliminary results, we found evidence of the association between the students test scores and, in order of importance, their scores on critical Reading (a positive relationship), the gender (men tend to have higher scores than women), the parents' education (the higher the level of education of the parents the higher the scores obtained by the students), the tuition fee of the University (the higher the tuition the higher the scores), the social strata (a positive relationship), and the socio-political region (the central region of the country, especially the capital, Bogotá tend to present higher students scores than the students from other regions of the country).

Concerning the spatial factors affecting the students' performance, we carry out a geospatial clustering analysis taking as units of the spatial analysis the departments of the country. Those are 32 areas in which the government is administrative and politically divided. We selected them as a unit of study because, in general terms, these are a good proxy of the slightly cultural and environmental differences that are present in Colombia.

This analysis aims to find similarities in groups or "clusters" in terms of spatial and non-spatial variables, specifically related to the educative level of the high school graduates. We are also interested in detecting spatial patrons regarding education levels in the country, allowing for beneficial externalities between departments. Among the spatial variables included in the geospatial clustering process are the latitude, longitude, and department shape. On the other hand, regarding the education variables, we analyze the number of the students, the student's results on Saber-Pro tests in the subjects of Quantitative thinking, English, Critical Reading, Citizenship competencies, and finally, the global scores.

Figure 13 we present some of the results of the spatial clusterization of the Saber-Pro tests by the different departments of the country. We represent the clusters by the different shades and colors. As the lighter colors reflect better results, it can easily identify the clusters of departments where the students' performance was better. Among these are the departments of the central region such as Cundinamarca, Antioquia, Santander, Valle del Cauca, Boyacá, Caldas,

Risaralda, and Armenia. After these departments, we can find the departments situated in the coastal region and the south of the country according to the level of performance. Finally, it is important to mention that the departments with deficient performance are Chocó, Vaupés, Guanía, Putumayo, Vichada y Guajira, which are departments located in the periphery region of the country. It is also worth highlighting that these patterns found coincided with the test results related to critical reading, quantitative reasoning, English, and citizenship skills.

Analyzing the results obtained through this geospatial clustering, the following can be concluded:

1) Colombia is divided into geographic regions with different levels of quality in education. 2) The central or Andean region and some departments of the Atlantic coast and the south of the country present a higher level of education quality. 3) The geographic areas of the country that present higher levels of education also show higher levels of development, economic growth, and presence of the state. 4) Through the spatial and educational structure identified thanks to spatial clustering, it is possible to locate neighboring regions for each department, which could result in beneficial externalities between departments. Considering that the activities carried out in a particular department may affect the decisions made in neighboring departments.

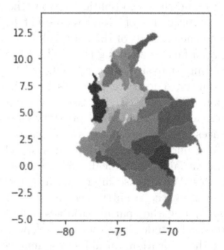

Fig. 13. Global score results of Saber-Pro test by departments. Similar colors represent the clusters of the departments. Lighter-colored clusters represent better scores in the overall results of Saber-Pro tests.

Visual inspection of the map pattern for the test results allows us to search for spatial structure. If the spatial distribution of the tests was random, then we should not see any clustering of similar values on the map. However, our visual system is drawn the lighter hues (higher performance on the tests). View Fig. 14.

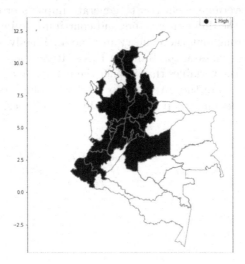

Fig. 14. Departments that perform above the average of the global score on the Saber-Pro tests

This visualization tool is not just reserved for the performance of the students on the tests. We can also visualize the distribution all over the country of other important education-related variables such as the rate of the approval, the rate of drop-out, the number of students, etc. Therefore, this type of tool allows central and state government entities to focus and prioritize their development plans towards the most disadvantaged departments and the departments that could most impact the development of their neighbors through externalities and reciprocities. See Fig. 15.

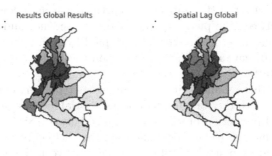

Fig. 15. Neighborhood or peer departments. A neighboring department can have direct and indirect effects on its neighbors or peers, impacting its development through various externalities and/or multiplier effects

In this sense, our solution contributes to effectively identify which department represents a neighbor or peer in terms of its similarity in the quality of education found and measured by the results of the Saber tests. In such a way, it is possible for government entities to generate impacts or externalities that positively influence the different clusters and contribute to improving the quality of education throughout the country in general. Finally, but not least, we present some of the results of the Random Forest Regression Model, in Fig. 16. According to these, the variables that impact the performance of the undergrads on the Saber-Pro test are those related to the background and the abilities of the individual on academic competencies, evaluated in Saber11 tests.

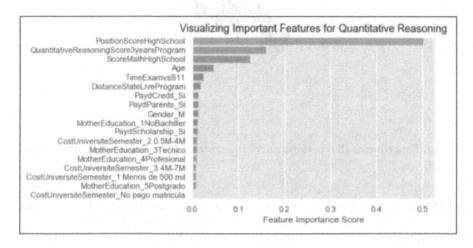

Fig. 16. Importance of the variables included in the Quantitative Reasoning Models

Other variables such as age, mother's education, the cost of the University, as a proxy for the quality of the education provided by this entity; the interval of time elapsed for a student between the presentation of the exam Saber 11 and Saber-Pro; the cluster of the states (or departments as are known in Colombia), the distance between the place of study and the residence and how the studies were paid (for instance, if the studies were paid by credit, by their parents, or by a scholarship), have a significant impact on the performance of students on the Saber-Pro tests.

On the other hand, it is important to highlight the great predictability of both the Random Forest and spatial models for our case. These models achieved prediction precision in a range between 88% and 93.6%. After tuning the parameters, using cross-validation that helped to reduce the chances of overfitting and keep similar and good results between the train and the test dataset.

To implement an additional validation procedure, we compare the results of the XGBM adn the Random Forest for each of the variables. By performing this process, we evaluated the performance of the model on the whole distribution of whole variables. In Fig. 17 can compare the behavior of actual observations versus the prediction score for quantitative reasoning tests results.

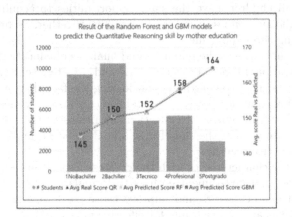

Fig. 17. Comparison of the performance of the two models, Random Forest Regression and Gradient Boosting Machine by mother education

Therefore students, universities, and government entities could get a very good idea of the future performance of potential higher education students if we maintain similar conditions. In the final solution, it has been included the results of the Spatial model and the Random Forest Regression Model results related to the Global score and the five skills evaluated (Fig. 18).

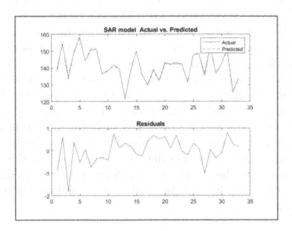

Fig. 18. This figure presents the prediction performance of the spatial model versus the real observations.

6   Conclusions

The objective of this research aims to contribute to the development of the strategy designed by the National Ministry to improve the quality of education In order that all children have the same opportunities to acquire knowledge, develop the skills and values necessary to live, live together, be productive and continue learning throughout life.

It is important to assess the potential and qualities of educational evaluation to improve educational processes at a general and private level to achieve beneficially goals. We expect to contribute considering the fact that our educational quality evaluation solution allows us to establish education, by means of holistic perspective of the phenomena of education, by means of the use of two tests (the standard state tests at the end of high school, Saber11, and undergraduate education, Saber-Pro, together).

Identifying the characteristics with the greatest impact on test results could serve universities and government entities to formulate policies that reinforce positive impact characteristics and improve those with negative impact. This tool would serve as an early warning for effective policy design.

The most relevant variables associated with the undergrads' performance on the Saber-Pro test are those related to the background and the abilities of the individual on academic skills, especially those related to quantitative reasoning. The other variables that have more impact on the students' performance on the Saber-Pro tests, according to our models are: age, mother's education, the cost of the University (as a proxy for the quality of the education provided by this entity), the interval of time elapsed for a student between the presentation of the exam Saber11 and sober-pro, the cluster of the state, the distance between the place of study and the residence, and finally the way in which students paid the studies (for instance, if the studies were paid by credit, by their parents, or by a scholarship).

Additionally, the spatiality of the data is taking into account. The fact of not considering it could lead to wrong conclusions of regression analysis, and specification problems. By the means of the SAR model we explore the spatial dependence of the phenomena under study. According to the results obtained by the spatial model, the quality of education in Colombia presents different levels according to geographic location. In general, the performance of higher education students measured by the Saber-Pro tests is superior in the central region and part of the north of the country. In contrast, the periphery regions present low levels of performance on average. On the other hand, the spatial model allows us to identify who would be the neighbors or peers whose development could impact through indirect effects to departments that need to reinforce the quality of their higher education.

References

1. Acceso a bases de datos y diccionarios - portal icfes. https://www.icfes.gov.co/investigadores-y-estudiantes-posgrado/acceso-a-bases-de-datos
2. Barrera Osorio, F., Maldonado, D., Rodríguez Orgales, C.: Calidad de la educación básica y media en colombia: diagnóstico y propuestas, Technical report, Universidad del Rosario (2012)
3. Camacho, A., Messina, J., Uribe Barrera, J.: The expansion of higher education in Colombia: bad students or bad programs? Documento CEDE (2017–13) (2017)
4. Carrascal, A.I.O., Giraldo, J.J.: Minería de datos educativos: Análisis del desempeño de estudiantes de ingeniería en las pruebas saber-pro. Revista Politécnica **15**(29), 128–140 (2019)
5. Castro-Ávila, M., Ruiz-Linares, J., Guzmán-Patiño, F.: Cruce de las pruebas nacionales saber 11 y saber pro en antioquia, colombia: una aproximación desde la regresión geográficamente ponderada (gwr). Revista Colombiana de Educación **74**, 63–79 (2018)
6. Garzón González, M.A., Vega Bonilla, S.: Modelo estadístico de correlación de resultados examen Saber 11 (ICFES) y Saber Pro (ECAES). Ph.D. thesis, Universidad del Rosario (2014)
7. Melo-Becerra, L.A., Ramos-Forero, J.E., Hernández-Santamaría, P.O.: La educación superior en colombia: situación actual y análisis de eficiencia. Revista Desarrollo y sociedad **78**, 59–111 (2017)
8. Saavedra, J.E.: Resource constraints and educational attainment in developing countries: Colombia 1945–2005. J. Dev. Econ. **99**(1), 80–91 (2012)

Development of Digital Competences of Elementary School Teachers with a Life-Long Learning Approach

Michał Czołombitko, Tomasz Grześ, Maciej Kopczyński,
Urszula Kużelewska$^{(\boxtimes)}$, Anna Lupińska-Dubicka, Dorota Mozyrska,
and Joanna Panasiuk

Faculty of Computer Science, Bialystok University of Technology, Wiejska 45a,
15-351 Bialystok, Poland
{u.kuzelewska,d.mozyrska}@pb.edu.pl

Abstract. The dynamic development of digital technology has an increasing influence on all areas of our lives. New technologies are also changing the face of education. Young people are particularly attracted to technological innovations. It is important that students consciously and constructively use the newest information technologies, which they should learn at school. The responsibility to take on new educational challenges lies with the teacher, who must have high digital competences and learn to act effectively in a rapidly changing reality. Between June 2017 and December 2019, more than 140 early-education school teachers were trained in the programming teaching course. Before 36-h training and after 30 h of lessons assessments among teachers based on pre- and post-questionnaires about digital competences were performed. The questionnaires were prepared accordingly to the Digital Competence Framework 2.0 (DigComp 2.0). Obtained results gave a picture of the effectiveness of developing the digital competences of the primary school teachers.

Keywords: Digital competences · ICT teaching · Early childhood education · Photon robot

1 Introduction

There are no doubts that we live in an information society. The Internet and digital technologies have become an integral part of everyday life in the 21st century. According to the European Commission [6,8] digital competence is a part of the eight key competences for lifelong learning. That is why digital competences are required as an indispensable condition for the quality of life of every citizen. They refer to the conscious and critical use of the entire spectrum of digital technologies enabling information acquisition, communication, digital content creation (including programming), safety (including cyber security competences) as well as problem solving in all aspects of life [8]. As the Eurydice

© Springer Nature Switzerland AG 2021
K. Saeed and J. Dvorský (Eds.): CISIM 2021, LNCS 12883, pp. 100–111, 2021.
https://doi.org/10.1007/978-3-030-84340-3_8

Report [5] points out, a national strategy on digital competence is available in almost all European countries.

High-level programming competencies are not easy to gain. Learning programming at a university is considered as the most difficult academic course [20]. Although there is no formal concept of the natural or acquired ability to learn programming easily [19], many researchers claim that starting to develop logical thinking and being familiar with basic programming concepts in early ages provide time enough for most of the people to get acquainted with advanced skills in adolescence. It means that the child taught problem solving skills in their early age has a great chance to become a highly skilled graduate in computer science. It may seem to not be difficult to fulfil these requirements and provide a good start to the programming future, however, according to Piaget's theory of cognitive development, the abstract, hypothetical thinking of children in primary school is immature and not developed enough. Thus, they are able to solve problems related to the real world only [21]. The solution can be to introduce an appropriate way for teaching programming - a cartoon-based program or toy-like tool that makes a lot of fun for the children and is associated with real world situations [11].

According to [7] promoting creativity, innovation, and digital competence through education in the early years of a child's life can benefit in later years, as it lays the foundation for further learning, enables a much higher level of knowledge and generally increases the child's ability to develop skills of creative and critical thinking. The effective and age-appropriate development of digital competences in early education can have important consequences for pedagogical assumptions, assessment, pedagogical resources, and the educational environment, as well as for reducing the differences in the level of digital competence.

Digital skills develop from a very young age by observing and mirroring parents and older siblings' behaviour [3]. However, decisions on the types of technology and the amount of time that is spent on learning of them should be taken with caution. As shown by research in the Nordic countries [3], schools can have a big impact on the acquisition of digital competences (including creative use), integrating digital technology as active learning tools.

The European Framework for the Digital Competence of Educators (DigCompEdu) published in 2017 describes the digital competences specific to the teaching profession [15]. It details 22 educator-specific digital competences organised in six different areas: (1) professional engagement, (2) digital resources, (3) teaching and learning, (4) assessment, (5) empowering learners, and (6) facilitating learners' digital competence. Areas 1–5 explain the teachers' digital pedagogical competences, i.e., those digital competences they need to apply effective, inclusive, and innovative teaching and learning strategies.

The main goal of this paper is to summarize the project "Programming from scratch – development of digital competences among teachers and students of grades 1–3 of the bialostocki and sokolski counties" – project implemented thanks to the European Union structural fund from the Digital Poland Operational Program 2014–2020, Measure 3.2 "Innovative solutions for digital activation". The project methodology, among others, assumed that teachers conduct the classes using given set of scenarios. Those scenarios, through teaching programming, made it possible to improve the other elements of digital competences listed in [8], such as supporting communication and collaboration, the use of different devices and software, the awareness of the legal and ethical principles, the ability to manage and protect information, data, and digital identities.

This paper is structured as follows. Section 2 provides an overview of related research. Section 3 contains a detailed description of the project. Section 4 explains the methodology, while Sect. 5 presents the analysis of the achieved results. Section 6 concludes the paper and gives some ideas for future research.

2   Related Work

In [2] the Lego Mindstorms EV3 robotics education kit was used as a programming teaching tool. The experiment lasted 10 days and a small group of children of ages 7 to 13 took part in it. Their competencies in logical problem solving were assessed before and after the experiment, which was done by evaluation their performance in a particular computer game: how many levels and how quickly they could be able to pass them. Then, the following skills were assessed, among others: computational thinking, handling complexity, project management, and team work. After the experiment, all children, despite one child, have improved their skills. For the half group, the progress was three levels.

The other study [16] examined the impact of robotics and programming through a visual programming language on understanding of the elements of logic and mathematics. The authors followed [12] and the constructionist theory of learning, stating strengthen this process by the engagement of students in the creation of meaningful artifacts that can be probed and shared. On the contrary to the common passive model of learning, in which the participants observe and listen most of the time, the use of specific tools such as robotics and computers activates learners and supports building knowledge [13]. The article presents the results of the experiments on 90 6-th grade pupils with the mBot robot. The group was divided into an experimental and a control group with, respectively, the active (with the robots) and the passive (traditional) learning model. Selected criteria related to science and mathematics from the Spanish educational curriculum for the 6-th grade were assessed. According to the results, there were statistically significant improvements in the mathematics curriculum area with the integration of programming and robotics, however, there were no improvements in sciences. Particularly, a positive impact had robot programming, working with sequences and conditionals.

The goal of the research in [9] was improvement of the coding abilities through Scratch activities. The 559 teachers were particularly focused on increasing either their or their students' competences in computational thinking, that is, an activity that promotes the application of logical, structured, and modular solutions to various problems. The level of difficulty of programs was gradually rising to achieve skills like abstraction, decomposition, and recursion.

3   Project Description

The main aim of the project was to support the development of competences in teaching programming basics and to create conditions for introducing programming to primary school students aged 6–10.

3.1   Basic Information

Research was performed in the suburban areas of Bialystok and Sokolka, where more than 140 teachers of primary schools took part in the study. This goal was achieved through training in programming techniques for teachers of public schools, employees of public libraries, and cultural institutions. The main result contributed to increasing the e-activation of peoples' basic digital competences and the development of digital competences. In addition, teachers were supported with the necessary teaching aids in the form of lesson scenarios and required tools, including mobile devices, educational robots, and educational mats.

3.2   Project Details

The main goal of the project was to introduce teaching programming in the form of extra-curricular activities, and in the longer term as a part of integrated education to the primary schools in rural and suburban municipalities of the bialostocki and sokolski counties. The detailed objectives were focused on delivering equipment with the skills necessary for teaching programming for early school education, teachers and other employees of a locally competent public teacher training facility, employees of public libraries, or employees of public culture centers. Another important task was related to providing teachers the necessary equipment, creating conditions (also in terms of raising awareness for school management) to continue teaching programming, also after the end of the project. In modern society, there is a great need to teach children problem solving skills from an early age. Pointing out solutions, as well as allowing critical thinking and the use of modern technology have great importance, especially at the time when information and communication technologies are used from early ages. Programming teaches many skills that are crucial in today's world, focusing on analyzing information, using knowledge in practice, creativity, independent approach to find solutions, and improve teamwork. By developing programming skills, children learn to understand the world around them. As a part of the classes, they learn programming in an intuitive way using Scratch Junior, Scratch, AppInventor as mobile and desktop applications, with a strong focus on programming of the Photon educational robot. Conducting training among early school education teachers and other people in the educational process enables them to be involved in the programming teaching process conducted for young children.

Authors achieved the planned objectives by implementing the following tasks:

1. Recruitment of project participants focusing on teachers.
2. Conducting an initial analysis of the digital competences of the project participants and determining how to conduct the classes.
3. Purchase the necessary equipment, i.e. mobile devices like tablets and robots and other teaching aids, i.e. educational mats.
4. Organization of specialized training activities.
5. Conducting the first stage of training for teachers and other adults in selected schools.
6. Recruiting children for additional classes with teachers.
7. Developing preliminary balance of competences of children in cooperation with teachers.
8. Preparation of the second stage of teacher training schedule including practical classes with students.
9. Conducting the second stage of training ensuring personal and remote participation of the trainer. This stage included computers available in schools, purchased mobile devices, educational robots and educational mats.
10. Conducting one classes for students outside the place of training,
11. Conducting a final competences assessment of teachers and students.
12. Summarizing of training results.

One of the main tasks was creating a blog providing substantive support and a forum for the exchange of information in the field of teaching programming and opinion for everyone involved in the project. The above tasks were carried out in cooperation between coordinators, principals, and trainers. At the same time, information and promotion activities were carried out.

As a final result of the project, teachers received the tools and knowledge necessary to conduct classes, thanks to which children developed their skills related to operating a computer, mobile devices, and educational robots. Teachers were equipped with tools and teaching materials including lesson scenarios, that were previously inaccessible to them. Substantive support did not end with the end of the training, as the project provides a forum for the exchange of knowledge and experience for project participants. The content of this forum is being developed by them. The aforementioned training was not only to provide teachers with knowledge how to conduct classes, but also to encourage further searching for modern solutions in the field of teaching programming in the future. Information on the objectives of the project and the importance of achievable results are addressed to a wide range of schools management, teachers, and parents. This allows to show the importance of children future development in the form of learning, algorithmic thinking, reasoning, problem solving, and using digital equipment (including computers and mobile devices). Big scale of the local project, both in the context of the number of participants and geographical dispersion in the bialostocki and sokolski counties, assumed that the direct effect of the project was the creation of conditions for the introduction of teaching programming in public primary schools.

4   Methodology

Methodology of the project assumed that teachers conduct the classes using the developed set of scenarios focusing on educational matt from Masters of Coding [10], Photon robot [14], Scratch application [17], AppInventor application [1] and ScratchJr application [18]. Authors prepared:

- 6 scenarios for educational matt from Masters of Coding,
- 11 scenarios for Photon robot,
- 8 scenarios for Scratch application,
- 4 scenarios for AppInventor application,
- 6 scenarios for ScratchJr application.

All teachers involved in the project had personal training regarding all mentioned tools and scenarios during the group weekend sessions, where each session was devoted to a different subject. The number of training hours was equal to the number of scenario topics for each main subject. The next step was the teachers' personal involvement in the project, where each of them had to perform 30 h of classes with their group of children, averaging from 10 to 28 kids. Each teacher had a personal trainer supporting her/him for 10 class hours. At the beginning, teachers had to perform a questionnaire with the children focusing on crucial questions related to their programming knowledge. They had to do the same task at the end of the process.

4.1   Pre- and Post-questionnaire Details

One of the obligatory conditions of this project was to prepare and conduce pre- and post-questionnaires among teachers about digital competences. The questionnaires were prepared accordingly to the framework known across Europe as the Digital Competence Framework 2.0 (DigComp 2.0) [4] identifying 6 areas of key components of digital competence: (1) professional engagement, (2) digital resources, (3) teaching and learning, (4) assessment, (5)empowering learners, and (6) facilitating learners' digital competence. Areas 1–5 relate to teachers' digital pedagogical competences, that is, those they need to apply effective, inclusive, and innovative teaching, and learning strategies, while the sixth area is connected to teaching how to use digital technologies in a creative and responsible way for information search, communication, creating content, and problem solving. For every question, teachers rate a level of their knowledge and skills on a scale of 0–7 (0 – very low, 7 – very advanced).

5   Results Analysis

In the beginning and in the end of the proposed course, the level of competence were different among teachers. One of the main goals of the project was to raise all digital competences in each of the five groups, and at a general level. To compare a complex/general level the box-plot was used, see Fig. 1.

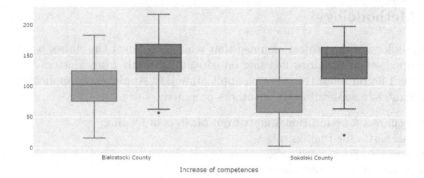

Fig. 1. Box-plots comparing initial (whiter) and final (darker) competences in bialostocki and sokolski counties.

In Fig. 1 the whiter boxes represent the values of the sum of competences in the beginning and the darker boxes are for the competences after course. It is seen that in bialostocki county medians and both quartiles are higher than in sokolski county. However, it is observed that final competences (darker boxes) are similar in both counties for teachers who took part in the project. Hence, it can be summarized that the goal was reached independently on the beginning level of the general set of competences. From box-plots it is seen that the group of teachers in the course was uniform (no outstanding points in the graph).

As the set of competences is divided into five groups, it is worth checking whether there is any correlation in raising competence in different groups. To observe the correlations between the levels of competence between groups of competences, the rise index of competence in each of a group and a county was used.

$$\Delta_i^k = Cf_i^k - Cb_i^k, \qquad (1)$$

where $k \in \{bialostocki, sokolski, together\}$, i is the number of a group of competences Cb_i^k-the level of competences in i-th group in the beginning and Cf_i^k - the level of competences in i-th group after course. Calculating vectors Δ^k, there were measured if there is a significant correlation between groups in the raising of competence.

Values of correlation coefficients between rise indices in groups of digital competences among the teachers are presented in Table 1 – bialostocki county, and in Table 2 – sokolski county. Both regions are taken under consideration in Table 3. It can be observed that all coefficients are greater than 0.5. In Table 1 for bialostocki county, there also can be observed lower values of correlation coefficients than those in Table 2 for sokolski county, which could mean that the competences among teachers involved in the project from bialostocki county are more scattered and in post-questionnaires they showed learning in different directions. In all Tables 1–3 it is seen that the highest correlation was diagnosed between the information and communication group. Moreover, all coefficients are positive. The latter is important to be stressed and means that the rising of any of the group competences causes a rising of the other level. From Table 3 a statistical significant test for correlation coefficients can be calculated, treating the teachers of the project as a probe from Podlaskie Voivodeship and all values then are significant.

Table 1. Correlation coefficients between results of rise indices: $\Delta_k^{bialostocki}$ in groups of digital competences among teachers in bialostocki county (based on results of 98 teachers).

	Information	Communication	Content creation	Security	Troubleshooting
Information	1	**0.8293**	0.6697	**0.4642**	0.5803
Communication		1	0.6685	0.4998	0.6195
Content creation			1	0.7288	0.7309
Security				1	0.7733
Troubleshooting					1

Table 2. Correlation coefficients between results of rise indices: $\Delta_k^{sokolski}$ in groups of digital competences among teachers in sokolski county (based on results of 42 teachers).

	Information	Communication	Content creation	Security	Troubleshooting
Information	1	**0.8705**	0.8047	0.765	**0.6428**
Communication		1	0.855	0.7976	0.7753
Content creation			1	0.8652	0.804
Security				1	0.8069
Troubleshooting					1

To observe the levels of raising different competences, a raising the ratio of competences was used

$$p_i^k\% = \frac{\Delta_i^k}{Cb_i^k} * 100\%, \tag{2}$$

where $k \in \{bialostocki, sokolski, together\}$, i is the number of a group of competences Cb_i^k-the level of competences in i-th group in the beginning and Cf_i^k - the level of competences in i-th group after course.

The raising ratio vectors were used to create again box-plots for different counties: bialostocki county - Fig. 2, sokolski county - Fig. 3, both counties together - Fig. 4. It is seen that in all figures the median remains at a similar level about $p\% = 50\%$, the third quartile for teachers from both counties is slightly less than 100% for competences such like: information, communication, security and troubleshooting. For content creation competencies, at least 75% teachers

Table 3. Correlation coefficients between results of rise indices in groups of digital competences among teachers - generally in both counties (based on results of 140 teachers).

	Information	Communication	Content creation	Security	Troubleshooting
Information	1	**0.8497**	0.7345	**0.6086**	0.623
Communication		1	0.7565	0.6336	0.6955
Content creation			1	0.7891	0.7667
Security				1	0.7927
Troubleshooting					1

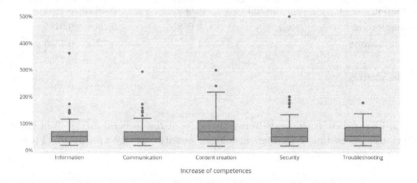

Fig. 2. Raising ratio of competences: $p_i^{bialostoki}$ in bialostocki county (based on results for 98 teachers).

from the project raise those skills to more that at least 100%. It is worth observing also, that there are results much more higher than the other, hence teachers who raise their competence to about 500%.

One might suspect that in the beginning teachers could have claimed themselves to have lower knowledge that they really had. All results from Fig. 1–4 underline that teachers in the project independently on the county raise their competence in each group.

There was an introduced one-way ANOVA test to check whether the raising ratio is depending on the region of teachers. The null hypothesis is stated that the difference between means of raising ratios is zero in a population of teachers in two regions: bialostocki and sokolski counties. In Table 4 there are raising rations $p_i^k\%$ of competences in counties bialostocki and sokolski used for one-way ANOVA test.

The critical significance coefficient for the test is equal $p_{value} = 0.151434$. It means that there is no base to reject the null hypothesis. And it can be claimed that if the same program of the course was applied among all teachers in both regions: bialostocki and sokolski counties, there would be no difference in raising digital competences accordingly to the questionnaires that were examined.

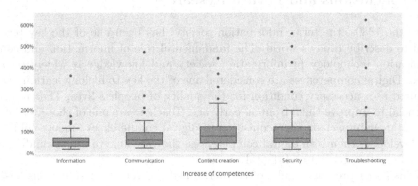

Fig. 3. Raising ratio of competences: $p_i^{sokolski}$ in bialostocki county (based on results for 42 teachers)

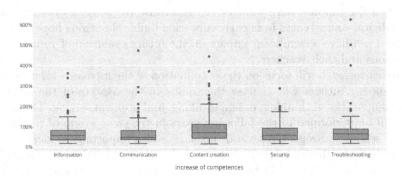

Fig. 4. Raising ratio of competences: $p_i^{together}$ in bialostocki county (based on results for 140 teachers)

Table 4. Raising rations $p_i^k\%$ of competences in counties bialostocki and sokolski.

Raising rations	Bialostocki county	Sokolski county
[0%; 20%]	28	6
(20% − 40%]	36	14
(40% − 60%]	21	11
(60% − 80%]	6	3
(80% − 100%]	4	3
more than 100%	3	5
	98	42

6   Conclusions and Future Research

Since the 1980s, the term 'information society' has been one of the key terms used to describe today's world. The fundamental role of information and communication technology in information society and knowledge is widely recognized. Digital competences are considered one of the key to lifelong learning and required as a necessary condition for the quality of people's lives. Therefore, it is crucial to improve them from an early age. Teachers are one of those who can have a great impact on the acquisition of digital competences among children. By developing their own digital competences, they are able to direct children to the safe and creative use of digital resources.

This paper presents results of the performed project. All assumptions based on the project were met. All teachers and all pupils, that took part in project, showed that their digital competences have increased. To be more precise, the distance of the school from the city of Bialystok was important. A level of competences was higher in the case of all schools from bialostocki county in comparison to the schools from sokolski county. Additionally, the increase was more significant when the children were younger. To generalise the project's results, introducing digital competences from early education builds the strong hope, that the outcomes will have a significant impact on the future evolution of young digital generations and their teachers.

Further research will focus on the examination of the increase of the children competences. Authors will analyse their skills in the aspects of the following fields: computational thinking, design thinking, and problem solving. The assessment will be performed in the following years in the same group of children in primary school and repeated several times. It is also important to identify connections between these aspects and the tools or resources used for teaching. The examination in this field will be performed twofold. Several teachers will continue using the programming tools in education. Some of them will focus only on web environment programming (Scratch, AppInventor) and others will use only the robot - Photon. Due to the rising age of the pupils, either Scratch Junior or the matt is not going to be used. Then the competences, mentioned above will be assessed at the end of the school. The other approach for the identification of the relation between the resource and skills improvement is to examine the most favourite tool of the particular child during the described project and then in the following years, its influence on his/her further education.

Other research activity is to extend the analysis to students from secondary schools. One of the projects the authors were involved in was directed to older pupils. It included programming in a web environment (AppInventor), programming the bash shell scripts (on the Raspberry Pi device), and mathematical quests. The results will be evaluated and described in further publications.

Acknowledgments. The work was supported by the grant WZ/WI-IIT/2/2020 from Bialystok University of Technology and funded with resources for research by the Ministry of Science and Higher Education in Poland.

References

1. App Inventor. https://appinventor.mit.edu/. Accessed 30 Mar 2020
2. Chaudhary, V., Agrawal, V., Sureka, P., Sureka, A.: An experience report on teaching programming and computational thinking to elementary level children using Lego robotics education kit, pp. 38–41 (2016)
3. Chaudron, S., DiGioia, R., Gemo, M.: Young children (0–8) and digital technology. a qualitative study across Europe (2017). https://ec.europa.eu/jrc/en/publication/eur-scientific-and-technical-research-reports/young-children-0-8-and-digital-technology-qualitative-study-across-europe. Accessed 30 Mar 2020
4. DigComp: The digital competence framework 2.0. https://ec.europa.eu/jrc/en/digcomp/digital-competence-framework. Accessed 30 Mar 2020
5. EACEA/Eurydice: Key Data on Education in Europe 2012 (2012). https://eurydice.org.pl/publikacja/the-system-of-education-in-poland-2018/. Accessed 30 Mar 2020
6. European Commission: European Council Recommendation of the European Parliament and the Council of 18 December 2006 on Key Competencies for Lifelong Learning (2006). Accessed 30 Mar 2020
7. European Commission: Council conclusions on the role of early childhood education and primary education in fostering creativity, innovation and digital competence (2015). Accessed 30 Mar 2020
8. European Commission: Council Recommendation of 22 May 2018 on key competences for lifelong learning (2018). Accessed 30 Mar 2020
9. Lazarinis, F., Karachristos, C.V., Stavropoulos, E.C., Verykios, V.S.: A blended learning course for playfully teaching programming concepts to school teachers. Education and Information Technologies 24(2), 1237–1249 (2019)
10. Masters of Coding (2015). https://mistrzowiekodowania.samsung.pl/ (in polish). Accessed 30 Mar 2020
11. Meluso, A., Zheng, M., Spires, H., Lester, J.: Enhancing 5th graders' science content knowledge and self-efficacy through game-based learning. Comput. Educ. **59**, 497–504 (2012)
12. Papert, S.: Mindstorms: Children, Computers, and Powerful Ideas. Basic Books, New York (1980)
13. Parmaxi, A., Zaphiris, P.: The evolvement of constructionism: an overview of the literature. In: Learning and Collaboration Technologies. Designing and Developing Novel Learning Experiences, pp. 452–461. Springer International Publishing (2014)
14. Photon. https://photonrobot.com/. Accessed 30 Mar 2020
15. Redecker, C.: European Framework for the Digital Competence of Educators: DigCompEdu (2017). https://doi.org/10.2760/159770
16. Sáez-López, J.M., Sevillano-García, M.L., Vazquez-Cano, E.: The effect of programming on primary school students' mathematical and scientific understanding: educational use of mbot. Education Tech. Research Dev. **67**, 1405–1425 (2019)
17. Scratch. https://scratch.mit.edu/. Accessed 30 Mar 2020
18. Scratch Junior. https://www.scratchjr.org/. Accessed 30 Mar 2020
19. Wadsworth, B.J.: Piaget's Theory of Cognitive and Affective Development: Foundations of Constructivism. Pearson (2004)
20. Yadin, A.: Reducing the dropout rate in an introductory programming course. ACM Inroads 2 (2011)
21. Zaharija, G., Mladenovic, S., Boljat, I.: Introducing basic programming concepts to elementary school children. Procedia Soc. Behav. Sci. **106**, 1576–1584 (2013). https://doi.org/10.1016/j.sbspro.2013.12.178

Design of Web Application with Dynamic Generation of Forms for Group Decision-Making

Zornitsa Dimitrova[1] , Daniela Borissova[1,2](✉) , and Vasil Dimitrov[1]

[1] Institute of Information and Communication Technologies, Bulgarian Academy of Sciences, 1113 Sofia, Bulgaria
{zornitsa.dimitrova,daniela.borissova,
vasil.dimitrov}@iict.bas.bg
[2] University of Library Studies and Information Technologies, 1784 Sofia, Bulgaria

Abstract. The primary role of software engineering is to apply engineering approaches to improve the processes and methods for software development. There are various different custom applications that could be generalized as a common application' tool. These applications are related to the problems of different group decision-making variants. In order to improve the software quality, modular architecture could be used to separate different functionality and to minimize the complexity of each individual module. For the goal, the current article deals with the problem of the dynamic generation of matrices that is the core of group decision-making. An algorithm for designing a web application to support group decision-making based on multi-attribute utility theory is proposed. This algorithm is implemented in a web-based software tool to support group decision-making. The main features of the described tool to support group-decision making are the ability to generate individual matrices for each expert and subsequent generation of aggregated group-decision matrix. These two types of matrices together with the completed data are stored as two components of the problem to be solved and can be reused. The proposed algorithm and software tool are applied in a case study for a group decision-making problem for the selection of videoconferencing software tool. The obtained results show the applicability of the dynamic generation of forms that support group decision-making.

Keywords: Dynamic generation of forms · Group decision-making · Software architecture · Software engineering · Web application

1 Introduction

The successful software systems are subject to constant change, as they must be constantly improved and adapted to ever-changing requirements. The primary goal of software engineering is to improve software quality and productivity (Wagner and Deissenboeck 2019). A possible way to avoid a major redesign of software is using software modularity. Using the modular software architecture allow separating different functionality into different units (Mustakerov and Borissova 2013). The goal of modular

K. Saeed and J. Dvorský (Eds.): CISIM 2021, LNCS 12883, pp. 112–123, 2021.
https://doi.org/10.1007/978-3-030-84340-3_9

design is to simultaneously minimize the complexity of each module and minimize the complexity of the overall system. Practically, each module should be as easy as possible to design, implement, test, deploy, upgrade and maintain. This makes it possible for the interfaces to be easily extensible with new functionalities (Mustakerov and Borissova 2017). In designing a complex software application, it is challenging to realize modularization and to create less coupled architectures using design patterns (Corral 2019). It should be noted the possibility to extend the functionality in SCADA systems could be done by using the novel architecture of the script component to incorporate the scripting language support (Anwar and Azam 2014). Some of the users prefer to be able to access applications any time using their smartphone. This determines the need for developing applications compatible with android service and related widgets (Tomov et al. 2019). One of the primary goals of software engineering is to improve processes and methods for software development. In this regard, an integrated framework able to guide software engineers in addressing sustainability concerns in software development processes is proposed (Saputri and Lee 2021). A systematic literature review of intelligent software engineering in the context of agile software development could be found in (Perkusich et al. 2020).

The main problem, the companies are currently facing is to motivate developers to develop robust and scalable applications by using the latest trends in software engineering. This corresponds with the authors' efforts related to developing a multi-objective robust possibilistic model for technology portfolio optimization (Shaverdi et al. 2020), multi-objective fuzzy robust optimization for designing sustainable and reliable power systems (Tsao and Thanh 2020), a framework of business intelligence system for decision making in efficiency management (Borissova et al. 2020a), etc. These scalable applications rely on the development of suitable models that in most cases are based on group decision-making (GDM). For example, group decision-making for distance collaboration software tools (Borissova et al. 2020b), group decision-making model for a selection of green building project (Borissova 2020), or personnel selections (Borissova 2018), or large-scale group decision making in a social network (Lu et al. 2021). In addition, when designing custom information systems some enterprise perspectives need to be considered too (Shishkov et al. 2020). It is worth mentioning that proper methods need to be used to increase the security of such web-based information systems (Trifonov et al. 2018).

The GDM is motivated by more and more complicated and complex problems that managers should cope with day by day. Such complex decisions require to involve many experts with different expertise. This will contribute to the credibility of the group decision-making considering different points of view. The GDM makes it possible to reduce to some degree the subjectivism considering multiple points of view toward the investigated domain area. A proved approach that is able to assist DM to make a reasonable and responsible choice among alternatives is the multi-attribute utility theory (MAUT) (Keeney and Raiffa 1993). It is based on different utility function to aggregate individual preferences of DMs into final preferable group decision (Triantaphyllou 2000). The most commonly used form of the utility function is the additive or multiplicative form (Triantaphyllou et al. 1998). Due to its simplicity, this multiple attribute decision-making technique has been used for different decision-making problems (Alinezhad and Khalili 2019).

In the current article, an approach based on MAUT is used to develop a web application for a dynamic generation of forms that support the group decision-making process. For the goal an algorithm for the sequence of requirements needed to realize the functionality of an application for dynamic forms generation is proposed. This algorithm is realized in three-layer software architecture. The numerically testing is done in a case study for a multi-criteria group decision-making problem for the selection of video conferencing software tool.

The rest of the article is organized as follows: Sect. 2 contains a description of the problem including the formulation of a utility function, Sect. 3 describes the proposed algorithm for designing a web application to support group decision-making, Sect. 4 present the software architecture of the developed application and provide some screenshots from the numerical testing including discussion of obtained results, and conclusions are given in Sect. 5.

2 Problem Description

The problem of group decision-making investigated in the current article could be represented by the following generalized matrix adapted from (Mustakerov and Borissova 2014).

Table 1. Generalized group decision matrix

Group of DMs	Weights for DMs expertize	Alternatives	Criteria, weights and evaluations		
			C_1	.....	C_n
DM^1	λ^1		w_1^1		w_n^1
		A_1	e_{11}^1		e_{1n}^1
		.....			
		A_m	e_{1m}^1		e_{nm}^1
....					
DM^k	λ^k		w_1^k		w_n^k
		A_1	e_{11}^k		e_{1n}^1
		.....			
		A_m	e_{1m}^k		e_{nm}^k

This matrix contains 3 basic vectors that express: 1) set of DMs $\{DM^k\}$ and corresponding weighted coefficients for each DM that express the importance of each DM in respect to the particular problem $\{\lambda^k\}$, 2) set of alternatives $\{A_m\}$, and 3) set of criteria $\{C_n\}$. The set of criteria are to be assessed by a DM using corresponding coefficients for their importance by $\{w_n^k\}$. The evaluations of alternative toward criteria are denoted by $\{e_{nm}^k\}$. These input data are used in the following utility function that determines the most preferable alternative incorporating the individual DMs' preferences:

$$A^* = max\left\{\left(\sum_{k=1}^{K} \lambda^k \sum_{j=1}^{J} w_j^k e_j^k\right), \forall m = 1, 2, \ldots M\right\} \tag{1}$$

where $\sum_{k=1}^{K} \lambda^k$ represents the weighted coefficients for DMs importance when aggregating final decision; while the second member of (1) expresses classical utility function of simple additive weighting for selection of the best alternative $\sum_{j=1}^{J} w_j^k e_j^k$.

To design a web application to support group decision making, it is necessary dynamically to generate the decision matrices, i.e. web forms, according to the dimension of the specific problem. This is a necessary condition that makes the web application to be universal and reusable. If the forms are static and are directly coded, then the application would work in the best case only for tasks with the same number of alternatives, criteria and DM, and in the worst case only for one specific problem. This requires the forms to be generated dynamically based on parameters entered by the user.

3   Algorithm for Designing of a Web Application to Support Group Decision-Making

Considering the input data from the generalized group decision matrix (Table 1), the following algorithm is proposed for designing a web application as a tool to support group decision-making as shown in Fig. 1.

On **Stage 1**, the user (DM) authentication is realized from the home page of the web application. Here the user can either log in or register. Two different roles are implemented: 1) a user that can act as expert (DM), and 2) a supra-DM (SDM) that act as an administrator, responsible for the overall definition and administration of the problems to be solved. It is possible for the supra-DM to be involved as a user (DM).

On **Stage 2** it is necessary to define the problem for group decision making. This activity can be done only from the supra-DM. In accordance with the defined problem (number of alternatives, number of criteria and number of DMs), it is necessary to be determined the dimensions of dynamic form generation. This includes determining the group of DMs, as well as their respective weighting factors, and the set of criteria and alternatives to be assessed.

Stage 3 uses the information from the previous stage that is considered as input data for the determination of dynamically generated individual matrices for each member of the group, where the DMs have to fill in their assessments of the alternatives and weights for the criteria. The dimensionality of the individual matrices depends on the parameters defined in Step 2 for the number of alternatives and the number of criteria for the particular problem.

Stage 4 requires the presence of completed assessments from all the DMs in order to be able to generate the generalized matrix. This matrix contains all the parameters describing the problem, including the assessment points for each alternative to the set of criteria, the weights of each of the criteria, and the weights for each DM.

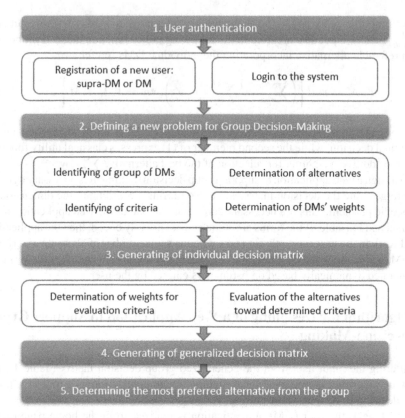

Fig. 1. Algorithm for designing of a web application to support group decision-making

On **Stage 5**, the most preferred alternative as a group decision is determined in accordance with the used utility function.

The use of web technologies allows the generation of multiple individual matrices for DMs where they can express their assessments at a time and remote place convenient for them. This advantage of the web applications especially now in a pandemic situation makes the web forms suitable for different usage. This is due to the ability to set up different levels of access to the web application itself. In such way, from the administrative account it is possible to manage all needed settings of web application including different roles and access of the participants in the group decision-making process. In order to implement such a web-based tool for dynamic form generation in support of GDM, three-layer client-server software architecture is selected, as shown in Fig. 2.

The user interface provides the required forms that SDM and DMs should fill to solve a particular decision-making problem. According to the layered architecture pattern, this is the so-called presentational layer that is visible to all users. The presence of support layers such as interaction control, authentication and session management ensures that the particular DM has the permissions to access only the individual matrices of the problems that he is supposed to evaluate as an expert, while the SDM has access to the additional and advanced activities like defining a new problem and aggregation of a generalized matrix. The second and most specific layer is the business layer that realizes the functional process logic, while the third layer refers to the data storage and data access. Both the main and supporting processes have access to the database, as the access of each process is limited only to the necessary data.

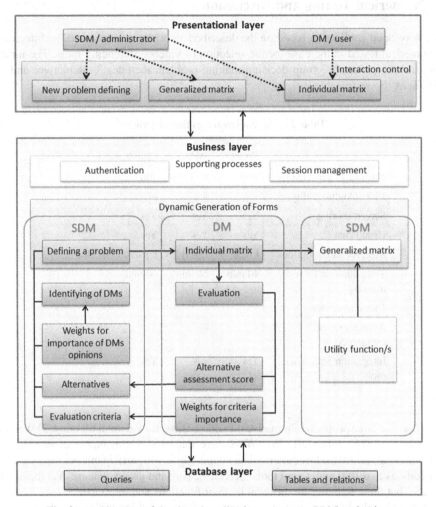

Fig. 2. Architecture of developed application to support GDM evaluations

The dynamic generation of forms for a new problem is initiated by SDM. First, the dimension of the problem should be set up – group of proper DMs and corresponding weighed coefficients for their expertise, alternatives and evaluation criteria. Once the problem is defined each DM should log in his account to determine the evaluations of the alternatives toward criteria, and to determine weighted coefficients according to his point of view about the importance of evaluation criteria. The final generalized group decision matrix can be generated from the SDM account. Using these data can be processed by the proposed modified utility function based on SAW (1) or by a different one in determining the aggregated group decision based on the individual estimations from each DM.

4   Numerical Testing and Discussion

The developed application based on the described algorithm and proposed architecture is numerical tested in the case for the selection of videoconferencing tools. The input data for this particular group decision-making problem includes 3 alternatives and 9 criteria as shown in Table 2.

Table 2. Alternatives and evaluation criteria

	Zoom	Webex	Google meet
Number of participants	100	100	100
Video/Audio quality	–	–	–
Screen sharing	Yes	Yes	Yes
Group chat	Yes	Yes	Yes
Meet recording options	Local	Local	Up to 15 GB cloud
Time duration limit per meeting	40 min	50 min	60 min
User experience	–	–	–
Administration experience	–	–	–
Integration with other tools	Yes	yes	Yes

There are three proposed alternatives: 1) Zoom Basic for Personal Meeting, 2) Webex Free plan, and 3) Google Meet – Free Workspace, that have to be evaluated in accordance with nine criteria. All the three alternatives support up to 100 participants per meeting and integrations to different external tools. Screen sharing and group chat are also included in each, but these features are different by their functions and interface.

Only Google Meet offer cloud recording of the meetings with limited capacity. Video and audio quality depends on the network infrastructure and the hardware used by the users, so it has to be evaluated by the experience of the DM. The experience has a subjective nature, so the criteria related to it are entirely evaluated by each user according to his perceptions.

The presented above alternatives need to be estimated toward evaluation criteria forms a group composed of 5 experts that include: Chief Information Officer (DM-1), Human Resource Officer (DM-2), Training leader (DM-3), and two experts from IT support office (DM-4) and (DM-5).

Considering the described problem together with the proposed algorithm and architecture for a web application, SDM should set up the input parameters using its profile with corresponding permission as shown in Fig. 3. Next, the SDM needs to describe every alternative that is a part of the problem (Fig. 4a) along with proper criteria (Fig. 4b) toward which the evaluation should be done by each group expert (DM).

There is one more submenu where SDM should enter the corresponding weighted coefficients for the opinion importance of all DMs forming the final group decision considering the utility function (1). When the problem is already defined form SDM, the individual experts can start their evaluation process.

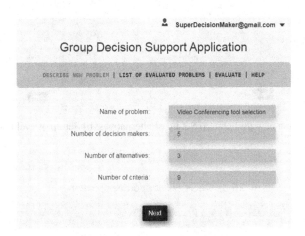

Fig. 3. Defining a new problem

Each DM should enter the coefficients for the criteria importance and evaluation score of alternatives toward all criteria. Knowing the performance of alternatives from different points of view given by the DMs, the final generalized decision-making matrix can be composed by the SDM profile. These input data are to be properly processes considering business logic with a determined utility function. After that, the result of the final group decision can be determined and visualized as shown in Fig. 5.

The obtained result shows that the most preferable alternative is alternative A-3 (2.808), i.e. the Google Meet video conferencing tool. It should be noted that all DMs take part in aggregated final decision with equal importance. The weighted coefficients for each DM have the same value equal to 0.2 (see Fig. 5).

The investigated problem is modified and solved in the case of a group of 3 DMs, namely the first three from the previous problem. The difference here is in the dimension of the overall problem that reflects in the generalized group decision matrix and respectively to weighed coefficients for the experts. In this case, all DMs take part also with equal importance expressed by a value of 0.33. The final group decision is also to select the alternative A-3 (2.8737) but the difference with A-2 (2.8395) in this case is much smaller.

All these prove the applicability of the proposed application for a dynamic generation of forms to support group decision-making. In both tested cases, the weighted

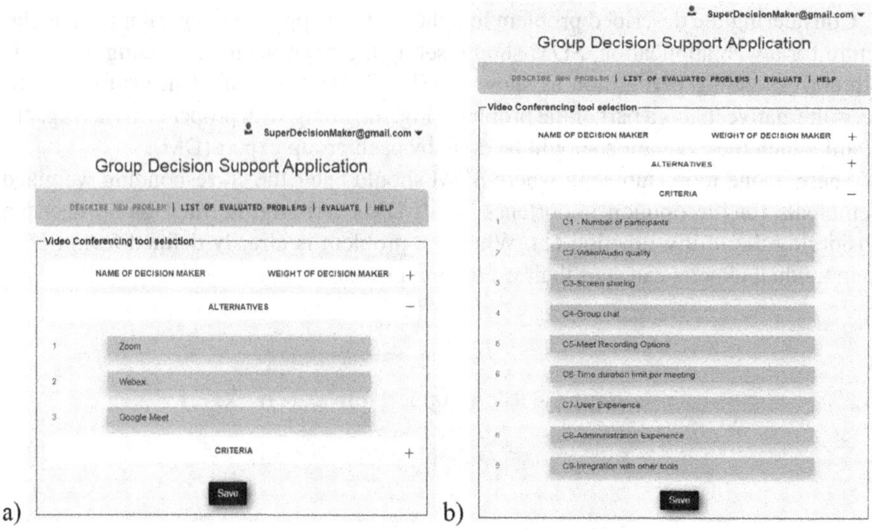

Fig. 4. Defining a new problem: a) Set up of alternatives; b) Set up of evaluation criteria

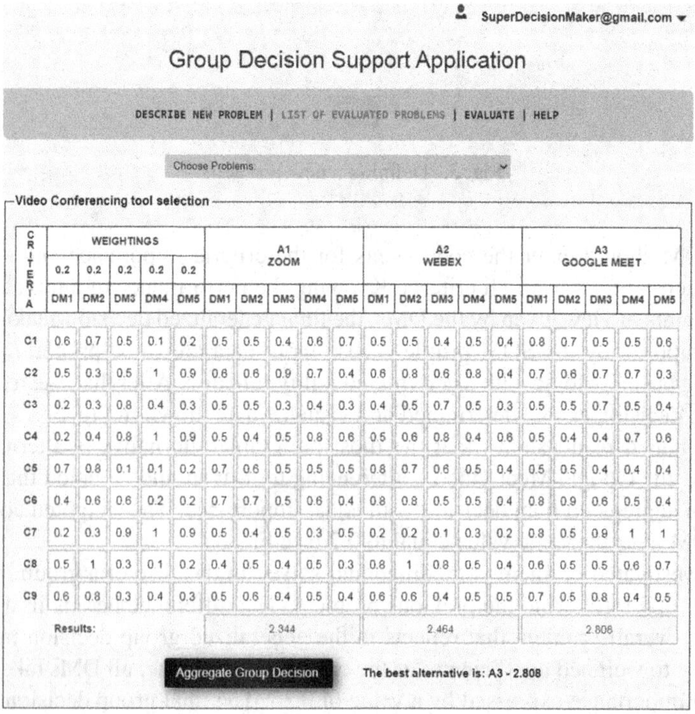

CRITERIA	WEIGHTINGS					A1 ZOOM					A2 WEBEX					A3 GOOGLE MEET				
	0.2	0.2	0.2	0.2	0.2															
	DM1	DM2	DM3	DM4	DM5	DM1	DM2	DM3	DM4	DM5	DM1	DM2	DM3	DM4	DM5	DM1	DM2	DM3	DM4	DM5
C1	0.6	0.7	0.5	0.1	0.2	0.5	0.5	0.4	0.6	0.7	0.5	0.5	0.4	0.5	0.4	0.8	0.7	0.5	0.5	0.6
C2	0.5	0.3	0.5	1	0.9	0.6	0.6	0.9	0.7	0.4	0.6	0.8	0.6	0.8	0.4	0.7	0.6	0.7	0.7	0.3
C3	0.2	0.3	0.8	0.4	0.3	0.5	0.5	0.3	0.4	0.3	0.4	0.5	0.7	0.5	0.3	0.5	0.5	0.7	0.5	0.4
C4	0.2	0.4	0.8	1	0.9	0.5	0.4	0.5	0.8	0.6	0.5	0.6	0.8	0.4	0.6	0.5	0.4	0.4	0.7	0.6
C5	0.7	0.8	0.1	0.1	0.2	0.7	0.6	0.5	0.5	0.5	0.8	0.7	0.6	0.5	0.4	0.5	0.5	0.4	0.4	0.4
C6	0.4	0.6	0.6	0.2	0.2	0.7	0.7	0.5	0.6	0.4	0.8	0.8	0.5	0.5	0.4	0.8	0.9	0.6	0.5	0.4
C7	0.2	0.3	0.9	1	0.9	0.5	0.4	0.5	0.3	0.5	0.2	0.2	0.1	0.3	0.2	0.8	0.5	0.9	1	1
C8	0.5	1	0.3	0.1	0.2	0.4	0.5	0.4	0.5	0.3	0.8	1	0.8	0.5	0.4	0.6	0.5	0.5	0.6	0.7
C9	0.6	0.8	0.3	0.4	0.3	0.5	0.6	0.4	0.5	0.4	0.6	0.6	0.4	0.5	0.5	0.7	0.5	0.8	0.4	0.5
Results:						2.344					2.464					2.808				

Fig. 5. Generalized GDM matrix with determined group decision

coefficients for the opinion importance of the DMs are the same, but these coefficients can be different. This is a distinguishing feature of the proposed algorithm and developed software architecture. The application requires the SDM to set weights that make it possible for more precisely to consider the opinions of DMs with different importance.

There are no obstacles to use different utility functions like well-known MAUT or to formulate a new one. It should be noted that in some cases where different evaluation scale is used, for example, the range from 0 to 100, the proper normalization has to be done. This is related to the specifics of the used utility function and some intermediate calculations have to be done that will not affect the application as a whole. Following the proposed algorithm for designing a web application different matrices with a variety of dimensions could be dynamically generation as web forms for different purposes.

The proposed algorithm shown in Fig. 1 is realized by using XAMPP that includes all the required components like Apache HTTP Server, MySQL and some other tools to use PHP and Perl. The advantages of modular three-tier software architecture are the fact that all of the three tiers can be upgraded or replaced independently in response to changes in requirements for technology.

This application could be used for an investigation of excessive use of smart technologies by formulation of proper multi-criteria decision analysis' problem. For the goal, a representative group from different ages need to be formed to evaluate the usage of different smart technologies at home and at the office.

5   Conclusions

The current article deals with problems arising in group decision-making. For the goal, an algorithm for the design of an application to support group decision-making is proposed. This algorithm is realized in a developed client-server architecture. The essence of the demonstrated approach to support group decision-making consists in the modified utility function based on the SAW method along with the possibility of the dynamic generation of forms. Each expert from the group needs to fulfill his evaluations for the investigated problem in such form. Using the information from all filled forms is used to generate a generalized decision matrix on which base the final group decision is realized. This matrix is based not only on the experts' evaluation but rely also on the proper utility function, which is realized by the business logic of the developed prototype. There are no obstacles to use different utility functions to generate the generalized group decision matrix.

The proposed algorithm for the design of a web-based tool to support group decision-making is demonstrated in a case study for the selection of videoconferencing tools. Formulated problem is composed of 3 alternatives, evaluated toward 9 criteria by a group of 5 experts. The usage of this application contributes to improving decision-making efficiency and reducing time consumption as the whole process is realized at a convenient time for each expert. Due to the used client-server architecture, the remote participation of the DMs is also an advantage of the proposed application. The SDM can easily modify the particular problem by adding/removing experts, alternatives, or evaluation criteria.

As future development of the described application to support group decision-making is planned to extend the functionality related to the option in the selection of different utility functions.

Acknowledgment. This work is supported by the Bulgarian National Science Fund, Project title "Synthesis of a dynamic model for assessing the psychological and physical impacts of excessive use of smart technologies", KP-06-N 32/4/07.12.2019.

References

Alinezhad, A., Khalili, J.: MAUT method. In: Khalili, J., Alinezhad, A. (eds.) New Methods and Applications in Multiple Attribute Decision Making (MADM). ISORMS, vol. 277, pp. 127–131. Springer, Cham (2019). https://doi.org/10.1007/978-3-030-15009-9_18

Anwar, M., Azam, F.: Proposing a novel architecture of script component to incorporate the scripting language support in SCADA systems. In: Saeed, K., Snášel, V. (eds.) CISIM 2014. LNCS, vol. 8838, pp. 351–362. Springer, Heidelberg (2014). https://doi.org/10.1007/978-3-662-45237-0_33

Borissova, D., Cvetkova, P., Garvanov, I., Garvanova, M.: A framework of business intelligence system for decision making in efficiency management. In: Saeed, K., Dvorský, J. (eds.) CISIM 2020. LNCS, vol. 12133, pp. 111–121. Springer, Cham (2020a). https://doi.org/10.1007/978-3-030-47679-3_10

Borissova, D., Dimitrova, Z., Dimitrov, V.: How to support teams to be remote and productive: group decision-making for distance collaboration software tools. Inf. Secur. Digital Transform. Cyber Secur. Resil. **46**, 36–52 (2020b)

Borissova, D.: A group decision making model considering experts competency: An application in personnel selections. Comptes rendus de l'Academie Bulgare des Sciences **71**(11), 1520–1527 (2018)

Borissova, D.: A multi-criteria group decision making model for selection of green building project. In: Ofluoglu, S., Ozener, O.O., Isikdag, U. (eds.) EBF 2019. CCIS, vol. 1188, pp. 137–146. Springer, Cham (2020). https://doi.org/10.1007/978-3-030-42852-5_11

Corral, T.: Mastering JavaScript Design Pattern - Third Edition: Create Scalable and Reliable Applications with Advanced JavaScript Design Patterns Using Reliable Code, 3rd edn., 439 p. Packt Publishing (2019)

Keeney, R.L., Raiffa, H.: Decisions with Multiple Objectives: Preferences and Value Trade-Offs, 569 p. Wiley, New York (1993)

Lu, Y., Xu, Y., Herrera-Viedma, E., Han, Y.: Consensus of large-scale group decision making in social network: the minimum cost model based on robust optimization. Inf. Sci. **547**, 910–930 (2021)

Mustakerov, I., Borissova, D.: Data structures and algorithms of intelligent Web-based system for modular design. Int. J. Comput. Sci. Eng. **7**(7), 87–92 (2013)

Mustakerov, I., Borissova, D.: A framework for development of e-learning system for computer programming: application in the C programming language. J. e-Learn. Knowl. Soc. **13**(2), 89–101 (2017)

Mustakerov, I., Borissova, D.: A web application for group decision-making based on combinatorial optimization. In: Proceedings of 4th International Conference on Information Systems and Technologies (ICIST 2014), pp. 46–56 (2014)

Perkusich, M., et al.: Intelligent software engineering in the context of agile software development: a systematic literature review. Inf. Softw. Technol. **119**, 106241 (2020)

Saputri, T.R.D., Lee, S.-W.: Integrated framework for incorporating sustainability design in software engineering life-cycle: an empirical study. Inf. Softw. Technol. **129**, 106407 (2021)

Shaverdi, M., Yaghoubi, S., Ensafian, H.: A multi-objective robust possibilistic model for technology portfolio optimization considering social impact and different types of financing. Appl. Soft Comput. **86**, 105892 (2020)

Shishkov, B., Bogomilova, A., Garvanova, M.: Four enterprise modeling perspectives and impact on enterprise information systems. In: Rocha, Á., Adeli, H., Reis, L.P., Costanzo, S., Orovic, I., Moreira, F. (eds.) WorldCIST 2020. AISC, vol. 1159, pp. 660–677. Springer, Cham (2020). https://doi.org/10.1007/978-3-030-45688-7_66

Tomov, P., Zankinski, I., Balabanov, T.: Training of artificial neural networks for financial time series forecasting in android service and widgets. Probl. Eng. Cybern. Robot. **71**, 50–56 (2019)

Triantaphyllou, E., Shu, B., Nieto Sanchez, S., Ray, T.: Multi-criteria decision making: an operations research approach. Encycl. Electr. Electron. Eng. **15**, 175–186 (1998)

Triantaphyllou (2000)Triantaphyllou, E.: Multi-criteria decision making methods. In: Multi-criteria Decision Making Methods: A Comparative Study. Applied Optimization, vol. 44. Springer, Boston (2000). https://doi.org/10.1007/978-1-4757-3157-6_2

Trifonov, R., Manolov, S., Yoshinov, R., Tsochev, G., Nedev, S., Pavlova, G.: Operational cyber threat intelligence supported by artificial intelligence methods. In: Proceedings of International Conference on Information Technologies (InfoTech-2018), pp. 1–9, Bulgaria (2018)

Tsao, Y.-C., Thanh, V.-V.: A multi-objective fuzzy robust optimization approach for designing sustainable and reliable power systems under uncertainty. Appl. Soft Comput. **92**, 106317 (2020)

Wagner, S., Deissenboeck, F.: Defining productivity in software engineering. In: Sadowski, C., Zimmermann, T. (eds.) Rethinking Productivity in Software Engineering. Apress, Berkeley (2019)

Neural Networks as Tool to Improve the Intrusion Detection System

Esmeral Ernesto[1]([✉]), Mardini Johan[1], Salcedo Dixon[1]([✉]),
De-La-Hoz-Franco Emiro[1], Avendaño Inirida[1,2], and Henriquez Carlos[2]

[1] Universidad de la Costa, Barranquilla, Colombia
{eesmera12,dsalcedo2}@cuc.edu.co
[2] Universidad del Magdalena, Santa Marta, Colombia

Abstract. Nowadays, computer programs affecting computers both locally and network-wide have led to the design and development of different preventive and corrective strategies to remedy computer security problems. This dynamic has been important for the understanding of the structure of attacks and how best to counteract them, making sure that their impact is less than expected by the attacker.

For this research, a simulation was carried out using the DATASET-KDD NSL at 100%, generating an experimental environment, where processes of pre-processing, training, classification, and evaluation of model quality metrics were carried out. Likewise, a comparative analysis of the results obtained after implementing different feature selection techniques (INFO.GAIN, GAIN RATIO, and ONE R), and classification techniques based on neural networks that use an unsupervised learning algorithm based on self-organizing maps (SOM and GHSOM), with the purpose of classifying bi-class network traffic automatically. From the above, a 97.09% hit rate was obtained with 21 features by implementing the GHSOM classifier with 10-fold cross-validation with the ONE R feature selection technique, which would improve the efficiency and performance of Intrusion Detection Systems (IDS).

Keywords: SOM neural networks · GHSOM neural networks · NSL_KDD · IDS

1 Introduction

Cyber-attacks continue to be a major problem in today's production context, as they lead to the loss or hijacking of sensitive information, which is usually used for decision making in organizations [1]. There are different techniques to prevent and correct malicious intrusive actions, among them: Access Control Lists (ACLs), Message Encryption, Port Blocking, Virtual Private Networks (VPNs) and Firewalls. The latter restrict traffic from unknown services by blocking ports. While they are useful in countering a wide variety of attacks, there is still a security gap from the outside, when attacks are encapsulated in the traffic of services allowed by the device, and firewalls and the other techniques mentioned do not control attacks generated from inside the network.

The validation of such environments requires the execution of a series of phases: pre-processing of the dataset, feature selection or extraction, construction of the classification

© Springer Nature Switzerland AG 2021
K. Saeed and J. Dvorský (Eds.): CISIM 2021, LNCS 12883, pp. 124–139, 2021.
https://doi.org/10.1007/978-3-030-84340-3_10

model and evaluation of the classifier detection rates. The proposed models are evaluated by running different experimentation scenarios where the detection quality metrics are analysed, to subsequently implement them in productive environments.

On the other hand, this work is mainly focused on bi-class classification processes, given their relevance in real application contexts [2], where the main goal is to detect attacks or possible attacks in computer networks, to take corrective actions when faced with the anomalous behaviour identified, and the identification of the attack category (denial of service - DoS, remote to local - R2L, user to root - U2R or probe) is not so relevant. Here we have applied the selection techniques based on information filtering: Info.Gain [3] Gain ratio [4] and One R [5], to identify the attributes that contribute the most to the subsequent classification process. Once the most appropriate selection technique was identified, the SOM (Self-Organizing Map) [6, 7] and GHSOM (Growing Hierarchical Self Organizing Maps) [8] classification techniques were applied. With the results obtained, a comparative analysis was made of the quality metrics generated. Subsequent paragraphs, however, are indented.

For a more detailed description of the procedures applied here, the article is organized as follows: in section one the introduction, in section two the pre-processing techniques, in section three the feature selection techniques, in section four the training and classification techniques, in section five the applied methodology, section six contains the simulation scenarios and results obtained, section seven the related work, section eight the conclusions, section nine the future work and at the end the references are presented.

2 Related Techniques

According to [9], feature selection refers to a concept used in data mining with the aim of reducing the size of the input data, to facilitate the processing and analysis of such information. Feature selection not only considers the reduction of cardinality, i.e., maintaining a partial or predefined limit on the number of attributes considered when creating a model, but also allows for the appropriate discarding of attributes based on their usefulness for a good analysis process.

In addition to this classification, feature selection methods can also be divided into three models according to [10].

According to [11] filter-based feature selection technique (filter) is used to find the best feature subset from the original set, filtering methods seem to be good in selecting a large subset of data, they do not depend on the classification algorithm and their computational cost is less for large datasets. Wrapper-based feature selection techniques defined in [12–16] use performance prediction of the learning algorithm for feature selection. It improves the results of the corresponding predictors, and achieves better recognition rates, in some cases outperforming filter-based techniques, however, they depend on the classification algorithm and for a large dataset, the computational cost is higher in the wrapper method.

Finally, embedded methods, also defined in [16], are based on the evaluation of the performance of the metrics calculated directly from the data, without direct reference to the results of the data analysis systems, in them there is a union of the feature selection techniques with the learning process for a given learning algorithm. Embedded methods are less prone to overfitting and depend on the classification algorithm.

The ability to employ feature selection is paramount for effective analysis because the data contains information that is not necessary for model generation. In this research, Info.Gain, Gain Ratio and One R techniques have been selected because in the preliminary exploration of the state of the art it was observed that when implementing them in issues related to anomaly detection, their results were promising. However, they will be implemented in conjunction with SOM and GHSOM neural networks to analyse the performance metrics of the proposed model.

Below, we introduce a brief description of the techniques used in this research, such as Info.Gain, Gain Ratio and One R feature selection techniques.

2.1   Feature Selection Techniques in IDS Systems

Info.Gain

It is a filter-based feature selection technique defined in [3]. It is also known as information gain and is used to identify the relevance level or ranking of features in a data collection. Equation 1 defines this relevance level. The attribute with the highest information gain is chosen as the partition attribute for node N. This attribute minimizes the information needed to rank the duplicates in the resulting partition and reflects the lowest randomness or impurity in these partitions.

$$IG(D, X_3) = entropy(D) - \sum_v \frac{|D_v| entropy(D_v)}{|D|} \tag{1}$$

Implementing the selection technique on the KDD NSL dataset, the order of features is as follows: src_bytes, service, dst_bytes, flag, diff_srv_rate, same_srv_rate, dst_host_srv_count, dst_host_same_srv_rate, dst_host_diff_srv_rate, dst_host_serror_rate, logged_in, dst_host_srv_serror_rate, serror_rate, count, srv_serror_rate, dst_host_srv_diff_host_rate, dst_host_count, dst_host_same_src_port_rate, srv_diff_host_rate, srv_count, dst_host_srv_rerror_rate, protocol_type, rerror_rate, dst_host_rerror_rate, srv_rerror_rate, duration, hot, wrong_fragment, num_compromised, num_root, num_access_files, is_guest_login, num_file_creations, su_attempted, root_shell, num_shells, num_failed_logins, land, is_host_login, num_outbound_cmds, urgent.

Gain Ratio

According to [4, 18], Gain ratio belongs to the category of filtering feature selection techniques and is a measurement method for weighting features in the dataset with high dimensionality. When there are many different values, the information gain ratio is used to consider these features. This method is widely used because it yields very good results, which are then used in the classification phase. Its main peculiarity is that the modification of the information gain reduces the bias. Gain ratio considers the number and size of branches to be chosen in an attribute.

Implementing the selection technique on the KDD NSL dataset, the order of features is as follows: logged_in, srv_serror_rate, flag, serror_rate, dst_host_srv_serror_rate, diff_srv_rate, dst_host_serror_rate, dst_bytes, src_bytes, same_srv_rate, service, dst_host_srv_diff_host_rate, wrong_fragment, dst_host_srv_count, dst_host_same_srv_rate, dst_host_diff_srv_rate, srv_diff_host_rate, dst_host_srv_rerror_rate count, dst_host_count, srv_rerror_rate, num_root, rerror_rate, dst_host_same_src_port_rate, num_access_files, protocol_type, num_compromised, su_attempted, hot, duration, is_host_login, dst_host_rerror_rate, num_file_creations, num_failed_logins, srv_count, root_shell, num_shells, is_guest_login, land, num_outbound_cmds, urgent.

One R

In [6] they define it as a method based and characterized by being based on the error rate of the rules generated from a set of attributes unlike other algorithms, the function contains only one attribute is induced by testing on the training set all combinations of attributes and value staying with the rule with fewer errors, it works as a classifier very quickly; in addition to all its results are very good compared to much more complex algorithms (Fig. 1).

```
1r (Example) {
  For each attribute (A)
    For each attribute (Ai)
      Count the number of occurrences of each class with Ai
      Obtain the most frequent class (Cj)
      Create a rule of type Ai->Cj
    Calculate the error of the rules of the attribute A
    Choose the rules with the lowest error.
}
```

Fig. 1. 1R algorithm pseudo code.

Similarly, this algorithm, also known in many documentary reviews as 1R [17–19], is a very simple classifier, which only uses one attribute for classification. Although the author calls it "Program 1R is ordinary in most respects", its results can be very good compared to much more complex algorithms and its average performance is below those of C4.5 by only 5.7% points of classification success according to studies carried out by the author of the algorithm.

The implementation of the 1R algorithm was performed using the pseudocode shown. This function only allows working with tables that have nominal attributes and in which there must be no attributes with unknown values to obtain the desired result.

According to [20], the function takes as input the name of the table and the class on which the analysis is to be performed and returns as output a set of rules for the attributes with the least number of errors.

Implementing the selection technique to the KDD NSL dataset, the order of features is as follows: src_bytes, service, dst_bytes, flag, same_srv_rate, diff_srv_rate, dst_host_same_srv_rate, dst_host_srv_count, dst_host_diff_srv_rate, logged_in, count, serror_rate, dst_host_serror_rate, dst_host_srv_serror_rate, srv_serror_rate, dst_host_count, dst_host_same_src_port_rate, dst_host_srv_diff_host_rate, srv_count, srv_diff_ host_rate, dst_host_srv_rerror_rate, dst_host_rerror_rate, rerror_rate, srv_rerror_rate, protocol_type, wrong_fragment, hot, num_compromised, duration, root_shell, num_outbound_cmds, is_guest_login, num_shells, num_access_files, is_host_login, urgent, su_attempted, num_root, land, num_file_creations, num_failed_logins.

2.2 Training and Classification Techniques

This type of techniques is used in this research to train the classifier, starting from the selected learning algorithm, and using the data set already normalised and reduced to the most relevant features, to generate a more efficient learning. Once the model has been trained, the classifier determines the normal and anomalous network traffic, performing the subsequent classification of each of the connections in the dataset (KDD-NSL). Quality metrics are then calculated to evaluate the performance of the classification technique.

In this Research we will deal with Artificial Neural Networks SOM and GHSOM. Therefore, it is necessary to define the concept of neural network, according to [21], neural networks are represented by a directed graph with four (4) conditions: (1) Links are called connections and operate as instantaneous one-way paths; (2)Nodes are called processing elements (PEs), which can have any number of connections and have a local memory; (3) All connections leaving the PE must have the same signal; (4) Each PE has a transfer function, which based on the inputs and the local memory, produces an output signal thus altering the local memory.

SOM Neural Networks (Self-organizing Map)

It is an efficient (unsupervised) neural algorithm that allows the projection of data from a multidimensional space onto a two-dimensional grid called a "map", while qualitatively preserving the organisation (topology) of the original set [22, 23].

In 1982 T. Kohonen [24] presented a network model called self-organising maps or SOM (Self-Organizing Maps), with which he wanted to show that an external stimulus (input) can force the formation of maps, assuming a certain structure and a functional description. According to [7], the most important characteristic of SOMs is that they learn to classify data by means of an unsupervised learning algorithm (a SOM learns to classify training data without any external control).

SOM Architecture

According to [24], a SOM network is made up of two lattices of neurons. The input layer (formed by N neurons, one for each input variable) oversees receiving and transmitting the information coming from the outside, to the output layer.

The output layer (consisting of M neurons) is responsible for processing the information and forming the feature map. Normally, the neurons in the output layer are organised in the form of a two-dimensional map as shown in Fig. 2.

SOM Training

According to Kohonen [7] a SOM does not need a target output to be specified unlike

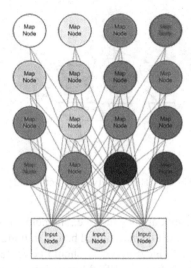

Fig. 2. SOM structure [17]

many other types of network. Instead, those nodes in which their weight vector matches the input vector, the lattice area is selectively optimised by further closing the data reassembly. The training of a SOM network occurs in six (6) steps, which have many iterations:

1. Each node is initialized with its respective vector of weights.

2. A vector is randomly chosen from the training data set and presented to the lattice (input vector).

3. Each node is examined to calculate which weight is the closest "match" to the input vector. The winning node is commonly referred to as the Best Matching Unit (BMU).

4. The radius of the BMU neighbourhood is calculated, which is an initially large value, associated with the size of the lattice, and decreases over time. Nodes located within this radius are considered BMU neighbours.

5. Each node neighbouring the BMU adjusts its weights to make it more like the input vector. The closer the node is to the BMU, the more its weight will be altered.

6. Step 2 is repeated for "n" iterations.

Neural Networks GHSOM (Growing Hierarchical Self Organising Maps)
According to [8], GHSOM is a hierarchical and dynamic structure, developed to overcome the weaknesses and problems presented by SOM (see Fig. 3). The GHSOM structure consists of multiple layers composed of several independent SOMs whose number and size are determined during the training phase. The process of adaptive growth is controlled by two parameters that determine the depth of the hierarchy and the breadth of each map. Therefore, these two parameters are the only ones that must be set initially in GHSOM.

This type of mapping is born as an improved version of the SOM architecture, according [8] there are two purposes for the GHSOM architecture:

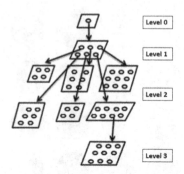

Fig. 3. GHSOM network structure [25]

1. SOM has a fixed network architecture, i.e., the number of units of use as well as the distribution of the units must be determined before training.

2. Input data that is hierarchical in nature should be represented in a hierarchical structure for clarity of representation. GHSOM uses a multi-layered hierarchical structure, where each layer consists of a few of independent SOMs. Only one SOM is used in the first layer of the hierarchy.

For each map unit, one SOM could be added to the next layer of the hierarchy. This principle is repeated with the third level of the map and the other layers of the GHSOM, as shown in Fig. 4.

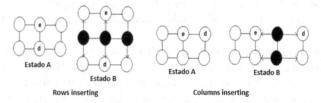

Fig. 4. Row insertion process in a GHSOM network [26]

GHSOM Learning Algorithm

According to [8] and [25], the training stage of the GHSOM algorithm starts with the initial configuration, in this step the "map" is created at level 0 with a single unit.

The vector m0 of weights of this unit is initialised, with the average of all the input vectors and the average quantization error mqe0 is calculated.

The growth of the structure starts by creating a new SOM under layer 0 of the map, with an initial size of 2 x 2 units. The growth process continues until the mean quantization error, known as MQE, in capital letters, reaches a certain fraction $\tau 1$ of the mqeu of the corresponding unit in the upper layer, i.e., the unit constituting map layer 0 for the first map layer.

The described conceptualisation has served as a basis for different simulation scenarios to define a model for intrusion detection in computer network systems, based on the phases of training, classification, and metric calculation.

3 Data Set Processing

This research was based on the NSL-KDD data set at 100% in its pure state and the SMOTE (Synthetic Minority Oversampling Technique) pre-processing and normalisation techniques were applied applying normalisation to zero mean.

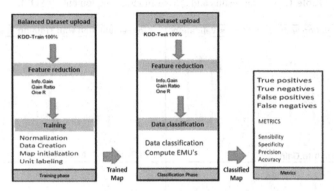

Fig. 5. Proposed functional model.

Once the cleaned data is obtained, we proceed to apply a series of feature selection techniques (Info.gain, Gain Ratio, One R), to identify the attributes that have the greatest impact on the performance of the classifier, we applied two (2) classification techniques based on artificial neural networks SOM and GHSOM.

The testing process was carried out by implementing a dataset for 100% testing by implementing cross-validation using 10 folds and the results obtained from this were represented in the respective confusion matrices, allowing us to calculate the quality metrics for each of the experimental scenarios. From this, the techniques (both selection and classification) that yielded the best results were identified (see Fig. 5).

4 Simulation Scenarios and Results

The development of this research involved the use of two (2) sets of experimental tests. The first set of tests used the SOM classifier, varying the previously mentioned feature selection techniques. Once the corresponding feature selection technique was applied, the order of the most relevant attributes was identified, and from this a series of experimental scenarios were simulated, varying the number of attributes for each of the selection techniques implemented, see Table 1.

For the second set of tests, the GHSOM classifier was used, also varying the feature selection techniques. After identifying the order of relevance of the attributes, the corresponding experimentation scenarios were performed, varying the number of attributes for each of the implemented selection techniques, see Table 2.

Table 1. Test set results and cross validation implementing SOM.

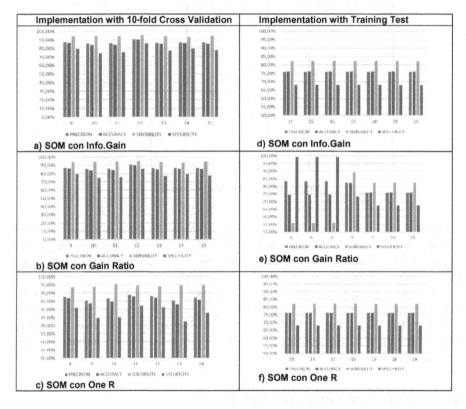

The different experiments were run on a DELL LATITUDE 3470 computer with an Intel Core i7 6500U processor at 2.5 Ghz, 8 GB of DDR 3 Ram at 2400 MHz and NVIDIA GeForce 920 M video card with a capacity of 2 GB DDR3. Each experiment was carried out 10 times, which resulted in the values of the metrics that allowed the quality of the processes to be evaluated. See Tables 3 and 4, which contain each quality metric by feature selection technique and by classification method, with their respective standard deviation.

Table 2. Test set results and cross validation implementing GHSOM.

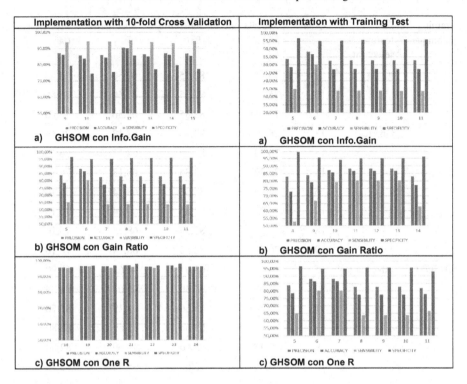

Table 3. Results with dataset test implementation for SOM and GHSOM classifiers

Training technique	T. feature selection	Quant	Success rate (%)	Sensibility (%)	Specificity (%)	Precision (%)
SOM	Info. Gain	14	76,22	82,35	68,13	76,10
		15	76,22	82,35	68,13	76,10
		16	76,22	82,35	68,13	76,10
		17	76,23	82,35	68,14	76,10
		18	76,23	82,35	68,14	76,10
		19	76,23	82,35	68,14	76,10
		20	76,23	82,35	68,14	76,10
	Gain Ratio	5	74,50	55,84	99,17	83,40
		6	74,50	55,84	99,17	83,40
		7	74,60	56,01	99,17	83,40
		8	82,30	89,04	73,39	82,40

(continued)

Table 3. (*continued*)

Training technique	T. feature selection	Quant	Success rate (%)	Sensibility (%)	Specificity (%)	Precision (%)
		9	75,95	82,35	67,50	75,80
		10	75,95	82,35	67,50	75,80
		11	75,95	82,35	67,50	75,80
	One R	13	76,22	82,35	68,13	76,10
		14	76,22	82,35	68,13	76,10
		15	76,22	82,35	68,13	76,10
		16	76,23	82,35	68,14	76,10
		17	76,23	82,35	68,14	76,10
		18	76,23	82,35	68,14	76,10
		19	76,23	82,35	68,14	76,10
GHSOM	Info. Gain	5	78,62	65,01	96,61	83,90
		6	86,64	80,30	95,01	88,20
		7	77,24	63,66	95,19	82,50
		8	77,45	63,66	95,69	82,80
		9	77,45	63,66	95,69	82,80
		10	77,44	63,55	95,78	82,90
		11	77,44	63,55	95,78	82,90
	Gain Ratio	8	73,00	52,92	99,53	83,00
		9	79,22	66,80	95,63	83,80
		10	85,67	79,34	94,04	87,20
		11	86,61	80,26	95,01	88,20
		12	86,61	80,26	95,01	88,20
		13	86,61	80,26	95,01	88,20
		14	77,19	62,84	96,15	82,90
	One R	5	78,62	65,01	96,61	83,90
		6	86,64	80,30	95,01	88,20
		7	86,64	80,30	95,01	88,20
		8	77,46	63,67	95,69	82,80
		9	77,46	63,67	95,69	82,80
		10	77,46	63,67	95,69	82,80
		11	77,89	66,52	92,92	81,90

Table 4. Results with cross validation fold 10 implementations for SOM and GHSOM classifiers

Training technique	T. feature selection	Quant	Success rate (%)	Sensibility (%)	Specificity (%)	Precision (%)
SOM	Info. Gain	9	86,21 ± 0,033	93,84 ± 0,009	79,56 ± 0,027	87,32 ± 0,047
		10	83,9 ± 0,030	94,50 ± 0,016	74,66 ± 0,024	85,82 ± 0,041
		11	84,35 ± 0,018	94,39 ± 0,012	75,59 ± 0,016	86,10 ± 0,027
		12	90,03 ± 0,019	95,05 ± 0,049	85,65 ± 0,014	90,56 ± 0,037
		13	85,03 ± 0,045	93,92 ± 0,043	77,24 ± 0,036	86,46 ± 0,059
		14	85,99 ± 0,023	93,29 ± 0,010	79,62 ± 0,018	87,01 ± 0,036
		15	85,37 ± 0,027	94,49 ± 0,008	77,42 ± 0,022	86,86 ± 0,037
	Gain Ratio	5	88,16 ± 0,021	79,84 ± 0,007	95,4 ± 0,017	88,8 ± 0,028
		6	88,15 ± 0,028	79,86 ± 0,009	95,37 ± 0,022	88,79 ± 0,036
		7	88,12 ± 0,022	79,8 ± 0,010	95,36 ± 0,018	88,76 ± 0,029
		8	88,35 ± 0,009	98,69 ± 0,003	79,35 ± 0,008	90,23 ± 0,013
		9	80,68 ± 0,002	85,11 ± 0,005	76,83 ± 0,003	81,2 ± 0,002
		10	83,23 ± 0,003	94,47 ± 0,009	73,44 ± 0,005	85,35 ± 0,001
		11	78,56 ± 0,002	84,59 ± 0,005	73,3 ± 0,003	79,35 ± 0,001
	One R	8	86,88 ± 0,048	93,62 ± 0,010	81,01 ± 0,037	87,77 ± 0,062
		9	83,59 ± 0,032	93,80 ± 0,010	74,71 ± 0,025	85,36 ± 0,048
		10	84,63 ± 0,029	95,52 ± 0,013	75,16 ± 0,023	86,66 ± 0,040
		11	87,88 ± 0,033	94,55 ± 0,017	82,08 ± 0,026	88,76 ± 0,053
		12	87,08 ± 0,028	93,92 ± 0,016	81,13 ± 0,022	88,00 ± 0,045
		13	82,87 ± 0,025	94,79 ± 0,013	72,49 ± 0,021	85,21 ± 0,040
		14	85,62 ± 0,017	94,79 ± 0,009	77,63 ± 0,015	87,13 ± 0,022
GHSOM	Info, Gain	5	96,45 ± 0,006	95,12 ± 0,005	97,61 ± 0,004	96,46 ± 0,011
		6	96,45 ± 0,008	95,68 ± 0,008	97,12 ± 0,005	96,45 ± 0,014
		7	94,98 ± 0,004	94,96 ± 0,006	95,01 ± 0,003	94,99 ± 0,016
		8	94,89 ± 0,005	95,12 ± 0,005	94,69 ± 0,005	94,90 ± 0,010
		9	95,19 ± 0,003	95,84 ± 0,006	94,63 ± 0,003	95,21 ± 0,007
		10	94,60 ± 0,011	94,59 ± 0,008	94,60 ± 0,006	94,60 ± 0,025
		11	93,86 ± 0,010	95,21 ± 0,007	92,68 ± 0,006	93,92 ± 0,019
	Gain Ratio	18	94,75 ± 0,005	94,80 ± 0,014	94,71 ± 0,007	94,75 ± 0,011
		19	95,41 ± 0,005	95,13 ± 0,012	95,65 ± 0,008	95,41 ± 0,014
		20	96,16 ± 0,004	96,12 ± 0,009	96,19 ± 0,004	96,16 ± 0,016
		21	96,24 ± 0,006	96,14 ± 0,009	96,32 ± 0,005	96,24 ± 0,010

(continued)

Table 4. (*continued*)

Training technique	T. feature selection	Quant	Success rate (%)	Sensibility (%)	Specificity (%)	Precision (%)
		22	95,76 ± 0,004	95,13 ± 0,008	96,30 ± 0,003	95,76 ± 0,007
		23	96,04 ± 0,003	95,41 ± 0,007	96,58 ± 0,011	96,04 ± 0,025
		24	95,77 ± 0,005	95,06 ± 0,009	96,38 ± 0,010	95,77 ± 0,019
	One R	18	86,88 ± 0,004	93,62 ± 0,010	81,01 ± 0,005	87,77 ± 0,005
		19	83,59 ± 0,007	93,80 ± 0,009	74,71 ± 0,008	85,36 ± 0,013
		20	84,63 ± 0,006	95,52 ± 0,007	75,16 ± 0,006	86,66 ± 0,009
		21	97,09 ± 0,007	96,11 ± 0,010	97,94 ± 0,008	97,09 ± 0,009
		22	87,08 ± 0,005	93,92 ± 0,007	81,13 ± 0,005	88,00 ± 0,008
		23	82,87 ± 0,005	94,79 ± 0,005	72,49 ± 0,006	85,21 ± 0,007
		24	85,62 ± 0,007	94,79 ± 0,010	77,63 ± 0,08	87,13 ± 0,009

In the classification process of both test sets, the 10-fold cross-validation technique was used, applied to the training NSL-KDD dataset, and generating simulations that allow evaluating the network traffic with a behaviour very similar to that of real computer attacks.

At the end of each experimental scenario, the evaluation of the proposed functional models was performed, calculating the evaluation metrics of sensitivity, specificity, precision, and accuracy.

5   Conclusions

Considering that the most appropriate metric to evaluate the performance of a classifier is the hit percentage (at the level of traffic detection in computer networks) because it is the ratio of true positives to true negatives.

For the set of tests performed with the SOM classifier, the best results have been obtained when using the Info gain feature selection technique with 12 attributes, reaching a hit rate of 90.03%, as shown in the table below.

The most significant simulation scenarios are provided in Table 5, where, using the GHSOM classifier, with the One R feature selection technique, better values are obtained in the metrics that allow to evaluate the quality of the proposed method.

With One R, the 21 features that best contribute to the classification process have been identified, in order of priority, from highest to lowest, they are: src_bytes, service, dst_bytes, flag, same_srv_rate, diff_srv_rate, dst_host_same_srv_rate, dst_host_srv_count, dst_host_diff_srv_rate, logged_in, count, serror_rate, dst_host_serror_rate, dst_host_srv_serror_rate, srv_serror_rate, dst_host_count, dst_host_same_src_port_rate, dst_host_srv_diff_host_rate, srv_count, srv_diff_host_rate, dst_host_srv_rror_rate.

Table 5. Results using GHSOM classifier, with the One R feature selection technique.

Training technique	T. feature selection	Quant	Success rate (%)	Liability (%)	Specificity (%)	Precision (%)
SOM + Croos V	Info. Gain	12	90,03 ± 0,019	95,05 ± 0,049	85,65 ± 0,014	90,56 ± 0,037
	Gain Ratio	8	88,35 ± 0,009	98,69 ± 0,003	79,35 ± 0,008	90,23 ± 0,013
	One R	11	87,88 ± 0,033	94,55 ± 0,017	82,08 ± 0,026	88,76 ± 0,053
GHSOM + Croos V	Info. Gain	5	96,45 ± 0,006	95,12 ± 0,005	97,61 ± 0,004	96,46 ± 0,011
	Gain Ratio	21	96,24 ± 0,006	96,14 ± 0,009	96,32 ± 0,005	96,24 ± 0,010
	One R	21	97,09 ± 0,007	96,11 ± 0,010	97,94 ± 0,008	97,09 ± 0,009
SOM + Test	Info. Gain	17	76,23	82,35	68,14	76,10
	Gain Ratio	8	82,30	89,04	73,39	82,40
	One R	16	76,23	82,35	68,14	76,10
GHSOM + Test	Info. Gain	6	86,64	80,30	95,01	88,20
	Gain Ratio	11	86,61	80,26	95,01	88,20
	One R	6	86,64	80,30	95,01	88,20

The quality metrics obtained with this distribution were: a hit rate of 97.09%, sensitivity of 96.11% and specificity of 97.94% and accuracy of 97.09%. Using only the 21 most relevant features out of the 41 possible attributes of the NSL-KDD dataset, contributes to generate a lighter IDS, which will require less hardware resources for the classification process.

The methods shown in Table 6, have been classified as: (1) methods that do not use feature selection, (2) filter-based methods, and (3) wrapper-based methods or wrapper method. In all the studies referenced here, the NSL-KDD dataset was used. Although there are studies with which very good results have been obtained, some of them superior to the proposed one, this research has identified a significant improvement in the detection rate of attacks and normal traffic in computer networks, using a smaller proportion of features than in other correlated studies, which demands the use of fewer computational resources. This is useful for a later solution on lower performance equipment and if real-time analysis is required. With the compilation described in Table 5, it is not intended to indicate that GHSOM + One R is the best solution. The aim is to provide an idea of the performance of the proposed procedure, compared to results provided by other authors. To be able to conclude this would require a comprehensive comparison, which is currently not possible, because the only available performance results refer to the hit rate, the standard deviation is not available in all cases, and not all specific implementations are available to be able to run and compare the obtained results in a much more thorough way.

Table 6. Results using the proposed method.

Methods	Features	Success rate (%)
No feature selection		
Naïve Bayes [25]	41	76.56
Random forest [25]	41	80.67
Decision tree (J48) [25]	41	81.05
AdaBoost [26]	41	90.31
GHSOM-pr [26]	41	99.59
GHSOM [27]	41	96.02
Filtering methods		
Naïve Bayes + N2B [26]	41	96.50
Naïve Bayes + *Gain ratio* [23]	30	89.03
Naïve Bayes + *Info.gain* [23]	30	93.49
IBK con Symmetric + Gain ratio [24]	15	98.50
Proposed GHSOM con One R	**21**	**97.09**
PCA	30	82.1
PART + Chi Squared [24]	30	97.57
PART + Consistency [24]	14	97.57
Wrapper Method		
GHSOM + multi-target feature selection [24]	25	99.12

References

1. Kimani, K., Oduol, V., Langat, K.: Cyber security challenges for IoT-based smart grid networks. Int. J. Crit. Infrastruct. Protect. **25**, 36–49 (2019)
2. Guerrero, C.D., Salcedo, D., Lamos, H.: A clustering approach to reduce the available bandwidth estimation error. IEEE Lat. Am. Trans. **11**(3), 927–932 (2013)
3. Kumar Kundu, M., Mohapatra, D.P., Konar, A., Chakraborty, A. (eds.): Advanced Computing, Networking and Informatics- Volume 1. SIST, vol. 27. Springer, Cham (2014). https://doi.org/10.1007/978-3-319-07353-8
4. Ibrahim, H.E., Badr, S.M., Shaheen, M.A.: Adaptive layered approach using machine learning techniques with gain ratio for intrusion detection systems. arXiv preprint arXiv:1210.7650 (2012)
5. Barletta, V.S., Caivano, D., Nannavecchia, A., Scalera, M.: Intrusion detection for in-vehicle communication networks: an unsupervised Kohonen SOM approach. Future Internet **12**(7), 119 (2020)

6. Holte, R.C.: Very simple classification rules perform well on most commonly used datasets. Mach. Learn. **11**(1), 63–90 (1993)
7. Kohonen, T.: Analysis of a simple self-organizing process. Biol. Cybern. **44**(2), 135–140 (1982)
8. Dittenbach, M., Merkl, D., Rauber, A.: Organizing and exploring high-dimensional data with the growing hierarchical self-organizing map. In: FSKD, pp. 626–630 (2002)
9. Sánchez-maroño, V.B.N.: A review of feature selection methods on synthetic data. Knowl. Inf. Syst. **34**, 483–519 (2013). https://doi.org/10.1007/s10115-012-0487-8
10. Spolâ, N., Monard, M.C.: Label construction for multi-label feature selection (2014). https://doi.org/10.1109/BRACIS.2014.52
11. Kaur, R., Kumar, G., Kumar, K.: A comparative study of feature selection techniques for intrusion detection. In: 2nd International Conference on Computing for Sustainable Global Development (2015)
12. Singh, R., Kumar, H., Singla, R.K.: Analysis of feature selection techniques for network traffic dataset. In: 2013 International Conference on Machine Intelligence and Research Advancement (ICMIRA), pp. 42–46. IEEE (2013)
13. Ghosh, M., Guha, R., Sarkar, R., Abraham, A.: A wrapper-filter feature selection technique based on ant colony optimization. Neural Comput. Appl. **32**, 7839–7857 (2019)
14. Ali, M.: An ensemble-based feature selection methodology for case-based learning. Doctoral dissertation, University of Tasmania (2018)
15. Osanaiye, O., Cai, H., Choo, K.-K., Dehghantanha, A., Xu, Z., Dlodlo, M.: Ensemble-based multi-filter feature selection method for DDoS detection in cloud computing. EURASIP J. Wirel. Commun. Netw. **2016**(1), 1 (2016). https://doi.org/10.1186/s13638-016-0623-3
16. Bolón-Canedo, V., Sánchez-Maroño, N., Alonso-Betanzos, A.: A review of feature selection methods on synthetic data. Knowl. Inf. Syst. **34**(3), 483–519 (2013). https://doi.org/10.1007/s10115-012-0487-8
17. Enache, A.-C., Sgarciu, V.: Anomaly intrusions detection based on support vector machines with bat algorithm. In: 2014 18th International Conference on System Theory, Control and Computing (ICSTCC), pp. 856–861 (2014). https://doi.org/10.1109/ICSTCC.2014.6982526
18. Ferles, C., Papanikolaou, Y., Naidoo, K.J.: Denoising autoencoder self-organizing map (DASOM). Neural Netw. **105**, 112–131 (2018)
19. Dai, J., Xu, Q.: Attribute selection based on information gain ratio in fuzzy rough set theory with application to tumor classification. Appl. Soft Comput. **13**(1), 211–221 (2013)
20. Aranda, Y.R., Sotolongo, A.R.: Integración de los algoritmos de minería de datos 1R, PRISM e ID3 a PostgreSQL. JISTEM-J. Inf. Syst. Technol. Manage. **10**(2), 389–406 (2013)
21. Chen, A.M., Lu, H.M., Hecht-Nielsen, R.: Sobre la geometría de las superficies de error de red neuronal de avance. Cálculo Neuronal **5**(6), 910–927 (1993)
22. Chiu, C. H., Chen, J.J., Yu, F.: An effective distributed ghsom algorithm for unsupervised clustering on big data. In: 2017 IEEE International Congress on Big Data (BigData Congress), pp. 297–304 (2017)
23. Kohonen, T.: Associative Memory: A System-Theoretical Approach, vol. 17. Springer, Heidelberg (2012)
24. Kohonen, T.: Essentials of the self-organizing map. Neural Netw. **37**, 52–65 (2013)
25. De La Hoz Franco, E., Ortiz Garcia, A., Ortega Lopera, J., De La Hoz Correa, E., Mendoza Palechor, F.: Implementation of an intrusion detection system based on self organizing map. J. Theor. Appl. Inf. Technol. **71**(3), 324–334 (2015)
26. Rauber, A., Merkl, D., Dittenbach, M.: The GHSOM Architecture and Training Process. Department of Software Technology, Vienna University of Technology (2016)
27. Dittenbach, M., Merkl, D., Rauber, A.: The growing hierarchical self-organizing map. In: Proceedings of the IEEE-INNS-ENNS International Joint Conference on Neural Networks. IJCNN 2000. Neural Computing: New Challenges and Perspectives for the New Millennium, vol. 6, pp. 15–19. IEEE (2000)

Anonymous Group Signature Scheme with Publicly Verifiable General Access Structure

Tomasz Hyla$^{(\boxtimes)}$ and Jerzy Pejaś

West Pomeranian University of Technology, Szczecin, Poland
{thyla,jpejas}@zut.edu.pl

Abstract. The group signature scheme allows a group member or defined subsets of all group members to sign a message on behalf of the group. Any party can verify the validity of the group signature, as well as whether it was created by member of the group or members of some subgroup. However, without the participation of the group manager it is not possible to determine exactly who is part of the group. This paper proposes a new generalised group signature scheme in which members of an authorised set can jointly create a group signature without revealing the identities of its members. Furthermore, the authorised sets can be dynamically modified. The scheme is existentially unforgeable against adaptively chosen message attacks assuming the hardness of Computational Diffie-Hellman problem and meets other requirements imposed on group signature schemes. The scheme has been implemented and performance tests have shown that the scheme is suitable for practical application.

Keywords: Group signature · Secret sharing · Digital signature · Anonymity · General access structure

1 Introduction

In a group signature scheme, the entity signs a message not on behalf of himself, but on the behalf of the group. A recipient of a group signature can verify its validity as well as verify whether a group member has created a signature or not. However, nobody knows (except the Group Manager, GM) who has generated the signature. In addition, it is difficult to determine whether the same group member generated two different signatures or not. These features of group signatures make them useful as a basic building block for many security applications such as electronic banking and electronic voting.

The term *group signature* or *group-oriented signatures* is sometimes used for another type of signature scheme in which signers form such groups that only the authorised members can cooperate to sign a message on behalf of the group. If a set of authorised signers form such groups that any set of $t-$out-of-n or more group members can together produce a signature, then the group signature is

© Springer Nature Switzerland AG 2021
K. Saeed and J. Dvorský (Eds.): CISIM 2021, LNCS 12883, pp. 140–155, 2021.
https://doi.org/10.1007/978-3-030-84340-3_11

called a threshold signature scheme. However, when the authorised set can be arbitrarily specified, it is called a generalised group signature scheme [1].

In threshold signature schemes and generalised group signature schemes, the dealer (group manager) splits a secret into different shares and transfers one share to each shareholder (a group member). However, if a dealer or some players are dishonest, an efficient verifiable secret sharing (VSS) schemes or publicly verifiable secret sharing (PVSS) schemes [15] are necessary in practice. In VSS scheme, the shareholder:

1. can verify the validity of the commitments to their shares and thus overcome the problem of dishonest dealers,
2. cannot submit wrong shares in the reconstruction phase.

For PVSS schemes (a) and (b) conditions can be verified publicly, i.e., the participants can verify their own shares and other participants' shares. The condition (b) means that it is possible to implicitly verify the shares without the need to reveal them.

1.1   Related Works

The concept of group signature was introduced by D. Chaum and E. van Heyst in 1991 [3]. After this work, many group signature schemes, e.g., [1,5] were presented. Many of them are built on a certificate-based traditional Public Key Cryptography (PKC), on an identity-based public key cryptography (ID-PKC) or on a certificateless public key cryptography (CL-PKC).

In many practical applications, the signature should be created for the information with different importance grades (or sensitivity levels). In such cases, the signatures can be generated by any subset of subjects, for example, by any group of any t or more subjects, chosen from the set of all n subjects. The conventional (t, n) threshold signature scheme is not applicable in this case. The reason is simple: the information is so important that it should be signed only by some special (qualified) subset of legal parities (signers) with proper rights. Thus, the generalised group signature schemes have wider potential application, than threshold schemes in the real world.

The group-oriented signature schemes with general access structure are more suitable to solve the problem of the group signature with authorised sets. An access structure describes which subsets of shareholders are qualified to recover the secret. In this type of scheme, the GM can specify, according to the message classification grade and the group signature policy, a set of distinct qualified subset of signers. The group signature for the message can be produced when and only when all signers in a specified combination work cooperatively. Nevertheless, most of proposed group-oriented signature schemes are threshold schemes, e.g.: [16,18]. Only a few generalised schemes are proposed (e.g., [17]).

Over the last few years, several more advanced group signature schemes not based on general access structures have been proposed. In 2018, Eom and Huh [6] proposed an efficient group signature scheme providing restrictive linkability.

The scheme proposed by Ishida et al. [7] uses verifier-local revocation. Also, Perera and Koshiba [11] proposed a fully dynamic group signature scheme that allows to both add and revoke member.

The novel generalised group signature scheme presented in this paper is conceptually closest to the threshold signature scheme based on the general access structure given in [12] and improved by Y. Cai et al. in [17]. However, in the contrast to the scheme of [17], the secrets $y^j, a^j \in Z_p^*$ are assigned to each authorised set A_j of the general access structure $\Gamma = \{A_j | j = 1, 2, ..., m\}$ separately and then implicitly associated with individual secrets $S_{i_j}^j$ of all shareholders $u_{i_j} \in A_j$ (cf. Eq. (1) and Eq. (15)).

$$\gamma_j - \sum_{u_{i_j} \in A_j} S_{i_j}^j \equiv y^j + a^j d_j \pmod{p} \tag{1}$$

1.2   Our Contribution

The proposed certificate-based generalised group signature (CB-GGS) is based on the secret sharing scheme [13] and Zhang et al. [19] certificate-based signature scheme and has the following features:

1. the scheme is a certificate-based generalised group signature scheme and meets the requirements for a generalised group signature;
2. the scheme preserves the anonymity of members of authorised set;
3. any authorised subset A_j is assigned a different private key y^j and a public key Pk_{A_j}, agreed as the result of protocol completion between all members in A_j; this approach has the advantage in comparison with a common access key for the whole access structure (cf. [17]), because disclosure of the key y^j affects only the members of subset A_j;
4. the designed publicly verifiable secret sharing scheme is based on bilinear pairings and allows owners of the secrets and all other members of the authorised set not only to verify the correctness of the shares, but also to evaluate the possibility of recovery of secret y^j by authorised set A_j in cooperation with the other members of that set;
5. the authorised set A_j is dynamic, i.e., neither the number of the participants nor the identity of the set A_j are fixed or known on the setup stage;
6. the access structure of the proposed signature system, as opposed to [17], do not have to be minimal – all members of an authorised set must always participate in a signature creation process; cancelling of this requirement allows defining the access structure as an arbitrary subset of the power set, i.e. $\Gamma \subseteq 2^U$;
7. in the event of dispute, the list of signers is publicly verifiable; this is possible because the opener (GM) publishes, together with the authorised set signature, some claims that particular signers produced a particular signature with a publicly verifiable evidences, which are available after the signature opening; it is evident that such solution protects against a corrupt opener.

To our knowledge, the generalised group signature scheme with above features has not been treated in the literature.

1.3   Paper Organisation

The reminder of the paper is structured as follows. The Sect. 2 contains a description of the algorithms that are part of our proposed scheme. The security analysis and performance evaluation are presented in Sect. 3. The paper ends with a conclusion.

2   Certificate-Based Group Signature Scheme with General Access Structure

For a given n-element set $U = \{u_1, u_2, ..., u_n\}$ containing all shareholders and m-element access structure $\Gamma = \{A_j | j = 1, 2, ..., m\} \subseteq 2^U$ we introduce three types of roles: Trusted Authority (TA), a Group Manager (GM) and a subset of group members (i.e. any authorised set $A_j \in \Gamma$, which members are entitled to sign the message). Hence, the proposed certificate-based generalised group signature (CB-GGS) consists of nine algorithms (cf. [9,10]): $Setup$, $CreateUser$, $GenerateCertificates$, $CreateQualifiedSet$, $JoinToQualifiedSet$, $RevokeFromQualifiedSet$, $Sign$, $Verify$, and $Open$.

Setup. For cyclic additive group $(G_1, +)$ and cyclic multiplicative group $(G_T, \times)$ of the same prime order p, TA chooses randomly its master secret key $s \in_R Z_p^*$, defines a bilinear pairing $\hat{e}$ and generates generalised group signature scheme parameters $params$:

$$
\begin{aligned}
&\hat{e} : G_1 \times G_1 \rightarrow G_T \\
&params = \{G_1, G_T, \hat{e}, p, P, P_0, H_0, H_1, H_2, H_3\}
\end{aligned}
\tag{2}
$$

where P is a generator of G_1^*, $P_0 = sP$ is a TA's public key, $H_0, H_1 : \{0,1\}^* \rightarrow Z_p^*$, $H_2 : \{0,1\}^* \rightarrow G_1^*$ and $H_3 : \{0,1\}^* \rightarrow 0, 1^n$ (n is a number of output bits) are secure hash functions.

CreateUser. Every shareholder $u_i \in U$ with an identity ID_i chooses a random number $s_i \in_R Z_p^* (i = 1, ..., n)$ as the private key, calculates the public key $Pk_i = s_i P$ and sends it to the TA. GM performs similar operations, $GM \notin U$: chooses the secret $s_{GM} \in_R Z_p^*$ and calculates the public key $Pk_{GM} = s_{GM} P$.

GenerateCertificates. For $i = 1, ..., n$, the TA randomly selects $r_i \in Z_p^*$ and calculates iteratively hash values $Q_i = H_0(ID_i, Pk_i, R_i)$, and then the corresponding shareholder's implicit and explicit certificates, i.e., $iCert_i = r_i + sQ_i$, $eCert_i = iCert_i P$, where $R_i = r_i P$. In similar way the GM's certificates $iCert_{GM}$ and $eCert_{GM}$ are calculated for $R_{GM} = r_{GM} P$ and ID_{GM}. The TA publishes all issued explicit certificates, i.e., $\{ID_i, (Pk_i, R_i, eCert_i)\}$ and records them on the registration list REG_{TA}. Then, TA sends implicit certificates to all users via a secure channel. Every shareholder with an identity ID_i tests authenticity of received certificates $iCert_i$ and $eCert_i$ using equation $\hat{e}(eCert_i, P) = \hat{e}(R_i, P)\hat{e}(Q_i P, P_0) = \hat{e}(iCert_i P, P)$. If the verification pass, then shareholder $u_i \in U (i = 1, ..., n)$ accepts the certificates and his public key Pk_i, else re-executes the $CreateUser$ algorithm. GM proceeds similarly.

CreateQualifiedSet. The GM chooses a random value $d_j \in_R Z_p \backslash \{1\}$ and assigns to the set $A_j \in \Gamma$ an unique identifier ID_{A_j}. Next, the GM registers the new authorised set $A_j \in \Gamma$ and appends the tuple $\{j, ID_{A_j}, d_j, A_j, \gamma_j, Pk_{A_j},$ $eCert_{A_j}, R_{A_j}, F_{A_j}(1), Z_{A_j}, \overline{R}_{A_j}\}$ to the GM's registration list REG_{GM}. The values of the variables $\gamma_j, Pk_{A_j}, eCert_{A_j}, R_{A_j}, F_{A_j}(1)$ and Z_{A_j} are initially equal to zero, while the sets A_j and $\overline{R}_{A_j}$ are empty. The contents of the sets and the values vary with each iteration of *JoinToQualifiedSet* or *RevokeFrom-QualifiedSet* protocol. For distinction, denote by $\gamma_{j,0}, Pk_{A_j,0}, eCert_{A_j,0}, R_{A_j,0},$ $F_{A_j,0}(1), Z_{A_j,0}$ and $R_{A_j,0}$ the initial authorised set A_j, public key $Pk_{A_j,0}$, its explicit certificate $eCert_{A_j,0}$ and the evidences $\gamma_{j,0}, F_{A_j,0}(1), Z_{A_j,0}, \overline{R}_{A_j,0}$. These parameters will be updated per joining or revocation operation.

JoinToQualifiedSet. We assume that any subject $u_w \in U$ joined to the authorised set A_j has the private key s_w, the public key Pk_w, implicit and explicit certificates $(iCert_w, eCert_w)$, and knows d_j - the parameter of the set A_j; this algorithm is executed by the entity $u_w \in U$ in cooperation with GM:

1. $u_w \rightarrow GM$: the shareholder u_w plays the role of initiator of this protocol.
   (a) the u_w chooses the function $f_i^j(x) = y_i^j + a_i^j x$ at random, where $f_i^j(x)$, $y_i^j, a_i^j \in Z_p^*$; an index i indicates the i-th member of the j-th set A_j and equals w when the entity $u_w \in U$ is joined, i.e. $i = w$;
   (b) the u_w chooses at random the value $r_i^j \in_R Z_p^*$ and calculates:

$$\widetilde{\gamma}_i^j = f_i^j(d_j) h_{1,i}^j + r_i^j h_{2,i}^j \tag{3}$$

$$R_{i,1}^j = r_i^j s_i^j P, R_{i,2}^j = s_i^j P, R_{i,3}^j = r_i^j P \tag{4}$$

$$R_{i,4}^j = \left(r_i^j + s_i^j h_{3,i}^j\right) P_0 \tag{5}$$

$$\widetilde{X}_i^j = y_i^j P, \widetilde{Z}_i^j = a_i^j P \tag{6}$$

$$\widetilde{F}_i^{\gamma,j}(1) = f_i^j(1) = \left(y_i^j + a_i^j\right) \tag{7}$$

where:

$$s_i^j = h_{2,i}^j \left(h_{1,i}^j\right)^{-1} \tag{8}$$

$$\left.\begin{array}{l} h_{1,i}^j = H_1\left(\hat{e}\left(eCert_{GM} + eCert_i, Pk_{GM}\right)^{s_i}, d_j\right) \\ h_{2,i}^j = H_1\left(\hat{e}\left(eCert_i, Pk_i\right)^{s_i}, d_j\right) \\ h_{3,i}^j = H_1\left(d_j, P\ k_i, R_{i,1}^j, R_{i,2}^j, R_{i,3}^j\right) \end{array}\right\} \tag{9}$$

Note. The value $S_i^j = r_i^j h_{2,i}^j \left(h_{1,i}^j\right)^{-1}$ will be henceforth called the share of shareholder $u_w \in U$ in the secret y^j of the set A_j.
   (c) the u_w sends $\widetilde{\gamma}_i^j, R_{i,1}^j, R_{i,2}^j, R_{i,3}^j, R_{i,4}^j, \widetilde{X}_i^j, \widetilde{Z}_i^j$ and $\widetilde{F}_i^j(1)$ to the GM; the value $r_i^j \in_R Z_p^*$ keeps in secret.
2. $GM \rightarrow REG_{GM}$: the GM plays the role of the responder for the shareholder u_w request and its response is placed in the public part of REG_{GM}.

(a) the GM checks, if values $\tilde{\gamma}_i^j, R_{i,1}^j, R_{i,2}^j, R_{i,3}^j, R_{i,4}^j, \tilde{X}_i^j, \tilde{Z}_i^j$ and $\tilde{F}_i^j$ (1) received from $u_w \in U$ meet the following:

$$\hat{e}\left(\tilde{\gamma}_i^j eCert_{GM}, P\right)^{\left(g_i^j\right)^{-1}} = \hat{e}\left(eCert_{GM}, \tilde{X}_i^j + d_j \tilde{Z}_i^j + R_{i,1}^j\right) \qquad (10)$$

$$\hat{e}\left(eCert_i, P\right) = \hat{e}\left(R_i, P\right)\hat{e}\left(H_0\left(ID_i, P\, k_i, R_i\right) P, P_0\right) \qquad (11)$$

$$\hat{e}\left(\tilde{F}_i^j\left(1\right), P\right) = \hat{e}\left(eCert_{GM}, \tilde{X}_i^j + \tilde{Z}_i^j\right) \qquad (12)$$

$$\left.\begin{aligned}\hat{e}\left(R_{i,4}^j, P\right) &= \hat{e}\left(R_{i,3}^j + h_{3,i}^j R_{i,2}^j, P_0\right) \\ \hat{e}\left(R_{i,1}^j, P\right) &= \hat{e}\left(R_{i,2}^j, R_{3,i}^j\right)\end{aligned}\right\} \qquad (13)$$

where:

$$g_i^j = h_{1,i}^j = H_1\left(\hat{e}\left(eCert_{GM} + eCert_i, X_i\right)^{s_{GM}}, d_j\right) \qquad (14)$$

Note. Before registering the user $u_w \in U$ as the member of the set A_j, the entity GM always checks in the register REG_{GM} if the user $u_w \in U$ is already the member of the set A_j. If the verification is positive, the GM rejects the registration request.

(b) If (10)–(14) hold for $u_w \in U$, then the GM chooses the function $\Delta f_i^j(x) = \Delta y_i^j + \Delta a_i^j x$ at random, where $\Delta f_i^j(x), \Delta y_i^j, \Delta a_i^j \in Z_p^*$ and updates the content of REG_{GM} (index k is the subsequent number of operation performed at the appropriate parameter related to the set A_j):

$$\gamma_j = \gamma_{j,k} = \gamma_{j,k-1} + \tilde{\gamma}_i^j\left(g_i^j\right)^{-1} + \Delta f_i^j(d_j)$$

$$= f_k^j(d_j) + \sum_{u_{i_j} \in A_{j,k}} r_i^j h_{2,i}^j\left(h_{1,i}^j\right)^{-1} \qquad (15)$$

$$X^j = y^j P = X_k^j = y_k^j P = X_{k-1}^j + \tilde{X}_i^j + \Delta\, y_i^j P \qquad (16)$$

$$Z^j = a^j P = Z_k^j = a_k^j P = Z_{k-1}^j + \tilde{Z}_i^j + \Delta\, a_i^j P \qquad (17)$$

$$Pk_{A_j} = Pk_{A_j,k} = X^j \qquad (18)$$

$$F_{A_j}(1) = F_{A_j,k}(1) = \left(y_k^j + a_k^j\right)$$

$$= F_{A_j,k-1}(1) + \tilde{F}_i^j(1) + \left(\Delta y_i^j + \Delta a_i^j\right) \qquad (19)$$

$$\overline{R}_{A_j} = \overline{R}_{A_j,k} = \overline{R}_{A_j,k-1} \cup \{i, R_{i,1}^j, R_{i,2}^j, R_{i,3}^j, R_{i,4}^j\} \qquad (20)$$

$$A_j = A_{j,k} = A_{j,k-1} \cup \{u_w\} \qquad (21)$$

It is evident that following equalities hold:

$$y^j = y_k^j = \sum_{u_{i_j} \in A_{j,k}} \left(y_i^j + \Delta y_i^j \right) \tag{22}$$

$$a^j = a_k^j = \sum_{u_{i_j} \in A_{j,k}} \left(a_i^j + \Delta a_i^j \right) \tag{23}$$

$$f_k^j (d_j) = y_k^j + a_k^j d_j \tag{24}$$

(c) the GM sends to TA the group's identity ID_{A_j}, the public key Pk_{A_j} and the evidence γ_j, and requests to issue the certificate for the authorized set $A_j \in \Gamma$; the TA randomly selects $r_{A_j} \in Z_p^*$ and according to *Generate-Certificates* algorithm calculates group's implicit and explicit certificates:

$$iCert_{A_j}x = iCert_{A_j,k} = r_{A_j} + sQ_{A_j}$$
$$= r_{A_j} + sH_0 \left(ID_{A_j}, \gamma_j, P\ k_{A_j}, R_{A_j} \right) \tag{25}$$
$$eCert_{A_j} = iCert_{A_j}P$$

where $R_{A_j} = r_{A_j}P$, $Pk_{A_j} = X^j = y^jP$ is the public key of the set A_j, and $y^j = \sum_{u_{i_j} \in A_j} \left(y_i^j + \Delta y_i^j \right)$ is its private key; if the previous value of certificate $eCert_{A_j,k-1}$ is not zero, then this certificate is revoked and placed on the Crl list in REG_{GM} (the entry of Crl contains the item $(Pk_{A_j,k-1}, eCert_{A_j,k-1}, t_{rev}, t_{inv})$, where t_{rev} and t_{inv} mean the notification time and Crl publication time, respectively; all signatures signed by the set A_j with $eCert_{k-1}^j$ are invalid from time t_{inv});

(d) the values: $d_j, \gamma_j, Pk_{A_j}, Z^j, eCert_{A_j}, R_{A_j}, F_{A_j}(1)$ and $\overline{R}_{A_j}$ are published by the GM in REG_{GM} and publicly available; the set $\overline{R}_{A_j}$ contains evidences of existing members of the set A_j and the evidence of its new member $u_w \in U$.

It should be noticed that any member $u_p \in A_j (p = 1, ..., |A_j|)$ can determine whether he has an appropriate share depending on his secret values (r_p^j, s_p^j):

$$\hat{e} \left(\gamma_j eCert_{GM}, P \right) = \hat{e} \left(eCert_{GM}, X^j + d_j Z^j \right)$$
$$\cdot \hat{e} \left(r_p^j s_p^j eCert_{GM}, P \right) \prod_{u_i \in A_j \setminus u_p} \hat{e} \left(eCert_{GM}, R_{i,1}^j \right) \tag{26}$$

$$\hat{e} \left(eCert_{A_j}, P \right) = \hat{e} \left(R_{A_j}, P \right) \hat{e} \left(H_0 \left(ID_{A_j}, \gamma_j, P\ k_{A_j}, R_{A_j} \right) P, P_0 \right)$$
$$\hat{e} \left(eCert_{GM}, P \right) = \hat{e} \left(R_{GM}, P \right) \hat{e} \left(H_0 \left(ID_{GM}, P\ k_{GM}, R_{GM} \right) P, P_0 \right) \tag{27}$$

and additionally the following must be hold for every $u_{i_j} \in A_j$:

$$\hat{e} \left(P, R_{i,1}^j \right) = \hat{e} \left(R_{i,2}^j, R_{3,i}^j \right) = \hat{e} \left(s_i^j P, r_i^j P \right) \tag{28}$$

$$\hat{e}(R_{i,4}^j, P) = \hat{e}(R_{i,3}^j + H_1(d_j, Pk_i, R_{i,1}^j, R_{i,2}^j, R_{i,3}^j)R_{i,2}^j, P_0) \tag{29}$$

Note. If the entity $u_i \notin U$, then the GM joins that entity to the set U before the execution of algorithm *JoinToQualifiedSet*.

RevokeFromQualifiedSet. The entity $u_i \in A_j$ is revoked from the set A_j if the further membership of this entity in the set A_j is no longer required or when his private keys are disclosed and it is necessary to revoke this entity from all sets $A_j (j = 1, ..., m)$. The revocation of the shareholder $u_i \in U$ from the group A_j is performed on request of the shareholder himself or request of an authorised entity (e.g. GM). The revocation algorithm revokes previous group public key $Pk_{A_j,k-1}$ and generates the new one $Pk_{A_j,k}$. The algorithm is executed by the GM in cooperation with the entity $u_i \in U$ and works as follows:

1. The entity u_i, which is revoked from the group A_j, performs actions in accordance with step 1(a) of $JoinToQualifiedSet$ protocol, then calculates (based on his secrets s_i and r_i^j):

$$\widetilde{\gamma}_i^j = f_i^j (d_j) h_{1,i}^j - r_i^j h_{2,i}^j \tag{30}$$

$$\widetilde{X}_i^j = y_i^j P, \widetilde{Z}_i^j = a_i^j P \tag{31}$$

$$\widetilde{F}_i^j (1) = f_i^j (1) = \left(y_i^j + a_i^j \right) \tag{32}$$

and sends them to the GM ($h_{1,i}^j$ and $h_{2,i}^j$ are defined as in Eq. (8)).

2. The GM picks the values $R_{i,1}^j, R_{i,2}^j, R_{i,3}^j, R_{i,4}^j$ from the register and checks whether $\widetilde{\gamma}_i^j, \widetilde{X}_i^j, \widetilde{Z}_i^j$, and $\widetilde{F}_i^j (1)$ received from $u_i \in U$ meet the following equalities:

$$\hat{e} \left(\widetilde{\gamma}_i^j eCert_{GM}, P \right)^{(g_i^j)^{-1}} = \hat{e} \left(Cert_{GM}, \widetilde{X}_i^j + d_j \widetilde{Z}_i^j \right) \hat{e} \left(eCert_{GM}, R_{i,1}^j \right)^{-1} \tag{33}$$

$$\hat{e} (eCert_i, P) = \hat{e} (R_i, P) \hat{e} (H_0 (ID_i, P k_i, R_i) P, P_0) \tag{34}$$

$$\hat{e} \left(\widetilde{F}_i^j (1), P \right) = \hat{e} \left(eCert_{GM}, \widetilde{X}_i + \widetilde{Z}_i \right) \tag{35}$$

3. If the verification of (33)–(35) is successful, the GM performs step 2(b)–(d) of $JoinToQualifiedSet$ protocol. The only difference is in the calculation of the value R_{A_j} and contents of the set A_j.

$$\overline{R}_{A_j} = \overline{R}_{A_j,k} = \overline{R}_{A_j,k-1} \backslash \left\{ i, R_{i,1}^j, R_{i,2}^j, R_{i,3}^j, R_{i,4}^j \right\} \tag{36}$$

$$A_j = A_{j,k} = A_{j,k-1} \backslash \{u_i\} \tag{37}$$

4. The GM updates the values: $\gamma_j, Pk_{A_j}, Z^j, eCert_{A_j}, R_{A_j}, F_{A_j} (1)$ and $\overline{R}_{A_j}$ in the register REG_{GM}.

5. The information concerning the revoked entity $u_i \in U$ are placed on the list of revoked entities Crl in REG_{GM}. The entry of Crl contains the tuple $(Pk_{A_j,k-1}, eCert_{A_j,k-1}, \gamma_{j,k-1}, ID_{A_j}, ID_i, t_{rev}, t_{inv})$, which means that a member $u_i \in U$ with identifier ID_i was revoked in time t_{rev} and all signatures signed by this user as a member of a set A_j with $eCert_{A_j,k-1}$ are invalid from time $t_{inv} \geq t_{rev}$.

Note. (1) In the case of an entity revocation from the authorised set A_j on request of the GM, when the cooperation of the GM and the entity is impossible, the GM revokes all members of the set A_j and the certificate of this set. Information about revoked entities and the certificate of authorised set are placed on entities revocation list Crl in REG_{GM}. All entries concerning this set are rejected from public and private parts of the registry REG_{GM} (the state of REG_{GM} is the same as after execution of *CreateQualifiedSet* algorithm for the group A_j with one exception – the new value d_j is generated). (2) If an adversary compromises the private key y_j of authorised set A_j, then the GM performs the same actions as in the case (1).

Sign. Assume that the authorised subset $A_j \in \Gamma$ wants to sign a message M. Then the creation of partial signature by the members of this set requires the GM cooperation and runs as follows.

1. For a message M the entity $u_i \in A_j$ creates a partial signature $\sigma_{i_j} = (U_{i_j}, R_{A_j})$, where:

$$U_{i_j} = r_i^j s_i^j h W$$
$$h = H_1(M, ID_{A_j}, Pk_{A_j}, R_{A_j}) \tag{38}$$
$$W = H_2(M, ID_{A_j}, Pk_{A_j})$$

and sends it to the GM. **Note.** It should be noted that anyone can verify the validity of $\sigma_{i_j} = (U_{i_j}, R_{A_j})$ signature share by checking Eqs. (37) and (38).

2. The GM takes all the partial signatures generated by each member of the set A_j and completes the signature by performing the following operations:
   (a) using REG_{GM} checks whether each signer is a valid member of the authorised group A_j; if the member was removed, then GM refuses partial signature immediately, otherwise GM checks correctness of the each partial signature $\sigma_{i_j} (i = 1, ..., |A_j|)$:

$$\hat{e}(U_{i_j}, P) = \hat{e}\left(W, h\, R_{i,1}^j\right)$$
$$\hat{e}\left(R_{i,4}^j, P\right) = \hat{e}\left(R_{i,3}^j + H_1\left(d_j, P\, k_i, R_{i,1}^j, R_{i,2}^j, R_{i,3}^j\right) R_{i,2}^j, P_0\right) \tag{39}$$

$$\hat{e}(eCert_{i_j}, P) = \hat{e}(R_{i_j}, P)\,\hat{e}\left(H_0\left(ID_{i_j}, Pk_{i_j}, R_{i_j}\right)P, P_0\right) \tag{40}$$

   (b) if (39) and (40) are valid for each $i = 1, ..., |A_j|)$, it means that the partial signatures were created by members of the authorised set A_j with the appropriate shares; the GM accepts partial signatures of members of this set and calculates:

$$\overline{U}_1 = -\sum_{u_i \in A_j} U_{i_j} + h\gamma_j W + iCert_{A_j} W$$
$$\overline{U}_2 = (F_{A_j}(1)h + iCert_{A_j})W \tag{41}$$

generates the digital group signature $\sigma = (\overline{U}, R_{A_j})$, wherein:

$$\overline{U} = \lambda_1 \overline{U}_1 + \lambda_2 \overline{U}_2 \tag{42}$$

where $\lambda_1 = \frac{-1}{d_j - 1} \in Z_p^*$, $\lambda_2 = \frac{d_j}{d_j - 1} \in Z_p^*$; both values are the coefficients of the Lagrange interpolation formula (42).

(c) the GM generates a new random value $k_{GM} \in Z_p^*$ and conceals identification data ID_{i_j} of each group members $u_i \in A_j (i = 1, \ldots, |A_j|)$ engaged in the signature creation and identification data ID_{A_j} of the authorised set A_j:

$$\overline{ID}_i = ID_i \oplus H_3\left(\hat{e}\left(eCert_{GM}, i \times k_{GM}P\right), \sigma, t_S\right) \tag{43}$$

where t_S is a system time stamp, and next, the GM generates an token-anonymity value $t_{k_{GM}}$ along with a covert identifier vector:

$$t_{k_{GM}} = k_{GM} + (s_{GM} \times iCert_{GM})H_1(\overline{A}_j, ID_{GM}, P_{GM}, R_{GM})$$
$$\overline{A}_j = \left\{\overline{ID}_{1_j}, \overline{ID}_{2_j}, \ldots, \overline{ID}_{|A_j|_j}\right\} \tag{44}$$

3. The GM uses the Zhang's et al. signature scheme [19] and generates the signature $\sigma_{GM} = (U_{GM}, R_{GM})$ for a message $\overline{U}$:
   (a) computes $h' = H_1(\overline{U}, ID_{GM}, Pk_{GM}, R_{GM})$, $W' = H_2(\overline{U}, ID_{GM}, Pk_{GM})$;
   (b) generates the digital signature $\sigma_{GM} = (U_{GM}, R_{GM})$, where:

$$U_{GM} = (s_{GM}h' + iCert_{GM})W' \tag{45}$$

Finally, the protocol outputs the full signature $\sigma_F = (M, \sigma, \sigma_{GM}, \overline{A}_j, t_{k_{GM}}, t_S)$ generated by the A_j group members.

Verify. To verify the correctness of the full signature $\sigma_F = (M, \sigma, \sigma_{GM}, \overline{A}_j, t_{k_{GM}}, t_S)$ a verifier check whether the signature was created by an authorised set of users A_j; for this purpose:

1. A verifier, based on the signature σ_F sends requests to GM to verify the concealed list of members of group A_j who are authorised to create the signature;
   (a) the GM opens the token-anonymity value $t_{k_{GM}}$ and calculates $\tau_{A_j} = k_{GM}P = t_{k_{GM}}P - s_{GM}\,H_1(\overline{A}_j, ID_{GM}, P_{GM}, R_{GM})eCert_G M$;
   (b) the GM can get identification data ID_i of every group member $u_i \in A_j (i = 1, \ldots, |A_j|)$ engaged in the creation of the signature $(M, \sigma, \overline{A}_j, t_{k_{GM}}, t_S)$:

$$ID_i' = \overline{ID}_i \oplus H_3\left(\hat{e}\left(eCert_{GM}, i \times k_{GM}P\right), \sigma, t_S\right) \tag{46}$$

If the user u_{i_j} with the identifier ID_i' is not a member of the group A_j or the list Crl includes a record $(Pk_{A_j,k-1}, eCert_{A_j,k-1}, \gamma_{j,k-1}, ID_{A_j}, ID_i, t_{rev}, t_{inv})$ and the two conditions are satisfied: $t_{rev} \leq t_{inv} \leq t_S$ and $ID_i' = ID_i$, then GM returns a message *invalid* to a verifier; a verifier refuses the signature;

2. If the GM returns a message *valid*, the verifier first checks the correctness of the signature σ_{GM}, and then the signature σ.
   (a) compute $h' = H_1(\overline{U}, ID_{GM}, Pk_{GM}, R_{GM})$, $W' = H_2(\overline{U}, ID_{GM}, Pk_{GM})$, and $Q_{GM} = H_0(ID_{GM}, Pk_{GM}, R_{GM})$;

(b) verify if:

$$\hat{e}(U_{GM}, P) = \hat{e}(W', h'Pk_{GM} + R_{GM} + Q_{GM}P_0) \qquad (47)$$

If the (45) holds return *valid*, else return *invalid*.
3. To verify the signature σ, the verifier computes:

$$\hat{e}(\overline{U}, P) = \hat{e}(W, hPk_{A_j} + R_{A_j} + Q_{A_j}P_0) \qquad (48)$$

where W, h and Q_{A_j} are defined in Eq. (36) and Eq. (23). The GM accepts a signature$(M, \sigma, A_j, t_{k_{GM}}, t_S)$ if and only if Eq. (46) holds.

Open. In the case of a dispute, the GM can open the signature $(\sigma, A_j, t_{k_{GM}}, t_s)$. This operation is based on the disclosure the value $\tau_{A_j} = k_{GM}P = t_{k_{GM}}P - s_{GM} H_1(\overline{A_j}, ID_{GM}, P_{GM}, R_{GM})eCert_{GM}$ from the token-anonymity $t_{k_{GM}}$. The publication of values τ_{A_j} allows each entity to reveal identification data of any member $u_i \in A_j (i = 1, \ldots, |A_j|)$ who was involved in the signature creation:

$$ID_i = \overline{ID}_i \oplus H_3\left(\hat{e}\left(eCert_{GM}, i\tau_{A_j}\right), \sigma, t_S\right) \qquad (49)$$

The knowledge of value τ_{A_j} allows also verifying the correctness of the signature σ and confirming the identity of the authorised set A_j:

$$\hat{e}\left(eCert_{A_j}, P\right) = \hat{e}\left(R_{A_j}, P\right)\hat{e}\left(H_0\left(ID_{A_j}, \gamma_j, Pk_{A_j}, R_{A_j}\right)P, P_0\right) \qquad (50)$$

as well as the identities of this set members:

$$\hat{e}\left(\gamma_j eCert_{GM}, P\right) = \hat{e}\left(eCert_{GM}, X^j + d_j Z^j\right) \prod_{u_i \in A_j} \hat{e}\left(eCert_{GM}, R_{i,1}^j\right) \qquad (51)$$

3 Discussion

3.1 Security Analysis

In this Section, security requirements for the scheme are listed. We discuss the requirements in the context of our proposed scheme. Due to page limits, security model and formal security proofs will be published in the full version of the paper.

Definition 1. *The certificate-based generalised group signature (CB-GGS) is secure if it is correct, unforgeable, anonymous, unlinkable, exculpable, traceable, coalition-resistant, and forward secure.*

The security requirements are as follow [1,4,20]:

- **Correctness.** Signatures produced by group members and GM must be accepted by any verifier.
- **Unforgeability.** Only group members and the GM (but not himself) are able to sign messages on behalf of the group. This feature should be publicly verifiable.

- **Anonymity**. Given a valid signature of a message, it is computationally hard for everybody (except GM) to identify the signers and the group of which they are members.
- **Unlinkability**. Unless to open signatures, it is computationally hard for anybody (except GM) to decide whether two different valid signatures were generated by the same group of members or not.
- **Exculpability** (non-framing). Neither a coalition of the authorised set members nor the group manager GM can generate a valid signature that will be opened by the *Open* procedure as generated from another group member.
- **Traceability**. GM can always open a valid signature using the *Open* procedure and identify the actual authorized group signers. This requirements prevents attacks where some group signature passes the verification procedure, but its opening by GM fails.
- **Coalition-resistance**. A colluding subset of group members (even if comprised of the whole group) cannot produce a valid signature that the group manager cannot open.
- **Forward security**. Signers who leave the group can no longer sign messages in behalf of the group. Removing the member from the group does not affect anything based on his secrets and shares from prior periods.

Correctness. A correctness requires showing that:

1. any entity (shareholder) $u_i \in A_j$ can check that he is able to recover the value of his concealed share S_i^j and it is the same as the values published by the GM;
2. any shareholder $u_i \in A_j$ can verify (without revealing shares) similar opportunities of other members of the set A_j;
3. each entity can create appropriate shares for the authorised set of which she or he is a member; these shares, in relation to the shares of the other members of the authorised set, allows recovering unambiguously (implicitly) the secret key of the authorised set and then use it to create the group signature;
4. the members of the authorised set are able to create the correct signature for any message M that can be properly open by the group manager (GM).

CB-GGS scheme meets the above mentioned properties, the proof will be in the full version of the paper.

Unforgeability. The proof of the unforgeability (Existential Unforgeability for Generalized Group Signature CB-GGS Against Adaptive Chosen Message Attacks) of our CB-GGS scheme is based on the concept of the simulatable adversary view. This idea was used by J. Baek and Y. Zheng [8] to define the simulatability of the ID-based threshold signature and to prove the relationship between the security of ID-based threshold signature and that of ID-based signature.

Anonymity. Given a valid generalised group signature $(M, \sigma, \sigma_{GM}, \overline{A_j}, t_{k_{GM}}, t_S)$ no one can determine either the identity of the authorised set A^j or the identity of its members. This was achieved due to randomly chosen factor k_{GM}

that blinds the confidential identifier vector A_j (cf. (44)), and does not allow to reveal the identity information to anyone except the authorised group A_j. From Eq.(44) follows that token-anonymity $t_{k_{GM}}$ is created according to Schnorr signature scheme [14]. This means that breaking the anonymity in CB-GGS scheme is a problem just as difficult as breaking the Schnorr signature scheme and requires to solve the DL_{G_1} problem in group G_1^*.

Unlinkability. Any two signatures $(M, \sigma, \sigma_{GM}, \overline{A_j}, t_{k_{GM}}, t_s)$ and $(M, \sigma', \sigma'_{GM}, \overline{A'_j}, t'_{k_{GM}}, t'_s)$ are related to two different sets of random numbers k_{GM} and k'_{GM} (cf. *Sign* algorithm). Hence, even if these signatures are generated for the same message and by the members of the same authorised set it is still computationally hard, for given $t_{k_{GM}}$ and $t'_{k_{GM}}$, to reveal the $k_{GM}P$ and $k'_{GM}P$ (cf. [43]) and deduce the signers list.

Exculpability. A distributed secrets share scheme applied in *JoinToQualified-Set* protocol) ensures that the GM does not know the shares (r_i^j, s_i^j) owned by the members u_i of any authorized set $A_j(i = 1, \ldots, |A_j|; j = 1, \ldots, m)$. Also, these shares are unknown to other members belonging to the same or another authorised set.

Traceability. The identity of the actual signer can be revealed from the procedure *Open*. Moreover, the signers list is publicly verifiable when the GM publishes the value $\tau_{A_j} = k_{GM}P$ (cf. (44) and (46)). No one (except GM) can open a generalised group signature.

Coalition-Resistance. The cooperation of the GM and the members of the authorised A_j set is required to create a valid signature $\sigma_F = (m, \sigma, \sigma_{GM}, \overline{A_j}, t_{k_{GM}}, t_s)$. The fact is that members of A_j are free to make the signature σ and generate $\overline{A_j}$ and $t_{k_{GM}}$, but they are unable to forge the signature σ_{GM} for the σ authentication. Hence, it is evident that proposed scheme CB-GGS is resisted against coalition attack efficiently.

Forward security. As we know (cf. *RevokeFromQualifiedSet* protocol), the information about removing the member u_i from authorised set A_j and the certificate $eCert_j$ revocation is recorded in the register REG_{GM} in the form of following tuple $(Pk_{A_j,k-1}, eCert_{A_j,k-1}, ID_{A_j}, ID_i, t_{rev}, t_{inv})$. Due to the t_{inv}, each partial signature made by a former member u_i of an authorised set cannot be longer accepted by GM. So, all signatures of each group A_j, in which the removed member u_i was involved, are invalid. However, any valid signature submitted with his participation and with corresponding time period before t_{inv} is still accepted and does not need to be re-signed.

3.2   Performance Evaluation

The CB-GGS scheme is computationally effective. Algorithms related to *Qualified Set* management has constant time complexity, which do not depend on the size of the set. The time complexity of *Sign, Verify* and *Open* algorithms is linear and depends on the number c of signers from the given authorised set A_j, i.e. $c = |A_j|$.

The time-consuming operations include scalar multiplication in G_1 (M_G), bilinear pairing on ($\hat{e}$) and exponentiation in G_T (P_{GT}). Other operations like: hashing, operations in (inversion, addition, multiplication), multiplication in G_T and addition in G_1 can be omitted in efficiency comparison, because they are several orders of magnitude faster when compared with pairings, scalar multiplications in G_1 and exponentiations in G_T.

The algorithms were tested using a laptop computer (Intel Core i7 3537U 2,00GHz, 16 GB RAM) and MIRACL library [2]. Type 1 symmetric pairing built on GF(p) curve was used (MR_PAIRING_SSP, AES-128 security GF(p) in MIRACL library). Time was measured using C++ chrono library and results are the average of five repetitions. Test results do not include data transfer time.

Table 1. CB-GGS PERFORMANCE (c - number of signers in the authorised set A_j)

Algorithm	Time Complexity	Time-consuming operations	Test results [s]
JoinToQualifiedSet	O(1)	$19M_G + 14\hat{e}$	1.36
RevokeFromQualifiedSet	O(1)	$15M_G + 11\hat{e}$	1.03
Sign	O(c)	$c(5M_G + 8\hat{e}) + 6M_G$	1.65 for $c = 2$ 2.30 for $c = 3$ 3.74 for $c = 5$ 7.40 for $c = 10$
Verify	O(c)	$c(M_G + \hat{e}) + 5M_G + 4\hat{e}$	0.64 for $c = 2$ 0.71 for $c = 3$ 0.86 for $c = 5$ 1.24 for $c = 10$
Open	O(c)	$c(M_G + 2\hat{e}) + 4M_G + 5\hat{e}$	0.78 for $c = 2$ 0.91 for $c = 3$ 1.21 for $c = 5$ 1.97 for $c = 10$

The execution time using the test computer is around one second for *Join*- and *RevokeFromQualifiedSet* algorithms (Table 1). The signing time varies from 1.7 (for two users in the set) to 7.4 s (for 10 users) and verification time from 0.6 to 1.2 s. The algorithms were tested using only a single thread and one computer (the worst-case scenario for implementation).

4   Conclusion

The CB-GGS scheme uses a double signature mechanism. The first signature provides authenticity and non-repudiation of a group signature, while the second guarantees that our scheme is coalition-resistant, i.e., any colluding subset of group members cannot produce a valid signature. Although the double signature mechanism reduces the effectiveness of the scheme, but it makes possible to meet all the security requirements for the group signature, which are specified

in Sect. 3. Of course, a double signature mechanism can be treated as optional
and should not be used if coalition-resistant is not needed.

In relation to recent group signature schemes [6,7,11], our scheme supports
dynamic access structure and therefore is more useful where there are many
groups and users. The scheme proposed by Eom and Huh [6] meets restrictive
linkability property. That property means that, among others things, signers
designate a linker who can check the linkability of the message. In contrast,
our scheme does not have that property but has unlikability property. Another
scheme, proposed by Ishida et al. [7], uses different approach (verifier-local revocation) for member revocation than our scheme. In our approach, group manager
must verify information about revoked users before generating the signature
and information about revoked users must be frequently updated. In verifier-
local technique [7], the signature can be generated without information about
revoked users. The scheme proposed by Perera and Koshiba [11] also support
verifier-local revocation.

The main limitation of the scheme is that infrastructure to manage certificates' revocation list is required and the trusted party (the group manager)
is necessary during signature generation and verification. During generation of
the group signature the group manager must verify if users' certificates are not
revoked. Also, the verifier cannot verify the group signature without using group
manager support, because only the group manager can internally open the signature and verify if the group certificate is not on the revocation list. Additionally, secure channels are required in *CreateUser*, *GenerateCertificates*, and *Verify*
algorithms.

The CB-GGS scheme was implemented and tested. The tests show that even
implementation without any optimization (like parallel and distributed processing) executed on a five year old computer is efficient enough for practical application. The most time-consuming operations in the scheme are bilinear pairings'
computations, which can be accelerated using techniques like precomputations
or secure computation outsourcing.

References

1. Camenisch, J.: Efficient and generalized group signatures. In: Fumy, W. (ed.)
   EUROCRYPT 1997. LNCS, vol. 1233, pp. 465–479. Springer, Heidelberg (1997).
   https://doi.org/10.1007/3-540-69053-0_32
2. CertiVox/MIRACL: MIRACL cryptographic SDK: multiprecision integer and
   rational arithmetic cryptographic library (2020). https://github.com/CertiVox/
   MIRACL. 7.0.0
3. Chaum, D., van Heyst, E.: Group signatures. In: Davies, D.W. (ed.) EUROCRYPT
   1991. LNCS, vol. 547, pp. 257–265. Springer, Heidelberg (1991). https://doi.org/
   10.1007/3-540-46416-6_22
4. Chen, X., Zhang, F., Kim, K.: New id-based group signature from pairings. J. Electron. (China) **23**(6), 892–900 (2006). https://doi.org/10.1007/s11767-005-0065-2
5. Cheng, X., Wang, J., Du, J.: A new revocation method for standard model group
   signature. J. Comput. **9**(5), 1053–1057 (2014)

6. Eom, S., Huh, J.H.: Group signature with restrictive linkability: minimizing privacy exposure in ubiquitous environment. J. Ambient Intell. Hum. Comput. 1–11 (2018)
7. Ishida, A., Sakai, Y., Emura, K., Hanaoka, G., Tanaka, K.: Fully anonymous group signature with verifier-local revocation. In: Catalano, D., De Prisco, R. (eds.) SCN 2018. LNCS, vol. 11035, pp. 23–42. Springer, Cham (2018). https://doi.org/10.1007/978-3-319-98113-0_2
8. Baek, J., Zheng, Y.: Identity-based threshold signature scheme from the bilinear pairings (extended abstract). In: Proceedings of the International Conference on Information Technology: Coding and Computing, 2004 (ITCC 2004), vol. 1, pp. 124–128, April 2004. https://doi.org/10.1109/ITCC.2004.1286437
9. Liang, X., Cao, Z., Shao, J., Lin, H.: Short group signature without random oracles. In: Qing, S., Imai, H., Wang, G. (eds.) ICICS 2007. LNCS, vol. 4861, pp. 69–82. Springer, Heidelberg (2007). https://doi.org/10.1007/978-3-540-77048-0_6
10. Park, S., Kim, S., Won, D.: ID-based group signature. Electron. Lett. **23**(19), 1616–1617 (1997)
11. Perera, M.N.S., Koshiba, T.: Fully dynamic group signature scheme with member registration and verifier-local revocation. In: Ghosh, D., Giri, D., Mohapatra, R.N., Sakurai, K., Savas, E., Som, T. (eds.) ICMC 2018. SPMS, vol. 253, pp. 399–415. Springer, Singapore (2018). https://doi.org/10.1007/978-981-13-2095-8_31
12. Qin, H.W., Dai, Y.W., Wang, Z.Q.: Threshold signature scheme based on the general access structure. Beijing Youdian Daxue Xuebao/J. Beijing Univ. Posts Telecommun. **32**, 102–104+119 (2009)
13. Sang, Y., Zeng, J., Li, Z., You, L.: A secret sharing scheme with general access structures and its applications. Int. J. Adv. Comput. Technol. **3**(4), 121–128 (2011)
14. Schnorr, C.P.: Efficient identification and signatures for smart cards. In: Brassard, G. (ed.) CRYPTO 1989. LNCS, vol. 435, pp. 239–252. Springer, New York (1990). https://doi.org/10.1007/0-387-34805-0_22
15. Schoenmakers, B.: A simple publicly verifiable secret sharing scheme and its application to electronic voting. In: Wiener, M. (ed.) CRYPTO 1999. LNCS, vol. 1666, pp. 148–164. Springer, Heidelberg (1999). https://doi.org/10.1007/3-540-48405-1_10
16. Wang, F., Chang, C.C., Harn, L.: Simulatable and secure certificate-based threshold signature without pairings. Secur. Commun. Netw. **7**(11), 2094–2103 (2014). https://doi.org/10.1002/sec.921
17. Yongquan, C., En, Z., Fula, C.: Analysis and improvement of a threshold signature scheme based on the general access structure. Procedia Eng. **15**, 4470–4475 (2011). https://doi.org/10.1016/j.proeng.2011.08.840
18. Zhang, Y., Wang, X., Qiu, G.: A secure and efficient threshold group signature scheme. In: Qin, S., et al. (eds.) Applied Mechanics, Mechatronics and Intelligent Systems - Proceedings of the 2015 International Conference (AMMIS2015), pp. 567–573. World Scientific Publishing Co., Pte. Ltd. (2016). ISBN #9789814733878
19. Zhang, Y., Li, J., Wang, Z., Yao, W.: A new efficient certificate-based signature scheme. Chin. J. Electron. **24**(4), 776–782 (2015). https://doi.org/10.1049/cje.2015.10.019
20. Zhu, J., Cui, G., Zhou, S.: Two group signature schemes with multiple strategies based on bilinear pairings. Int. J. Inf. Technol. Comput. Sci. **1**, 16–22 (2009). https://doi.org/10.5815/ijitcs.2009.01.03

A Novel Proposal of Using NLP to Analyze IoT Apps Towards Securing User Data

Raghunath Maji[1], Atreyee Biswas[2], and Rituparna Chaki[1(✉)]

[1] AKC School of Information Technology, Calcutta University, Kolkata, India
[2] Maulana Abul Kalam Azad University of Technology, West Bengal, Kolkata, India

Abstract. The evolution of Internet of Things over the years has led to all time connectivity among us. However, the heterogeneity of the constituent layers of IoT makes it vulnerable to multiple security threats. One of the typical vulnerability of IoT involves the endpoint, i.e. the apps that are used by end users for enabling IoT services. Generally, the users have to authorize the app, during installation time, to perform certain tasks. Often the apps ask for permissions to access information which are not related to the IoT services provided by them. These over-privileged apps have the chance to turn malicious at any moment and use such information for their benefit. Sometimes, the users are naive enough to trust the apps and grant permissions without caution, thus leading to unintended exposure of personal information to malicious apps. It is important to analyze the app description for understanding the exact meaning of a stated functionality in the app description. In this paper, we have focused on the use of NLP in securing user data from malicious IoT apps by analysing their privacy policies and user reviews. This is followed by a novel proposal that supports cautious decision making of users based on a careful analysis of app behaviour.

Keywords: Natural language processing · Internet of Things · Malicious app · Endpoint security · HDBSCAN · Lda2vec · Isolation forest

1 Introduction

The internet of Things (IoT) environment is becoming increasingly popular in the present era due to the flexibility it offers. The applications of IoT cover almost all the facades of human existence. The applications involving IoT include a variety of entities and actors. The actors may be end-point users such as doctors or patients in a smart healthcare system, the farmers using a smart farming system, etc. In all the applications of IoT, smart phone apps play the role of enablers of the IoT services. Consequently, the use of smart app has been increased to great extent. From educational institutes to healthcare systems and financial sectors, everyone takes help of various apps which facilitate users to get smooth services.

© Springer Nature Switzerland AG 2021
K. Saeed and J. Dvorský (Eds.): CISIM 2021, LNCS 12883, pp. 156–168, 2021.
https://doi.org/10.1007/978-3-030-84340-3_12

However, the ease of use comes with a price – the price of security. Whenever an app is used for procuring some service, the users need to share their personal data to some extent like location, phone number, their likes and dislikes, etc. These information are necessary for better service delivery. The installation of any app requires the user to agree to a series of permissions being granted to the app. Generally, the users have no time to go through these lengthy documents and they agree to them immediately-without much thought. This thoughtless behavior exposes the users to unintended disclosure of their private information. Often the apps seek permissions which are not relevant to their executions. These over-privileged apps have the chance of turning security breaches. IoT users need to exercise caution while granting these permissions to avoid severe misuse of their personal information. Therefore, giving permissions to the mobile applications in a righteous way is a very important issue for securing data over the IoT environment. Thus it becomes essential to develop techniques for checking an app's behaviors prior to installing. According to the report released by McAfee [1] in November 2020, 419 threats are observed per minute in Q2 2020 showing an increase of almost 12% over the previous quarter.

The challenge faced by researchers in this domain is to identify the malicious apps out of all the available apps so as to protect the IoT user's personal information. There are two types of techniques that have been used to detect malicious apps so far. The first one is static data flow analysis and the second one is dynamic data flow analysis or runtime behavior analysis. Static analysis method detects the malicious app based on string feature or structural feature. The string feature uses the Android application information, source code, and API call. The structural features mainly consider about the structural relationship within the app such as CFG (Control Flow Graph). The static method consumes less time and resource as compared to dynamic method because it does not need to run the app.

In this paper, we consider an in-depth study of static analysis methods for predicting app behaviour. The focus is mainly on methods that used NLP based techniques for accurately classifying apps as malicious or safe. Based on our study, we have presented a novel proposal for app behaviour analysis aimed to protect users from unwanted access to personal information. This new technique will be useful in securing the user's information in a more efficient manner. In this connection we like to mention that we thought to develop this technique keeping security of IOT users only in mind, because, with rapid increase of people's affinity towards IOT gadgets, people's personal and important information are being put at stake through these apps mostly. The rest of the paper is organized as follows: Sect. 2 consists of the reviews of state of the art research work which would be required to understand the research gaps. Section 3 presents the research gaps in this field as obtained from the literature survey. Section 4 discusses the basics of proposed technique to classify apps as malicious or safe depending on its behavior analysis. Section 5 discusses future scope before concluding the paper.

2   Related Work

In this section we review some significant recent works on different techniques and approaches for identifying malicious app behaviour with the help of NLP and will figure out the research gap.

The authors in [2] proposed a framework, called SmartPI, that collects the functionality-relevant user reviews from noisy crowd sourced user reviews using Natural Language Processing (NLP) techniques and estimated the permissions effects of applications to reduce the gap between functionality and the actual behavior of an app. To do this, they used some NLP analysis techniques such as words lemmatization (for the normalization of words in texts), Word2Vec (a word embedding technique for identifying functiona lity-relevant user reviews), Biterm topic model (a topic model technique for building the permission inference model). For new applications, SmartPI compares the declared permissions in manifest files with the inferred permissions of apps that provide similar functionalities from user reviews with the help of NLP techniques and then identifies whether the new application asks for supererogatory permissions from users. However, this SmartPI approach for predicting malicious app behavior relies entirely on user reviews assuming that all the users are trustworthy and therefore fails to detect malicious attackers who appear in guise of user reviewers.

In an another work by A. Gorla et al. [3] a prototype called CHABADA was introduced that detects mobile applications with irrational behavior. In CHABADA approach, the authors checked app's behaviour in five steps: 1) downloading collection of apps from Google -Play store, 2) topic modelling 3) clustering applications by related topic, 4) identifying the APIs which each app statically accesses and 5) identifying outliers with respect to API usage. In particular, they used LDA (Latent Dirichlet Allocation) as topic modelling technique for identifying the main topics of each android application from app description and K-mean clustering algorithm to separate all applications into some clusters (Cluster 1 Map, Traffic, Routes Cluster 2 Cities, Travel, Visits). In the Android application, the API can perform their tasks automatically if the user has already granted permission. They used Apktool to extract and detect sensitive APIs used in Android applications and unsupervised One-Class SVM anomaly classification technique (OC-SVM) to identify outliers. However, in order to test application behavior, in this work only the app description has been considered, but context of IoT is also an important aspect of verifying the application behavior and can be an interesting research topic.

In CHABADA the author creates a data flow pattern by extracting semantic meaning from its description and on the basis of this they detect abnormally sensitive API uses. The description of the app in Google Play has a character limit, thus it does not describe the behavior of an app in detail. Hence prediction of behaviour lacks accuracy as the description is not complete. In [4] the authors proposed a Text-based Application Verification system called TAPVerifier to overcome the above problem. The TAPVerifier system analyzes four types of software artifacts, including, privacy policy, bytecodes, description and permissions. The author has prepared a table here where the results of VirusTotal, CHABADA, and TAPVerifier have been compared. It has been shown that TAPVerifier can analyze privacy policy with a high accuracy and recall rate and more importantly, integrating privacy policy and bytecode level information can remove up to 59.4% false alerts of the state-of-the-art systems, such as AutoCog, CHABADA, etc.

In [5] the authors have made some changes in their previous paper on CHABADA to get better results. They made some improvements in their previous approach to detect outliers in each cluster with respect to their API usage and the improvements are mainly related to filtering outliers, optimal selection of OC-SVM kernel sizes, and weights in APIs using IDF that can produce better results than their previous paper [3]. The authors had shown that the updated algorithm now predicts 74% of malware's (previously it was 56%), and the false positives rate 11% (previously 15%). It is to be mentioned here that the apps they have tested in both papers [3] and [5] are all free apps that earn money through advertising or donations. In this paper, the authors have not tested on any paid app. So further study is needed to check it's effectiveness on paid apps.

In CHABADA the author's have identified malicious activity in an app using app description. However, this information (about the maliciousness of the app) is not reusable in the context of checking behavior of another application. In [6] the authors proposed an improved version of CHABADA that detects malicious apps by comparing app description and app behavior using semi-supervised learning and active learning. The results published by the authors showed that the updated method could achieve a higher F-measure than the previous method. The updated method also achieved higher accuracy with minimum number of labeled data.

In CHABADA the authors decide whether the application is corrupted or benign, based on the presence of privileged API calls, whereas Demissie et al. [7] considered only the execution paths from public entry points to privileged API calls. In [7] the authors proposed a framework to detect permission re-delegation vulnerabilities in Android apps. The methodology is a combination of four techniques: static analysis, natural language processing, machine learning, and genetic algorithm-based test generation techniques. A simple code is used to identify the over privileged API calls. To find out the data flow patterns of the Android application, the authors used only the similar type of application, not all applications.

The authors in [8] proposed a prototype to raise awareness among users about malware while installing an application. In general, when we install an Android app, it shows all its permissions on one page and these are quite long in length prompting users to strike the "accept" button without really going through the details. In [8] The author assigned each permission a separate box to draw the user's attention. They showed the individual relationship between an app's permissions and the concrete pieces of personal and private information that can be accessed. They created a modified permission display that they thought will alert users more than Google's permission display. For example, the Google play store permission display dialog box displays the message "full internet access......accept" while modified permission display dialog box displays "this app can download file like a virus to your phone or upload your private information.......accept". In this work Amazon's Mechanical Turk service had been used to perform this mapping. It showed that participants spent less time (3.1 s) on the modified version over the old permission box (7.6 s). The authors succeeded in bringing more clarity to the permission set. However, habituation and general changes in behavior may occur with respect to privacy may occur with this modified permission display approach and therefore it requires to do more research on long term affects associated with increased attention of users due to this modification.

ContexIoT [9] is a context-based permission system for appified IoT platforms. IoT systems are built with some sensor node appified IoT Platforms and programming framework. The appified IoT Platforms refers to a smart device or mobile device and the programming framework refers to an app. Smart application is useful in handling these smart sensors. They also provide permission to smart devices through the appified IoT platforms. The permission system plays an important role in IoT security. The authors in [9] created a context-based permission system for the IoT system and used it to check the app's behavior. For example, let us consider two different commands: 'open the door-When the homeowner wants to enter the house' (context1) and 'open the door-When no one is present in the house' (context2). In both the cases the task is same but context is different. They used the Samsung Smart Things platform and pitch the Context with the app before they are submitted for execution. The proposal aimed to detect malicious behavior of the app with static analysis. This means they do not enforce access control at runtime which is essential to improve the efficiency.

The approaches proposed in [2,3,9] used static data flow analysis to identify the malicious activity in android app. In [10], the author proposed a machine learning approach where they used a combination of static and dynamic data flow analysis to detect malicious apps. Static analysis extracts the manifest.xml file from the APK file and test it using the Machine Learning technique while the dynamic analysis checks the behavior of a file while it is running. Thus combined application of static and dynamic data flow analysis develop ed an efficient and effective android mobile application with a high success rate of distinguishing malicious from benign applications.

Static data flow analysis and dynamic data flow analysis are used to identify malicious activity in an android application. However in these detection technologies the uncertainty of the features are not considered. MADFU [11] is a features uncertainty based malicious application detection model. Here the author used logistic regression function to describe the relationship between permission and labels. The Markov chain Monte Carlo (MCMC) algorithm was used to measure features' uncertainty. An experiment with 20337 samples was conducted that resulted in an accuracy of up to 95.5%, and the false-positive rate (FPR) is 1.2%. It is to be mentioned here that though MADFU used dangerous permissions to detect the behavior of Android applications, but it is impossible to identify the behavior of apps only by permission.

The authors in [12] proposed a mobile privacy nudges that could increase user awareness of data collection practices and effectively could motivate users to review and often revise their app permissions.

The authors in [13] proposed a framework for security analysis of the emerging smart home programming platform. Authors used some third-party apps to make it easier to access the smart home device. These third-party apps largely increases the security risk of the device. They experimented on a total of 499 Samsung Smart Themes apps and found that 55% of the apps were over-privileged. They discovered security-critical design flaws in two cases: the Smart Things capability model and the event subsystem. They also had shown how various security issues conspire to weaken home security. In particular, they used static analysis on Smart App source code to check whether the app is over privileged or not. The main drawback of this framework is that they cannot analyze the app presented in binary format. The use of only static analysis also puts a restriction on the capability of the proposed framework.

The author's in [14] proposed a technology called MAPPER (Mapping Application Description to Permissions) that checks whether the application's permission is completely covered in the application description or not. Here the authors used Android manifest files of 1100+ Android applications to extract the API details. In [15] the author proposes a technical tool called APPA (automatic app privacy assessment) that generates personalized privacy scores for each application which help the user during the app selection phase.

An user-centered authorization and system-level enforcement mechanism called SmartAuth was introduced in [16]. SmartAuth system collects and evaluates all security-related data of all apps installed on the smart device (like smart phone) to minimize the gap between a user's expectations of what an IoT app will do and the app's true functionality. The authors compared the actual functionality of the application (determined by program analysis) with the functionality that the developers present. This is achieved by using NLP techniques to analyze app details provided by developers on the Google Play Store. Specifically, in SmartAuth [16] Samsung smart-Things had been used for obtaining app description. The authors then tried to mitigate security risk of extra privileged IoT applications. Now, the SmartAuth authorization mechanism is basically a context-sensitive security policy with low overhead. A malicious developer can fool this technique using custom-defined methods and property names mirroring Smart-Things commands.

Story et al. [17] framed a methodology using NLP techniques to compare the practices described in privacy policies of smartphone apps to the practices actually performed by these apps covered by those policies in compliance with Government regulations. They framed the identification of privacy practice statements in privacy policies as a classification problem, addressed with a three-tiered approach: a privacy practice statement which is classified based on a data type (e.g., location), party (i.e., first or third party), and modality (i.e., whether a practice is explicitly described as being performed or not performed). The performance results of this three-tiered classification methodology suggested an improvement over the state-of-the-art with negative F1 scores ranging from 78% to 100%. They argued that their NLP analysis of privacy policies to be an integral part of Mobile App Privacy System (MAPS), which they used to analyze 1,035,853 free apps on the Google Play Store. Potential compliance issues appeared to be widespread, particularly, when it comes to the disclosure of third party practices. These and similar results may be of interest to app developers, app stores, privacy activists, and regulators.

Tao et al. [18], in order to provide a detailed overview of apps' security issues for users, introduced SRR-Miner, a novel review summarization approach that automatically summarizes security issues and users' sentiments through NLP techniques. In this methodology, SRR-Miner followed a keyword-based approach to extracting security-related review sentences. Basically it summarized security issues and users' sentiments with <misbehavior-aspect-opinion> triples, which made full use of the deep analysis of sentence structures. SRR-Miner also provided visualized review summarization through a radar chart. The authors applied their methodology on 17 mobile apps and their evaluation had shown that SRR-Miner achieves higher F1-score and MCC than Machine Learning-based classification approaches in extracting security-related review sentences.

3   Research Gap

From the study of state of the art research in the previous section, we have arrived at the following research gaps that demand attention.

It is observed that, context analysis of app description plays significant role in accurate interpretation of the intention of an app. Unfortunately, this aspect is mostly missing in the reviewed works. Therefore context based framework equipped with improved algorithms may serve remarkably to distinguish malware from benign apps.

The NLP technologies and their different combinations are not explored extensively. In order to understand the semantic relationships among the various keywords used in the app descriptions and user reviews, suitable combinations of NLP technologies may prove to be significant.

IT is also observed that the previous works considered mostly app descriptions and API provided by the app developer for identifying malicious app behaviour. However, due to the character limit in Google Play, the description of an app may not contain detailed information about the app behaviours. Thus it becomes important to consider other sources such as user reviews along with app description for improved detection of malicious apps.

In the following section we propose a novel frame work where the above mentioned research gaps are addressed and may proved to be a better technique in identifying malicious apps.

4   Proposed Framework

In this section we have proposed a new framework for detecting malicious apps in IOT context using combinations of different NLP technologies. This framework consists of the following steps:

- Pre-processing android application privacy policy and user review with NLP technique.
- Topic modeling with lda2vec.
- Clustering android application with HDBSCAN.
- API analysis.
- Outlier detection with Isolation forest algorithm.

We describe each steps in detail as follows (Fig. 1):

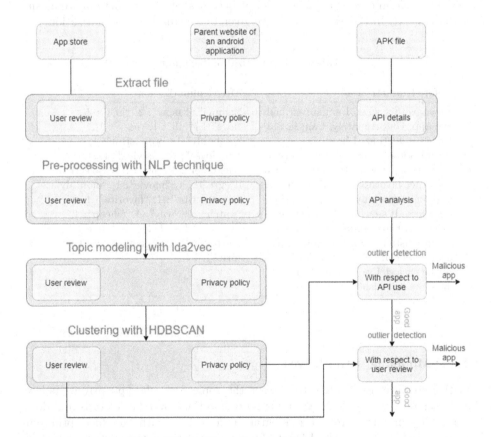

Fig. 1. The system architecture

Pre-processing Android Application Privacy Policy and User Review with NLP Technique

Initially, as We are considering texts in only English language here, all application privacy policies and reviews that are not written in English will be removed from the database. Next, all HTML tags and punctuation stop words (it, a .... on ....) have to be removed from the user reviews and app privacy policy because they do not provide any relevant information from the perspective of NLP strategies. During this step, we reduce the word to their root word, i.e., similar words are reduced to the same root word using lemmatization technique. One major difference of lemmatization with stemming is that it takes a part of speech parameter, "pos" if not supplied. Lemmatization has higher accuracy rate compared to stemming because it always gives the dictionary meaning word while converting into root-form. For example, stemming converts "Studies" to "Studi" while in case of lemmatization it becomes "Study" giving a more meaningful context. In the Table 1, we have given one example of lemmatization.

Table 1. Lemmatization technique

Before lemmatization	After lemmatization
I love Netflix when I am subscribed to the app. Unfortunately, I am not at this current time. I have it downloaded however. There's just a lot of cheaper ways to watch most of my other favorite T.V. Shows movies without a monthly bill. But Netflix does have it's own great selection of shows that my Hubby and I miss. Their Customer Service Employees are wonderful. They are probably one of the easiest I've ever worked with. Just the price isn't for me	"lemma": "show": 2, "just": 2, "love":1, "bill": 1, "easy": 1, "probably":1, "wonderful": 1, "employee": 1, "service": 1, "customer": 1, "miss": 1, "selection": 1, "great": 1, "movie": 1, "monthly": 1, "subscribe": 1, "favorite": 1, "watch": 1, "way": 1, "cheap": 1, "lot": 1, "download": 1, "time": 1, "current": 1, "unfortunately": 1, "price": 1

Topic Modeling with lda2vec

In this step we use lda2vec to extract the topic from the app privacy policy and user review. The lda2vec builds representations over both words and documents by mixing word2vec's skipgram architecture with Dirichlet-optimized sparse topic mixtures. The LDA technique cannot guess the context word but by providing an additional context vector in the lda2vec model, it is possible to better guess the context word. For example, if we use this technique on a food related document, it will put apples, bananas, mangoes, and oranges in a group and if we use this technique on any city related document, it will put Kolkata,

Delhi, Ahmedabad, Bangalore, these cities in another group. Therefore when used this technique in an android application's privacy policy and reviews, it gives complete information about how much it is related to a topic.

Clustering Android Application with HDBSCAN

The result of topic modeling is a vector of affinity value to each topic for each application. The main purpose of clustering is to place similar applications in the same group for further use. Here we use the HDBSCAN clustering technique to group the similar type of topics. The HDBSCAN clustering technique perform the work in five simple steps:

1 Transform the space according to the density/sparsity.
2 Build the minimum spanning tree of the distance weighted graph.
3 Construct a cluster hierarchy of connected components.
4 Condense the cluster hierarchy based on minimum cluster size.
5 Extract the stable clusters from the condensed tree.

API Analysis

The most important thing to identify a malicious app is to identify the malicious APIs, first you have to download an Android APK file for which different authors use different toolkits. Here we have used the APK tool. The apps made with Android have all the details of the APIs in their manifest.xml file. So we first extract all the details of APIs from the manifest.xml file. We only tested the APIs specified in the manifest.xml file here because, if the permissions are not declared in the manifest.xml file of the Android app, the API call will fail to execute, so it is not relevant to the analysis of the application behaviour. Then to find out which permissions each of these APIs are using, we relied on the work of Felt et al., who identified and used the mapping between permissions and Android methods [19]. The main goal of this app analysis is to identify what APIs these applications are using and what permissions those APIs are using, which will then be used to identify malicious apps by comparing them to their privacy policies.

4.1 Outlier Detection with Isolation Forest Algorithm

Here the outlier detection technique collects data as input from topic modeling, such as the topic the application belongs to, the group the application belongs to, and the minimum permissions requested by each Android application in a group. It also collects data from API analysis as to which API it is using and what permissions its API is seeking. Based on this data, the outlier detection technique identified which apps are seeking to use extra permissions. Here we have used Isolation forest algorithm technique for outlier detection. The Isolation forest algorithm is a tree-based anomaly detection algorithm. It takes advantage of two anomalies' quantitative properties: a) they are the minority consisting of fewer instances and b) they have attribute-values that are very different from those of normal instances.

5   Comparative Analysis with CHABADA

CHABADA and its extensions have used the stemming techniques for preprocessing, LDA for Topic modeling, K-Means for clustering, and One class-SVM for
outlier detection. The computational complexity of LDA algorithm is $O(Nd^2)$ if
$N > d$ otherwise $O(d^3)$ where 'd' indicates the number of features and 'N' indicates the number of applications under consideration. The K-Means algorithm
is NP hard problem but if k and d are fixed then the complexity is $O(n^{dk+1})$
where n is the number of entities to be clustered, d is the dimension of each
point and k is number of cluster and the time complexity of One class-SVM [20]
is $O(n^3)$. Thus CHABADA results in a minimum complexity of order $O(n^2)$.

Our aim is to design a light-weight tool for fast and accurate detection of security breach in IoT application. In order to achieve this objective, we have used
lemmatization technique instead of stemming for pre-processing because Lemmatization has higher accuracy rate compared to stemming. For example, stemming
converts "Studies" to "Studi" while in case of lemmatization it becomes "Study"
giving a more meaningful context. We have used Lda2vec model which combines
both LDA and Word2vec in a single framework where the computational com-
plexity of Word2vec is $O(log2(|V|))$, here 'V' indicates the vocabulary size. We
have used HBDSCAN for clustering and the average time complexity of this algorithm in case of accelerating index structure (e.g. All points within a distance
less than) is $O(logn)$. We have used the Isolation Forest algorithm (iForest)
for outlier detection and it has a linear time complexity $O(n)$. Thus the total
complexity is of order $O(n)$. This is definitely an improvement over CHABADA
and its' enhancements.

6   Conclusion

The IoT environment, consisting of heterogeneous operating layers, suffers from
security vulnerabilities at each layer. The authors in this paper have focused on
endpoint security in IoT. A state of the art literature survey in this domain have
been presented here. We have provided a comprehensive survey in a structured
manner that detects the Android malicious application more accurately. We have
identified a number of research gaps following the study. The work of [3] has been
observed to be a motivating one as it took up the use of NLP in an interesting
manner for identifying the maliciousness of an app. Based on our findings, we
have tried to solve some of the problems of their approach. It has been observed
that some of the applications are falsely identified as malicious since CHABADA
considers only the APIs related to the network and device ID.

In reality, however, the applications under consideration have explain the
use of all requested permissions in their respective privacy policies. To overcome
this type of problem, we have considered the Android application privacy policy
in our proposed method for analysis. The clustering technique of K-means as
used in CHABADA has certain drawbacks, (The K-means clustering does not
work well with outliers and noisy data sets, where the HDBSCAN is specifically

designed to handle outliers and noisy data sets.) hence we propose to replace it with a better clustering strategy (HDBSCAN) that clusters the Android applications based on user reviews and privacy policies. This is aimed to increase the accuracy of analysis. We use lda2vec, an advanced topic modelling technique that takes advantage of both LDA and Word2vec to generate better thematic clusters. Finally, we used a tree-based anomaly detection algorithm called "Isolation Forest" to detect outlier.

In future, we plan to validate the proposed model and present the comparative performance evaluations.

References

1. McAfee Labs Threats Report, November 2020. https://www.mcafee.com/enterprise/en-us/assets/reports/rp-quarterly-threats-nov-2020.pdf
2. Wang, R., Wang, Z., Tang, B., Zhao, L., Wang, L.: SmartPI: understanding permission implications of android apps from user reviews. IEEE Trans. Mob. Comput. **19**(12), 2933–2945 (2020). https://doi.org/10.1109/TMC.2019.2934441
3. Gorla, A., Tavecchia, I., Gross, F., Zeller, A.: Checking app behavior against app descriptions. In: Proceedings of the 36th International Conference on Software Engineering, pp. 1025–1035, May 2014
4. Yu, L., Luo, X., Qian, C., Wang, S., Leung, H.K.N.: Enhancing the description-to-behavior fidelity in android apps with privacy policy. IEEE Trans. Softw. Eng. **44**(9), 834–854 (2018). https://doi.org/10.1109/TSE.2017.2730198
5. Kuznetsov, K., Gorla, A., Tavecchia, I., Groß, F., Zeller, A.: Mining android apps for anomalies. In: Bird, C., Menzies, T., Zimmermann, T. (eds.) The Art and Science of Analyzing Software Data, pp. 257–283. Morgan Kaufmann (2015). https://doi.org/10.1016/B978-0-12-411519-4.00010-0. ISBN 9780124115194
6. Ma, S., Wang, S., Lo, D., Deng, R.H., Sun, C.: Active semi-supervised approach for checking app behavior against its description. In: IEEE 39th Annual Computer Software and Applications Conference, Taichung, Taiwan, pp. 179–184 (2015). https://doi.org/10.1109/COMPSAC.2015.93
7. Demissie, B.F., Ceccato, M., Shar, L.K.: Security analysis of permission re-delegation vulnerabilities in android apps. Empir. Softw. Eng. **25**, 5084–5136 (2020). https://doi.org/10.1007/s10664-020-09879-8
8. Harbach, M., Hettig, M., Weber, S., Smith, M.: Using personal examples to improve risk communication for security & privacy decisions. In: Proceedings of the SIGCHI Conference on Human Factors in Computing Systems, pp. 2647–2656, April 2014
9. Jia, Y.J., et al.: ContexIoT: towards providing contextual integrity to appified IoT platforms. In: 21st Network and Distributed Security Symposium (NDSS 2017), February 2017
10. Shibija, K., Joseph, R.V.: A machine learning approach to the detection and analysis of android malicious apps. In: International Conference on Computer Communication and Informatics (ICCCI), pp. 1–4 (2018). https://doi.org/10.1109/ICCCI.2018.8441472
11. Yuan, H., Tang, Y.: MADFU: an improved malicious application detection method based on features uncertainty. Entropy **22**(7), 792 (2020). https://doi.org/10.3390/e22070792

12. Almuhimedi, H., et al.: Your location has been shared 5,398 times! A field study on mobile app privacy nudging. In: Proceedings of the 33rd Annual ACM Conference on Human Factors in Computing Systems, pp. 787–796, April 2015
13. Fernandes, E., Jung, J., Prakash, A.: Security analysis of emerging smart home applications. In: IEEE Symposium on Security and Privacy (SP) 2016, pp. 636–654 (2016). https://doi.org/10.1109/SP.2016.44
14. Solanki, R.K., Laxmi, V., Gaur, M.S.: MAPPER: mapping application description to permissions. In: Kallel, S., Cuppens, F., Cuppens-Boulahia, N., Hadj Kacem, A. (eds.) CRiSIS 2019. LNCS, vol. 12026, pp. 84–98. Springer, Cham (2020). https://doi.org/10.1007/978-3-030-41568-6_6
15. Wettlaufer, J., Simo, H.: Decision support for mobile app selection via automated privacy assessment. In: Friedewald, M., Önen, M., Lievens, E., Krenn, S., Fricker, S. (eds.) Privacy and Identity 2019. IAICT, vol. 576, pp. 292–307. Springer, Cham (2020). https://doi.org/10.1007/978-3-030-42504-3_19
16. Tian, Y., et al.: Smartauth: user-centered authorization for the internet of things. In: Proceedings of the 26th USENIX Conference on Security Symposium (SEC 2017), pp. 361–378. USENIX Association, USA (2017)
17. Story, P., et al.: Natural language processing for mobile app privacy compliance. In: AAAI Spring Symposium on Privacy-Enhancing Artificial Intelligence and Language Technologies (2019)
18. Tao, C., Guo, H., Huang, Z.: Identifying security issues for mobile applications based on user review summarization. Inf. Softw. Technol. **122**, 106290 (2020)
19. Felt, A.P., Chin, E., Hanna, S., Song, D., Wagner, D.: Android permissions demystified. In: ACM Conference on Computer and Communications Security (CCS), pp. 627–638. ACM, New York (2011)
20. Abdiansah, A., Wardoyo, R.: Time complexity analysis of support vector machines (SVM) in LibSVM. Int. J. Comput. Appl. **128**(3), 28–34 (2015). https://doi.org/10.5120/ijca2015906480

Addressing the Permutational Flow Shop Scheduling Problem Through Constructive Heuristics: A Statistical Comparison

Javier Velásquez Rodriguez[1], Dionicio Neira Rodado[1(✉)], Alexander Parody[2],
Fernando Crespo[3], and Laurina Brugés-Ballesteros[1]

[1] Universidad de la Costa CUC, Calle 54 No 55-66, Barranquilla, Colombia
{jvelasqu3,dneira1}@cuc.edu.co
[2] Universidad Libre, Carrera 46 No 48 – 170, Barranquilla, Colombia
[3] Universidad Alberto Hurtado, Santiago de Chile, Chile

Abstract. Flow shop problem has been addressed by many researchers around the world. Different heuristic methods has been developed to deal with this kind of problems. Nevertheless, it is necessary to explore the impact that the bottleneck machine has on the performance of each heuristic. In this article an F6 ‖ Cmax (Makespan) flow shop is tackled with different well-known heuristics in open literature, such as Palmer, Johnson, Gupta, CDS, NEH and PAS and their impact on Cmax was measure. The methodology used seeks to find the possible relationship between the different bottleneck machines and the result obtained from each of the heuristics. For this experiment, there were 302 scenarios with six machines in series, in which each machine had a parity number of scenarios in which it was the bottleneck. The values of Cmax obtained for each heuristic were compared against the result of corresponding MILP (Mixed Integer Liner Problem) problem. The results show that the performance of the NEH heuristic is superior in each scenario, regardless of the bottleneck, but also shows a variable behavior in each heuristic, taking into account the bottleneck machine.

Keywords: Flow shop · Heuristics · Makespan

1 Introduction

The current globalized markets has forced companies all around the world to find different ways to operate in a more efficient way and remain competitive [1–3]. The search for ways to increase the companies' competitiveness include the optimization of the production process. In general, it can be said that there are two main categories for the type of the production process arrangement. These two categories are the flow shop and job shop and the way to addressed them in the scheduling problem is very different between each other.

The first one is the flow shop where n jobs have to be sequenced to enter a line of m machines each one performing a different operation (Fig. 1). All the jobs should pass through all operations following the same pattern. (i.e. all jobs must go first to machine one, then to machine two and so on).

© Springer Nature Switzerland AG 2021
K. Saeed and J. Dvorský (Eds.): CISIM 2021, LNCS 12883, pp. 169–181, 2021.
https://doi.org/10.1007/978-3-030-84340-3_13

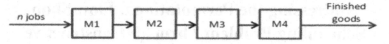

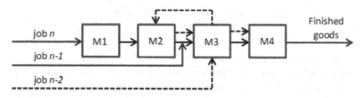

Fig. 1. General flow shop scheme

This type of shops is useful to represent high standardized processes that not required much flexibility.

On the other hand, is the job shop problem in which the jobs to be sequenced have to go to different work stations but the flow pattern in the shop floor is different for each job (Fig. 2).

Fig. 2. General job shop scheme

In the case of the simplest flow shop layout, there is only one machine per operation. In the cases that there is more than one machine per operation the problem is known as flexible flow shop problem. Another variant of the flow shop problem appears when the sequencing order can be modified downstream within the flow shop. Nevertheless, considering that this kind of scenario is rare, this paper focuses only on permutational flow shops, i.e. flow shops in which the sequencing order remains downstream within the flow shop.

The flow shop problem has been addressed for years by many researchers. This problem has been proved to be in the NP-hard category [4–7]. Therefore in order to solve it quickly and avoiding high computational times many heuristics and metaheuristics have been developed to address this problem [4–7]. The complexity increases when adding more machines to each work station. Nevertheless, as it was mentioned before this paper will focused only in the simplest form of flow shop, considering that the heuristics available to address the hybrid or flexible flow shop problems, have its roots in the heuristics developed for the simple flow shop problem. In this sense, it is important in the context of high complex problems, in which many jobs and machines are involved, to determine if the performance of a particular heuristic varies depending on the position of the bottleneck machine in the flow shop. This might reduce the computational time of metaheuristics, considering that having a good initial feasible solution might reduce the time the metaheuristic will converge.

This paper is organized as follows, in Sect. 2 a literature review of the more relevant heuristics is performed. Section 3 describes the process carried out. Section 4 drive some conclusions of the solution of the flow shop with simulated data through the different heuristics.

2 Literature Review

The flow shop scheduling problem is one of the most addressed topics in literature [8], because of its many economic and industrial applications. In its simplest form, the flow shop problem consists of two main elements: (1) a group of M machines and (2) a set of N jobs to be processed on this group of machines. Each job can be processed on one and only one machine at a time (which means no job splitting), and each machine can process only one job at a time. Each job is processed only once on each machine. Operations are not preemptable and set-up times of operations are independent of the sequences and therefore can be included in the processing time. The scheduling problem specifies the order and timing of the processing of the jobs on machines, with an objective or objectives respecting above-mentioned assumptions [8].

In general, the common objectives of these flow shop systems are the minimization of the average tardiness, the average flow time, number of tardy jobs, maximum tardiness and makespan [9]. The flow shop problem with makespan criterion can be defined as completion time at which all jobs complete processing or equivalently as maximum completion time of jobs. The makespan is the most frequent objective in flow shop problems. The search space in a permutational flow shop (number of possible sequences) can be determined with n!, where n is the number of jobs considered in the problem. On the other hand, in the classical flow shop, an infinite buffer is assumed and jobs may wait on or between the machines [10].

Many heuristics have been proposed to tackle the problem of minimizing the makespan in a flow shop considering its difficulty to be solved. In this sense it is important to mention the proposals by Palmer [11], Gupta [12, 13], Nawaz et al. [14], Campbell et al. [15]. These works tackle the problem in similar way implementing heuristics approaches that vary in their accuracy and solution time. The importance of these approaches lies on the fact that they allow to have good quality solution in small computing times considering as it was mentioned before that the problem is considered as NP-hard. Nevertheless some of these approaches base on the work by Johnson [10], in which a heuristic can give the optimal solution of a two machine flow shop problem.

When considering more complex problems, for example sequence-dependent set up times, multiple machines, zero buffer between machines and other, the problems increases in size and it becomes harder to solve. In these cases the adequate approaches include metaheuristics, such as Ant Colony Optimization, Genetic Algorithms, among others and the combination of these metaheuristics [8].

2.1 Johnson's Rule

According to Alharkan [16], Johnson's rule for addressing the flow shop problem, when minimizing the makespan has become a standard in the scheduling theory and many heuristics reduce the size of the problem to a two machine flow shop, in order to solve it at end with Johnsons rule.

The steps stated by Johnson in 1954 for his heuristic for constructing the optimal schedule can be summarized as follows [16]:

- Step 1: Form set-I containing all the jobs with $p_{1j} < p_{2j}$
- Step 2: Form set-II containing all the jobs with $p_{1j} > p_{2j}$
  The jobs with $p_{1j} = p_{2j}$ can be put in either set.
- Step 3: Form the sequence as follows:

a) The jobs in the set-I will be schedule following SPT rule.
b) The jobs in the set-II will be schedule following LPT rule. Ties are broken arbitrarily
c) The final schedule will be obtained listing the schedule of set-I and then the schedule of set-II. This type of schedule is referred to as SPT (1) – LPT (2) schedule.
Where p_{ij} corresponds to the processing time of job j in machine i.

2.2 Palmer Heuristic

Palmer [11], suggested the concept of a 'slope index' for each job. This slope index is a measure of whether a job proceeds from a shorter to a longer processing time in the sequence. The sequence is then constructed with the descending slope indices, with the idea that jobs that tend to proceed from shorter to longer processing times in the sequence of operations are processed earlier. While there might be several ways of implementing this precept, Palmer proposed a slope index for job j, SI_j, as:

$$SI_j = -\sum_{i=1}^{m}[m - (2i - 1)] * p_{ij}/2$$

Where p_{ij} corresponds to the processing time of job j in machine i, and m corresponds to the number of machines in the flow shop.
Then a permutation schedule is determined using the job ordering:

$$SI_{[1]} \geq SI_{[2]} \geq SI_{[3]} \geq \ldots \geq SI_{[n]}$$

2.3 Gupta Heuristic 1

Gupta [13], proposed a first heuristic for the minimization of the makespan in 1971. In his proposal Gupta calculates a slope index S_j for each job j. This slope index depends on the processing times of the job j in each machine k, and a gradient of the flow e_j that depends on the comparison of the processing times of job j in the first and last machine.

$$S_j = \frac{e_j}{min_{t \leq k \leq m-1}\{p_{ki} + p_{k+1,i}\}}$$

$$e_j = \begin{cases} -1 sip_{1,i} < p_{m,i} \\ +1 sip_{1,i} \geq p_{m,i} \end{cases}$$

The sequence is determined by ordering the jobs considering an increasing value of S_j.

2.4 Gupta Heuristic 2

Gupta [12], proposed a second heuristic for the minimization of the makespan on 1975, that requires the calculation of some parameters that will be used in the process. The process used by Gupta to address the m-machine flow shop problem implies breaking down the problem into K- auxiliary two machine problems. The processing times of the kth auxiliary two-machine problem are obtained from the original problem as follows: the sum of the processing times for the first k machines is treated as the processing time of a job on machine 1 of the auxiliary problem, while the sum of the processing times for the last k machines forms the processing time of a job on machine 2 of the auxiliary problem.

Gupta [12] set $p_k(j, 1)$ and $p_k(j, 2)$ as the processing times of job j for the kth auxiliary problem and calculates them as follows:

$$
\left.
\begin{aligned}
p_k(j, 1) &= \sum_{i=1}^{k} p_{ij}, \\
p_k(j, 2) &= \sum_{i=m+1-k}^{m} p_{ij},
\end{aligned}
\right|
\begin{aligned}
& j = 1, 2, 3, \ldots, n \\
& k = 1, 2, \ldots, K
\end{aligned}
$$

where $K = m - 1$, and represents the number of auxiliary problems to be solved.

Then Gupta [12] calculates the value $R(k, j)$ for the kth auxiliary problem as follows:

$$
R(k, j) = A_{kj}/\min(p_k(j, 1), p_k(j, 2))
$$

where,

$$
A_{kj}
\begin{cases}
= 1 & if \ \ p_k(j, 1) \geq p_k(j, 2) \\
= -1 & otherwise
\end{cases}
$$

Once all these calculations are made the heuristic implies the fulfillment of the following steps:

- Step 1: Calculate all the $R(k, j)$ for each k and j.
- Step 2: For each k create the sequence in an ascending order of the values of $R(k, j)$
- Step 3: For each k auxiliary problem, calculate the makespan.
- Step 4: Select the sequence with the lesser makespan.

2.5 CDS Heuristic

Campbell et al. [15] proposed a heuristic to address makespan problems, which is known the CDS algorithm. Using two main principles, this procedure yields good solutions: (1) it uses Johnson's rule in a heuristic way and (2) it generally creates several schedules, the best one of which should be chosen.

The CDS algorithm creates m-1 auxiliary two-machine problems and then solves them by implementing Johnson's two-machine algorithm. Then, the best m-1 obtained solution becomes the best solution for the main m-machine makespan problem. Processing times for the auxiliary two-machine subproblems for jth job on ith machine at kth auxiliary two machine problem can be calculated as follows:

$$p_k(j, 1) = \sum_{i=1}^{k} p_{ij}, \quad j = 1, 2, 3, \ldots, n$$

$$p_k(j, 2) = \sum_{i=m+1-k}^{m} p_{ij}, \quad k = 1, 2, \ldots, K$$

where $K = m - 1$, and represents the number of auxiliary problems to be solved.

2.6 NEH Heuristic

Nawaz et al. [14] proposed a heuristic, that constructs the flow shop sequence in an iterative manner. Two jobs having the largest values of total processing times (called total work content) are arranged in the two possible partial sequences. The partial sequence having the smaller makespan value is then selected for subsequent iteration. Then, next job from the work content list is picked and placed alternately at all possible locations in the partial sequence. This will generate 3 new sequences. For each one the value of the makespan is calculated, and the sequence giving the smallest value is kept. This process continues until all the jobs are placed in the partial sequence. The steps required to execute NEH are described as follows:

- Step 1: Find total work content for each job using expression:

$$T_j = \sum_{i=1}^{m} p_{ij}$$

- Step 2: Arrange all jobs in a work content list in a decreasing order of the value of T_j.
- Step 3: Select the two first jobs from the list and form two sequences by interchanging its positions. Compute the makespan for each sequence and discard the partial sequence with the highest value of makespan.
- Step 4: Pick next job from work content list, and construct all possible partial sequences, starting from selected partial sequence in the previous iteration and placing the new job in all possible locations within the previously selected sequence.
- Step 5: Calculate makespan for each partial sequence and keep the sequence with the lowest value of makespan. Continue this process until there is no jobs left in the work content list.

2.7 PAS Heuristic

Pugazhenthi et al. [17] proposed a heuristic, that generates m sequences and selects the sequence with the lesser makespan. The heuristic constructs the m sequences ordering the jobs in an ascending order considering the processing time of the jobs in the different machines. Each one of the m sequences is then evaluated and its makespan calculated selecting the sequence with the lesser makespan.

3   Study Case

The purpose of these study was to simulate some scenarios and evaluate the performance of the different heuristics Vs the mixed integer programming formulation for the flow shop. In this sense it is important to point out that this study was aimed also to assess if the performance of the different heuristics and to identify if the position of the bottleneck machine affects the performance of each one of them.

For this purpose, a 6-machine flow shop was simulated considering 20 jobs to be sequenced. The processing times for each job in each machine were simulated with a uniform distribution in excel ®. The minimum value of the uniform distribution was 5 and the maximum was 10000. The number of simulated scenarios was 302, and the distribution of the bottleneck machine can be observed on table No1:

Table 1. Number of scenarios in which each machine was the bottleneck.

	Number of scenarios as bottleneck
Machine 1	43
Machine 2	56
Machine 3	53
Machine 4	54
Machine 5	58
Machine 6	38

Then the different scenarios were tackled using the different heuristics and linear programming formulation. In each case the makespan (C_{max}) was calculated. The model used to represent and optimize the flow shop was a mix integer formulation based on the position each job has in the sequence.

The variables considered in the model were the following:

x_{jk} → *denotes if job j is assigned to position k*
C_{km} → *denotes completion time of position k on machine m*
C_{max} → *denotes the makespan*

The parameters considered in the model were:

p_{jm} → *denotes the processing time of job j on machine m*
K → *denotes the total number of positions*
M → *denotes the total number of machines*

These parameters and variables were used to formulate the following optimization problem:

$$Z_{min} = C_{max}$$

Subject to:

$$C_{km} \geq \sum_j (x_{jk} * p_{jm}) + C_{(k-1)m} \quad ; \forall(k, m)$$

$$C_{km} \geq \sum_j (x_{jk} * p_{jm}) + C_{k(m-1)} \quad ; \forall(k, m)$$

$$C_{0m} = 0 \quad ; \forall(m)$$

$$C_{K0} = 0 \quad ; \forall(k)$$

$$C_{max} \geq C_{KM}$$

This model was written in AMPL® and solved with Gurobi® through the Neos Server®. Each scenario was solved using this formulation and the value obtained for C_{max} was used as the basis for the comparison of the performance of the different heuristics.

4   Conclusions and Analysis of Results

As it was mentioned before the value of C_{max} was obtained for each scenario, with the MILP model and each one of the heuristics. In each case the percentage of difference between the heuristic and the MILP was calculated. Then the mean and the standard deviation of the differences were calculated for each heuristic in each case a particular machine acts as the bottleneck. This process drives to the calculation of six means and six standard deviation for the difference between MILP formulation and the heuristics. Each mean and standard deviation correspond to the cases in which each machine acts as the bottleneck machine.

Table 2. Summary of the performance of each heuristic

Bottleneck machine	Parameters	Heuristic					
		CDS	Gupta2	NEH	Palmer	Pugazhenthi	Gupta 1
M1	Mean	9.31%	9.31%	2.15%	10.88%	18.21%	15.50%
	Standard deviation	3.15%	3.15%	1.54%	4.69%	4.50%	6.30%
M2	Mean	8.79%	8.79%	2.07%	12.06%	20.42%	15.78%
	Standard deviation	4.20%	4.20%	1.71%	5.33%	5.39%	5.98%
M3	Mean	9.36%	9.36%	2.21%	12.94%	19.74%	16.62%
	Standard deviation	3.64%	3.64%	2.89%	5.02%	5.84%	6.44%
M4	Mean	7.94%	7.95%	2.04%	10.15%	16.37%	15.14%
	Standard deviation	3.72%	3.73%	1.55%	3.78%	5.50%	5.84%
M5	Mean	8.49%	8.49%	2.41%	10.95%	17.56%	17.30%
	Standard deviation	3.69%	3.69%	2.43%	3.95%	5.08%	6.96%
M6	Mean	8.19%	8.19%	1.92%	11.58%	17.88%	15.01%
	Standard deviation	3.30%	3.30%	1.75%	4.69%	4.84%	5.79%

The next step is to perform statistical tests in order to evaluate if there is a significant difference between the performance of the different heuristics. In this regard the first thing to do is to check if the data follow a normal distribution. Using the R® language the Anderson Darling test was used to evaluate normality. The results of the test can be observed on Table 2.

Table 3. P-value for Anderson Darling test for normality

| Bottleneck machine | p-value for Anderson Darling test for normality | | | | | |
	CDS	Gupta2	NEH	Palmer	Pugazhenthi	Gupta 1
M1	0.2764	0.2764	0.0111	0.0135	0.7488	0.0221
M2	0.0297	0.0297	0.0206	0.597	0.8915	0.6162
M3	0.4189	0.4189	0.0000	0.2051	0.617	0.0625
M4	0.532	0.5577	0.0238	0.4371	0.3914	0.6288
M5	0.5227	0.5227	0.0000	0.0261	0.7066	0.2554
M6	0.4481	0.4481	0.0136	0.4106	0.557	0.4492

The ANOVA comparison was not possible considering that normality condition was not met in all the samples (Table 3). Therefore, multiple comparison of the results of the medians was made in each of the methodologies by means of the Kruskall-Wallis test, accompanied by the box-and-whisker plot with notch on the median in order to establish between which methodologies there were significant differences when each of the analyzed machines (from M1 to M6) was placed as bottleneck. A total of 11 of the 36 samples analyzed did not comply with the data normality condition, given that the p-value of the Anderson Darling test showed a value less than 0.05. On the other hand, homoscedasticity condition was not met either. P-values for Levene's test were lesser than significance level of 0,05 (Table 4).

Table 4. P-values of the Levene's test

Machine	Test		*Valor-P*
M1	Levene's	14,62	1,36791E-12
M2		9,74	1,06071E-8
M3		7,43	0,00000131251
M4		9,75	1,11239E-8
M5		13,59	4,11449E-12
M6		7,59	0,00000131814

None of the p-values of the Levene's test presented a value above 0.05, therefore all the results of the analyzed methodologies show statistically significant differences in terms of the variances. Therefore, it was necessary to perform the comparison with the

Kruskal – Wallis test to compare the results of the different methods as the machine that would take the role of being the bottleneck was changed.

The values of Kruskall – Wallis test for the comparison within each machine, when being the bottleneck can be observed on Table 5.

Table 5. P-values of the Kruskal Wallis test for bottleneck machines

Bottleneck machine	Kruskal-Wallis Test statistic	p-value
Machine 1	158.68	0.00
Machine 2	213.75	0.00
Machine 3	199.17	0.00
Machine 4	192.55	0.00
Machine 5	212.52	0.00
Machine 6	147.36	0.00

On Table 5 can be observed that the results within each machine are statistically different, considering that in each case p-values are lesser than significance level of the test. This means that in each case in which a particular machine is the bottleneck there is a difference in the performance between the different heuristics. This highlights the relevance of selecting a particular heuristic to tackle the flow shop problem when minimizing the makespan.

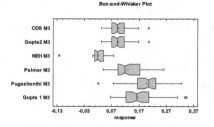

Fig. 3. Box and whisker plot - machine 1

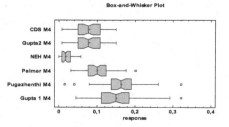

Fig. 4. Box and whisker plot - machine 2

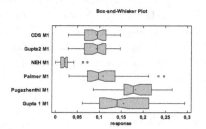

Fig. 5. Box and whisker plot - machine 3

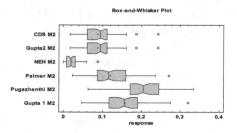

Fig. 6. Box and whisker plot - machine 4

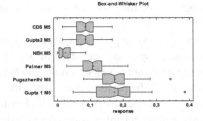

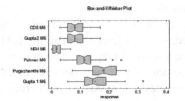

Fig. 7. Box and whisker plot - machine 5   **Fig. 8.** Box and whisker plot - machine 6

According to the test performed in each case (Fig. 3, 4, 5, 6, 7, 8 and Fig. 9), the best heuristic is NEH in all scenarios, followed by Gupta 2 and CDS. The tests show that there is no significant difference between these two heuristics. These results are common for the six cases. The next heuristic in the rank would be Palmer in all cases. Nevertheless, when the bottleneck is machine 1 and 4 there is no statistical difference with respect CDS.

On the other hand it is important to point out that the worst heuristic is the Pugazhenthi. Nevertheless, its performance also varies depending on the bottleneck. In the case that the bottleneck machine is 4, 5 and 6 there is no significant difference with Gupta 2.

This study shows how the position of the bottleneck machine affects the performance of the heuristic. This could be useful in the case for the solution of bigger problems where for the use of metaheuristics approach it is necessary the generation of an initial feasible solution. The quality of this initial feasible solution could affect the outcome of the metaheuristic. It is necessary to explore if this pattern is similar in problems with more and less machines, and to explore if the position will also affect other heuristics. On Fig. 9 it can also be observed the fact that the performance of CDS, Gupta 2, and NEH heuristic remains stable, no matter which machine the bottleneck is. On the other hand, in the case of Palmer and Pughazhenti their performance increases when machine 4 is the bottleneck. Additionally, these two heuristics have a better performance when the bottleneck is on the second half of the flow shop (machines 4, 5 and 6) rather than the

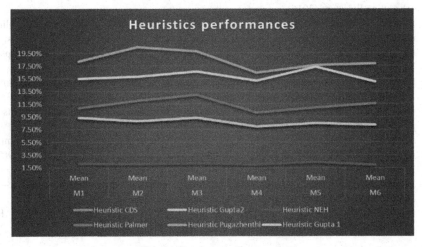

Fig. 9. Heuristic performances

cases when the bottleneck is in one of the machines of the first half of the flow shop (machines 1, 2, and 3).

For further research, tt is important to carry out more experiments, including more heuristics, such as Dannenbring [18], hybrid flow shops, and scenarios in which the maximum and minimum values of the processing times are smaller, in order to check if the variability of the processing times could also affect the performance of the different heuristics. Additionally, a multicriteria comparison could be carried out, in which criteria such as computational time, precision, variability, and others are considered and in doing so, a general rank for the heuristics could be made. For this purpose methodologies such as AHP and TOPSIS could be useful and could help to make better decisions related to the heuristic to use in a particular problem considering criteria such as the number of machines, the size of the problem, the variability of processing times, the objective function among others.

References

1. Neira Rodado, D., Escobar, J.W., García-Cáceres, R.G., Niebles Atencio, F.A.: A mathematical model for the product mixing and lot-sizing problem by considering stochastic demand. Int. J. Ind. Eng. Comput. **8**(2), 237–250 (2016)
2. Salcedo Miranda, R., Crespo, F., Ramirez, D., Neira, D., Castro Bolaño, L.J., Puello, N.: Estrategias de cooperación como fuente de competitividad: Caso de estudio del clúster de muebles del departamento del Atlántico (Colombia) (2017)
3. Ortiz, M., Neira, D., Jiménez, G., Hernández, H.: Solving flexible job-shop scheduling problem with transfer batches, setup times and multiple resources in apparel industry. In: Tan, Y., Shi, Y., Li, L. (eds.) ICSI 2016. LNCS, vol. 9713, pp. 47–58. Springer, Cham (2016). https://doi.org/10.1007/978-3-319-41009-8_6
4. Rossit, D.A., Tohmé, F., Frutos, M.: The non-permutation flow-shop scheduling problem: a literature review. Omega **77**, 143–153 (2017)
5. Wilson, J.M.: Alternative formulations of a flow-shop scheduling problem. J. Oper. Res. Soc. **40**(4), 395–399 (1989)
6. Neufeld, J.S., Gupta, J.N.D., Buscher, U.: A comprehensive review of flowshop group scheduling literature (2016)
7. Ronconi, D.P., Birgin, E.G.: Mixed-integer programming models for flowshop scheduling problems minimizing the total earliness and tardiness. In: Ríos-Mercado, R., Ríos-Solís, Y. (eds.) Just-in-Time Systems. SOIA, vol. 60, pp. 91–105. Springer, New York (2012). https://doi.org/10.1007/978-1-4614-1123-9_5
8. Reza Hejazi, S., Saghafian, S.: Flowshop-scheduling problems with makespan criterion: a review. Int. J. Prod. Res. **43**(14), 2895–2929 (2005)
9. Phanden, R.K., Jain, A.: Assessment of makespan performance for flexible process plans in job shop scheduling. IFAC-PapersOnLine **48**(3), 1948–1953 (2015)
10. Semančo, P., Modrák, V.: A comparison of constructive heuristics with the objective of minimizing makespan in the flow-shop scheduling problem. Acta Polytech. Hungarica **9**(5), 2012–177 (2012)
11. Palmer, D.S.: Sequencing jobs through a multi-stage process in the minimum total time—a quick method of obtaining a near optimum. J. Oper. Res. Soc. **16**(1), 101–107 (1965)
12. Gupta, J.N.D.: A heuristic algorithm for the flowshop scheduling problem. Rev. Fr. d'Automatique Inform. Rech. Oper. **10**(2), 63–73 (1976)

13. Gupta, J.N.D.: A Functional heuristic algorithm for the flowshop scheduling problem. J. Oper. Res. Soc. **22**(1), 39–47 (1971)
14. Nawaz, M., Enscore, E.E., Ham, I.: A heuristic algorithm for the m-machine, n-job flow-shop sequencing problem. Omega **11**(1), 91–95 (1983)
15. Campbell, H.G., Dudek, R.A., Smith, M.L.: A HEURISTIC ALGORITHM FOR THE n JOB, m MACHINE SEQUENCING PROBLEM* f, no. 10 (1970)
16. Alharkan, I.M.: Algorithms for Sequencing and Scheduling
17. Pugazhenthi, R., Anthony Xavior, M., Somasundharam, E.: Minimizing makespan of a permutation flowshop by, pp. 110–112 (2014)
18. Nurprihatin, F., Jayadi, E.L., Tannady, H.: Comparing heuristic methods' performance for pure flow shop scheduling under certain and uncertain demand. Manag. Prod. Eng. Rev. **11**, 50–61 (2020)

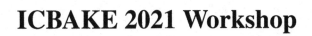

ICBAKE 2021 Workshop

Search for a Flavor Suited to Beverage by Interactive Genetic Algorithm

Makoto Fukumoto$^{(\boxtimes)}$ ⓘ and Seishiro Yoshimitsu

Fukuoka Institute of Technology, Fukuoka, Japan
fukumoto@fit.ac.jp

Abstract. Interactive evolutionary computation (IEC) is a method to optimize media contents suited to user's subjective feelings and preferences. Previous IECs employed various evolutionary algorithms, and most of them employed Genetic Algorithm (GA). The interactive type of GA is called IGA, and the IGA is applied to create user's media content such as computer graphics, music, and sound. As a special application of the IGA, the creation of the scent was already proposed. In the IGA related to the scent, the intensity of the source aromas was treated as variable of GA individuals. In this study, the IGA is applied to create the flavor suited to beverage. The soda water with no sugar is treated as the beverage. It is popular among health-minded people, and some of the soda waters wear a flavor. In other words, the purpose of this study is to create a good flavor suited to soda water by reflecting each user's feeling using IGA. In the use of the IGA, the user looks at the soda water with no sugar and smells the mixed flavor. In the mixture of the source aromas, Aromageur is used in the system. To investigate the fundamental efficiency of the IGA, a smelling experiment was conducted. The target of creation was "delicious" flavor for soda water, and six aroma oils were used as the source oils. The significant increase in fitness value was observed.

Keywords: Interactive Evolutionary Computation · Genetic Algorithm · Flavor · Beverage · Subjective evaluation

1 Introduction

Various media contents move our minds in terms of enjoyment, excitement, and impressment. Most of these contents are related to the sense of sight and hearing. In addition, recent information technology enables us to use the contents related to smell. Using the contents related to smelling is important from viewpoints of not only multi-modality but also the strong connection of smelling and brain. The human sense of smell is believed as weak long time, however, recent studies revealed that the sense of smell is not weak [1].

From a different perspective, using contents related to smell is important for the development of products. A recent trend of a lifestyle keeping healthy by restricting carbohydrate intake, some of foods and drinks contains flavor. One of the examples, some of the makers flavor soda water to be flavored beverages and sell them. These

© Springer Nature Switzerland AG 2021
K. Saeed and J. Dvorský (Eds.): CISIM 2021, LNCS 12883, pp. 185–192, 2021.
https://doi.org/10.1007/978-3-030-84340-3_14

flavored soda waters are expected to keep us healthy by avoiding sugar and satisfied us with their flavor.

This study aims to create a flavor that will be attached to the soda water. The flavors described above are defined by the makers. Creating the flavors suited to each person is an ideal concept of this study. To realize the concept, Interactive Evolutionary Computation (IEC) [2, 3] is used in this study. IEC is an approach where solution evaluation must be performed by human users, while EC employs mathematical or certain functions to evaluate solutions. As a famous EC, Genetic Algorithm (GA) [4, 5] is well known as a search method. Thus, the flavor is treated as a solution candidate, GA individuals, in this study.

The scent has been treated as a target of optimization of IEC. For example, search methods of preferable scent for each user were proposed [6–8]. GA, Differential Evolution, and Tabu Search were used as EC in these studies respectively. The target was just a creation of scent. No-application of the scent was considered in these studies. By following these studies, some previous IECs tried to create scents suited to a certain product. For example, a previous study proposed IEC creating the scent suited to a deodorizer [9]. However, no previous study applied IEC creating scent suited to food and drinks which do not have scent originally.

The purpose of this study is to investigate the effect of IGA on the creation of flavor suited to a beverage. Especially, soda water is treated as the beverage in this study (Fig. 1). If we can easily obtain flavor suited to the beverage based on each user's feelings (Kansei), it will enrich our life. Additionally, a smelling experiment is conducted to investigate the efficiency of IGA for creating the flavor. The target of creation is a "delicious" flavor suited to the soda water.

The remainder of this manuscript is as follows. Section 2 describes GA and IGA with a flowchart. Section 3 explains a method of the smelling experiment, and Sect. 4 shows the results of the experiment. Based on the results, Sect. 5 has discussion. Finally, Sect. 6 concludes this study.

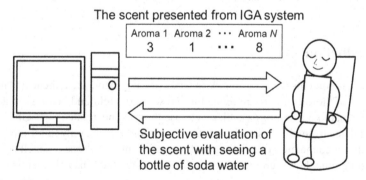

The scent presented from IGA system

Aroma 1	Aroma 2	$\cdots$	Aroma N
3	1	$\cdots$	8

Subjective evaluation of the scent with seeing a bottle of soda water

Fig. 1. Outline of the IGA for creating flavor suited to the soda water.

2 Interactive Genetic Algorithm Creating Scents Suited to User's Feelings

In this section, GA and IGA are explained. After that, IGA creating flavor as the scent is described.

2.1 Genetic Algorithm and Interactive Genetic Algorithm

GA is the most famous method of evolutionary algorithms which is a stochastic search for obtaining optimal solution [4, 5]. GA imitates the evolution process of living things with the phenotype and genotype of individuals, and it is applied for various problems. The fitness value of GA individuals is calculated by a mathematical function. A typical flowchart of GA is shown in Fig. 2.

IGA is the interactive version of GA, and human user participates in the evaluation. This means that the search of IGA is performed by the user's subjective evaluation as Kansei which cannot be represented as an obvious function. Repeating IGA processes will find good solutions for each user.

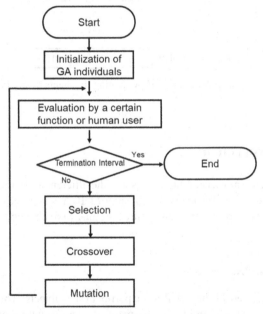

Fig. 2. A flowchart of GA and IGA. In IGA, a human user subjectively evaluates the GA individuals.

2.2 IGA Creating Scents

With the search ability of GA and the framework of IGA introducing human user's evaluation into the search, many previous studies proposed methods creating various media contents. According to a survey of IEC, CG, sound, and music are major objectives of the search with IGA [3].

The creation of scents by IGA was proposed by the author [6]. As the objective of creation by IGA, it is a rare case. In this IGA, the scent is created by mixing several aromas as shown in Fig. 3. The values of the GA individuals show the intensity of each aroma. In this case, three aromas are used. As shown in GA individual 2, no effect of a certain aroma is permitted, however, GA individual having all zero values is prohibited. In the previous IGA [6], six aromas were used, and Aromageur was used as a diffuser that mixes six aromas via special software. By following the IGA, several IECs with different evolutionary algorithms were proposed [7–9].

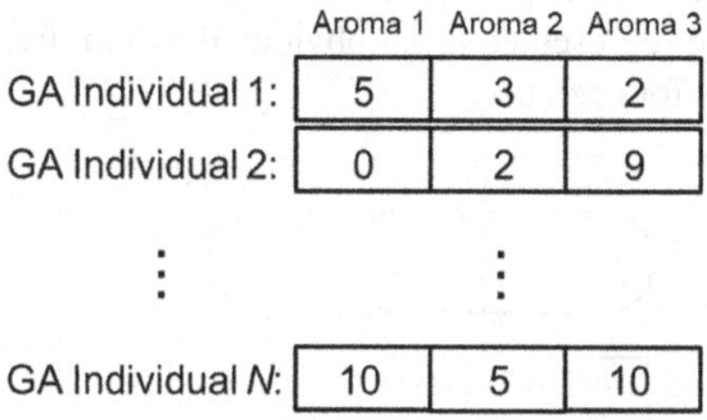

	Aroma 1	Aroma 2	Aroma 3
GA Individual 1:	5	3	2
GA Individual 2:	0	2	9
⋮	⋮		
GA Individual N:	10	5	10

Fig. 3. Examples of GA individuals in IGA creating the scents by mixing three aromas.

3 Smelling Experiment

The smelling experiment was conducted to show the efficiencies of the IGA for creating good flavor for each user. Basically, the system of IGA was almost the same as the previous IGA study [6]: parameters and source aromas were changed from the previous study.

3.1 Experimental Procedure

Ten persons participated in the smelling experiment as subjects. The experiment was composed of two steps: a searching experiment and an evaluating experiment. In the searching experiment, the subjects evaluated the scent afforded from the IGA system repeatedly: its flow was shown in Fig. 2. After the searching experiment, the best GA individuals were picked up from the initial and the final generations. The subjects evaluated the two GA individuals again in the evaluating experiment: the sequence of the presentation of the two GA individuals was randomized and counter-balanced. The evaluating experiment was needed to definite evaluation because the evaluation criterion of the subjects seems to be relative in each generation, and it was performed on a different day from the searching experiment.

In both experiments, the subjects smelled scents created the IGA system with Aromageur. In front of the subjects, a bottle of soda water is placed. In the evaluation process, the subjects were told to score the scents by seeing the bottle of soda water. The score is defined by the Semantic Differential method [10] with the 7-point scale: 1 meant "undelicious" for the soda water, 4 meant "neither", and 7 meant "delicious" for the soda water. As the beverage, Wilkinson's soda water made from Asahi [11] was used in the experiment. The subjects could have a rest freely and smell coffee beans or their clothes to refresh their olfactory.

3.2 Settings of IGA and Source Aromas

The settings of IGA were summarized in Table 1. Each GA individual has six variables, and the range of these variables was from 0 to 100 in integer. In the initialization, random values were used in the range. As selection methods, tournament selection and elitism strategy were employed. Aroma oils used in the experiments are also included in this table. These aroma oils are explained as having effects of appetite promotion and digesting. Additionally, GA operations of 1-point crossover and mutation were used in the IGA.

Table 1. Settings of GA and aroma oils in the smelling experiment.

The number of generations	10
The number of GA individuals	8
Crossover	1-point cross over with 90%
Mutation	Change of variables from 0 to 50 with 10%
Aroma oils	Lemon, Orange sweet, Juniper, Cinnamon leaf, Black pepper, Fennel sweet

4 Results

4.1 Results of the Searching Experiment

Figure 4 shows the progress of mean and maximum fitness values between the 10 subjects: these values were obtained after calculating each subject's fitness values. Error bars in the graphs mean standard deviation. Gradual increases are found in both mean and maximum fitness values in accordance with the progress of the generation, and the increases from the initial to the final generations were about 1 point.

Figure 5 shows two examples of the progress of aroma sources' intensity. The values are mean intensities between the eight GA individuals in each generation. In some aroma sources such as Orange sweet, one direction change in its intensity was observed. Between the two examples, the obtained mean intensities in the final generation were similar to each other. However, a quite different trend was observed in Lemon.

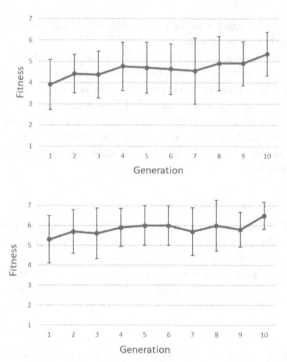

Fig. 4. The progresses of fitness value in the searching experiment. Upper graph shows the mean fitness value, lower graph shows the maximum fitness value.

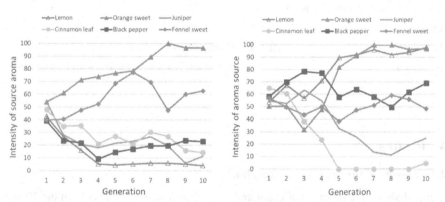

Fig. 5. Examples of the progress of aroma sources' intensity: the mean intensity of the eight GA individuals in each generation. Left one is the result of subject a, and right one is the result of subject b.

4.2 Result of the Evaluating Experiment

Figure 6 shows mean and standard deviation obtained in the evaluating experiment where the definite efficiency of the IGA creating flavor suited to the soda water was investigated. Obviously, the mean fitness value for the 10th generation was higher: it almost reached 6 point. Statistical analysis was performed with a sign test. A significant difference between them was observed ($P < 0.05$).

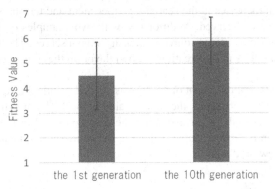

Fig. 6. The fitness values of the representative GA individuals from the 1st and the 10th generations in the evaluating experiment.

5 Discussion

The gradual increases in the searching experiment and the significant increase in the evaluating experiment were observed in the fitness values. The authors thought that the investigation in the evaluating experiment is more important, and the meaningful result showing the efficiency of the IGA could be observed in the evaluating experiment. The six aroma sources were changed from the previous study, and the change seems to be effective for obtaining good results in this study: the authors do not say that the IGA is effective for finding various sets of aroma sources composing good flavors suited to the soda water.

In the evaluation process of the subjects in the experiment, the subjects smelled afforded scents with seeing the bottle of the soda water. However, the obtained scent via the search process is attached to the soda water in the application: the users smell the scent with the taste and aroma of the soda water itself. Therefore, in further studies, the evaluation process should be reconsidered with the thought of the taste and aroma of the soda water because the evaluation on the scent searched by the IGA might be affected by the taste and scent of the soda water itself.

From a property of IGA, the obtained intensities are expected to reflect each subjects' feelings. Related to the change in the aroma sources' intensity, the authors did not finish the analysis. From the results showing the one direction changes as a movement the search space of the individuals, the efficient search seems to be performed in the limited evaluation times.

6 Conclusion

This study applied the IGA creating the scent for each user by mixing several aroma sources on creating good flavor on beverages. As the concrete beverage, soda water with no flavor was selected. In the use of the IGA for the creation of the flavor, the user repeatedly mixed flavor by seeing the soda water. With this situation, the smelling experiment was performed to show the efficiency of the IGA in the creation of the flavor. The gradual increases in the searching experiment and the statistical increase in the fitness value were observed. Additionally, with two examples of the subjects, one direction change in some aroma sources' intensity was observed. These results showed the efficiency of the IGA in the creation of good flavor on the soda water suited to each user's feelings.

In future studies, improvement of the IGA is needed. While the significant increase in the fitness value was observed, the fitness value in the 10th generation did not reach 7 point. As a further analysis, investigating the common trend in the intensity of the aroma sources is an interesting topic. Knowing the common trend can be used for the development of new products.

References

1. McGann, J.P.: Poor human olfaction is a 19th-century myth. Science **356**(6338), eaam7263 (2017)
2. Dawkins, R.: The Blind Watchmaker, Norton (1986)
3. Takagi, H.: Interactive evolutionary computation: fusion of the capabilities of EC optimization and human evaluation. Proc. IEEE **89**(9), 1275–1296 (2001)
4. Holland, J.H.: Adaptation in Natural and Artificial Systems: An Introductory Analysis with Applications to Biology, Control and Artificial Intelligence. The University of Michigan Press, Ann Arbor (1975)
5. Goldberg, D.: Genetic Algorithms in Search, Optimization and Machine Learning. Addison-Wesley Professional, Reading (1989)
6. Fukumoto, M., Imai, J.: Design of scents suited with user's Kansei using interactive evolutionary computation. In: Proceedings of the International Conference on Kansei Engineering and Emotion Research 2010, pp. 1016–1022 (2010)
7. Fukumoto, M., Inoue, M., Imai, J.: User's favorite scent design using paired comparison-based interactive differential evolution. In: Proceedings of the IEEE Congress on Evolutionary Computation 2010, pp. 4519–4524 (2010)
8. Fukumoto, M., Koga, S., Inoue, M., Imai, J.: Interactive differential evolution using time information required for user's selection: in a case of optimizing fragrance composition. In: Proceedings of the IEEE Congress on Evolutionary Computation 2015, pp. 2192–2198 (2015)
9. Fukmoto, M., Wakiyama, R., Nomura, K.: Creation of fragrance suited to a product based on interactive tabu search. In: Proceedings of the FIT 2017, pp.159–162 (2017). (in Japanese)
10. Osgood, C.E., Suci, G.K., Tannenbaum, P.: The Measurement of Meaning. University of Illinois Press, Champaign (1957)
11. ASAHI web site. https://www.asahigroup-holdings.com/en/brand/wilkinson/

Investigation of Facial Preference Using Gaussian Process Preference Learning and Generative Image Model

Masashi Komori[1]($\boxtimes$)(ID), Keito Shiroshita[2], Masataka Nakagami[1],
Koyo Nakamura[3,4](ID), Maiko Kobayashi[5], and Katsumi Watanabe[5](ID)

[1] Faculty of Information and Communication Engineering,
Osaka Electro-Communication University, 18-8 Hatsucho, Neyagawa,
Osaka 572-8530, Japan
{komori,gp17a085}@oecu.jp
[2] Graduate School of Engineering, Osaka Electro-Communication University,
18-8 Hatsucho, Neyagawa, Osaka 572-8530, Japan
mi20a005@oecu.jp
[3] Faculty of Psychology, Department of Cognition, Emotion, and Methods
in Psychology, University of Vienna, Liebiggasse 5, 1010 Vienna, Austria
koyo@fennel.sci.waseda.ac.jp
[4] Japan Society for the Promotion of Science, 5-3-1, Kojimachi, Chiyoda-ku,
Tokyo 102-0083, Japan
[5] Faculty of Science and Engineering, Waseda University, 3-4-1, Okubo, Shinjuku-ku,
Tokyo 169-8555, Japan
maikokobayashi@aoni.waseda.jp, katz@waseda.jp

Abstract. This study introduces a novel approach to investigate human facial attractiveness's intrinsic psychophysical function using a sequential experimental design with a combination of Bayesian optimization (BO) and StyleGAN2. To estimate a facial attractiveness function from pairwise comparison data, we used a BO that incorporates Gaussian process preference learning (GPPL). Fifty female Japanese university students provided facial photographs. We embedded each female facial image into a latent representation (18 × 512 dimensions) in the StyleGAN2 network trained on the Flickr-Faces-HQ (FFHQ) dataset. Using PCA, the latent representations' dimension is reduced to an 8-dimensional subspace, which we refer to here as the Japanese female face space. Nine participants participated in the pairwise comparison task. They had to choose the more attractive facial images synthesized using StyleGAN2 in the face subspace and provided their evaluations in 100 trials. The stimuli for the first 80 trials were created from randomly generated parameters in the face subspace, while the remaining 20 trials were created from the parameters calculated using the acquisition function. We estimated the facial parameters corresponding to the most, the least, 25, 50, 75 percentile rank of attractiveness and reconstructed the faces based

This work was supported by JSPS KAKENHI (No. 17H02651, 19K03375, 17H06344) and Strategic Japanese-Swiss Science and Technology Programme from JSPS to K.W.

K. Saeed and J. Dvorský (Eds.): CISIM 2021, LNCS 12883, pp. 193–202, 2021.
https://doi.org/10.1007/978-3-030-84340-3_15

on the results. The results show that a combination of StyleGAN2 and GPPL methodologies is an effective way to elucidate human *kansei* evaluations of complex stimuli such as human faces.

Keywords: Bayesian optimization · Gaussian process preference learning · StyleGAN2 · ICBAKE

1 Introduction

We can intuitively make evaluations in one-dimensional quantities for stimuli that consist of complex physical features in multiple dimensions. A typical example is the perception of facial attractiveness. The human face characteristics consist of a large number of variables, and facial attractiveness is evaluated by assessing the multidimensional variables [1,2]. Several studies have investigated the influence of facial characteristics on facial attractiveness. Clarifying the relationship between multidimensional physical features and one-dimensional psychological evaluations, that is, multidimensional psychophysical functions is essential for elucidating the mechanism of intuitive judgment. However, it is difficult to collect psychological evaluations of multidimensional physical quantities in a brute-force manner because of its high cost. This study applies Bayesian optimization to the elucidation of multidimensional psychophysical functions to solve this problem.

Bayesian optimization is a method of global sequential optimization that searches for the maximum/minimum value of a black-box function or estimates an unknown function [3]. Bayesian optimization combines Gaussian process regression with the determination of the search point using the acquisition function. Bayesian optimization estimates the unknown function by repeating (1) collection of responses, (2) Gaussian process regression, and (3) determination of the search point and collection of responses.

However, there are problems in applying Bayesian optimization to the estimation of psychophysical functions. In a typical Bayesian optimization method, the response from an unknown function is expected to be continuous. However, it is difficult for humans to respond continuously. It is desirable to use discrete responses To estimate psychophysical functions based on natural human responses. In this study, we use the Gaussian process with preference learning (GPPL) [4,5], which can estimate nonlinear functions from sparse pairwise preference datasets (Fig. 1).

2 Gaussian Process Preference Learning

GPPL can be considered a combination of Thurstones pairwise comparison model (probit model) [6] and Gaussian process regression. Here, we assume that a participant has a certain intrinsic psychophysical utility function $f(\mathbf{x})$ that maps the multivariate input $\mathbf{x}$ to a scalar value representing the evaluation of a given stimulus.

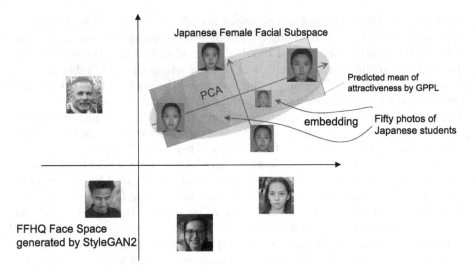

Fig. 1. Schematic illustration of the procedures of this study

Consider a set of m observed pairwise preference relations for the stimuli, denoted as

$$\mathcal{D} = \{v_k \succ u_k; k = 1, \ldots, m\}$$

where $v_k \succ u_k$ means the stimulus v_k is preferred to u_k.

By assuming Gaussian noise $\mathcal{N}(\delta; \mu, \sigma^2)$ on participants responses, the likelihood of a pairwise comparison $v_k \succ u_k$ becomes

$$\mathcal{P}(v_k \succ u_k \mid f(v_k), f(u_k))$$
$$= \iint \mathcal{P}_{\text{ideal}}(v_k \succ u_k \mid f(v_k) + \delta_v, f(u_k) + \delta_u) \mathcal{N}(\delta_v; 0, \sigma^2) \mathcal{N}(\delta_u; 0, \sigma^2) d\delta_v d\delta_u$$
$$= \Phi(z_k)$$

where $z_k = \frac{f(v_k) - f(u_k)}{\sqrt{2}\sigma_{\text{noise}}}$, $\Phi(z) = \int_{-\infty}^{z} \mathcal{N}(\gamma; 0, 1) d\gamma$

We assume that the intrinsic psychophysical function f follows a Gaussian process prior, $f \sim \mathcal{GP}(0, \mathcal{K})$, where $\mathcal{K}$ is a kernel function. Here, we used an RBF ARD kernel [7]. Following previous studies, the posterior distribution $\mathcal{P}(f \mid \mathcal{D})$ was approximated as a Gaussian using a Laplace approximation [4,5].

3 Facial Image Generation

3.1 StyleGAN2

Previous studies on facial attractiveness have relied mainly on two techniques. The first is a method that uses digitally blended composite faces created by photographic superimposing techniques or 2D/3D morphing techniques [2,8,9]. The problem with these methods is that the expression of hair and facial texture differs greatly from natural facial photographs. The unnaturalness of the photographs might affect the judgment of the participants. The other method is a measurement-based technique that examines the relationship between the measured data of individual faces and evaluates the attractiveness of individual facial photographs [1]. This approach requires the use of facial photographs of real people, which raises the issue of violating face providers' privacy and the ethical issue of evaluating the attractiveness of real people's faces.

Recent developments in deep learning-based image generation models should be an effective method for solving the above problems. StyleGAN is a variant of the generative adversarial network (GAN) machine learning framework [10]. It is a generator architecture that excels in generating images. Both local and global features are important, such as human faces, and can generate completely fake but realistic and convincing face images. StyleGAN2 [11] is the second version of StyleGAN that removes various artifacts, improves the quality of the generated images, and fixes the water-splotches issue in StyleGAN.

This study attempts to solve both the ethical problem of using real facial images and the ecological validity problem of using unnatural facial images that have been problematic in conventional attractiveness research using StyleGAN2 to generate face stimulus images. The relationship between the generated face images and subjective attractiveness evaluations can be investigated using a Gaussian process regression model with the latent representations of StyleGAN2 as the explanatory variables and subjective attractiveness evaluation as the response variable.

3.2 Construction of Latent Facial Subspace

Kerras et al. [11], the authors of StyleGAN2, introduced a dataset of human faces called Flickr-FacesHQ (FFHQ), which is a dataset of human faces of various races that consists of 70,000 high-quality images at a resolution of 1024×1024. We used the StyleGAN2 network, which was trained with FFHQ for our study.

In the StyleGAN2 latent face space, the vector has 18×512 dimensions, which is an enormous space for searching with GPPL. Additionally, the latent facial space consists of other racial groups' faces, so it is not suitable for Japanese people's experiments. Therefore, we created a low-dimensional subspace of the latent space using a reference face image. Moreover, the latent facial space consists of male and female faces of other races and is not suitable for female facial attractiveness surveys in Japan. Therefore, we created a low-dimensional subspace of the latent space consisting of only Asian female faces using reference facial images.

Fifty Japanese female university students provided facial photographs at a resolution of 1024×1024. The neutral expression of each face was captured using a digital camera. A gray screen was set up in the background. The foreheads of the models were exposed using a headband after removing accessories such as eyeglasses.

First, the facial images of the 50 females were embedded into the latent space of StyleGAN2 using the method of Kerras et al. [11]. Then, principal component analysis (PCA) was performed on the resulting 18×512 dimensional latent representation. Since the contribution ratios of the 9th and higher PCs were very small, we used up to the 8th PCs. The cumulative contribution ratio by the 8th PC was 29.5%. Changes in the facial image along each principal component are illustrated in Fig. 2 to identify the facial features linked to each component. The 1st PC was related to the height of the forehead and the eyes' shape: The 2nd PC was linked to the thickness of the eyebrows and the face's length. The 3rd, the 4th, 5th, and the 6th were related to the shape of the cheekbones, eyes, eyelids, and jaw. The 7th PC is linked to the width of the face. The 8th PC was related to the shape of the face and the color and texture of the face.

In this study, the 8-dimensional space obtained by the above procedure is referred to as the face subspace. We used GPPL to regress the subjective attractiveness evaluations of the 8-dimensional facial vectors of this subspace.

4   Assessment of Attractiveness

4.1   Methods

Participants. All of the procedures employed in this study were approved by the Ethics Committee of the Osaka Electro-Communication University. Participants ($n = 9$; mean age $= 22.11$, SD$= .57$) participated in the experiment.

Procedure. Participants were instructed to select an attractive face from two images in 100 trials. Participants were requested to respond in terms of esthetics, not preference—the model was considered a sexual partner or a companion.

In the first 95 trials of the 100 trials, the stimulus images were generated from parameters randomly selected from a range of ± 2 SD in the eight-dimensional face subspace. In the next five trials, one of the image pairs was generated from the parameter corresponding to the posterior mean's current maximum attractiveness. The other image was generated from the parameter corresponding to the maximum expected improvement (EI) [5].

Each participant completed one session. Stimuli were presented on an LCD monitor. Further, participants responded with a keyboard, and the application used in the experiments was implemented in a PsychoPy environment [12].

5   Results and Discussion

Based on all pairwise preferences, the attractiveness function of each participant was estimated using the GPPL. The latent variables corresponding to the maximum posterior mean of each participant's attractiveness evaluations are listed in Table 1. The 1st and the 3rd principal components showed the least variability among participants indicating that these components are the most important in attractiveness evaluation.

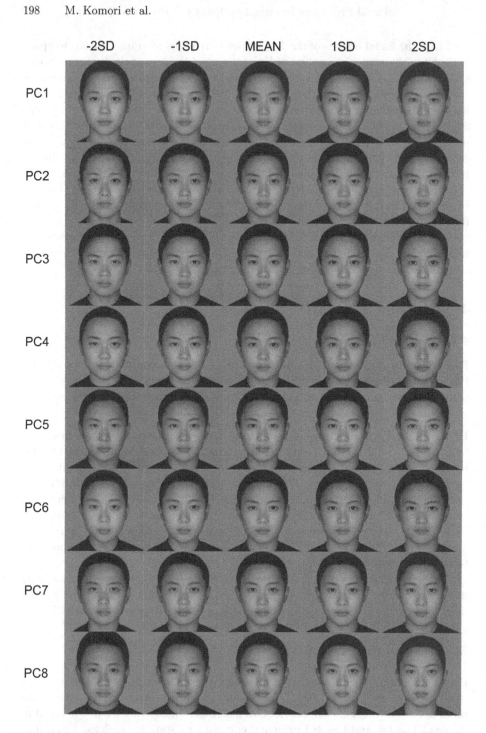

Fig. 2. Facial image variation along each dimension of the face subspace (−2SD/Mean/+2SD).

The 1st PC is related to the height of the forehead. The third principal component is the component related to the cheekbones. It is known that the forehead shape is related to baby schema [13], and the cheekbone shape is related to sexual dimorphism [14]. The similarity of preferences among these PCs participants suggests that preferences with evolutionary origin strongly influenced judgments concerning the 1st and 3rd principal components. On the other hand, the second principal component with the highest variability was the component related to eyebrow shape, which might be culturally rather than evolutionarily derived.

The predicted mean and variance of the whole subspace were obtained with an interval of 0.25 for each participant's dimensions, resulting in 43,046,721 points. Figure 3 shows an example of the predicted mean map of participant 1 on PC1 and PC2. Further, for each participant, the predicted mean maximum, third quartile, median, first quartile, and minimum points were determined, and the corresponding images were generated (Fig. 4).

Table 1. Posterior mean maximum points, means and SDs

Participant	1st PC	2nd PC	3rd PC	4th PC	5th PC	6th PC	7th PC	8th PC
1	−1.08	−1.35	0.79	1.42	1.16	1.7	0.19	1.14
2	−0.6	−0.65	−0.48	−0.28	1.25	0.96	−0.21	1.14
3	−0.79	0.39	0.32	1.32	1.22	0.47	1.02	0.25
4	−0.69	0.67	0.7	0.6	1.23	1.11	1.08	0.28
5	−1.26	1.48	0.02	1.29	1.14	0.36	−0.08	−1.06
6	0.08	−0.75	0.31	0.59	0.57	0.06	1.02	−0.11
7	−0.92	0.62	1.48	1.54	0.82	0.81	0.78	0.12
8	−1.15	−0.12	−0.96	0.14	0.98	1.21	−0.3	−0.84
9	−0.09	1.53	1.36	0.45	0.3	2	1.52	0.48
Mean	−0.72	0.2	0.39	0.78	0.96	0.96	0.56	0.15
S.D.	0.44	0.94	0.75	0.6	0.32	0.59	0.63	0.72

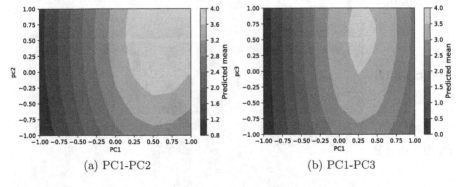

(a) PC1-PC2　　　　　　　　　　　　(b) PC1-PC3

Fig. 3. Examples of predicted mean contours of attractiveness on the PC1-PC2 and PC1-PC3. The height of each surface describes the attractiveness strength.

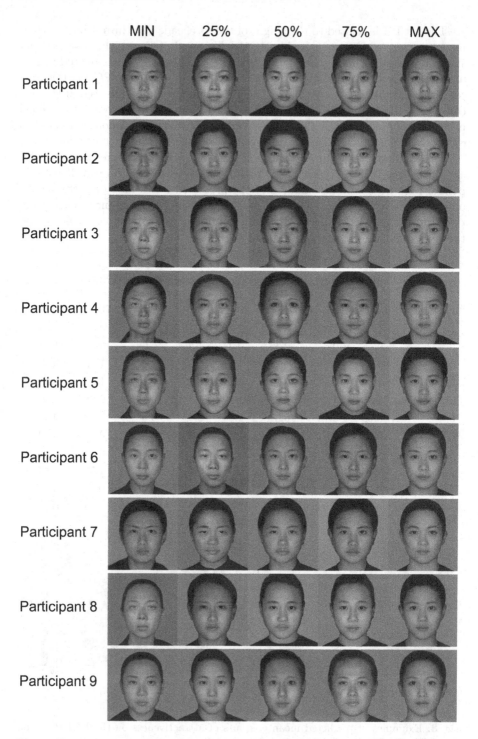

Fig. 4. Face images corresponding to the ranking of the predicted mean value for each experimental participant (the least attractive/1st quartile/middle/3rd quartile/the most attractive)

Figure 4 shows that the faces corresponding to the maximum and minimum predicted mean values are similar among the participants, suggesting that there is a common trend in face attractiveness evaluation.

6 Conclusion

This study provides a novel approach to clarify human facial attractiveness's intrinsic psychophysical function using a sequential experimental design that combines Bayesian optimization (BO) with GPPL and StyleGAN2 methods. This is the first study on facial attractiveness using GPPL. Further, the results show that GPPL is an effective method for investigating complex human judgments of multivariate physical stimuli such as faces. We used StyleGAN2 to generate facial images in this study. In conventional facial attractiveness studies, there are ethical problems of using real face images and ecological validity problems using unnatural face images. However, by using StyleGAN2, we have solved these problems. Furthermore, the dimensional reduction technique used in this study, which embeds the reference images into the latent space and then performs PCA, has adequately reduced the enormous search space of StyleGAN— indicating our method's effectiveness in using trained deep learning networks for psychological studies. Although this study focuses on facial attractiveness, our proposed method can be applied to research in product design, experimental esthetics, and other fields.

Ethical Approval

All of the procedures employed in this study were approved by the Ethics Committee of the Osaka Electro-Communication University (18-004) and the institutional review board of Waseda University (2015-033).

References

1. Cunningham, M.R.: Measuring the physical in physical attractiveness: quasi-experiments on the sociobiology of female facial beauty. J. Pers. Soc. Psychol. **50**(5), 925 (1986)
2. Benson, P.J., Perrett, D.I.: Extracting prototypical facial images from exemplars. Perception **22**(3), 257–262 (1993)
3. Mockus, J.: Bayesian Approach to Global Optimization: Theory and Applications. Kluwer Academic Publishers (1989)
4. Chu, W., Ghahramani, Z.: Preference learning with Gaussian processes. In: Proceedings of the 22nd International Conference on Machine Learning, pp. 137–144 (2005)
5. Brochu, E., Cora, V.M., DeFreitas, N.: A tutorial on Bayesian optimization of expensive cost functions, applying active user modeling and hierarchical reinforcement learning. arXiv preprint arXiv:1012.2599 (2010)
6. Thurstone, L.L.: A law of comparative judgment. Psychol. Rev. **34**(4), 273 (1927)

7. MacKay, D.J.: Bayesian methods for backpropagation networks. In: Models of Neural Networks III, pp. 211–254. Springer (1996). https://doi.org/10.1007/978-1-4612-0723-8_6

8. Langlois, J.H., Roggman, L.A.: Attractive faces are only average. Psychol. Sci. **1**(2), 115–121 (1990)

9. Oosterhof, N.N., Todorov, A.: The functional basis of face evaluation. Proc. Nat. Acad. Sci. **105**(32), 11087–11092 (2008)

10. Karras, T., Laine, S., Aila, T.: A style-based generator architecture for generative adversarial networks. In: Proceedings of the IEEE/CVF Conference on Computer Vision and Pattern Recognition, pp. 4401–4410 (2019)

11. Karras, T., Laine, S., Aittala, M., Hellsten, J., Lehtinen, J., Aila, T.: Analyzing and improving the image quality of stylegan. In: Proceedings of the IEEE/CVF Conference on Computer Vision and Pattern Recognition, pp. 8110–8119 (2020)

12. Peirce, J.W.: PsychoPy–psychophysics software in python. J. Neurosci. Methods **162**(1–2), 8–13 (2007)

13. Farkas, L.G.: Anthropometry of the Head and Face. Lippincott Williams & Wilkins (1994)

14. Enlow, D.H.: A morphogenetic analysis of facial growth. Am. J. Orthod. **52**(4), 283–299 (1966)

Evaluation of Strong and Weak Signifiers in a Web Interface Using Eye-Tracking Heatmaps and Machine Learning

Kitti Koonsanit$^{(\boxtimes)}$ ⓘ, Taisei Tsunajima, and Nobuyuki Nishiuchi

Department of Computer Science, Graduate School of Systems Design,
Tokyo Metropolitan University, Tokyo, Japan
{koonsanit-kitti,tsunajima-taisei}@ed.tmu.ac.jp,
nnishiuc@tmu.ac.jp

Abstract. The eye-tracking heatmap is a quantitative research tool that shows the user's gaze points. Most of the eye-tracking heatmap is a 2D visualization comprising different colors. The heatmap colors indicate gaze duration, and the color cell's position indicates gaze position. The eye-tracking heatmap has often been used to evaluate the usability of web interfaces to understand user behavior. For example, web designers have used heatmaps to obtain actual evidence for how users use their website. Further, the collection of eye-tracking heatmap data during website viewing facilitates measurement of improvements in site usability. However, although the eye-tracking heatmap provides rich information about how users watch, focus, and interact with a site, the high informational requirements substantially increase computational burden. In many cases, the distribution of gaze points in an eye-tracking heatmap may not be easily understood and interpreted. Accordingly, manual evaluation of heatmaps is inefficient. This study aimed to evaluate web usability by focusing on signifiers as an interface element using eye-tracking heatmaps and machine learning algorithms. We also used the dimensionality reduction technique to reduce the complexity of heatmap data. The results showed that the proposed classification model that combined the decision tree and PCA technique provided more than 90% accuracy when compared with the other nine classical machine learning methods. This finding indicated that the machine learning process reached the correct decision about the interface's usability.

Keywords: Eye-tracking Heatmap · Signifier · Usability · Web interface · Classification · Machine learning

1 Introduction

The eye-tracking heatmap is the first imaging technique to play an essential role in analyzing web interfaces [1]. The eye-tracking heatmap is a data visualization which comprises different color spectra that display on the part of the web page receiving the most interest from website visitors. Most web designers used eye-tracking heatmaps to make datasets comprehensible and applicable in usability evaluation.

© Springer Nature Switzerland AG 2021
K. Saeed and J. Dvorský (Eds.): CISIM 2021, LNCS 12883, pp. 203–213, 2021.
https://doi.org/10.1007/978-3-030-84340-3_16

Because eye-tracking heatmaps consist of meta-information, including user interaction, focused location and time spent looking, the eye-tracking heatmap analysis is essential for usability research. Generally, there are three kinds of eye-tracking heatmap, all of which show where users focus their attention on a web page [2]. First, click heatmaps are a basic visualization that records all clicks during a visit to a page. Second, scroll heatmaps display the level of interest from the top of a page to the bottom. Third, mouse movement heatmaps provide the best representation for eye-tracking by collecting mouse movements which occur during the visit to a page [3].

As described above, most eye-tracking heatmap visualizations are displayed as a 2D data visualization which comprises different colors. Different colors indicate gaze duration, and the color cell's position refers to the gaze position.

The eye-tracking heatmap's color shade reflects a user's interest level in different parts of the page, with different levels of interest represented using different colors. For example, hot colors indicated where the users spent the most time, and soft colors indicated a reduced interest level. Generally, the color red indicates that the zone received the most attention and green indicates the second-greatest degree of attention. In contrast, colorless elements represent areas on the webpage which attract the least interest from users. Figure 1 provides an example of an eye-tracking heatmap for evaluating a web interface.

Fig. 1. Example of a superimposed eye-tracking heatmap for evaluating a web interface [4].

The eye-tracking heatmap also shows significant visual focus suggestive of the user's heightened engagement with the web page and its relevance to the user. This research assumes that the eye-tracking heatmap is a valid expression of actual focus and can be used as a source of precise usability data reflecting a user's visit to a website without awareness of tracking.

Several papers have proposed that eye-tracking heatmaps provide rich information showing which parts of a page receive the most attention [5, 6]. With the growth of the Internet, however, the increasing size of websites and the need for usability evaluation has led to large workloads for web designers. The interpretation of eye-tracking heatmaps remains a manual job that requires human input and evaluation. However, these in turn open the possibility of both human bias and system factors, which may lead to erroneous or missed findings [7, 8].

Accordingly, this study proposes a new method of evaluating web usability which focuses on the signifier as an interface element which can be utilized by automated machine learning techniques. In addition, the use of eye-tracking heatmap data and machine learning techniques may allow the evaluation of web usability using an interface which is both effective and comfortable for target users.

The paper is organized as follows: related works will be described in Sect. 2; the methodology of this study will be described and explained in Sect. 3; the results and discussion will be described in Sect. 4; and our conclusion will be summarized in Sect. 5.

2 Related Works

This section reviews web site usability evaluation using eye-tracking, related machine learning, and principal component analysis (PCA). It presents a discussion of relevant issues of the study regarding the eye-tracking heatmap processing and related studies.

2.1 Usability Evaluation Using Eye-Tracking

The eye-tracking heatmap identifies and accumulates the gaze points gathered by the eye tracker. The eye tracker consists of high-resolution cameras, light sources, and image processing algorithms. The eye tracker's basic concept is to use the light source to create a pattern of near-infrared light on the eyes which the high-resolution cameras use to record an image of the user's eye movement. Lastly, specific details in the user's eyes and reflection patterns are obtained with an image processing algorithm. An outline of the eye tracker is shown in Fig. 2.

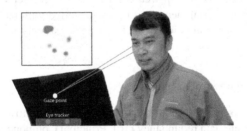

Fig. 2. Basic concept of the eye tracker adopted from TobiiPro [9]

Most web designers used eye-tracking heatmaps to make datasets which are comprehensible and actionable within the field of usability evaluation [10]. For example, Moran et al. [11] proposed a comparison of user attention between a web interface with strong signifiers and a web interface with weak signifiers. They evaluated the effectiveness of strong signifiers (traditional clues such as underlined, blue text) and weak signifiers (e.g. static text or a ghost button) and how they affect the way users process and understand web pages. They used an eye-tracking device to generate eye-tracking heatmaps from webpages with strong or weak signifiers. The results showed that user attention was significantly different between the two versions of the web interface.

2.2 Machine Learning

Several machine learning techniques which perform preliminary eye-tracking heatmap classification have been developed. Several papers have proposed the use of machine learning models for eye-tracking heatmap classification. For example, Duan et al. [12] proposed a machine learning model that predicts which part of a picture would be viewed by children with Autism Spectrum Disorder (ASD). They developed a machine learning model using 500 eye-tracking heatmaps collected from 13 children with ASD, and then compared the performance of five kinds of deep neural networks (DNN) on the collected dataset. The results indicated that the machine learning model could be applied in children with autism.

In another study, Fujii et al. [13] analyzed eye-tracking heatmaps and eye gaze movements related to watching English movies with subtitles. They proposed a machine-learning algorithm, namely a random forest algorithm, to classify participants' English ability level through tracking eye movement.

Another example of the use of machine learning with eye-tracking data involves the comparison of a visual system of human differences between normal adults and adults with high-functioning autism captured through eye-tracking data. Yaneva et al. [14] proposed using eye-tracking data and machine learning classifier to detect high-functioning autism in adults. Results showed that machine learning could detect high-functioning autism automatically with 74% accuracy from eye-tracking data.

In 2019, Salminen et al. [15] proposed using machine learning and eye-tracking data (gaze movements on the screen) to predict user confusion. They reported that a random-forest algorithm achieved more than 70% accuracy when predicting user confusion using only fixation features of gaze movements.

Machine learning can comprehend and learn from existing data. The results of the machine learning process will help web designers make correct web interface usability decisions. Our eye-tracking heatmap challenge started with building machines that performed a preliminary evaluation of web interface usability at the level of at least entry-level usability workers.

2.3 Principal Component Analysis

Dimension reduction is a transformation technique from a high to a low order dimension which aims to eliminate data redundancy [16]. Principal Component Analysis (PCA), a widely known dimension reduction technique, is the optimal linear scheme for reducing high-dimensional vectors into a set of lower-dimensional vectors.

PCA consists of all the information of an "N" feature original data set into a smaller number than "N" of new features (or principal components) in such a way that maximizes the covariance and reduces redundancy to achieve lower dimensionality. Principle component analysis is a standard feature extraction that filters only a limited number of significant features needed for training. The number of components that hold the importance of the information is called the intrinsic dimensionality.

3   Methodology

3.1   Proposed Procedure

We built a machine learning process to classify eye-tracking heatmaps into classes that belong to either class A, a web interface with strong signifiers; or class B, a web interface with weak signifiers. Moreover, we applied the dimension reduction technique that was used to reduce data dimension. On completion of these tasks, machine learning would be able to understand and learn from existing data. The machine learning process results would then help web designers make correct web interface usability decisions. The steps for eye-tracking heatmap classification using the proposed procedure are as follows in Fig. 3.

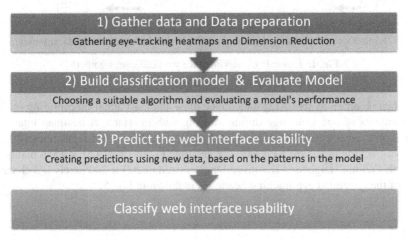

Fig. 3.   Proposed procedure of eye-tracking heatmap classification

3.2   Gathering of Dataset

Eye-tracking heatmaps in this study were obtained from 11 university students aged 22–24 years. They were first entered into a preliminary experiment in which they were divided into two groups, the first of five participants who visited a webpage with a strong signifier, and the second of six participants who visited a webpage with a weak signifier.

The two versions differed in the use of signifiers as interactive elements, namely as text and links. The strong signifier version (left) included underlined blue text used on interactive elements only, whereas the weak signifier version (right) used plain text instead, as shown in Fig. 4.

The 11 participants were initially informed of the experimental task to make sure they understood the instructions. Before starting task, we explained them to find and then click on the shopping link for the pearl necklace in the webpage of jewelry store. They were then requested to set the eye-tracking device (Tobii Pro X3-120) [9] to record their eye behavior while they visited the e-commerce website. Eye-tracking heatmaps

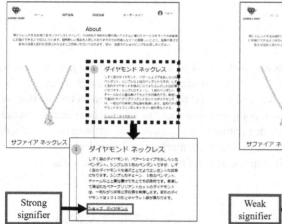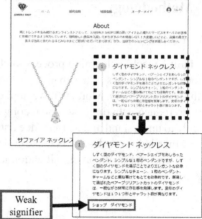

(a) Web interface with a strong signifier   (b) Web interface with a weak signifier

Fig. 4. Example of web interface with different signifiers

were then recorded by gathering data on the most and least attention capturing sections and elements of one web page during viewing web interface. A heatmap image is a three-dimensional byte array that explicitly stores a color value for each pixel [9, 17]. The eye-tracking heatmaps were initially generated with size 1920×1536 pixels $\times 3$ channels (Width, Height and Depth) and then resized to 200×200 pixels $\times 3$ channels. Each of the generated eye-tracking heatmaps is shown in Fig. 5.

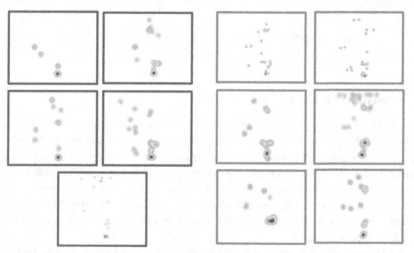

(a) Web interface with a strong signifier   (b) Web interface with a weak signifier

Fig. 5. Example of a generated eye-tracking heatmap

After data collection, each generated eye-tracking heatmap was identified by the web interface's usability before modeling. For example, five eye-tracking heat maps were labeled as obtained from a web page with a strong signifier, and six were labeled as obtained from a web page with a weak signifier.

3.3 Data Preparation

In this study, an essential phase in machine learning was data preparation, in which the eye-tracking heatmap was appropriately transformed to a feature matrix before we started using it. Moreover, the dimension reduction technique was used to reduce computation resources using PCA.

Data preparation was done in three main steps. First, we resized all images to reduce processing time and make them suitable for processing. Second, we converted eye-tracking heatmap files (3 dimensions) of individual images to a feature matrix (multi-dimension arrays). Third, we used PCA to reduce high-dimensional vectors into a set of lower-dimensional vectors. Our process flattens a feature matrix and keeps its data as one-dimension array. PCA computed the eigenvectors and eigenvalues of the covariance matrix from data to identify the principal components [18]. The step of PCA transformed those set of one-dimension arrays to PCA dataset. Each of the eye-tracking heatmaps was processed and transformed by these techniques before modeling.

We then transformed the eye-tracking heatmap into two kinds of dataset, namely the original eye-tracking heatmap dataset and a PCA dataset. First, the original eye-tracking heatmap dataset was transformed using the original eye-tracking heatmap collected from the 11 participants. Second, the original eye-tracking heatmap was transformed by reduction from a high dimension to a low dimension, which was called the PCA dataset.

3.4 Building Classification Models

First, 10 appropriate machine learning algorithms were selected: SVM [19], namely SVM linear, SVM sigmoid, SVM RBF and SVM polynomial; Logistics Regression [20]; K-Nearest Neighbors (KNN) [21]; Multi-Layer Perceptron (MLP) [22]; Decision tree [23]; AdaBoost [24]; and random forest techniques [23]. Classification models were then created. Finally, each model was trained by these algorithms using the two datasets.

3.5 Model Evaluation

In the evaluation step, the conventional leave-one-out, cross-validation method was used to evaluate performance of the classification model [25]. The concept of the leave-one-out approach is to leave 1 data out of the training data; in this study, for example, the original sample consisted of 11 heatmap data sets; 10 of these were used to train the model, and one was used as the validation set. The leave-one-out cross-validation procedure is often appropriate for small datasets because its result are reliable and unbiased in estimating model performance [26].

4 Results and Discussion

Firstly, we compared the 10 created machine learning models, namely SVM with a polynomial kernel, SVM with a linear kernel, SVM with an RBF kernel, SVM with a sigmoid kernel, K-nearest neighbors, logistic regression, multi-layer perceptron, decision tree, AdaBoost, and the random forest technique. We then measured their performance on the two datasets (including the original eye-tracking heatmap dataset and the PCA dataset) by leave-one-out cross-validation. The accuracy score of Fig. 6 contains percentages between 0 to 100, in which a higher value indicates better accuracy.

Overall, the bar chart below shows the classification model's cross-validation accuracy compared with the ten machine learning algorithms. The vertical data of the bar chart is given as a percentage of the cross-validation accuracy, while the horizontal data shows the 10 created machine learning algorithms. Among the machine learning algorithms, cross-validation accuracy of the eye-tracking heatmap classification differed considerably between the two datasets (original heatmap dataset and PCA dataset). Moreover, cross-validation accuracy increased significantly after using the PCA dataset.

With regard to overall trends, the bar chart showed an improvement in classification accuracy after using the PCA dataset. The decision tree algorithm classification on the PCA dataset gave the highest accuracy, at 90%. Similarly, the decision tree algorithm classification provided better accuracy with the PCA dataset than with the original eye-tracking heatmap dataset.

Moreover, logistic regression and AdaBoost gave the second-rank accuracy, at 81%. Logistic regression can also perform better with PCA dataset because PCA creates a new set of features which maximally preserve information and more features of the heatmap data that help to separate different classes. Only AdaBoost shows the same result accuracy between original heatmap dataset and PCA dataset. Because AdaBoost algorithm has already embedded a feature selection mechanism based on training a classifier for each feature [27]. As a result, AdaBoost also picks best features (like feature selection) from data apart from weighting weak classifiers and use them in testing phase to perform classification efficiently. Hence, there is no difference in the accuracy of AdaBoost algorithm between original heatmap dataset and PCA dataset.

This study's findings indicated that the use of dimension reduction maintains the significant representation of the feature and maximally preserves information that helps to appropriately evaluate the apparent signifier in the web interface.

In summary, machine learning evaluated the usability of eye-tracking heatmap data which focused on signifier strength as an element of the web interface. The combination of dimension reduction and machine learning techniques proposed in this study can help achieve better practical performance in classifying web interface usability from eye-tracking heatmaps.

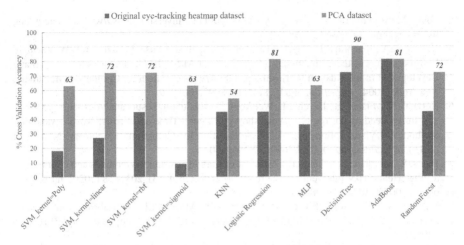

Fig. 6. Performance of each technique on two datasets

5 Conclusion

This paper proposes a method to evaluate web usability using eye-tracking heatmap data and machine learning algorithms. The dimensionality reduction technique was used to reduce the complexity of eye-tracking heatmap data. It also maximally maintained the feature's major representation, and appropriately evaluated the apparent signifier in the web interface. The results show that the proposed classification model that combined the decision tree and PCA technique achieved greater than 90% accuracy when compared with nine other classical machine learning methods. This study's findings indicated that the machine learning process helped in decision making on web interface usability.

Two limitations of our study warrant mention. First, the created model was developed from only a small dataset; accordingly, future experiments should expand to a bigger dataset to confirm this classification model's effectiveness. A large dataset could improve model training reliability. Second, because our study used eye-tracking heatmap data only, it may be possible to incorporate additional data and features to improve the performance classification.

Acknowledgment. This work was supported by JSPS KAKENHI Grant Number JP20K12511.

References

1. Tula, A.D., Kurauchi, A., Coutinho, F., Morimoto, C.: Heatmap explorer: an interactive gaze data visualization tool for the evaluation of computer interfaces. In: Proceedings of the 15th Brazilian Symposium on Human Factors in Computing Systems, pp. 1–9 (2016)
2. Blascheck, T., Kurzhals, K., Raschke, M., Burch, M., Weiskopf, D., Ertl, T.: State-of-the-art of visualization for eye tracking data. In: EuroVis (STARs) (2014)
3. Birkett, A.: Heat Maps: What Are They Good For (Besides Looking Cool)? https://cxl.com/blog/heat-maps/. Accessed 15 Feb 2021

4. Tokyo Metropolitan University: Tokyo Metropolitan University. https://www.tmu.ac.jp/eng lish/index.html. Accessed 23 Apr 2021
5. Granka, L.A., Joachims, T., Gay, G.: Eye-tracking analysis of user behavior in WWW search. In: Proceedings of the 27th Annual International ACM SIGIR Conference on Research and Development in Information Retrieval, pp. 478–479. Association for Computing Machinery, New York (2004). https://doi.org/10.1145/1008992.1009079
6. Kurzhals, K., Fisher, B., Burch, M., Weiskopf, D.: Evaluating visual analytics with eye tracking. In: Proceedings of the Fifth Workshop on Beyond Time and Errors: Novel Evaluation Methods for Visualization, pp. 61–69. Association for Computing Machinery, New York (2014). https://doi.org/10.1145/2669557.2669560
7. Davis, R., Gardner, J., Schnall, R.: A review of usability evaluation methods and their use for testing eHealth HIV interventions. Curr. HIV/AIDS Rep. **17**(3), 203–218 (2020). https://doi.org/10.1007/s11904-020-00493-3
8. Hussain, A., Mkpojiogu, E.O.C., Jamaludin, N.H., Moh, S.T.L.: A usability evaluation of Lazada mobile application. AIP Conf. Proc. **1891**, 020059 (2017). https://doi.org/10.1063/1.5005392
9. Tobiipro: Tobii Pro X3–120 screen-based eye tracker. https://www.tobiipro.com/product-lis ting/tobii-pro-x3-120/. Accessed 18 Feb 2021
10. Prendinger, H., Hyrskykari, A., Nakayama, M., Istance, H., Bee, N., Takahasi, Y.: Attentive interfaces for users with disabilities: eye gaze for intention and uncertainty estimation. Univ. Access Inf. Soc. **8**, 339–354 (2009)
11. Moran, K.: Heatmap Visualizations from Signifier Eyetracking Experiment. https://www.nng roup.com/articles/heatmap-visualizations-signifiers/. Accessed 16 Feb 2021
12. Duan, H., et al.: Learning to predict where the children with asd look. In: 2018 25th IEEE International Conference on Image Processing (ICIP), pp. 704–708. IEEE (2018)
13. Fujii, K., Rekimoto, J.: SubMe: an interactive subtitle system with English skill estimation using eye tracking. In: Proceedings of the 10th Augmented Human International Conference 2019, pp. 1–9. Association for Computing Machinery, New York (2019). https://doi.org/10.1145/3311823.3311865
14. Yaneva, V., Ha, L.A., Eraslan, S., Yesilada, Y., Mitkov, R.: Detecting high-functioning autism in adults using eye tracking and machine learning. IEEE Trans. Neural Syst. Rehabil. Eng. **28**, 1254–1261 (2020). https://doi.org/10.1109/TNSRE.2020.2991675
15. Salminen, J., Nagpal, M., Kwak, H., An, J., Jung, S., Jansen, B.J.: Confusion prediction from eye-tracking data: experiments with machine learning. In: Proceedings of the 9th International Conference on Information Systems and Technologies, pp. 1–9. Association for Computing Machinery, New York (2019). https://doi.org/10.1145/3361570.3361577
16. Koonsanit, K., Jaruskulchai, C., Eiumnoh, A.: Band selection for dimension reduction in hyper spectral image using integrated information gain and principal components analysis technique. Int. J. Mach. Learn. Comput. **2**, 248 (2012)
17. Van den Boom, B., et al.: Analysis of Eye-Tracking Data by Combining Visualizations Interactively
18. Kherif, F., Latypova, A.: Chapter 12 - Principal component analysis. In: Mechelli, A., Vieira, S. (eds.) Machine Learning, pp. 209–225. Academic Press (2020). https://doi.org/10.1016/B978-0-12-815739-8.00012-2
19. Schölkopf, B., Smola, A.J., Williamson, R.C., Bartlett, P.L.: New support vector algorithms. Neural Comput. **12**, 1207–1245 (2000)
20. Pedregosa, F., et al.: Scikit-learn: machine learning in Python. J. Mach. Learn. Res. **12**, 2825–2830 (2011)
21. Zhang, M.-L., Zhou, Z.-H.: A k-nearest neighbor based algorithm for multi-label classification. In: 2005 IEEE International Conference on Granular Computing, pp. 718–721. IEEE (2005)

22. Haykin, S.S.: Neural Networks and Learning Machines. Prentice Hall, New York (2009)
23. Sharma, R., Cecotti, H.: Classification of graphical user interfaces through gaze-based features. In: Santosh, K. C., Hegadi, Ravindra S. (eds.) RTIP2R 2018. CCIS, vol. 1035, pp. 3–16. Springer, Singapore (2019). https://doi.org/10.1007/978-981-13-9181-1_1
24. Zhu, B., Zhang, P.Y., Chi, J.N., Zhang, T.X.: Gaze estimation based on single camera. In: Advanced Materials Research, pp. 1066–1076. Trans Tech Publ (2013)
25. Ng, A.Y.: Preventing "overfitting" of cross-validation data. In: ICML, pp. 245–253. Citeseer (1997)
26. Yadav, S., Shukla, S.: Analysis of k-fold cross-validation over hold-out validation on colossal datasets for quality classification. In: 2016 IEEE 6th International conference on advanced computing (IACC), pp. 78–83. IEEE (2016)
27. Sun, C., Hu, J., Lam, K.-M.: Feature subset selection for efficient AdaBoost training. In: 2011 IEEE International Conference on Multimedia and Expo, pp. 1–6 (2011). https://doi.org/10.1109/ICME.2011.6011905

Applying Artificial Bee Colony Algorithm to Interactive Evolutionary Computation

Hiroshi Takenouchi[1]([✉]) and Masataka Tokumaru[2]

[1] Fukuoka Institute of Technology, 3-30-1 Wajiro-higashi, Higashi-ku,
Fukuoka 811-0295, Japan
h-takenouchi@fit.ac.jp
[2] Kansai University, 3-3-35 Yamate-cho, Suita-shi, Osaka 564-8680, Japan
toku@kansai-u.ac.jp

Abstract. In this study, we apply an artificial bee colony (ABC) algorithm to the interactive evolutionary computation (IEC) method for the multimodal retrieval of candidate solutions. Previous works have proposed IEC systems using a parallel interactive tabu search algorithm (PITS) that generates multiple tabu search (TS) retrievals and a hybrid genetic algorithm (GA) involving a global retrieval method and a TS involving a local retrieval method for multimodal retrieval. However, the PITS cannot efficiently retrieve candidate solutions and it has a complicated algorithm. The hybrid GA–TS also finds it hard to retrieve candidate solutions if the user has a more multimodal preference. We propose herein an IEC method with the ABC algorithm for the multimodal and simultaneous retrieval of candidate solutions. We perform a numerical simulation with a pseudo user that imitates multimodal preferences as target candidate solutions instead of a real user. The results show that the proposed method can retrieve multimodal candidate solutions in conditions with limited numbers of candidate solutions and bees.

Keywords: Artificial Bee Colony · Interactive Evolutionary Computation · ICBAKE2021

1 Introduction

The interactive evolutionary computation (IEC) method is a technique that optimizes and retrieves candidate solutions using the Kansei information of users [1]. Systems using the IEC method include the color scheme search system [2], music recommendation system [3], and big data searching support system [4], among many others. IEC systems usually use a genetic algorithm (GA) for EC operation. The GA method performs a unimodal retrieval that globally searches only for a single goal. However, real users have multimodal preferences in various objects (e.g., clothes and music). Hence, an IEC system must not only have a unimodal searching performance, but also a multimodal searching performance.

Supported by JSPS KAKENHI Grant Number 20K19912.

K. Saeed and J. Dvorský (Eds.): CISIM 2021, LNCS 12883, pp. 214–224, 2021.
https://doi.org/10.1007/978-3-030-84340-3_17

Previous studies used a parallel interactive tabu search algorithm (PITS) with multiple tabu search (TS) retrievals and a hybrid GA–TS algorithm for the multimodal retrieval of candidate solutions [5,6]. However, the PITS method generates multiple TS retrievals at the same time, retains TS retrievals with a higher user evaluation, and deletes TS retrievals with a lower user evaluation. Therefore, the PITS algorithm is complicated and cannot simply retrieve candidate solutions. The hybrid GA–TS method performs only a single TS search in GA searching. If a user has various multiple preferences, this method retrieves only approximately two kinds of candidate solutions.

To solve this problem, IEC systems must use an algorithm that performs multimodal searches and simultaneously retrieves candidate solutions. This study applies an artificial bee colony (ABC) algorithm to the IEC method for retrieving candidate solutions multimodal. The ABC algorithm is a kind of swarm intelligence method that is effective for the optimization of multivariable and multimodal functions [7]. It has three kinds of bees; namely employed, onlooker, and scout bees, and searches for candidate solutions multimodal using this bee collaboratory. If the parameters of the ABC method for the IEC system are tuned, the IEC method can retrieve candidate solutions multimodal.

We investigate whether the proposed method can retrieve candidate solutions multimodal by a numerical simulation that uses a pseudo user instead of real user. The pseudo user in the simulation has multiple target candidate solutions (preferences in a real user). In the simulation, we measure evolutionary performance when changing parameters of the proposed method, the Hamming distances between target candidate solutions and generated candidate solutions at the last generation, and the rate for the number of candidate solutions that nearest each target candidate solution.

2   Proposed Method

2.1   ABC Algorithm

The ABC algorithm retrieves various candidate solutions collaborative using three kinds of bees (i.e., employed, onlooker, and scout bees). Accordingly, some studies have investigated the high performance of the ABC algorithm method, regardless of the optimization targets [8–10]. Note that the titles of Refs. [8] and [9] include the words "interactive artificial bee colony," but these words do not represent the IEC systems with ABC algorithms. These studies improved the evolutionary performances of the ABC algorithm with the universal gravity concept or Newton's law.

Figure 1 shows the ABC algorithm flow. The details of the ABC algorithm are as follows:

1. **Initialization of food sources (candidate solutions):** The ABC algorithm randomly generates the target food sources of each employed bee.

2. **Phase of the employed bee:** Each employed bee randomly generates a new food source for their retrieval food source. When a new food source has a higher (lower) evaluation than their retrieval food source, the ABC algorithm replaces (does not replace) their retrieval food source with the newly generated food source. It then counts the number of obtained food source by each employed bee.

3. **Phase of the onlooker bee:** Each onlooker bee decides to support the employed bee based on the evaluation information of each employed bee. Equation (1) shows the selection probability $p(b_k)$ of the kth employed bee.

$$p(b_k) = \frac{v(f_k)}{\sum_{i=0}^{n} v(f_i)}, \tag{1}$$

where, f_k and b_k are the kth food source and the employed bee, respectively. $v(f_i)$ is the evaluation value of the food source that targets the food source of the kth employed: and n shows the number of employed bees. After calculating each evaluation value, the ABC algorithm counts the number of the obtained food source by each onlooker bee.

4. **Phase of the scout bee:** When the number of each obtained food source reaches a predefined upper limit, the ABC algorithm deletes the food source and randomly generates a new food source.

5. **End condition:** If the ABC algorithm obtains a target food source or reaches the final generation, it finishes the retrieval of the candidate solutions.

6. **Output of the optimized candidate solution:** The ABC algorithm outputs an optimized candidate solution.

In the ABC algorithm, the algorithm can retrieve around each candidate solution widely (locally) when the upper limited number of obtained each food source is large (small).

2.2   Flow of the Proposed Method

Figure 2 shows the schematic of the proposed method. First, it randomly generates the initial candidate solutions. Each employed bee randomly selects a candidate solution from the initial candidates and generates a new candidate solution. A user then evaluates the candidate solutions, including the initial and randomly generated candidate solutions of each employed bee. The ABC algorithm compares each initial candidate solution with the newly generated candidate solution of each employed bee and selects a candidate solution of a higher evaluation value as the selected candidate solution of the employed bee. The algorithm also counts the number of selections by every employed bee. Next, each onlooker bee selects a candidate solution of a higher evaluation value based on the evaluation values of each candidate solution and counts the number of selections for every candidate solution. Finally, each scout bee replaces the candidate solutions that reach the upper limit of the selections of each employed and onlooker bee with the newly generated candidate solutions. The ABC algorithm repeats these operations and optimizes the candidate solutions.

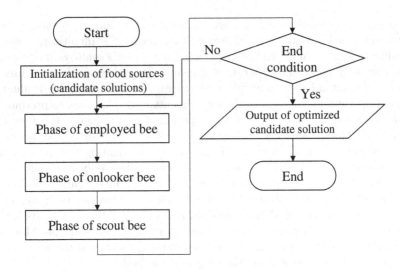

Fig. 1. Flow of the ABC algorithm

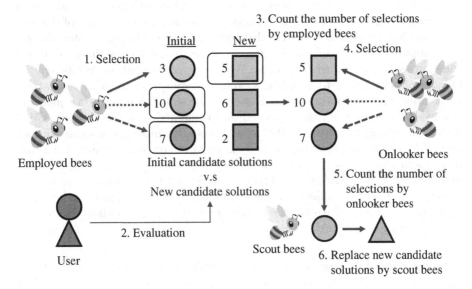

Fig. 2. The schematic of the proposed method

3 Numerical Simulations

3.1 Outline of the Simulation

We applied the ABC algorithm to an IEC system and investigated whether or not the proposed method can retrieve the candidate solutions multimodal using a numerical simulation that sets multiple target candidate solutions (i.e., preference in a real user). The simulations use a pseudo user that imitates the multimodal preferences of a real users. Ideally, evaluation experiments should be performed using real users. However, this makes the quantitative evaluation difficult. For example, the elements affecting a user's evaluation or loadings can significantly affect the experimental results. It is also rare for real users to perfectly understand their multiple preferences. For a quantitative evaluation, the same subjects participate in the experiments multiple times to produce the experiment results. However, such an experiment can influence the user evaluation load. Moreover, with real users, we must create an actual system to retrieve objects, such as clothes. In this case, investigating the versatility of the proposed method is difficult because the real system only retrieves clothes. Therefore, we based our quantitative evaluation and investigation of versatility on pseudo users. We verified the evolutionary performance of changing the numbers of candidate solutions, employed and onlooker bees, and rate for the number of candidate solutions nearest each target candidate solution. Moreover, we used the GA method as a compared method and conducted the performance comparisons with the proposed and compared methods.

Table 1 shows the simulation parameters. When the gene length increases, the retrieval space is generally widely spread, and the IEC methods find it hard to search for optimized solutions. However, we assume to application of the proposed method to a real IEC system that retrieves various clothing or shoe designs from approximately 1 million designs. Accordingly, 20 bits of the gene length can express 1,048,576 various designs. We set the gene length to 20 bits and the number of generations to 100. IEC systems generally use 10 to 20 generations considering user evaluation loads. However, the simulation performs quantitative evaluations between the proposed and compared methods. In a real IEC system, it is possible that the IEC system operates more generations without increasing the user evaluation loads by improving how users evaluate the candidate solutions. We set various numbers of candidate solutions and employed and onlooker bees of the proposed method in Sect. 4.1. In the Kansei space of a pseudo user described in Sect. 3.2 the area of higher (lower) evaluation by a user shows peaks (valley). We show the number of peaks (target candidate solutions) as the number of user preferences.

3.2   Multimodal Kansei Evaluation Model

The evaluation characteristics of the pseudo user capture the Kansei of a real user as close as possible. Real users generally do not evaluate clothing designs or color combinations using a single preference (i.e., typically have several different preferences). Moreover, the strength of the preference of real users varies for each design. For example, users evaluate clothing designs on a rating scale that ranges from "like" to "do not like at all." Thus, the evaluation characteristics of real users are complex. Accordingly, we use herein a multimodal Kansei evaluation model for the Kansei space of a pseudo user [11].

Figure 3 shows an example of a multimodal Kansei space visualization. The multiple peaks of the Kansei representation are caused by the nonlinear evaluation process used in the original Kansei space. To visually confirm this, we

Table 1. Simulation parameters

	Proposed method (ABC)	Compared method (GA)
Gene length	20 bits	
Generations	100	
Candidate solutions	10 – 100	20
Employed bees	10 – 100	–
Onlooker bees	10 – 100	–
Collection upper limit	$\frac{Employed\,bee + Onlooker\,bee}{Candidate\,solutions} + 10$	–
Selection	–	Roullet selection
Elite preservation	–	Available
Crossover	–	Uniform crossover
Mutation rate	–	5%
Target candidate solutions	2 – 5	
Simulation trials	100	

represent a multidimensional Kansei space in a three-dimensional space as follows:

The number of bits of the pseudo user (i.e., the number of dimensions of the Kansei space) is 20. The x (y) axis represents the value that converts the first (latter) 10 bits of the bit string of the pseudo user into a decimal number. The z axis represents the evaluation value. In Fig. 3, the region with lower evaluation values forms a valley. In this region, the user preference is weak. Regions with higher evaluation values form mountains. In these region, the user preference is strong.

We now describe the calculation method of the evaluation value in the multimodal Kansei space. First, the model sets some weights $w_i = 1.0$ to the bit patterns of the target candidate solutions of a pseudo user as the preferences. The number of weights is equal to the number of target candidate solutions. The model sets the lower weights $w_i = 0.1$ to bit patterns that express valleys in the Kansei space. We used the three lower weights regardless of the number of target candidate solutions. The model then calculates evaluation values of the bit patterns with the weighted average of the assigned weighted values and the Hamming distances between each weighted bit pattern and the bit pattern of the evaluation object. We set the distances of each target candidate solution to more than 6 bits because if each target candidate solution is close to each other, the difference of the peaks hardly appear. Finally, to express a 10–stage evaluation of real users, the calculated evaluation values are quantized into integers of 1 to 10.

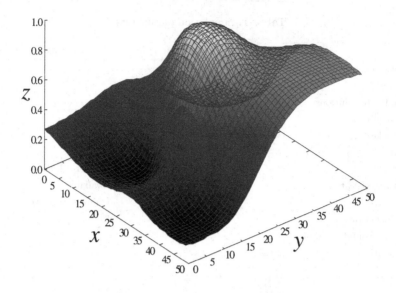

Fig. 3. Example of multimodal Kansei space

4   Results and Discussion

4.1   Tuning of Each Parameter

In the proposed method, it is important to decide on the parameters of the numbers of candidate solutions, and employed and onlooker bees for a higher evolutionary performance. This section describes the parameter tuning results.

Figure 4 shows the evolutionary performance when the number of candidate solutions is changed. In this simulation, the number of employed and onlooker bees was 100, while the number of target candidate solutions was 2. Figure 4 confirmed that the evaluation values of all cases increased when passing the generations. The evolutionary performance was greater when the numbers of the candidate solutions were 20 and 30. In contrast, the evolutionary performance was smaller when the number of candidate solutions was large. This result is attributable to the collection upper limit being too small and the proposed method quickly replacing the candidate solutions in areas that have not been sufficiently searched.

Figure 5 depicts the evolutionary performance when changing the number of employed bees. In this simulation, the numbers of the candidate solutions and the onlooker bees were 20 and 100, respectively. The number of target candidate solutions was 2. Figure 5 confirmed that the evaluation values of all cases similarly increased when passing the generations.

Figure 6 demonstrates the evolutionary performance when the number of onlooker bees is changed. In this simulation, the numbers of candidate solutions and employed bees were 20. The number of the target candidate solutions was 2. Figure 6 confirmed that the evaluation values of all cases increased when passing

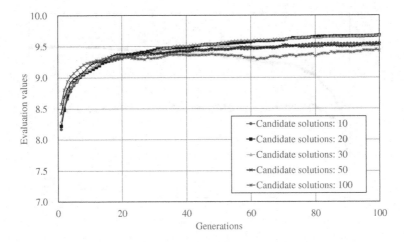

Fig. 4. Results of evolutionary performance (changing candidate solutions)

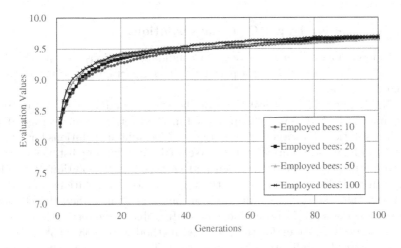

Fig. 5. Results of evolutionary performance (changing employed bees)

the generations. However, when the number of onlooker bees was 10, the evolutionary performance was smaller than those of the other cases because the collection upper limits was high against the total number of employed and onlooker bees. The proposed method cannot end any candidate solution retrievals and cannot search around for new candidate solutions.

From these results for the best performance of the proposed method, we set the numbers of candidate solutions and employed and onlooker bees to 20, 20, and 100, respectively, at the simulation in Sect. 4.2.

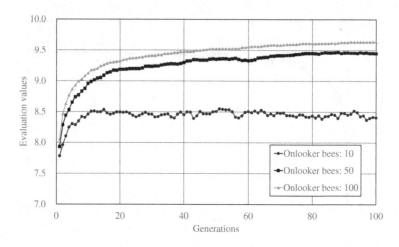

Fig. 6. Results of evolutionary performance (changing onlooker bees)

4.2   Retrieval for Target Candidate Solutions

The proposed method aims to retrieve candidate solutions multimodal. This section describes the results of a performance comparison of the proposed and compared methods.

Table 2 shows the retrieval rates of the target candidate solutions. When the number of targets was 2, the proposed method retrieved an average of 10.5 candidate solutions for target 1, an average of 7.5 candidate solutions for target 2, and two candidate solutions for neither. We used the Hamming distances between the nearest target candidate solution and each candidate solution at the final generation to judge whether or not the target candidate solutions were found. We judged that the target candidate solutions were found when the Hamming distance was 5 bits (25% of the gene length). In Table 2, the retrieval rates of the target candidate solutions for the proposed method were 0.53 : 0.38. Note that the number of all candidate solutions was 20. The proposed method retrieved two kinds of candidate solutions multimodal. However, the compared method retrieved an average of 17.7 candidate solutions for target 1, an average of 1.9 candidate solutions for target 2, and 0.4 candidate solutions for neither. The retrieval rates of the target candidate solutions for the compared method were 0.89 : 0.02. These results show that the compared method found it hard to retrieve two kinds of candidate solutions multimodal.

When the number of the target candidate solutions was 3, the retrieval rates of the target candidate solutions for the proposed method were 0.62 : 0.24 : 0.14. The proposed method also retrieved three kinds of candidate solutions multimodal. The retrieval rates of the target candidate solutions for the compared method were 0.83 : 0.01 : 0. Similarly, the compared method retrieved only a single target when the number of targets was 2.

Table 2. Results of retrieval rate for target candidate solutions

	Targets				
	1	2	3	4	5
Proposed method, Targets: 2	0.53	0.38	–	–	–
Compared method, Targets: 2	0.89	0.02	–	–	–
Proposed method, Targets: 3	0.62	0.24	0.14	–	–
Compared method, Targets: 3	0.83	0.01	0	–	–
Proposed method, Targets: 4	0.56	0.26	0.16	0.10	–
Compared method, Targets: 4	0.84	0.02	0	0	–
Proposed method, Targets: 5	0.51	0.25	0.16	0.10	0.04
Compared method, Targets: 5	0.90	0.04	0	0	0
#Proposed method, Targets: 5	0.35	0.19	0.18	0.16	0.10

When the number of targets was 4, the retrieval rates of the target candidate solutions for the proposed and compared methods were 0.56 : 0.26 : 0.16 : 0.10 and 0.84 : 0.02 : 0 : 0. Moreover, when the number of targets was 5, the retrieval rates of the target candidate solutions for the proposed and compared methods were 0.51 : 0.25 : 0.16 : 0.10 : 0.04 and 0.90 : 0.04 : 0 : 0 : 0. These results show that when the number of targets were more than three, the retrieval rates of the proposed method had a bias. However, when the number of targets was four, the proposed method can retrieve four kinds of target candidate solutions more than once in average. Moreover, when number of the targets was 5, the proposed method can retrieve only four kinds of target candidate solutions more than once in average. The compared method retrieves only a single target when the numbers of targets were 4 and 5.

When the number of target candidate solutions increases, the proposed method finds it hard to retrieve every target candidate solution because the number of candidate solutions is not sufficient for achieving a higher evolutionary performance. We then performed a simulation with 100 candidate solutions. The bottom line attached # in Table 2 shows the simulation result. In this case, the retrieval rates of the target candidate solutions for the proposed method were 0.35 : 0.19 : 0.18 : 0.16 : 0.10. Therefore, we confirmed that when the number of candidate solutions increases, the proposed method can retrieve target candidate solutions multimodal even if the number of the target candidate solutions increases. However, if the number of candidate solutions increases, the evaluation loads of users becomes large in the IEC system. When applying the proposed method to a real IEC system, the user must be able to divide the evaluation into small pieces. In addition, it is efficient to build an IEC system that can evaluate candidate solutions from the user's daily behavior.

5 Conclusion

In this study, we proposed the IEC method applying the ABC algorithm and investigated its effectiveness for the multimodal retrieval of candidate solutions using a numerical simulation. The simulation used a pseudo user that imitates the Kansei evaluation of real users on a computer, tunes each parameter, and verifies whether the proposed method can retrieve multimodal candidate solutions. The results showed that the target retrieval rate of the proposed method is higher than that of the compared method. We will perform numerical simulations in more detail in the future.

References

1. Takagi, H.: Interactive evolutionary computation: fusion of the capabilities of EC optimization and human evaluation. Proc. IEEE **89**(9), 1275–1296 (2001)
2. Ishibashi, K., Miyata, K.: Statistics-based interactive evolutionary computation for color scheme search. Int. J. Affect. Eng. **14**(1), 33–41 (2015)
3. Yamaguchi, G., Fukumoto, M.: A music recommendation based on melody creation by interactive genetic algorithm with user's intervention. In: The 20th International Symposium on Advanced Intelligent Systems and International Conference on Biometrics and Kansei Engineering (ISIS2019&ICBAKE2019), pp. 146–151 (2019)
4. Hao, G.S., Guo, N., Wang, G.G., Zhang, Z.J., Zou, D.X.: Scheme of big-data supported interactive evolutionary computation. In: 2nd International Conference on Information Technology and Management Engineering, Issue 1, pp. 14–19 (2017)
5. Domae, S., Takneouchi, H., Tokumaru, M.: Parallel retrieval interactive Tabu search. In: 14th International Symposium on Advanced Intelligent Systems (ISIS 2013), T3f-2 (2013)
6. Takenouchi, H., Tokumaru, M.: Applying hybrid genetic algorithm-Tabu search method to an interactive evolutionary computation with gaze information. In: The 20th International Symposium on Advanced Intelligent Systems and International Conference on Biometrics and Kansei Engineering (ISIS2019&ICBAKE2019), pp. 253–260, T10-4 (2019)
7. Karaboga, D.; Artificial bee colony algorithm. Scholarpedia, vol. 5, no. 3 (2010)
8. Tsai, P.-W., Khan, M.K., Pan, J.-S., Liao, B.-Y.: Interactive artificial bee colony supported passive continuous authentication system. IEEE Syst. J. **8**(2), 395–405 (2014)
9. Anto, D., Nair, A.V.: Enhancement of sensor deployment using interactive artificial bee colony algorithm. Int. J. Eng. Res. Electron. Commun. Eng. (IJERECE) **2**(5), 16–21 (2015)
10. Li, J.-Q., Pan, Q.-K.: Solving the large-scale hybrid flow shop scheduling problem with limited buffers by a hybrid artificial bee colony algorithm. Inf. Sci. **316**, 487–502 (2015)
11. Takenouchi, H., Tokumaru, M., Muranaka, N.: Tournament-style evaluation using Kansei evaluation. Int. J. Affect. Eng. **12**(3), 395–407 (2013)

Emotion Estimating Method by Using Voice and Facial Expression Parameters

Kimihiro Yamanaka[✉]

Intelligence and Informatics, Konan University, Okamoto 8-9-1, Higashinada-ku, Kobe, Japan
kiyamana@konan-u.ac.jp

Abstract. This study aimed to propose a method of emotion estimation using facial expression and speech features for machine learning with fewer parameters than in previous studies. In the experiment, emotions were evoked in participants by displaying emotion-activation movies. Facial expressions and voice parameters were then extracted. These parameters were used to estimate emotions by machine learning. In machine learning, six types of learning were performed by combining objective variables and explanatory variables. It was shown that classification can be performed with an accuracy of 93.3% when only voice parameters are used in two-category classification, such as positive and negative.

Keywords: Emotion estimation · Audiovisual parameters · Machine learning

1 Introduction

In Japan, the numbers of nursing care workers have recently increased with an increase in the elderly population. However, the number of nursing care workers is not enough compared to the increase in the elderly population. Figure 1 illustrates the changes in the number of care recipients and nursing care workers. From this figure, it is evident that the workload of nursing care workers is heavy [1]. To solve this problem, the Ministry of Health, Labor, and Welfare is attempting to increase nursing care by robots. However, care recipients experience a difference in the responses received from humans and robots [2]. Therefore, it is necessary for robots to accurately grasp the emotions of the care recipient and respond according to the emotions of the other person. Therefore, many studies on emotion estimation have been conducted.

Previous studies used facial expressions and voices as well as both facial expressions and voices. However, problems such as many parameters and high calculation cost remain [3]. From these studies, it is also known that facial expressions are good at estimating positive emotions, and voice is effective in estimating negative emotions [4, 5].

The purpose of this study is to propose a method of emotion estimation using facial expression and voice parameters for machine learning with fewer parameters than those used in previous studies.

© Springer Nature Switzerland AG 2021
K. Saeed and J. Dvorský (Eds.): CISIM 2021, LNCS 12883, pp. 225–231, 2021.
https://doi.org/10.1007/978-3-030-84340-3_18

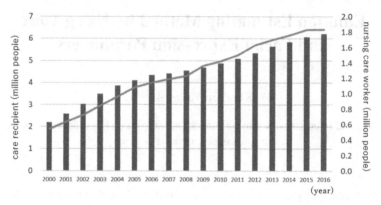

Fig. 1. Changes in number of care recipients and nursing care workers.

2 Experiment

2.1 Outline of Experiment

Participants were 12 university students (nine males and three females) aged 20 to 22 years, and the experiment was conducted with their consent after explaining the contents of the experiment.

The experiment was conducted using six pairs of two participants. Participants watched three types of emotional activation: positive, negative, and neutral. Then, participants responded to the PANAS (Positive and Negative Affect Schedule) [6], which is a questionnaire about comfort and discomfort, for each video. Subsequently, the impression of the video is discussed for each pair, as shown in Fig. 2. The situation was photographed from the front of the two participants using a facial expression estimation camera (HVC-P2, OMRON). The state of the experiment was recorded using a video camera (GZ-F270, JVC). This was set as one set, and three sets were performed with a break. The procedure for one set is as illustrated in Fig. 3, and the order of viewing was random for each pair, considering the influence of the order of the emotional activation movies.

Fig. 2. Snapshot of experiment.

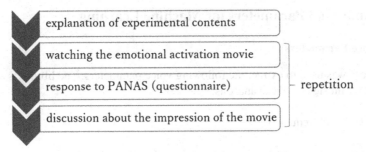

Fig. 3. Schematic diagram of the experiment.

2.2 Parameter Extraction

Figure 4 illustrates the procedure for parameter extraction. First, the video of the situation during the discussion was divided into silent sections. Next, the divided video was viewed by two participants and a third party and they evaluated the degree of comfort/discomfort, emotion, and excitement that can be felt from each video. Based on the evaluation results, the video clips that the three people evaluated as pleasant were used as positive data for the videos divided for the positive arousal activation movie. Similarly, a video clip that matches discomfort in negative data was used as negative data, and other video clips were used as neutral data.

Finally, three voice parameters were calculated from the video clip used as the data. Four facial expression parameters were simultaneously calculated from the facial expression estimation camera at the same time.

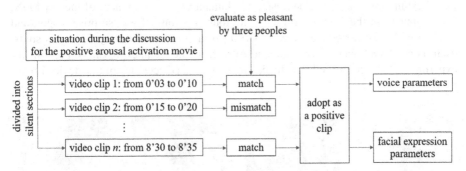

Fig. 4. Procedure of parameter extraction in case of positive.

3 Audiovisual Parameters for Machine Learning

3.1 Voice Parameters

The librosa was used to extract the following voice parameters. The librosa is a python package for music and audio analysis.

1) Fundamental frequency

The fundamental frequency is the frequency of the lowest frequency component when the signal is represented by a composite of sine waves. In this study, the fundamental frequency was obtained using the YIN algorithm [7], which is an autocorrelation method.

2) Loudness

Loudness is a sensory measure of loudness that considers human auditory characteristics (units are sone).

3) Mel-frequency cepstrum coefficient

The Mel scale is a sense of pitch and is a scale that considers human perception of pitch (unit is Mel). This Mel scale is then used to convert to the Mel frequency and then normalize the low-order components of the logarithmic cepstrum (12-dimensional) to calculate the average.

3.2 Facial Expression Parameters

Facial estimation was performed using the human vision component of the OMRON. The output from the device represents the four emotions of joy, surprise, anger, and sadness with scores ranging from 0 to 100 [8], as illustrated in Fig. 5. In this study, each score was used as a parameter calculated from the facial expressions. Preliminary experiments have confirmed that the positive's estimated accuracy of this device is over 85%.

(a) Joy   (b)Surprise   (c) Anger   (d) Sadness

Fig. 5. An example of emotion estimation by facial expression

4 Proposal Method of Emotion Estimating Using Machine Learning

4.1 Analysis Conditions for Support Vector Machine (SVM)

In the SVM, the RBF network kernel was used to construct the nonlinear evaluation function, and the hyperparameters were determined using the grid search method [9]. In the classification, only four facial expression parameters, joy, surprise, anger, and sadness, were used as explanatory variables, and only three voice parameters of fundamental frequency, loudness, and Mel-frequency cepstrum were used as explanatory variables, and seven in total. Three types of learning and classification were performed using parameters as explanatory variables. The objective variables were performed in two patterns: positive, negative, and neutral, and two categories of positive and negative.

For the evaluation, the training data were divided into 70%, and the evaluation data were divided into 30% holdout verification. This was randomly replaced and performed five times to check the accuracy of the emotion estimation. The mean of the correct answer rate for the five times evaluation data was used as the accuracy.

4.2 Classification Results and Consideration

Table 1 summarizes the results of the six types of machine learning. In all three categories, positive and negative were often discriminated as neutral, and the overall classification accuracy was low. In contrast, the accuracy of the two-category classification was high, with 86.7% for facial expression and voice, 86.9% for facial expressions, and 93.3% for voices, which is similar to those in previous studies using many parameters. From this result, the highest value was obtained when voice alone was used as a parameter.

From the classification results in Table 1, the discriminant rate was high for the two-category classification of positive and negative. In contrast, the discriminant rate was low for the three-category classification, including neutral. Although the values of positive and negative are evidently different, the neutral values are considered to overlap in the positive and negative ranges. There was a marked overlap between positive and negative in the expression parameters "anger" and the voice parameter " Mel-frequency cepstrum coefficient" For this problem, the accuracy of the three-category classification can be improved by examining the parameters that are sensitive to neutral emotions and adding them to the parameters of machine learning.

In the future, it should compare between the accuracy of previous methods and proposal method. Also, It is necessary to consider the reason why does the negative belong to the neutral more than the positive in the three-category classification.

Table 1. SVM classification results (confusion matrix). (Rows: actual, Columns: predicted)

(a) Facial expression + voice
three-category classification (Accuracy: 72%)

	positive	negative	neutral
positive	36	0	22
negative	4	2	18
neutral	2	2	84

two-category classification (Accuracy: 87%)

	positive	negative
positive	46	6
negative	4	19

(b) Facial expression
three-category classification (Accuracy: 73%)

	positive	negative	neutral
positive	38	0	19
negative	2	0	15
neutral	10	0	86

two-category classification (Accuracy: 87%)

	positive	negative
positive	54	2
negative	9	19

(c) Voice
three-category classification (Accuracy: 75%)

	positive	negative	neutral
positive	40	0	17
negative	1	0	19
neutral	5	0	88

two-category classification (Accuracy: 93%)

	positive	negative
positive	52	2
negative	3	18

5   Conclusions

The following results were obtained:

- When classifying emotions by machine learning, it was shown that highly accurate classification can be performed with a small number of parameters by using the

fundamental frequency, loudness, and Mel-frequency cepstrum coefficients as voice parameters.
- In the emotion classification method using machine learning, we suggested the possibility of highly accurate three-category classification such as positive, negative, and neutral by adding sensitive parameters specializing in neutral emotions.

Acknowledgments. I gratefully acknowledge the work of past and present members of laboratory. This work is supported in part by MEXT, Japan.

References

1. Statistics Bureau Home Page/Statistics. https://www.stat.go.jp/english/data/index.html. Accessed 27 Dec 2020
2. Ito, T., Sugiya, M.: Mihabilly: voice calling robot for rehabilitation according with the emotion estimation with biological information. In: IPSJ Interaction 2018, pp. 1068–1071 (2018)
3. Abe, W., Makabe, D., Kosaka, T.: Study on training data for emotion recognition in spontaneous dialogue speech using SVM. IPSJ Tohoku Branch SIG Technical report, 7-A3–3, 13 p. (2016). (in Japanese)
4. Neagoe, V., Barar, A., Robitu, P.: A deep learning approach for subject independent emotion recognition from facial expressions. In: Recent Advances in Image, Audio and Signal Processing, pp. 93–98 (2013)
5. Okada, A., Uemura, J., Mera, K., Kurosawa, Y., Takezawa, T.: Construction of real-time emotion recognition system from facial expression, voice, and text information. In: Proceedings of the 31st Annual Conference of the Japanese Society for Artificial Intelligence, 1B1-OS-25a, 4 p. (2017). (in Japanese)
6. Crawford, R., Henry, D.: The positive and negative affect schedule (PANAS): construct validity, measurement properties and normative data in a large non-clinical sample. Br. J. Clin. Psychol. **43**(3), 245–265 (2004)
7. de Cheveigné, A., Kawahara, H.: YIN, a fundamental frequency estimator for speech and music. J. Acoust. Soc. Am. **111**(4), 14 (2002)
8. OKAOTM Vision | Technology | OMRON's Image Sensing Site. https://plus-sensing.omron.com/technology/. Accessed 5 Jan 2021
9. Claesen, M., De Moor, B.: Hyperparameter search in machine learning. In: Proceedings of the XI Metaheuristics International Conference, 5 p. (2015)

Industrial Management and other Applications

Multilayer Perceptron Applied to the IOT Systems for Identification of Saline Wedge in the Magdalena Estuary - Colombia

Paola Patricia Ariza-Colpas[1]([✉]), Cristian Eduardo Ayala-Mantilla[2],
Marlon-Alberto Piñeres-Melo[3], Diego Villate-Daza[2], Roberto Cesar Morales-Ortega[1],
Emiro De-la-Hoz-Franco[1], Hernando Sanchez-Moreno[4], Shariq Butt Aziz[5],
and Carlos Collazos-Morales[6]

[1] Universidad de la Costa, CUC, Barranquilla, Colombia
{pariza1,rmorales1,edelahoz}@cuc.edu.co
[2] Escuela Naval de Suboficiales ARC "Barranquilla", Barranquilla, Colombia
{cristian.ayala,diego.villate}@armada.mil.co
[3] Universidad del Norte, Barranquilla, Colombia
pineresm@uninorte.edu.o
[4] Universidad Simón Bolivar, Barranquilla, Colombia
hsanchez13@unisimonbolivar.edu.co
[5] University of Lahore, Lahore, Pakistan
shariq2315@gmail.com
[6] Universidad Manuela Beltrán, Bogotá, Colombia
carlos.collazos@docentes.umb.edu.co

Abstract. Maritime safety has become a relevant aspect in logistics processes using rivers. In Colombia, specifically in the Caribbean Region, there is the Magdalena River, a body of water that broadly borders the Colombian territory and is a tributary of various economic and public health activities. At its mouth, this river interacts with the sea directly, which generates a phenomenon called saline wedge, which is directly related to the sediments that must be continuously extracted and which threatens the proper functioning of the port from the city of Barranquilla, Colombia. Through this research, a network of sensors located in strategic places at the mouth of this river was generated, which allows predicting the behavior of the salt wedge. Using artificial neural networks, more specifically, the Multilayer Perceptron algorithm, it was possible to analyze the results of the implementation in light of the indicators or quality metrics, generating a highly reliable scenario that can be replicated in other sections of the river and in other aquifers.

Keywords: IOT systems · Machine learning · Salt wedge · Aquifers · Magdalena river estuary · Multilayer Preceptron

© Springer Nature Switzerland AG 2021
K. Saeed and J. Dvorský (Eds.): CISIM 2021, LNCS 12883, pp. 235–244, 2021.
https://doi.org/10.1007/978-3-030-84340-3_19

1 Introduction

The Colombian Caribbean plain is in South America in the northernmost part. The limits are delimited in the east from the Darien jungle, on the border that communicates with Panama, to the Guajira Peninsula that connects directly with the Caribbean Sea and the vicinity of the Andes mountain range to the south. In South America, the crust blocks emerge and move horizontally, thus forming the mountain ranges that are part of the Andes mountain range [1]. That is why this plain has plains with heights that do not exceed 100 m, and with plateaus and mountain ranges between 200 and 1000 m, among which the Sierra Nevada de Santa Marta stands out with an altitude of 5,000 m. In these plains the savanna climate predominates, and they are generally used for livestock and agriculture.

Among the main rivers that have an impact on the plain, we can highlight: Sucío, Mulatos, Sinú, Magdalena, Aracataca, Fundación, Frío, Palomino, Ranchería, among others. In the specific case of the estuary object of study of this research. The Magdalena River is one of the most important rivers in Colombia, due to its extensive extension of 1,540 km. Considering the high importance of this river, it constitutes a driver of different factors around the economy, including port activities. That is why sedimentation processes bring with them wide consequences and generate a negative impact on both the security and the financial aspect of this economic sector. This article shows the automatic detection process of the saline wedge in the Magdalena River estuary, using the Multilayer Preceptron algorithm through time series analysis. The paper is distributed as follows, first a brief review of the literature is shown, second each of the components of the solution is described and third the results of the experimentation are shown.

2 Literature Review

In Colombia, the estimation of sediment transport in deltaic areas, as well as the study of the processes that control it have been incipient. Some authors have stood out for research related to sediment transport [2, 3] other authors have focused on analyzing the behavior of the dynamics of the different rivers of Colombia [4, 5] These studies indicated that the deltas located in the Colombian Pacific can be classified as tidal dominance, although exhibit some typical characteristics of wave-dominated deltas, such as the presence of barriers and littoral cords. The Magdalena and Sinú rivers have been categorized according to their swell [4]. Other types of investigations related to suspended sediments were carried out in the Magdalena, San Juan, Sinú, Patia, Atrato and Mira rivers [3] which are an important aspect in the morphology of rivers. Restrepo [4], carried out research aimed at analyzing highly relevant characteristics in terms of flow and width of the Magdalena River. Also, the same relationship that exists between this estuary and the influence it receives from other bodies of water.

Regarding the use of automatic processing to discover the relationships between the factors that generate sedimentation. Bhattacharya [6], uses Machine Learning to help reduce the different existing inaccuracies in models previously mentioned in the literature. This type of analysis is carried out by means of regression techniques, in which it also implements artificial neural networks for the characterization of the different variables in the sediment transport models. Fisher [7], performs an analysis of images of the rivers to be able to identify and process characteristics from the images for the assurance of use in the decision-making of the aquifers. Other authors such as Alizamir [8], use artificial neural networks to perform an analysis of the existing temperatures in aquifers, to determine the different changes that can be detrimental to both the fauna and the flora that are part of the ecosystem, they are also compared the results with multilinear regression models based on the mean-square error analysis, showing effectiveness when analyzing the data from different depth levels.

Li [9], carries out research based on the analysis of spectral image processing through data mining techniques to be able to automatically identify the impact of the residues left by the animals in the lagoons, which can affect in a preponderant way in public health. Alfonso [10], conducts research concerning the change generated by the flooding of the Dique channel in the southern vicinity of the Magdalena River, using the data generated in different aspects of the aquifer and its impact on the community. Ren [11], defines a scheme based on image analysis to be able to identify the way in which trees should be planted along the river in such a way that it can benefit when floods occur. Anfuso [12], performs the analysis based on aerial images in an area of 120 km of coastline that ranges from the coast of Galerazanba and Puerto Caiman, which collected a data set of frames during the years 1935 and 1947. By means of This study was able to identify the different settlements that were generated during those years that previously did not exist as Puerto Velero sandy shoals drifted rapidly. As a result, a spit in Puerto Colombia. Phillips [13], makes use of unsupervised learning through the implementation of clustering to perform the analysis on 2 major rivers in Canada, using remote sensing systems, the K Nearest Neighbors algorithm was used to identify different ecosystem variables of the aquifer. Adad [14], used LandSat satellite images to identify the quality of the soil and thermal variables to be able to identify in the Iranian desert, which were the characteristics that could affect the quality of the soil for crops and different activities related to the adequacy of the soil to improve the quality of life of the population.

3   Materials and Methods

3.1   Software Architecture Details

For the development of this application, a client-server architecture was considered that would allow real-time interaction of the information from the devices installed in the buoys in the Magdalena River and the processing of these using time series, see Fig. 1. In this architecture, in the first phase the location and correct number of sensors are defined at kilometers 3 and 5, which is the critical point to determine the presence of saline intrusion (or saline wedge) in the Magdalena River, because It is the gateway for exchange between the water of the Caribbean Sea and the fresh water of the river. These sensors emit data of high relevance for the identification of saline wedge, such as temperature, pressure, and conductivity, which send data every 15 min. The data that is sent by the sensors is sent and received by a gateway, which makes the interface between the sensor system that is in the river and the application that is processing this data remotely.

This data is then organized for the export of a data set, allowing data mining techniques to discover the relationship between the data. After analyzing the characteristics of each of the data, the application of data mining techniques based on time series such as MultiLayer Perceptron is carried out. For the development of the application, the Enterprice Architect tool was used in the modeling and design phase and the MySQL workBrench database. Regarding the support operating system, Ubuntu Server, and the backup of processing in the cloud of Amazon web service were used. For the development of the application, node and react were used. As for the model based on data mining techniques, Phyton was used, see Fig. 2.

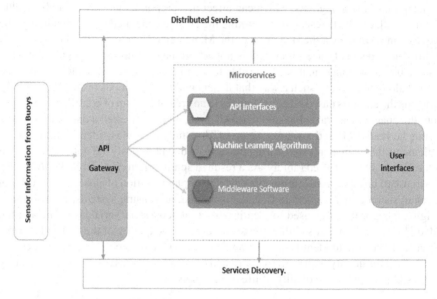

Fig. 1. Software architecture scheme.

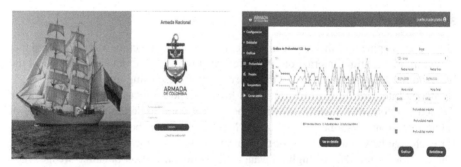

Fig. 2. a) Initial screen of the software. b) Data extraction interface.

3.2 Machine Learning Approach

ML is a scientific discipline in the field of AI, which is responsible for creating systems that learn automatically; This means that it identifies complex patterns in millions of data, using algorithms that review the information and predict future behavior. In our increasingly complex world, the field of analytics has dramatically increased in importance. Intuition is no longer sufficient in decision-making, but it must be combined with the support of the vast amount of data available today. In [15], problems arise in at least two situations: when the data is imprecise by nature and when the data is incomplete. Both situations are problematic and must be addressed appropriately. According to [16], deep learning allows computational models, made up of multiple processing layers, to learn data representations with different levels of abstraction. In recent years, artificial neural networks have been widely used in research that seeks to carry out pattern recognition and machine learning processes; Schmidhuber [17] there is a review of supervised deep learning, in addition to unsupervised learning and evolutionary calculus. A variety of knowledge engineering and data processing methods can be used to analyze the information, the most referenced methods are decision trees [18], vector support machines - SVM [19], Naive Bayesian classifiers [20], hidden Markov models [21], classifiers based on fuzzy logic [18], artificial neural networks - ANN [22], decision tables [23], and logistic model trees - LMT [24].

For the case of this experimentation, the Multilayer Perceptron (MLP) algorithm was used, which is a model that uses the artificial neural network scheme. This algorithm performs its relationships based on the graphical scheme of directed graphs, which is made up of a set of input data to finally deliver a set of appropriate output data. This algorithm has been programmed based on supervised learning. It is an evolution of the linear MultiLayer and is considered one of the most popular neural network-based algorithms and is a unidirectional type of network, see Fig. 3.

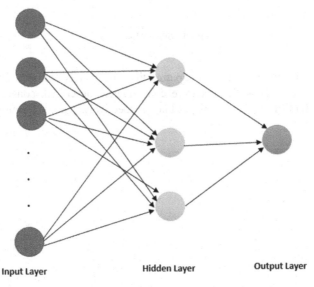

Input Layer   **Hidden Layer**   **Output Layer**

Fig. 3. Structure of the Multilayer Perceptron algorithm.

4 Model and Materials

With the data supplied from the sensors, it will be possible to consolidate a dataset, which includes the information from the two buoys located at kilometers 3 and 5, respectively. In order to define the place where each of the buoys would be installed, the sectors of the Magdalena River where the greatest presence of sediments can be evidenced were taken into account and different factors were taken into account for the definition of the types of sensors, see Fig. 4.

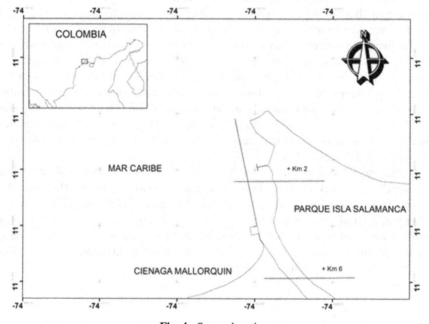

Fig. 4. Sensor location.

This experimentation scenario captures the data that is emitted at hours 00 and 15 during the sensing. 4 datasets were consolidated, described, considering what is described in Table 1. Two datasets per buoy respectively, one for training and one for testing.

Table 1. Dataset description.

File	Boya_3.csv	Boya_7.csv
Fields (data columns)	Date, Time, Battery Voltage, Conductivity Depth. Maximum, Average Depth Conductivity, Minimum Depth Conductivity, Maximum Depth Pressure, Average Depth Pressure, Minimum Depth Pressure, Maximum Depth Temperature, Depth Temperature. Medium, Minimum Depth Temperature	Date, Time, Battery Voltage, Conductivity Depth. Maximum, Average Depth Conductivity, Minimum Depth Conductivity, Maximum Depth Pressure, Average Depth Pressure, Minimum Depth Pressure, Maximum Depth Temperature, Depth Temperature. Medium, Minimum Depth Temperature
Number of fields	70	70
Time frame	From 09/18/2019 at 12:06:17 pm to 12/5/2019 at 1:31:45 pm	From 09/25/2019 at 10:58:38 am to 12/5/2019 at 1:39:39 pm
Number of instances (rows of data)	15.683	13.988

For the validation of the experimentation scenario, the model described in Fig. 5 was considered.

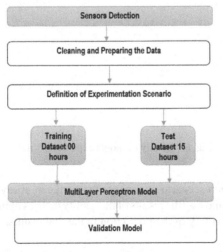

Fig. 5. Scheme of the experimentation model.

After the data preparation and adaptation phase, the construction of the two dataset groups was prepared for both training and testing, as input to the MultiLayer Perceptron algorithm. To validate this model, metrics based on the mean square error were used to identify the quality of the results obtained, see Table 2 and Fig. 6.

Table 2. Quality metrics.

Metrics	Real	Prediction	Scenario results
Media	0,0613490	0,0623860	−0,0010370
Standard deviation	0,0126820	0,0118150	0,0043640
Minimum	0,0410000	0,0457710	−0,0142630
First quartile (25%)	0,0478750	0,0484590	−0,0036140
Second quartile (50%)	0,0626670	0,0610450	−0,0010030
Third quartile (75%)	0,0723960	0,0734490	0,0020510
Maximum	0,0891670	0,0838290	0,0128460

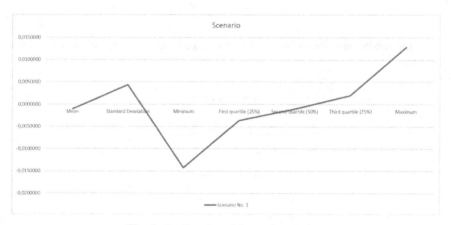

Fig. 6. Quality of model experimentation.

This experimentation scenario guarantees that you can always work with different data instances, in the same way the results of the quality metrics of independent evaluation of the data and the proximity of the prediction to the real results.

5 Conclusions

Among the most important conclusions of the implementation of this model focuses on the validation of the model based on neural networks, to support data from systems based on the Internet of Things. The implementation of this model has allowed us to know relevant aspects of the saline wedge, which results in maritime safety, on the banks of the Rio Magdalena. Among the future works that can be highlighted the generation of new scenarios and validation of the model with data from other hours of interaction with the data from the sensors.

References

1. Kellog, J.: Cenozoic tectonic history of the Sierra de Perijá, Venezuela-Colombia, and adjacent basins. Geol. Soc. Am. Mem. **162**, 239–261 (1984)
2. Restrepo, J.D., Kjerfve, B.: Magdalena river: interannual variability (1975–1995) and revised water discharge and sediment load estimates. J. Hydrol. **235**, 137–149 (2000)
3. Restrepo, J.D., Kjerfve, B.: The pacific and Caribbean rivers of Colombia: water discharge, sediment transport and dissolved loads. In: Lacerda, L., Santelli, R., Duursma, E., Abrao, J. (eds.) Environmental Geochemistry in Tropical and Subtropical Environments, pp. 169–187. Springer, Berlín (2004). https://doi.org/10.1007/978-3-662-07060-4_14
4. Restrepo, J.D.: Applicability of LOICZ catchment-coast continuum in a major Caribbean basin: the Magdalena River, Colombia. Estuar. Coast. Shelf Sci. **77**, 214–229 (2008)
5. Restrepo, J.C., Otero, L., Lopez, S.: Clima de oleaje en el Pacifico sur de Colombia, delta del Río de Mira: Comparaciones Estadísticas y Aplicación a procesos Costeros. Revista de la Academia Colombiana de Ciencias Exactas, Físicas y Naturales. **128**(33), 339–357 (2009)
6. Bhattacharya, B., Price, R.K., Solomatine, D.P.: Machine learning approach to modeling sediment transport. J. Hydraul. Eng. **133**(4), 440–450 (2007)
7. Fisher, L.H.: Sediment dynamics in the Magdalena river basin, Colombia: implications for understanding tropical river processes and hydropower development (2020)
8. Alizamir, M., et al.: Advanced machine learning model for better prediction accuracy of soil temperature at different depths. PLoS ONE **15**(4), e0231055 (2020)
9. Li, Y., Wang, X., Zhao, Z., Han, S., Liu, Z.: Lagoon water quality monitoring based on digital image analysis and machine learning estimators. Water Res. **172**, 115471 (2020)
10. Alfonso, L., Tefferi, M.: Effects of uncertain control in transport of water in a river-wetland system of the Low Magdalena River, Colombia. In: Ocampo-Martinez, C., Negenborn, R.R. (eds.) Transport of water versus transport over water, pp. 131–144. Springer, Cham (2015). https://doi.org/10.1007/978-3-319-16133-4_8
11. Ren, J., et al.: Multi-objective optimization of wave break forest design through machine learning. J. Hydroinf. **21**(2), 295–307 (2019)
12. Anfuso, G., Rangel-Buitrago, N., Arango, I.D.C.: Evolution of sandspits along the Caribbean coast of Colombia: natural and human influences. In: Randazzo, G., Jackson, D.W.T., Andrew, J., Cooper, G. (eds.) Sand and Gravel Spits, pp. 1–19. Springer, Cham (2015). https://doi.org/10.1007/978-3-319-13716-2_1
13. Phillips, A.: Modelling riverine dissolved silica on different spatial and ttemporal scales using statistical and machine learning methods. Doctoral dissertation (2020)
14. Adab, H., Morbidelli, R., Saltalippi, C., Moradian, M., Ghalhari, G.A.F.: Machine learning to estimate surface soil moisture from remote sensing data. Water **12**(11), 3223 (2020)
15. Björk, K.-M., Eirola, E., Miche, Y., Lendasse, A.: A new application of machine learning in health care, pp. 1–4 (2016). https://doi.org/10.1145/2910674.2935861
16. Ariza Colpas, P., Vicario, E., De-La-Hoz-Franco, E., Pineres-Melo, M., Oviedo-Carrascal, A., Patara, F.: Unsupervised human activity recognition using the clustering approach: a review. Sensors **20**(9), 2702 (2020)

17. Schmidhuber, J.: Deep learning in neural networks: an overview. Neural Netw. **61**, 85–117 (2015)
18. Amiribesheli, M., Benmansour, A., Bouchachia, A.: A review of smart homes in healthcare. J. Ambient. Intell. Humaniz. Comput. **6**(4), 495–517 (2015). https://doi.org/10.1007/s12652-015-0270-2
19. Fleury, A., Vacher, M., Noury, N.: SVM-based multimodal classification of activities of daily living in health smart homes: sensors, algorithms, and first experimental results. IEEE Trans. Inf Technol. Biomed. **14**(2), 274–283 (2010). https://doi.org/10.1109/TITB.2009.203731
20. McCallum, A., Nigam, K.: A comparison of event models for Naive Bayes text classification. In: AAAI-98 Workshop on Learning for Text Categorization, vol. 752, no. 1, pp. 41–48, July 1998
21. Eddy, S.R.: Profile hidden Markov models. Bioinformatics **14**(9), 755–763 (1998). https://academic.oup.com/bioinformatics/article-abstract/14/9/755/259550. Envejecimiento y salud (5 February 2018). https://www.who.int/es/news-room/fact-sheets/detail/envejecimiento-y-salud
22. Murata, N., Yoshizawa, S., Amari, S.: Network information criterion-determining the number of hidden units for an artificial neural network model. IEEE Trans. Neural Networks **5**(6), 865–872 (1994). https://doi.org/10.1109/72.329683
23. Du, W.S., Hu, B.Q.: Approximate distribution reducts in inconsistent interval-valued ordered decision tables. Inf. Sci. **271**, 93–114 (2014). https://doi.org/10.1016/j.ins.2014.02.070
24. Chen, W., et al.: A comparative study of logistic model tree, random forest, and classification and regression tree models for spatial prediction of landslide susceptibility. CATENA **151**, 147–160 (2017). https://doi.org/10.1016/j.catena.2016.11.032

Assessment of Organizational Policies in a Retail Store Based on a Simulation Model

Jairo R. Coronado-Hernández[1]([✉]) [iD], Mayra A. Macías-Jiménez[1] [iD],
Joned D. Chica-Llamas[2], and José I. Zapata-Márquez[2]

[1] Universidad de la Costa, 080001 Barranquilla, Colombia
{jcoronad18,mmacias3}@cuc.edu.co
[2] Universidad Tecnológica de Bolívar, 130001 Cartagena, Colombia

Abstract. This paper evaluates three organizational policies in a retail store by a discrete simulation model in Simio®. The policies implemented were using one, two, or three express checkouts, cross-trained workers, and allocating one, two, or three weighing counters in the produce section (fruit and vegetables). These policies were evaluated during days with low, medium, and high demand over critical performance metrics such as the queue length, waiting time, active and idle time rate, the average time in the system, average service time, and sales. Our results demonstrated that all policies are beneficial for the studied system but in days with high demand. In days with low or medium demand, there were good improvements for some indicators, but this conflicted with others. As the simulation model was implemented to evaluate each policy independently, a future direction should include studying the performance simultaneously.

Keywords: Organizational policies · Retail industry · Simulation model · Express checkouts · Cross-trained workers · Weighing counters · Queuing theory

1 Introduction

Service quality and satisfaction are key factors affecting customer retention [1, 2]. Due to the positive relationship between retention and productivity, many companies must increase their capability to retain customers [3].

A strategy to improve customer satisfaction and retention is reducing their waiting time [4]. Customers use to wait because of the limited capacity of a resource that provides a product or service. In the retail industry, waiting time increases as the number of available checkout points decreases [5]. In this sector, a reduction in waiting time represents a big task to deal with due to the different demand patterns, which could vary among customers (express and regular shoppers) and days in an observed period.

This paper presents the evaluation of organizational policies which aim to reduce waiting time in a retail company using a simulation model. Queuing phenomena have been studied before in many sectors, including retail one using simulation techniques [5–7]. However, the papers which attempted to address this problem usually emphasized checkout process optimization. This paper's main contribution is assessing cross-trained

© Springer Nature Switzerland AG 2021
K. Saeed and J. Dvorský (Eds.): CISIM 2021, LNCS 12883, pp. 245–258, 2021.
https://doi.org/10.1007/978-3-030-84340-3_20

workers' policy, weighting counter policy in the produce section (fruits and vegetables), and supermarket express lane implementation, over some queuing indicators in a retail store.

Theoretical analysis on quick queues or express lane settings is limited in the literature [8]. Also, little attention has grown around strategies to balance customer demand with workforce capacity in real-time, where cross-trained workers have demonstrated some benefits [9]. Simultaneously, supermarkets' weighing policy has been implemented with cashier service or by the customers independently [10]. Most of the papers about it studied this policy isolated [10, 11].

The remainder of the paper is organized as follows. Section 2 presents a brief literature review about simulation models and queuing studies in supermarkets. Section 3 and 4 describe the research methodology and the case study application, respectively. Finally, the main conclusions and further research directions are presented in Sect. 5.

2 Brief Literature Review

Several approaches have been applied to assess the impact of some policies in the retail industry. For instance, a queuing study to assess the effect of quick queues was developed in a supermarket [8]. The paper results allowed determining the number of quick queues to minimize customer losses. Another approach was conducted using a simulation model to investigate the impact of express checkouts over some key indicators [12]. According to the authors, there was no evidence that express checkout lanes would reduce the waiting time. However, it was proved to reduce the average number of customers in the queue for small-buying customers.

On the other hand, a computational model was used to evaluate the effect of a premium pricing for express checkout policy between two companies who sold the same products [13]. This policy was based on the principle that impatient customers who buy few products tend to prefer a smaller store for quick service. But the paper results suggest that this strategy causes a decrease in market prices and reduces seller profits.

Quick queues are not the only policy implemented by retail stores to retain customers. Cross-trained workers are usually hired by companies who carried out back and front room operations, allowing switching workers among tasks depending on the demand in each of the duties [14]. Due to the variable demand over a day experimented in the retail industry, cross-trained worker policy has been implemented.

Some research has explored the impact of this policy using deterministic and stochastic approaches. A deterministic approach was used to study servers' policy in front and back rooms [15]. The results indicated that a reduction in productivity happens when workers return to the back room. Also, it was possible to solve two problems: 1. Minimize the queue length, and 2. Minimize the worker complement. However, the increase in the use of cross-trained workers does not necessarily generate improvements for a store. The above was demonstrated in a work where the authors designed a stylized retail store simulation with RTLA practice (real-time labor allocation) [9]. The cause is because it can generate an excess in non-value-added changeovers.

Another policy that is commonly implemented in retail stores is the use of weighing machines in sections with products like fruit and vegetables. It has taken some relevance because of the trends around healthy lifestyles that have increased their demand [11]. Some products from the fruit and vegetable section are previously packed or labeled with their respective price. However, due to the properties of these products, most are exhibited in their traditional form. For that, stores have provided weighing points or counters to determine a product's price in advance. However, it causes weighing queues [16].

Hence, reviewing the available literature, we can infer that the retail sector is a dynamic industry that implements organizational policies to improve customer satisfaction. But there are still some perspectives to explore for supporting the decision-making process, especially in assessing several policies together.

3 Methodology

A methodology based on four stages was conducted to fulfill the objectives of the research.

- Problem description: In this stage, based on a diagnosis of the company's current state, the potential policies to implement were defined.
- Input and output variables: The second stage in the research consisted of defining the simulation goals by selecting input and output variables to measure. In this step, interviews and technical visits were carried out. Therefore, most of the data were collected by direct observation and from historical data sets.
- Model design: In this phase, the conceptual and simulation models were proposed based on the buying process performance in the selected company.
- Policy assessment: In this stage, each policy was evaluated. For express lanes policy, scenarios with one, two, and three quick queues were considered. In cross-trained workers policy, a comparison before and after the implementation of the policy was made. Finally, we considered using one, two, and three weighing points for the weighing policy.

4 Case Study

4.1 Problem Description

The selected retail has experienced customer complaints due to the long waiting times in peak days, delays because of a deficient tagging in the produce section (fruit and vegetables), and the lack of quick queues dedicated to express shoppers who buy 10 products or less. Service level in this type of industry usually is influenced by several dimensions such as the quality and speed of the attention and a short time waiting in the queue. Companies use to apply organizational policies that enable increase customer satisfaction to achieve a high service level.

The selected retail wants to implement the following policies:

- Express lanes: This policy uses checkouts exclusively for customers with few products (less than 10). This solution helps to decongest the queues in the regular checkouts.

- Cross-trained workers: This policy implies that free regular workers from Operations & Logistics or Commercial Department move to specific checkouts during hours or entire days of high demand. To fulfill this policy, the manager of the point of sale is responsible for checking the operations and requesting additional workers in case of need. This policy is also applicable when a cashier is absent during working hours for any reason.
- Weighing policy: This policy consists of using points for register products without bar codes. With this solution, people who bring fruits, vegetables, or other bulk products use the weighing points to get a ticket with their price.

However, in the retail industry, a challenge for a policy implementation consists of handle the changing demand in each period, which influences the stability of an organizational decision.

Therefore, before applying a known policy, it is essential to assess the potential impact over key service indicators against different demand behaviors. For this purpose, a simulation model was proposed.

4.2 Variables

In general terms, the following independent variables were considered:

- Population size (N): Number of potential clients.
- Arrival rate (λ)
- Time between arrivals ($1/\lambda$)
- Service average time ($1/\mu$)
- Service rate (μ): Served clients in a period.

The output variables measured were: (1) Average number of customers in the queue, (2) Average time in the queue (min), (3) Active/busy time (%), (4) Idle time (%), (5) Average time in the system (min), (6) Average service time (min), and (7) Sales[1] (USD/day).

4.3 Model Design

Conceptual Model. There are two sources from arrival entities (primary and secondary entry); both are assumed as infinite population. Customers who arrive could use a shopping cart or not. After this decision, they spend some time picking items among the supermarket sections. Figure 1 represents the buying process in the selected company.

Figure 2 illustrates the conceptual model. Customers who arrive can go into any section. The produce section (fruit and vegetables) and the dairy section works like a self-service system M/M/∞. The meat section works under a FIFO (first-in, first-out) discipline. Then, when the customer finishes the selection of items goes to the checkout to pay. The checkout system works as an M/M/n system in parallel.

---

[1] The total sales per day are estimated from the number of customers in a day multiplied by the average sale amount in the point of sale (24.054 USD) which is calculated based on historical data.

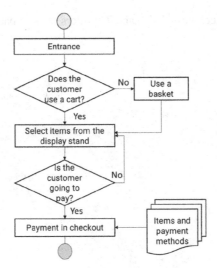

Fig. 1. Buying process

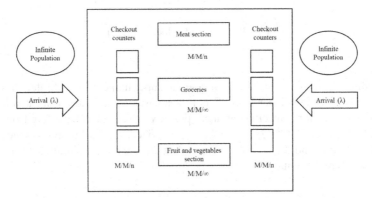

Fig. 2. Conceptual model

Simulation Model. Simio® [17], a discrete simulation software, was used for implementing the simulation model. The entities used in the simulation model were the customers who entered the store and split the flow according to the use or not of shopping carts and weighing points.

The locations employed in the simulation model were the main entrance, secondary entrance, general zones of the store, weighing points, and checkouts (Fig. 3).

In the store, there are three checkout zones called:

a. Fruit and vegetables: checkouts 1–8, and 8 cashiers with 13 packers[2].
b. Customer service: checkouts 9–20, and 12 cashiers with 15 packers.

---

[2] The role of the packers is negligible for performance purposes considering that before any policy simulation their idle time was more than 60%.

c. Back checkouts: checkouts 21–27, and 7 cashiers with 17 packers.

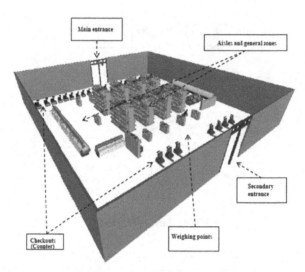

Fig. 3. Supermarket locations [18]

Arrival Rate. A timer was used to simulate the supermarket's arrival rate, allowing to change arrivals' behavior per hour. This process was represented using two kinds of schemes, each one for a specific entrance (primary or secondary), starting from hour 0 (7.00 am) until hour 12 (20.00), as Table 1 summarized. Figure 4 represents the process in Simio software, and the rest of the input data considered for simulation purposes is included in a supplementary file [19].

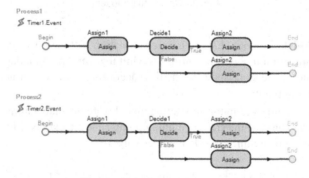

Fig. 4. Arrival rate process [18]

Table 1. Arrival time distribution in the primary and secondary entrance

Time	Primary		Secondary	
	No. customers.	Distribution (min)	No. customers.	Distribution (min)
07.00–08.00	44	exp (1.39)	41	exp (1.49)
08.00–09.00	52	exp (1.17)	46	exp (1.25)
09.00–10.00	82	exp (0.7)	66	exp (0.75)
10.00–11.00	79	exp (0.77)	64	exp (0.82)
11.00–12.00	77	exp (0.77)	55	exp (0.82)
12.00–13.00	67	exp (0.91)	58	exp (0.97)
13.00–14.00	65	exp (0.92)	59	exp (0.98)
14.00–15.00	68	exp (0.88)	61	exp (0.94)
15.00–16.00	67	exp (0.89)	58	exp (0.95)
16.00–17.00	82	exp (0.73)	63	exp (0.78)
17.00–18.00	54	exp (1.15)	58	exp (1.23)
18.00–19.00	39	exp (1.57)	52	exp (1.68)
19.00–20.00	34	exp (1.81)	33	exp (1.94)

Departure of Weighing Points. A process in Simio software was used to identify the entities before and after using a weighing point. Therefore, to split the flow, the property affected for the entities was the picture. Figure 5 illustrates how this change was implemented in the model.

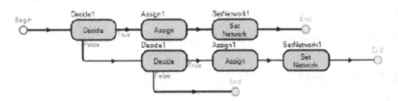

Fig. 5. Departure of weighing points process [18]

Change the Queue. When the end of a work shift happens, the checkout involved closes. In this situation, probably a customer or a group may stay in the queue. Therefore, the supermarket implements the change of this customer or group to an available checkout. Hence, to model this scenario, a process was set in the simulation tool.

The process interrupts the checkout process when the capacity reaches 0 (the signal that a work shift ends), then we used a counter to search the entities in the queue and transfer them to another checkout point. Figure 6 shows how the process works.

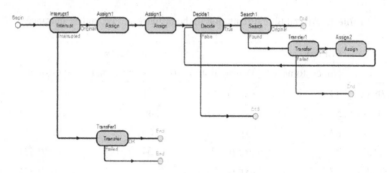

Fig. 6. Change between queues due to end of a turn [18]

Assumptions. The time between arrivals was utterly random, and they came from a finite population. Also, we assumed that the supermarket capacity is infinite and that every customer needs a basket or a shopping cart. Therefore, the model does not include the possibility of carrying the products in their hands.

Regarding the customer traveling in the supermarket store, it is assumed that the time using to selecting items for the basket or cart is entirely random.

Finally, the customer election of the checkout and the time spend on it are entirely random.

Statistical Validity. Three variables were selected to validate the model: a) customers served by a cashier in a day, b) active/busy time (%) in a day, and c) the total time using for payment (h). These variables were measured in three days: I) low demand, II) regular demand, and III) high demand. Two hypothesis tests were conducted for each day: homoscedasticity test and comparison of means using Statgraphics® [20]. These results are included in a supplementary file [19]. We inferred that the simulation model was adjusted to the actual system behavior at a 95% confidence level from these test results.

The simulation model was run with 50 replications.

4.4 Policy Assessment

Express Lanes

Category I: Days with Low Demand. Table 2 shows critical improvements in some indicators (1, average customers in the queue, and 2, the average time in queue), even some increase in others representing a notorious drawback.

Analyzing advantages and disadvantages, the recommended policy in this category consisted of using two express lanes cashier checkouts. Implementing this, the average number of customers in the queue and the average time in queue decreased by 50% and 54.1%. However, indicators such as idle time, average service time, and the system's total time increased.

This alternative showed less impact than others in these critical indicators among every scenario (1, 2, and 3 express lanes).

Table 2. Results of express lanes (EL) in days type I.

Indicator	Current	1 E.L	Change	2 E.L	Change	3 E.L	Change
1	2.0	1.0	−50.0%	1.0	−50.0%	1.0	−50.0%
2	8.7	4.0	−54.0%	4.0	−54.1%	1.4	−84.3%
3	54.2	42.4	−21.9%	43.1	−20.6%	37.6	−30.7%
4	45.8	57.6	25.9%	56.9	24.4%	62.4	36.3%
5	30.3	42.1	39.0%	41.9	38.4%	41.9	38.4%
6	3.0	3.6	17.2%	3.4	13.5%	3.5	13.9%
7	44400.6	45604.5	2.7%	46413.6	4.5%	46265.2	4.2%

Category II: Average Demand/Regular Day. These days, the impact over the studied indicators is even more than in the previous section. It is expected because, on a regular day, the potential demand is more significant than type 1 days.

According to the results, one express lane checkout is highly recommended over two or three lanes. The above is due to the comparison among decrease and increase in the studied indicators (Table 3). This single change generated a reduction of congested queues. The average queue length and the average waiting time decreased by 66.7% and 79.5%, respectively, even though there is a slight increment in the idle time.

Table 3. Results of express lanes (EL) in days type II.

Indicator	Current	1 E.L	Change	2 E.L	Change	3 E.L	Change
1	3.0	1.0	−66.7%	1.0	−66.7%	1.0	−66.7%
2	23.5	4.8	−79.5%	3.2	−86.4%	2.4	−89.8%
3	55.4	51.9	−6.3%	51.8	−6.6%	49.8	−10.1%
4	44.6	48.1	7.8%	48.2	8.2%	50.2	12.6%
5	35.0	45.8	30.8%	42.3	21.0%	42.4	21.1%
6	3.3	3.5	4.5%	3.2	−3.9%	3.2	−2.7%
7	54552.3	55372.6	1.5%	55515.4	1.8%	55658.2	2.0%

Category III: High Demand. During days type III, the implementation of an express lane policy is highly beneficial. Simulation results suggested that using quick queues, the average number of customers in the queue (Indicator 1), average time in queue (Indicator 2), and the average service time (Indicator 6) experience a significant decrease (Table 4).

A slight increase in other indicators such as idle time and the average time in the system happened. Among all the scenarios, the best option consists of using two express lanes because of the comparison among positive and negative effects. With this alternative, indicators 1, 2, and 6 reduce their performance by 66.7%, 87.5%, and 46.1%, respectively.

Table 4. Results of express lanes (EL) in days type III.

Indicator	Current	1 E.L	Change	2 E.L	Change	3 E.L	Change
1	3.0	2.0	−33.3%	1.0	−66.7%	1.0	−66.7%
2	35.1	5.3	−84.8%	4.4	−87.5%	4.2	−88.1%
3	58.4	59.7	2.2%	56.7	−2.8%	56.3	−3.5%
4	41.6	40.3	−3.2%	43.3	3.9%	43.7	4.9%
5	35.1	47.7	35.9%	45.1	28.6%	42.4	21.0%
6	5.8	3.3	−43.5%	3.2	−46.1%	3.5	−39.9%
7	73598.7	73626.7	0.0%	74399.5	1.1%	74256.7	0.9%

Cross-Trained Workers. To assess this policy, we analyzed data from the Operations & Logistics Department about when workers of this division move to checkout operations due to the high demand. From this analysis, the peak hours were set at 10.00–12.00 and 16.00–18.00.

Tables 5 and 6 include the impact of applying cross-trained workers policy during the three types of days. As we expected, the benefits of the policy were negligible on days I and II. While in days III, the goodness was more significant, finding changes in the average number of customers (indicator 1) and average time in the queue (indicator 2) and the percentage of idle time (indicator 4) by 33%, 77%, and 26%, respectively.

Table 5. Results of cross-trained workers' policy in days type I and II

Indicator	Category I			Category II		
	Current	Improved	Change	Current	Improved	Change
1	2.0	2.0	0.0%	3.0	3.0	0.0%
2	8.7	7.4	−14.7%	23.5	17.2	−27.0%
3	54.2	51.0	−5.9%	55.4	65.0	17.3%
4	45.8	49.0	7.0%	44.6	35.0	−21.5%
5	30.3	32.3	6.9%	35.0	37.5	7.3%
6	3.0	4.4	45.3%	3.3	4.1	23.1%
7	44400.6	44571.4	0.4%	54552.3	57030.1	4.5%

Table 6. Results of cross-trained workers' policy in days type III.

Indicator	Current	Improved	Change
1	3.0	2.0	−33.3%
2	35.1	8.2	−76.6%
3	58.4	69.3	18.7%
4	41.6	30.7	−26.3%
5	35.1	32.6	−7.0%
6	5.8	6.7	13.9%
7	73598.7	75720.9	2.9%

Weighing Policy. One, two, and three weighing points were considered to assess this policy. Simulation results are shown in Tables 7, 8 and 9.

According to the results in days type I, the weighing policy looks poor in terms of benefits. Although implementing one weighing point, the queue length, and the average time queuing decrease by 50% and 43.1%, the sales and other relevant indicators worse.

On the contrary, in days type II, the benefits are worthy even though the drawbacks. In this case, one weighing point allows a decrease in the waiting indicators (average number of customers and average time in queue). It reduces these metrics by 33.3% and 60%, respectively.

Finally, on average, the best option was to implement one weighing point in days type III, improving every critical indicator. For instance, the average number of customers in the queue and the queue's average time decreased by 33.3% and 75.5%. While the effect on the active time was by 13.1%, increasing sales by 5.4%. This change is the highest registered in the simulation in this last indicator.

Table 7. Results of weighing policy in days type I

Indicator	Current	1 point	Change	2 points	Change	3 points	Change
1	2.0	1.0	−50.0%	1.0	−50.0%	1.0	−50.0%
2	8.7	5.0	−43.1%	5.8	−33.4%	6.6	−24.6%
3	54.2	46.6	−14.1%	46.0	−15.2%	47.4	−12.6%
4	45.8	53.4	16.6%	54.0	18.0%	52.6	14.9%
5	30.3	30.2	−0.1%	31.1	2.8%	32.2	6.3%
6	3.0	3.1	1.0%	3.3	9.9%	3.2	5.9%
7	44400.6	42670.4	−3.9%	43053.9	−3.0%	44137.4	−0.6%

Table 8. Results of weighing policy in days type II

Indicator	Current	1 point	Change	2 points	Change	3 points	Change
1	3.0	2.0	−33.3%	2.0	−33.3%	1.0	−66.7%
2	23.5	9.4	−60.0%	13.7	−41.9%	10.8	−54.1%
3	55.4	60.7	9.5%	60.2	8.7%	58.6	5.7%
4	44.6	39.3	−11.9%	39.8	−10.7%	41.4	−7.2%
5	35.0	33.1	−5.3%	39.8	13.8%	35.1	0.5%
6	3.3	3.7	10.2%	3.2	−3.6%	3.2	−5.4%
7	54552.3	55129.1	1.1%	56789.3	4.1%	53734.8	−1.5%

Table 9. Results of weighing policy in days type III

Indicator	Current	1 point	Change	2 points	Change	3 points	Change
1	3.0	2.0	−33.3%	2.0	−33.3%	2.0	−33.3%
2	35.1	8.6	−75.5%	7.6	−78.3%	11.2	−68.0%
3	58.4	66.1	13.1%	62.0	6.2%	64.4	10.2%
4	41.6	33.9	−18.5%	38.0	−8.7%	35.6	−14.4%
5	35.1	32.9	−6.2%	32.8	−6.6%	36.1	2.9%
6	5.8	4.5	−23.1%	4.4	−25.0%	4.2	−27.7%
7	73598.7	77549.1	5.4%	73458.8	−0.2%	75720.9	2.9%

5 Conclusion

This article evaluated the benefits and drawbacks of a set of organizational policies in a retail store. Express lanes policy showed to be helpful in days with high demand. This policy presented the best performance during these days, improving most of the assessed metrics such as queue length and the average time in queue. But, among the scenarios considered (with one, two, or three lanes), use two express lanes was the most suitable because it does not significantly affect other metrics such as idle time and generates an increase in sales.

Moreover, cross-trained workers policy also demonstrated benefits in the same indicators during the same type of days simulated. It was expected because when the store experienced low or medium demand, there is no need to allocate workers from other functional areas to checkout zones, allowing specialized workers to have a focus on their tasks.

Finally, weighing policy presents good results in days with medium and high demand, despite the drawbacks experienced in some indicators. But among these two categories of days, the convenient time to implement the policy was in days with high demand, which is demonstrated from the improvement rate in queuing indicators.

Therefore, the implementation of these policies in the selected store must be on days with high demand. In contrast, it is better to switch among individual policies according to a specific goal set by the manager during the other days. The study's main limitation is that the policies were evaluated one each time and not simultaneously, and it was selected just one store to pursue the research. Hence, further research need to include these points and the model implementation with another input dataset.

References

1. Alkitbi, S.S., Alshurideh, M., Al Kurdi, B., Salloum, S.A.: Factors affect customer retention: a systematic review. In: Hassanien, A.E., Slowik, A., Snášel, V., El-Deeb, H., Tolba, F.M. (eds.) AISI 2020. AISC, vol. 1261, pp. 656–667. Springer, Cham (2021). https://doi.org/10.1007/978-3-030-58669-0_59
2. Dahm, M., Wentzel, D., Herzog, W., Wiecek, A.: Breathing down your neck!: the impact of queues on customers using a retail service. J. Retail. **94**, 217–230 (2018). https://doi.org/10.1016/j.jretai.2018.04.002
3. Penceliah, D.S., Noel, D.T., Adat, N.: Customer satisfaction within pharmacies in a supermarket: a South African perspective. Probl. Perspect. Manag. **13**, 452–459 (2015)
4. Zhang, Q.: Multi-agent based supermarket queuing model and optimization. Adv. Intell. Soft Comput. **129**, 635–640 (2011). https://doi.org/10.1007/978-3-642-25986-9_99
5. Antczak, T., Weron, R., Zabawa, J.: Data-driven simulation modeling of the checkout process in supermarkets: insights for decision support in retail operations. IEEE Access **8**, 228841–228852 (2020). https://doi.org/10.1109/ACCESS.2020.3045919
6. Chai, C.-F.: Problem analysis and optimizing of setting service desks in supermarket based on M/M/C queuing system. In: Qi, E., Shen, J., Dou, R. (eds.) The 19th International Conference on Industrial Engineering and Engineering Management, pp. 833–841. Springer, Heidelberg (2013). https://doi.org/10.1007/978-3-642-38391-5_88
7. Pereira Junior, J.V., da Silva, A.M., de Moraes, D.G.: Discrete simulation applied to queue management in a supermarket. Indep. J. Manag. Prod. **11**, 1667 (2020). https://doi.org/10.14807/ijmp.v11i5.1296
8. Li, K., Pan, Y., Liu, B., Cheng, B.: The setting and optimization of quick queue with customer loss. J. Ind. Manag. Optim. **16**, 1539–1553 (2020). https://doi.org/10.3934/JIMO.2019016
9. Mou, S., Robb, D.J.: Real-time labour allocation in grocery stores: a simulation-based approach. Decis. Support Syst. **124**, 113095 (2019). https://doi.org/10.1016/j.dss.2019.113095
10. Luo, R., Shi, Y.: Analysis and optimization of supermarket operation mode based on queuing theory: queuing and pricing of personalized service. In: ACM International Conference Proceeding Series, pp. 221–224 (2020). https://doi.org/10.1145/3380625.3380635
11. Zhou, H., Chen, X., Wang, X., Wang, L.: Design of fruits and vegetables online inspection system based on vision. J. Phys. Confe. Ser. **1074**, 012160 (2018). https://doi.org/10.1088/1742-6596/1074/1/012160
12. Kwak, J.K.: Analysis on the effect of express checkouts in retail stores. J. Appl. Bus. Res. **33**, 765–772 (2017). https://doi.org/10.19030/jabr.v33i4.9998
13. Deck, C., Kimbrough, E.O., Mongrain, S.: Paying for express checkout: competition and price discrimination in multi-server queuing systems. PLoS ONE **9**(3), e92070 (2014). https://doi.org/10.1371/journal.pone.0092070

14. Terekhov, D., Christopher Beck, J.: An extended queueing control model for facilities with front room and back room operations and mixed-skilled workers. Eur. J. Oper. Res. **198**, 223–231 (2009). https://doi.org/10.1016/j.ejor.2008.08.013
15. Wang, J.: An optimal deterministic control policy of servers in front and back rooms with a variable number of switching points and switching costs. Sci. China Ser. F Inf. Sci. **52**(7), 1113–1119 (2009). https://doi.org/10.1007/s11432-009-0130-9
16. Rengarajan, V., Vijay Anand, V., Vijayabanu, C., Thiyagarajan, S.: Customer perception on waiting time in super markets – an exploratory study using one way anova. Int. J. Sci. Technol. Res. **8**, 2649–2659 (2019)
17. Simio LLC: Simio 9.147 (2016)
18. Chica Llamas, J.D., Zapata Márquez, J.I.: Modelo de simulación para la evaluación del impacto de las políticas de pesaje, personal polivalente y cajas rápidas en el rendimiento operacional de empresas minorista. Caso Megatiendas Express - Sector Prado (2012). http://biblioteca.utb.edu.co/notas/tesis/0063077.pdf
19. Coronado-Hernández, J.R., Macías-Jiménez, M.A., Chica-Llamas, J.D., Zapata-Márquez, J.I.: Additional files. Assessment of organizational policies in a retail store based on a simulation model (2020). https://doi.org/10.6084/m9.figshare.14608113
20. Statgraphics Technologies Inc.: Statgraphics Centurion XVIII, statgraphics.com (2019)

Locating Sea Ambulances to Respond to Emergencies of Vulnerable Populations. Case of Cartagena Bay in Colombia

Jairo R. Coronado-Hernández[1]([✉])([iD]), Marly Rico-Carrillo[2,3],
Katherine Rico-Carrillo[2,3], and Orlando Zapateiro Altamiranda[2,3]

[1] Universidad de la Costa, Barranquilla, Colombia
jcoronad18@cuc.edu.co
[2] Armada Nacional, Cartagena, Colombia
{marly.rico,katherine.rico}@armada.mil.co
[3] Escuela Naval de Catedes "Almirante Padilla", Cartagena, Colombia

Abstract. Emergency services are an important element for healthcare assistance because its rapid response to transportation is essential for saving lives. Cartagena de Indias presents some weaknesses in terms of covering the demand for emergency transfers from insular areas due to the non-existence of terrestrial routes to hospitals and healthcare facilities. This study aims to determine the optimal location for sea ambulances using a mixed-integer linear programming model. A three-staged methodology allowed to select optimal locations, reducing response times of emergencies for vulnerable populations considering available healthcare facilities and maritime safety requirements.

Keywords: Location · Sea ambulances · Mixed integer linear programming · Healthcare

1 Introduction

Emergency services are an important element for healthcare assistance because its rapid response in transportation is essential for saving lives [4,20].

A critical aspect for these services is the physical location of the ambulances. The typical service provided by an ambulance involves: (i) receiving an incoming emergency call and assessing the situation, (ii) dispatching an ambulance to the emergency site, if required, (iii) providing assistance at the site by the emergency medical team, and (iv) transferring the patient to the nearest hospital [1].

Location problems have received substantial attention in the literature because they are very useful in practice, and because of the difficulty in finding optimal solutions [19]. These problems are classified into three major groups: (i) Flat models, in which demand sites are located at discrete points on the plain and the facilities can be located on any point [3]; network models, in which demand is produced in the nodes of a network and the facilities may be located

© Springer Nature Switzerland AG 2021
K. Saeed and J. Dvorský (Eds.): CISIM 2021, LNCS 12883, pp. 259–269, 2021.
https://doi.org/10.1007/978-3-030-84340-3_21

on the network's nodes [7,13]; and discrete models, in which demand is produced in the nodes of the supply chain, and the facilities can be located based on a set of nodes and the distance between the locations of the facilities and the demand points are represented by a distance matrix [10]. These are the most common models used in the facility location literature.

Discrete location models are sub-divided into four major groups: (i) The median-p models, whose objective is to minimize the total or average distance between the demand nodes and the location of the facility to which they are assigned [14]; (ii) p-center models, which minimize the maximum distance between a demand node and the nearest facility, also known as a minimax location problem; (iii) Maximum coverage models, which are aimed at maximizing the coverage of a facility to cover demand by location [13,15]; and (iv) Fixed cost models, which seek to minimize the cost of opening while ensuring coverage for all demand points [2].

A literature review on healthcare facility location is provided by [1]. Ambulance location problems are generally considered as Maximum Expected Coverage Location Problems (MEXCLP), developed by [11].

Schmid et al. [17] studied the problem of locating ambulance vehicles, allowing covering and responding to emergencies efficiently, depending on the time of travel. To solve the problem, they used the metaheuristic "Variable Neighborhood Search" (VNS).

Zaffar et al. [20] presented a simulation model to assess different policies on coverage, survival and response times as a function of ambulance location.

Dibene et al. [12] presented an application of ambulance location in the city of Tijuana, Mexico, considering the information on possible locations for ambulance bases, demand and priorities, demand scenarios, possible points of demand, and average travel times. This study demonstrated improvements in response and coverage.

Belanger et al. [5] presented a review of optimization models and trends regarding location, relocation and dispatching of medical emergency vehicles.

The literature also includes the problem of helicopter location for the healthcare sector. [8] studies the case of locating helicopters and transfer points to receive patients from land ambulances to then transfer them to hospitals. [16] studies the problem of ambulance vehicle location but considering unique stochastic demands in different time periods and at different points.

Shahriari et al. [18] proposed a dual-objective model for the location of ambulance bases, air bases and heliports subject to uncertainty in transfer times between demand points and hospitals, with penalties based on time windows. The first objective was minimizing the maximum time of transfer under the assumption that the times are stochastic.

Overall, the reviewed literature indicates that the problem of location of ambulance boats has not yet been considered. This topic is only mentioned in some studies about healthcare services in remote islands [9]. This article is intended to be a contribution to the scientific literature, proposing a three-stage methodology that allows the selection of optimal locations for ambulance boats, considering the available healthcare facilities and marine safety requirements.

The aim of this paper is showing the results for the definition of optimal locations for ambulance boats, ensuring coverage and a faster response for vulnerable populations in case of emergencies in the insular area of Cartagena Bay (Colombia) using an MIP optimization model.

This papers is organized as follows: Sect. 2 shows a brief explanation of the implemented methodology, Sect. 3 shows the main results for every stage. Finally, Sect. 4 exposes the main conclusions and opportunities for further research.

2   Methodology

A three-stage methodology allowed to identify and characterize vulnerable populations and healthcare centers with access to the bay and proposing optimal location for ambulance boats using an MIP model:

2.1   Characterization of Healthcare Facilities

This stage involved identifying and characterizing the hospitals that have access by sea to the Cartagena Bay and have the capacity to respond to emergencies by sea. Basic requirements for ambulance boats and regulations established by maritime authorities were considered and the possible docks were identified using the Directorate General Maritime (DIMAR) registry.

2.2   Characterization of Vulnerable Populations

In this stage, the vulnerable populations that can be covered by sea in case of an emergency was identified. Information was gathered through interviews and historical records of assistance provided to the communities by the Coast Guard. In this case, the term "vulnerable" refers to populations with the highest emergency occurrence and accidental rates. Statistics for emergencies and assistance covered by sea were calculated.

2.3   Optimal Location for Ambulance Boats

This stage aimed to determine the location of the sea ambulances of Cartagena Bay, taking into consideration the available healthcare facilities and vulnerable populations identified the first two stages. An Mixed Integer Linear Programming model (MILP) is proposed to define the optimal location for the ambulance boats, considering a from/to travel time matrix.

3   Results

Two hospitals with access to the Cartagena Bay by sea were identified:

- Hospital Nuevo de Bocagrande is a high-complexity healthcare provider that offers emergency services, general hospitalization for adults, intensive and intermediate care units for adults, and other services. This hospital is rated with levels III and IV of assistance complexity.
- Hospital Naval de Cartagena is a Military Healthcare facility, whose declared mission is to provide quick and good services to users when required. In addition to the services offered by other hospitals in the city, Hospital Naval offers multi-stage hyperbaric medicine, specialized treatment of degenerative diseases, traumas, burns, Parkinson's, diving accidents, diabetes complications, encephalopathies, wound healing and ulcers. Hospital Naval de Cartagena is rated as Complexity Level III–IV.

The identified vulnerable populations are shown in Table 1.

Table 1. Insular vulnerable populations

Town	Area	Inhabitants	Risk
Tierra Bomba	Rural district	1460	Middle
Punta arenas	Rural district	352	Middle
Caño de Oro	Rural district	1239	Middle
Bocachica	Rural district	3028	High
Isla de manzanillo	Comuna 10	2180	Middle
Bosque	Comuna 10	12902	Middle
Bocagrande	Comuna 1	14376	Low
Manga	Comuna 1	16005	Low
Contecar-Mamonal	Comuna 11	1900	High
Cotecmar-Mamonal	Comuna 11	1800	High
Centro	Comuna 1	4173	Low
Castillo Grande	Comuna 1	7330	Low

Table 2 shows the historical data on support for evacuations provided by the Coast Guard Unit to these communities, for a total of 186 evacuations assisted between 2013 and 2017. The community that most assistance has received in recent years was Bocachica, with a total of 137 evacuations, followed by the community at Caño de Loro, with 22 evacuations assisted.

The Emergency Regulation Center (CRUE, by its acronym in Spanish) provided data on the activities performed by the Sea Ambulance 'DADIS' since 2016, as indicated in Table 3. The sum of events assisted by the ambulance in the Cartagena community in 2016 and 2017 was 1087 transfers by sea.

Overall, in these populations from 2013 to 2017 there were 1273 evacuations by sea, the great majority of which took place in the towns of Bocachica, Caño de Loro and Punta Arenas. It should be noted that the Cartagena Bay area includes the Mamonal industrial park and CONTECAR, which have large numbers of employees, as well as other neighborhoods along the Cartagena Bay. Table 4

Table 2. Evacuation support provided by the coast guard in 2013–2017

Town	2013	2014	2015	2016	2017	Total
Bocachica	62	57	10	6	2	**137**
Caño de Loro	0	16	5	1	0	**22**
Punta Arenas	0	8	2	0	0	**10**
Basurto	0	1	0	0	0	**1**
Tierra Bomba	0	0	0	10	5	**15**
Bocagrande	0	1	0	0	0	**1**
Total	**62**	**83**	**17**	**17**	**7**	186

Table 3. CRUE statistics per year for sea assistance in 2016–2017

Town	2016	2017	Total
Bocachica	351	381	**732**
Bocagrande		1	**1**
Caño de Loro	152	176	**328**
Centro	1		**1**
Punta Arenas	7	18	**25**
Total	**511**	**576**	**1087**

displays the geographic coordinates of the hospitals with access by sea and the vulnerable populations.

Given the geography of the city itself and the travel times in the city of Cartagena de Indias, combined with heavy vehicle traffic, it is necessary to locate ambulance boats to respond to maritime emergencies in order to improve response times in emergencies. A mixed integer linear programming model was implemented to optimally determine the location of the sea ambulances to cover emergencies of the vulnerable populations and to minimize response and travel times to the main hospitals. This kind of model was selected considering that MIP models are one of the most used in literature for solving ambulance location problems.

The model variables and parameters are listed in Table 5. The objective function seeks to maximize coverage of the vulnerable population according to the risk level of each town (Eq. 1).

$$Max \; Z \; = \sum_{j \in P} w_j * p_j * x_j \tag{1}$$

$$\sum_{i \in L} y_i \leq q \tag{2}$$

$$x_j \leq \sum_{i \in L} y_i * a_{i,j} \forall (j \in P) \tag{3}$$

$$y_i \in \{0, 1\} \forall i \in L; x_j \in \{0, 1\} \forall j \in P \tag{4}$$

Table 4. Geographic coordinates of the hospitals with access by sea and the vulnerable populations

Type	Place	Latitude	Longitude
Hospitals	Nuevo Hospital Bocagrande	10 23' 40.89"N	75 33' 21.14"W
	Hospital Naval	10 25' 02.51"N	75 32' 58.87"W
Vulnerable Populations	Isla Manzanillo	10 23' 34.29"N	75 31' 57.41"W
	Punta Arenas	10 21' 58.04"N	75 33' 13.29"W
	Contecar – Mamonal	10 22' 28.46"N	75 30' 34.14"W
	Coctemar – Mamonal	10 19' 34.79"N	75 30' 36.05"W
	Caño de Loro	10 20' 30.09"N	75 32' 40.78"W
	Bocachica	10 19' 27.01"N	75 34' 40.53"W
	Tierra Bomba	10 22' 39.76"N	75 34' 25.56"W
	Castillo Grande	10 23' 43.62"N	75 33' 02.61"W
	Bosque	10 23' 53.98"N	75 31' 27.27"W
	Manga	10 24' 41.15"N	75 32' 25.12"W
	Centro	10 25' 19.44"N	75 32' 57.16"W
	Bocagrande	10 24' 10.90"N	75 33' 07.83"W

Table 5. Variables and parameters of the proposed model

Symbol	Description
P	Set of indexes identifying vulnerable populations to be covered by sea ambulances
H	Set of hospitals with maritime access
L	Set of indexes identifying all possible locations for sea ambulances. $L = P \cup H$
i	Index for possible locations, where $i \in L$,
j	Index for vulnerable populations locations, where $j \in P$
p_j	Number of inhabitants for population j
w_j	Weight associated to the risk of population j
$t_{i,j}$	Travel time from potential location $i \in L$ to town $j \in P$
$tr_{i,j}$	Travel time from potential location $i \in L$ to town $j \in P$,
	Plus travel time to the nearest hospital from town $j \in P$ (i.e., $t_{i,j} + Min_{k \in P}(t_{j,k})$)
NS	Service level
q	Number of available sea ambulances
$a_{i,j}$	Binary variable that is equals to 1 if $tr_{i,j} \leq NS$, and 0 otherwise
y_i	Binary variable that is equals to 1 if a sea ambulance if located in location $i \in L$, and 0 otherwise
x_i	Binary variable that is equals to 1 if vulnerable population $j \in P$ can be covered by an ambulance in less than NS, and 0 otherwise

The first constraint (Eq. 2) controls the number of available ambulances, this is, no additional ambulances than the existing ones can be added.

The second constraint (Eq. 3) helps to meet the response time defined for covering an emergency in a vulnerable population.

The travel routes were determined for all the nodes, based safety standards established by DIMAR, and considering that the emergency boat seeks to perform the transportation as quickly as possible, depending on its technical characteristics and the zone of operations. These routes are shown in Fig. 1.

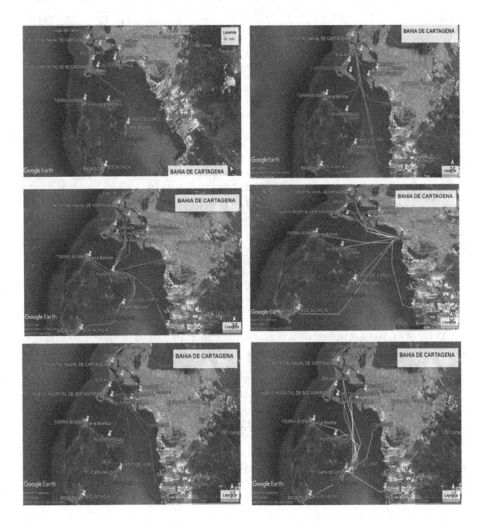

Fig. 1. Map of sea routes of the vulnerable populations in the inner Cartagena Bay

Based on the route distances and the maximum speed of travel (30 knots), a FROM/TO travel time matrix was developed, as displayed in Table 6.

Table 6. FROM/TO matrix of travel time (in minutes) by route between all the nodes. Note: 1) Nuevo Hospital Bocagrande, 2) Hospital Naval, 3) Isla Manzanillo 4) Punta Arenas, 5) Contecar -Mamonal 6) Cotecmar - Mamonal, 7) Caño de loro, 8) Bocachica 9) Tierra Bomba, 10) Castillo grande, 11) Bosque, 12) Manga, 13) Centro and 14) Bocagrande.

From/To	1	2	3	4	5	6	7	8	9	10	11	12	13	14
1	0	6,04	3,46	3,42	6,32	9,9	7,88	12,3	2,98	2,6	4,6	4,6	6	3,6
2	5,56	0	3,64	6,54	8	12,1	10,1	16,2	7,58	2,9	3,9	1,54	0,62	2,24
3	3,6	8,04	0	5,34	5,28	10	8,42	13,4	5,84	2,2	1,7	2,54	4,2	2,6
4	3,38	6,8	4,7	0	5,32	8,06	5,68	11	2,76	4,4	5,9	5,76	7,6	5
5	6,04	8,26	5,14	5,38	0	6,88	6,42	11,1	7,66	5,5	6,5	7,12	8,36	6,26
6	9,74	12,6	9,72	7,58	6,84	0	4,6	8,14	11	10	12	11,42	13,4	11,3
7	8,68	12,6	8,28	5,38	5,74	4,76	0	4,7	8,26	8,3	9,4	9,24	11,1	8,54
8	12,8	17	13,4	10	11,1	8,12	4,72	0	13,1	13	14	13,77	15,5	13,1
9	2,98	3,6	6,58	2,66	7,84	11,5	8,48	12,6	0	5,6	6,8	6,64	8,42	5,78
10	2,78	3,04	2,24	4,3	5,76	10,2	7,94	12,9	6,22	0	3,4	2,3	3,56	0,92
11	4,48	4,22	1,72	6	6,64	11,2	9,14	14,1	7,16	3,3	0	2,9	4,82	3,44
12	4,6	1,72	2,74	5,8	7	12	9,7	14,2	6,98	2,3	3	0	2,32	1,78
13	5,78	0,64	3,7	7,18	8,22	13,2	11,1	15,6	8,3	3,5	4,8	2,14	0	2,82
14	3,72	2,36	2,62	4,98	6,62	11,3	8,92	13,9	5,9	0,9	3,5	1,74	2,9	0

The model was programmed in MATHPROG and solved with solver LPSOLVE [6].

When two sea ambulances are available, the application of the mixed integer linear programming algorithms yields an optimal solution:

- Ambulance boat No. 1 should be located in the town of Cotecmar – Mamonal, at coordinates (10 19' 34.79" N, 75 30' 36.05" W).
- Ambulance boat No. 2 should be located in the town of Castillo Grande, at coordinates (10 23' 43.62" N, 75 33' 02.61" W).

As shown in Fig. 2, these ambulance boat locations minimize the response times to emergencies that may arise in the vulnerable populations in the insular area and the Cartagena Bay.

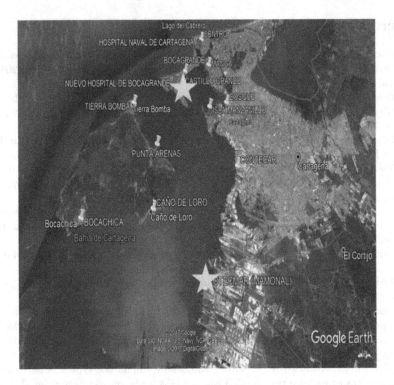

Fig. 2. Optimal location for two ambulance boats in Cartagena Bay

4 Conclusions

An optimal location for ambulance boats was obtained to ensure coverage for vulnerable populations in case of emergencies in the insular area of Cartagena Bay using an MIP model.

The boat location was performed as a function of predefined routes that follow safety standards established by DIMAR, and takes into account a maximum speed of 30 knots.

Two locations were defined: the first one is located on one of the vulnerable populations (towns) in the insular area and the second one is located at a hospital with docks.

These locations provide coverage to any point in the insular area, achieving improvements in response times.

Further research opportunities include expanding the MIP model considering terrestrial ambulances and helicopters, as an interconnected emergency system that optimizes displacements in cities with maritime routes. Additionally, simulation and dynamic location approaches should be considered, including stochastic demand scenarios.

References

1. Ahmadi-Javid, A., Seyedi, P., Syam, S.S.: A survey of healthcare facility location. Comput. Opera. Res. **79**, 223–263 (2017). https://doi.org/10.1016/j.cor.2016.05.018

2. Alcaraz, J., Landete, M., Monge, J.F., Sainz-Pardo, J.L.: Strengthening the reliability fixed-charge location model using clique constraints. Comput. Operat. Res. **60**, 14–26 (2015). https://doi.org/10.1016/j.cor.2015.02.003

3. Ballou, R.H.: Logística: Administración de la cadena de suministro, 5th edn. Pearson Educación, Ciudad de México (2004)

4. Bélanger, V., Kergosien, Y., Ruiz, A., Soriano, P.: An empirical comparison of relocation strategies in real-time ambulance fleet management. Comput. Ind. Eng. **94**, 216–229 (2016). https://doi.org/10.1016/j.cie.2016.01.023

5. Bélanger, V., Ruiz, A., Soriano, P.: Recent optimization models and trends in location, relocation, and dispatching of emergency medical vehicles. Eur. J. Oper. Res. **272**(1), 1–23 (2019). https://doi.org/10.1016/j.ejor.2018.02.055

6. Berkelaar, M., Eikland, K., Notebaert, P.: lpsolve: open source (mixed-integer) linear programming system, version 5.5.0.15. (2005)

7. Berman, O., Simchi-Levi, D.: Conditional location problems on networks. Transp. Sci. **24**(1) (1990)

8. Bozorgi-Amiri, A., Tavakoli, S., Mirzaeipour, H., Rabbani, M.: Integrated locating of helicopter stations and helipads for wounded transfer under demand location uncertainty. Am. J. Emerg. Med. **35**(3), 410–417 (2017). https://doi.org/10.1016/j.ajem.2016.11.024

9. Caliskan, C., Altintas, K.H.: Time, island and ambulance type characteristics of patient transfers from two Turkish islands: Gökçeada and Bozcaada. Int. J. Emerg. Serv. **9**(1), 47–55 (2019). https://doi.org/10.1108/IJES-12-2018-0065, https://www.emerald.com/insight/content/doi/10.1108/IJES-12-2018-0065/full/html

10. Dantrakul, S., Likasiri, C., Pongvuthithum, R.: Applied p-median and p-center algorithms for facility location problems. Expert Syst. Appl. **41**(8), 3596–3604 (2014). https://doi.org/10.1016/j.eswa.2013.11.046

11. Daskin, M.: A maximum expected covering location model: formulation, properties and heuristic solution. Transp. Sci. **17**(1), 48–70 (1983)

12. Dibene, J.C., Maldonado, Y., Vera, C., de Oliveira, M., Trujillo, L., Schütze, O.: Optimizing the location of ambulances in Tijuana, Mexico. Comput. Biol. Med. **80**, 107–115 (2017). https://doi.org/10.1016/j.compbiomed.2016.11.016

13. Farahani, R.Z., Hekmatfar, M., Fahimnia, B., Kazemzadeh, N.: Hierarchical facility location problem: models, classifications, techniques, and applications. Comput. Ind. Eng. **68**, 104–117 (2014). https://doi.org/10.1016/j.cie.2013.12.005

14. Hakimi, S.L.: Optimum locations of switching centers and the absolute centers and medians of a graph. Oper. Res. **12**(3), 450–459 (1964). https://doi.org/10.1287/opre.12.3.450

15. He, Z., Fan, B., Cheng, T., Wang, S.Y., Tan, C.H.: A mean-shift algorithm for large-scale planar maximal covering location problems. Eur. J. Oper. Res. **250**(1), 65–76 (2016). https://doi.org/10.1016/j.ejor.2015.09.006

16. Nickel, S., Reuter-Oppermann, M., Saldanha-da Gama, F.: Ambulance location under stochastic demand: a sampling approach. Oper. Res. Health Care **8**, 24–32 (2016). https://doi.org/10.1016/j.orhc.2015.06.006

17. Schmid, V., Doerner, K.F.: Ambulance location and relocation problems with time-dependent travel times. Eur. J. Oper. Res. **207**(3), 1293–1303 (2010). https://doi.org/10.1016/j.ejor.2010.06.033

18. Shahriari, M., Bozorgi-Amiri, A., Tavakoli, S., Yousefi-Babadi, A.: Bi-objective approach for placing ground and air ambulance base and helipad locations in order to optimize EMS response. Am. J. Emerg. Med. **35**(12), 1873–1881 (2017). https://doi.org/10.1016/j.ajem.2017.06.026
19. Villegas, J.G.: Problemas de localización multiobjetivo. Ph.D. thesis (2004)
20. Zaffar, M.A., Rajagopalan, H.K., Saydam, C., Mayorga, M., Sharer, E.: Coverage, survivability or response time: a comparative study of performance statistics used in ambulance location models via simulation-optimization. Oper. Res. Health Care **11**, 1–12 (2016). https://doi.org/10.1016/j.orhc.2016.08.001

Toward a Unique IoT Network via Single Sign-On Protocol and Message Queue

Tran Thanh Lam Nguyen[1(✉)], The Anh Nguyen[2], Hong Khanh Vo[2], Hoang Huong Luong[2], Huynh Tuan Khoi Nguyen[2], Anh Tuan Dao[2], and Xuan Son Ha[3]

[1] VNPT Information Technology Company, Ho Chi Minh City, Vietnam
[2] FPT University, Can Tho, Vietnam
[3] University of Insubria, Varese, Italy

Abstract. Internet of Things (IoT), currently, is one of the most rapidly developing technology trends. However, at present, users, devices, and applications using IoT services mainly connect to IoT service providers in a client-server model. Each IoT service provider has its own management mechanism and internal message exchange method. This results in the isolation between IoT service providers, and it is challenging to connect these organizations into an IoT network. Besides, one of the most popular protocols in IoT deployments, Message Queuing Telemetry Protocol (MQTT), also has significant security and privacy issues. Therefore, in this paper, we propose an IoT Platform Model capable of improving the MQTT protocol's security problem by using a Single Sign-On. Also, this model allows the organizations to provide the IoT services to connect into a single network but does not change too much of each organization's current architecture. We describe the evaluation to prove the effectiveness of our approach. Specifically, we check the number of concurrent users who can publish messages simultaneously for two internal communication and external communication; furthermore, a complete code solution is publicized on the authors' GitHub repository to engage further reproducibility and improvement.

Keywords: Internet of Things · MQTT · OAuth · Single Sign-On · Kafka

1 Introduction

In recent years, the Internet of Thing applications has grown and applied in most fields such as smart cities, healthcare, supply chains, industry, and agriculture. According to several authors estimation, by 2025, the whole world have approximately 75.44 billion IoT-connected devices [1,2]. However, the current systems still have many weaknesses in the ability to connect IoT service providers as well as the security issues.

IoT systems are often centrally designed according to a client-server model [3,4], which can be easily understood. When an organization deploys its own IoT

© Springer Nature Switzerland AG 2021
K. Saeed and J. Dvorský (Eds.): CISIM 2021, LNCS 12883, pp. 270–284, 2021.
https://doi.org/10.1007/978-3-030-84340-3_22

system, they require all devices and users to authenticate exchange information through one or more of the organization's servers. This architecture may be suitable when the number of devices is limited because it has the advantage of communication latency [5]. However, when millions of users and devices join the IoT network, millions of organizations provide Internet of Thing service, this model cannot meet needs for expanding and abilities to communicate between various components using IoT services of organizations.

In terms of protocols, devices in the IoT network often have limited network connectivity, power, and processing capabilities [6,7], so there is a specific requirement for separate machine-to-machine (M2M) protocols, unlike standard communication protocols. The five most prominent protocols used for IoT are Hypertext Transfer Protocol (HTTP), Constrained Application Protocol (CoAP), Extensible Messaging and Presence Protocol (XMPP), Advanced Message Queuing Protocol (AMQP), and Message Queuing Telemetry Protocol (MQTT) [8,9]. For communications in limited networks (constrained networks), MQTT and CoAP are proposed to be used [10]. We found that the MQTT protocol has faster packet creation time, and packet transmission time is twice as fast as the CoAP protocol [11]. Furthermore, for developers of low bandwidth and memory devices, MQTT is the most preferred protocol [12]. Therefore, in this paper, we apply the MQTT protocol to our approach.

Nevertheless, the current MQTT model still contains some security problems, namely data confidentiality, availability, integrity, and privacy [13]. This model only provides identity, authentication, and authorization for the security mechanism [14] but it is very simple.

The security risks of the MQTT protocol are also common in systems with an internet connection. In particular, the MQTT's security flaws are generally vulnerable to attack due to user behavior. Users often ignore security issues, especially privacy, until the loss of critical data [15]. Statistics from the article [16] show that a significant proportion of IoT users are not fully aware of where their pieces of information are shared. Therefore, with IoT systems having billions of users and devices, it is quite challenging to manage all user's behavior, especially when users among IoT systems exchange information with each other.

To address the risk of security and availability of MQTT, our proposal designs management databases which manages users, things and channels (topic). This approach allows the users to own, use, and exchange messages through ensuring precisely on which channels they are sharing information. To improve the Authentication and Authorization protocol of the MQTT protocol, we propose a combination of MQTT and OAuth protocol. Implementing the OAuth protocol is achieved by adding a centralized authentication management system (Single Sign-On system). Finally, we use Kafka to build a message queue system that connects discrete IoT systems into an IoT network. To engage further reproducibility or improvement in this topic, we share the completely code solution which is publicized on the our Github[1].

The remainder of the paper is organized as follows. In Sect. 2 we provide knowledge about the technology used in the article. In Sect. 3, we discuss related

---

[1] https://github.com/thanhlam2110/iot-platform-paper.

work. In Sect. 4, we introduce our proposed IoT Platform and in Sect. 5 we build a prototype system to test the proposed solution in Sect. 4. In Sect. 6, we discuss our test results. In Sect. 7, we conclude the key points paper and discuss further work directions.

2 Background

2.1 MQTT Protocol

MQTT (Message Queue Telemetry Transport) is a messaging protocol in a publish-subscribe model, using low bandwidth and high reliability. MQTT architecture consists of two main components: Broker and Client.

MQTT Broker is the central server. It is the intersection point of all the connections coming from the client. The broker's main task is to receive messages from all clients and then forward them to a specific address. Clients are divided into two groups: publisher and subscriber. The publisher is the client that publishes messages on a specific topic. Subscribers are clients that subscribe to one or more topics to receive messages going to these topics.

2.2 OAuth Protocol and Single Sign-On

Oauth is an authentication mechanism that enables third-party applications to be authorized by the user to access the user's resources located on another application. OAuth version 2, an upgrade of OAuth version 1, is an authentication protocol that allows applications to share a portion of resources without authenticating via username and password as the traditional way. Thereby limiting the hassle of having to enter the username, password in too many places or register too many accounts for many applications that they cannot remember. According to the OAuth document[2], there are four basic concepts, namely Resource owners, Resource server, Clients, and Authorization server.

Single Sign-On (SSO) is a mechanism that allows users to access multiple applications with just one authentication. SSO simplifies administration by managing user information on a single system instead of multiple separate authentication systems. It makes it easier to manage users when they join or leave an organization [17]. SSO supports many authentication methods such as OAuth, OpenID, SAML, and so on.

2.3 Kafka

Kafka is a distributed messaging system. Kafka is capable of transmitting a large number of messages in real-time. In case the kernel has not received the message, this message is still stored on the message queue and on the disk to ensure safety.

Kafka includes the four components: producer, consumer, topic, and partition. Kafka producer is a client to publish messages to topics. Data is sent to

---

[2] https://oauth.net/2/.

the partition of the topic stored on the broker. Kafka consumers are clients that subscribe and receive messages from the topic. Group names identify consumers, whereas many consumers can subscribe to the same topic. Data is transmitted in Kafka by topic. Once it is necessary to transmit data for various applications, it can create many different topics. Partition is the data storage on a topic. Each topic can have one or more partitions. For each partition, the data is stored permanently and assigned an ID called offset. Besides, Kafka servers are also called a broker, and the zookeeper is a service to manage the brokers.

3 Related Work

3.1 OAuth and MQTT

Paul Fremantle et al. [18] used OAuth to enable access control in the MQTT protocol. The paper results show that IoT clients can fully use OAuth token to authenticate with an MQTT broker. The article demonstrates how to deploy the Web Authorization Tool to create the access token and then embed it in the MQTT client. However, the article does not cover the control of communication channels, so when the properly authenticated MQTT client is able to subscribe to any topic on the MQTT broker, this creates the risk of data disclosure. The paper presents the combined implementation of OAuth and MQTT for internal communication between MQTT broker and MQTT client in the same organization, but not the possibility of applying for inter-organization communication. Therefore, in our article, we implement a strict management mechanism for users, devices, and communication channels. We also present the mechanism of combining MQTT and OAuth protocols to authenticate users when communicating among organizations.

Benjamin Aziz et al. [19] investigated OAuth to manage the registration of users and IoT devices. These papers also introduce the concept of Personal Cloud Middleware (PCM) to perform internal communication between the device and a third-party application on behalf of the user. PCM is an MQTT broker that isolates and operates on a Docker or operating system. Each user has their PCM, and this can help limit data loss. However, Benjamin Aziz et al. also said that they do not have a mechanism for revoking PCM when users are no longer using IoT services, nor have they clearly stated the mechanism to ultimately connect PCMs to form a network for users of various organizations to communicate with each other.

3.2 Kafka and MQTT

A.S. Rozik et al. [20] found that the MQTT broker does not provide any buffering mechanism and cannot be extended. When large amounts of data come from a variety of sources, both of these features are essential. In the Sense Egypt IoT platform, A.S. Rozik et al. have used Kafka as an intermediary system to transport messages between the MQTT broker and the rest of the IoT system, which improves the overall performance of the system as well as provides easy scalability.

Moreover, in the previous studies [21], the authors presented Kafka Message Queue and MQTT broker's combined possibilities in Intelligent Transportation System. The deployment model demonstrates the ability to apply to bridge MQTT with Kafka for low latency and handle messages generated by millions of vehicles. They used MQTT Source Connector to move messages from MQTT topic to Kafka Topic and MQTT Sink connector to move messages from Kafka topic to MQTT topic. In the implementation of the IoT Platform, we also adopt and extend this technique by building APIs that allow users to map their topics.

4   IoT Platform Proposal

The IoT Platform is a set of APIs combined with system architecture such as Single Sign-On system, Kafka Message Queue, and MQTT broker that provide the following capabilities:

- Authenticate information believes the user, thereby granting OAuth access token and refresh token for the user.
- Create and manage user information in the tree model and the unlimited number of user levels created.
- Allowing users to participate in an IoT system capable of creating logical information management of physical devices/applications and communication channels.
- Allows sending and receiving messages locally when correctly defining a user, a thing, and a specific communication channel.
- Allow users to send and receive messages between two various organizations through the Kafka message queue.

4.1   System Architecture

Figure 4 presents an architectural proposal model of the IoT framework. Let's consider Org 1 and Org 2 are two separate organizations in the system. Each organization is a set of MQTT brokers that are interconnected to form a cluster MQTT broker. These MQTT brokers play two roles as follows:

- Internal MQTT broker: is responsible for transporting messages communicating between users, IoT devices
- External MQTT broker: is in charge of transporting messages communicating between two organizations

The IoT Platform Proposal system also includes the Single Sign-On server and the Single Sign-On service's database cluster to perform the following tasks:

- Authenticate user according to OAuth protocol
- Manage user registration information, channels (public and local), and things.

Finally, the IoT Platform Proposal system uses the Kafka Message Queue to transport messages between two organizations' external brokers.

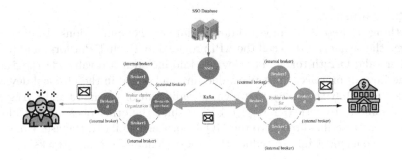

Fig. 1. IoT Platform proposal

4.2   Software Architecture

To meet the goals set out by the IoT Framework, we provide several definitions of the components involved in the system and the interaction of these components.

4.2.1   Users

Users participate in an organization and use IoT services provided by that organization. They have two types (corresponding to the parameter field *"usertype"* in the database): a representation user and a normal user.

Each organization has only one representation user that created when an organization registers information of the organization with the IoT Platform. Representation users are not allow to send or receive messages through the MQTT broker or Kafka message queue. A representation user only creates an organization's public channel and the normal users use this channel to communicate with other organizations in the IoT network. Also, they manage the normal users of the organization.

The purpose in creating a representation user concept is to efficiently manage (e.g., send or receive) messages as well as the organization's (e.g., join or leave) the IoT network. All normal users have to send and receive public messages on the public channel that created and not allowed to create a public channel. Besides, the IoT Platform manager efficiently manages the entry and exit of an organization's IoT network via the organization's status (i.e., the userstatus parameter field in the database). When an organization leaves the IoT network or may be attacked, the IoT Platform administrator switches the userstatus from ACTIVE to DISABLE.

A normal user registers to use the IoT services of a particular organization. They can create things, channels and assign things to channels to manage which things allowed to send and receive messages on a predefined channels. Each user has a unique user_id value, conforming to the UUID[3] standard created by the API and managed by the IoT Platform (user is not aware of this value).

---

[3] https://tools.ietf.org/html/rfc4122.

4.2.2 Things

The things represent the physical devices info or the applications. To create the things, the owners need to call the API provided by the IoT Platform and pass in his/her valid OAuth token. The device's info includes two values thing_id and thing_key. In practice, these two values are embedded in the physical device or application. Only the things that own the valid pair of thing_id and thing_key, can communicate with the MQTT broker since the other ones are not able to publish or subscribe directly to the MQTT broker. Similarly, the user can create device management info to reduce the risk of denial-of-service attacks.

4.2.3 Channels and Assign Things to Channels

In the IoT Platform, we propose, channels are the logical concept that governs topics where users and things publish and subscribe to messages. There are two types of channels: public channel and local channel.

The local channel is an MQTT topic that is created and managed by a normal user. Each normal user can create one or more local channels. Besides, the user has to assign things to this channels by calling the API and pass in thing_id, channel_id and his valid OAuth token. The purpose of this process is to only allow a thing with a valid thing_id and thing_key to publish and subscribe to messages on a predefined channel. From there, this help to avoid the client can subscribe to any topic.

The public channel is a Kafka topic are created by the representation user. Each organization has a unique public channel. All of the normal users of the organization have to communicate with another organization through the public channel.

4.2.4 Publish and Subscribe Message Locally

After creating the things, the users (owners) have enough information including channel_id, thing_id and thing_key generated by the API layer of IoT Platform Proposal and returned to the user. Users embed three values thing_id, thing_key and their refresh token into the things (physical device or application).

The information of token, thing_id, thing_key and channel_id are validated by the API services. If all information is correct, the message is sent to the MQTT broker; otherwise, the message is discarded. Similarly, for the Subscribe process, things also send information of token, thing_id, thing_key, channel_id to connect to the MQTT Broker through the API. If the information is not valid, the API are not allow the things to connect to the MQTT Broker.

4.2.5 Publish and Subscribe Message Publicly

The process of publishing and subscribing to the message is described in Fig. 2.

To support the communication among the users in the different organizations, our platform applies a public channel (or Kafka topic). In particular, we assign a local topic (MQTT topic) with a public channel (Kafka topic). For instance, organization A has a public channel with channel ID "95ce1a32-2136-417e-85b4-46b432f1c9ad". A user of organization A, called ''user-a'', wants to send a

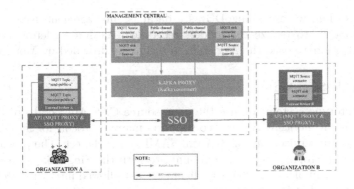

Fig. 2. Process publish a message to the public

message to any user of another organization, called ''user-b'', he must go through this public channel and perform two steps as follows:

- Step 1: ''user-a'' creates a dedicated local channel to send messages to the public, assuming it is called ''send-public-a''. This channel is created via the API that creates a local channel, as shown in Sect. 4.2.3. In fact, the API uses channel_id, but for brevity, we cover the channel's name.
- Step 2: ''user-a'' uses the IoT Platform's API to assign the local channel just created above to the public channel. This process is equivalent create the MQTT Source Connector. After the mapping complete, ''user-a'' publishes the message to the ''send-public-a'' channel. Finally, the message is automatically routed to the public channel.

On the IoT Platform Proposal, we build the Kafka consumer service, which receive the message sent by ''user-a'', check the destination address (defined in body of public message), then forward it to the public channel of the ''user-b''. At that time, the message is on the public channel (Kafka topic) of ''user-b''. Therefore, to receive the message, the ''user-b'' must previously create a local channel (MQTT topic), called ''receive-public-b'' and map it to the public channel of ''user-b''. This is equivalent create an MQTT sink connector. The ''user-b'' uses an API provided by IoT Platform Proposal to create MQTT sink connector.

5   Implementation

5.1   Database

As explained in Sect. 4.2, the IoT Platform allows to manage the information of users, things, channels and implement assign things to channel. In practical implementation, we use MongoDB as a database management system belonging to NoSQL. To realize the model tree (select, update, delete) outlined in Sect. 4.2.1, we have used the Aggregation technique provided by MongoDB[4].

5.2   Single Sign-On

In the prototype system, we use the open source CAS Apereo[5] to provide the Single Sign-On service. CAS Apereo supports many protocols for implementing Single Sign-On services such as OAuth, SAML, OpenID, ect. The protocol that IoT Platform Proposal used to communicate with the Single Sign-On server is OAuth. In our implementation, the clients are not allowed interact directly with the CAS server but instead we provide the API for request OAuth token.

5.3   Mosquitto MQTT Broker

Mosquitto is an open source to implement MQTT broker that allows to transmit and receive data according to MQTT protocol. Mosquitto is also part of the Eclipse Foundation, the project iot.eclipse.org[6]. Mosquitto is very light and has the advantages of fast data transfer and processing speed, high stability.

5.4   Prototype System Deployment Model

We deploy prototype system as shown in Fig. 3.

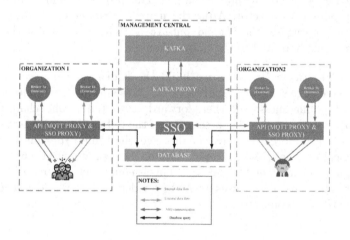

Fig. 3. Prototype system deployment model

The Prototype system we deployed on Amazon EC2 infrastructure consists of seven servers as shown in Table 1.

---

[4] https://docs.mongodb.com/manual/reference/operator/aggregation/graphLookup/.
[5] https://apereo.github.io/cas/6.3.x/index.html.
[6] https://iot.eclipse.org/.

Table 1. List of infrastructure info in the prototype

Zone	Server	Role	Server configuration
Organization 1	Broker 1a	Deploy service MQTT broker for local communication	CPU 1
		Deploy service API (MQTT Proxy & SSO Proxy)	RAM 1 GB
	Broker 1b	Deploy service MQTT broker to serve public communication	CPU 1 RAM 1 GB
Organization 2	Broker 2a	Deploy service MQTT broker for local communication	CPU 1
		Deploy service API (MQTT Proxy & SSO Proxy)	RAM 1 GB
	Broker 2b	Deploy service MQTT broker for public communication	CPU 1 RAM 1 GB
Management central	Management central	Deploy Single Sign-On service Deploy the Kafka service Deploy Kafka Proxy service Deploy the Database service	CPU 2 RAM 8 GB

In Table 1, Organization 1 consists of two servers. The first server deploys the MQTT Broker 1a service for local communication. Second server, deploying MQTT Broket 1b service for public communication. In addition, we deploy MQTT Proxy API service and SSO Proxy to provide APIs for users and devices to communicate with MQTT brokers and SSO through APIs in the first server. The implementation of organization 2 is similar to Organization 1.

Management Central is a single server deploying 4 services: Kafka, Kafka Proxy, Single Sign-On and database. Single Sign-On service creates access token and refresh token for users according to OAuth protocol. The Kafka service acts as the message queue to transport messages between Organization 1 and Organization 2. The Kafka Proxy service acts as the Kafka consumer to receive messages from Organization 1's public channel and forward it to the Organization's public channel 2. Database service to store information of users, things, channels, etc. presented in Sect. 5.1.

6 Evaluation

After completing the deployment of the prototype system on the Amazon EC2 infrastructure, we conduct performance test scenarios of the IoT Framework. We check the number of concurrent users that can publish messages simultaneously for two cases of internal communication and external communication. We measure the time it takes to create a public channels. The test tool we use is the Apache Jmeter[7].

---

[7] https://jmeter.apache.org/.

Firstly, Jmeter makes requests and sends them to the server according to the predefined method, in this case it is REST. Then, it receives responses from the server, collects them and displays information in the report. Jmeter has many report parameters, but when performing system load test, we are mainly interested in two parameters: throughput and error, where the former is the number of requests processed by the server in a second and the latter is the percentage of the number of failed requests over the total number of requests. For our IoT Platform Proposal, the system crashed because the API layer is overload and can't handle request lead to crash API service.

For the local communication test scenario, we compare the case where the user publishes the message through the MQTT Proxy API, i.e., the authentication process with Single Sign-On, checked by the MQTT Proxy and SSO Proxy, then passed to the local MQTT broker and finally received by the MQTT subscriber with case the user publishes the message directly to the MQTT broker. For two cases in the internal communication test scenario, we use Jmeter to call the API publish message locally then record the number of concurrent users and the number of requests processed per second. For MQTT Broker we use Mosquitto. The test model for internal communication is shown in the Fig. 4 and the test results are shown in Table 2.

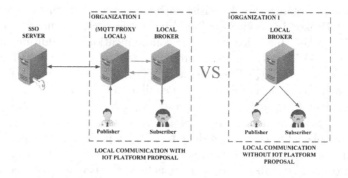

Fig. 4. Test Scenerio for the performance of local communication

Through the results obtained, we found that with a server configuration of 1 GB RAM and 1 CPU, the IoT Platform Proposal provides the ability to connect 400 concurrent users with a processing speed of 23.6 requests/s without error. Correspondingly, when publishing messages directly to the MQTT broker, Mosquitto can provide the ability to connect 500 concurrent users with a processing speed of 36.9 requests/s. This is reasonable and the result is completely acceptable because our IoT Platform proposal has added the inspection and authentication mechanisms as outlined in Sect. 4.2.4.

Table 2. Test results of internal communication

Scenario	Result	100 CCU	200 CCU	300 CCU	400 CCU	500 CCU	600 CCU
With IoT platform	Through put (request/s)	22	23.9	24.2	23.6	19.8	–
	Error (%)	0	0	0	0	10.8	–
Without IoT platform	Through put (request/s)	49	49.5	41.5	39.9	36.9	33.3
	Error (%)	0	0	0	0	0	30.67

For the test scenario for public communication between organizations, we use Jmeter to call the API publish message publicly then record the number of concurrent users and the number of requests processed per second. Test model of communication between two organizations is similar Fig. 4. Test results are shown in Table 3.

Table 3. Test results of external communication

Result	40 CCU	60 CCU	80 CCU	100 CCU	120 CCU	140 CCU	160 CCU
Through put (request/s)	9.1	19.8	25.9	30.3	31.8	32.8	34.7
Error (%)	0	0	0	0	0	0	46.25

According to aforementioned results, we found that with a server configuration of 1GB RAM and 1 CPU, the IoT Platform provides the ability to connect 140 concurrent users with a processing speed of 32.8 requests/s without error. To the best of our knowledge, we do not find any similar implementation models, so in this section we only record the measured parameters. This test result is reasonable and this result is completely acceptable because when sending messages between two organizations, the IoT Platform must perform more processing and authentication steps as we have presented in Sect. 4.2.5. The processing speed and the number of concurrent users can be improved by deploying the IoT platform on a higher configuration server. In fact, APIs of the Iot Platform Proposal such as MQTT Proxy, SSO Proxy, SSO service and Kafka services should also be deployed as cluster to enhance processing capacity and high availability.

7   Conclusion

With the combination of OAuth protocol, single sign on system, model of management user , things and channels, our IoT Platform proposal provides significant improvements in the security capabilities of the MQTT protocol. The procedure of assigning things to channels, strict management of local and public communication channels helps to minimize careless behavior of users when sharing data. The Kafka system allows us to easily connect organizations providing IoT services to the IoT network without changing too much of the available IoT system architecture of each organization.

To develop a larger scenario and increase the number of devices/users authorized quickly, other security issues such as security, privacy, availability for objects are still the challenges. For the security aspect, further works will be deployed in different scenarios like healthcare environment [22–24], cash on delivery [25,26]. For the privacy aspect, we will exploit attribute-based access control (ABAC) [27,28] to manage the authorization process of the IoT Platform via the dynamic policy approach [29–31]. Finally, we will apply the blockchain benefit to improve the availability issues [32–34].

References

1. Alam, T.: A reliable communication framework and its use in internet of things (IoT). CSEIT1835111— Received, vol. 10, pp. 450–456 (2018)
2. Morfino, V., Rampone, S.: Towards near-real-time intrusion detection for IoT devices using supervised learning and apache spark. Electronics **9**(3), 444 (2020)
3. Atlam, H.F., Alenezi, A., Alassafi, M.O., Wills, G.: Blockchain with internet of things: benefits, challenges, and future directions. Int. J. Intell. Syst. Appl. **10**(6), 40–48 (2018)
4. Novo, O.: Blockchain meets IoT: an architecture for scalable access management in IoT. IEEE Internet Things J. **5**(2), 1184–1195 (2018)
5. Ccori, P.C., De Biase, L.C.C., Zuffo, M.K., da Silva, F.S.C.: Device discovery strategies for the IoT. In: 2016 IEEE International Symposium on Consumer Electronics (ISCE), pp. 97–98. IEEE (2016)
6. Karagiannis, V., Chatzimisios, P., Vazquez-Gallego, F., Alonso-Zarate, J.: A survey on application layer protocols for the internet of things. Trans. IoT Cloud Comput. **3**(1), 11–17 (2015)
7. Weissman, D., Jayasumana, A.: Integrating IoT monitoring for security operation center. In: 2020 Global Internet of Things Summit (GIoTS), pp. 1–6. IEEE (2020)
8. Niruntasukrat, A., Issariyapat, C., Pongpaibool, P., Meesublak, K., Aiumsupucgul, P., Panya, A.: Authorization mechanism for MQTT-based internet of things. In: 2016 IEEE International Conference on Communications Workshops (ICC), pp. 290–295. IEEE (2016)
9. Mishra, B., Kertesz, A.: The use of MQTT in M2M and IoT systems: a survey. IEEE Access **8**, 201071–201086 (2020)
10. Jaikar, S.P., Iyer, K.R.: A survey of messaging protocols for IoT systems. Int. J. Adv. Manage. Technol. Eng. Sci. **8**(II), 510–514 (2018)
11. Çorak, B.H., Okay, F.Y., Güzel, M., Murt, Ş., Ozdemir, S.: Comparative analysis of IoT communication protocols. In: 2018 International Symposium on Networks, Computers and Communications (ISNCC), pp. 1–6. IEEE (2018)
12. Hillar, G.C.: MQTT Essentials-A lightweight IoT protocol. Packt Publishing Ltd, Birmingham (2017)
13. Anthraper, J.J., Kotak, J.: Security, privacy and forensic concern of MQTT protocol. In: Proceedings of International Conference on Sustainable Computing in Science, Technology and Management (SUSCOM), Amity University Rajasthan, Jaipur-India (2019)
14. Mena, D.M., Papapanagiotou, I., Yang, B.: Internet of things: survey on security. Inf. Secur. J. Global Perspect. **27**(3), 162–182 (2018)
15. Tawalbeh, L., Muheidat, F., Tawalbeh, M., Quwaider, M., et al.: IoT privacy and security: challenges and solutions. Appl. Sci. **10**(12), 4102 (2020)
16. Subahi, A., Theodorakopoulos, G.: Detecting IoT user behavior and sensitive information in encrypted IoT-app traffic. Sensors **19**(21), 4777 (2019)

17. Radha, V., Reddy, D.H.: A survey on single sign-on techniques. Procedia Technol. **4**, 134–139 (2012)
18. Fremantle, P., Aziz, B., Kopecký, J., Scott, P.: Federated identity and access management for the internet of things. In: 2014 International Workshop on Secure Internet of Things, pp. 10–17. IEEE (2014)
19. Fremantle, P., Aziz, B.: OAuthing: privacy-enhancing federation for the internet of things. In: 2016 Cloudification of the Internet of Things (CIoT), pp. 1–6. IEEE (2016)
20. Rozik, A.S., Tolba, A.S., El-Dosuky, M.A.: Design and implementation of the sense Egypt platform for real-time analysis of IoT data streams. Adv. Internet Things **6**(4), 65–91 (2016)
21. Hugo, Å., Morin, B., Svantorp, K.: Bridging MQTT and Kafka to support C-ITS: a feasibility study. In: 2020 21st IEEE International Conference on Mobile Data Management (MDM), pp. 371–376. IEEE (2020)
22. Son, H.X., Chen, E.: Towards a fine-grained access control mechanism for privacy protection and policy conflict resolution. Int. J. Adv. Comput. Sci. Appl. **10**(2), 507–516 (2019)
23. Duong-Trung, N., Son, H.X., Le, H.T., Phan, T.T.: Smart care: integrating blockchain technology into the design of patient-centered healthcare systems. In: Proceedings of the 2020 4th International Conference on Cryptography, Security and Privacy, ICCSP 2020, pp. 105–109, New York, NY, USA, 2020. Association for Computing Machinery. https://doi.org/10.1145/3377644.3377667
24. Duong-Trung, N., Son, H.X., Le, H.T., Phan, T.T.: On components of a patient-centered healthcare system using smart contract. In: Proceedings of the 2020 4th International Conference on Cryptography, Security and Privacy, pp. 31–35, New York, NY, USA, 2020. Association for Computing Machinery (2020). https://doi.org/10.1145/3377644.3377668
25. Le, H.T., Le, N.T.T., Phien, N.N., Duong-Trung, N.: Introducing multi shippers mechanism for decentralized cash on delivery system. Money **10**(6), 13 (2019)
26. Le, N.T.T., et al.: Assuring non-fraudulent transactions in cash on delivery by introducing double smart contracts. Int. J. Adv. Comput. Sci. Appl. **10**(5), 677–684 (2019)
27. Hoang, N.M., Son, H.X.: A dynamic solution for fine-grained policy conflict resolution. In: Proceedings of the 3rd International Conference on Cryptography, Security and Privacy, pp. 116–120 (2019)
28. Son, H.X., Hoang, N.M.: A novel attribute-based access control system for fine-grained privacy protection. In: Proceedings of the 3rd International Conference on Cryptography, Security and Privacy, pp. 76–80 (2019)
29. Xuan, S.H., Tran, L.K., Dang, T.K., Pham, Y.N.: Rew-XAC: an approach to rewriting request for elastic ABAC enforcement with dynamic policies. In: 2016 International Conference on Advanced Computing and Applications (ACOMP), pp. 25–31. IEEE (2016)
30. Thi, Q.N.T., Dang, T.K., Van, H.L., Son, H.X.: Using JSON to specify privacy preserving-enabled attribute-based access control policies. In: Wang, G., Atiquzzaman, M., Yan, Z., Choo, K.-K.R. (eds.) SpaCCS 2017. LNCS, vol. 10656, pp. 561–570. Springer, Cham (2017). https://doi.org/10.1007/978-3-319-72389-1_44
31. Son, H.X., Dang, T.K., Massacci, F.: REW-SMT: a new approach for rewriting XACML request with dynamic big data security policies. In: Wang, G., Atiquzzaman, M., Yan, Z., Choo, K.-K.R. (eds.) SpaCCS 2017. LNCS, vol. 10656, pp. 501–515. Springer, Cham (2017). https://doi.org/10.1007/978-3-319-72389-1_40

32. Ha, X.S., Le, H.T., Metoui, N., Duong-Trung, N.: DeM-CoD: novel access-control-based cash on delivery mechanism for decentralized marketplace. In: 2020 IEEE 19th International Conference on Trust, Security and Privacy in Computing and Communications (TrustCom), pp. 71–78. IEEE (2020)

33. Ha, X.S., Le, T.H., Phan, T.T., Nguyen, H.H.D., Vo, H.K., Duong-Trung, N.: Scrutinizing trust and transparency in cash on delivery systems. In: Wang, G., Chen, B., Li, W., Di Pietro, R., Yan, X., Han, H. (eds.) SpaCCS 2020. LNCS, vol. 12382, pp. 214–227. Springer, Cham (2021). https://doi.org/10.1007/978-3-030-68851-6_15

34. Son, H.X., Le, T.H., Quynh, N.T.T., Huy, H.N.D., Duong-Trung, N., Luong, H.H.: Toward a blockchain-based technology in dealing with emergencies in patient-centered healthcare systems. In: Bouzefrane, S., Laurent, M., Boumerdassi, S., Renault, E. (eds.) MSPN 2020. LNCS, vol. 12605, pp. 44–56. Springer, Cham (2021). https://doi.org/10.1007/978-3-030-67550-9_4

Machine Learning and Artificial Neural Networks

Multi-objective Approach for Deep Learning in Classification Problems

Jerzy Balicki[(✉)] and Witold Sosnowski

Faculty of Mathematics and Information Science, Warsaw University of Technology,
Warsaw, Poland
{jerzy.balicki,witold.sosnowski.dokt}@pw.edu.pl

Abstract. We study the possibility of using a distributed multi-objective differential evolutionary algorithms with tabu mutation (DMD+) to optimize classification deep learning models. We discuss conflicts between three metrics used for evaluating the quality of some classifiers: an accuracy, F1-score, and Area Under the ROC Curve. Because a smart city is a place where economic mechanisms are intensively supported by modern computational methods, including deep learning, we select some datasets to verify the quality of designed classifiers. As a result, we develop an effective approach for determining the key parameters of Convolution Neural Networks and Long Short Term Memory models with using computing cloud.

Keywords: Classification · Deep learning models · Multi-objective evolutionary algorithms

1 Introduction

For the classification problems, most of deep learning models are trained by optimization with one criterion such as an accuracy, F1-score, Area Under the ROC Curve, Area Under the Precision-Recall Curve or the others. Let x be a set of classifier parameters that are decision variables for an adequate optimization problem. For example, x is a matrix of a synaptic weights for a multi-layer neural network with the given structure. If a model of classifiers $C(x)$ is trained regarding the accuracy (ACC), the best classifier $C^* = C(x^*)$ maximizes ACC for all feasible solutions $x \in X$. Because the accuracy measures how many observations are correctly classified, a decision-maker can select another metrics if a dataset is imbalanced. For instance, F1-score can replace the accuracy if a decision-maker prefer a precision and a recall.

However, F1-score for C^* can be smaller than F1-score for C^{**} obtained for F1-score maximization. It means that there is a conflict between criteria ACC and F1-score, and increasing of ACC may decreases F1-score and vice versa. In this paper, we present some numerical examples to confirm above conflict situations. Besides, we analyze the other criteria, too.

© Springer Nature Switzerland AG 2021
K. Saeed and J. Dvorský (Eds.): CISIM 2021, LNCS 12883, pp. 287–298, 2021.
https://doi.org/10.1007/978-3-030-84340-3_23

To solve this research problem, we propose Distributed Multi-objective Differential Evolution Algorithm with Tabu Mutation (DMD+) that can be used for optimization deep learning models by maximization several criteria such as an accuracy, F1-score, Area Under the ROC Curve or Area Under the Precision-Recall Curve.

By maximization selected criteria it is possible to train a machine learning model to consider preferences of decision makers. Above observations open us a perspective to revise an approach for machine learning with one metric. Therefore, the goal of this paper is to analyze a new multi-objective evolutionary approach for deep learning based on Pareto-optimal model.

For using by DMD+, we select datasets that include knowledge about a smart city because the development of large cities drives the economy. Cities have to cope with some open important issues like growing population, a traffic congestion or a spread of the pandemic Covid-19. Besides, there is a huge problem with a lack of city resources like water and energy in some regions of the world. Therefore, an efficient management of resources is strongly required. What is more, it is predicted that global warming and carbon emissions will be probably considered as the most critical factors for living conditions.

In a smart city, Internet of Things (IoT) provides data streams from sources to computing cloud [2]. Some various steps are supposed to be performed: data collection, aggregation, filtration, machine learning (classification by DMD+), and decision making. Unquestionably, development of a smart city using DMD+ is an innovative approach. It is meaningful to underline the significance of the Internet of Things, DMD+ and Big Data in a smart city.

Social media, smart education, financial support, and health protection are crucial pillars of a smart city. DMD+ provides valuable outcomes from text analysis due to emotion recognition without reading personally by experts or city authorities. Particularly, a stream of tweets can be a valuable text source for opinion mining from a micro-blogging platform. We present examples from emotion recognition based on text analysis related to dataset sentiment140 [11] and a pre-trained model BERT [7]. In a smart city, it is possible to prevent undesirable situations in the education process before they happen. The efficient decisions about the further activities can be made by taking into account some recommendation provided by a Convolutional Neural Network (CNN) that can improve the situation. The system aims to delivery of instructions in smart environments. The processing of sensitive data requires security measures to detect network intrusions, too.

Besides, DMD+ can be developed for prediction the credit scoring for citizens. We developed DMD+ for providing models that detects the Covid-19 cases from X-ray images, too. A key measure in the fight against SARS-CoV-2 is the effective screening of infected patients, and an effective diagnosis in hospitals includes radiological examination using chest radiography. We present an effective deep learning model of diagnosis of SARS-CoV-2 virus infection based on remote analysis of X-rays taking into account comorbidity, too.

Furthermore, we consider face image datasets to verify the quality o models provided by DMD+. Especially, we tested a population of models such as multilayer perceptrons, support vector machines and convolutional neural networks. For evaluation of Pareto-optimal classifiers, some datasets from a variety of databases were selected such as Georgia Tech Face Database [9] and The MUCT Face Database [13]. In addition, feature extraction techniques are discussed for face image analysis - landmark points prediction with model and embedding of facial images generated with FaceNet network, as well as three CNN architectures: VGG16, ResNet-50 and SENet-50 [12].

To order many important issues in this paper, related work is described in Sect. 2. Then, Distributed Multi-objective Differential Evolution Algorithm with Tabu mutation DMD+ is studied in Sect. 3. Next, Sect. 4 presents results of experiments with deep learning models for some selected datasets. Finally, remarks and conclusions are presented in Sect. 5.

2   Related Work

Fernandez, Carbonero, Gutierrez, and Hervas-Martinez proposed multi-objective evolutionary optimization using the relationship between F1 and accuracy metrics in classification tasks [8]. This work analyses the complementarity and contrast between two metrics commonly used for evaluating the quality of a binary classifier: the correct classification rate and the F1-score metric. Based on this analysis, a set of constraints are defined as a function of the ratio of positive patterns in the dataset. They evaluate the possibility of using a multi-objective evolutionary algorithm guided by this pair of metrics to optimize binary classification models. To check the validity of the constraints, we perform an empirical analysis considering 26 benchmark datasets obtained from the UCI repository and an interesting liver transplant dataset. The results show that the relation is fulfilled and that the use of the algorithm for simultaneously optimizing the pair (C, F1) leads to a generally balanced accuracy for both classes. The experiments also reveal that, in some cases, better results are obtained by using the majority class as the positive class instead of using the minority one, which is the most common approach with imbalanced datasets.

Lv, Chen, Lou, and Wang considered intelligent edge computing based on machine learning for smart city [14]. They proposed a method to conduct calculations in a collaborative way by encouraging devices to cooperate. This method answers the following question: how can calculations be conducted when there are privacy problems in machine learning tasks? In view of the above challenges, a mobile edge server is taken as the focus, and the available resources around the mobile edge server are used for collaborative computing. Machine learning is applied in the distributed task scheduling algorithm and distributed device coordination algorithm.

Kuru and Khan characterized a framework for the synergistic integration of fully autonomous ground vehicles with smart city [17]. Currently, most of the vehicle manufacturers aim to deploy level-5 fully autonomous ground vehicles on city roads by leveraging extensive existing knowledge about sensors, actuators, and deep learning gained from the level-4 autonomy. They consider non-trivial sequences of events with decimeter-level accuracy. Autonomous ground vehicles are supposed to be integrated with all the components and domains of a smart city using real-time data analytic. The set of vehicles can be modeled as a swarm intelligent system in a smart environment enabling cooperative agents. The integration of vehicles with a smart city helps improve the sustainability of a city towards the next-generation driverless society. The Authors built a simulation platform both to model the varying penetration levels of vehicles into mixed traffic and to perform the optimal self-driving behaviors of vehicle swarms. The results show that autonomous vehicles improves the urban traffic flow significantly without huge changes to the traffic infrastructure.

Pattern matching provides theory and tools for new domains such as smart city, social media analysis and smart education. The proliferation of user-generated content on social media is important because a micro-blogging platform Twitter is being used to collect views about products, trends, and politics. Sentiment analysis is developed to analyze the attitude, emotions and opinions of citizens, and it can be carried out on tweets to analyze public opinion on news, policies, social movements, and personalities. In [19], it was proposed a voting classifier to predict sentiment from tweets.

In the field of smart academic education, Mitrofanova et al. identified numerous techniques for intellectual assessment in the smart education industry. Moreover, several classes have been formulated based on the applications and goals for intelligent education development. Furthermore, numerous beneficial aspects of smart education have been presented for research exploration. Besides, it was presented a novel system for the identification of several didactic techniques for incorporating smart technologies in the education sector. Comprehensively, numerous paradigms were considered for the development of the smart education industry including IoT, Cloud Computing, and Artificial Intelligence [16].

Lyapina et al. investigated the classical education system in the universities and compared it with the remote assessment procedure using smart ICT technologies. The authors assessed the beneficial aspect of smart education technology in terms of data analysis, synthesis, abstraction, and logic. Moreover, it was analyzed the teacher's trust for the incorporation of smart medical devices in the education industry. The authors acquired the data instances from nearly 400 primary and secondary teachers for determining the acceptance rate of smart technology in academics. Based on the experimental questionnaire, 5 important factors were identified for the teacher's belief. These include interactivity, instability, inconvenience, interest, and immediacy [15].

Basset et al. proposed an IoT-based supportive framework for smart education. The presented system contributes to making decisions effectively and efficiently regarding the quality of education provided to the students. Moreover, challenges like security, better management, and cost reduction were handled using the presented system. Besides, it was discussed the use of smart technologies in mathematical education. The authors surveyed teachers and experts to analyze curriculum effectiveness. The results of the study depicted that the use of Smart Education Technologies motivates the students to handle or solve mathematical problems quickly [4].

Verma and Sood developed an IoT-based framework for evaluating the performance of students. The presented framework generates the results of the student's performance by analyzing the data collected based on spatial-temporal patterns. Furthermore, it was discussed the role of IoT in education. The authors presented the challenges, impact, and the latest research works in future learning. They proposed a smart computing framework for evaluating the performance of engineering students. The authors developed 5-layer architecture to generate results by analyzing the performance of students. The results captured by the proposed system were efficient for improving the learning skills of the students in comparison to the results generated by the manual method [18].

Zhu et al. provided a research framework for smart education. The authors developed a 4-layer framework with 10 vital features of an intelligent learning environment. The presented framework also discussed the concept of smart education using different techniques. They proposed a smart system for ubiquitous learning in a smart campus. The proposed method acquired prevalent resources of education that meet the expectations of both teachers and students of a smart campus. They explores how students learn linguistic skills using adaptive influences. The analysis students are assessed by questionnaires on their cognitive factors, such as motivation, attitude, extra-version, extrusion, fear, and self-esteem. The gathered results were then used to model students with a particular collection of parameters [20].

Bhatia et al. discussed the healthcare industry as the leading area revolutionized by IoT technology that has led to the introduction of intelligent medical applications. The authors have introduced an efficient home-centered urine-based diabetes monitoring system. Besides, it was proposed an integrated IoT-based system for tracking and forecasting parameters for air pollution such as benzene utilizing the application of machine learning [5].

Smart education systems are affected by the progress of deep learning that provides the real-time decision making related to Big Data that is collected upon students' behavior within knowledge acquisition and skills improvements. Therefore, classification models for emotions recognition are crucial to predict possible actions. We distinguish three main logic channels to collect important information. We can control the interest level of volunteer students during the learning by a text channel, a video channel, and an audio channel. Besides, we can develop channels related to brain waves analysis in medicine.

Moreover, camera systems can analyze movement and fidgeting to increase the accuracy or the other measures of the interest level. An audio channel can support prediction by providing a noise around student, too. Wearable sensors send data about temperature and pulse to deep learning systems. In consequences, the lecture can moderate the presented content to take into account recommendation from deep learning prediction. Of course, the standard method based on an analysis partial grades of students provides additional data to prevent undesirable situations before they happen, i.e. a student fails an exam [2].

Internet of Things supports a smart classroom with smartphones, cameras, microphones and wearable sensors for an identification of the physiological responses while assimilating educational content. We believe above technique can improve the final grades. This system aims to identify student qualities to predict the probability of passing the exams.

3   Distributed Multi-objective Differential Evolution and Tabu Mutation DMD+

If we construct several machine learning models for classification, it arises an issue of selection. Therefore, this issue of classifier selection can be studied in context of smart education. Multilayer perceptron, support vector machines, convolutional neural networks, as well as hybrid and team classifiers are supposed to be compared for different datasets regarding several criteria such as: accuracy, precision, recall, F1-score, Area Under Curve ROC, training time, and testing time).

Cetiner, Koçak, and Güngör analyzed credit risk based on hybrid classification. They introduced two case studies on German and Turkish credit datasets [6]. Because a finance sector is connected with the city economy, credit risk analysis plays a major role in decision process. Banks and finance institutions gather large amounts of raw data from their customers, and data mining techniques can be employed to obtain useful information from this raw data. The Authors propose hybrid classification approaches, which try to combine several classifiers and ensemble learners to boost accuracy on classification results with respect to their classification accuracy. Experimental results provided three important consequences. First, feature selection stage has a major role both on result accuracy and calculation complexity. Second, hybrid approaches have better generalability over single classifiers. Third, using SVM-Radial Basis Function (RBF) as the base classifier and a hybrid model member gives the best accuracy results among others.

However, we discovered some conflicts between pairs of criteria within the classification model training for German Credit Dataset [10]. It means that training regarding accuracy can maximize accuracy only and the other criteria may achieve the smaller value than their maximal level [3]. Figure 1 presents several conflicts observed during training artificial neural networks by an evolutionary algorithm with an accuracy consideration in the fitness function. The other metrics are measured within the training, but their have no influence on optimization process.

We observe that usually improvements of accuracy is accompanying with the improvements of F1-score and AUC. However, there are epochs during training with the conflicts between criteria under consideration. For instance, the value of accuracy decreases at the iteration denoted as A, when artificial neural network is trained due to the maximization F1-score, only. The value of F1-score increases at A, and AUC is neutral. At the iteration B, the values of AUC and F1-score increase in conflict to an accuracy that decreases. In results, we can expect that trained neural networks have different parameters such number of neurons, activation functions, synaptic weights, biases, and feedback connections regarding conflicts between above criteria.

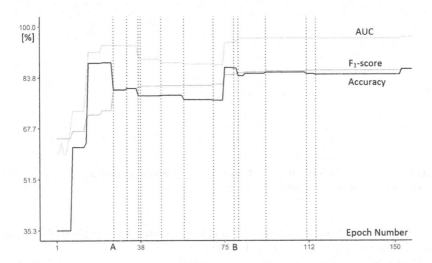

Fig. 1. Conflicts between criteria within training of artificial neural networks on German Credit Dataset for F1-score maximization.

Another case with conflicts between metrics is presented on Fig. 2. An evolutionary algorithm optimizes a population of artificial neural networks regarding an accuracy. In this case, increasing of the accuracy causes decreasing AUC at an iteration denoted as A. Both F1-score and AUC decreases at epoch B, when an accuracy still increases. At C, AUC decreases in contrast to Accuracy and F1-score.

To find the Pareto-optimal artificial neural network we propose Distributed Multi-objective Differential Evolution with Tabu Mutation (DMD+). Let a pre-trained model due to one criterion is given. For instance, Bidirectional Encoder Representations from Transformers (BERT) is the most efficient machine learning pre-trained model for natural language processing (NLP) [7]. In DMD+, we create an initial population of the BERT models that are trained by adding layers of new neurons with the cross-validation entropy as a goal function by solver ADAM (Adaptive Moment Estimation). However, each model is trained by different sub-datasets. The sentiment140 consists of 16,000,000 tweets denoted as positive or negative. Each sub-dataset is constructed from sentiment140 by random selection from 50,000 tweets. Each subset is assigned to the BERT model from the current population, and then the training is made, concurrently. After 10 epochs, the training of all models is stopped and the evaluation of BERT models is calculated regarding Fonseca-Flemming ranking procedure [2]. Then, the highest value of rank R_{max} is assigned to the most dominated solution. Besides, a

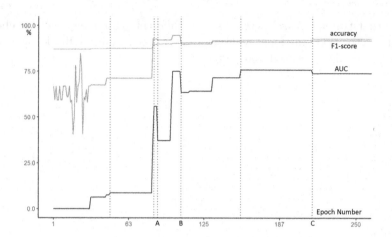

Fig. 2. Conflicts between criteria within training of artificial neural networks on German Credit Dataset for accuracy maximization.

density award $d(x)$ is calculated according to preferring some separated solutions than solutions very close to the others [2].

However, differential evolution has a problem to reach the Pareto set fpr large datasets. Therefore, the new mutation based on tabu search has been introduced [3]. This tabu mutation maximizes one criterion that is chosen, randomly. A tabu mutation avoid cycles by the matrix of the recently visited solutions (a short therm memory) and the list of the most frequently used observations (a long term memory). The rate of the tabu mutation is usually ten times smaller than a differential mutation.

Let the identification of an observation $id(i)$ be an average value from all numbers in this observations. Then, we can determine the average value for the subset of observations by calculations all ids from this subset. The matrix of the recently visited solutions is constructed by entering the identification of each subset of observations assigned to the BERT models in the current population. Let $S2TM$ be a size of a short therm memory. We maintain matrix stm with $S2TM$ rows and L columns. The element $stm[j, l]$ is the identification of the observation subset that was assigned to the lth BERT model in the population number $(t - j)$. If the new subset has the same identification as any element of matrix stm, it is mutated to avoid a cycle in searching. The list of the most frequently used observations (a long term memory) is constructed to avoid the frequent repeating the same observations at the end of calculations. In above tabu mutation improves the quality of obtained solutions produced by the differential evolution algorithm.

Each observation $id(i)$ is characterized by the number of using it for training $ida(i)$. If a subset with the ith observation is assigned to the BERT model x, the penalty is calculated calculation average value on all $ida(i)$. By normalization, the $ltm(x)$ is between 0 and 1. The fitness of the model x with the given rank $r(x)$ is calculated according to the following formula:

$$fitness(x) = R_{max} - r(x) + 1 + d(x) - ltm(x) \qquad (1)$$

To avoid changing the Bert model that is very efficient according to one criterion, we crossover subsets of data that are related to the models in a current population. Two subsets are selected according to the roulette rule, and then the fraction of the first subset with the rate 0.5 is exchanged randomly with the fraction of the second subset of data. We assume the crossover probability $p_c = 1/L$, where L is the size of the population. Besides, a mutation is carried out with the probability pm that increases with the number of population t, as follows $p_c = 0.1(t/T_{max})$, where T_{max} is the maximal value of iterations. A succession to the new population is related to adding the population of parents and a population of offspring. Afterwards, the extended population is verified regarding Pareto definition of non-dominated solutions [2]. The subset with front rank is sorted regarding the $d(x)$ values. This elitism provides the non-dominated solutions to the next population.

A cycle with the selection, crossover, mutation, and the succession is repeated until T_{max} is exceeded or there is no improvements for an assumed number of populations. In a cycle with the period 10 populations, the standard mutation is substituted by the tabu mutation. We explore the neighborhood of the current subset of data by verifying the NM mutated subsets. We select the best subset due to the fitness value and the memories about the past exploration.

Figure 3 shows the Pareto-optimal evaluations obtained by DMD+ for the emotion recognition on the text analysis with the BERT individuals.

4   Experimental Results

Distributed Multi-objective Differential Evolution (DMD+) with Tabu Mutation produces Pareto-optimal representation of models of deep learning for the selected dataset. The following criteria are minimized by DMD+: **ACC** - *accuracy*, **FSC** - *F_1 score*, and **AUC** - *area under ROC curve*. Table 1 includes characteristics of obtained classifiers due to Face Recognition Data provided by University of Essex. Additionally, four metrics are presented, as below: **PRC** - *precision*, **REC** - *recall*, **TRT** - *training time*) in seconds, **TST** - *testing time*) in seconds.

Table 2 includes characteristics for a comparison of classifiers due to three datasets: Face Recognition Data (University of Essex), Georgia Tech Face Database and The MUCT Face Database. The overall ranking winner was the FaceNet with support vector machine (SVM-FN) trained on datasets with *embedding*. Further, the FaceNet with the multilayer perceptron is recommended (MLP-FN).

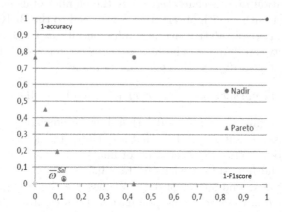

Fig. 3. Pareto-optimal evaluations obtained by the DMD+ for emotion recognition by the text analysis.

Table 1. Comparison of classifiers due to Face Recognition Data (University of Essex)

	MLP-LP	#	MLP-FN	#	SVM-LP	#	SVM-FN	#	VGG16	#	RESNET	#	SENET	#
ACC	0.843	7	0.982	2	0.853	6	0.983	1	0.913	5	0.952	3	0.951	4
PRC	0.899	6	0.988	1	0.885	7	0.982	2	0.921	5	0.952	3	0.952	3
REC	0.828	7	0.982	2	0.853	6	0.983	1	0.973	3	0.952	4	0.951	5
FSC	0.844	6	0.984	1	0.844	6	0.980	2	0.909	5	0.949	3	0.948	4
AUC	0.918	7	0.996	2	0.962	5	0.998	1	0.975	4	0.925	6	0.977	3
TRT	210.87	2	495.66	3	209.54	1	496.57	4	1340.00	5	2733.27	7	1581.82	6
TST	48.23	1	122.66	6	49.83	2	124.10	7	62.36	5	59.93	3	61.51	4
$=$	36	7	17	1	33	6	18	2	32	5	29	3	29	3

Table 2. Comparison of classifiers due to three datasets

	MLP-LP	#	MLP-FN	#	SVM-LP	#	SVM-FN	#	VGG16	#	RESNET	#	SENET	#
ACC	0.500	6	0.992	1	0.374	7	0.981	2	0.757	5	0.967	3	0.962	4
PRC	0.529	6	0.992	1	0.355	7	0.974	2	0.856	5	0.972	3	0.968	4
REC	0.500	6	0.991	1	0.374	7	0.981	2	0.757	5	0.967	3	0.962	4
FSC	0.481	6	0.991	1	0.336	7	0.976	2	0.742	5	0.963	3	0.958	4
AUC	0.623	6	1.000	1	0.505	7	1.000	1	0.847	5	0.990	3	0.989	4
TRT	664.28	2	761.41	3	655.34	1	764.41	4	1657.61	5	3056.78	7	2347.68	6
TST	158.64	1	189.06	6	159.46	2	190.36	7	161.57	3	162.36	4	163.40	5
$=$	33	5	14	1	38	7	20	2	33	5	26	3	31	4

Above methodology can be developed by using an ideal point and calculation Euclid distance to it from characteristics evaluated for all datasets. In this case, the shortest distance to an ideal point was obtained by the deep network FaceNet with support vector machine trained on datasets with *embedding*.

The last example of verifying a multi-criteria approach for supporting models for a smart city is related to the COVID-19 pandemic that has a devastating impact not only on health and the economy, but also on people's sense of security, well-being and satisfaction. For numerical experiments, we developed the benchmark COVIDx X-ray collection includes 13,975 chest X-ray images (CXR). This collection is systematically expanded in the project based on selected photo collections of CXR. Distributed Multi-objective Differential Evolution (DMD+) with Tabu Mutation provided a model with an accuracy 0.97, F1-score 0.98, and ROC AUC 0.99.

5   Conclusions and Remarks

Credit scoring, emotion recognition, identification of citizens, diagnosis of Covid-19 can be performed by models trained by Multi-objective Differential Evolution (DMD+) with Tabu Mutation. Several criteria such as: accuracy, F1-score, Area Under Curve ROC, training time, and testing time can be applied for evaluation Pareto-optimal models. A proposed approach is a very general and it can be extended on several new deep learning models.

Our future work will be related to extend DMD+ to the selected models based on deep learning. Besides, we are going to consider larger datasets that are useful in emergent domains.

References

1. Ahanger, T.A., Tariq, U., Ibrahim, A., Ullah, I., Bouteraa, Y.: ANFIS-inspired smart framework for education quality assessment. IEEE Access **8**, 175306–175318 (2020)
2. Balicki, J., Korlub, W., Krawczyk, H., Paluszak, J.: Genetic programming for interaction efficient supporting in volunteer computing systems. Issues Challenges Artif. Intell. **559**, 129–139 (2014)
3. Balicki, J.: Tabu programming for multiobjective optimization problems. Int. J. Comput. Sci. Netw. Secur. **7**, 44–50 (2007)
4. Basset, M.A., Manogaran, G., Mohamed, M., Rushdy, E.: Internet of things in smart education environment: supportive framework in the decision-making process. Concurr. Comput. Pract. Exper. **31**, e4515 (2019)
5. Bhatia, M., Sood, S.K.: Internet of things based activity surveillance of defence personnel. J. Ambient Intell. Humaniz. Comput. **9**(6), 2061–2076 (2017). https://doi.org/10.1007/s12652-017-0507-3
6. Cetiner, E., Koçak, T., Güngör, V.Ç.: Credit risk analysis based on hybrid classification: case studies on German and Turkish credit datasets. In: SIU, pp. 1–4 (2018)

7. Devlin, J., Chang, M.-W., Lee, K., Toutanova, K.: BERT: Pre-training of Deep Bidirectional Transformers for Language Understanding, arXiv:1810.04805v2 (2019)
8. Fernandez, J.C., Carbonero, M., Gutierrez, P.A., Hervas-Martınez, C.: Multi-objective evolutionary optimization using the relationship between F1 and accuracy metrics in classification tasks. Appl. Intell. **49**, 3447–3463 (2019)
9. Georgia Tech face database. http://www.anefian.com/research/. Accessed 4 Feb 2021
10. German Credit Data - part of UCI Repository of machine learning databases. https://archive.ics.uci.edu/ml/datasets/Statlog+%28German+Credit+Data%29. Accessed 4 Feb 2021
11. Go, A., Bhayani, R., Huang, L.: Twitter sentiment classification using distant supervision, CS224N Project Report, Stanford, vol. 1, p. 12 (2009)
12. Hu, J., Shen, L., Albanie, S., Sun, G., Wu, E.: Squeeze-and-Excitation Networks, arXiv:1709.01507v4 (2019)
13. Milborrow, S., Morkel, J., Nicolls, F.: The MUCT Landmarked Face Database, Pattern Recognition Association of South Africa (2010)
14. Lv, Z., Chen, D., Lou, R., Wang, Q.: Intelligent edge computing based on machine learning for smart city. Future Gener. Comput. Syst. **115**, 90–99 (2021)
15. Lyapina, I., Sotnikova, E., Lebedeva, O., Makarova, T., Skvortsova, N.: Smart technologies: perspectives of usage in higher education. Int. J. Educ. Manag. **33**, 454–461 (2019)
16. Mitrofanova, Y.S., Glukhova, L.V., Tukshumskaya, A.V., Popova, T.N.: Modeling of residual knowledge estimation in smart university. Smart Educ. e-Learn. **188**, 220–227 (2020)
17. Kuru, K., Khan, W.: A framework for the synergistic integration of fully autonomous ground vehicles with smart city. IEEE Access **9**, 923–948 (2021)
18. Verma, P., Sood, S.K.: Internet of things-based student performance evaluation framework. Behav. Inf. Technol. **37**, 102–119 (2018)
19. Yousaf, A., Umer, M., Sadiq, S., Ullah, S., Mirjalili, S., Nappi, V.R.M.: Emotion recognition by textual tweets classification using voting classifier (LR-SGD). IEEE Access **9**, 6286–6295 (2021)
20. Zhu, Z.-T., Yu, M.-H., Riezebos, P.: A research framework of smart education. Smart Learn. Environ. **3**(1), 1–17 (2016). https://doi.org/10.1186/s40561-016-0026-2

A First Step Towards Automated Species Recognition from Camera Trap Images of Mammals Using AI in a European Temperate Forest

Mateusz Choiński[1], Mateusz Rogowski[1], Piotr Tynecki[1(✉)], Dries P. J. Kuijper[2], Marcin Churski[2], and Jakub W. Bubnicki[2]

[1] Faculty of Computer Science, Bialystok University of Technology, Bialystok, Poland
`m.choinski@pb.edu.pl, p.tynecki@doktoranci.pb.edu.pl`
[2] Mammal Research Institute, Polish Academy of Sciences, Bialowieza, Poland

Abstract. Camera traps are used worldwide to monitor wildlife. Despite the increasing availability of Deep Learning (DL) models, the effective usage of this technology to support wildlife monitoring is limited. This is mainly due to the complexity of DL technology and high computing requirements. This paper presents the implementation of the light-weight and state-of-the-art YOLOv5 architecture for automated labeling of camera trap images of mammals in the Białowieża Forest (BF), Poland. The camera trapping data were organized and harmonized using TRAPPER software, an open-source application for managing large-scale wildlife monitoring projects. The proposed image recognition pipeline achieved an average accuracy of 85% F1-score in the identification of the 12 most commonly occurring medium-size and large mammal species in BF, using a limited set of training and testing data (a total of 2659 images with animals).

Based on the preliminary results, we have concluded that the YOLOv5 object detection and classification model is a fine and promising DL solution after the adoption of the transfer learning technique. It can be efficiently plugged in via an API into existing web-based camera trapping data processing platforms such as e.g. TRAPPER system. Since TRAPPER is already used to manage and classify (manually) camera trapping datasets by many research groups in Europe, the implementation of AI-based automated species classification will significantly speed up the data processing workflow and thus better support data-driven wildlife monitoring and conservation. Moreover, YOLOv5 has been proven to perform well on edge devices, which may open a new chapter in animal population monitoring in real-time directly from camera trap devices.

Keywords: Computer vision · Deep learning · YOLOv5 · Camera trap · TRAPPER · Wildlife

1 Introduction

To conserve and manage diverse mammalian communities in a way that their population status is secured and conflict with humans is minimized, requires in the first place

© The Author(s) 2021
K. Saeed and J. Dvorský (Eds.): CISIM 2021, LNCS 12883, pp. 299–310, 2021.
https://doi.org/10.1007/978-3-030-84340-3_24

comprehensive data-derived knowledge of their status. There is a growing awareness that standard wildlife monitoring methods are not effective and difficult to scale-up (e.g. snow-tracking or hunting-bag data). Therefore, numerous new initiatives to monitor mammals using camera traps are currently being developed across Europe, collectively generating enormous amounts of pictures and videos. However, a large amount of available data is not effectively exploited, mainly because of the human time required to mine the data from collected raw multimedia files.

Camera trapping has already proved to be one of the most important technologies in wildlife conservation and ecological research [1–5]. Rapid developments in the application of AI speed up the transformation in that area and contribute to the fact that most of the recorded material will be automatically classified in the future [6-8, 11-13]. However, despite the increasing availability of deep learning models for object recognition [14, 15, 17, 18], the effective usage of this technology to support wildlife monitoring is limited, mainly because of the complexity of DL technology, the lack of end-to-end pipelines, and high computing requirements.

In this study, we present the preliminary results of applying the new AI standalone model for both object detection and species-level classification of camera trapping data from a European temperate lowland forest, the Białowieża Forest, Poland. Our model was built using an extremely fast, light-weight and flexible deep learning architecture based on recently published YOLOv5 (pre-trained YOLOv5l) [9] and trained on 2659 labeled images accessed via the API built in TRAPPER [10]. To the best of our knowledge, this is the first YOLOv5 implementation for automated mammal species recognition using camera trap images.

2 Materials and Methods

2.1 Dataset Preparation and Preprocessing

As the main data source in our research we used species-classified images originating from camera trapping projects from Białowieża Primeval Forest stored in TRAPPER [10]. This consisted of 2659 images. Bounding boxes were manually added to all images with the animal's presence to determine the exact position of each individual. When multiple individuals were present in the image, several bounding boxes were created for each individual. Example annotations and images are shown in Fig. 3. We did not use empty images in our dataset.

We have 12 classes in our dataset, 11 species of animals and 1 class "Other", which represents birds and small rodents. Images in our dataset were of various sizes. Most of them are 12 Mpixel high-resolution images. The distribution of the sizes can be found in Fig. 1. In our dataset we identified 11 common species occurring in Białowieża Primeval Forest.

Observations are not balanced across these species and we have species with larger and smaller support of samples (Fig. 2). Example annotations and images are shown in Fig. 3.

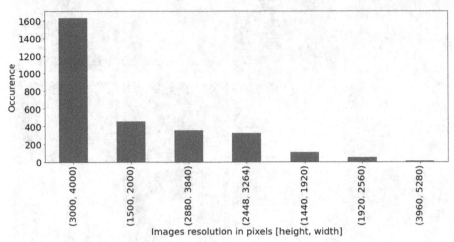

Fig. 1. The distribution of the image sizes (pixels) in the dataset.

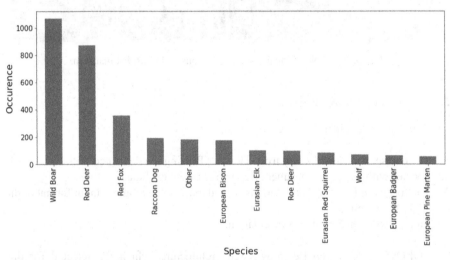

Fig. 2. The distribution of species in the dataset.

In our experiments we decided to perform cross-validation. This is the process of splitting the dataset into k equal size parts and process k training runs. For each training run, one split of the data was used for validation, and the rest was used for training the network. Images to each split were selected randomly using stratification on animal species - each separate data split had the same proportions of the observed species.

Fig. 3. Example of images and annotations in TRAPPER platform.

2.2 Deep Learning Architecture

The following data pipeline was adopted:

1. The dataset was downloaded from TRAPPER using the dedicated API.
2. Species with less than 40 camera trap images were excluded.
3. The format of the image annotations was adapted to the required input format of the YOLOv5 architecture.
4. Model testing in 5-fold cross validation.

YOLOv5 is the Deep Learning-based architecture, which we selected for this research. It achieves state-of-the-art results in the object detection field. In comparison to other Deep Learning architectures, YOLOv5 is simple and reliable. It needs much less computational power than other architectures, while keeping comparable results [14, 15] and performing much faster than other networks (Fig. 4). YOLOv5 strongly utilizes the architecture of YOLOv4 [18]. The encoder used in YOLOv5 is CSPDarknet [18]. Along with Path Aggregation Network [17] (PANet) they make up the whole network architecture. In comparison to the YOLOv4, activation functions were modified (Leaky ReLU and Hardswish activations were replaced with SiLU [19] activation function).

The selection of YOLOv5 architecture for this research was motivated by several reasons:

1. The network is currently state-of-the-art in the fast objects detection field.
2. The architecture is light-weight; this allows us to train the model using small computational resources and keep it cost-effective.
3. Small size of the model has the potential to be used in mobile devices (i.e. camera traps).

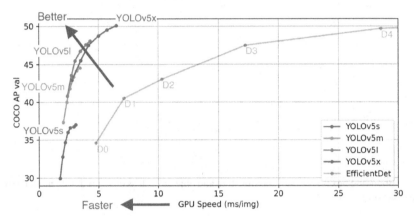

Fig. 4. Comparisons between YOLOv5 models and EfficientDet. Published within author permission.

2.3 Model Training Process

The first stage of model training was the hyper-parameter tuning. For that purpose, we have used evolutionary hyper-parameter tuning methods from YOLOv5 on the training and validation data. This has given us more optimal parameters for our dataset. In the next step, we have trained the model using the optimal hyper-parameters, starting from an already trained YOLOv5l model checkpoint.

Using a pre-trained model is a common technique in computer vision called Transfer Learning [20]. It speeds up the training process and keeps the generalization at the high level. During our experiments we have observed that the optimal number of epochs is 60, after that there are negligible changes in the model. Figure 5 shows how the YOLOv5 loss functions changed during the training. The results are shown on one of the training cross-validation splits.

YOLOv5 loss function is a sum of three smaller loss functions:

- Bounding Box Regression Loss - penalty for wrong anchor box detection, Mean Squared Error calculated based on predicted box location (x, y, h, w);
- Classification Loss - Cross Entropy calculated for object classification;
- Objectness Loss - Mean Squared Error calculated for Objectness-Confidence Score (estimation if the anchor box contains an object).

Below plots (Figs. 5 and 6) shows that after 51 epochs there is a minimal change in the loss functions as well as in F1-score.

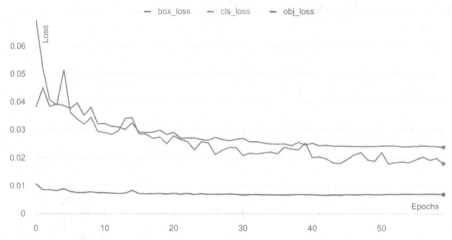

Fig. 5. Bounding box regression, classification and objectness loss changes during model training on the 1-st split from cross-validation.

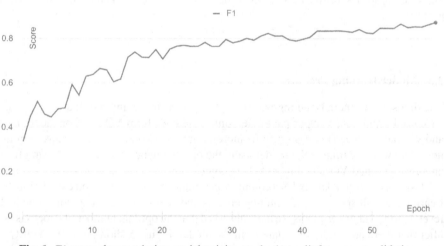

Fig. 6. F1-score changes during model training on the 1-st split from cross-validation.

The main software used in the training of the models was Python 3.8, with PyTorch 1.7, CUDA 11.2 and Jupyter Notebook. All AI model iterations, as well as the final one, were trained using cloud computing on Microsoft Azure. We executed the experiment on a virtual machine with preinstalled Linux software and a single NVIDIA Tesla K80 GPU. The training time for a single training run (60 epochs) on the train data took 2h (8.5h for the whole cross-validation).

3   Results and Discussion

The preliminary results using a limited amount of training data showed on average 85% F1-score in identification of 12 most commonly occuring medium-size and large mammal species in BF (including "other" class). The results presented in this study are the averaged results from all of the 5 validation splits from the cross-validation process. Table 1 shows the results of the combined evaluation. From the data we can see that the detection precision for species is cut down with decreasing sample size. Furthermore, for example, "roe deer" class has the lowest F1-score (0.58) because of the low abundance of this species in our data-set. As a result, this species is often not detected by our model, as shown in Figs. 7 and 8. Future experiments should address this issue.

Another insight from Fig. 7 is that "roe deer" class is often misclassified as "red deer" (15%). These species are similar in size and coloration and the reason for those mistakes might be caused by the low number of the targets - "red deer" occurs 872 times, where there are only 97 instances of "roe deer" in the dataset. To address this issue, we suggest to re-run these analyses on larger samples of classified images with bounding boxes.

Table 1. The combined results of the 5-fold cross-validation process.

Class (Species)	Targets	F1	Precision	Recall	mAP@.5	mAP@.5:.95
All	3143	0.85	0.88	0.82	0.88	0.66
Wild Boar	1070	0.89	0.92	0.86	0.91	0.68
Red Deer	872	0.86	0.88	0.85	0.89	0.68
Red Fox	356	0.94	0.93	0.94	0.97	0.75
Raccoon Dog	193	0.94	0.93	0.95	0.95	0.71
European Bison	176	0.81	0.89	0.76	0.85	0.68
Eurasian Elk	103	0.85	0.89	0.81	0.89	0.76
Roe Deer	97	0.58	0.67	0.53	0.61	0.47
Eurasian Red Squirrel	84	0.89	0.93	0.84	0.91	0.59
Wolf	71	0.87	0.89	0.85	0.91	0.73
European Badger	63	0.89	0.93	0.86	0.94	0.70
European Pine Marten	58	0.76	0.83	0.72	0.80	0.54

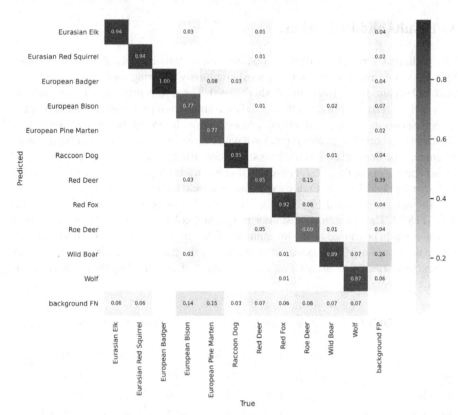

Fig. 7. Confusion matrix of the predictions on the test data from the 1-st cross-validation split.

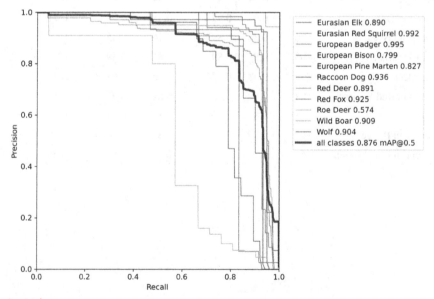

Fig. 8. Precision-Recall curve of the first split of the 1-st cross-validation. Values in the plot legend show the AUC score for each species.

3.1   Incorrect Classification Examples

We are aware of the disadvantages of our classification model. Three most common registered issues are: misclassifying animals with trees (Fig. 9), classifying animals with incorrect classes and not detecting animals at all (Fig. 10).

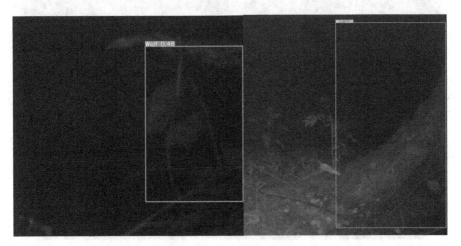

Fig. 9. Example of trees misclassified as animals.

Fig. 10.   Incorrect species classification. European bison is classified as "red deer" and wild boar as "wolf". The last-right image is an example of an unrecognized red fox sample.

3.2   Correct Classification Examples

The tested solution works with expected accuracy level with partially visible animals on images. Figure 11. shows correct detection and classification of a red fox that has only half of its body visible in the frame. Next examples (Fig. 12) prove that the model is able to detect animals that are blended with the background.

Fig. 11. First-left image presents correct detection of partially visible animals, the center and last, correct detection of barely visible animals.

Fig. 12. Correct detection of animals blended with the background.

4   Conclusions

Our achievement of the preliminary results presented in this study evidently proves a large potential in using YOLOv5 deep learning architecture to train AI models for automatic species recognition. Moreover, it can be directly incorporated into the camera trapping data processing workflows. Extended camera trap images dataset would allow for higher metrics and better detection of species from the Białowieża Forest.

As a future step, we see that the inclusion of additional training data sets from multiple European forest areas would greatly improve generalization of the Deep Learning model. However, this work suggests that there is room for improvement in case of the selected YOLOv5 network architecture and the inference pipeline. The encoder network may be changed for deeper structure to be able to extract more specific features from the images. Another common practice to improve the results is the usage of the Test Time Augmentation (TTA) on the inference process.

Pre-trained YOLOv5l model is fast enough, accurate and light-weight to be deployed on a well functional Edge AI computing platform. This advantage opens a new chapter for species classification in real time using camera-traps in the field.

Data Availability
Jupyter Notebook, which implements this experiment pipeline, includes TRAPPER integration and YOLOv5 usage for species recognition. It has been released as open-source code and is available on GitLab: https://gitlab.com/oscf/trapper-species-classifier.

Authors' Contributions
MCH, MR and PT from Bialystok University of Technology designed, developed and tested ML infrastructure. JB, MCH and DK from Polish Academy of Sciences delivered training and testing data, shared domain support and verified research results.

Conflict of Interest
The authors declare that they have no conflicts of interest.

Ethical Approval
All applicable, international, national, and/or institutional guidelines for the care and use of animals were followed.

Acknowledgment. This work was supported by Microsoft AI for Earth research grant funded by Microsoft and by the grant WZ/WI-IIT/3/2020 from Bialystok University of Technology. We thank Open Science Conservation Fund for making this article open access. We also thank all the people from MRI PAS and Kamil Kuijper for their help with drawing bounding boxes that were used for training and validation of our model.

References

1. Ripple, W.J., et al.: Collapse of the world's largest herbivores. Sci. Adv. **1**, e1400103 (2015)
2. Chapron, G., et al.: Recovery of large carnivores in Europe's modern human-dominated landscapes. Science **346**, 1517–1519 (2014)
3. Kuijper, D.P.J., et al.: Keep the wolf from the door: How to conserve wolves in Europe's human-dominated landscapes? Biol. Conserv. **235**, 102–111 (2019)
4. Lamb, C.T., et al.: The ecology of human–carnivore coexistence. Proc. Natl. Acad. Sci. U.S.A. **117**, 17876–17883 (2020)
5. Wearn, O.R., Glover-Kapfer, P.: Snap happy: camera traps are an effective sampling tool when compared with alternative methods. R. Soc. Open Sci. **6**, 181748 (2019)
6. Norouzzadeh, M.S., et al.: A deep active learning system for species identification and counting in camera trap images. Methods Ecol. Evol. **12**, 150–161 (2021)
7. Whytock, R.C., et al.: Robust ecological analysis of camera trap data labelled by a machine learning model. Methods Ecol. Evol. 13576 (2021). https://doi.org/10.1111/2041-210X.13576
8. Gilbert, N.A., Clare, J.D.J., Stenglein, J.L., Zuckerberg, B.: Abundance estimation of unmarked animals based on camera-trap data. Conserv. Biol. **35**, 88–100 (2020)
9. YOLOv5 official GitHub repository: https://github.com/ultralytics/yolov5. Accessed 13 Mar 2021
10. Bubnicki, J.W., Churski, M., Kuijper, D.P.J.: Trapper: an open source web-based application to manage camera trapping projects. Methods Ecol. Evol. **7**, 1209–1216 (2016)

11. Beery, S., Morris, D., Yang, S.: Efficient pipeline for camera trap image review. arXiv (2019)
12. Beery, S., Van Horn, G. Perona, P.: Recognition in Terra Incognita. In: Lecture Notes in Computer Science, vol. 11220, pp. 472–489 (2018)
13. Swanson, A. et al.: Snapshot Serengeti, high-frequency annotated camera trap images of 40 mammalian species in an African savanna. Sci. Data **2**, 150026 (2015)
14. Ren, S., He, K., Girshick, R., Sun, J.: Faster R-CNN: towards real-time object detection with region proposal networks. IEEE Trans. Pattern Anal. Mach. Intell. **39**, 1137–1149 (2017)
15. Szegedy, C., Ioffe, S., Vanhoucke, V., Alemi, A.A.: Inception-v4, inception-ResNet and the impact of residual connections on learning. In: 31st AAAI Conf. Artificial Intelligence, pp. 4278–4284 (2017)
16. YOLOv5 official release note: https://github.com/ultralytics/yolov5/releases/tag/v4.0. Accessed 13 Mar 2021
17. Liu, S., Qi, L., Qin, H., Shi, J., Jia, J.: Path aggregation network for instance segmentation. In: Proceedings of the IEEE Computer Society Conference on Computer Vision and Pattern Recognition, pp. 8759–8768. IEEE (2018). https://doi.org/10.1109/CVPR.2018.00913.
18. Bochkovskiy, A., Wang, C.Y., Liao, H.Y.M.: YOLOv4: optimal speed and accuracy of object detection. arXiv (2020)
19. Elfwing, S., Uchibe, E., Doya, K.: Sigmoid-weighted linear units for neural network function approximation in reinforcement learning. Neural Netw. **107**, 3–11 (2018)
20. Zhuang, F., et al.: A comprehensive survey on transfer learning. Proc. IEEE **109**, 43–76 (2021)

Battle on Edge - Comparison of Convolutional Neural Networks Inference Speed on Two Various Hardware Platforms

Kristian Dokic[1]([✉]) [iD], Dubravka Mandusic[2] [iD], and Lucija Blaskovic[2] [iD]

[1] Polytechnic in Pozega, Pozega, Croatia
kdjokic@vup.hr
[2] Faculty of Agriculture, University of Zagreb, Zagreb, Croatia
{simunovic,lmarkic}@agr.hr

Abstract. Several reasons influenced the tendency to move the first level of machine learning data processing to the edge of the information system. Edge-generated data is typically processed by so-called edge devices with low processing power and low power consumption. In addition to well-known SoC (System on Chip) manufacturers that are usually used as an edge device, some manufacturers in this market base their processor design on open source. This paper compares two different SoC, one based on the ARM (Advanced RISC Machines) architecture and the other on the open-source RISC-V (Reduced Instruction Set Computer) architecture. The specificity of the analysed SoC based on the RISC-V architecture is an additional processor for speed up calculations common in neural networks. Since the architectures differ, we compare two SoC of similar price. The comparison's focus is an analysis of the inference performance with the different number of filters in the first layer of the convolutional neural network used to detect handwritten digits. The process of convolutional neural network's training occurs in the cloud and uses a well-known database of handwritten digits – MNIST (Modified National Institute of Standards and Technology). In the SoC based on the RISC-V architecture, a reduced dependence of the inference speed on the number of filters at the first level of the convolutional neural network was observed.

Keywords: RISC-V · CNN · MNIST · K210

1 Introduction

There are several reasons why some tasks are easier and more reasonable to do on edge. Zhang et al. analysed different neural network architectures for keyword spotting on SoCs used for easier interaction with consumer electronic devices. They state that these devices use predefined keywords whose utterance activates full-scale speech recognition either on a device or in a cloud. Constantly enabled speech recognition would consume significantly more electricity, and if speech is recognised in the cloud, unnecessary network traffic would be generated. The authors also mention the problem of privacy in case the audio is continuously being sent to the cloud, as well as the problem of

© Springer Nature Switzerland AG 2021
K. Saeed and J. Dvorský (Eds.): CISIM 2021, LNCS 12883, pp. 311–322, 2021.
https://doi.org/10.1007/978-3-030-84340-3_25

delays due to the physical distance between the device and the cloud [1]. Sakr et al. also cite several benefits of moving computation toward the edge, such as response latency, energy consumption, security, bandwidth occupancy and expected privacy [2].

On the other hand, most machine learning and artificial intelligence algorithms are generally "hungry" for computing resources, especially in the training phase. This is one of the main reasons that neural networks inference phases take place on edge, while training is performed on much stronger processors.

This paper aims to compare two different SoC, one based on the ARM architecture and the other on the open-source RISC-V architecture. The specificity of the analysed SoC based on the RISC-V architecture is an additional processor called The Knowledge Processing Unit (KPU). It is a neural network processor with built-in convolution, pooling, batch normalisation and various activation operations. The comparison's focus is an analysis of the inference performance with a different number of filters in the first layer of the convolutional neural network used to detect handwritten digits. The process of defining the parameters of a convolutional neural network occurs in the cloud and uses a well-known database of handwritten digits - MNIST.

2   Literature Overview

2.1   Hardware on the Edge

It isn't easy to make a boundary that defines a device as an edge or non-edge device. Regarding the use of machine learning on edge devices, from the paper of different authors, edge devices are generally used for inference. At the same time, training of neural network or some other algorithm usually takes place on other more powerful computers.

Various microcontrollers and SoCs have been used as edge devices, and below are some examples where the emphasis is on the implementation of convolutional neural networks on edge devices.

Zhang et al. presented an object detector trained with the Caffe framework that used a convolutional neural network. The model was deployed on a development board based on Cortex-A9 Quad-Core SoC with 1 GB RAM. Inference speed was 1.13 frames/s [3]. Cerutti et al. presented a human detection model that used CNN (Convolutional Neural Network) in work and was developed using the CMSIS-NN library that allows deployment of neural networks to Cortex-M SoC. With 8-bit quantisation of the parameters, the model used 20 kB of flash memory and 6 KB of RAM [4]. Alameh et al. presented a tactile sensing system implemented with CNN on the Raspberry Pi4 and NVidia's Jetson TX2 platforms. The authors state that these two platforms are used as edge devices, and they have 4 and 8 GB of RAM and ARM® Cortex®-A57 and Cortex-A72 (ARM v8) processors. NVidia's Jetson TX2 also has a 256-core NVIDIA Pascal™ GPU (Graphics processing unit) implemented [5].

Finally, some authors tested RISC-V based SOC (Kendryte K210) as an edge device and used various models with CNN implemented. They concluded that the hardware accelerator's performance is acceptable and real-time object recognition speed at 13 frames/s. The authors made their models and used a previously developed surveillance camera application [6].

2.2 Software on the Edge

The implementation of machine learning on SoCs is primarily done by large corporations well known in the field. Cortex Microcontroller Software Interface Standard Neural Network (CMSIS-NN) is an open-source library published by ARM for neural network implementation on the Cortex-M platform [7]. STMicroelectronics also published an AI Expansion Pack for STM32CubeMX named X-CUBE-AI, which enables conversion and optimisation of pre-trained Neural Networks easy implementation on microcontrollers [8].

Google has been developing a Tensorflow lite for microcontrollers for years. This is an upgrade to the existing Tensorflow and allows optimisation and conversion of previously developed models to microcontrollers [9, 10]. Microsoft has released EdgeML, which includes implementing neural networks on devices with modest resources [11].

Many authors, with their papers, have influenced the optimisation of machine learning algorithms on microcontrollers trying to maximally overcome the limitations related to speed and a limited amount of memory. Fedorov et al. suggest the Sparse Architecture Search method, which allows convolutional neural networks on platforms with only 2 kB RAM. The authors use several optimisation methods [12]. Liberis and Lane work on optimising memory usage to implement convolutional neural networks on microcontrollers, proposing changes in the order of operations. In doing so, they demonstrate the use of a tool that significantly reduces the convolutional neural network's size. The authors use microcontrollers with 512 kB of RAM [13].

Capotondi et al. propose quantisation of tensors at 2, 4, and 8 bits to make the best use of microcontroller memory. The paper's result is the library that the authors call CMix-NN and report an increase in precision of up to 8% compared to previous results by other authors [14, 15]. The same approach was used by Cheng et al. They used quantisation and compression of CNN parameters and thus achieved an acceleration of 4–6 times, while the amount of memory used was reduced to as much as 20 times with a loss of accuracy of 1%. They did not use microcontrollers in their work but a smartphone [16]. Mocerino and Calimera proposed the use of 8-bit quantisation and binarisation, with their integration increasing speed by 81.48% and accuracy by 3.8% compared to separately used methods [17].

Louis et al. are aware of edge devices' importance and have introduced software infrastructure for optimising neural network execution on RISC-V with ISA extensions. Their implementation reduces the executed instruction count by 8× in comparison to baseline implementation. They also added optimised functions to the TensorFlow Lite source code [9].

3 Methods

3.1 Hardware Part

As mentioned above, in this paper, we wanted to compare SoC based on ARM architecture with SoCs based on RISC-V architecture that has started to appear on the market. In the beginning, we were aware that we would be forced to compare two SoC with significantly different characteristics. Still, the goal was to choose similar SoC in price and to test the same convolutional neural network in both cases.

nRF52840 SoC was selected on the ARM architecture, with a price of €5.65. The development board's price was €27.00, and the development board used in the research was the Arduino nano 33 BLE sense. This development board was chosen because of its support by the Tensorflow development team, which guarantees simpler development and code examples. There are several examples and instructions on the official website [18].

Kendryte K210 SoC was chosen as an SoC representative based on the RISC-V architecture, priced at $8.64. The development board's price was $23.90, and it is a development board Sipeed Maixduino Kit for RISC-V AI + IoT. The development board includes a GC0328 camera module and a 2.4-inch TFT (Thin Film Transistor) display. This development board was chosen because of the relatively good support from Seeed Technology Co., Ltd. One of the many features by which the K210 SoC differs from the nRF52840 is a Neural Network processor with built-in convolution, batch normalisation, activation, and pooling operations. Table 1 lists the SoC basic characteristics, and a more detailed description is available in the datasheets [19, 20].

Table 1. SoC basic characteristics

	nRF52840	Kendryte K210
Producer	Nordic semiconductors	Canaan Inc.
Bit width	32 bit	64 bit
CPU clock	64 MHz	400 MHz
RAM	256 kB	6 MB
FLASH	1 MB	16 MB

3.2 Software Part

As mentioned above, in this paper, we wanted to compare two SoCs with different characteristics but with a similar price. The well-known handwritten digit problem of classification and digit database MNIST (Modified National Institute of Standards and Technology database) was used as the base model. It is a dataset of 60,000 square 28 × 28-pixel grayscale images of handwritten digits between 0 and 9. The size of all images is initially reduced to 14 × 14-pixel images. The same convolutional neural network has been used to solve this problem for both microcontrollers, and it can be seen in Fig. 1. It is simple, and it includes a single convolution layer (Conv2D) with a small filter size (3 × 3) and without max pooling. The number of filters was changed from one to nine, which affected the model's speed, accuracy, and memory usage. A used activation function is Rectified Linear Unit (ReLU), and the optimiser is Adam. The model was developed on Google Colaboratory, and Jupyter files can be found on GitHub (https://github.com/kristian1971/TFML_RACE1). The file named *Arduino_14x14FINAL.ipynb* includes Python code for Arduino nano 33 BLE sense board model, and the file named *Maixduino_14x14FINAL.ipynb* contains Python code for the Sipeed Maixduino board.

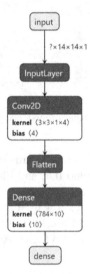

Fig. 1. The model schema

The models were trained for only 12 epochs. After training, the models were exported in standard formats (h5 and tflite) for comparison. Still, to use them on SoC, we had to export them in different formats depending on the development board. For the Arduino Nano 33 BLE Sense development board, the model was converted to C code using the EloquentTinyML library. In this way, the model is very easily imported on an SoC [21].

To prepare a model for Sipeed Maixduino, the process is somewhat more complex. After conversion to standard formats (h5 and tflite), the model should be converted to kfpkg format with a special conversion tool NNCase. This model is transferred to the development board separately from the main program itself, whereby the address in the FLASH memory where the model will be located is defined. Figure 2 shows the different stages of model conversion, where red models are not necessary but were used for comparison.

Fig. 2. Stages of model conversion

The model is deployed on development boards using various tools. In the Arduino Nano 33 BLE Sense case, the Arduino IDE and EloquentTinyML library were used. The specified development board does not have a connected camera, so instead of a captured picture, an array of 196 bytes was used as input in the neural network. This array simulated an image of 14 × 14-pixels. The program that used the model was written in the C programming language. In Fig. 3, Arduino IDE can be seen.

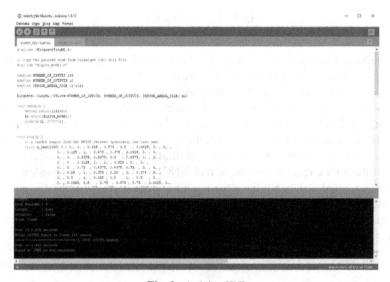

Fig. 3. Arduino IDE

In the case of the Sipeed Maixduino development board, the model was deployed using the KFlash tool. After that, the MaixPy IDE and the Python programming language were used, in which a script was written that used the transferred model. Unlike the Arduino Nano 33 BLE Sense development platform, the Sipeed Maixduino has an implemented camera, so a picture from the camera was used in the neural network's feedforward process. In Fig. 4, MaixPy IDE can be seen.

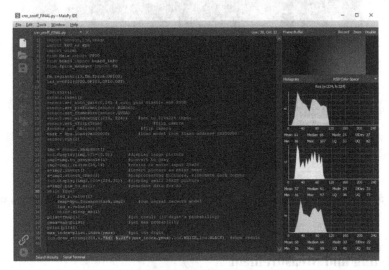

Fig. 4. MaixPy IDE

After transferring the convolutional neural network model to both development boards, it remained to choose a suitable way to measure the feedforward process's duration. Some authors have used built-in timing functions in such situations, such as the *micros()* function, which counts microseconds from an SoC reset [22]. Since two different development tools and programming languages were used, the method with an oscilloscope was chosen. Before feedforward through the neural network, one pin is raised from LOW to HIGH, and immediately after feedforward, the value on the pin is lowered from HIGH to LOW. In the case of the C programming language on the Arduino IDE, this code looks like this:

digitalWrite(2, HIGH);
ml.predict(x_test, y_pred);
digitalWrite(2, LOW);

In the case of the Python programming language on the MaixPy IDE, this code looks like this:

led_r.value(1)
fmap=kpu.forward(task,img2)
led_r.value(0)

By measuring the HIGH pin state's duration, we obtain the feedforward propagation duration through the neural network with a slight error that occurs by changing the pin state, which is significantly less than the feedforward propagation duration itself. The measurement process can be seen in Fig. 5.

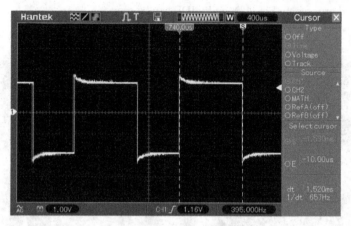

Fig. 5. Process of measuring the duration of forwarding propagation with an oscilloscope

4 Testing and Measurement

As mentioned above, we are aware that two different SoC whit differs in architecture and in characteristics are compared, and finally in the tools used for neural network deployment. Nevertheless, to draw some conclusions, we chose SoC of similar cost, and we used the same model of a convolutional neural network on both development boards.

To find the difference between the SoCs, we used a different number of filters in the convolution layer, between 1 and 9. For each of these values, we recorded the size of the stored model in different formats and the actual duration of feedforward propagation. Also, we recorded the model's accuracy concerning the number of filters in the convolutional layer. Since it was the same model in both cases, as expected, these values did not differ, as seen in Fig. 6. The only difference is in the different versions of the TensorFlow that we were forced to use due to the incompatibility of the other tools used. For Arduino board, TF 2.x was used, but for Miaxduino version TF 1.x.

In Tables 2 and 3, the values shown in Fig. 6 (accuracy) can be seen, and in the third and fourth columns, the model sizes in different formats for both development boards can be seen. In Table 2, data from the Arduino nano 33 BLE sense can be seen, and in Table 3 data from the Sipeex Maixduino. There was no significant difference, as might be expected. However, in the last column, significant differences in feedforwarding propagation speed through the neural network can be observed. This difference could also be expected when comparing the two SoC clock speed on the development boards, with the nRF52840 (Arduino nano 33 BLE sense) running at 64 MHz while the Kendryte K210 (Sipeex Maixduino) running at 400 MHz.

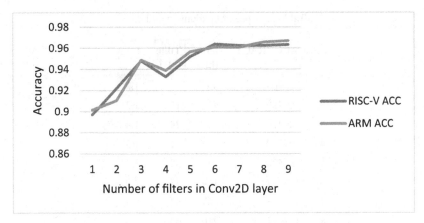

Fig. 6. Accuracy of the models

Table 2. Arduino nano 33 BLE sense board data

	ACCURACY	h5 (kB)	Tflite (kB)	t (ms)
1	0.9015	48	9	5.5
2	0.9104	71	16	10.9
3	0.9487	94	24	16.3
4	0.9388	117	32	21.6
5	0.9566	140	40	27.2
6	0.9608	163	47	32.4
7	0.9606	186	55	37.8
8	0.9658	209	63	43.2
9	0.9669	232	70	49.0
10	0.9705	255	78	–

However, if we look at the data in more detail, we notice a difference depending on the feedforward propagation duration growth and the number of filters in the convolutional layer. To illustrate this difference, we will define the feedforward propagation duration with only one filter in the convolution layer as t_1, while we will define the feedforward propagation duration with x filters as t_x. The ratio of the values of t_x and t_1 tells us how much the number of filters affects the feedforward propagation duration in our model, and the calculated values are shown in Fig. 7.

Table 3. Sipeex Maixduino board data

	ACCURACY	h5 (kB)	Tflite (kB)	t (ms)
1	0.8969	49	8	1.2
2	0.9220	72	16	1.3
3	0.9479	95	24	1.4
4	0.9330	118	31	1.5
5	0.9520	141	39	1.6
6	0.9637	164	47	2.0
7	0.9623	187	54	2.3
8	0.9624	210	62	2.3
9	0.9632	233	70	2.6
10	0.9620	256	78	2.6

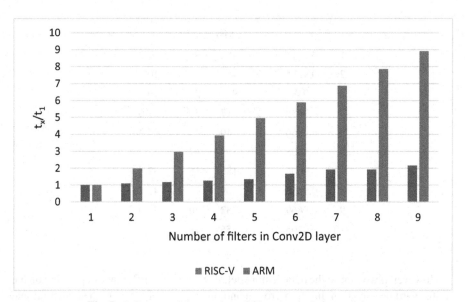

Fig. 7. Influence of the number of filters on the inference time

5   Discussion and Conclusion

A simple convolutional network was used to compare the feedforward propagation duration on two different SoC. At the time of writing, one development platform was not available on which both SoC could be tested under the same conditions, it was decided to use the same model, but different tools would be used in the deployment phase.

Given that the model was developed on the Google Collaborative platform using Keras and Tensorflow in both cases, there was no difference in the model's level and accuracy, as expected. Furthermore, the feedforward propagation duration differs because the SoC operate at different clock speeds, and this difference was also expected.

Finally, the most exciting part of the research is the influence of increasing the number of filters in the convolutional layer on the feedforward propagation duration. In the nRF52840 SoC (Arduino nano 33 BLE sense), there is practically a linear relationship between the number of filters in the convolutional layer and the feedforward propagation duration for this simple model. Of course, we can conclude this only for the above case in which most of the calculations also carry the calculations of parameters in the convolutional layer, and we must not generalise this conclusion.

On the other hand, with the Kendryte K210 SoC (Sipeex Maixduino), increasing the number of filters by nine times caused the feedforward propagation duration to increase slightly more than two times. This difference is caused by a Neural Network processor in K210 with built-in convolution, batch normalisation, activation, and pooling operations, as stated in the documentation.

In future research multiple SoCs using the same development platform will be compared because using different platforms is one of the significant drawbacks of this paper. On the other hand, an attempt will be made to explore in detail the capabilities of the K210 SoC as documentation in English on it is a little scarce.

References

1. Zhang, Y., Suda, N., Lai, L., Chandra, V.: Hello Edge: Keyword Spotting on Microcontrollers (2018)
2. Sakr, F., Bellotti, F., Berta, R., De Gloria, A.: Machine learning on mainstream microcontrollers. Sensors **20**, 2638 (2020)
3. Zhang, Y., Bi, S., Dong, M., Liu, Y.: The implementation of CNN-based object detector on ARM embedded platforms. In: Proceedings of the 2018 IEEE 16th International Conference on Dependable, Autonomic and Secure Computing, 16th International Conference on Pervasive Intelligence and Computing, 4th International Conference on Big Data Intelligence and Computing and Cyber Science and Technology Congress (DASC/PiCom/DataCom/CyberSciTech) (2018)
4. Cerutti, G., Prasad, R., Farella, E.: Convolutional neural network on embedded platform for people presence detection in low resolution thermal images. In: Proceedings of the 2019 IEEE International Conference on Acoustics, Speech and Signal Processing (ICASSP 2019) (2019)
5. Alameh, M., Abbass, Y., Ibrahim, A., Valle, M.: Smart tactile sensing systems based on embedded CNN implementations. Micromachines **11**, 103 (2020)
6. Torres-Sánchez, E., Alastruey-Benedé, J., Torres-Moreno, E.: Developing an AI IoT Application with Open Software on a RISC-V SoC. In: Proceedings of the 2020 XXXV Conference on Design of Circuits and Integrated Systems (DCIS) (2020)
7. Suda, N., Loh, D.: Machine Learning on ARM Cortex-M Microcontrollers. Arm Ltd., Cambridge (2019)
8. ST Microelectronics: AI Expansion Pack for STM32CubeMX, 5 January 2021. [Online]. https://www.st.com/en/embedded-software/x-cube-ai.html
9. Louis, M.S., et al.: Towards deep learning using tensorflow lite on risc-v. In: Third Workshop on Computer Architecture Research with RISC-V (CARRV) (2019)

10. Google Inc.: TensorFlow Lite for Microcontrollers, 7 January 2021. [Online]. https://www. tensorflow.org/lite/microcontrollers

11. Dennis, D.K., et al.: EdgeML: Machine Learning for Resource-Constrained Edge Devices (2020). https://github.com/Microsoft/EdgeML

12. Fedorov, I., Adams, R.P., Mattina, M., Whatmough, P.N.: SpArSe: Sparse Architecture Search for CNNs on Resource-Constrained Microcontrollers (2019)

13. Liberis, E., Lane, N.D.: Neural networks on microcontrollers: saving memory at inference via operator reordering (2020)

14. Capotondi, A., Rusci, M., Fariselli, M., Benini, L.: CMix-NN: mixed low-precision CNN library for memory-constrained edge devices. IEEE Trans. Circuits Syst. II Express Briefs **67**, 871–875 (2020)

15. Rusci, M., Capotondi, A., Benini, L.: Memory-Driven Mixed Low Precision Quantization for Enabling Deep Network Inference On Microcontrollers (2019)

16. Cheng, J., Wu, J., Leng, C., Wang, Y., Hu, Q.: Quantised CNN: a unified approach to accelerate and compress convolutional networks. IEEE Trans. Neural Netw. Learn. Syst. **29**, 4730–4743 (2017)

17. Mocerino, L., Calimera, A.: Fast and accurate inference on microcontrollers with boosted cooperative convolutional neural networks (BC-Net). IEEE Trans. Circuits Syst. I. Regul. Pap. **68**, 77–88 (2020)

18. TensorFlow: How-to Get Started with Machine Learning on Arduino, 7 January 2021. [Online]. https://blog.tensorflow.org/2019/11/how-to-get-started-with-machine.html

19. Nordic Semiconductors: nRF52840 Product Specification v1.1, 8 January 2021. [Online]. https://infocenter.nordicsemi.com/pdf/nRF52840_PS_v1.1.pdf

20. KENDRYTE Canaan Inc.: K210 Datasheet, 12 September 2020. [Online]. https://kendryte. com/downloads/

21. Simone: 12 January 2021. [Online]. https://eloquentarduino.github.io/category/progra mming/eloquent-library/

22. Dokic, K., Martinovic, M., Mandusic, D.: Inference speed and quantisation of neural networks with TensorFlow Lite for Microcontrollers framework. In: Proceedings of the 2020 5th South-East Europe Design Automation, Computer Engineering, Computer Networks and Social Media Conference (SEEDA-CECNSM) (2020)

Efficient Hair Damage Detection Using SEM Images Based on Convolutional Neural Network

QiaoYue Man[(✉)], LinTong Zhang, and Young Im Cho

Gachon University, Seongnam, Korea
zhanglintong1@naver.com, yicho@gachon.ac.kr

Abstract. With increasing interest in hairstyles and hair color, bleaching, dyeing, straightening, and curling hair are widely used worldwide, and the chemical and physical treatment of hair is also increasing. As a result, the hair suffered a lot of damage, and the degree of damage to the hair was measured only by the naked eye or touch. This has led to serious consequences, such as hair damage and scalp diseases. However, although these problems are serious, there is little research on hair damage. With the advancement of technology, people began to be interested in preventing and restoring hair damage. Manual observation methods cannot accurately and quickly identify hair damage areas. With the rise of artificial intelligence technology, a large number of applications in various scenarios have given researchers new methods. In the project, we created a new hair damage data set based on SEM (Scanning Electron Microscope) images. Through various physical and chemical analyses, we observe the changes in the hair surface according to the degree of hair damage, find the relationship between them, and use intelligence the convolutional neural network recognizes and confirms the degree of hair damage, and divides the degree of damage into weak damage, damage and extreme damage.

Keywords: Hair damage detection · Convolution neural network · Data analysis

1 Introduction

Hair is an important part of human body image. Modern people's aesthetic desire for beauty, with the continuous growth and diversification of hair, the continuous development of hair shape, color, and texture are trying to change, and you can use your own personality to change the image to follow the ever-changing trends. Hair is composed of 1–8% external hydrophobic lipid epidermis, 80–90% α-helix or β-sheet conformation of parallel polypeptide chains to form water-insoluble keratin, less than 3% melanin pigment, and 0.6–1.0% trace elements, Moisture 10–15%, etc. The normal cuticle has a smooth appearance, reflecting light and limiting friction between hair shafts. It's responsible for the shine and texture of the hair. The keratin layer of the hair becomes fragile and cracked under the influence of the external environment, temperature, humidity, and chemical and physical treatments, thus affecting hair quality. Although most people's hair is prone to various damage problems because the hair is inconvenient to observe,

© Springer Nature Switzerland AG 2021
K. Saeed and J. Dvorský (Eds.): CISIM 2021, LNCS 12883, pp. 323–330, 2021.
https://doi.org/10.1007/978-3-030-84340-3_26

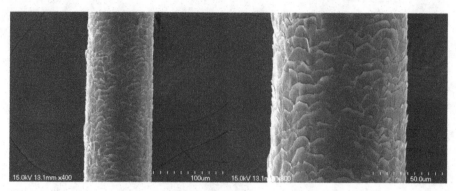

Fig. 1. Scanning electron microscope (SEM) to observe hair magnification 400× and 800× micrographs.

it is impossible to conduct a detailed analysis, and there are few studies on related hair damage.

Hair damage can be used as an indicator of health. Its evaluation relies on the measurement of morphological characteristics through microscopic analysis. However, few studies classify the degree of damage, but simply qualitatively analyze specific functions based on whether they exist. In this paper, we propose a novel hair damage detection network (Fig. 2). Based on artificial intelligence algorithms, which is used for scanning electron microscope (SEM) hair surface image (Fig. 1) damage to automatically identify and divide the damage. At the same time, we established a new hair damage data set based on SEM microscopic image data. To summarize, the contributions of this work are as follow:

1. We created a new hair microscopy data set based on SEM (Scanning Electron Microscope) image data and performed a quantitative analysis to classify the degree of hair damage according: weak damage, damage, and high damage.
2. We propose a novel and effective convolutional network model for hair damage detection: SACN-Net (Spatial attention convolutional neural networks).
3. We designed and introduced a spatial attention mechanism into the hair damage detection model to gather hair features to improve the accuracy of detection and recognition.

2 Related Work

Hair micro-detail detection and recognition can find use in many disciplines such as medicine and forensics. In the context of forensic science, microscopic hair analysis (a qualitative method) has shown effective discrimination [2, 3], and detailed examination of hair under the microscope is helpful for forensic identification. Clinically, microscopic analysis can be used as a tool to assess hair damage, as an indicator of health status [1, 4], but the analysis needs to be performed under certain conditions. Hair is subjected to various physical and chemical agents, including detergents, dyes, combing, and ultra-violet rays, which will change the structure of the hair [7, 8, 10]. The morphological characteristics of damaged hair can be identified through qualitative methods. The diagnosis is of great interest. However, there are few studies to quantify the degree of hair damage based on morphological characteristics [5, 6, 9]. It is worth noting that Kim et al. A hair damage classification system was developed. The system has five damage levels to characterize the damage to the hair surface caused by weathering [6]. Later, Lee et al. extended it to 12 classifications [9]. The grading system depends on the scan Electron microscope (SEM) images are based on subjective assessment of the severity of the structural irregularities of the hair. Through visual assessment, microscopic analysis is still the main qualitative technique. Few have developed more objective indicators of hair damage analysis and even fewer quantitative analyses of the severity of hair damage. Although it provides the potential to detect and compare image features more objectively, digital image analysis fails to make full use of various microscopic methods to objectively and automatically classify hair fibers. In these studies, most of the studies focused on the morphological features detected by optical microscope and analyzed using commercial software [11, 12], and there is little research on objective and efficient automatic hair damage detection schemes.

The detection and recognition of hair microscopic features is a challenging task. In recent decades, with the continuous development of microscopic examination technology, the microstructure of the hair that can be observed is clearer, more precise, and the sample preparation is simple and high-resolution, which makes the study of the microscopic morphology of the hair more in-depth. For example, Enrico et al. [13], used SEM image data to study the relationship between hair damage that may be caused by repeated cosmetic treatments and the absorption of cocaine from a wettable solution into the hair matrix (simulating external contamination). Over the years, researchers have been developing a fast and accurate method to automatically detect the degree of hair damage and have made many useful attempts. These methods mainly include optical microscope and scanning electron microscope (SEM) observation and analysis, image processing and computer vision.

In recent years, with the emergence of convolutional neural networks and a large number of applications, The method based on image processing and computer vision are the current research hotspot, more and more researchers have focused on the field of hair detection. For example, Umar Riaz et al. [15] proposed a convolutional model that uses convolutional neural network algorithms from an unconstrained perspective and uses only texture information to achieve complete hair analysis (detection, segmentation, and hairstyle classification). Chang et al. [16] proposed a smart scalp inspection and diagnosis system based on deep learning used to detect and diagnose the four common scalp and hair symptoms (dandruff, folliculitis, hair loss, and oily hair), an effective inspection and diagnosis system for scalp and hair physiotherapy as part of scalp health care. In the early days, people mainly used image processing technology to measure the geometric parameters of hair, such as hair diameter and hair uniformity. Recently, some scholars have begun to use computer vision technology to extract abstract detailed features from hair microscopic images in order to recognize them. For example, Jiang et al. [14]. Propose a convolutional network algorithm based on artificial intelligence: XI-Net, which performs feature analysis, extraction, and classification of hair microscopic SEM images to deal with forensic criminal investigation cases. The efficiency of investigation work is greatly improved, and it will be limited from the scene. Extract more valuable information from hair forensic evidence.

3   Proposed Methods

3.1   Residual Network

Reset introduces a residual block in the traditional convolutional neural network and superimposes a constant mapping layer on the basis of a shallow network to perform residual learning, which improves the accuracy of deep feature extraction and solves the problem of gradient disappearance. The residual block as shown as Fig. 2.

ResNet consists of many staked Residual Units and each Residual Unit could be generally given by:

$$X_{t+1} = h(x_t) + F(x_t) \tag{1}$$

When x_t and x_{t+1} denote the input and output of the t-th Residual Unit, $h(x_t) = x_t$ is an identity mapping and F is a non-liner residual function.

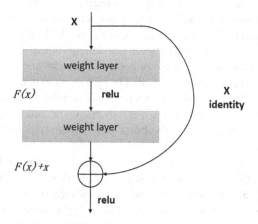

Fig. 2. Residual block

3.2   SACN-Net: Spatial Attention Convolutional Neural Networks

Our SCAN network is based on the residual network [14]. On this basis, we deal with complex and difficult-to-detect hair damage feature areas by stacking multiple spatial attention modules, to build a spatial attention residual network framework for hair damage detection.

We propose the SACN network is based on ResNet, under this network framework, we design a spatial attention model and add it to the residual module to efficiently focus on

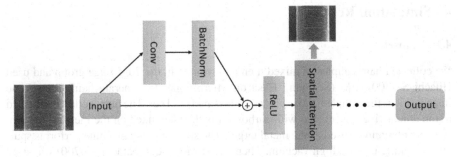

Fig. 3. SACN: Spatial Attention Convolutional Network Framework.

hair damage features and improve detection efficiency. First, the residual convolutional network is used to process the SEM hair microscopic data. After multi-layer convolution processing, the hair feature map is generated. After that, the hair feature map enters the spatial attention module we designed. Focus on the hair damage features and extract the detailed features of the hair damage that are of interest. Finally, complete the detection and classification of the degree of hair damage.

3.3 Attention Mechanism Module

When processing hair SEM microscopic image data, due to the small differences in hair surface characteristics, ordinary algorithm models cannot accurately identify the subtle differences in hair damage. In this paper, we design a spatial attention mechanism module suitable for hair microscopic images. To improve the accuracy of hair SEM microscopic image detection and damage feature identification (Fig. 4).

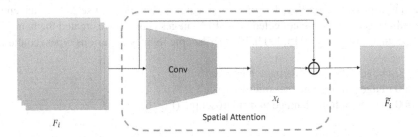

Fig. 4. Spatial attention module.

We apply an importance mask X_i the image feature F_i of the i-th frame to obtain attended image features by element-wise multiplication:

$$\widetilde{X}_i = F_i \cdot X_i \tag{2}$$

for $1 \leq i$, each entry of X lies in [0,1]. This operation attenuates certain regions of the feature map based on their estimated importance. Here we simply use three convolutional layers to learn the importance mask.

4 Simulation Results

4.1 Dataset

We collected hair samples of mixed men and women in the 20–55 age group and used Hitachi S-4700 SEM (Scanning Electron Microscope) to generate hair microscopic images. First, the sample hair is screened, classified, and cut. The hair section is attached to the conductive tape coated with carbon on both sides, fixed on the metal aluminum rod, and platinum is used as the metal target. The spray coating machine performs sputtering coating under a high vacuum. Then, an SEM (model: Hitachi S-4700) was used to scan the coated hair sample at 15 kV. Scan multiple sections of each axis to ensure that the changes in the surface of the hair sample seen are uniform and not isolated. The damage to the hair shaft under the scanning electron microscope is divided into three grades: weak damage, damage, and high damage (Fig. 3.).

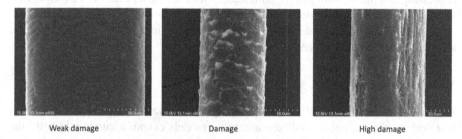

Weak damage   Damage   High damage

Fig. 5. Classification of hair damage.

Since the collection of SEM microscopic images of hair is complicated and expensive, it is impossible to collect data on a large scale. To this end, we use data enhancement algorithms to enhance the collected hair SEM images (Fig. 5). we created the hair SEM data set that has a total of 15,000 hairs microscopic images of various types, contains:

- 5000 images of weakly damage hair microscopic.
- 5000 images of damage hair microscopic.
- 5000 images of high damage hair microscopic (Fig. 6).

4.2 Implementation Details

In the experiment, we divided the data into a training set and a test set, 80% as a training set and 20% as a test set. Crop the image size to 224*224 by using center cropping. The network is trained using a stochastic gradient descent algorithm (SGD) [15]. Set the initial learning rate to 0.1 and gradually decrease. Used a Nesterov momentum [6] of 0.9 and a 10–4 weight decay without dampening for all the weights.

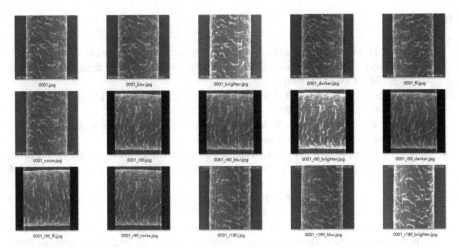

Fig. 6. Hair SEM microscopic image data augmentation

4.3 Compared with Other Advanced Methods

We selected other excellent network models to compare with our proposed model algorithm and used the SEM-based hair microscopy data set we created to detect the accuracy of the algorithm. The experimental surface, our proposed SACN-Net compared to other models Have better accuracy (Table 1).

Table 1. Comparison of accuracy of different models.

Model	Accuracy
AlexNet	**0.8310**
VGG16	**0.9055**
InceptionV3	**0.9545**
MobileNet	**0.9430**
ResNet50	**0.9685**
SACN-Net	**0.9845**

5 Conclusions

In this paper, we created a hair data set based on SEM microscopy and developed a classification based on the degree of hair damage. For this data set, we also proposed a novel residual convolutional network based on the spatial attention module and verified it with our data set. The experiment shows that our network model is efficient and robust.

References

1. Aut Rice, R.H., Wong, V.J., Price, V.H., Hohl, D., Pinkerton, K.E.: Cuticle cell defects in lamellar ichthyosis hair and anomalous hair shaft syndromes visualized after detergent extraction. Anat. Rec. **246**, 433–441 (1996)
2. National Research Council USA: Strengthening Forensic Science in the United States: A Path Forward. National Academies Press, Washington (2009)
3. Birngruber, C., Ramsthaler, F., Verhoff, M.A.: The color(s) of human hair—forensic hair analysis with SpectraCube®. Forensic Sci. Int. **185**, e19–e23 (2009)
4. Zhang, Y., Alsop, R.J., Soomro, A., Yang, F.-C., Rheinstädter, M.C.: Effect of shampoo, conditioner and permanent waving on the molecular structure of human hair. PeerJ **3**, e1296 (2015)
5. Kaliyadan, F., et al.: Scanning electron microscopy study of hair shaft damage secondary to cosmetic treatments of the hair. Int. J. Trichol. **8**, 94–98 (2016)
6. Kim, Y.-D., Jeon, S.-Y., Ji, J.H., Lee, W.-S.: Development of a classification system for extrinsic hair damage: standard grading of electron microscopic findings of damaged hairs. Am. J. Dermatopathol. **32**, 432–438 (2010)
7. Richena, M., Rezende, C.A.: Effect of photodamage on the outermost cuticle layer of human hair. J. Photochem. Photobiol. B Biol. **153**, 296–304 (2015)
8. Takada, K., Nakamura, A., Matsuo, N., Inoue, A., Someya, K., Shimogaki, H.: Influence of oxidative and/or reductive treatment on human hair (I): analysis of hair-damage after oxidative and/or reductive treatment. J. Oleo Sci. **52**, 541–548 (2003)
9. Lee, S.Y., Choi, A.R., Baek, J.H., Kim, H.O., Shin, M.K., Koh, J.S.: Twelve-point scale grading system of scanning electron microscopic examination to investigate subtle changes in damaged hair surface. Skin Res. Technol. **22**, 406–411 (2016)
10. Lee, Y., Kim, Y.-D., Hyun, H.-J., Pi, L.-Q., Jin, X., Lee, W.-S.: Hair shaft damage from heat and drying time of hair dryer. Ann. Dermatol. **23**, 455–462 (2011)
11. Verma, M.S., Pratt, L., Ganesh, C., Medina, C.: Hair-MAP: a prototype automated system for forensic hair comparison and analysis. Forensic Sci. Int. **129**, 168–186 (2002)
12. Park, K.H., Kim, H.J., Oh, B., Lee, E., Ha, J.: Assessment of hair surface roughness using quantitative image analysis. Skin Res. Technol. **24**, 80–84 (2018)
13. Gerace, E., Veronesi, A., Martra, G., Salomone, A., Vincenti, M.: Study of cocaine incorporation in hair damaged by cosmetic treatments. Forensic Chem. **3**, 69–73 (2017)
14. Xiaojia, J., Mengjing, Y., Yongzhi, Q., Ya, H.: Hair microscopic image classification method based on convolutional neural network. In: 2019 IEEE International Conference on Power, Intelligent Computing and Systems (ICPICS), Shenyang, China, pp. 433–438 (2019)
15. Muhammad, U.R., Svanera, M., Leonardi, R., Benini, S.: Hair detection, segmentation, and hairstyle classification in the wild. Image Vis. Comput. **71**, 25–37 (2018)
16. Chang, W.-J., Chen, L.-B., Chen, M.-C., Chiu, Y.-C., Lin, J.-Y.: ScalpEye: a deep learning-based scalp hair inspection and diagnosis system for scalp health. IEEE Access **8**, 134826–134837 (2020)

Why Do Law Enforcement Agencies Need AI for Analyzing Big Data?

Aleksandra Pawlicka[1](✉), Michał Choraś[1,4], Marcin Przybyszewski[1],
Laurent Belmon[2], Rafał Kozik[1,4], and Konstantinos Demestichas[3]

[1] ITTI, Poznań, Poland
apawlicka@itti.com.pl
[2] Thales Research Technology, Cannes, France
[3] Institute of Communication and Computer Systems, Athens, Greece
[4] UTP University of Science and Technology, Bydgoszcz, Poland

Abstract. The aim of the article is to give the rationale behind employing AI tools to help Law Enforcement Agencies analyze data, based on the existing solution, i.e., the MAGNETO (Multimedia Analysis and correlation enGine for orgaNised crime prevention and investigation) platform. In order to do this, the challenges Law Enforcement Agencies (LEAs) face with regard to data handling are presented. Then, the paper presents the key features of the MAGNETO platform, which is an innovative AI-based approach to empowering LEAs with the capabilities to process, manage, analyse, correlate and reason from the voluminous heterogeneous datasets; the underlying technologies are mentioned, too. It then discusses the innovative potential of the solution. The article proposes an array of technologies and methods that may be applied in order to facilitate LEAs in their handling of large amounts of heterogeneous data. Owing to the study, it has been shown that in the long run, the application of the platform will contribute to safer, more secure Europe. Additionally, it may even help save lives during the COVID-19 pandemic.

Keywords: Law enforcement agencies · Artificial intelligence · Big data · Innovation · Data processing

1 Introduction

At present, almost every entity which operates based on vast amounts of digitalized data encounters problems related to big data processing, knowledge understanding and interoperability. This is also true for Law Enforcement Agencies (LEAs); the common understanding of information among cooperating LEAs and external parties, as well as the flexible tools for sharing and exchanging data (or the lack thereof) affect the effectiveness and successfulness of law enforcement and prosecution. Actually, no matter the location, LEAs have to deal with very similar challenges: "Budgets are getting tighter and resources scarcer. And

This research was funded by H2020 786629 project MAGNETO.

© Springer Nature Switzerland AG 2021
K. Saeed and J. Dvorský (Eds.): CISIM 2021, LNCS 12883, pp. 331–342, 2021.
https://doi.org/10.1007/978-3-030-84340-3_27

yet agencies are expected to deal with these cuts and deliver an equal if not higher level of service than before" [2,20]. The solution to this issue is surprisingly easy – LEAs should use their greatest asset – i.e., the vast amounts of various kinds data they collect and possess - number plate data, crime records, HR records and so on, to the fullest. Sadly, "agencies are not exploiting the full value of the data they have" [20]. It is clear that "without effective data analysis, Law Enforcement Agencies will struggle to counter the criminal actors they are charged with targeting" [19] and LEAs "do not always effectively use the data available to them to improve their operations, measure their effectiveness and make the community safe" [2]. For that reason, a number AI-based solution projects were conceived, the main ambition of which being the empowerment of LEAs with the capabilities to process, manage, analyze, correlate and reason from the voluminous heterogeneous datasets. Apart from the support they would provide for the fight against crime and terrorism, they may contribute to the overall security of Europe. This paper will discuss the abovementioned issues in the light of a particular AI-based solution for LEAs, i.e., the MAGNETO project, the acronym standing for Multimedia Analysis and correlation enGine for orgaNised crime prevention and investigation. Although it is still an ongoing project, after two years of development it has entered the validation phase and already shows great promise as the way of catering for the LEAs' specific needs, that will transfer into better capabilities to serve the society. In terms of enhancing the security and safety of Europe, the potential of such a solution seems to be limitless [6,7]. This paper is structured as follows: firstly, the State of the Art approach to employing AI tools in Law Enforcement Agencies' work is being presented, then in Sect. 3, the LEAs' needs, challenges and required solutions are shown. Then, in Sect. 4 the MAGNETO platform is introduced, its innovative potential is discussed, followed by the final remarks in Sect. 5.

2   State of the Art

The potential of the application of the artificial intelligence tools for the needs of the Law Enforcement Agencies, although being a relatively recent issue, has already been mentioned, discussed and explored in a number of papers. Back in 2014, Suhaib et al., in a review study, concluded that AI will be significant as supportive technology in law enforcement [1]. In [12], the authors note that many AI-based tools have already been tested and are used worldwide; they comprise solutions for analyzing video and image data, recognizing faces, identifying people by their biometric traits, etc. They also mention using AI in drones and robots, as well as utilizing it in forecasting future crimes. The authors also suggest always giving into consideration the fact that criminals are fast to embrace novel technologies, as well. Tim Dees recommends the application of AI for law enforcement activities, especially in the three cases where it may prove the most useful: editing video material in a quicker way (e.g., removing personal or unwanted data from the dashcam footage before publication), supporting the analysis of verbal statements (detecting whether the interrogated person is lying), and recognizing and tracking vehicles or faces in live footage. The article mentions the ever more popular concerns about facial recognition systems, which have led to the solution being banned in San Francisco, for example. However, the author emphasizes the fact that it is still worth employing AI solutions despite the concerns, as the application of such tools makes the LEAs work smarter, by shortening the processing time from hundreds of hours to minutes, and thus saving taxpayers' money [3]. Marr refers to the fact that there have already been arrests made based on the data sourced from connected smart devices. The author also mentions the usefulness of switching to the data-driven way of fighting crime, by employing AI to identify patterns and discerning a modus operandi of a wrongdoer. Finally, they believe AI may be of use in detecting serial crimes, by finding the relations that would take humans much more time to uncover [10]. In her paper, Lalley says that (AI-based technology) "can help provide legitimacy for an agency, accountability to citizens, and the foundation for trusting relationship [8]." At the same time, she emphasizes the importance of ensuring transparency, community involvement and regular review and feedback, in order for the solutions to play their role to the fullest. Hisham mentions the ways AI-based tools may be applied in Law Enforcement Agencies' work, and emphasizes the immense potential they have. The author even says that LEAs using AI will "help us live safer lives." They also remind of the significance of ensuring explainability of the solutions [5]. Quest et al. discuss in detail the benefits and drawbacks of employing AI-based tools for solving crimes, and conclude that if the advantages outweigh the risks, then it is worth applying the tools. They also note that AI can identify areas of potential fraud and "serious crimes", but also help solve "mundane crimes", such as faking invoices or committing cyber fraud; eventually contributing to helping "public agencies with prosecuting these offenses much more effectively and efficiently". According to the authors, if managed correctly, "AI will eventually have a hugely positive impact on reducing crime in the world [16]".

3   Law Enforcement Agencies and Data Analysis

Various LEAs express different needs and goals and no solution is able to satisfy all the numerous needs. Thus, the AI solution should address this by being adapted to the most significant use cases that various kinds of LEAs share. It has been determined that LEAs actually need tools which will enable processing and correlating vast amounts of data as well as enriching the data across a plethora of sources of heterogeneous nature [18]. This may make the investigation process faster. Thus, instead of being forced to waste time on technical aspects and correlating data in a manual way, they would be able to focus on the actual investigation. LEAs have determined five most significant use cases in which there occur problems with processing large volumes of heterogeneous information:

1. Crime against persons and property
2. Economic organized crime

3. Prevention and investigation of terrorist attacks
4. Parallel illegal economic circuits of organized crime
5. Identity crime

A successful AI-based project has the potential to change the capabilities of Law Enforcement Agencies as far as dealing with enormous amounts of exceptionally diverse data is concerned. This will lead to crime prevention and investigation becoming more efficient and effective.

3.1   The Technology in Demand

In order to address the expressed needs of LEAs, it has been determined that the most optimal and effective array of tools to be employed in order to discover new, unsuspected relations within large datasets in an automatic way should comprise of:

1. Advanced correlation engine. This technology would enable automatic finding of new relations within large datasets; the relations that has not been suspected before.
2. Sophisticated representational model. In order to represent knowledge in an open, standardized manner; this would lead to discovering relations and enabling interoperability.
3. Evidence collection platform. Such a platform would be used for mining heterogeneous data and indexing multimedia content. Thus, it would become available for the processing at next stages.
4. Threat prediction engine by semantic reasoning. This technology would enable analyzing trends and assessing the levels of threat.
5. Augmented intelligence tools. They would be applied so as to deliver Human Machine Interfaces (HMIs) that are both immersive and interactive, and enhance the awareness of the situation.

The fundamental concept of a successful AI-based solution for LEAs is to establish a crime prevention and investigation scheme that will be perpetually self-improving. The heterogeneous data flows within the scheme are to be changed into knowledge bases in accordance with a complex representational model. Then, they should be processed and fused by means of semantic technologies. HMIs would represent their results and significance in a visual manner. Such HMIs would enable decision making that is timely and accurate; make it possible to extract court-proof evidence; they would also allow for situational awareness. An innovative, successful AI-based solution should thus be designed to concentrate on five abovementioned representative use cases. They all complement one another and cover actual and relevant needs of LEAs. They comprise:

1. Crime against persons and property
The amount of data, both of textual and multimedia nature, related to terrorist attacks makes the already daunting task even more complicated. An AI solution should aim at facilitating digital forensic investigations. This would help to:

collect and process relevant data concerning the event; identify suspects; comprehend and associate the chain of events, as well as the roles the participants played; give evidence, which can be used in a court of law, to charge suspects.

2. Economic Organized Crime

It has been established that cases of economic organized crime and corruption produce about 5–15 Terabytes of data per case on average. The AI-based solution should allow seamless exchange of data owing to the integration of an array of tools. This, in turn, would enable quicker processing of the exceptionally vast amounts of information in supraregional and international cases. Furthermore, it would enable identifying the relations among the different groups that engage in criminal activities. Consequently, future criminal actions might be prevented whilst still being planned.

3. Prevention and investigation of terrorism

As terrorism is a kind of crime of complex and multifaceted character, the data about it must be sought and gathered from many sources; it comes in a variety of formats. The solutions are needed that would enable performing cross searches, regardless of the hindering issues, such as formats and volumes of data or multilingualism. The framework of an AI solution could be designed to facilitate biometric information. An example of this may be gathering fingerprints at borders. Such a solution should also aim at achieving complete interoperability of the components. The basis for those must be constituted by EU and national legal frameworks.

4. Parallel illegal economic circuits of organized crime

They bypass taxes, state monopolies or quality inspection. Thus, they comprise a primary source of income for many branches of organized crime. At present, Police forces, when collecting all the necessary data, are forced to contact several entities and institutions. This makes the investigation processes be very complex. The goal of a proper AI-based solution should be supporting smart managing, exploiting and correlating the data the LEAs are able to access. The Police would thus be supported in their fight against illegal trade by the following functions: correlating the available information followed by extracting from it the patterns which verify suspicions and indicate that a crime either has been committed or is still in progress.

5. Identity crime

As identity crime data is collated by LEAs using multiple various formats, the examination thereof might prove to be too challenging or even impossible to share with other LEAs. An AI solution is being sought after that aims at defining open common data models with minimum interfaces. This would lead to processing data and extracting evidence. As a result, interoperable tools and standard interfaces will enable crossing boundaries and borders.

Table 1 shows a more specific look on the problems and challenges that LEAs face along with the propositions of values that a successful AI-based solution should provide and respond to. The issues that have been identified so far fall into four groups as presented in Table 1. In addition to the value AI-based solutions

Table 1. The problems LEAs face and the solutions to them that the AI-based solution could provide.

LEA problem statement	Value proposition
Quality and quantity of data: Data quality and accuracy; non-operability of existing tools on some project spectra, irrelevant data indexing, frequently poor-quality data storage and intangibility, limited data accuracy – e.g., geo-location accuracy, etc. Data quantity – often must contact dozens of differentinstitutions and entities, in order to collect the necessary information	Identification of information sources and collection of data among heterogeneous sources. Advanced searching and meaningful, multimodal presentation of the results. Reduced processing time through seamless heterogeneous data integration.Full source-merging capability allowing cross searches, despite possible obstacles such as data volumes, heterogeneous formats, multilingualism, and alphabets (Latin, Cyrillic, Arabic, Korean, Chinese ideograms, etc.). Support the intelligent management, exploitation and correlation of the data that are accessible by the LEA. Common information ingest mode associated with visualization and summarization methods
Comprehensiveness and performance of analysis. Hard to correlate data with limited resources. Due to the volume of data, the computerized evidence has to be divided into multiple evaluation units for processing	Improved innovative processes and procedures, allowing more efficient handling of cases. Analysis and correlation of the information. Processing and verification of hypotheses. The extraction of relevant information and generation of case-related knowledge, as well as of hidden relationships and correlation between the different pieces of information. The generation of cross-case knowledge networks and easy, secure access to it via intuitive HMIs (Human-machine interface) and a portal
Knowledge and data sharing. Currently, LEAs collate, e.g., identity crime data in many differing formats, making the examination of these data challenging and preventing the sharing with other LEAs	Defines open common data models and minimum interfaces, which enable data to be processed and evidence extracted. Significantly standard interfaces and interoperable tools that allow for crossing of boundaries and borders. Fosters Security Union through facilitating knowledge transfer between LEAs
Legal compliance. Hard to find tools that take into account all the EU and national legal frameworks (Penal Code, Privacy and Data Protection, etc.)	Data management module ensures the traceability, transparency and verifiability of the actions performed on the data contained in the system

may offer to LEAs, they should also make it available for third party developers to join. The model that would be applied here is the multi-sided market model; more specifically a two-sided model, between LEAs and third party developers, with the solution's platform/community enabling them to connect with each other. Being a kind of intermediary between those two distinct sides of the market, the solutions would actually produce additional value for both of them. The values, most of them coming from the cross-side network effects, would consist in:

- Giving the ability to verify third-party developers' business concepts with LEA practitioners, against real-world scenarios (this may be useful especially for new market entrants).
- Reducing the total cost by means of avoiding duplication; that is, if one framework were used, there would be no need for investing in developing any in-house solutions.
- Cutting the transaction costs, that is giving access to LEAs whilst enjoying the benefits of guidance to follow the technical/organizational/legal and ethical standards, and good practices.

Finally, apart from addressing the challenges that LEAs face by giving technical solution, an AI-based solution should prepare the market (by building the community and making standardization effort) and address development of other significant supporting services. The said services include, amongst others, giving LEA workers new, relevant skills through training them to utilize the AI-based tool.

3.2 The Crucial Aspects of Privacy and Data Protection – GDPR Compliance

The information processed by such a tool would most probably fall into the category of sensitive data and thus must be handled properly, i.e., following ethical guidelines, legal principles and societal acceptance. In fact, the legal order of a specific country allows several situations in which the authorities are allowed to reach for this kind of data and use it. Generally speaking, the most significant principles and rules that determine the obtaining and processing of sensitive data comprise purposefulness, secrecy, gratuitousness, selectivity and monitoring. Moreover, a system which processes data must be GDPR-compliant [13]. GDPR stands for General Data Protection Regulation, and it is an EU regulation that came into force on May 25, 2018. According to the GDPR, anyone who processed data must adhere to the principles outlined in the regulation:

1. lawfulness, fairness and transparency
2. purpose limitation
3. data minimization
4. accuracy
5. storage limitation
6. integrity and confidentiality
7. accountability.

According to the regulations, personal data may be legally processed if the data subject has given unambiguous concept or the processing is necessary to:

- execute a contract to which the data subject is a party
- comply with a legal obligation
- save a person's life

– perform a task in the public interest or carry out some official functions, or
– when there is a legitimate interest to process a person's personal data.

GDPR compliance means that data protection is considered by design and
default, i.e., data protection is considered when developing any new product or
solution. Thus, when designing an AI-based solution, data protection principles
must not be casually considered at the end of the project. On the contrary: they
must be central to the way it was planned and operated, and the required ethical,
societal and legal considerations must be well-thought and embedded into the
design and development of any AI-based solution for LEAs [4].

4   The MAGNETO Platform

Having considered the aforementioned needs of LEAs, as well as the available
technology, the MAGNETO project was born [14]. It is an ongoing project
funded under Horizon 2020 (Grant Agreement 786629, Call: SEC-12FCT-2016-
2017; Technologies for prevention, investigation, and mitigation in the context
of fight against crime and terrorism). It has been coordinated by Institute of
Communication and Computer Systems (ICCS; Greece), there are 23 partners
from 11 European countries. It lasts 36 months; it started on May 1st, 2018 and
will finish on 30th April 2021. Its budget is 5,320,475 EUR. Under the project,
the cooperation of 11 Law Enforcement Agencies (PSNI, WSPol, KWP, CAST,
MINT, FHVR, PPM, IGPR, SAB, PSP, AGS), Research Centres (ICCS, IOSB),
Universities (KUL, UPV, QMUL) and For-profit entities (Thales, ITTI, CBRNE,
PAWA, EUROB, VML, SIV) has been established [9,11]. The leading concept of
MAGNETO is to 'augment the capabilities of LEAs in managing, correlating and
reasoning upon huge volumes of heterogeneous and disjoint multimedia data'.
The MAGNETO platform provides LEAs with considerable high-level value that
comprises:

– improved abilities to deal with vast volumes of heterogeneous data and to
  correlate it
– expanded capacity to fight organized crime and terrorism
– investigations being more effective and streamlined
– enhancing trend analysis/situation awareness thus leading to the improvement in preventing well-organized crimes
– information becoming more relevant (for example by presenting knowledge in
  a way that is open and standardized; this in turn may lead to the recognition of relations and enabling interoperability; and also by discovering new,
  unsuspected relations within voluminous data sets in an automatic way)
– accuracy and precision in data having been improved (by performing heterogeneous and multimedia data mining by means of indexing leading to making
  it able to be further
– reducing the amounts of data (for example by means of discovering new,
  unsuspected relations within large datasets in an automatic way)

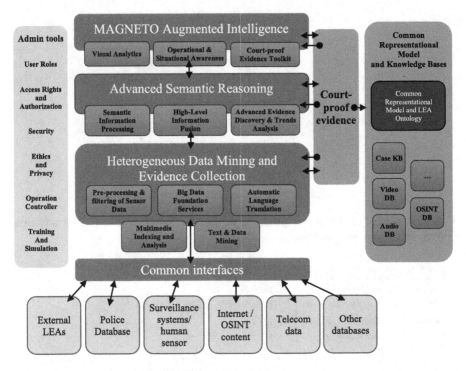

Fig. 1. The logical architecture of the MAGNETO platform addressing the needs of LEAs, source: authors' own work.

- increasing the number of well-trained staff (after having applied MAGNETO training that will allow using tools in an effective way)
- demonstrating being compliant with the law
- fostering Security Union with the help of knowledge transfer among LEAs, within the MAGNETO community, for example.

Figure 1 presents the logical and technical architecture of the platform and the elements which aim at addressing the needs of LEAs. Figures 2 and 3 show a fragment of the platform in use; here it has been used for call detail record (CDR) analysis [7].

It is worth mentioning, that apart from addressing the needs expressed by LEAs and contributing to the overall safety and security of Europe, the project also seems promising in business terms, i.e., it shows considerable commercial potential. Figure 4 presents the process of the initial concept of the MAGNETO platform becoming a finished product that brings revenue.

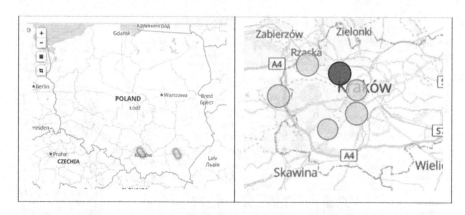

Fig. 2. A screen of the actual platform in use; call detail record (CDR) advanced feature extraction and analysis.

CDR

number_A	number_B	duration	time
04834677419	04834657459	15	10:00
04834677419	04834657459	50	10:01
04834677419	04834677559	15	10:03
04834677430	04834677419	150	12:11

Feature Extraction

Window
(A=04834677419, Time = from 10:00 to 10:15)

N(*)	N(distinct B)	Duration Max	Duration Avg	Duration Min
3	2	50	26.7	15

Fig. 3. A screen of the actual platform in use; call detail record (CDR) advanced feature extraction and analysis.

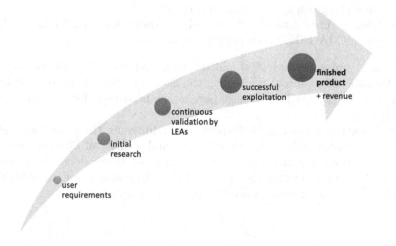

Fig. 4. The process from the concept to the finished product and revenue, source: authors' own work.

5 Conclusions

All in all, it must be stated that the successful application of an innovative AI-based solution will vastly enhance the way LEAs function nowadays, and the MAGNETO platform has the potential to do it, as "for Law Enforcement Agencies, data analytics can help officers lower crime rates and expand social services' [16]. The validation phase of the project has already shown promise in enhancing the capabilities of the LEAs testing it (indeed, currently the solution is being validated by over 10 Police Departments (LEAs) involved in MAGNETO project). Undoubtedly, the improvement in crime investigation and prevention, as well as in the fight against terrorism will contribute to a more secure, citizen-friendly Europe. In addition to this, artificial intelligence and machine learning solutions that the platform encompasses may prove to be the source of considerable revenue and a product being in great demand with the public. Moreover, the actual impact of the solution may be far greater, as the outcomes of the MAGNETO project have already proven useful as part of other solutions, e.g., the Prevision (Prediction and Visual Intelligence for Security Information) project [15,17]. Lastly, it has to be emphasized that the (as of October 2020) ongoing COVID-19 pandemic has made many jobs remote, so as to try to slow the spread of the disease down. Thus, implementing digital software may be the main factor to allow Law Enforcement Agencies continue performing their task without risking their employees' lives (Research and Markets, 2020).

Acknowledgements. This research was funded by H2020 786629 project MAGNETO.

References

1. Alzou'bi, S., Alshibly, H., Al-ma'aitah, M.: Artificial intelligence in law enforcement, a review. Int. J. Adv. Inf. Technol. (IJAIT) **4**(4) (2014). https://doi.org/10.5121/ijait.2014.4401
2. Boehmer, R.: 5 Ways to Improve the Use of Data by Police Departments. Hillard Heintze (2017)
3. Dees, T.: 3 ways artificial intelligence can work for your agency. Police 1 (2019). https://tinyurl.com/rv9s8nyt
4. Dove, E.S.: The EU general data protection regulation: implications for international scientific research in the digital era. J. Law Med. Ethics **46**(4), 1013–1030 (2018). https://doi.org/10.1177/1073110518822003
5. Hisham, S.: AI will be used for all forms of policing in future. Geospatial World (2019)
6. Kozik, R., et al.: Common representational model and ontologies for effective law enforcement solutions. Vietnam J. Comput. Sci. **07**(01), 1–18 (2020). https://doi.org/10.1142/S2196888820020017. https://tinyurl.com/w9baunvc
7. Kozik, R., Choraś, M., Pawlicki, M., Pawlicka, A., Warczak, W., Mazgaj, G.: Proposition of innovative and scalable information system for call detail records analysis and visualisation. In: Herrero, Á., Cambra, C., Urda, D., Sedano, J., Quintián, H., Corchado, E. (eds.) CISIS 2019. AISC, vol. 1267, pp. 174–183. Springer, Cham (2021). https://doi.org/10.1007/978-3-030-57805-3_17

8. Lalley, A.Z.: Introducing artificial intelligence into the United States law enforcement community: learning from foreign law enforcement agencies (2019)
9. MAGNETO: MAGNETO - fighting against crime and terrorism. http://www. magneto-h2020.eu
10. Marr, B.: How Robots, IoT and Artificial Intelligence are Transforming the Police. Bernard Marr and co. https://bernardmarr.com/default.asp?contentID=1170
11. Mills, M.: Using Big Data to Improve Law Enforcement. Datafloq (2017). https:// datafloq.com/read/using-big-data-to-improve-law-enforcement/3485
12. OSCE: Law enforcement agencies should embrace Artificial Intelligence to enhance their efficiency and effectiveness, say police experts at OSCE meeting (2019). https://www.osce.org/chairmanship/432152
13. Pawlicka, A., Jaroszewska-Choraś, D., Choraś, M., Pawlicki, M.: The guidelines for stego/malware detection tools achieving GDPR compliance. IEEE Technol. Soc. Mag. (2020)
14. Pérez, F.J., et al.: Multimedia analysis platform for crime prevention and investigation. Multimedia Tools Appl. (2021). https://doi.org/10.1007/s11042-020-10206-y
15. PREVISION: PREVISION - Prediction and Visual Intelligence for Security Information. http://www.prevision-h2020.eu
16. Quest, L., Charrie, A., Roy, S.: The risks and benefits of using AI to detect crime. Harvard Bus. Rev. (2018)
17. Research and Markets: Opportunities for Emerging Technologies in the Law Enforcement Software Market - Demand for Big Data, Data Analytics, OSINT, SIGNIT Rises. GlobeNewswire (2020). https://tinyurl.com/5c4w9csb
18. Rigano, C.: Using artificial intelligence to address criminal justice needs. NIJ J. **280** (2019)
19. Santos, A., Jenkins, I., Mariani, J., Gelles, M., Mirkow, A.: Investigative analytics leveraging data for law enforcement insights. Deloitte Insights (2019). https:// tinyurl.com/hjf6tzcr
20. SAS: How big data analytics can be the difference for law enforcement. https:// tinyurl.com/5384t7es

Deep Learning Bio–Signal Analysis from a Wearable Device

Mikołaj Skubisz[iD] and Łukasz Jeleń[✉][iD]

Department of Computer Engineering,
Wrocław University of Science and Technology,
Wybrzeże Wyspiańskiego 27, 50-370 Wrocław, Poland
lukasz.jelen@pwr.edu.pl

Abstract. World Health Organization reports that cardiovascular diseases are the main cause of death worldwide. To prevent the premature death rate it is important to ensure appropriate treatment. This is one of the most important WHO targets related to cardiovascular diseases. In this work we present a framework that is able to detect cardiovascular abnormalities with an application of specially prepared Android application that is capable of taking patient's input data. Such an interface allows for bio-parameters (e.g. sex, weight, etc.) input by the user. Furthermore, in this study we describe an artificial neural network model that is trained on the data collected by the wearable device that was also connected with the application with a specially prepared API.

Moreover, this paper highlights the possibility of utilization of a smartwatch with blood-pressure capabilities to deliver real-time measurements, which are added to input feature vector. Presented results show that the proposed scheme is capable of performing real-time data analysis. Achieved accuracy values are promising and allow for further examination of the application of off the shelf device in the detection of cardiovascular diseases.

Keywords: Signal processing · Artificial neural networks · Bio–signal analysis · Cardiovascular disease · Deep learning · Smartwatch

1 Introduction

Data provided by the World Health Organization (WHO) [28] cardiovascular diseases are the main cause of death worldwide. It is estimated they result in about 19.9 million deaths each year. To ensure appropriate treatment that can prevent premature deaths it is crucial to diagnose and predict the abnormal heart functions. The described framework allows for a real-time data monitoring with a simple of the shelf device that is connected with a mobile application. The proposed scheme can be a step forward in rapid disorder identification.

In recent years smartwatches have become one of the most popular sport assistant devices on the market [23]. Information provided by this type of devices such as user's blood pressure, heart rate, amount of burned calories, etc. can

© Springer Nature Switzerland AG 2021
K. Saeed and J. Dvorský (Eds.): CISIM 2021, LNCS 12883, pp. 343–353, 2021.
https://doi.org/10.1007/978-3-030-84340-3_28

be extremely useful in training assessment. Moreover, delivered data is a great source for various bio-analyses and can also be used for health monitoring. Apart from a simple approach that is based on comparing measurements to established norms, the area of machine learning could draw everyone's attention.

Literature review shows that ECG measurements have a very wide range of applications beside heart disorders determination [7,9,14]. One of the most popular utilization of the ECG recording is emotion and emotional states classification [9,24]. Nevertheless, in 2018 Liu et al. in [20] described a scheme for ECG monitoring in the form of a wearable device with an additional use of accelerometer. Such a device was used for activity recognition. Authors report that the described framework is able to achieve the overall accuracy of 96.92% and can further be used to monitor user's activities.

Further studies showed that heart conditions can also be classified with heart rate measurements [3,6,22]. Radha it et al. showed that heart rate variability allows for the determination of sleep stages with a decent accuracy of about 80% [22]. Different approach was described by Lin and Yang [19] where authors describe a scheme for heartbeat classification based on heart rate values. Authors were able to achieve accuracy as high as 75% and their heart rate values were calculated from ECG measurements. Another approach for heartbeat classification was described by Carrara et al. where authors used a set linear classifiers [10]. Their approach was able to achieve a positive predictive value of 99%.

As mentioned earlier as described by Liu et al. wearable devices can be used for bio–signal recording [20]. This is why in this study we took an advantage of such a scenario and decided to use an off the shelf device that is capable of measuring several body signals. The wrist–band was able to measure blood pressure, heart rate and blood oxygen level. Furthermore, we focus on feed–forward artificial neural networks (ANNs) which showed to be a structure that can be successfully used for signal processing. They consist of layers of parallel connected mathematical neurons [18], where a single neuron (as well as a whole network structure) is an object loosely patterned after biological structure. It receives an input vector and transforms it into an output values with a defined activation function. Typically this is performed by calculating weighted sum of all input values with corresponding weights. These weights are crucial components of properly functioning ANN structure. Furthermore, the process of learning (e.g. by using back–propagation algorithm [13]) is defined by adjusting all weights' values, so that they work properly for a given task. The number of layers, however, depends on a type of problem to be solved by the model. Aside from the "zero" layer, that is not responsible for any action other than collecting input parameters, single-layered networks are capable of solving only linearly separable problems. Multilayered structures, on the other hand, can be used in more complex, non-linearly separable tasks.

Artificial neural networks are commonly used in a wide range of medical applications [5]. Some of the problems that could be solved by these types of systems may include patient's health condition assessment, through analysis of symptoms [2] or disease detection based on image processing [29]. As already mentioned, this study focuses on a proposition of a feed–forward neural network that is used for medical data classification. More specifically, the purpose of a designed model is to estimate presence of a cardiovascular disease based on user's biological data as shown in Table 1). To implement, train and test proposed neural network scheme, a Python language with Keras API has been used [11]. The user's input information is provided via dedicated authorial Android application. The data was collected with an of the shelf wrist band connected with the application and analyzed with pre–trained ANN model that was previously exported to the mobile device. Furthermore, additional data was collected with various types of GUI forms. Such a setup allowed for a collection of a real–time measurements of systolic and diastolic blood pressure what resulted in the analysis that is based not only on user's input, acquired from previous medical examinations, but also from current, "freshly–measured" parameters.

2   Materials and Methods

2.1   Dataset

To create a properly working model, a sufficient dataset needs to be provided [4]. More specifically, in the process of supervised learning, adequate number of learning examples is required to be processed by the system where network's output error is verified after each epoch. This can be achieved with a validation set. When learning process is complete, the accuracy of the system is evaluated on a testing set. Measurements in that test were not seen by the network weight adjustment.

To be able to prepare a reliable and useful database based only on collected measurements, thousands of patients with every single combination of symptoms needed to be examined. Only such a scenario would provide sufficient dataset size. Undoubtedly, this process is extremely time–consuming and takes weeks or even years to collect. For this reason, many online services (e.g. [12]) provide publicly accessible datasets allowing for the various types of analyzes.

Taking that into consideration, in this study network training was performed on the "Cardiovascular Disease dataset" publicly available from Kaggle service [27]. This data base is a collection of 70000 records that were obtained during medical examination. What needs to be pointed out, is that input vector, defined by selected dataset, consists of biological parameters that are either known to most of patients (e.g. weight, height, alcohol intake) or are easily measurable with a wearable device that works with a created Android application. The described approach allowed us to design an ANN model that is able to classify data for a wide range of application users, that do not posses complex measurement instruments nor have previous medical history. Table 1 shows parameters that are stored in the database and each entry (besides examination result) is assigned one of three groups of features - objective, examination or subjective. Furthermore, each parameter can be assigned with a range of possible values and cholesterol, and glucose level can be described with only 3 possible values (normal, above normal and well above normal).

With input and output parameters defined, the dataset was split into learning, validation and testing set. In order to achieve best classification performance, every subset consists of respectively 54000, 6000 and 10000 records.

Table 1. Database parameter description.

Parameter	Group	Value type
Age	Objective	Integer [days]
Height	Objective	Integer [cm]
Weight	Objective	Float [kg]
Gender	Objective	Binary [Male/Female]
Systolic blood pressure	Examination	Integer [mmHg]
Diastolic blood pressure	Examination	Integer [mmHg]
Cholesterol	Examination	Multiclass
Glucose	Examination	Multiclass
Smoking	Subjective	Binary [Yes/No]
Alcohol intake	Subjective	Binary [Yes/No]
Physical activity	Subjective	Binary [Yes/No]
Presence of cardiovascular disease	Result	Binary [Yes/No]

2.2 Data Collection

As already mentioned, in this study a framework for real–time patient data is analyzed with deep neural network scheme. Presented model requires a user's input data that will be then passed to the ANN. Unfortunately, here we were unable to measure all of the required parameters (see Table 1). Our application allows a user to provide all objective and subjective data through user's profile mechanism created in the system. Moreover, it is compulsory to enter information about cholesterol and glucose level as they can not be measured with a wearable device. As mentioned earlier, these parameters stem from more advanced medical examinations and there are only three possible broad term values that determine them, so the user is able to easily define these features.

On the other hand, values of systolic and diastolic blood pressure are obtained from a wristband cooperating with a created software via API with Bluetooth Low Energy protocol [15]. A measurement is triggered by a user and lasts for 40 s. When a measurement is completed, the values are saved and all partial blood pressure values are displayed for the user in a form of a live–graph, which presents trajectory of the currently performed measurement.

2.3 Deep Learning Classification

The next stage of the described framework is classification of the incoming measurement. The described machine learning scheme performs classification always when the final result of both systolic and diastolic blood pressured is determined. It means, that every time the user triggers blood pressure measurement, he or she receives a result that consists not only with a desired blood pressure values, but also prediction of a likelihood of having a cardiovascular disease.

To be able to make real–time predictions, a previously trained ANN had to be transferred to the mobile device and therefore the model should be easy to integrate. For that reason it was created and trained using Keras API and later exported to Tensorflow Lite model [1]. This procedure allowed for the utilization of the model nside created Android application.

Structure of the Model

As described in Sect. 1 neural networks are commonly used in various classification tasks based on correctly labeled set of input features which describe objects. Model created in this study is dedicated to detect presence of a cardiovascular disease based on patients bio–signals. These parameters automatically define input size of the system to be 11 neurons and a single output that makes the classification a binary decision problem. This is due the fact that a goal of this study is to assign each patient only one of the two classes (no disease/disease).

To choose an appropriate topology of ANN, various selection tactics might be used. Apart from very sophisticated methods like pruning algorithms or the use heuristic, a trial and error approach is also a very popular technique applied to network parameters estimation [25]. It was proven that only one hidden layer is able to provide universal approximation but introduction of additional hidden layers are often used to boost model performance, especially when a number of neurons in a single-layered network could be large [30]. Taking this into consideration, in our setup several ANNs with different number of layers and nodes have been tested in order to achieve an optimal design.

Empirical studies of possible network inner structures showed that a model build of 3 hidden layers provides best performance for a described problem. For further experiments we continued to use the above mentioned structure. Moreover, each layer is built from respectively 9, 6 and 3 neurons, what is depicted in Fig. 1. The exit layer activation function is defined by the nature of the classification problem. Intuitively it shows that a simple Heaviside step function could be used, where value "1" defines presence of a disease and "0" its absence. The problem of this choice is that the approach does not provide any information about a level of affiliation of a given feature to a particular group. More precisely, network is able to access single patient as diseased with probability no other than 1.0 or 0.0. To grant a model ability to detect diseases with certain "likelihood" of its presence, a sigmoidal function was used. That way the output layer values are able to range between 0.0 and 1.0 which shows a probability of having a cardiovascular disease.

Moreover, each neuron in hidden layers needs to be defined with its own activation method. In order to achieve good performance, a Rectified Linear Unit (ReLU) function was assigned to every element in the network [21].

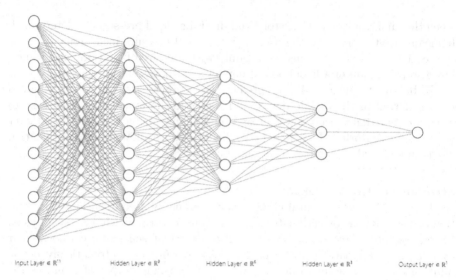

Fig. 1. Structure of the proposed neural network.

Training Process

Another crucial step in any classification framework is a correctly performed training of the created model. It can be easily acclaimed the most optimal structure will not perform well when training won't be able to provide correct generalization of the problem. For this reason the dataset of 70000 records was split into training, validation and testing sets. Since supervised learning process is based on back–propagation algorithm, the loss function needs to be determined. In described classification case, a binary cross–entropy method was used as a cost indicator. Moreover, the whole process was optimized using Adam optimizer [17].

Duration of the learning phase was 4000 epochs, where each epoch defines situation when all of training examples were passed to the network creating batches from 64 samples [8]. What it means, is that after passing 64 records, weights of the network were adjusted based on the value of accumulated weight correction.

3   Results

In this section we present the results obtained by the proposed scheme. The accuracy of a constructed model was defined as a quality indicator of training and was calculated on a validation set. As shown in Fig. 2, the selected performance rate, calculated after each epoch, converges at approximately 73%. One might say that such a rate might not be satisfactory, since only around 3 from 4 examples are classified correctly. The reason for that however stems from ambiguity of patient's symptoms meaning i.e. identical symptoms do not guarantee the same output every time. To give an intuitive example, not everyone that smokes cigarettes and has diabetes, has got medical heart problems, even though these factors contribute to the coronary heart disease presence and are noticed in a majority of afflicted patients [16]. Hence, the task of medical classification is an extremely difficult problem and its accuracy depends on the number of considered input symptoms, which often derive from sophisticated measurement techniques. Since the purpose of the described framework is to detect cardiovascular diseases based on parameters that are known to the user or are easily measurable (like: weight, blood pressure, etc.), it was concluded that final epoch accuracy of 73% is sufficient. It was also established that for our problem it is not connected to any training or network structural faults.

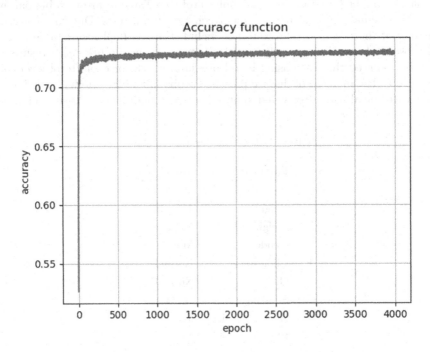

Fig. 2. Classification accuracy calculated after each epoch.

The final step of network's accuracy evaluation was a verification of its behaviour on a testing set. A value of the described quality indicator was evaluated and its level was recorded to be 72.57%. The result in this approach is similar to the one calculated on a validation set and for this reason, it was concluded that the model works properly and is ready to be used within an authorial Android application.

To test network's ability of detecting features that contribute to disease presence we performed 3 tests. More precisely, the model's reaction to increasing values of blood pressure, weight and cholesterol level was assessed. It needs to be highlighted that at each measurement only one of the parameters was manipulated, so its influence could be assessed. The controlled change of input features was achieved by user profile manipulation (in the case of weight and cholesterol examination) or by enhancement of blood pressure through physical exercises. Moreover, it is almost impossible to receive the same result of blood pressure in all measurements. Nevertheless, in examinations where this parameter should be constant, only records where blood pressure values didn't vary significantly were analyzed.

To mimic a testing environment, a test user was created inside the application. The information collected for that user are presented in Table 2. Information in the table does not include measurements of blood pressure that was obtained with a wearable device. Furthermore, since only blood pressure (see Table 3), weight (see Table 4) and cholesterol (see Table 5) are variable parameters, the remaining features were kept constant in all tests. Due to a constant manner of the features, they were not included in the final result tables, same as those that are not currently used for testing. From the presented results, it can be observed that increasing blood pressure, weight or cholesterol level contributes to the increase of disease presence probability. This model behaviour is similar to the already discovered knowledge that a high blood pressure, elevated

Table 2. Test user basal parameters.

Parameter	Value
Age	22 [years]
Height	175 [cm]
Weight	75 [kg]
Gender	Male
Cholesterol	Normal
Glucose	Normal
Smoking	No
Alcohol intake	Yes
Physical activity	Yes

Table 3. Network's output for increasing blood pressure values.

No.	Sys BP [mmHg]	Dia BP [mmHg]	Disease probability
1	127	74	0.0751
2	130	77	0.0927
3	132	78	0.1073
4	135	73	0.1330
5	138	77	0.1637

Table 4. Network's output for increasing user's weight values.

No.	Sys BP [mmHg]	Dia BP [mmHg]	Weight [kg]	Disease probability
1	124	77	75	0.0739
2	125	78	85	0.0832
3	124	76	95	0.1004
4	125	75	105	0.1390
5	125	77	115	0.1772

Table 5. Network's output for increasing cholesterol level values.

No.	Sys BP [mmHg]	Dia BP [mmHg]	Cholesterol	Disease probability
1	124	77	Normal	0.0739
2	125	71	Above normal	0.1449
3	124	76	High above normal	0.2801

levels of cholesterol as well as obesity are risk factors for many types of heart diseases [26]. That information allow to draw a conclusion that the proposed framework and implemented ANN works correctly and a created model reacts properly accordingly to established medical knowledge.

4 Conclusions and Further Work

The main objective of this study was to create a cardiovascular disease detection framework that employs deep learning techniques. As described in Sect. 2.3 model was created and trained using Keras API and to provide user input an Android application with wearable device communication API was designed.

The deep learning model consisted of 3 hidden layers and was trained using backpropagation algorithm with Adam optimization. As described in Sect. 2.3, empirical tests showed that the training process with 4000 epochs is sufficient to maintain the training accuracy around 73%. This accuracy level was confirmed with evaluation using testing set.

We can conclude that the model accuracy of around 73% is sufficient to build a bio–signal analysis framework. Furthermore, another conclusion that can be drawn here is that early misclassifications stem from ambiguity of patients' symptoms and real–time measurements are providing good information for further classification. Taking into consideration all the above conclusions, application with a trained network was tested to verify whether it reacts appropriately according to common medical knowledge [26]. The influence of three variable parameters (blood pressure, weight and cholesterol) whose excessive values contribute to heart diseases occurrence, have been tested. Results from these experiments clearly show that the model returns higher chance of disease presence when values the parameters rise. This observation allows us to draw a final conclusion that the proposed mobile framework works properly and can be used for the analysis of bio-signal retrieved from a wearable of the shelf device. It can also be noted that the system behaviour is comparable with accepted medical research.

Results presented in this paper are promising and allow us to plan further research on cheap wearable device usefulness in a prediction of cardiovascular diseases. In the future, it is planned to collect a reasonable size proprietary database of signals recorded with wearable devices. Such a database should help to achieve higher accuracies. Furthermore, as mentioned in Sect. 1 heart rate variability can be used not only for the estimation of cardiovascular disease risk, but also for the determination of emotional condition of a patient. Additionally, it is planned to research a possibility of certain cardiac conditions prediction.

References

1. Abadi, M., et al.: TensorFlow: large-scale machine learning on heterogeneous systems (2015). https://www.tensorflow.org/
2. AbuSharekh, E.K., Abu-Naser, S.S., et al.: Diagnosis of hepatitis virus using artificial neural network. Int. J. Acad. Pedagog. Res. 2(11), 1–7 (2018)
3. Acharya, R., et al.: Classification of cardiac abnormalities using heart rate signals. Med. Biol. Eng. Comput. 42(3), 288–293 (2004)
4. Ajiboye, A., Abdullah-Arshah, R., Hongwu, Q.: Evaluating the effect of dataset size on predictive model using supervised learning technique. Int. J. Softw. Eng. Comput. Sci. 1, 75–84 (2015)
5. Al-Shayea, Q.K.: Artificial neural networks in medical diagnosis. Int. J. Comput. Sci. Issues 8(2), 150–154 (2011)
6. Aziz, W., Rafique, M., Ahmad, I., Arif, M., Habib, N., Nadeem, M.: Classification of heart rate signals of healthy and pathological subjects using threshold based symbolic entropy. Acta Biologica Hungarica 65(3), 252–264 (2014)
7. Brás, S., Ferreira, J., Soares, S., Pinho, A.: Biometric and emotion identification: an ECG compression based method. Front. Psychol. 9, 467 (2018)
8. Brownlee, J.: What is the difference between a batch and an epoch in a neural network? Deep Learning; Machine Learning Mastery: Vermont. VIC, Australia (2018)
9. Bulagang, A., Weng, N., Mountstephens, J., Teo, J.: A review of recent approaches for emotion classification using electrocardiography and electrodermography signals. Inform. Med. Unlocked 20, 100363 (2020)
10. Carrara, M., et al.: Classification of cardiac rhythm using heart rate dynamical measures: validation in MIT-BIH databases. J. Electrocardiol. 48(6), 943–946 (2015)
11. Chollet, F.: Keras (2015). https://github.com/fchollet/keras
12. Dua, D., Graff, C.: UCI machine learning repository (2017). http://archive.ics.uci.edu/ml
13. Hameed, A.A., Karlik, B., Salman, M.S.: Back-propagation algorithm with variable adaptive momentum. Knowl.-Based Syst. 114, 79–87 (2016)
14. Hatzinakos, D., Agrafioti, F., Anderson, A.K.: ECG pattern analysis for emotion detection. IEEE Trans. Affect. Comput. 3(1), 102–115 (2012)

15. Heydon, R., Hunn, N.: Bluetooth low energy. CSR Presentation, Bluetooth SIG (2012). https://www.bluetooth.org/DocMan/handlers/DownloadDoc.ashx
16. Khot, U.N., et al.: Prevalence of conventional risk factors in patients with coronary heart disease. Jama **290**(7), 898–904 (2003)
17. Kingma, D.P., Ba, J.: Adam: a method for stochastic optimization. arXiv preprint arXiv:1412.6980 (2014)
18. Krogh, A.: What are artificial neural networks? Nat. Biotechnol. **26**(2), 195–197 (2008)
19. Lin, C.C., Yang, C.M.: Heartbeat classification using normalized RR intervals and morphological features. Math. Probl. Eng. **2014**, 712474 (2014)
20. Liu, J., Chen, J., Jiang, H., Jia, W., Lin, Q., Wang, Z.: Activity recognition in wearable ECG monitoring aided by accelerometer data. In: 2018 IEEE International Symposium on Circuits and Systems (ISCAS), pp. 1–4 (2018)
21. Nwankpa, C., Ijomah, W., Gachagan, A., Marshall, S.: Activation functions: comparison of trends in practice and research for deep learning. arXiv preprint arXiv:1811.03378 (2018)
22. Radha, M., et al.: Sleep stage classification from heart-rate variability using long short-term memory neural networks. Sci. Rep. **9**(1), 14149 (2019)
23. Rawassizadeh, R., Price, B.A., Petre, M.: Wearables: has the age of smartwatches finally arrived? Commun. ACM **58**(1), 45–47 (2014)
24. Selvaraj, J., Murugappan, M., Wan, K., Yaacob, S.: Classification of emotional states from electrocardiogram signals: a non-linear approach based on hurst. BioMed. Eng. OnLine **12**(1), 44 (2013)
25. Stathakis, D.: How many hidden layers and nodes? Int. J. Remote Sens. **30**(8), 2133–2147 (2009)
26. Thayer, J.F., Yamamoto, S.S., Brosschot, J.F.: The relationship of autonomic imbalance, heart rate variability and cardiovascular disease risk factors. Int. J. Cardiol. **141**(2), 122–131 (2010)
27. Ulianova, S.: Cardiovascular disease dataset (2019). https://www.kaggle.com/sulianova/cardiovascular-disease-dataset
28. WHO: World Health Organization (2019). https://www.who.int/health-topics/cardiovascular-diseases#tab=tab_1. Accessed 10 Feb 2021
29. Yıldırım, Ö., Pławiak, P., Tan, R.S., Acharya, U.R.: Arrhythmia detection using deep convolutional neural network with long duration ECG signals. Comput. Biol. Med. **102**, 411–420 (2018)
30. Zhang, G.P.: Avoiding pitfalls in neural network research. IEEE Trans. Syst. Man Cybern. Part C (Appl. Rev.) **37**(1), 3–16 (2006)

Modelling and Optimization

Big Data from Sensor Network via Internet of Things to Edge Deep Learning for Smart City

Jerzy Balicki[1]([⊠]), Honorata Balicka[2], and Piotr Dryja[3]

[1] Warsaw University of Technology, Warsaw, Poland
jerzy.balicki@pw.edu.pl
[2] Sopot University of Applied Sciences, Sopot, Poland
honorata.balicka@ssw-sopot.pl
[3] Gdańsk University of Technology, Gdańsk, Poland
piodryja@pg.gda.pl

Abstract. Data from a physical world is sampled by sensor networks, and then streams of Big Data are sent to cloud hosts to support decision making by deep learning software. In a smart city, some tasks may be assigned to smart devices of the Internet of Things for performing edge computing. Besides, a part of workload of calculations can be transferred to the cloud hosts. This paper proposes benchmarks for division tasks between an edge layer and a cloud layer for deep learning. Results of some numerical experiments are presented, too.

Keywords: Deep learning · Edge computing · Computing cloud · Smart city

1 Introduction

An approach based on Multi-objective Decision-Making can be developed for Deep Learning (DL), which has a significant impact on the design of smart city infrastructures. The selected task of DL can be performed by edge computing (EC) at the intelligent devices, but the other tasks can be calculated at the cloud hosts. This specific distributed computing system should be supported by using teleportation of virtual machines via Internet of Things (IoT) to optimize several criteria such as workload of the bottleneck computer, energy consumption or cost of hardware. In this way, a smart city will efficiently enable various applications and introduce many market innovations. However, the dramatic increase in wireless devices and network traffic puts many bounds. The smart city system should be scalable with no degradation in computing cloud performance. Therefore, the current systems deploy edge computing to support cloud computing [2].

Sensor Networks (SNs) produce Big data (BD) that is very useful to achieve high-value information related to decision support, business intelligence, classification, estimation or forecasting in a city. Data is usually transferred via Internet of Things to cloud hosts, where machine learning is applied. Citizens of large cities should live in the smart environment that can be effectively supported by smart clouds used the Internet of Things. In consequence, a huge number of almost unlimited data sources may provide Big Data about different features of human expectations and behaviors. Some of them are

© Springer Nature Switzerland AG 2021
K. Saeed and J. Dvorský (Eds.): CISIM 2021, LNCS 12883, pp. 357–368, 2021.
https://doi.org/10.1007/978-3-030-84340-3_29

related to city environments. In results, it is possible to understand some reasons of city behaviors, what is important to prevent some crisis situations. Besides, DL can be used to prepare an efficient annual expenditure budget to satisfy a community expectation. Moreover, some disadvantages of the city infrastructure can be identified and improved [13].

The main contribution of this paper is to present solutions how sensor networks, Internet of Things, Deep Learning and edge computing can improve processing of Big Data by the computing cloud of smart city. Therefore, a manuscript is organized, as follows. Related work is presented in Sect. 2, and then, a network of sensors and Internet of Things for a smart city ecosystem are characterized in Sect. 3. Next, Sect. 4 presents some studies under deep learning and edge computing. Moreover, multi-objective approach for an edge computing infrastructure design is analyzed in Sect. 5. Finally, some numerical results are considered in Sect. 6.

2 Related Work

The concept of a smart city can be recognized as representing a crucible for invention. Besides, the smart city is an area for developing global integration. It is also a pattern answer for addressing the existing global issues related to environmental, societal, governance and economic areas [16]. There is a reasonable expectation that developing information and communication technologies such as sensor networks, Internet of Things, Deep Learning, and edge computing can be applied for integration smart city facilities and innovations. Besides, cloud computing has been developed for many strategic e-government initiatives as some global government clouds.

The most populated cities in the world: Tokyo (37.5 million residents), Delhi (29.4), Shanghai (26.3), Sao Paulo (21.9), and Mexico City (21.7) have to cope with some open important issues such as growing population or traffic congestion [18]. Of course, many other, much smaller cities suffer from these problems, too. These factors cause that home and public spaces are used in the more efficient way in large cities. Even currently, there is a huge issue with a deficiency of city resources like water and energy. Therefore, an efficient management of resources is strongly required by automatic way. What is more, global warming and carbon emissions are some critical factors for future conditions in cities. That is why, the city infrastructure should be rapidly adjusted to the new ecosystems. For instance, tighter city budgets should be prepared and controlled in more sophisticated way [22].

To solve these open dilemmas, some projects have been implemented effectively. Masdar City is a highly planned and specialized research project that is based on the high technology that incorporates a living environment in this artificial city [10]. A smart vision of Masdar City is based on an efficient use of resources. A road infrastructure is designed to be very friendly to pedestrians and cyclists.

Citizens are supposed to be well informed and educated by the smart city environment. Some limited data sources, such as logs from email servers or web browsers can be supported by many intensive sources like cameras, microphones and social networks. Furthermore, the Internet of Things increases the data capacity about the behavior of the citizens from the real-life sensors. Specifically, this data is coming with an extended system such as SmartSantander that is a city-scale experimental research with several applications and services. Its goal is to enable horizontal and vertical federation with other experimental city facilities. Besides, it stimulates development of some mobile applications based on data from over 20,000 sensors [11].

Another an efficient approach is the United Kingdom's nationwide fault-reporting website called FixMyStreet, where residents can report various comments such as broken streetlights, car accidents, not cleared of snow streets, road potholes, or other inconvenience in the local area. System recognizes and redirects citizen complaints to the right page of the council website that accelerate an information transfer to responsible centers for getting things fixed [14].

SN and IoT provide data for monitoring a growth of CO_2 emissions and an increase of energy consumption [9]. It causes better protection of natural environment and more efficient use of it. Besides, citizens expect better urban planning. A quality of data depends on services provided by some public platforms and places of sensors' locations. BD services provided by some public cloud computing platforms can offer real-time insights about large-scale multimedia data for smart city systems. In addition, a query to BD database can be performed for multi-terabyte datasets in few seconds [4].

The Internet of Vehicles connects a wide variety of devices such as cars with built-in sensors [7]. The Internet of Medical Things uses heart monitoring implants, wearables and medical monitors, which are located on the body, in the home, or in community, clinic or hospital settings. Sensors such as activity trackers, bands, wristbands, sports watches, and smart garments are mainly associated with real-time location or telehealth services. Besides, IoT support biochip transponders on animals or field operation devices that assist fire-fighters [12]. These devices collect useful data and then autonomously flow data between other devices. Moreover, there are smart thermostat systems and washer with Wi-Fi for remote monitoring in homes and buildings. Radio-frequency identification (RFID) can support all objects and citizens in daily life. Furthermore, the tagging of things may be achieved through such additional technologies as barcodes, QR codes, or digital watermarking [25].

Lee, Silva, and Han presented an algorithmic implementation of deep learning for edge computing at smart city environment [16]. Supporting deep learning by IoT is a very difficult issue because of a limited computing resources. However, edge computing can support such hardware by transferring and processing bottlenecks. To allocate appropriate loads, they proposed transferring modules from the deep learning layers to edge nodes. A constructed algorithm determines the number of deep learning layers to be assigned to each edge considering computing capacity and bandwidth of each edge.

Some additional experiments with smart city that were carried out in Tsukuba Science City, Japan, permits to focus on some the most important elements of a smart city: education, research, environment, governance, and economy. Besides, several others aspects are considered: healthcare, employment opportunities, mobility, energy, buildings, infrastructures, and technology [5].

3 Network of Sensors and Internet of Things

Networks of Sensors and the Internet of Things are patterned on some technological trends that will reshape the Internet over the next years. Researchers analyze this technologies while contributing to making the future internet more human-centric. Increasingly these technological trends influence each other. For instance, they provide Big Data to the edge of the cloud, what can improve some criteria of city system by moving processing of data for the sources of it. These technologies will allow users to access, process and deliver information in more natural, efficient and less intrusive ways, providing enhanced and personalized experiences. Furthermore, advances in artificial intelligence are critical to turn information into knowledge that permits for embedding autonomy and intelligence into the connected devices in a smart city.

Internet of Things and applications alter the way users, services and applications interact with the city environment in a trusted way. The social networks, media and platforms transform the way residents produce, consume and interact with content, services and objects, within and across users' groups and become the way city societies operate for communication, exchange, business, creation and knowledge acquisition. City services should be multilingual and inclusive. Advances in language technologies help eliminate language barriers. New technologies also help to provide a new quality in digital learning as smart, open, and personalized learning solutions that are tailored to each citizen's needs, competences and abilities.

Internet of Things consists of smart devices that are commonly used in daily life with using protocol IPv6. Technology G5 supports increasing the mobile communication rate up to 100 Gb/s. Things can be supported by quick access to the large databases. The 128-bit IPv6 addressing system distinguishes about 3×10^{38} devices for city services [19]. IPv6 is implemented for Low Power Wireless Personal Area Networks (6LoWPAN) with the 2.4 GHz frequency that can be applied even to the smallest devices. In results, some low-power devices with limited processing capabilities are able to participate in the IoT. Low-power radio communication need wireless web connectivity at lower data rates 250 kbps for devices such as home automation, entertainment applications, office and factory environments. They use wireless sensors networks or the cellular networks. Currently, these devices are used to separate purposes and part of them can be developed to the common goals related to the smart city.

Besides, the protocol Routing Over Low power and Lossy networks (ROLL or RPL) determines routes for the networks with low power consuming and minimization energy losses. Also, the nano Internet Protocol (NanoIP) implements the efficient versions of the wireless TCP/IP algorithms with minimal latency and the memory capacity for addressing. Security and privacy are supported by the protocol Datagram Transport Layer Security (DTLS) that inhibits message forgery for client/server communication. In results, spying and data restrictions in IoT are constrained, too. Because packets can be misplaced or reordered, the DTLS introduces the transport layer security procedures on datagram transport [14].

Important roles play low cost air-interfaces, and systematic reduction of costs and sizes for the electronic chipsets. Some smart embedded things (devices or sensors) have capabilities to communicate and interact with the environment and other smart objects. They are smart, because they can act intelligently with an autonomous behavior.

Smart things support an extended range of solutions based on cellular infrastructure and wireless sensor networks [27].

Figure 1 shows how the Internet of Things can support smart city applications. Data are gathered from sensors connected via IoT (Fig. 1). Big Data mining is required to use data by smart city applications. There are some levels of integration of sensors, data, machine learning and applications. In consequence, we can expect new models of healthcare, social protection, transport, energy delivery, recycling, water management, and monitoring [24]. In addition, education of citizens is the most crucial to achieve higher level of collective intelligence in a city. A well-educated society is able to adjust quicker to new challenges and it can make efficient decisions for some difficult problems [28].

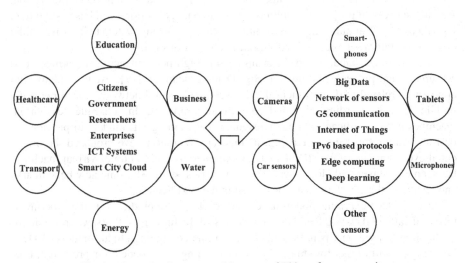

Fig. 1. Network of sensors and Internet of Things for a smart city.

Gathering data by a Network of Sensors in a city is very important. For example, the quick classifications of video can allow counteracting many extreme situations on city streets. This Deep Learning model can learn the Human Motion DataBase (HMDB) with 6,849 clips divided into 51 action categories, each containing a minimum of 101 clips [15]. The application based on the trained Long Short Term Memory Artificial Neural Network (LSTM) can detect smoking and drinking citizens in the forbidden areas, pedestrians falling on the floor, or the dangerous situations in the park with the accuracy over 95%.

4 Deep Learning and Edge Computing

Deep Learning requires scalable solutions for parallel training with large datasets. MapReduce is upfront designed to be the fault-tolerant and universal concepts related to Big Data [23]. One of the most commonly used implementation is the open-source alternatives offered by the Apache Hadoop project [20]. MapReduce is especially useful in processing massive historical data but may not be the optimal solution for real-time processing. Because thousands smart devices could provide huge amount of valuable data, which would need to be processed in a fast and efficient manner, an edge computing could be developed. For example, monitoring of cars by RFID tags is the smart way to detect traffic issues. An initial proceeding can be performed by edge computing closed to tags to shorten the latency of transmission. Results can support planning the road infrastructure, too. Other example is the monitoring of energy consumption in houses or calculation of people density in the means of public transportation.

An interesting example of such Big Data analytics was the project made by IBM. The goal was to introduce a traffic management system as a response to a fast growing population of the city. With the data collected from many sources including buses and roads, this system can reduce a traffic congestion by optimizing traffic lights synchronization. Another successful project in Dublin is related to data collection form bus system (e.g. GPS data), CCTV monitoring system, and weather monitoring system to improve public bus transportation services and reduce traffic congestions [8].

On the other hand, Deep Learning using high-performance computing cloud resources can process multimedia Big Data, efficiently [21]. Achievements and approaches related to development the deep artificial neural networks can support the mobile devices regarding edge and core cloud computing. In consequences, virtual machines need significant computer resources for training DL models to provide the best algorithms for decision making in smart city. Therefore, we proposed the differential evolution algorithm MDE+ that can optimize live migration of virtual machines between edge layer and cloud layer in a smart city system [3]. Some new benchmarks and results of the simulations are described in the next Section.

Several Deep Learning models have been developed for prediction in the experimental cloud called GUT-WUT (Gdańsk University of Technology – Warsaw University of Technology) based on OpenStack platform. In this computing cloud, models of Deep Learning perform tasks for smart city and e-learning. The models for prediction traffic congestion and web clip recognition are embedded into separate virtual machines. The other virtual machines support training of DL models related to waste management, energy supply and demand governance. Models use mostly LSTM networks or the Convolutional Neural Networks (CNNs).

For instance, the LSTM can classify some city objects from the web camera monitoring system by using the Cityscapes Dataset with 25,000 stereo videos about the street scenes from 50 cities [6]. There are classes such asroads, sidewalks, parking, and rail tracks. Besides, we can identify a person, riders, cars, trucks, buses, motorcycles, bicycles, trailers, traffic signs, and traffic lights. City constructions can be recognized like walls, fences, guardrails, bridges, and tunnels. For this DL model, the virtual machine on the smartphone is too weak for the practical using because an average accuracy on 10 times more powerful computer is approximately 62% after a training within 70 h of the CPU elapsed time. However, a smartphone has enough resources for using pre-trained Deep Learning model [26].

5 Benchmarks for Multi-objective Smart Cloud Design

An efficient computer infrastructure of a smart city can be designed by metaheuristics [4]. To verify the quality of some selected metaheuristics, we propose four benchmarks that contain numerical data on measurements in the experimental environment of GUT-WUT for Big Data collected by a sensor network. This BD is sent via Internet of Things to an edge or cloud computing systems to train Deep Learning Models. Some intelligent agents in virtual machines can be moved to the edge of the cloud and reduce the latency of the big data receiving. These benchmarks are available at the URL https://www.researchgate.net/project/Optimization-of-cloud-computing-resources-using-intelligent-agents-in-remote-teaching-2#. There are four instances for 90, 306, 855 and 1020 decision variables. Input data is provided, and the adequate Pareto optimal solutions are presented, too.

Decision makers can select criteria to define the goal of optimization. For this set of benchmarks, we recommend multi-criteria differential evolution algorithm with tabu mutation (MDE+). An introduction of tabu search algorithm as an additional mutation supports the diversity of the population. Tabu search algorithms have been applied for solving several optimization problems in scheduling, computer-aided design, quadratic assignment, training and designing of neural networks [4].

In the mutation with tabu search, there is a long-term memory. Within a long searching, there is an opportunity to count frequency measures of selected attributes that characterize visited solutions. Often performed movements should be outlawed to take a chance rarely performed alternatives after extensive calculations. Frequency measures of selected attributes are respected in a selection function of the next solution from the current neighborhood. An evolutionary mutation is substituted through the tabu search mutation for randomly chosen chromosome very rarely. A tabu search results an additional complexity $O(n^3)$.

MDE+ can find the Pareto-optimal solutions, and then we can select the compromise solution. In the *benchmark0306*, 24 Deep Learning based virtual machines migrate to 9 cloud nodes. Besides, 10 types of hosts can be chosen at each node. A decision making situation is characterized by two criteria [5]. The first criterion is the CPU workload of the bottleneck computer (denoted as $\hat{Z}_{max}$), and the second one is the communication workload of the bottleneck server $\left(\tilde{Z}_{max} \right)$.

Moreover, we can consider the other benchmark with 855 binary decision variables. In the *benchmark855*, 45 DL based virtual machines migrate to 15 nodes. Besides, 12 types of hosts can be selected at each node. In this case, a binary searched space contains $2.4 * 10^{257}$ items. The number of integer decision variables is 60, and the number of all solutions - $1.3 * 10^{69}$. A decision-maker can consider four criteria in this situation. In addition, the energy consumption E(x) [watt] for each infrastructure x can be analyzed. However, omitting the cost of computers seems unwise, so we are introducing a fourth criterion representing the cost of hosts in the infrastructure $\varXi$ [$].

In consequences, there are six evaluation cuts with two criteria: $\left(\hat{Z}_{max}, \tilde{Z}_{max}\right)$, $\left(\hat{Z}_{max}, \varXi\right)$, $\left(\hat{Z}_{max}, E\right)$, $(\tilde{Z}_{max}, \varXi)$, $\left(\tilde{Z}_{max}, E\right)$, and $(\varXi, E)$. Figure 2 shows the evaluations of Pareto-optimal solutions $\{P_1, P_2, ..., P_{200}\}$ obtained for four criteria. The Pareto set of 4D evaluations is represented in the two criteria space cut $\left(\hat{Z}_{max}, \tilde{Z}_{max}\right)$. Points $P_4 = (448; 25{,}952; 82{,}626; 19{,}640)$ and $P_5 = (587; 25{,}221; 78{,}010; 20{,}300)$ are non-dominated due to two criteria $\hat{Z}_{max}$, $\tilde{Z}_{max}$. Also, points P_1, P_2, and P_3 are efficient regarding two basic criteria. However, the 2D Pareto set with 5 elements is substituted by the 4D Pareto set with 200 elements if a decision maker considers four criteria. All solutions from the 2D Pareto set are included in the 4D Pareto set, too.

We can observe during many simulations that an extension of the criteria set causes a significant increase of the Pareto set because some dominated solutions due to two criteria $\hat{Z}_{max}$, $\tilde{Z}_{max}$ can change status to be non-dominated if four criteria $\hat{Z}_{max}$, $\tilde{Z}_{max}$, $\varXi$, E are introduced. Similarly, the Pareto set can be affected by the adding a new criterion. We can explain it by formulation the following lemma and theorem.

Lemma 1. A set of Pareto solutions $X_{\bar{N}}^{\leq}(2) \subseteq X$ for two criteria F_1 and F_2 in the multi-criteria optimisation problem $(X, F, \vdash_{\leq})$ is included in the set of Pareto solutions $X_{\bar{N}}^{\leq}(3) \subseteq X$ for three criteria F_1, F_2 and F_3, the same admissible solution set X, and a domination relation $\vdash_{\leq}$ in R^3.

Proof: Let $X_{\bar{N}}^{\leq}(2)$ be a set of Pareto solutions for two criteria F_1 and F_2. If we add the third criterion F_3, all solutions from $X_{\bar{N}}^{\leq}(2)$ are still Pareto-optimal regardless their values related to F_3. The other admissible solutions $x \in X, x \notin X_{\bar{N}}^{\leq}(2)$ cannot dominate solutions from the set $X_{\bar{N}}^{\leq}(2)$ because of their values related to F_1 and F_2. Besides, the admissible solutions $x \in X, x \notin X_{\bar{N}}^{\leq}(2)$ could exist that are become non-dominated regarding their values related to F_3. So, $X_{\bar{N}}^{\leq}(2) \subseteq X_{\bar{N}}^{\leq}(3)$, which ends the proof. □

Theorem 1. A set of Pareto solutions $X_P^{\leq}(N) \subseteq X$ for N ($N \geq 2$) criteria in the multi-criteria optimisation problem $(X, F, \vdash_{\leq})$ is included in the set of Pareto solutions $X_P^{\leq}(N + k) \subseteq X$ for $N + k$ criteria, $k = 1, 2, 3,...$, the same admissible solution set X, and a domination relation $\vdash_{\leq}$ in R^{N+k}.

Proof is based to the proof of Lemma 1.

Multi-criteria differential evolution algorithm MDE+ founded the compromise solution characterized by $\omega^{p=2} = (1{,}240; 25{,}952; 10{,}244; 11{,}630)$ with the smaller distance 0.49 to an ideal point $P^{inf} = (442; 25{,}221; 6{,}942; 6{,}750)$ than P_5 with the distance 1.32 in the four criteria space. The point $\omega^{p=2} = (1{,}240; 25{,}952; 10{,}244; 11{,}630)$ is dominated by $P_4 = (448; 25{,}952; 82{,}626; 19{,}640)$ due to basic criteria, but two additional criteria change the domination between these two points. The infrastructure characterized by $\omega^{p=2}$ saves energy and is cost-efficient, what cannot be said about the solution with the evaluation P_4. In consequences, above solutions are non-dominated between themselves.

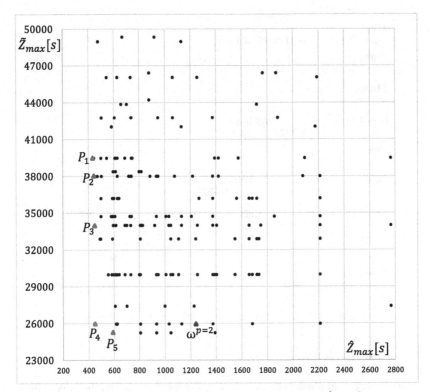

Fig. 2. Pareto front of the solution evaluations for criteria $\hat{Z}_{max}$, $\tilde{Z}_{max}$.

Figure 3 shows evaluations of Pareto teleportation of virtual machines for five meta-heuristics. We use *benchmark*306 to compare the crucial approaches. Results obtained by Multi-criteria Differential Evolution (MDE+) dominates the other solutions provided by Multi-criteria Particle Swarm Optimization (MPSO), Multi-criteria Genetic Programming (MGP), Multi-criteria Harmony Search (MHS), and Non-dominated Sorting Genetic Algorithm II (NSGA-II).

In a smart city, an optimization of an infrastructure can be done iteratively with the given period of time, i.e. 3 min. During this time virtual machines with DL models can migrate to the better adjusted hosts for task performing. Besides, the more efficient trade-off between cloud and edge computing can be achieved. These efforts can increase the decision-making aid by allowing it to make intelligent and effective decisions in real time [17].

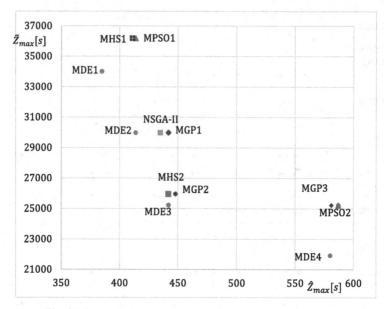

Fig. 3. Outcomes provided by five multi-criteria metaheuristics.

6 Concluding Remarks

Some intelligent virtual machines in the edge computing can significantly support the efficiency of the processing Big Data by using Deep Learning model and Internet of Things in a smart city. Multi-objective differential evolution with tabu mutation (MDE+) is a relatively new paradigm of artificial intelligence that can be used for finding Pareto-optimal infrastructures of edge and loud computing systems. The major contributions of this paper are:

- A development a concept of transmission Big Data from sensors by the Internet of Things to the edge of the cloud to minimize the delay of data transmission;
- A multi-criteria approach for live migration of virtual machines with Deep Learning models among edge and cloud computing devices and hosts;
- A presentation some benchmarks and outcomes obtained upon data sampled at the laboratory cloud GUT-WUT.

Our future works will focus on testing the other metaheuristics to find the compromise infrastructures for new sets of additional criteria. Besides, some new quantum-inspired algorithms will be considered for decision making in a smart city.

References

1. Agarwal, M., Al-gaashani, M.S.A., Khakimov, A., Muthanna, A., Kirichek, R.: Intelligent system architecture for smart city and its applications based edge computing. In: ICUMT, pp. 269–274 (2020)

2. Ayed, B., Halima, A.B., Alimi, A.M.: Big data analytics for logistics and transportation. In: 4th International Conference on Advanced Logistics and Transport, pp. 311–316 (2015)
3. Balicki, J., Korlub, W., Krawczyk, H., Paluszak, J.: Genetic programming for interaction efficient supporting in volunteer computing systems. Issues Chall. Artif. Intell. **559**, 129–139 (2014)
4. Balicki, J.: Tabu programming for multiobjective optimization problems. Int. J. Comput. Sci. Netw Secur. **7**, 44–50 (2007)
5. Bloom, J.L., Asano, S.: Tsukuba science city: Japan tries planned innovation. Science **212**(4500), 1239–1247 (1981)
6. Cordts, M., et al.: The cityscapes dataset for semantic urban scene understanding. In: Proceedings of the IEEE Conference on Computer Vision and Pattern Recognition (2016)
7. Cui, Q., et al.: Big data analytics and network calculus enabling intelligent management of autonomous vehicles in a smart city. IEEE Internet Things J. **6**(2), 2021–2034 (2019)
8. Galligan, S.D., O'Keeffe, J.: Big Data Helps City of Dublin Improves its Public Bus Transportation Network and Reduce Congestion. IBM Press, USA (2013)
9. Ghoneim, O.A., Doreswamy, Manjunatha, B.R.: Forecasting of ozone concentration in smart city using deep learning. In: International Conference on Advances in Computing, Communications and Informatics, Udupi, pp. 1320–1326 (2017)
10. Gutiérrez, V., et al.: SmartSantander: Internet of Things research and innovation through citizen participation. In: Galis, A., Gavras, A. (eds.) FIA 2013. LNCS, vol. 7858, pp. 173–186. Springer, Heidelberg (2013). https://doi.org/10.1007/978-3-642-38082-2_15
11. Hassan, S.-U., et al.: Leveraging deep learning and SNA approaches for smart city policing in the developing world. Int. J. Inf. Manag. **56**, 102045 (2021)
12. Khan, Z.A., Abbasi, A.G., Pervez, Z.: Blockchain and edge computing–based architecture for participatory smart city applications. Concurr. Comput. Pract. Exp. **32**(12), e5566 (2020)
13. Kuehne, H., Jhuang, H., Garrote, E., Poggio, T., Serre, T.: HMDB: a large video database for human motion recognition. In: ICCV (2011)
14. Lee, K., Silva, B.N., Han, K.: Algorithmic implementation of deep learning layer assignment in edge computing based smart city environment. Comput. Electr. Eng. **89**, 106909 (2021)
15. Lingani, G.M., Rawat, D.B., Garuba, M.: Smart traffic management system using deep learning for smart city applications. In: CCWC, pp. 101–106 (2019)
16. Liu, Q., et al.: Analysis of green spaces by utilizing big data to support smart cities and environment: a case study about the city center of Shanghai. ISPRS Int. J. Geo Inf. **9**(6), 360 (2020)
17. Liu, Y., Zhang, W., Pan, S., Li, Y., Chen, Y.: Analyzing the robotic behavior in a smart city with deep enforcement and imitation learning using IoRT. Comput. Commun. **150**, 346–356 (2020)
18. Mardani, S., Akbari, M.K., Sharifian, S.: Fraud detection in process aware information systems using MapReduce. In: International Proceedings on Information and Knowledge Technology, pp. 88–91 (2014)
19. Marz, N., Warren, J.: Big Data – Principles and Best Practices of Scalable Realtime Data Systems. Manning, Shelter Island (2014)
20. Sun, M., Zhang, J.: Research on the application of block chain big data platform in the construction of new smart city for low carbon emission and green environment. Comput. Commun. **149**, 332–342 (2020)
21. Vavilapalli, V.K.: Apache Hadoop yarn: yet another resource negotiator. In: International Proceedings on Cloud Computing, New York, USA, pp. 5:1–5:16 (2013)
22. Viegas, J.: Big data and transport. International Transport Forum (2013)
23. Wang, A., Zhang, A., Chan, E.H.W., Shi, W., Zhou, X., Liu, Z.: A review of human mobility research based on big data and its implication for smart city development. ISPRS Int. J. Geo Inf. **10**(1), 13 (2021)

24. Wu, H., Zhang, Z., Guan, C., Wolter, K., Xu, M.: Collaborate edge and cloud computing with distributed deep learning for smart city Internet of Things. IEEE Internet Things J. **7**(9), 8099–8110 (2020)
25. Zhang, H., Zhang, Z., Zhang, L., Yang, Y., Kang, Q., Sun, D.: Object tracking for a smart city using IoT and edge computing. Sensors **19**(9), 1987 (2019)
26. Zhao, Z., Zhang, Y.: Impact of smart city planning and construction on economic and social benefits based on big data analysis. Complexity **2020**, 8879132:1-8879132:11 (2020)

A Tale of Four Cities: Improving Bus and Waste Collection Schedules in Practical Smart City Applications

Jan Dünnweber[1](✉), Amitrajit Sarkar[2], Vimal Kumar Puthiyadath[3], and Omkar Barde[3]

[1] Ostbayerische Technische Hochschule Regensburg, Regensburg, Germany
jan.duennweber@othr.de
[2] Ara Institute of Canterbury, Christchurch, New Zealand
amit.sarkar@ara.ac.nz
[3] Birlasoft Limited®, Pune, India
{Vimal.Puthiyadath,Omkar.Barde}@birlasoft.com

Abstract. Computer-based Improvements of waste collection and public transport procedures are often a part of smart city initiatives. When we envision an ideal bus network, it will primarily connect the most crowded bus stops. Similarly, an ideal waste collection vehicle will arrive at every container exactly at the time when it is fully loaded. Beyond doubt, this will reduce traffic and support environmentally friendly intentions like waste separation, as it will make more containers manageable. A difficulty of putting that vision into practice is that vehicles cannot always be where they are needed. Knowing the best time for arriving at a position is not insufficient for finding the optimal route. Therefore, we compare four different approaches to optimized routing: Regensburg, Christchurch, Malaysia, and Bangalore. Our analysis shows that the best schedules result from adapting field-tested routes frequently based on sensor measurements and route optimizing computations.

Keywords: Smart city · Bus schedules · Waste management

1 Introduction

Even with the latest IoT technology the behavior of the population of megacities, practical implementations of on-demand public transport and smart waste collection still have difficulties in keeping up with the prognosticated improvements. A vehicle that drives obstinately from the most crowded bus stop (respectively, the most heavily filled container) to one with the fill-grade closest to that will obviously need more time in the majority of cases than a vehicle following a fixed plan, since the crowded bus stops and the heavily filled containers are probably positioned far apart from each other. Finding a smarter route leads us to the classic vehicle routing problem (VRP [1]), an instance of the Travelling Salesman Problem (TSP) with the added constraint that we need to return to the starting

© Springer Nature Switzerland AG 2021
K. Saeed and J. Dvorský (Eds.): CISIM 2021, LNCS 12883, pp. 369–380, 2021.
https://doi.org/10.1007/978-3-030-84340-3_30

point after visiting a fixed number of points, since the collection vehicle has a limited capacity. Thus, we do not need to find the minimum Hamiltonian circle through all the points but multiple circles forming clover leaf. However, finding the best route does not only require considering the distances between the single stops. Busses should leave out stops where no passengers are waiting and waste collectors should skip containers which are filled only to a certain level, i. e. we are dealing with an instance of a dynamic route planning problem, which is also the subject of more recent [2].

There are $\frac{n!}{2}$ different routes connecting n positions. For comparing all possible routes between only 10 stops, this means 3628800 routes must be analyzed. While a typical bus line might comprise 10 stops, a modern waste collection vehicle can be loaded with ≈400 containers of 120 l [3]. 400! is a 882-digit number. Skipping containers with little load means, the vehicle has to pickup an other one, where it usually does not drive to. Thus, solving the dynamic VRP requires to solve a new problem of that size, every time when the fill level measurements are updated. Nowadays, supercomputers can deal with such problem sizes [4]. However, this work presents four projects based on approximate solvers, which can run a standard PC or an on-board computer. Therefore, the presented work is relevant for automating the navigation of autonomous busses and robotic garbage trucks, like the one Volvo started testing in Brussels recently [5].

Section 2 of this paper motivates our work in the context of design science. Section 3 explains the ant colony optimization (ACO) and shows how Regensburg and Christchurch benefit from ACO and fill level sensing for collecting their waste containers. Section 4 introduces a different approach to minimizing routes be means of a greedy algorithm and shows two more practical implementations: The waste collection in Malaysia and the employee transport service of Bangalore. Section 5 discusses the lessons learned and points out some future perspectives.

2   Design Science Research and Artifact Development

Our literature analysis revealed that there is still a lack of design knowledge for creating vehicle routing problem related forecasting and data-driven decision making. Design science has been also described to assist in understanding, explaining, and improving the behavior of existing systems by creating innovative and unique artifacts and frameworks in a well-defined manner [6]. Such Artifacts include theories, frameworks, instruments, constructs, models, methods, and instantiations are considered as major outputs of the design process [7].

Many research projects were conducted in active cooperation between researchers and various stakeholders who will be impacted by the TSP and VRP. In this paper, we discuss smart city solutions similar to others which are also implemented currently in various countries. However, in our design-science inspired presentation, the creation process of these applications is not a "black box": We cooperate with expert professionals and developers, two research institutes, two city councils and one multinational company. We incorporated the experts' knowledge in our problem identification, definition of solution objectives, the derivation of the requirements, and the design of our artifacts.

We conducted both semi-structured individual interviews and group interviews. All meetings took between 30 and 60 min and all conversations were carefully recorded and transcribed. Our development process includes all the necessary steps that were defined for design science [8]: (1) problem identification and motivation, (2) definition of solution objectives, (3) design and development, (4) demonstration, (5) evaluation and (6) communication. It is necessary to mention that in our design processes, these steps are not linear but rather iterative.

3 Intelligent Routing by Means of the Ant Colony Optimization (ACO)

The *ant colony optimization* is an approximate solution for TSP instances (ACO [9]). This approach has also been proven suitable for dynamic VRP instances in a simulation, where the road network and the related traffic were taken into account [10]. ACO is a *swarm intelligence* procedure, i. e. not an individual (a simulated ant in the case of ACO) solves the problem but a group. For finding optimal routes, the simulation starts with letting the ants take random paths until they reach their destination. In higher iterations, the paths are no more randomly chosen but influenced by the most successful ants from preceding iterations. These are the ants whose pheromone trails did not evaporate until their followers reached them, since they were on the shortest paths.

Fig. 1. Container (left) and electronics (right)

3.1   Application 1: The Collection of Biological Waste in Regensburg

Our work in Regensburg focuses on improving the collection of biological waste [11]. While other approaches toward the computer-aided routing of waste collection vehicles rely only on fill level sensing [12] or only on ACO-based path computations [14], we combined both ideas.

Practical Implementation. In Regensburg, we recently started applying route optimization and fill level sensing to the collection of the containers for biological waste. Figure 1 (left) shows one such container and the protection casing on the back which houses our electronics. Actually, the right part of the picture with the detail view of the electronics shows an earlier prototype where the electrical parts were placed in the lid. The new box is smaller (making it more difficult to recognize single parts like our LoRa transmitter) and delivers correct data, even if the lid of the container is not properly closed.

Regensburg established its novel program for the collection of biological waste in 2018. The city and its surrounds were equipped with 700 new containers. While the number of possible thorough paths, connecting all containers is tremendous ($\frac{n!}{2}$ is a 1719-digit number), there are only $\binom{700}{2}$ ways to choose an interconnecting route between an unordered pair of containers. Numerically, there are $\frac{700!}{2!(700-2)!} = \frac{700!}{2\times(698)!} = \frac{699\times700}{2} = 244650$ possible interconnections. The Combinations may vary, but the single interconnections are static and can be stored in a database.

Preliminary Work. We set up a database, which holds for half of the 700 containers (*one-way*) a file with the distances connecting it to the remaining 699 candidates.

After accompanying the waste collectors and recording the GPS positions of the containers and the time needs for emptying them with a fitness tracking app on the smart phone, we requested the distances for all possible pairs from the *Google Maps* Web service by means of a Java program, which the students have developed to export the distance data into the popular TSPLIB-format [17]. With this representation, our data can be processed using Open-Source ACO-code and other TSP-solvers. Our routing software makes use of the Thomas Stützle Implementation [9] and we used the exact TSP-solver *Concorde* [18] as a reference. Experimentally, we found out, that running the approximation algorithm for 10 s is enough to obtain a solution for the 700 container problem which is close to the optimal solution.

Overfull and Underfull Containers. To integrate fill-level sensing with the ACO-based route computations, we started to cope with underfilled containers. While overfilled containers seem to be a more urgent problem, it is difficult (or almost impossible) to send a vehicle instantaneously, when an overfilled container is detected. Planning collection routes such that underfilled containers are skipped is much easier and saves time and the saved time is used to collect new containers. The recorded data about overfilled containers helps the Regensburg city council with positioning the new containers where they are needed. Thus, our waste management software, tackles both problems, underfilled containers directly (by leaving them our during the collection) and overfilled containers as well, by finding the best positions for new containers in the long run. Instead of resetting the route computations when a container is added, removed or repositioned, we keep the ACO software continuously running, since it is known that the swarm algorithm adapts to its input [19].

Fill Level Prediction. Regensburg currently has 10 containers readily equipped with sensors. The project is still ongoing and in 2021, there will be at least 20 more containers with sensors or even more, depending on the funding we receive. However, for most of the 700 containers, we do not have measurements but we use a simulation. To compute a trustworthy prediction for the fill levels of all containers, we compute for each container i, from a set of containers which were emptied on the same route, the fill level using the formula: $P(x_i) = q_i * \frac{c_i}{d_i}$. The value for q_i ranges between 0.1 (overfull), 0.2 (full), 0.3 (half-full) and 0.5 (empty) and was set accordingly to the average fill level of that container which we observed on the collection tours. Parameter d_i takes account for the fact that waste containers located near the city center are more likely found full and is 1.2 for a container withing a 2 km circle around the center; 1.1 withing 4 km and 0.9 for containers located more than 6 km away from the center. Parameter c_i is weighted accordingly to the number of waste containers next to it and 0.9 when there is none; 1.1 for up to 5 neighboring containers and 1.3 for 6 or more. With these values, the routes are shortened, such that they include only containers with a measured or predicted fill level above 0.3, which allows for time savings of approximately one hour per route.

3.2 Application 2: Smart Garbage Collection in Christchurch

Smart garbage collection is only a part of a larger smart city initiative in New Zealand [13] which comprises efficient street and traffic lighting, water and wastewater management and energy-saving as well. In reply to the disastrous earthquakes of 2010/11, Christchurch City Council (CCC) put aside funds for 'Sensing Cities' initiatives.

A Versatile Level Sensor. Christchurch is using smart sensors to ensure that rubbish bins are emptied at the right time. The LevelSense™ product was developed by Christchurch company PiP IoT to check rubbish levels. The sensors allow city council's contractors to recognise optimal waste collection times. Its key features are

- Tilt sensing
- GPS position and movement monitoring
- Tampering and orientation detection

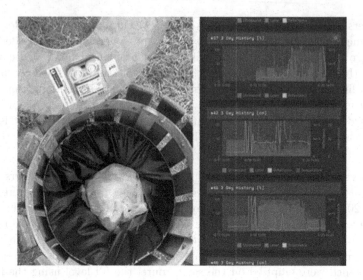

Fig. 2. LevelSense™ in container lid (left) and the Christchurch online monitoring app (right)

- Shock and vibration sensing
- Temperature measurement
- An expected battery life of 5 years
- Low power network/LPWAN connectivity
- Real time analytics
- Mobile/Web reporting
- SIGFOX class 0 certification.

Project Outcomes. Christchurch's rubbish collection contractors work constantly to empty the city's bins but when they arrived at a bin, before the introduction of LevelSense™, they did not know whether it was empty, full one or an overflowing mess. PiP IoT developed LevelSense™ primarily to avoid overflowing public rubbish bins, which where a frequent source of complaints from residents. Though, with the LevelSense™ devices, multiple other enhancements are anticipated.

- A reduction of CO_2 emissions and pollution: Fewer rubbish collection trucks on the road for less time means lower fuel consumption and lower greenhouse gas emissions. Fewer collection trucks on the road will also mean less noise pollution, air pollution, and less wear and tear on the road network.
- A reduction in operational costs: Bin level sensors and monitoring solutions have been known to reduce waste collection costs by up to 50% (fewer collections mean less money spent on driver hours, fuel and truck maintenance).
- Improved hygiene: overflowing rubbish is a breeding ground for bacteria, insects and pests because of accumulated rubbish. It's a public nuisance and unpleasant for residents and tourists.

- Identification of misuse of public rubbish bins: for example, sudden spikes in rubbish levels at night can indicate that household rubbish is being dumped illegally from residents or campers.

IoT Mobile Waste Monitoring App. Christchurch selected the local company PiP IoT to develop and test sensor and software technology with the objective of creating operational efficiencies and an enhanced streetscape.

PiP IoT has rolled out LevelSense™ devices to bins around rubbish trouble spots, including a city park and a retail area. Notifications are sent to contractors' phones and bin status across the city can be viewed in an online dashboard telling them how full each bin is (see Fig. 2, right). Rubbish levels are also being tracked, providing a graphic illustration of when the bins are used most.

Updating and Distributing Information. For finding the optimal route connecting the full (or almost full) containers, Christchurch pioneered in the use of ACO (Actually, the Christchurch implementation served as an exemplar for the Regensburg project described in Sect. 3.1).

$$p_k(i,j) = \frac{\tau(i,j)^\alpha \cdot \eta(i,j)^\beta}{\sum_{l \in N_k} \tau(i,l)^\alpha \cdot \eta(i,l)^\beta}$$

Fig. 3. The probability formula

The formula in Fig. 3 shows how an ant k (in m ants) at position i, when Nk is the set of k's unvisited positions, chooses position j to visit next in a probabilistic way, according to the classic ACO algorithm [9]. $\eta(i,j)$ represents the reciprocal of the distance between i and j, $\tau(i,j)$ represents the pheromone value. α and β are non-negative weights and $\tau(i,j)$ is updated according to the formula shown in Fig. 4, where T^k represents the set of all routes from the start to the goal position and L^k represents the collective distance from the start to the goal.

$$\tau(i,j) \leftarrow (1-\rho)\tau(i,j) + \rho \cdot \sum_{k=1}^{m} \Delta\tau^k(i,j)$$

$$\Delta\tau^k(i,j) = \begin{cases} \dfrac{1}{L^k} & \text{if } (i,j) \in T^k \\ 0 & \text{otherwise} \end{cases}$$

Fig. 4. Updating pheromone values

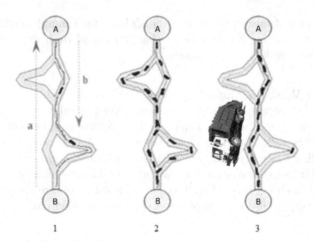

Fig. 5. Three iterations of ACO

Our implementation of the algorithm relies on indirect communication mediated by the environment, which is called *stigmergy* and is typical of social insects. Figure 5 shows how the information updates are used for routing the garbage truck: it will take path b from $A \to B$ already after the third iteration, since in the second iteration more simulated ants have returned from this path, leading to a stronger pheromone concentration than on the longer return path a from $B \to A$.

4 The Greedy Approach to the Travelling Salesman Problem

Regensburg's project partner Birlasoft has been working on the use of TSP solvers for vehicle routing problems in two former projects: One was focused on collecting waste and another one was focused on scheduling busses.

Both projects started from a brute-force method, i.e., a computer program that compares all possible routes. This method was improved using a greedy approach. Similarly to ACO, the main idea in the greedy algorithm is *local* optimization, i.e., the algorithm picks what seems to be the best thing to do at a particular time, instead of considering the global situation. In comparison with ACO, the greedy algorithm finds approximate solutions using a more coarsely granular procedure leading to an increase of inaccuracy but also to an increase in performance The greedy algorithm can be sketched as follows

1. Calculate transport times and distances between all stops, e.g. pickup and destination locations, as well as vehicle start locations.
2. Based on the information collected in step 1, generate routes and assign vehicles. The primary constraint is that the total travel time for the first

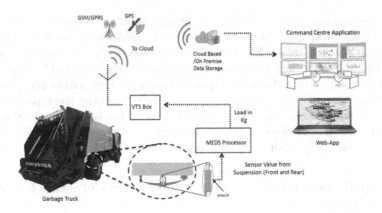

Fig. 6. Suspension Monitoring for Routing Malaysia's Trucks Optimally using the Greedy Approach

person to board the vehicle should not exceed 1.5 times the time taken for him to reach the destination had he chose his direct transport option.

3. For each node (stop), the eligible (satisfying time & capacity constraints) neighbors are evaluated to form paths and the ones which meet the criteria (serve maximum demand with shortest path) are selected. The acceptance criteria considers aspects like remaining capacity, direction deviation from the destination and total travel time.

4. Since this is a greedy approach, this algorithm is susceptible to choice of first route. We run it for a set of feasible origins and best possible solution (i. e. the one which requires the minimum number of resources) is chosen.

The first route is chosen by picking the farthest location from the office. We draw a circle with the office as the center and the farthest location as radius, thus, capturing all the stops.

The above description is about routing busses collecting employees. However, it can be fine tuned for routing waste collection vehicles as well. Interestingly, Birlasoft implemented this use case in Malaysia without container sensors. Instead of monitoring the containers, the collection vehicle load was monitored, allowing for a predictive estimation of the container fill grades.

4.1 Application 1: The Malaysia Garbage Initiative

Like New Zealand, Malaysia is another trend-setter concerning smart city activities and their garbage collection initiative is unique in multiple aspects [15]. Figure 6 shows how the components of this IoT infrastructure work together: the MEDS (*Mechanical Engineering Design Service*) is was developed by Birlasoft's engineering team to connect a microcontroller to the VTS (*Vehicle Tracking System*). This microcontroller converts the measured deflection on the leaf suspension to payload weight and uses the GSM network to transmit the data back to the backend server.

For monitoring the garbage collection, Malaysia's garbage trucks are equipped with leaf spring sensors measuring the vehicles' suspension levels. The measured data and the GPS positions of the respective trucks can be visualized in a Web App and they are also used as input of the command center application for coordinating the trucks dynamically. The other parameters processed by this application comprise static information, such as the truck parking locations, the bin locations and time estimates before a bin is full. Using these data, the Malaysian authorities can observe the amount of the loaded garbage at each location, which helps them to avoid vehicle overloading and truck breakdowns.

4.2   Application 2: Optimized Bus Routing for Collecting Employees in Bangalore

The costs of transporting employees is a concern for many companies [16]. Especially in India, where the number of employees is high in many companies these costs are huge: employee transport costs are the third highest cost after employee salaries and rentals. Therefore, minimizing these costs is of vital importance.

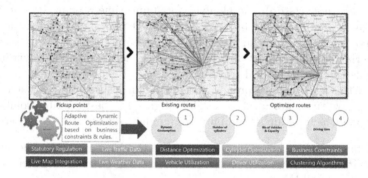

Fig. 7. Employee collection

As shown in Fig. 7, Birlasoft has implemented the greedy approach to finding minimal routes and also minimize the number of vehicles required to transport employees located at various locations in the metro city of Bangalore. The software makes sure that the total demand never exceeds the maximum capacity of the vehicles. In Bangalore, there are 39 employee busses with a capacity range between 6 and 30 passengers. There are 106 bus stops and 191 employees are using the bus transport.

5   Conclusion and Future Perspectives

In this work, we have analyzed and compared the vehicle routing procedures used in four practical smart city implementations. Our analysis has shown that the fundamental IoT approach, allowing people to order on-demand (using their phone or a signal button at the bus stop), can be improved significantly by route optimization algorithms. The analysis of the waste collection projects has also shown that the combination of processing fill level signals with route optimization leads to the best collection times.

However, there is also a trade-off between finding the best schedule or route and taking into account the specific requirements of a particular application. While ACO can lead to a shorter route than the greedy algorithm, applications like the employee collection must cope with time windows [20]. A better utilization of busses is no more beneficial, when it comes for the price of employees arriving late at work. A specific characteristic of both, the Bangalore and the Malaysia use case was that arbitrary deviations from the collections plans cannot be tolerated. This additional constraint is always given, when a route planning algorithm is applied to a vehicle with a limited load capacity or operating distance [21]. This observation from project that were all (at least partially) implemented in practice distinguishes our work from simulation experiments that are often aimed at improving route plans at all costs.

The analysis of the waste management in Christchurch has revealed more benefits of the networked sensors. At the same time, when the routes between the full bins were minimized, Christchurch experienced: (1) a reduction in operational cost; (2) a reduction of CO_2 emissions and pollution; (3) improved hygiene and (4) a reduction of misuse of public rubbish bins.

Our next plans contain an improvement of the reliability of the employed forecasts by the use of more sensors and more detailed data (including e. g. loop ways and one-way streets). Especially in the narrow lanes of the Regensburg city center, the shortest way is not always the fastest and the traveling times predicted by the Google Web service can be infeasible for a garbage truck. However, the time saving which we could prove for all projects let already rate all of them as a success. Our next stage of research is to go beyond the pilot stage and implement the optimisation at the entire city level, tune the implementation to address the needs of the specific cities and to extend our initiatives to multiple other cities around the globe.

References

1. Dantzig, G.B., Ramser, J.H.: The truck dispatching problem. Manag. Sci. **6**(1), 80–91 (1959)
2. Chen, J., Bai, R., Dong, H., Qu, R., Kendall, G.: A dynamic truck dispatching problem in marine container terminal. In: Symposium Series on Computational Intelligence (SSCI), pp. 1–8 (December 2016)
3. Hyundai Motor Company: Garabge Truck Press Pack. Online e-Brochure (2018). http://www.hyundai.com/gd/en/find-a-car/garbage-truck/press-pack.html
4. Burkhovetskiy, V.V., Steinberg, B.Y.: Parallelizing an exact algorithm for the traveling salesman problem. Procedia Comput. Sci. **119**(C), 97–102 (2017)
5. Volvo Group: Volvo pioneers autonomous, self-driving refuse truck in the urban environment. Press release (2017). http://www.volvogroup.com/en-en/news/2017/may/news-2561936.html

6. Simon, H.A.: The Sciences of the Artificial, 3rd edn. MIT Press, Cambridge (1996)
7. Hevner, A.R., March, S.T., Park, J., et al.: Design science in information systems research. MIS Q. **28**(1), 75–105 (2004)
8. Peffers, K., Rothenberger, M., Tuunanen, T., Vaezi, R.: Design science research evaluation. In: Peffers, K., Rothenberger, M., Kuechler, B. (eds.) DESRIST 2012. LNCS, vol. 7286, pp. 398–410. Springer, Heidelberg (2012). https://doi.org/10.1007/978-3-642-29863-9_29
9. Dorigo, M., Gambardella, L.M.: Ant colonies for the travelling salesman problem. Biosystems **43**, 73–81 (1997)
10. Karadimas, N.V., Doukas, N., Kolokathi, M., Defteraiou, G.: Routing optimization heuristics algorithms for urban solid waste transportation management. Trans. Comput. **7**(12), 2022–2031 (2008)
11. Burger, D., Sarkar, A., Kirsch, K., Dünnweber, J.: Combining fill-level sensing with route optimization for a more efficient waste collection. In: 18th European Conference on Digital Government (2018)
12. Lundin, A.C., Özkil, A.G., Schuldt-Jensen, J.: Smart cities: a case study in waste monitoring and management. In: 50th Hawaii International Conference on System Sciences (2017)
13. Taylor, S., Sharplin, N., Williams, D.F., et al.: PIP IoT - real-time data for better business outcomes. http://www.pipiot.com
14. Ismail, Z., Loh, S.L.: Ant colony optimization for solving solid waste collection scheduling problems. J. Math. Stat. **5**, 199–205 (2009)
15. Omar, M.F., et al.: Implementation of spatial smart waste management system in Malaysia. In: IOP Conference On Earth and Environmental Science, vol. 37 (2016)
16. Kochar, M.: Smart transportation: a key building block for a smart city. In: Forbes India (July 2018)
17. Reinelt, G.: TSPLIB - a t.s.p. library. Tech. rep. 250, Universität Augsburg, Institut für Mathematik, Augsburg (1990)
18. Applegate, D.: Concorde - a code for solving traveling salesman problems. http://www.math.princeton.edu/tsp/concorde.html
19. Angus, D., Hendtlass, T.: Dynamic ant colony optimisation. Appl. Intell. **23**, 33–38 (2005)
20. Kirci, P.: An optimization algorithm for a capacitated vehicle routing problem with time windows. Sādhanā **41**, 519–529 (2016)
21. Yu, L., Wei, Z., Wang, Z., Hu, Y., Wang, H.: Path optimization of AUV based on smooth-RRT algorithm. In: 2017 IEEE International Conference on Mechatronics and Automation (ICMA), pp. 1498–1502 (August 2017)

Fractional-Order Nonlinear System Identification Using MPC Technique

Wiktor Jakowluk[1] ⓘ and Sjoerd Boersma[2](✉)

[1] Bialystok University of Technology, Bialystok, Poland
w.jakowluk@pb.edu.pl
[2] Wageningen University, Wageningen, Holland
sjoerd.boersma@wur.nl

Abstract. Many real-world processes exhibit fractional-order dynamics and are described by the non-integer order differential equations. In this paper, we quantify the fitting of the Oustaloup approximation method to the fractional-order state-space system to be obtained in the specified narrow frequency range and order. A novel method of the plant model state estimation using the model predictive control (MPC) technique has been verified on the approximated fractional-order water tanks system. To improve the system tracking and reduce the experimental effort, the Kalman filter (KF) has been connected to the MPC structure. The main objective is to design a control system of the linearized fractional-order system with the tuning of its parameters concerning an additive white noise affecting the output of the system. The presented scheme has been verified using numerical examples, and the results of the prediction of the state are discussed.

Keywords: Fractional calculus · Model predictive control · Kalman filtering · Oustaloup approximation

1 Introduction

Considering a derivative of non-integer order, the fractional calculus offers a new modeling tool for accurate system identification, and controller tuning tasks [1, 2]. It has been reported that fractional-order models guarantee a more exact description of the system dynamics than models designated using ordinary differential equations [3, 4]. However, fractional calculus is a generalization of the ordinary differential equations by partial order differentiation [5]. Many papers have been published to show the accuracy of the fractional calculus applied to solving problems in various domains, such as: bioengineering [6], physics [7], chaos theory [8], control systems [9, 10], and fractional processes [11]. The fractional calculus has become a helpful tool in mechatronics and control engineering areas where the non-integer system representation has been used for more accurate process control [12]. It has been reported that fractional-order controllers exactness varies from the integer-order controllers, and in some applications, fractional PID controllers have become better compared to the classic PID's [13].

© Springer Nature Switzerland AG 2021
K. Saeed and J. Dvorský (Eds.): CISIM 2021, LNCS 12883, pp. 381–393, 2021.
https://doi.org/10.1007/978-3-030-84340-3_31

It has been verified that the model development absorbs about 75% of the costs related to real-life control processes [14]. Therefore, one of the trends in the system identification area is to sequentially improve the system fitting by more accurate estimates of the model parameters. Such problems can be solved using Model Predictive Control (MPC) method where the input signal obtained by the MPC algorithm is designed to provide the acceptable control performance [15, 16]. The MPC method enables to control of multivariable nonlinear processes and allows to impose constraints on inputs, states, and output signals. The model of the system and the acquired measurement data are used to predict a future plant output concerning a future input signal [17, 18]. The objective function operates on the estimated input and output signals and then is optimized concerning the future input signal sequence.

The MPC model parameter estimates depend on conditions under which the experiments are performed, including the proper input signal selection. The input signal design has substantial meaning in the task of the precise model parameter estimates. The main goal of the input design is to maximize the sensitivity of the state variable to the unknown parameters [19]. A great effort has been made to discover identification methods for robust control where a nominal model is estimated concerning the established limitations on the model uncertainty set [20]. However, such an approach cannot guarantee the precise model parameter estimates. This problem can be solved using the least-costly identification method for control purposes. In this method, the constraints are not imposed on the experiment cost (i.e. input energy, experiment duration) but the cost of the experiment is associated with the objective function [21]. Another approach for experimental cost minimization is the so-called 'plant-friendly' input design task [22, 23]. Then the goal of the identification experiment is to find a trade-off between minimal working point displacement, and the estimated model parameters accuracy. The methods for designing excitation signals in the economic, plant-friendly, and application-oriented frameworks, where the objective is to minimize the displacement from the normal operating conditions, are presented in [23, 24].

In this paper, we introduce the data-driven, and model-based scheme for the robust controller design to predict the water flow in the nonlinear tanks interacting system. The control diagram contains the linearized discrete-time model of the water tanks system with unknown parameters, the MPC optimizer, and the Kalman filter used for a model state estimation. In the paper, the non-integer order model of the gravitational water tanks system, from the interval $0.5 \leq \alpha < 1.0$, has been studied. The main objective of the experiment has been to estimate the fractional-order model states and compare them with the integer-order model state waveforms. The problems of the input design for integer and fractional-order models excitation have been considered in the following works [25, 26].

2 Fractional-Order Optimal Control Problem

The concept of the fractional calculus is a generalization of integral and differential operators to a non-integer operator $_aD_t^\alpha$. The continuous operator of the fractional-order α is given by:

$$
_aD_t^\alpha =
\begin{cases}
\frac{d^\alpha}{dt^\alpha} & \Re(\alpha) > 0 \\
1 & \Re(\alpha) = 0 \\
\int\limits_a^t (d\tau)^{-\alpha} & \Re(\alpha) < 0
\end{cases},
\tag{1}
$$

where: a, t - denote the integration limits, and α is the operator order. Presently many different forms of the fractional integrodifferential operator exists [1]. We consider one specific definition, which is then used to estimate a non-integer order system. The Grünwald - Letnikov definition is as follows:

$$
_aD_t^\alpha f(t) = \lim_{h \to 0} \frac{1}{h^\alpha} \sum_{j=0}^{k} (-1)^j \binom{\alpha}{j} f(t - jh),
\tag{2}
$$

where: $\omega_j^\alpha = (-1)^j \binom{\alpha}{j}$ denotes polynomial coefficients, which can be obtained recursively from:

$$
\omega_0^\alpha = 1, \omega_j^\alpha = \left(1 - \frac{\alpha + 1}{j}\right)\omega_{j-1}^\alpha, j = 1, 2, \ldots,
\tag{3}
$$

Using Eq. (3) the fractional-order derivative (2) can be written as:

$$
_aD_t^\alpha f(t) \approx \frac{1}{h^\alpha} \sum_{j=0}^{k} \omega_j^\alpha f(t - jh),
\tag{4}
$$

where $a = 0, t = kh$ is the step number and h is the step duration. The Laplace transform, with zero initial conditions, of derivative (4) where $\alpha \in R^+$ is given by [1]:

$$
L\{_0D_t^\alpha f(t)\} = s^\alpha F(s).
\tag{5}
$$

The non-integer order calculus is the special case of a traditional ordinary differential equations ODE approach. Linear-fractional order continuous-time SISO dynamic system is comensature-order if all powers of a derivative are integer multiples of the order q in such a way that $\alpha_k, \beta_k = kq, q \in R^+$, and can be written as [1, 2]:

$$
\sum_{k=0}^{n} a_k D_t^{\alpha_i} y(t) = \sum_{k=0}^{m} b_k D_t^{\beta_i} u(t),
\tag{6}
$$

where: a_k, b_k are model constant coefficients. The LTI system is of rational order if $q = r^{-1}$, and $q \in R^+$. Using the Laplace transform to formula (6), with zero initial conditions, the input-output description of the fractional-order model can be presented as the transfer function form:

$$G(s) = \frac{Y(s)}{U(s)} = \frac{b_m s^{\beta_m} + b_{m-1} s^{\beta_{m-1}} + \ldots + b_0 s^{\beta_0}}{a_n s^{\alpha_n} + a_{n-1} s^{\alpha_{n-1}} + \ldots + a_0 s^{\alpha_0}}. \tag{7}$$

The system with commensurate order q can be reformulated to obtain the pseudo-rational transfer function $H(\lambda)$ in the form:

$$H(\lambda) = \frac{\sum\limits_{k=0}^{m} b_k \lambda^k}{\sum\limits_{k=0}^{n} a_k \lambda^k}, \tag{8}$$

where: $\lambda = s^q$. The pseudo-rational version of the non-integer order linear time-invariant system can be easily expressed using state-space equations:

$$\begin{aligned} {}_0 D_t^\alpha x(t) &= Ax(t) + Bu(t), \\ y(t) &= Cx(t) + Du(t). \end{aligned} \tag{9}$$

The state-space representation enables multiple-input and multiple-output (MIMO) fractional-order system specification.

3 Fractional-Order Operator Approximation

The possibilities of estimating fractional-order models have been reported in [1]. The Oustaloup methods, which have a good fitting to non-integer zero-pole transfer function approximation are often used in practical implementations. The Oustaloup recursive approximation (ORA) method has been considered in this paper. Fixing a permissible frequency fitting range the problem of a fractional differentiator, and fractional integrator can be solved using the following formula:

$$s^\alpha \approx K \prod_{k=1}^{N} \frac{s + \omega_k'}{s + \omega_k}, \tag{10}$$

where: poles, zeros, and the gain of this filter is obtained from:

$$\omega_k' = \omega_b \cdot \omega_u^{(2k-1-\alpha)/N}, \tag{11}$$

$$\omega_k = \omega_b \cdot \omega_u^{(2k-1+\alpha)/N}, \tag{12}$$

$$K = \omega_h^\alpha, \tag{13}$$

$$\omega_u = \sqrt{\frac{\omega_h}{\omega_b}}. \tag{14}$$

where: N is the order of the approximation, and (ω_b, ω_h) is chosen pulsation interval. Considering the higher orders of the filter $2N + 1$ the obtained results of the approximation become more precise.

For the fractional-order operators, where $\alpha \geq 1$, the non-integer order component should be separated according to the following formula:

$$s^{\alpha} = s^n s^{\gamma}, \tag{15}$$

where: $n = \alpha - \gamma$ is the integer part of α, and s^{γ} can be estimated using the Oustaloup method. The transfer function obtained from the ORA method is then used to transform the external model into the integer-order internal state-space form. For a general n-th order transfer function received from the pole-zero formula is given by:

$$H(s) = \frac{Y(s)}{U(s)} = \frac{b_0 s^n + b_1 s^{n-1} + \ldots + b_{n-1} s + b_n}{s^n + a_1 s^{n-1} + \ldots + a_{n-1} s + a_n}, \tag{16}$$

where: a and b are the coefficients of the polynomials in descending powers of s, and $a_0 = 1$. Then, it is possible to solve the problem of the fractional-order system identification using the integer state-space formulation.

4   An Interacting Water Tanks Process

The nonlinear double-tanks water system is presented in Fig. 1. The plant model is defined by the dependence of the volumetric flow $Q_{in}(t)$ into the first tank to the outflow of water $Q_{out}(t)$ through the valve at the second tank. The balance of water flow in each tank can be expressed using the following equation:

$$A \frac{dh(t)}{dt} = Q_{in}(t) - Q_{out}(t), \tag{17}$$

where: A denotes the cross-sectional surface of the tank, and $h(t)$ indicates the height of the fluid level in the tank.

When the cross-sectional area of the tank outlet hole, assuming an ideal sharp-edged orifice, is given the outflow of water of each tank can be determined using Torricelli's principle as follows:

$$Q_{out}(t) = a \cdot \sqrt{2gh(t)}. \tag{18}$$

where: a is the cross-sectional surface of the hole, and g is the gravitational constant value (9.8 m/s^2).

Substituting Eq. (18) to (17), and assuming that the output of the first tank is connected to the input to the second one, it is possible to formulate the following nonlinear differential equations:

$$\begin{cases} A_1 \frac{dh_1(t)}{dt} = -a_1 \cdot \sqrt{2gh_1(t)} + Q_{in}(t) & h_1(0) = h_{10}, \\ A_2 \frac{dh_2(t)}{dt} = a_1 \cdot \sqrt{2gh_1(t)} - a_2 \cdot \sqrt{2gh_2(t)} & h_2(0) = h_{20}. \end{cases} \tag{19}$$

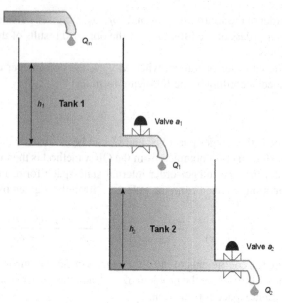

Fig. 1. The interacting water tanks process diagram

where: $n = 1, 2$ represents one of the system's tanks. The following substitutions have been made $Q_{in}(t) = u(t), x_1(t) = h_1(t), x_2(t) = h_2(t), y(t) = h_1(t)$ to receive classical form of the state-space equations:

$$\begin{cases} \dot{x}_1 = -\frac{a_1}{A_1} \cdot \sqrt{2gx_1} + \frac{1}{A_1}u & x_1(0) = h_{10}, \\ \dot{x}_2 = \frac{a_1}{A_2} \cdot \sqrt{2gx_1} - \frac{a_2}{A_2} \cdot \sqrt{2gx_2} & x_2(0) = h_{20}. \end{cases} \tag{20}$$

where: $x_1 = x_1(t, a_1), x_2 = x_2(t, a_1, a_2)$. The water levels in the tanks have the real working constraints:

$$h_{i, max} \geq x_i(t) \geq 0 \quad i = 1, 2. \tag{21}$$

The double-tank system parameters and the physical constraints are summarized in Table 1.

To control the water levels of the tanks (Fig. 1), the MPC method can be applied. In the case of the MPC application, the controlled system should be linear and discrete-time. Generally, the model of the discrete system can be written as:

$$\begin{aligned} x(t+1) &= A_d \hat{x}(t) + B_d u(t) + w(t), \\ y(t) &= C_d \hat{x}(t) + v(t). \end{aligned} \tag{22}$$

where: $\hat{x}(t) \in \Re^n$ is a predicted state vector, $u(t) \in \Re^n$ denotes an input signal, $y(t)$ signifies a measured output, whereas $v(t)$ and $w(t)$ represent zero-mean Gaussian process noise, and measurement noise, respectively. The nonlinear process (20) has been

Table 1. The physical constraints and the model parameters.

Parameter	Value	Unit	Description
$h_{1,\text{max}}$	4.00	m	Max. water level of tank 1
$h_{1,\text{min}} = h_{2,\text{min}}$	0.00	m	Min. water level of tanks 1, 2
$h_{2,\text{max}}$	2.00	m	Max. water level of tank 2
h_{10}	0.75	m	Initial condition of tank 1
h_{20}	0.50	m	Initial condition of tank 2
$a_1 = a_2$	0.05	m^2	Area of water outlet holes
A_1	1.50	m^2	Cross-section of tank 1
A_2	0.75	m^2	Cross-section of tank 2
u_0	0.05	m^3/s	Initial water inflow

linearized around the steady-state values x^0, u^0, and then discretized. The state-space matrices obtained using a first-order Taylor expansion are:

$$A_l = \begin{bmatrix} -\tau_1 & 0 \\ \tau_3 & -\tau_4 \end{bmatrix}, \quad B_l = \begin{bmatrix} \frac{1}{A_1} \\ 0 \end{bmatrix}, \quad C_l = \begin{bmatrix} 1 & 0 \end{bmatrix},$$

$$\tau_1 = \frac{a_1}{A_1} \sqrt{\frac{g}{2x_1^0}}, \quad \tau_3 = \frac{a_1}{A_2} \sqrt{\frac{g}{2x_1^0}}, \quad \tau_4 = \frac{a_2}{A_2} \sqrt{\frac{g}{2x_2^0}}. \tag{23}$$

The discretization using the zero-order hold on the input, and a 1 Hz sampling rate subject to (22), yields:

$$A_d = e^{A_l}, \quad B_d = \int_0^1 e^{A_l(1-t)} B_l \, dt, \quad C_d = C_l. \tag{24}$$

The matrices obtained using (24) are then implemented to MPC algorithm to predict the future system output.

5 The MPC Implementation for Water Level Control

To control the water level of the interacting water tanks system, the MPC controller has been used [26]. The MPC diagram containing the Kalman filter is shown in Fig. 2.

The discrete-time matrices of the linearized double tank model obtained for the integer-order derivative (i.e. $\alpha = 1$) with sample period 1 Hz, are as follows:

$$A_d = \begin{bmatrix} 0.918 & 0 \\ 0.147 & 0.812 \end{bmatrix}, \quad B_d = \begin{bmatrix} 0.639 \\ 0.052 \end{bmatrix}, \quad C_d = \begin{bmatrix} 1 & 0 \end{bmatrix}. \tag{25}$$

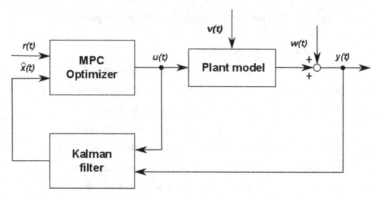

Fig. 2. The block diagram of the system (plant model) governed by (20) and the controller (MPC and Kalman filter).

To estimate the future output of the system from time t, knowledge of a system's state estimate $\hat{x}(t)$ is needed:

$$\hat{y}(t + k|t) = C_d A_d^k \hat{x}(t) + \sum_{i=0}^{k-1} A_d^{k-i-1} B_d u(t + i). \tag{26}$$

with $k \geq 0$. The state estimation $\hat{x}(t)$ is provided by the Kalman filter (see Fig. 2) by using the measurement $y(t)$ from the true system. The performance can be estimated by the following objective function:

$$J(t) = \sum_{i=0}^{N_y} \left\| \hat{y}(t + i|t) - r(t + i) \right\|_Q^2 + \sum_{i=0}^{N_u} \left\| \hat{u}(t + i) \right\|_R^2, \tag{27}$$

where:$\hat{y}(t + i|t)$ is the estimated output of the model (22), $r(t)$ is the reference for the water level in the first tank, $\hat{u}(t)$ is the input excitation signal. The Q and R are weighting matrices, N_y signifies the prediction region, and N_u is the control horizon. The MPC input sequence is found by minimizing the control performance index (27) subject to constraints using the sqp method, i.e.,:

$$\begin{aligned} \underset{u(t)}{\text{minimize}} \quad & J(t) \\ \text{subject to} \quad & \hat{y} \in Y \\ & \hat{u} \in U. \end{aligned} \tag{28}$$

where: Y and U signify the constraint sets of the outputs and inputs, respectively.

6   The MPC Results of the Interacting Water Tanks System

The Matlab/Simulink are used for the simulation results presented in this section. Simulink is a block diagram environment for model-based design. All simulation experiments have been performed using low-cost PC (Intel®, 2.40 GHz, 4 GB RAM) running Windows 10 and Matlab 9.3 (R2017b).

The results of the Oustaloup approximation of the linearized water tanks model (20) for orders from the interval $0.5 \leq \alpha < 1.0$, and arbitrary selected bandwidth $\omega = [10^{-1}, 10^1]$, are given by:

$$\alpha = 0.9, \ A_d = \begin{bmatrix} 0.85 & 0.13 & 0.20 & 0.30 & 0.45 \\ 0 & 0.76 & 0.33 & 0.49 & 0.72 \\ 0 & 0 & 0.51 & 0.43 & 0.63 \\ 0 & 0 & 0 & 0.19 & 0.23 \\ 0 & 0 & 0 & 0 & 0.02 \end{bmatrix}, \ B_d = \begin{bmatrix} 0.31 \\ 0.53 \\ 0.57 \\ 0.37 \\ 0.13 \end{bmatrix}, \tag{29}$$

$$C_d = \begin{bmatrix} 0.09 & 0.19 & 0.31 & 0.49 & 0.77 \end{bmatrix}, \ D_d = [0.08].$$

$$\alpha = 0.8, \ A_d = \begin{bmatrix} 0.86 & 0.12 & 0.18 & 0.26 & 0.36 \\ 0 & 0.74 & 0.28 & 0.40 & 0.54 \\ 0 & 0 & 0.49 & 0.36 & 0.48 \\ 0 & 0 & 0 & 0.17 & 0.18 \\ 0 & 0 & 0 & 0 & 0.01 \end{bmatrix}, \ B_d = \begin{bmatrix} 0.26 \\ 0.42 \\ 0.46 \\ 0.31 \\ 0.12 \end{bmatrix}, \tag{30}$$

$$C_d = \begin{bmatrix} 0.11 & 0.22 & 0.36 & 0.57 & 0.91 \end{bmatrix}, \ D_d = [0.10].$$

$$\alpha = 0.5, \ A_d = \begin{bmatrix} 0.87 & 0.08 & 0.11 & 0.14 & 0.15 \\ 0 & 0.71 & 0.160. & 0.19 & 0.20 \\ 0 & 0 & 0.44 & 0.18 & 0.18 \\ 0 & 0 & 0 & 0.13 & 0.08 \\ 0 & 0 & 0 & 0 & 0.01 \end{bmatrix}, \ B_d = \begin{bmatrix} 0.12 \\ 0.21 \\ 0.33 \\ 0.53 \\ 0.85 \end{bmatrix}, \tag{31}$$

$$C_d = \begin{bmatrix} 0.10 & 0.17 & 0.27 & 0.44 & 0.70 \end{bmatrix}, \ D_d = [0.21].$$

Considering the Oustaloup filter of order $N = 2$, we obtain the state equations with five state variables. It should be noted that the physical meaning of the states has been lost during the Oustaloup approximation process. Figure 3 presents the chosen state variables of the models (25, 29–31) controlled with the system shown in Fig. 2 designed using a five-dimensional model. The reference trajectory has been chosen according to [16], it has the shape of the zero-one square wave with the period of 10 [s], and the duration of the high value (1 [m]) equal to 4 [s]. The Kalman filter gains are obtained using weighting matrices of the process and observation noise covariance $Q = \text{diag}[1.0]$ and $R = \text{diag}[1.0]$, respectively. The upper tank water level has been controlled by applying the MPC linear technique. The process zero-mean Gaussian noise signals $v(t)$, and $w(t)$ have the same arbitrarily chosen variance 1e−5.

The prediction of the state variable $x_1(t)$ has been performed for established values of parameters: $a_1 = 0.05$, $a_2 = 0.05$ using the sequential quadratic programming algorithm with a termination time of 20 s. The equations describing the water tanks dynamics have been obtained with the following initial conditions: $x_1(0) = 0.75$, $x_2(0) = 0.50$. The KF response sequence has been calculated using the fixed-step, 4th-order Runge-Kutta algorithm, with a grid interval of 0.1 s. The main reason for the MPC application has been to ensure the reference tracking of the water level in the first tank of the system.

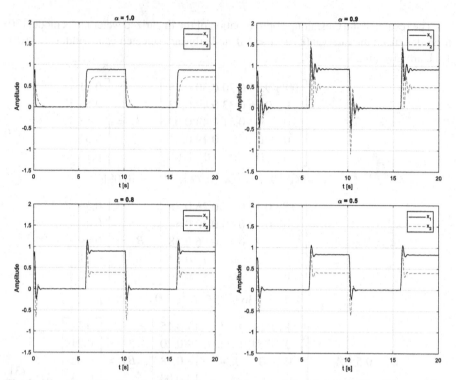

Fig. 3. The states of the linearized double tank model controlled with the MPC for different values of α, and noise variance values $v(t) = 1e-5$, $w(t) = 1e-5$ (Color figure online)

The water levels in the upper and lower tanks obtained using the MPC method are displayed in Fig. 3. The black (solid) line represents the water level in the first tank and the red (dashed) line illustrates the water flow in the second tank. These curves are identified for the noise variance values $v(t) = 1e-5$, and $w(t) = 1e-5$, respectively. For greater variances the plots are similar but the curves are more distorted by the noise. The slight first tank water level changes observed for different α values are definitely caused by the low order of the approximation performed in this study. However, sufficient reference tracking of the first tank water level can be observed. Figure 4 shows the estimated input signals of the integer ($\alpha = 1$), and the fractional-order models ($\alpha < 1$) controlled with the MPC law.

The blue curves shown in Fig. 4 represent input signals $u(t)$ obtained for the integer and fractional-order models using MPC controller (Fig. 2). The input signal fluctuations observed during signal switching are the result of the chosen Outsaloup approximation discretization range.

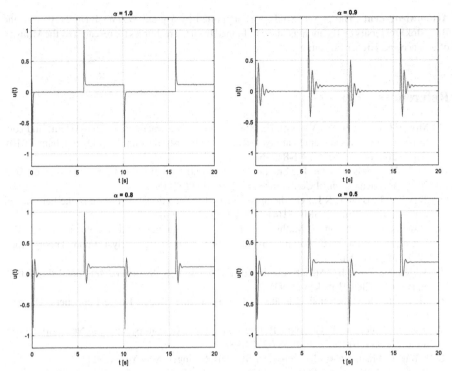

Fig. 4. The input signals to the linearized double tank model controlled with the MPC for different values of α, and noise variance values $v(t) = 1e-5$, $w(t) = 1e-5$ (Color figure online)

7 Conclusions

In this paper, the accuracy of the approximation of the integer-order state equations using the Outsaloup method for the given fractional-order double tank system has been studied. It should be noted that the application of the presented model-based strategy for the system state prediction purposes improves the system tracking and reduces the experimental costs. The experiments show the acceptable reference tracking of the first tank water level. The simulation results have confirmed that the increasing value of the noise variance makes the predicted states of the approximated models more distorted. However, the designed control system ensures the stability of the integer and fractional-order double tank system for different order values.

The proposed methodology requires further investigations to obtain a more precise fitting of the predicted state variable to the reference input signal. The oscillating nature of the predicted state variable in the first period of the control may be disturbing. This inconvenience can be reduced by increasing the order, and the frequency range of the approximation. However, such a procedure will certainly increase the computational effort required for the model of the system state prediction. An interesting issue for further research would be the nonlinear MPC algorithm implementation for the above model-based design.

Acknowledgment. The present study was supported by a grant WZ/WI-IIT/4/2020 from the Bialystok University of Technology and was funded from the resources for research by the Ministry of Science and Higher Education.

References

1. Monje, C.A., Chen, Y., Vinagre, B., Xue, D., Feliu, V.: Fractional orders systems and controls: fundamentals and applications. Advances in Industrial Control. Springer, Cham (2010). https://doi.org/10.1007/978-1-84996-335-0
2. Chen, Y., Petráš, I., Xue, D.: Fractional order control - a tutorial. In: Proceedings of ACC 2009. American Control Conference, pp. 1397–1411 (2009)
3. Torvik, P.J., Bagley, R.L.: On the appearance of the fractional derivative in the behavior of real materials. Trans. ASME **51**(4), 294–298 (1984)
4. Oustaloup, A., Levron, F., Mathieu, B., Nanot, F.: Frequency-band complex noninteger differentiator: characterization and synthesis. IEEE Trans. Circuits Syst. Fund. Theory Appl. **47**(1), 25–40 (2000)
5. Miller, K., Ross, B.: An introduction to the fractional calculus and fractional differential equations. Wiley, Hoboken (1993)
6. Magin, R., L.: Fractional Calculus in Bioengineering. Begell House Publishers, Danbury (2006)
7. West, B., Bologna, M., Grigolini, P.: Physics of Fractal Operators. Springer, New York (2003). https://doi.org/10.1007/978-0-387-21746-8
8. Petras, I.: Fractional-Order Nonlinear Systems. Springer, New York (2011)
9. Podlubny, I.: Fractional Differential Equations. Academic Press, San Diego (1999)
10. Valério, D., Costa, J.: An Introduction to Fractional Control. IET, London (2013)
11. Sheng, H., Chen, Y.D., Qiu, T.S.: Fractional Processes and Fractional-order Signal Processing. Springer, London (2012). https://doi.org/10.1007/978-1-4471-2233-3
12. Tepljakov, A., Petlenkov, E., Belikov, J.: FOMCON: a MATLAB toolbox for fractional-order system identification and control. Int. J. Microelectron. Comput. Sci. **2**(2), 51–62 (2011)
13. Monje, C., Vinagre, B., Feliu, V., Chen, Y.: Tuning and autotuning of fractional order controllers for industry applications. Control Eng. Pract. **16**(7), 798–812 (2008)
14. Hussain, M.: Review of the applications of neural networks in chemical process control–simulation and on–line implementation. Artif. Intell. Eng. **13**, 55–68 (1999)
15. Maciejowski, J.M.: Predictive Control with Constraints, pp. 108–115. Prentice-Hall, Englewood Cliffs (2002)
16. Jakowluk, W.: Design of a state estimation considering model predictive control strategy for a nonlinear water tanks process. In: Saeed, K., Chaki, R., Janev, V. (eds.) CISIM 2019. LNCS, vol. 11703, pp. 457–468. Springer, Cham (2019). https://doi.org/10.1007/978-3-030-28957-7_38
17. Rawlings, J.B., Mayne, D.Q.: Model Predictive Control: Theory and Design, 5th ed., Nob Hill Pub., Madison (2012)
18. Bernardini, D., Bemporad, A.: Stabilizing model predictive control of stochastic constrained linear systems. IEEE Trans. Autom. Control **57**, 1468–1480 (2012)
19. Atkinson, A.C., Donev, A.N., Tobias, R.D.: Optimum Experimental Designs, with SAS, pp. 119–147. Oxford University Press, Oxford (2007)
20. Schoukens, J., Ljung, L.: Nonlinear system identification. A user-oriented roadmap. IEEE Control Syst. Mag. **39**(6), 28–99 (2019)
21. Rojas, C.R., Agüero, J.C., Welsh, J.S., Goodwin, G.C.: On the equivalence of least costly and traditional experiment design for control. Automatica **44**(11), 2706–2715 (2008)

22. Jakowluk, W.: Plant friendly input design for parameter estimation in an inertial system with respect to D-efficiency constraints. Entropy **16**(11), 5822–5837 (2014)
23. Kumar, A., Nabil, M., Narasimhan, S.: Economical and plant friendly input design for system identification. In: Proceedings 2014 European Control Conference (ECC), Strasbourg, France, pp. 732–737 (2014)
24. Annergren, M., Larsson, C.A., Hjalmarsson, H., Bombois, X., Wahlberg, B.: Application-oriented input design in system identification: optimal input design for control. IEEE Control Syst. Mag. **37**(2), 31–56 (2017)
25. Jakowluk, W.: Optimal input signal design for fractional-order system identification. Bull. Polish Acad. Sci. Tech. Sci. **67**(1), 37–44 (2019)
26. Jakowluk, W., Świercz, M.: Application-oriented experiment design for model predictive control. Bull. Polish Acad. Sci. Tech. Sci. **68**(4), 883–891 (2020)

ToMAL: Token-Based Fair Mutual Exclusion Algorithm

Debdita Kar, Mandira Roy$^{(\boxtimes)}$, and Nabendu Chaki

University of Calcutta, JD 2, Sector 3, Bidhannagar, Kolkata 700106, India
mrcomp_rs@caluniv.ac.in, nabendu@ieee.org

Abstract. Token-based mutual exclusion (ME) algorithms for distributed systems have gained much attention over the years due to their inherent safety property. Safety property ensures that only one process executes the critical section at any instant of time. Raymond, et al. have proposed a token-based ME algorithm that uses an inverted-tree topology. The solution is simple, fast, and widely accepted by the community. However, a major drawback of Raymond's algorithm is that it fails to satisfy the fairness property in terms of the first-come-first-serve policy among equal-priority processes requesting the token. Several attempts have been initiated to resolve this issue. In this work, we provide a new token-based ME algorithm (*ToMAL*) that, similar to Raymond's algorithm, works on inverted tree topology. The proposed solution not only ensures the fairness property but also requires very little additional storage in a node. We have compared our proposed approach *ToMAL* with another existing work. The comparative performances are studied in terms of storage space and control messages.

1 Introduction

In distributed systems, mutual exclusion is an important concern. The safeness property of the concurrency control mechanism ensures that only one process can enter the critical section (CS), at any given instance of time. A good distributed mutual exclusion algorithm must be safe, fair and fault-tolerant. Token-based mutual-exclusion algorithms have gained considerable attention over the years as these inherently guarantee the safety property. Raymond's algorithm [10] is one such token-based algorithm that is efficient and requires only O(log N) messages to gain access to the CS. However, in token-based algorithms, fairness-criteria, that is responding to token request in a FCFS (First-come-first-serve) manner, is not always ensured. This is observed in case of Raymond's algorithm too.

The problem of ensuring fairness for mutual exclusion algorithms for distributed systems has drawn considerable attention over the years. There have been attempts [5,7] to overcome this deficiency. We have observed that in [7] authors have proposed a Modified Raymond's algorithm (MRA) that solves the fairness problem of Raymond's algorithm. Though Modified Raymond's Algorithm solves the fairness issue of Raymond's algorithm, the storage complexity

© Springer Nature Switzerland AG 2021
K. Saeed and J. Dvorský (Eds.): CISIM 2021, LNCS 12883, pp. 394–405, 2021.
https://doi.org/10.1007/978-3-030-84340-3_32

for MRA is quite high. The algorithm in [7] not only requires more storage but also some additional processing time.

In this research work, we propose a new token-based mutual exclusion approach *ToMAL* (that includes the basics of Raymond's algorithm [10]) such that fairness condition is ensured with lower storage complexity. We have also experimentally evaluated that *ToMAL* does not incur any extra control message overhead and requires much less storage space.

The structure of the paper is as follows. Section 2 provides a brief overview of distributed mutual exclusion algorithms. Section 3.1 illustrates our proposed approach along with algorithms. Section 3.2 compares *ToMAL* with the algorithm in [7]. Section 4 illustrates on the experimental evaluation of our approach. Finally Sect. 5 concludes the paper.

2   Related Works

A large number of mutual exclusion algorithms for distributed systems have been proposed over the years. There are both centralized approach and distributed token-based approaches. In a centralized mutual exclusion algorithm [2], a single site acts as the sole arbiter to resolve conflicts among all sites. This algorithm is highly skewed as far as symmetry is concerned. Raymond's algorithm is a tree-based distributed mutual exclusion algorithm that uses tokens for resolving the conflict between the sites. In Raymond's Algorithm [10] the fairness is not assured. This is because this algorithm stores the identifier (id) of the nodes that request to enter the CS but it never stores the order in which the request arrives. So even though all the nodes that request the CS gets it but, the order is not maintained. In [4] authors have proposed a tokenized mutual exclusion algorithm based on priority groups. Sites with the same priority are organized into a group and each group is organized in a tree structure like in [10]. Within the group, it uses Raymond's algorithm [10] and in the inter-group level it uses Ricart-Agrawala's algorithm [11]. In [8] authors have proposed an efficient token-based distributed algorithm for solving the group mutual exclusion problem. The proposed algorithm has a message complexity of $2n - 1$ per CS entry request. In [9] authors proposes a prioritized algorithm for distributed mutual exclusion with an average message overhead of $O(log(n))$ and a worst-case overhead of $n+1$ message per request, respectively. This approach requires an extra overhead of forwarding queues between the sites and local bookkeeping. In [1] authors proposes an efficient and fault-tolerant algorithm for generating quorums to solve the distributed mutual exclusion problem. The request sets are formed based on a binary-tree configuration of system sites. Sites are logically organized as a binary tree and the request set of a site contains all the sites on a path from the root to the leaf, containing that node. However, the algorithm violates the spirit of "equal responsibility" because some sites appear in more request sets than others. The Modified Raymond's algorithm in [7] resolves the issue of fairness in distributed mutual exclusion algorithm. In [7], processes requesting to enter in the CS are allowed to enter the CS based on their priorities. Any two processes with the same priority are granted token in FCFS order. When a node requests for the CS, the request is forwarded in the tree untill it reaches the node that holds the token. Each node that receives the request stores it in its local queue. Each entry of the queue contains 3-tuples for a single requesting node that is, the id of the requesting node, the 1 hop neighbor between the requesting node and the node that receives the request, and the priority. This process increases the storage complexity of the algorithm. In [13] authors propose a token-based mutual exclusion approach for Soft Real Time Systems. This approach uses the concepts of priority queue, dynamic request set and the process state. The algorithm maintains FCFS order in selecting processes for executing the CS having the same priority levels. In [3] a Hybrid Distributed Mutual Exclusion Algorithm for Cluster-Based Systems was proposed, called Raysuz. Raysuz's algorithm uses a clustered graph infrastructure. Suzuki-Kasami's [12] algorithm is used at intra-cluster level and Raymond's algorithm [10] at inter-cluster level. It provides better synchronization delay than pure Raymond's algorithm and better message complexity than pure Suzuki-Kasami's algorithm.

We have observed that over the years several distributed mutual exclusion algorithms have been proposed for different scenarios. However, we did not observe any approach that proposes token-based mutual exclusion for equal priority process that tends to improve the storage space complexity.

3   Approach and Analysis

In this section, we have described our token-based algorithm *ToMAL*, followed by a compaartive analysis of the algorithm. It is to be noted that *ToMAL* approach uses some of the concepts of Raymond's algorithm [10] that is widely studied. However, one major of limitation of Raymond's algorithm is that it does not ensure fairness. This issue is well researched [5,6] in the literature. *ToMAL* ensures fairness in concurrency control while reducing storage overhead.

3.1   ToMAl: The Proposed Algorithm

ToMAL is developed for a distributed environment where sites (or nodes) are logically connected as an inverted spanning tree that is each node have a single outgoing edge directed to its parent node. In the proposed approach (*ToMAL*) each node in the distributed environment have its own local queue (denoted as qe) and a local *store* (denoted as st) variable. This *store* variable is used whenever a node forwards a token to its child node while its queue is non-empty. The child node stores the id of the parent node in its local *store* variable. The token holder node either executes its own CS or forwards it to some other node. The algorithm further ensures that the token holder node returns the token to the node whose id is stored in its local *store* variable after using the token once. This process of token returning ensures that the token requests are served in an FCFS manner.

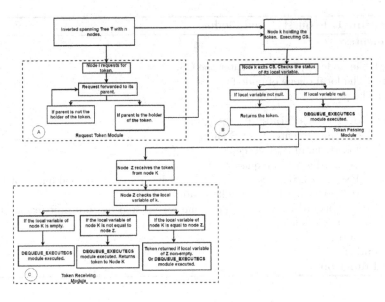

Fig. 1. Concurrency control in ToMAL

The block diagram in Fig. 1 demonstrates the flow of access-control in a distributed system using *ToMAL*.

Now we illustrate the different steps of *ToMAL* as follows:

1. Initially the *store* variable of every node is set to null.
2. When a node wants to enter the CS it sends a request for the token to its one-hop neighbor (that is the parent node) within the spanning tree. If the parent node does not hold the token, it stores the request in its local queue (qe) and forwards it to its one-hop neighbor. This process continues until the request reaches the node that holds the token. The stepwise detailing is illustrated in Algorithm 1. The portion marked as A in Fig. 1 illustrates the steps of token request module.
3. When a node P_i finishes executing the CS it checks the value of its local *store* (st_i) variable.
   (a) If value of st_i is null, then it invokes the module DEQUEUE_EXECUTECS. The module DEQUEUE_EXECUTECS performs the following steps:
      – Let P_x be the element at the front of the local queue of P_i (qe_i).
      – If P_i is equal to P_x then P_i executes the CS otherwise does the following steps:
      • Reverses the edge $P_x \rightarrow P_i$ as $P_i \rightarrow P_x$ in the spanning tree.
      • Forwards the token to P_x.
      • If qe_i is not empty then sets st_x as P_i. So that after executing the CS it shall return the token.
   (b) If value of st_i is not null, and suppose it contains the site P_y then node P_i returns the token to site the P_y. If P_i received new request while executing CS it enqueues its id in the queue of P_y.

Algorithm 1. Request Token Module

Arguments:

(a) P_m: The node requesting to enter the CS.
(b) qe_m: The local queue of node P_m.
(c) P_k: The parent node of P_m.

```
1: function REQUESTTOKEN(P_m, qe_m, P_k)
2:     if P_m wants to enter the CS then
3:         Insert the id P_m into qe_m
4:         Forward a token request to P_k
5:         ENQUEUE(qe_k, P_m)                ▷ Inserts P_m into local queue of P_k- qe_k
6:         if P_k does not hold the token then
7:             Forward the token request and repeat step 5 & 6 utill it reaches the
               token holder
8:         end if
9:     end if
10: end function
```

Algorithm 2 illustrates the set of steps of token passing between the nodes of the spanning tree (refer to the portion marked as B in Fig. 1).

4. Finally in Algorithm 3 we have demonstrated the steps performed when a node (P_r) receives a token from a node (P_z). There are three scenarios that may occur (refer to the portion marked as C in Fig. 1):

(a) P_r received the token from P_z whose local *store* (st_z) variable is empty. That is token need not be returned. In such a case P_r simply invokes the DEQUEUE_EXECUTECS module.

(b) P_r received the token from P_z whose local *store* (st_z) variable is not empty and also not equal to P_r. This implies that the parent node (P_z) has been granted the token but it has to return it after using it once. In such scenario P_r invokes DEQUEUE_EXECUTECS module and stores the id P_z in st_r. This is to ensure that the token is returned to P_z after executing the CS.

These two scenarios show that the token is forwarded in the tree from the parent to the child.

(c) P_r receives the token from a node whose local *store* (st_z) variable is not empty and is equal to P_r. This implies that the token is sent back after using it once. It implies the backward traversal of the token. In such a scenario (P_r) checks its own (st_r) and does the subsequent decison making. If (st_r) is empty it invokes DEQUEUE_EXECUTECS module else returns the token to the node whose id is in st_r (say P_y). If P_r received any new token request while it had the token then it enqueues the id of the new requesting node in the local queue of P_y.

Algorithm 2. Token Passing Module

Arguments:

1. P_h: The node presently holding the token.
2. st_h: It represents the local *store* variable of node P_h.
3. qe_h: The local queue of node P_h.
4. $\mathcal{T}$: The directed spanning tree representing the links between the nodes of the distributed system.

```
1: function TOKENPASSING(Pₕ, stₕ, qeₕ, 𝒯 )
2:     if Pₕ exits the CS then
3:         if stₕ=∅ then DEQUEUE_EXECUTECS(Pₕ, qeₕ)
4:         else if stₕ ≠ ∅ then
5:             Let the node id in stₕ be Pᵧ
6:             Reverse the edge Pᵧ → Pₕ as Pₕ → Pᵧ in 𝒯
7:             Forward the token to Pᵧ
8:             Set stₕ ← ∅
9:             if qeₕ is not empty ∧ qeₕ has new entry then
10:                 ENQUEUE(qeᵧ, Pₕ)          ▷ Inserts Pₕ into qeᵧ for each new request
11:             end if
12:         end if
13:     end if
14: end function
```

3.2 Comparative Analysis

In this section we have illustrated the steps of *ToMAL* using a use case and also compared it with the Modified Raymonds Algorithm [7] in terms of number of control messages and storage complexity.

In Modified Raymonds Algorithm (MRA) each node maintains a local request queue (denoted as RQ) to store the ids of the neighbors from which it has received a token request. In addition to this, the node that holds the token maintains an original request queue (denoted as ORQ) to store the id of the node from where the token request has been originated. In MRA when a node requests for the CS, then each node that receives the token request makes an entry in its local request queue (RQ). Each entry of the queue (RQ) contains 3-tuples for a single requesting node. Now let us compare *ToMAL* with MRA using a simple use case:

1. Let us consider the spanning tree in Fig. 2 with node **A** holding the token. We assume that the queues and local variables corresponding to each node in our approach (*ToMAL*) are set to null. Similarly, for MRA the local Request Queues(RQ) and the Original Request Queue(ORQ) are also null. In the figures, we have marked the node that holds the token as green and nodes having non-empty queues with yellow.
2. When node **A** executes the CS node **C**, **B** and **F** sends their request for token respectively.
   ToMAL: When **C** initiates a token request, it stores its own id in the local queue (qe_C) and forwards the request to its one-hop neighbor **A**. Node **A**

Algorithm 3. Token Receiving Module

Arguments:

1. P_r: An intermmediate node that receives the token.
2. P_z: The node that passes the token to P_r.
3. st_z: The local store variable of node P_z.
4. $\mathcal{T}$: The directed spanning tree representing the links between the nodes of the distributed system.

1: **function** TOKENRECEIVE(P_r, P_z, st_z, $\mathcal{T}$)
2:     **switch** st_z
3:         **case:** $st_z = \emptyset \wedge qe_z$ is empty   ▷ Forward passing the token
4:             DEQUEUE_EXECUTECS(P_r, qe_r)
5:             **break**
6:         **case:** $st_z \neq \emptyset \wedge st_z \neq P_r$ ▷ Forward passing the token
7:             Set $st_r \leftarrow P_z$
8:             DEQUEUE_EXECUTECS(P_r, qe_r)
9:             **break**
10:         **case:** $st_z = P_r$ ▷ Backward passing the token
11:             Set $st_r \leftarrow \emptyset$
12:             **if** $st_r \neq \emptyset$ **then**
13:                 Let the node id in st_r be P_y
14:                 Reverse the edge $P_y \rightarrow P_r$ as $P_r \rightarrow P_y$ in $\mathcal{T}$
15:                 Forward the token to P_y
16:                 **if** (qe_r not empty) $\wedge$ (qe_r has new entry) **then**
17:                     ENQUEUE(qe_y, P_r)   ▷ Inserts P_r into qe_y for each new request
18:                 **end if**
19:             **else**
20:                 DEQUEUE_EXECUTECS(P_r, qe_r)
21:             **end if**
22:             **break**
23: **end function**

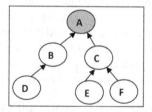

Fig. 2. Inverted spanning tree (Color figure online)

on receiving the token request, inserts it in the local queue (qe_A). When **F** requests for token, it forwards the request to **C** which in turn makes another request to **A**. So qe_A has two entries for **C**: one its own, another for node **F**. *MRA:* In MRA when node **C** requests for the token a 3-tuple entry $< C, C, 1 >$ is inserted into RQ_C (RQ_C denotes request queue of **C**), where 1 is the priority of node **C**. Then the request is forwarded to **A**. The 3-tuple $<C,C,1>$ is also added to RQ_A (RQ_A denotes request queue of **A**). The id **C** is added to the ORQ that records the fact that **C** has requested the token. Similarly for node **B** the 3-tuples $<B,B,1>$ is added into RQ_B and RQ_A respectively. The id **B** is also added to the ORQ. When node **F** requests the token, $<F,F,1>$ is added to RQ_F and RQ_C. The 3-tuples $<F,C,1>$ is added into RQ_A, where **F** is the node who requested the token, **C** is the one hop neighbor that can lead to **F** and 1 is the priority. The id **F** is added to the ORQ Fig. 3(a) and 3(b) shows the status of *ToMAL* and *MRA* respectively.

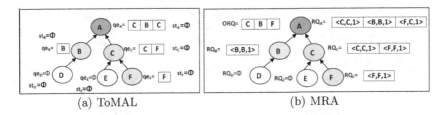

(a) ToMAL   (b) MRA

Fig. 3. Status of queues after **C**, **B**, **F** makes their requests.

3. Node **A** comes out of the CS.
   ToMAL: Node **A** checks the value of its local variable st_A. Since st_A is null it performs dequeue operation on qe_A and retrieves the id **C**. It reverses the edge between node **A** and **C** (Refer to red marked edge in Fig. 4(a)). Forwards the token to **C**. Since qe_A is not empty, sets st_C as **A**. Node **C** enters the CS. Figure 4(a) shows the status when token is sent to node **C**.
   MRA: Node **A** retrieves the front element of its queue (RQ_A). The edge between **A** and **C** is reversed and the token is sent to **C** along with the queue ORQ. Since the RQ_A is non-empty, a dummy request is sent to process **C**. On receiving such request **C** retrieves the first element of its queue (RQ_C) and replaces it with the dummy request. As the element retrieved from the queue is **C** itself, it enters the CS. Figure 4(b) shows the status when token is forwarded to node **C**.

4. Node **C** finishes executing the CS.
   ToMAL: Node **C** checks the status of its local variable (st_C). As (st_C) contains the id **A**, the edge between **C** and **A** is reversed and the token is returned back to **A**. After **A** gets the token from **C** it sets (st_C) to null. Since (st_A) is null, node **A** again performs dequeue operation. Node **A** forwards the token to node **B**.
   MRA: Here when node **C** comes out of the CS, it dequeues the first element of (RQ_C), and forwards the token to **A** along with the ORQ.
   Fig. 5(a) and 5(b) shows the status when the token returns to node **A**. In both cases, node **A** then forwards the token to node **B**. The edge between **A** and **B** is reversed. The status of the queues and local variables are modified.

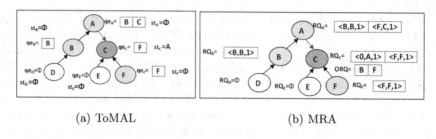

(a) ToMAL   (b) MRA

Fig. 4. Status when token is forwarded to **C**. (Color figure online)

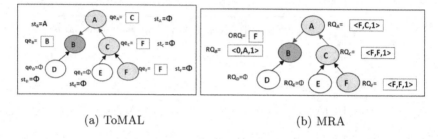

(a) ToMAL   (b) MRA

Fig. 5. Status when token is forwarded to **B**.

5. Finally when **B** comes out of the CS it returns the token to **A**, which then forwards it to **C** and **C** then grants the token to **F**. In *ToMAL* since qe_C is empty **F** is not bound to return the token. Figure 6(a) and 6(b) shows the status when the token is forwarded to **F**.

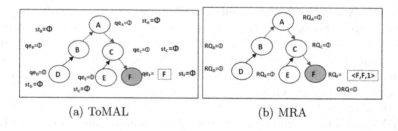

(a) ToMAL   (b) MRA

Fig. 6. Status when token is forwarded to **F**.

From the above comparison, it can be observed that both approaches generate the same number of control messages to serve a token request. In this example the total number of control messages generated in serving token request of **C**,

B and **F** for both the algorithm is 8. In *ToMAL* for every token request the local queues (qe) stores only a single value. In case of MRA each cell of the queue stores 3 elements that increase its storage complexity by three times. In addition to this, an extra queue is stored and forwarded in MRA whenever a token is granted to any node.

Storage Space Analysis: In *ToMAL* and MRA [7] a token request is propagated in the tree traveling one-hop at a time until it reaches the node that holds the token. Every node that gets a token request from its one-hop neighbor maintains a record in its local queue.

Let us consider that the height of the inverted spanning tree at any time instant be h, and all the token requests arrive from the leaf nodes of the spanning tree. This is to compute the maximum storage space complexity. Since when leaf node request token all other intermediate nodes in the path to root store its id in their local queue. Then for a single request, at most h number of nodes has to perform an enqueue operation. Now let's assume that the total number of leaf nodes requesting for the token at a time instant be m. Thus, a maximum $m * h$ number of data insertion can take place.

ToMAL: In *ToMAL* whenever the token holder passes the token to some other node and its queue is non-empty, then the token must come back. The local variable *store* at every node stores the id of the node to which token has to be returned. If there are a total n number of nodes in the spanning tree, we require extra storage of size n (this extra storage is for n number of local *store* variables). So the maximum storage complexity is of order $(m * h) + n$.

MRA: For MRA each record in the local queue requires 3 entries. So, storage complexity is of the order $(3 * m) * h + n$ where n is the storage space required for ORQ.

Table 1 illustrates the total storage space required for both approaches. We have considered the maximum length of request queue for each node. Suppose for node **A**, the maximum length can be 5 since it has that number of descendants in total. The total storage required for node **A** in *ToMAL* is 6, where the extra storage is for the local *store* variable. As for MRA total storage for A is 15 since each cell of the queue stores 3 tuples. The total storage required for *ToMAL* is 19 whereas for MRA it is 45. The extra 6 added to the total storage in MRA is for the length of the ORQ. In this simple use case, it can be noted that the storage required for *ToMAL* is less than 50% as compared to MRA .

4   Experimental Evaluation

The proposed approach *ToMAL* is implemented using Java and is available at https://github.com/concurrencyControl/ToMAL. We have evaluated our algorithm against some randomly generated spanning trees to check whether fairness is ensured in all possible conditions of request generation. The steps of our experimental evaluation are as follows:

Table 1. Storage space requirement

Node ID	Maximum length of request queue	Storage space required	
		ToMAL	MRA
A	5	6	16
B	2	3	7
C	3	4	10
D	1	2	4
E	1	2	4
F	1	2	4
TOTAL	13	19	45

- A connected graph with n nodes is produced by the system. Here n can take any value based on user choice.
- Now considering any one of the nodes from the n nodes as the initiator or token-holder node a spanning tree is generated.
- Then requests for token are generated by all the other nodes in the spanning tree in different possible ways. Suppose let us consider a situation where three token requests are generated in successive time instant. Then we check our algorithm for the following scenarios:

• Request 1, 2 and 3 are all generated from the same branch of the tree.
• Request 1 and 2 from the same branch while 3 from an alternate branch.
• Request 1 and 3 from the same branch and 2 from an alternate branch.
• Request 2 and 3 from the same branch and 1 from an alternate branch.

In all these scenarios our algorithm checks whether the token request is served in an FCFS manner.

- The order of execution of CS, the status of local queues and local variables by the nodes are recorded by the system. The recorded data are analyzed for any inconsistency in the execution.
- This process is again repeated by selecting another node of the graph as initiator and building a different spanning tree from it. We have repeated the same process by building n different spanning trees from the graph.
  This process of evaluation is used to ensure that the algorithm satisfies fairness for different possible ways of token-request generation.

5 Conclusion

The main contribution of this work is in proposing *ToMAL*, a new token-based mutual exclusion algorithm that ensures fairness in serving the token request of the nodes. We have used a very simple data structure for the implementation of *ToMAL*. The proposed algorithm also complies with the two constituent elements of correctness, namely safety, and liveness. Besides, we have compared our approach with the Modified Raymond's Algorithm (MRA) in [7] in an experimental approach using the same data-set. The existing *MRA* approach offers a priority-based token assignment. This is beyond the scope of *ToMAL*. However, the storage complexity of the *ToMAL* is lower as compared to the *MRA* algorithm. The number of control messages required for the job is the same for both algorithms. We have also evaluated our approach by implementing the algorithm against different randomly generated spanning trees of random sizes.

References

1. Agrawal, D., Abbadi, A.E.: An efficient and fault-tolerant solution for distributed mutual exclusion. ACM Trans. Comput. Syst. **9**(1), 1–20 (1991)
2. Buckley, G.N., Silberschatz, A.: A failure tolerant centralized mutual exclusion algorithm, pp. 347–356 (1984)
3. Challenger, M., Haytaoglu, E., Tokatli, G., Dagdeviren, O., Erciyes, K.: A hybrid distributed mutual exclusion algorithm for cluster-based systems. Math. Prob. Eng. 1–15 (2013)
4. Housni, A., Trehel, M.: Distributed mutual exclusion token-permission based by prioritized groups, pp. 253–259 (2001)
5. Kanrar, S.., Chaki, N..: Modified Raymond's Algorithm for priority (MRA-P) based mutual exclusion in distributed systems. In: Madria, Sanjay K.., Claypool, Kajal T.., Kannan, Rajgopal, Uppuluri, Prem, Gore, Manoj Madhava (eds.) ICD-CIT 2006. LNCS, vol. 4317, pp. 325–332. Springer, Heidelberg (2006). https://doi.org/10.1007/11951957_29
6. Kanrar, S., Chaki, N.: FAPP: a new fairness algorithm for priority process mutual exclusion in distributed systems. J. Netw. **5**(1), 11–18 (2010)
7. Kanrar, S., Chattopadhyay, S., Chaki, N.: A new link failure resilient priority based fair mutual exclusion algorithm for distributed systems. J. Netw. Syst. Manag. **21**(1), 1–24 (2013)
8. Mittal, N., Mohan, P.K.: A priority-based distributed group mutual exclusion algorithm when group access is non-uniform. J. Parallel Distrib. Comput. **67**(7), 797–815 (2007)
9. Mueller, F.: Prioritized token-based mutual exclusion for distributed systems. In: Proceedings of the First Merged International Parallel Processing Symposium and Symposium on Parallel and Distributed Processing, pp. 791–795 (1998)
10. Raymond, K.: A tree-based algorithm for distributed mutual exclusion. ACM Trans. Comput. Syst. **7**(1), 61–77 (1989)
11. Ricart, G., Agrawala, A.K.: An optimal algorithm for mutual exclusion in computer networks. Commun. ACM **24**(1), 9–17 (1981)
12. Suzuki, I., Kasami, T.: A distributed mutual exclusion algorithm. ACM Trans. Comput. Syst. **3**(4), 344–349 (1985)
13. Swaroop, A., Singh, A.K.: A distributed group mutual exclusion algorithm for soft real time systems. In: World Academy of Science, Engineering and Technology, International Journal of Computer, Control, Quantum and Information Engineering, vol. 1, no. 8 (2007)

FPGA in Core Calculation for Big Datasets

Maciej Kopczyński[✉]

Faculty of Computer Science, Bialystok University of Technology,
Wiejska 45A, 15-351 Bialystok, Poland
m.kopczynski@pb.edu.pl
http://www.wi.pb.edu.pl

Abstract. The rough sets theory developed by Prof. Z. Pawlak is one of
the tools used in intelligent systems for data analysis and processing. In
modern systems, the amount of the collected data is increasing quickly,
so the computation speed becomes the critical factor. This paper shows
FPGA and softcore CPU based hardware solution for big datasets core
calculation focusing on rough set methods. Core represents attributes
cannot be removed without affecting the classification power of all condition attributes. Presented architectures have been tested on real datasets
by running presented solutions inside two different FPGA chips. Datasets
had 1 000 to 1 000 000 objects. The same operations were performed in
software implementation. Results show the up to 15.83 times increase
factor in computation time using hardware supporting core generation
in comparison to pure software implementation.

Keywords: Rough sets · FPGA · Hardware · Core · Altera · Xilinx

1 Introduction

The rough sets theory developed by Prof. Z. Pawlak [19] is a powerful tool for data
analysis. That theory extends the concept of a set and allows processing the uncertain data. It is one of the tools that can be used in intelligent systems. Banking [2],
medicine [5], image recognition [1] and security [18] are possible fields of utilization. In all those fields the amount of either produced, as well as collected data, is
increasing quickly. The biggest challenge associated with creating optimal rough
sets based systems is the time needed to process input data, with particular emphasis on large datasets (big data). In practical applications, the concept of a large
dataset is relative and means a situation when the set cannot be processed using
simple and commonly available methods [15]. Depending on the purpose of the chosen method and the complexity of the algorithm, this may mean a dataset, which
size is calculated in megabytes, gigabytes, or terabytes.

There exist many software implementations of rough set methods and algorithms. However, they require significant amount of resources of a computer system, including CPU's, RAM and storage memories, especially during processing

© Springer Nature Switzerland AG 2021
K. Saeed and J. Dvorský (Eds.): CISIM 2021, LNCS 12883, pp. 406–417, 2021.
https://doi.org/10.1007/978-3-030-84340-3_33

large amount of data [16]. To improve the performance hardware acceleration methods can be used, e.g. Field Programmable Gate Arrays (FPGAs). FPGAs are a group of integrated circuits, whose functionality is defined by the user, using e.g. a hardware description language, such as VHDL.

At the moment there are some hardware implementation of specific rough set methods. Paper [26] presents the design for generating reduct from binary discernibility matrix. Reduct block was synthesized and downloaded into FPGA. The idea of sample processor generating decision rules from decision tables was described in [20]. Paper describes theoretical hardware approach to this issue. In [13] the authors presented architecture of rough set processor based on cellular networks described in [17]. Architecture was focusing on exiting programmable devices. In [6] a concept of hardware device capable of minimizing the large logic functions created on the basis of discernibility matrix was developed. More detailed summary of the existing ideas and hardware implementations of rough set methods can be found in [7,8].

Previous authors' research results focused on the subject of hardware implementations of rough sets methods can be found in the following papers covering the idea of the processor for rough sets methods [24], combinational type approach supporting operations for reduct and core calculation [3], hardware-supported reduct calculation [9], hardware units for a core calculations [10] or a two-stage algorithm for calculating the reduct [4]. All of presented approaches were implemented and tested on real FPGA units confirming acceleration in data processing comparing to software implementation, but mostly limited to small datasets due to combinational approach to the hardware module design.

The paper is organized as follows. In Sect. 2 some information about the notion of core and datasets used during research are provided. The Section 3 focuses on description of hardware solution, while Sect. 4 is devoted to the experimental results. Section 5 describes final conclusions and plan for future work.

Main goal of the paper is to compare efficiency of Altera and Xilinx comparable FPGA units in hardware supported core calculation focused on big datasets basing on author's version of algorithm.

2   Introductory Information

2.1   Core in the Rough Set Theory

Let $DT = (U, A \cup \{d\})$ be a decision table, where U is a set n of objects, A is a set of k condition attributes and d is a decision attribute. In decision table some of the condition attributes from A may be superfluous (redundant in other words). This means, that their removal cannot worsen the classification. The set $C \subseteq A$ of all indispensable condition attributes is called the core. None of its elements can be removed without affecting the classification power of all condition attributes. In order to compute the core, discernibility matrix $[DM(x,y)]_{x,y \in U}$ can be used, where $DM(x,y) = \{a \in A : a(x) \neq a(y) \text{ and } d(x) \neq d(y)\}$. The core is the set of all single element entries of the discernibility matrix, i.e.

$CORE = \bigcup_{x,y \in U, cardinality(DM(x,y))=1} DM(x,y)$. A much more detailed description of the concept of the core can be found, for example, in the article [21] or in the book [23].

2.2   CORE-HIDM Algorithm

The main concept of CORE-HIDM (**CORE** **H**ardware **I**ndirect **D**iscernibility **M**atrix) algorithm (described for the first time in [12]) is based on a property of singleton, which is a cell from discernibility matrix representing a set with only one attribute (element). This property tells that any singleton cannot be removed without affecting the classification power. Biggest problem with using discernibility matrix based algorithms, when dealing with big datasets, is amount of memory needed to store the matrix. Direct solution cannot be run in hardware because of FPGA resources limitations. Usage of FPGA available resources in correlation with dataset size is shown in author's papers, e.g. [3,9] or [10].

Main idea of CORE-HIDM algorithm is to divide the entire dataset into parts stored in two independent memory units providing information for hardware modules. These parts are subsequently processed by the unit. Pseudocode for the algorithm is given below:

CORE-HIDM Algorithm
INPUT: decision table $DT = (U, A \cup \{d\})$, one natural number $N > 0$
OUTPUT: core $C \subseteq A$

```
 1: C ← ∅
 2: M ← |U|/N
 3: for cnt₁ ← 0 to M − 1 do
 4:     RAM1 ← {x ∈ U : x_{cnt₁·N} to x_{(cnt₁+1)·N−1}}
 5:     for cnt₂ ← cnt₁ to M − 1 do
 6:         RAM2 ← {x ∈ U : x_{cnt₂·N} to x_{(cnt₂+1)·N−1}}
 7:         for x ∈ RAM1 do
 8:             for y ∈ RAM2 do
 9:                 if d(x) ≠ d(y) then
10:                     count ← 0
11:                     for a ∈ A do
12:                         if a(x) ≠ a(y) then
13:                             count ← count + 1
14:                             candidate ← a
15:                         end if
16:                     end for
17:                     if count = 1 and candidate ∉ C then
18:                         C ← C ∪ {candidate}
19:                     end if
20:                 end if
21:             end for
22:         end for
23:     end for
24: end for
```

Input to the CORE-HIDM algorithm is decision table DT, and output is core C. In the first steps, core C is initialized as empty set and M value is calculated. Decision table DT is divided into M parts, where each of them have the size of N objects. Dataset is prepared in the way, that $N \cdot M = |U|$. Two loops in lines 3 and 5 are responsible for choosing parts of input decision table. Lines 4 and 6 are responsible for loading chosen parts of dataset into RAM memories implemented in FPGA. Two loops in lines 7 and 8 take subsequent objects from decision table parts for comparison. Line 8 performs the comparison between decision attribute's value of two objects x and y. If these two objects belong to different decision classes, the algorithm is continued. *count* variable, responsible for storing the number of differences on condition attributes values between objects x and y is set to 0 in line 10. Loop in line 11 iterates over set of condition attributes A. Value of a condition attribute is compared between objects x and y in line 12. In case of difference, the *count* variable is incremented and a attribute is stored in *candidate* variable. When the attribute loop finishes, attribute in *candidate* variable is added to the core if *count* variable is equal to 1 and this attribute is not in core (lines 17 to 19).

2.3 Data to Conduct Experimental Research

In this paper, results of the experiments on two datasets are presented: Poker Hand Dataset (created by Robert Cattral and Franz Oppacher) and data about children with insulin-dependent diabetes mellitus (type 1) (created by Jaroslaw Stepaniuk).

First dataset was obtained from UCI Machine Learning Repository [14]. Each of 1 000 000 records is an example of a hand consisting of five playing cards drawn from a standard deck of 52. Each card is described using two attributes (suit and rank), for a total of 10 predictive attributes. There is one decision attribute that describes the "Poker Hand". Decision attribute describes 10 possible combinations of cards in descending probability in the dataset.

Insulin-dependent diabetes mellitus is a chronic disease of the body's metabolism characterized by an inability to produce enough insulin to process carbohydrates, fat, and protein efficiently. Treatment requires injections of insulin. Twelve condition attributes, which include the results of physical and laboratory examinations and one decision attribute (microalbuminuria) describe the database used in experiments. The data collection so far consists of 107 cases. The database is shown at the end of the paper [22]. A detailed analysis of the above data (only with the use of software systems) is part of the Chap. 6 of the book [23].

The Poker Hand database was used for creating smaller datasets consisting of 1 000 to 500 000 of objects by selecting given number of first rows of original dataset. Diabetes database was used for generating bigger datasets consisting of 1 000 to 1 000 000 of objects. New datasets were created by multiplying the rows of original dataset.

Created datasets had to be transformed to binary version. Numerical values were discretized and each attributes' value was encoded using four bits for both datasets. Every single object was described on 44 bits for Poker Hand and 52 bits for Diabetes. To fit to memory boundaries in both cases, objects descriptions had to be extended to 64 bits words filling unused attributes with binary 0's.

3   Hardware Implementation

Solution created by the author uses combination of softcore processor for Altera and ARM Cortex A9 core for Xilinx along with hardware unit designed to calculate the core. Functional diagram is shown on Fig. 1.

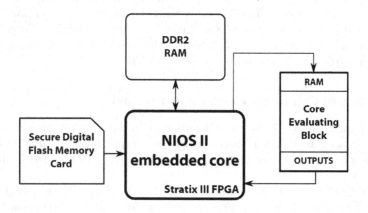

Fig. 1. System architecture diagram

Purpose of the processor is to:

- Control the process of dividing large input decision table.
- Control the core hardware calculation blocks.
- Reload the data between internal and external RAM memories.
- Process the results returned by core hardware calculation block.
- Perform operations on sets.

Selected processors are NIOS II for the Altera chip and ARM Cortex A9 for the Xilinx. NIOS II is the proprietary softcore unit provided by Altera for its FPGAs which can be instantiated as a block in the design. Xilinx Zynq XC7Z020 has dual-core CPU integrated in the FPGA.

DDR memories (DDR2 for Altera and DDR3 for Xilinx) store the large input decision table. SD card is the temporary solution for transferring data from PC to FPGA-based solution. Data from SD card is copied to FPGAs DDR memory in the beginning of calculation process.

Each subsequent part of data ready to be processed is stored in FPGA's built-in memories. This is MLAB, M9k and M144k for Altera and Block RAM for Xilinx device. Those types of memory are synchronous, dual-port memories with configurable organization, like 32×20 or 64×10 for Altera MLABs. Dual-port memories can be read and written simultaneously what makes operations faster. These type of memory blocks give a wide possibility of preparing memories capable of storing almost every type of the objects (words) – from small ones to big ones.

3.1   Hardware Modules for CORE-HIDM Algorithm

Core calculation unit is responsible for hardware support related to calculating subcores for given parts of decision table. This is modified version of sequential core hardware calculation unit described in paper [10]. This unit has been extended in order to allow processing large datasets, because previous one was limited to datasets that fit totally in the input register.

Inputs of the module are:

- **RAM1** and **RAM2** – memories storing parts of decision table,
- **Attribute Mask Register (AMR)** – register holding value corresponding to conditional attributes that have to be processed,
- **clock** – clock signal for synchronization purposes,
- **reset** – reset signal for setting initial values of internal registers in hardware module.

Outputs of the CORE-HIDM block are the value of calculated core given on *CORE* and *ready* signal providing the information that calculations performed by the block were finished.

The architecture of the modified sequential hardware core calculation unit is shown on Fig. 2.

In order to process large datasets two blocks of fast static RAM memories were added to the solution. RAM were created as instances of dedicated FPGA blocks. Both data memories used in module, denoted as RAM1 and RAM2, store parts of input decision table to comparison. In the beginning, memories contain the same part of decision table. When objects from RAM2 were compared with all objects from RAM1, then RAM2 is reloaded with next part of decision table, until decision table has any not compared elements in it. Then RAM1 and RAM2 are loaded with second part of dataset and whole process continues.

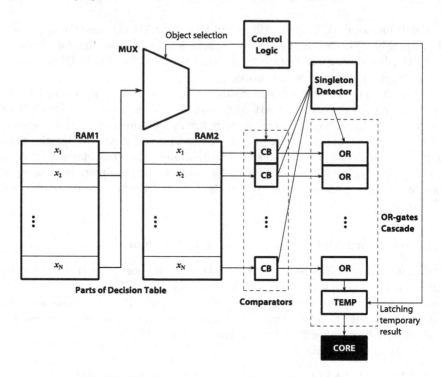

Fig. 2. Diagram of the CORE-HIDM block

Primary processing blocks of the circuit are five functionally separated blocks:

- **Comparators (CB)** – block of identical comparators which calculate the single row of discernibility matrix.
- **OR gates cascade** – block of OR gates connected in a cascade. Every gate calculates logical OR operation on two elements: one from previous gate in a cascade and second from corresponding comparator from CB block.
- **Singleton Detector (SD)** – block for checking if single row in discernibility matrix is a singleton (contains only one logical '1'). Outputs from this block are connected to OR gates cascade.
- **Multiplexer (MUX)** – in every turn selects the following object from decision table and puts it into the comparators in order to calculate single row of discernibility matrix.
- **Control Logic (CL)** – responsible for storing calculation data and controls overall operations of the module.

Required discernibility matrix entries are calculated by comparators very quickly, mostly because of simplicity of each comparator architecture. Then all entries go to OR gates cascade. The time to calculate the result depends on the size of discernibility matrix, increasing with its size. Last gate in cascade stores the result of calculations in the **CORE** register.

Sequential type of the core calculation module decreases number of used logical elements in FPGA. Number of cycles needed to complete the calculation is equal to the number of objects in the input decision table.

4   Experimental Results

Software version of CORE-HIDM algorithm described in Sect. 2.2 was implemented in C language. The results of the software implementation were obtained using a PC equipped with an 8 GB RAM and 4-core Intel Core i7 3632QM with maximum 3.2 GHz in Turbo mode clock speed running Windows 10 operational system. The source code of application was compiled using the GNU GCC 10.1 compiler with –O2 optimization level.

Quartus II 13.1 was used for design, compilation, synthesis and verifying simulation of the hardware implementation in Altera chip, while Xilinx Vivado 2020.1 was used for Zynq. In both cases VHDL language was used for hardware part. Synthesized hardware blocks were downloaded and run on TeraSIC DE-3 equipped with Stratix III EP3SL150F1152C2N FPGA chip and PYNQ-Z2 equipped with Zynq XC7Z020 chip. FPGA clocks was running at 50 MHz for the sequential parts of the project. Software part for NIOS II and ARM Cortex A9 was implemented in C language.

Timing results were obtained using LeCroy waveSurfer 104MXs-B (1 GHz bandwidth, 10 GS/s) oscilloscope. For longer times, hardware time measurement units instantiated inside FPGAs were used.

It should be noticed, that PCs clock is $\frac{clk_{PC}}{clk_{FPGA}} = 64$ times faster than development boards clock source.

All calculations were performed using datasets described in Sect. 2.3 with sizes between 1 000 and 1 000 000 objects. Data was preprocessed on PC in terms of binary transformation and discretization for all cases. Time needed for performing any of those operations was not taken into consideration.

Table 1 presents results of the time elapsed for hardware and software solution using indirect row-by-row discernibility matrix calculation (algorithm CORE-HIDM described in Sect. 2.2) for both datasets. Column labeled as t_{HA} represents time taken for hardware solution running in Altera, t_{HX} is for Xilinx, t_S is for software, while C_A and C_X represent speedup factors for Xilinx and Altera. Abbreviations in objects number are: $k = 10^3$, $M = 10^6$.

Table 1. Comparison of execution time between hardware and software implementation of CORE-HIDM algorithm for both datasets

$|U|$	t_{HA}	t_{HX}	t_S	$C_A = \frac{t_S}{t_{HA}}$	$C_X = \frac{t_S}{t_{HX}}$	$\frac{t_{HX}}{t_{HA}}$
—	[s]	[s]	[s]	—	—	—
Poker Hand dataset						
1k	0.003	0.003	0.033	10.875	12.946	1.190
2.5k	0.013	0.011	0.143	11.119	12.929	1.163
5k	0.055	0.046	0.603	10.951	13.194	1.205
10k	0.207	0.174	2.410	11.623	13.837	1.190
25k	1.225	1.066	14.721	12.015	13.810	1.149
50k	4.710	4.050	58.726	12.469	14.499	1.163
100k	21.737	18.476	237.942	10.946	12.878	1.176
250k	130.947	109.995	1 515.449	11.573	13.777	1.190
500k	506.225	435.354	6 092.916	12.036	13.995	1.163
1M	1 850.523	1 535.934	24 313.094	13.138	15.830	1.205
Diabetes dataset						
1k	0.003	0.003	0.018	5.911	7.037	1.190
2.5k	0.013	0.011	0.078	6.044	7.028	1.163
5k	0.055	0.046	0.328	5.953	7.172	1.205
10k	0.207	0.174	1.31	6.318	7.521	1.190
25k	1.225	1.066	8.002	6.531	7.507	1.149
50k	4.710	4.050	34.216	7.265	8.448	1.163
100k	21.737	18.476	135.309	6.225	7.323	1.176
250k	130.947	109.995	861.781	6.581	7.835	1.190
500k	506.225	435.354	3 464.821	6.844	7.959	1.163
1M	1 850.523	1 535.934	13 825.976	7.471	9.002	1.205

FPGA resources utilization is fixed and is independent of the input dataset size. Datasets are divided into parts which are processed by the module. Module for CORE-HIDM uses 21 562 Logical Elements (LE) of 113 600 available on Altera and 16 452 Programmable Logic Cells for Xilinx of 85 000 available. Number for Altera also include resources consumed by NIOS II processor.

It is worth to mention, that Xilinx processing speed comparing to Altera device is in average 1.18 times faster. The main reason for this is the fact, that Xilinx Zynq XC7Z020 is a newer design than Altera Stratix III EP3SL150F1152C2N. Additional and very important fact is that ARM Cortex A9 core in Xilinx device is a real core (instead of softcore) and is clocked faster that NIOS II Altera softcore CPU.

Figure 3 presents a plot showing the relationship between the number of objects and execution time for hardware and software solution using CORE-HIDM algorithm. Both axes on plot have the logarithmic scale.

Presented results show big increase in the speed of data processing for both implementations. Hardware module execution time compared to the software implementation using row-by-row discernibility matrix calculation (CORE-HIDM algorithm) is 5 to 12 times faster. Speed-up factor is almost constant for presented algorithms and is similar for all sizes of processed datasets.

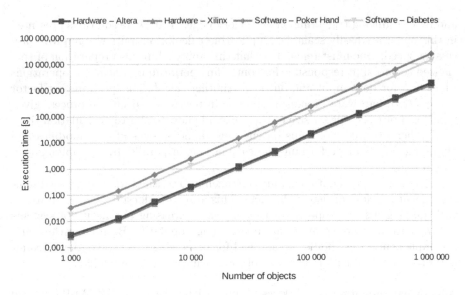

Fig. 3. Relationship between number of objects and calculation time for hardware and software implementation of CORE-HIDM algorithm

Hardware processing times for both datasets are the same - it doesn't matter what is the width in bits of single object from dataset, unless it doesn't fits in assumed memory boundary. Hardware processing unit takes the same time to finish the calculation for every object size, because it always performs the same type of operation.

Let comparison of attribute value between two objects or retrieving the element from discernibility matrix be an elementary operation. k denotes number of conditional attributes and n is the number of objects in decision table. Computational complexity of software implementation for the core calculation is using CORE-HIDM algorithm is $\Theta(kn^2)$. Using hardware implementation, complexity of core calculation is $\Theta(n^2)$. The k is missing in both hardware implementations, because presented solution performs comparison between all attributes in $\Theta(1)$ - all attributes values between two objects are compared in single clock cycle. Additionally, core module performs comparisons between many objects at time. In most cases $k \ll n$, so it can be said, that computational complexity for software and hardware implementations are the same.

5   Conclusions and Future Research

Performing core calculations using hardware implementations gives a big acceleration in comparison to software solution. This approach is the main direction of using scalable rough sets methods in solutions demanding real-time execution.

Core hardware calculation units were not optimized for performance. Processing time can be substantially reduced by increasing FPGA clock frequency and by introducing triggering on both clock edges. Hardware solutions presented in this paper are easily scalable. Duplicating calculation units will improve processing speed. One must remember that this approach needs preparation of specialized control unit responsible for controlling performing concurrent operations (data flow for both input and output). Another calculation speed impact factor is the size of hardware processing module in terms of capacity to process given number of objects. Bigger size of the unit will allow to shorten calculation time.

Further research will focus on checking different sizes of core modules and obtaining results of performing the calculations in parallel by multiplying execution units.

Type of processed data must also be taken into consideration. Presented solution is suitable for consistent datasets. This approach doesn't handle databases with missing values properly. In recent years increasing popularity of systems dealing with incomplete information is gaining popularity. Both algorithms and it's implementations should be modified for processing this type of data. Examples of such approach for software solutions can be found in e.g.[25].

Acknowledgements. The work was supported by the grant WZ/WI-IIT/2/2020 from Bialystok University of Technology and funded with resources for research by the Ministry of Science and Higher Education in Poland.

References

1. Banerjee, A., Maji, P.: Segmentation of bias field induced brain MR images using rough sets and stomped-t distribution. Inf. Sci. **504**, 520–545 (2019)
2. Chen, Y.S., Cheng, C.H.: Hybrid models based on rough set classifiers for setting credit rating decision rules in the global banking industry. Knowl.-Based Syst. **39**, 224–239 (2013)
3. Grześ, T., Kopczyński, M., Stepaniuk, J.: FPGA in rough set based core and reduct computation. In: Lingras, P., Wolski, M., Cornelis, C., Mitra, S., Wasilewski, P. (eds.) RSKT 2013. LNCS (LNAI), vol. 8171, pp. 263–270. Springer, Heidelberg (2013). https://doi.org/10.1007/978-3-642-41299-8_25
4. Grzes, T., Kopczynski, M.: Hardware implementation on field programmable gate array of two-stage algorithm for rough set reduct generation. In: Mihálydeák, T., Min, F., Wang, G., Banerjee, M., Düntsch, I., Suraj, Z., Ciucci, D. (eds.) IJCRS 2019. LNCS (LNAI), vol. 11499, pp. 495–506. Springer, Cham (2019). https://doi.org/10.1007/978-3-030-22815-6_38
5. Jiang, H., Zhan, J., Sun, B., Alcantud, J.C.R.: An MADM approach to covering-based variable precision fuzzy rough sets: an application to medical diagnosis. Int. J. Mach. Learn. Cybern. **11**(9), 2181–2207 (2020). https://doi.org/10.1007/s13042-020-01109-3
6. Kanasugi, A., Yokoyama, A.: A basic design for rough set processor. In: The 15th Annual Conference of Japanese Society for Artificial Intelligence (2001)
7. Kopczyński, M., Stepaniuk, J.: Rough set methods and hardware implementations. Zeszyty Naukowe Politechniki Białostockiej. Informatyka Zeszyt **8**, 5–18 (2011)
8. Kopczyński, M., Stepaniuk, J.: Hardware implementations of rough set methods in programmable logic devices. In: Rough Sets and Intelligent Systems - Professor Zdzisław Pawlak in Memoriam, Intelligent Systems Reference Library, vol. 43, pp. 309–321 Heidelberg, Springer (2013)

9. Kopczyński, M., Grześ, T., Stepaniuk, J.: FPGA in rough-granular computing : reduct generation. In: WI 2014: The 2014 IEEE/WCI/ACM International Joint Conferences on Web Intelligence, Warsaw, IEEE Computer Society, vol. 2, pp. 364–370 (2014)

10. Kopczynski, M., Grzes, T., Stepaniuk, J.: Generating core in rough set theory: design and implementation on FPGA. In: Kryszkiewicz, M., Cornelis, C., Ciucci, D., Medina-Moreno, J., Motoda, H., Raś, Z.W. (eds.) RSEISP 2014. LNCS (LNAI), vol. 8537, pp. 209–216. Springer, Cham (2014). https://doi.org/10.1007/978-3-319-08729-0_20

11. Kopczynski, M., Grzes, T., Stepaniuk, J.: Computation of cores in big datasets: An FPGA approach. In: Ciucci, D., Wang, G., Mitra, S., Wu, W.-Z. (eds.) RSKT 2015. LNCS (LNAI), vol. 9436, pp. 153–163. Springer, Cham (2015). https://doi.org/10.1007/978-3-319-25754-9_14

12. Kopczyński, M., Grześ, T., Stepaniuk, J.: Core for large datasets : rough sets on FPGA. Fundamenta Informaticae 147, 241–259 (2016)

13. Lewis, T., Perkowski, M., Jozwiak, L.: Learning in hardware: architecture and implementation of an FPGA-based rough set machine. euromicro, vol. 1, 25th Euromicro Conference (EUROMICRO 1999), vol. 1, 1326 (1999)

14. Lichman, M.: UCI Machine Learning Repository. Irvine, CA: University of California, School of Information and Computer Science (2013). [http://archive.ics.uci.edu/ml]

15. Marz, N., Warren, J.: Big Data: Principles and Best Practices of Scalable Realtime Data Systems. Manning Publications Co. (2015)

16. Mehdipour F., Noori H., Javadi B.: Energy-efficient big data analytics in datacenters. Adv. Comput. 100, 59–101 (2016)

17. Muraszkiewicz, M., Rybiński, H.: Towards a parallel rough sets computer. In: Rough Sets, Fuzzy Sets and Knowledge Discovery. Springer-Verlag, pp. 434–443 (1994)

18. Penmatsa, R.K.V., Kalidindi, A., Mallidi, S.K.R.: Feature reduction and optimization of malware detection system using ant colony optimization and rough sets. Int. J. Inf. Secur. Privacy 14, 95–114 (2020)

19. Pawlak, Z.: Rough Sets. Theoretical Aspects of Reasoning about Data. Kluwer Academic, Dordrecht (1991)

20. Pawlak, Z.: Elementary rough set granules: toward a rough set processor. In: Rough-Neurocomputing: Techniques for Computing with Words, Cognitive Technologies, Springer-Verlag, Berlin, Germany, pp. 5–14 (2004)

21. Pawlak, Z., Skowron, A.: Rudiments of rough sets. Inf. Sci. 177(1), 3–27 (2007)

22. Stepaniuk, J.: Knowledge discovery by application of rough set models. In: Rough Set Methods and Applications. New Developments in Knowledge Discovery, Information Systems, Physica-Verlag, Heidelberg, pp. 137–233 (2000)

23. Stepaniuk, J.: Rough–Granular Computing in Knowledge Discovery and Data Mining. Springer (2008)

24. Stepaniuk, J., Kopczyński, M., Grześ, T.: The first step toward processor for rough set methods. Fundam. Informaticae 127, 429–443 (2013)

25. Sun, L., Xu, J., Li, Y.: A feature selection approach of inconsistent decision systems in rough set. J. Comput. 9, 1333–1340 (2014)

26. Tiwari, K.S., Kothari, A.G., Keskar, A.G.: Reduct generation from binary discernibility matrix: an hardware approach. Int. J. Future Comput. Commun. 1(3), 270–272 (2012)

Resource-Wokflow Petri Nets with Time Tokens and Their Application in Process Management

Ivo Martiník[✉] [iD]

VSB-Technical University of Ostrava, 17. listopadu 2172/15,
708 00 Ostrava-Poruba, Czech Republic
ivo.martinik@vsb.cz

Abstract. Resource-workflow Petri nets with time tokens (RWPNTT) are the newly-introduced class of low-level process Petri nets in this article. The theory of RWPNTT can be successfully applied especially in modeling processes for which the lower and upper limits of the duration of their activities are specified and in determining their lower and upper duration limits of the time-optimal critical steps and paths. RWPNTT theory also generalizes the original process model used by the CPM method in the direction that each activity may require a limited set of resources (e.g., energy, financial, material, etc.) for its exclusive use and successful completion that are shared by other activities of the same process. The concept of global network time is not explicitly introduced in the definition of the class of RWPNTT and it is then used only implicitly within the mechanism of the transition firing. The new RWPNTT class also enables the analysis of other process properties by using well-known methods of Petri nets theory. These properties of RWPNTT class are demonstrated on the simple process examples in this article.

Keywords: Resource-Workflow Petri Nets with Time Tokens · Critical path method · Discrete time · Process management · Resource sharing

1 Introduction

A number of defined classes of Petri nets are currently available [2] for the needs of modeling generally parallel systems of all the types. Modeling of time variables associated with individual system events, duration of activities, time history of the modeled system and many other time characteristics also play an important role when studying systems of various types. Time Petri nets and timed Petri nets [2, 11] are the two most important classes of low-level Petri nets that use the concept of discrete time in their definition. In the case of these and many other classes of discrete-time Petri nets [3, 4, 8] it can be stated that most of them use only relative time variables usually related to the specific marking of a given Petri net. This can then cause problems when modeling complex systems in which their components must be synchronized with a given external time source.

Workflow Petri nets (WPN) [1] were defined as the subclass of low-level process Petri nets [5] for their using primarily in the area of workflow management. WPN is a connected Petri net that includes within the set of all its places the unique input place with

© Springer Nature Switzerland AG 2021
K. Saeed and J. Dvorský (Eds.): CISIM 2021, LNCS 12883, pp. 418–430, 2021.
https://doi.org/10.1007/978-3-030-84340-3_34

no input arcs and the unique output place with no output arcs. *Resource-workflow Petri nets with time tokens* (RWPNTT) are the newly-introduced class of low-level process Petri nets whose definition and selected properties are the main topics of this article. RWPNTT are based in their meaning on the definition of the class of *workflow Petri nets with time stamps* (WPNTS) [7]. RWPNTT are specifically designed for their use in modeling processes for which the lower and upper limits of the duration of their activities are specified and in determining their lower and upper duration limits of the time-optimal critical steps and paths. The main difference between RWPNTT and WPNTS classes of Petri nets is the fact that the definition of global network time is not explicitly introduced in the definition of RWPNTT which greatly simplifies its implementation and proof of its properties. The concept of global network time is worked only implicitly within the mechanism of the transition firing in this case.

The critical path of the process is generally defined as the (temporally) longest possible path from the process start point to the process end point. Each critical path consists of the list of activities that the project manager should focus most on to ensure timely completion of the given process. The completion time of the last mission on the critical path is also the process completion time. The Critical Path Method (CPM) [9, 10] is used by default for this purpose. The RWPNTT allows not only modeling processes composed of individual time-dependent activities and determining their lower and upper duration limits of the time-optimal critical steps and paths, but, in addition to the standard CPM method, it also enables the analysis of other process properties with using of the standard methods of Petri nets analysis and it also has the possibility to analyze the processes whose activities share a finite set of different resources that are necessary to successfully complete any of them. These behaviors of RWPNTT are demonstrated on the simple project examples and its properties specification in this article.

2   Resource-Workflow Petri Nets with Time Tokens and Their Properties

Let N denotes the set of all *natural numbers*, $N := \{1, 2, \ldots\}$; N_0 denotes the set of all *non-negative integer numbers*, $N_0 := \{0, 1, 2, \ldots\}$; $\varnothing$ denotes the *empty set*; $|A|$ denotes the *cardinality* of the given set A; $A \times B := \{(x, y) \mid (x \in A) \wedge (y \in B)\}$ denotes the *cartesian product* of the sets A and B; $\neg$ denotes the *logical negation* operator; $f: A \rightarrow B$ denotes the *function* f with the *domain* A and the *codomain* B. Let $(A \subset N_0) \wedge (\exists n \in N: |A| = n) \wedge (A \neq \varnothing)$, then $max(A) := x$, where $(x \in A) \wedge (\forall y \in A: x \geq y)$, $min(A) := z$, where $(z \in A) \wedge (\forall y \in A: y \geq z)$. Let A be the non-empty set; by the (non-empty finite) *sequence* σ over the set A we understand the function $\sigma: \{1, 2, \ldots, n\} \rightarrow A$, where $n \in N$, that is denoted by $\sigma := <a_1, a_2, \ldots, a_n>$, where $a_i = \sigma(i)$ for $1 \leq i \leq n$. Function $\varepsilon: \varnothing \rightarrow A$ is called the *empty sequence* over the set A. We denote the set of all finite sequences over the set A by the A_{SQ}. If $\sigma \in A_{SQ}$, $\sigma := <a_1, a_2, \ldots, a_n>$, then the set *ELEMS*$_\sigma := \{a \mid \exists i, 1 \leq i \leq n: a = \sigma(i)\}$ and the function *length*: $A_{SQ} \rightarrow N_0$ is defined as follows: $length(\varepsilon) := 0$, $length(\sigma) := n$.

Definition 1. Let $(x_1, y_1), (x_2, y_2), \ldots, (x_n, y_n) \in N_0 \times N_0$, $n \in N$, are the arbitrary couples. Then:

1. $\oplus$: $(N_0 \times N_0) \times (N_0 \times N_0) \to (N_0 \times N_0)$; $(x_1, y_1) \oplus (x_2, y_2) := (x_1 + x_2, y_1 + y_2)$,

2. $<<$ $\subseteq (N_0 \times N_0) \times (N_0 \times N_0)$; $(x_1, y_1) << (x_2, y_2) \Leftrightarrow (x_1 \le x_2) \wedge (y_1 \le y_2)$,

3. $>>=$ $\subseteq (N_0 \times N_0) \times (N_0 \times N_0)$;
    $(x_1, y_1) >>= (x_2, y_2) \Leftrightarrow ((x_1 = x_2) \wedge (y_1 \ge y_2)) \vee ((x_1 \ge x_2) \wedge (y_1 = y_2))$,

4. $MIN(\{(x_1, y_1), (x_2, y_2), ..., (x_n, y_n)\}) := (min(\{x_1, ..., x_n\}), min(\{y_1, ..., y_n\}))$,

5. $MAX(\{(x_1, y_1), (x_2, y_2), ..., (x_n, y_n)\}) := (max(\{x_1, ..., x_n\}), max(\{y_1, ..., y_n\}))$. $\square$

Remark 1. Both $(N_0 \times N_0, <<)$ and $(N_0 \times N_0, >>=)$ are partially ordered sets (properties of reflexivity, antisymmetry and tranzitivity of the relations $<<$ and $>>=$ follow directly from Definition 1), but they are *not totally ordered sets* (e.g., $\neg((2, 3) << (1, 5)) \wedge \neg((1, 5) << (2, 3))$, etc.). $\square$

Definition 2. *Net NET* is an ordered triple $NET := (P, T, A)$, where P is finite non-empty set of the *places*; T is finite set of the *transitions*, $P \cap T = \varnothing$; and A is finite set of the *arcs*, $A \subseteq (P \times T) \cup (T \times P)$. $\square$

Some commonly used notations for the nets are $\bullet y = \{x \mid (x, y) \in A\}$ for the *preset* and $y\bullet = \{x \mid (y, x) \in A\}$ for the *postset* of the net node y (i.e., place or transition). The *path* leading from the node x_1 to the node x_k of the net is the non-empty sequence $<x_1, x_2, ..., x_k>$ of net nodes, where $k \in N$, which satisfies $(x_1, x_2), (x_2, x_3), ..., (x_{k-1}, x_k) \in A$. We will denote the set of all such paths of the given net *NET* by $PATHS_{NET}(x_1, x_k)$. The path of the net *NET* leading from its node x to its node y is the *circuit* if $(y, x) \in A$. We will denote the set of all the circuits of the given net *NET* by $CIRCUITS_{NET}$.

Definition 3. *Workflow net with time tokens* (WNTT) *WNTT* is the ordered tuple *WNTT* $:= (P, T, A, TI, IP, OP)$, where:

1. (P, T, A) is the *net*,
2. $TI: (T \times P) \to N_0 \times N_0$ is the *time interval function*, $\forall a \in T \times P$: $TI(a) := (TI_L(a), TI_U(a)))$, where $(TI_L(a) \in N_0) \wedge (TI_U(a) \in N_0) \wedge (TI_L(a) \le TI_U(a))$,
3. IP is the *input place*, $(IP \in P) \wedge (\bullet IP = \varnothing) \wedge (|IP\bullet| = 1)$,
4. OP is the *output place*, $(OP \in P) \wedge (OP\bullet = \varnothing) \wedge (|\bullet OP| = 1) \wedge (OP \ne IP)$,
5. $\forall p \in P \setminus \{IP, OP\}$: $(|\bullet p| = 1) \wedge (|p\bullet| = 1)$,
6. $\forall x \in (P \cup T) \exists \sigma \in PATHS_{WNTT}(IP, OP)$: $x \in ELEMS_\sigma$,
7. $CIRCUITS_{WNTT} = \varnothing$. $\square$

The WNTT *WNTT* consists of the net (P, T, A); the *time interval function TI* then assigns with each arc $a \in A$ of the type *(transition, place)* the ordered couple of non-negative integer numbers $(TI_L(a), TI_U(a)))$, where $TI_L(a) \le TI_U(a)$ (with the default value of $(0, 0)$ in the net diagram) that expresses the lower $(TI_L(a))$ and upper $(TI_U(a))$ bound of minimum time interval during which the token has to remain in the *place* instead of being able to participate in the next firing of some transition; the *input place IP* is the only one place of *WNTT* with no input arc(s) and with one output arc; the *output place OP* that is the only one place of *WNTT* with no output arc(s) and with one input arc. It must also be fulfilled for the *WNTT* that every of its non-input and non-output places has exactly one input arc and one output arc (see 5 of Definition 3); every node x (i.e., place or transition) must be the element of some path σ from the input place IP to the output place OP (i.e., every WNTT is the connected net - see 6 of Definition 3); *WNTT* then must not contain any circuits that could cause a state of deadlock during its firing of the transitions.

Definition 4. *Resource-workflow net with time tokens.* (RWNTT) $RWNTT$ is the ordered tuple $RWNTT := (P, T, A, TI, IP, OP, RP)$, where:

1. (P, T, A, TI, IP, OP) is the WNTT denoted by $\underline{RWNTT}$,
2. RP is finite set of the *resource places*, $RP \subseteq (P \setminus \{IP, OP\})$,
   $\forall rp \in RP : \bullet rp = rp \bullet \neq \varnothing$. $\qquad \qquad \qquad \square$

The RWNTT $RWNTT$ consists of the WNTT $\underline{RWNTT} := (P, T, A, TI, IP, OP)$; the finite set RP of the *resource places* is used for expressing the conditions of the modeled process containing some initial resources and we use circles with the double line for their representation; the preset of the given resource place rp is the same as its postset, i.e., $RWNTT$ can contain so called *loops*, generally $\boldsymbol{CIRCUITS}_{RWNTT} \neq \varnothing$ and therefore every circuit of the $RWNTT$ must contain at least one resource place rp.

Definition 5. Let $RWNTT := (P, T, A, TI, IP, OP, RP)$ be the RWNTT. Then:

1. *marking M* of the RWNTT $RWNTT$ is the function $M: P \to (N_0 \times N_0) \cup \{\varnothing\}$; $\forall p \in P: (M(p) = \varnothing) \vee (M(p) = (M_L(p), M_U(p)))$, where $M_L(p) \leq M_U(p)$,
2. transition $t \in T$ is *enabled* in the marking M of the RWNTT $RWNTT$, that is denoted by t enM, if $\forall p \in \bullet t: M(p) \neq \varnothing$,
3. *firing of the transition* $t \in T$ results in changing the marking M of the RWNTT $RWNTT$ into its marking M' that is denoted by M $[t\rangle$ M', where
   - $\forall p \in \bullet t: M'(p) := \varnothing$,
   - $\forall p \in t\bullet: M'(p) := \boldsymbol{MAX}(\{M(p) \mid p \in \bullet t\}) \oplus TI(t, p)$,
   - $\forall p \in P \setminus (\bullet t \cup t\bullet): M'(p) := M(p)$,
4. if the mutually different transitions $t_1, t_2, ..., t_n \in T$ are enabled in the marking M of the RWNTT $RWNTT$ (i.e., $(t_1$ $enS) \wedge (t_2$ $enS) \wedge ... \wedge (t_n$ $enS))$ we say that these transitions are *enabled in parallel* in the marking M that is denoted by the statement $\{t_1, t_2, ..., t_n\}$ enM,
5. finite non-empty sequence $\sigma := <t_1, t_2, ..., t_n>$ of the transitions $t_1, t_2, ..., t_n \in T$ for which the following is valid in the marking M_1 of the RWNTT $RWNTT$:

$$M_1 [t_1\rangle M_2 [t_2\rangle ... [t_n\rangle M_{n+1},$$

is called *step σ* and it is denoted by $M_1 [\sigma\rangle M_{n+1}$,
6. we will say that the marking M' of the RWNTT $RWNTT$ *is reachable* from its marking M if there exists the finite sequence $\sigma := <t_1, t_2, ..., t_n>$ of the transitions $t_1, t_2, ..., t_n \in T$ such that $M [\sigma\rangle M'$,
7. the set of all the markings M' of the RWNTT $RWNTT$ that are reachable from its marking M is be denoted by $[M\rangle$,

8. the set of all the finite sequences $\sigma := <t_1, t_2, ..., t_n>$ associated with all the reachable markings $M' \in [M\rangle$ is denoted by $[M\rangle\rangle$, i.e.,

$$[M\rangle\rangle := \{<t_1, t_2, ..., t_n> \,|\exists M' \in [M\rangle \,:\, M[t_1t_2 ... t_n\rangle M', n \in \mathbf{N}\},$$

9. *input marking* M_i of the RWNTT *RWNTT* is such marking where $(\forall p \in (RP \cup \{IP\}))$: $M_i(p) = (0, 0)) \wedge (\forall p \in (P \setminus (RP \cup \{IP\}))$: $M_i(p) = \varnothing)$,

10. *output marking* M_o of the RWNTT *RWNTT* that is reachable from its input marking M_i is every of its markings M_o where $(M_o \in [M_i\rangle) \wedge (\forall p \in (RP \cup \{OP\}))$: $M_o(p)$ $\neq \varnothing) \wedge (\forall p \in (P \setminus (RP \cup \{OP\}))$: $M_o(p) = \varnothing)$,

11. the set of all the output markings M_o of the RWNTT *RWNTT* that *are reachable* from its input marking M_i is denoted by $[M_i\rangle_o$,

12. the set of all the finite sequences $\sigma := < t_1, t_2, ..., t_n >$ associated with all the output markings $M_o \in [M\rangle$ is denoted by $[M_i\rangle\rangle_o$, i.e.,

$[M_i\rangle\rangle_o := \{ <t_1, t_2, ..., t_n> \,|\, \exists M_o \in [M_i\rangle_o: M_i \, [t_1t_2 ... t_n\rangle \, M_o, n \in \mathbf{N} \}$.   □

Definition 6. *Resource-workflow Petri net with time tokens* (RWPNTT) *RWPNTT* is the ordered couple *RWPNTT* $:= (RWNTT, M_i)$, where *RWNTT* $:= (P, T, A, TI, IP, OP, RP)$ is the RWNTT and M_i is the input marking of the *RWNTT*.

RWPNTT *RWPNTT* is said to be *proper* RWPNTT if the following is satisfied:
$\forall t \in T \; \forall rp \in t\bullet: TI(t, rp) \leq TI(t, p)$, where $(p \in P \setminus (RP \cup \{IP\})) \wedge (\bullet p = t)$.
The class of all the RWPNTTs will be denoted by **RWPNTT**, the class of all the proper RWPNTTs will be denoted by **pRWPNTT**.   □

Definition 7. Let *RWPNTT* $:= ((P, T, A, TI, IP, OP, RP), M_i)$ be a RWNTT.

1. Let $(t \in T) \wedge (t' \in T) \wedge (t \neq t')$; *COST*: $\mathbf{PATHS}_{RWPNTT}(t, t') \rightarrow N_0 \times N_0$ is the *cost of path* function defined as follows: $\forall \rho \in \mathbf{PATHS}_{RWPNTT}(t, t')$, $\rho := <t, p_1, t_1,$ $p_2, ... t_{n-2}, p_{n-1}, t'>)$: $COST(\rho) := TI(t, p_1) \oplus TI(t_1, p_2) \oplus ... \oplus TI(t_{n-2}, p_{n-1})$, where $\{p_1, p_2, ..., p_{n-1}\} \subset P, \{t_1, t_2, ..., t_{n-2}\} \subseteq T, n \in N$,

2. *ETI*: $[M\rangle\rangle_o \rightarrow N_0$ is the step *execution time interval* function defined as follows: $\forall \sigma \in [M_i\rangle\rangle_o, M_i \, [\sigma\rangle \, M_o: ETI(\sigma) := M_o(OP)$,

3. *MINETI*$_{RWPNTT}$ is the *minimum execution time interval* of *RWPNTT* defined as follows: *MINETI*$_{RWPNTT} := \mathbf{MIN}(\{ETI(\sigma) \,|\, \sigma \in [M_i\rangle\rangle_o\})$,

4. *TOSTEPS*$_{RWPNTT}$ is the set of the *time-optimal steps* of *RWPNTT* defined as follows: *TOSTEPS*$_{RWPNTT} := \{\sigma \,|\, (M_i \, [\sigma\rangle \, M_o) \wedge (M_o(OP) >>= MINETI_{RWPNTT})\}$,

5. *TOCP*$_{RWPNTT}$ is the set of the *time-optimal critical paths* of *RWPNTT* defined as follows: *TOCP*$_{RWPNTT} := \{\rho \,|\, (\rho \in \mathbf{PATHS}_{RWPNTT}(IP, OP)) \wedge (COST(\rho) >>= MINETI_{RWPNTT})\}$.   □

The theory of RWPNTT can be successfully applied especially in modeling processes for which the lower and upper limits of the duration of their activities are specified and in determining their lower and upper duration limits of time-optimal critical steps and paths. RWPNTT theory also generalizes the original process model used by the CPM method in the direction that each activity may require a limited set of resources (e.g., energy, financial, material, etc.) for its exclusive use and successful completion that are shared by other activities of the same process. The simple resource sharing model based on RWPNTT will be described in which each of these resources is represented by the separate token (0, 0) that is located at the appropriate resource place in the input marking M_i of the given RWPNTT, i.e., each of these resources is immediately available to the appropriate activity for its completion in the input marking M_i of the given RWPNTT and (in the case of proper RWPNTT) also for its further use by another activity once the previous activity has been successfully completed. The simple example of such process whose activities need to share selected resources for their successful completion is described in the following table of its activities (see Table 1) and it is represented by RWPNTT *RWPNET1* in Fig. 1.

Table 1. Table of activities, their time durations, dependencies and shared resources.

Activity	Time duration	Previous activities	Shared resources
A	2, 8	–	R1, R2
B	1, 2	–	R2
C	4, 5	B	–

The RWPNTT *RWPNET1* := $((P, T, A, TI, IP, OP, RP), M_i)$ is shown in Fig. 1, where $P := \{IP, P1, A, B, C, OP\}$; $T := \{T1, T2, T3, T4\}$; $A := \{(IP, T1), (T1, P1), (T1, B), (P1, T2), (B, T3), (T2, A), (T3, C), (A, T4), (C, T4), (R1, T2), (T2, R1), (R2, T2), (T2, R2), (R2, T3), (T3, R2), (T4, OP)\}$; $TI := \{((T1, P1), (0, 0)), ((T1, B), (1, 2)), ((T2, A), (2, 4)), ((T3, C), (4, 7)), ((T2, R1), (2, 4)), ((T2, R2), (2, 4)), ((T3, R2), (4, 7)), ((T4, OP), (0, 0))\}$; $IP := IP$; $OP := OP$, $RP := \{R1, R2\}$ (it should be noted that $TI(T2, R1) = TI(T2, R2) = TI(T2, A) = (2, 4)$ and $TI(T3, R2) = TI(T2, C) = (4, 7)$, i.e., *RWPNET1* is the *proper* RWPNTT).

Places A, B and C in RWPNTT *RWPNET1* represent individual activities of the studied process, the respective values of the time interval function TI (i.e., the couples (TI_L, TI_U)) associated with the input arcs of these places then express the lower (i.e., the value TI_L) and upper (i.e., the value TI_U) limits of the durations of individual activities (i.e., for example the activity B is represented by the place B, lower and upper limit of its time duration is given by the value $TI(T1, B) = (1, 2)$ and it has no previous activities). The place P1 then has the character of an auxiliary activity with the lower and upper limit of its time duration of $TI(T1, P1) = (0, 0)$. Each of the tokens (0, 0) located in the resource places R1 and R2 in the input marking M_i of the *RWPNET1* models the shared resource R1, resp. R2. Both resources can be used immediately after the whole process starts (because both are modeled by the token (0, 0)) and all of them will also be immediately available for further use by other process activities as soon as the respective activity using this shared resource is successfully completed (because *RWPNET1* is the proper RWPNTT).

RWPNTT *RWPNET1* is in its input marking $M_i := (M_i(IP), M_i(P1), M_i(A), M_i(B), M_i(C), M_i(R1), M_i(R2), M_i(OP)) = ((0, 0) \varnothing, \varnothing, \varnothing, \varnothing, (0, 0), (0, 0), \varnothing)$. Marking

M of any RWPNTT expresses the current time state of the modeled system using the ordered couples of the time stamps associated with each of its token. Individual values of the time stamps associated with the token that is located at the given place $p \in P$, informally said, represent the lower and upper bound values of the *implicit net time* (the net time *is not explicitly introduced* in the definition of RWPNTT) at which the respective token can first participate in the firing of the selected enabled transition $t \in T$ of the given RWPNTT. The transition T1 is enabled in the input marking M_i of the RWPNTT *RWPNET1* because $\forall p \in \bullet T1: M_i(p) \neq \varnothing$, i.e., $(\bullet T1 = \{IP\}) \wedge (M_i(IP) = (0,$ $0) \neq \varnothing)$ (see 2 of Definition 5). Firing of the transition T1 changes the input marking M_i of the *RWPNET1* into its marking $M_1 = (\varnothing, (0, 0), \varnothing, (1, 2), \varnothing, (0, 0), (0, 0), \varnothing)$ (i.e., M_i [T1⟩ M_1), where (see 3 of Definition 5) $M_1(IP) := \varnothing$; $M_1(P1) := MAX(\{M_i(IP) \mid IP \in \bullet T1\}) \oplus TI(T1, P1) = MAX(\{(0, 0)\}) \oplus (0, 0) = (0, 0)$; $M_1(B) := MAX(\{M_i(IP) \mid IP \in \bullet T1\}) \oplus TI(T1, B) = MAX(\{(0, 0)\}) \oplus (1, 2) = (1, 2)$.

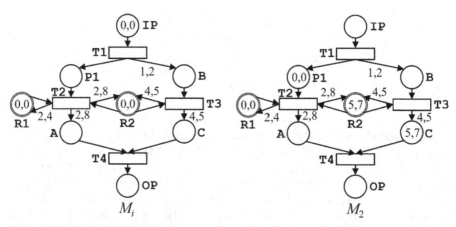

Fig. 1. RWPNTT *RWPNET1* in its input marking M_i and in the marking M_2 (M_i [T1 T3⟩ M_2).

The transitions T2 and T3 are enabled in the marking M_1 and so called *conflict* occurs at their enabling, i.e., both transitions T2 and T3 have at least one common (resource) place R2 in their presets, each of the these transitions is individually enabled in the marking M_1, but these transitions are not enabled in parallel in this marking (see 4 of Definition 5) and enabling of one of them will prevent enabling of the other (i.e., $(\bullet T2 \cap \bullet T3 \neq \varnothing) \wedge (T2\ enM_1) \wedge (T3\ enM_1) \wedge \neg(\{T2, T3\}\ enM_1))$. Since no explicit rule has been defined which of the conflicting transitions T2 and T3 to fire in this case, we will randomly select the transition T3 to fire. Firing of the transition T3 changes the marking M_1 into the marking $M_2 = (\varnothing, (0, 0), \varnothing, \varnothing, (5, 7), (0, 0), (5, 7), \varnothing)$ (i.e., M_1 [T3⟩ M_2) (see Fig. 1). The marking M_2 then models the situation in which the activity C is performed with using of the resource R2 and the activity A is waiting for the release of the resource R2. The token (5, 7) located in the place C expresses the fact that the lower, resp. the upper, bound value of the *implicit net time* when the activity C may be terminated is 5, resp. 7, time units and the token (5, 7) located in the resource place R1 that is shared by the activity C throughout this time interval have a similar meaning.

There is enabled transition T2 in the marking M_2 and firing of this transition changes the marking M_2 into the marking $M_3 = (\varnothing, \varnothing, \varnothing, (7, 15), (5, 9), (7, 15), (7, 15), \varnothing)$ (i.e., M_2 [T2⟩ M_3). Finally, there is enabled transition T4 in the marking M_3 and firing of this transition changes the marking M_2 into the output marking $M_o = (\varnothing, \varnothing, \varnothing, \varnothing, \varnothing, (7, 15), (7, 15), (7, 15))$ (i.e., M_3 [T4⟩ M_o). The single token $(7, 15)$ that is located in the output place OP in the output marking M_o of the *RWPNET1* then expresses *lower and upper bound of execution time interval* of the firing sequence $\sigma_1 = $ <T1, T3, T2, T4> (see 2 of Definition 7) required to implement the whole process, i.e., $ETI(\sigma_1) = M_o(OP) = (7, 15)$. There is another alternative firing sequence $\sigma_2 = $ <T1, T2, T3, T4>, i.e., M_i [T1 T2 T3 T4⟩ M_o, where $M_o = (\varnothing, \varnothing, \varnothing, \varnothing, \varnothing, (2, 8), (3, 10), (3, 10))$, $ETI(\sigma_2) = M_o(OP) = (3, 10)$. Therefore $MINETI_{RWPNET1} = MIN(\{(7, 15), (3, 10)\}) = (3, 10)$ is the *minimum execution time interval* of *RWPNET1* (see 3 of Definition 7). Finally $TOSTEPS_{RWPNET1} = \{\sigma_2\}$ is the set of *time-optimal steps* of *RWPNET1* (see 4 of Definition 7) because $(M_i$ [σ_2⟩ $M_o) \wedge (M_o(OP) = (3, 10) >> = (3, 10) = MINETI_{RWPNET1})$.

It is not without interest that in the case of RWPNTT *RWPNET1* no time-optimal critical path of this net can be found in the case of which its total time reserve is equal to zero, i.e., $TOCP_{RWPNET1} = \varnothing$ (because $PATHS_{RWPNET1}(IP, OP) = \{$<IP, T1, P1, T2, A, T4, OP>, <IP, T1, B, T3, C, T4, OP>$\}$, $COST($<IP, T1, P1, T2, A, T4, OP>$) = TI(T1, P1) \oplus TI(T2, A) \oplus TI(T4, OP) = (0, 0) \oplus (2, 8) \oplus (0, 0) = (2, 8), \neg((2, 8) >> = (3, 10) = MINETI_{RWPNET1}); COST($<IP, T1, B, T3, C, T4, OP >$) = TI(T1, B) \oplus TI(T3, C) \oplus TI(T4, OP) = (1, 2) \oplus (4, 5) \oplus (0, 0) = (5, 7), \neg((5, 7) >> = (3, 10) = MINETI_{RWPNET1})$. It is thus certainly worth noting that a given RWPNTT *RWPNET* can contain *several different time-optimal critical steps* but it *does not have to contain any time-optimal critical path* (in the sense of the classic CPM method)!!!

3 Basic Types of RWPNTT Reductions

Performing an analysis of a given RWPNTT with the primary goal of finding the members of the $TOSTEPS_{RWPNTT}$ and $TOCP_{RWPNTT}$ sets can be quite computationally intensive in the case of a large and complicated nets and in general the construction of its *state space* [2] may be necessary. One way to decrease the computational complexity of this task is to apply the so-called *reductions* above a proper RWPNTT. The reduction Φ: **pRWPNTT** $\rightarrow$ **pRWPNTT** is the function that transforms the given *proper* RWPNTT *RWPNTT* into a simpler proper one while preserving the values of $MINETI_{RWPNTT}$, $TOSTEPS_{RWPNTT}$ and $TOCP_{RWPNTT}$. We will present the basic types of such reductions in the following paragraphs for which it is obvious to preserve the values of $MINETI_{RWPNTT}$, $TOSTEPS_{RWPNTT}$ and $TOCP_{RWPNTT}$ after their application.

Definition 8. Let $RWPNTT := ((P, T, A, TI, IP, OP, RP), M_i)$ be a *proper* RWPNTT. Reduction Φ: **pRWPNTT** $\rightarrow$ **pRWPNTT** is defined as follows:

1. *if* $\exists rp \in RP \, \exists t \in T$: $\bullet rp = rp\bullet = \{t\}$

   then $\Phi_{rp}(RWPNTT) := ((P \setminus \{rp\}, T, A \setminus \{(rp, t), (t, rp)\}, TI \setminus \{((t, rp), TI(t, rp))\},$
   $IP, OP, RP \setminus \{rp\}), M_i')$, where $M_i'(p) = (0, 0)$
   $\qquad$ if $p \in (RP \cup \{IP\}) \setminus \{rp\}$; $M_i'(p) = \emptyset$ otherwise,

2. *if* $\exists rp \in RP \, \exists t \in rp\bullet \, \forall t' \in (rp\bullet \setminus \{t\}) \, \exists \sigma \in PATHS_{RWPNTT}(t, t')$

   then $\Phi_{rp,t}(RWPNTT) := ((P, T, A \setminus \{(rp, t), (t, rp)\}, TI \setminus \{((t, rp), TI(t, rp))\},$
   $IP, OP, RP), M_i)$,

3. *if* $\exists rp \in RP \, \exists t \in rp\bullet \, \forall t' \in (rp\bullet \setminus \{t\}) \, \exists \sigma \in PATHS_{RWPNTT}(t', t)$

   then $\Phi_{rp,t}(RWPNTT) := ((P, T, A \setminus \{(rp, t), (t, rp)\}, TI \setminus \{((t, rp), TI(t, rp))\},$
   $IP, OP, RP), M_i)$,

4. *if* $\exists p \in P \setminus (RP \cup \{IP, OP\}) \, \exists t \in T \, \exists t' \in T \, \exists \rho \in PATHS_{\underline{RWPNTT}}(t, t')$: $(\bullet p = \{t\}) \wedge$
   $(p\bullet = \{t'\}) \wedge (TI(t, p) << COST(\rho)) \wedge (p \notin ELEMS_\rho)$,

   then $\Phi_p(RWPNTT) := ((P \setminus \{p\}, T, A \setminus \{(t, p), (p, t')\},$
   $TI \setminus \{((t, p), TI(t, p)), ((p, t'), TI(p, t'))\}, IP, OP, RP), M_i)$,

5. *if* $\exists p \in P \setminus (RP \cup \{IP\}) \, \exists t \in T \, \exists t' \in T \, \exists \rho \in PATHS_{RWPNTT}(t, t')$,
   $\rho := <t, p_1, t_1, p_2, ..., p_n, t_n, p, t>$: $(p\bullet = \{t'\}) \wedge (|\bullet t_1| = |t_1\bullet| = ... = |\bullet t_n| = |t_n\bullet| = 1)$,

   then $\Phi_{p,t,t'}(RWPNTT) := ((P \setminus \{p_1, p_2, ..., p_n\}, T \setminus \{t_1, t_2, ..., t_n\},$
   $(A \setminus \{(t, p_1), (p_1, t_1), ..., (t_n, p)\}) \cup \{(t, p)\},$
   $(TI \setminus \{((t, p_1), TI(t, p_1)), ..., ((t_n, p), TI(t_n, p))\}) \cup \{((t, p), COST(\rho))\},$
   $IP, OP, RP), M_i)$,

6. *otherwise* $\Phi(RWPNTT) := ((P, T, A, TI, IP, OP, RP), M_i)$. $\qquad\qquad$ □

$\qquad$ All of the above types of reductions of a proper RWPNTT *RWPNTT* will be informally described in the following paragraphs and also demonstrated on the specific case of a simple proper RWPNTT *RWPNR1* (see Fig. 2). The Φ_{rp} reduction can be applied to a selected resource place *rp* of the given *RWPNTT* if it is associated only with a single input and a single output arc. The removal of this resource place *rp* and all of its associated arcs from the original *RWPNTT* is realized by application of the Φ_{rp} reduction and it is clear (see Definition 5) that the removal of this resource place *rp* containing the token $(0, 0)$ in the input marking M_i has no effect on the change of the $MINETI_{RWPNTT}$, $TOSTEPS_{RWPNTT}$ and $TOCP_{RWPNTT}$ values. It is therefore possible to apply the reductions $\Phi_{R1}(RWPNET1)$ (see Fig. 1) and $\Phi_{R1}(RWPNR1) = RWPNR2$ (see Fig. 2). The reduction $\Phi_{rp,t}$ can then be applied when the selected resource place *rp* is associated through its input and output arcs with the transition *t* and generally also with several other transitions $t_1, t_2, ..., t_n, n \in N$. If there is always for each of the transitions t_i ($1 \leq i \leq n$) a path connecting the transition *t* with the transition t_i, resp. the transition t_i with the transition *t*, it is possible to remove from the *RWPNTT* both the arcs connecting the resource place *rp* with the transition *t*. The firing of the transition *t* always takes place before, resp. after, the execution of any of the transitions $t_1, t_2, ..., t_n$ and due to the properties of proper *RWPNTT*, removing the respective arcs does not change the values of $MINETI_{RWPNTT}$, $TOSTEPS_{RWPNTT}$ and $TOCP_{RWPNTT}$. The application of the reduction $\Phi_{R2,T1}(RWPNR2)$ is shown in Fig. 2, where it holds that $rp = R2$, $t = T1$ and $t_1 = T3$ in the *RWPNR2*. It is worth mentioning that in this case it is of course also possible to apply the reduction $\Phi_{R2,T3}(RWPNR2)$, where $rp = R2$, $t = T3$ and $t_1 = T1$.

The reduction Φ_p can be applied if there exists a place $p \in P \setminus (RP \cup \{IP, OP\})$ (i.e., this is the place is B in *RWPNR3*) and the transitions t a t', where ($\bullet p = \{t\}$) $\wedge$ ($p\bullet = \{t'\}$) in *RWPNTT* (i.e., these are the transitions T1 and T3 in *RWPNR3*). If there exists an alternative path ρ that does not contain the place p between these two transitions in the *RWPNTT* (i.e., $\rho = $ <T1, A, T2, C, T3> in *RWPNR3*) and for which the condition $TI(t, p) <<COST(\rho)$ applies (i.e., $(2, 3) = TI(\text{T1, B})<<COST(<\text{T1, A, T2, C, T3}>)$ $= TI(\text{T1, A}) \oplus TI(\text{T2, C}) = (1, 4) \oplus (4, 7) = (5, 11)$ in *RWPNR3*). Then it is obvious that the removal of the place p with all of its associated arcs (i.e., the place B and the arcs (T1, B) and (B, T3) in *RWPNR3*) cannot have an effect on the change of the values $MINETI_{RWPNTT}$, $TOSTEPS_{RWPNTT}$ and $TOCP_{RWPNTT}$ due to the existence of an alternative path ρ with the longer time interval of execution.

The reduction $\Phi_{p,t,t'}$ can be applied in *RWPNTT* if there exists a place $p \in P \setminus (RP \cup \{IP\})$ and further the transitions t and t', where $p\bullet = \{t'\}$ (i.e., it is the place C and the transitions T1 and T3 in *RWPNR4*). If there exists a path $\rho = $ <t, p_1, t_1, p_2,..., p_n, t_n, p, t'> between the transitions t and t', where $|\bullet t_1| = |t_1\bullet| = ... = |\bullet t_n| = |t_n\bullet| = 1$ in the *RWPNTT* (i.e., $\rho = $ <T1, A, T2, C, T3> in *RWPNR4*), it is obvious that the places p_1, p_2,..., p_n, p can be "merged" into the single place p where $TI(t, p) := COST(\rho)$ (i.e., the reduction $\Phi_{C,T1,T3}$ "merges" the places A and C into the single place C where $TI(\text{T1, C})$ $:= COST(<\text{T1, A, T2, C, T3}>) = TI(\text{T1, A}) \oplus TI(\text{T2, C}) = (1, 4) \oplus (4, 7) = (5, 11)$ in *RWPNR4*). It is also obvious that the implementation of this reduction generally does not change the value of $MINETI_{RWPNTT}$, but the values $TOSTEPS_{RWPNTT}$ and $TOCP_{RWPNTT}$ are generally no longer preserved in this case (because they could potentially contain the places p_1, p_2,..., p_n and the transitions t_1, t_2,..., t_n; however, in this case it is very easy to restore both the original $TOSTEPS_{RWPNTT}$ and $TOCP_{RWPNTT}$ values of the *RWPNTT* by adding of the appropriate deleted places and transitions).

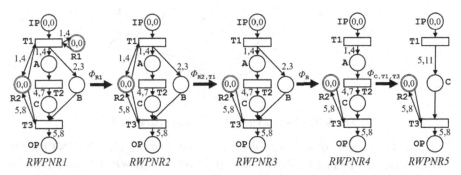

Fig. 2. Reductions Φ_{R1}, $\Phi_{R2,T1}$, Φ_B and $\Phi_{C,T1,T3}$ of RWPNTT *RWPNR1*.

The more complicated example of the process is given in the following table of its activities (see Table 2) and it is represented by proper RWPNTT *RWPNET2* in Fig. 3.

Table 2. Table of activities, their time durations, dependencies and shared resources.

Activity	Time duration	Previous activities	Shared resources
A	6, 8	–	R1, R2
B	3, 6	A	–
C	4, 7	–	R1, R3
D	1, 2	–	–
E	1, 3	B, D	R4
F	2, 4	A	R2
G	5, 6	A	R2, R4
H	6, 9	E, I	–
I	7, 9	C	–
J	5, 8	C	R3

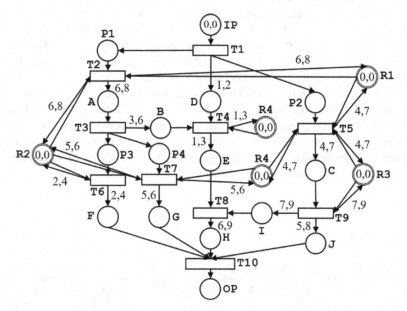

Fig. 3. RWPNTT *RWPNET2* in its input marking M_i.

Gradual application of selected reductions over *RWPNET2* gives RWPNTT *RWP-NET3* = $\Phi_{I,T5,T8}(\Phi_{E,T3,T8}(\Phi_J(\Phi_D(\Phi_{R4}(\Phi_{R3}(\Phi_{R3,T5}(\Phi_{R2,T2}(RWPNET2)))))))))$ that can be shown in Fig. 4. Let σ_1 = <T1, T2, T5, T3, T6, T7, T8, T10> and σ_2 = <T1, T5, T2, T3, T6, T7, T8, T10> in *RWPNET3*, where the transitions T6, T7, T8 are enabled in parallel in both sequences σ_1 and σ_2 and can be fired in any order. It can be shown that $ETI(\sigma_1)$ = (23, 32), $ETI(\sigma_2)$ = (20, 33), i.e., $MINETI_{RWPNET3}$ = $MIN(\{(23, 32), (20, 33)\})$ = (20, 32). $TOSTEPS_{RWPNET3}$ = $\{\sigma_1, \sigma_2\}$, because $ETI(\sigma_1)$ = (23, 32) $>>=$ (20, 32) = $MINETI_{RWPNET3}$ (i.e., the value 32 represents the *minimum upper bound of execution time interval* which can be achieved by performing the sequence σ_1); $ETI(\sigma_2)$ = (20, 33) $>>=$ (20, 32) = $MINETI_{RWPNET3}$ (i.e., the value 20 then represents the *minimum lower bound of execution time interval* which can be achieved by performing the

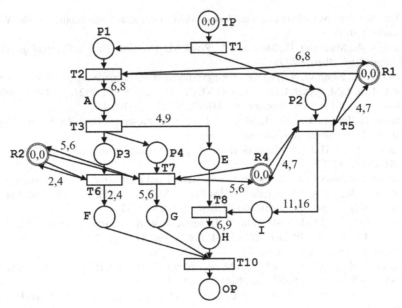

Fig. 4. RWPNT $RWPNET3 = \Phi_{I,T5,T8}(\Phi_{E,T3,T8} (\Phi_J(\Phi_D(\Phi_{R4} (\Phi_{R3}(\Phi_{R3,T5}(\Phi_{R2,T2}(RWP\text{-}NET2))))))))$.

sequence σ_2). Similar to the network $RWPNET1$, it can be shown that also the $RWPNET3$ (i.e., and also $RWPNET2$) does not contain the time-optimal critical path in the case of which its total time reserve is equal to zero, i.e., $TOCP_{RWPNET3} = \varnothing$.

4 Conclusions

The definition of RWPNTT presented in this article can be further generalized and their modeling capabilities for applications in the area of processes control and their optimization can be extended, especially for modeling the temporary unavailability of individual shared resources, the possibility to enter the duration of individual process activities in the form of fuzzy numbers, etc. The issue of RWPNTT reductions can also be significantly extended, especially by introducing the concept of RWPNTT subnets, determining their properties and their application in simplifying the shape of the given RWPNTT. Finding the time-optimal critical sequences and paths of such a process and verifying the properties of the RWPNTT that models this process is generally not a trivial problem and the use of Petri net theory plays a crucial role here.

This paper was supported by the Student Grant Competition project No. SP2021/86 by the Ministry of Education, Science, Research and Sport of the Czech Republic.

References

1. van der Aalst, W., van Hee, K.: Workflow Management: Models, Methods and Systems, 2nd edn. MIT Press, Massachusetts (2009)

2. Diaz, M.: Petri Nets: Fundamental Models, Verification and Applications, 1st edn. Willey, London (2013)

3. Furia, C.A., Mandrioli, D., Morzenti, A., Rossi, M.: Modeling Time in Computing, 1st edn. Springer, Heidelberg (2012)

4. van Hee, K., Sidorova, N.: The right timing: reflections on the modeling and analysis of time. In: Colom, J.-M., Desel, J. (eds.) PETRI NETS 2013. LNCS, vol. 7927, pp. 1–20. Springer, Heidelberg (2013). https://doi.org/10.1007/978-3-642-38697-8_1

5. Huang, H., Jiao, L., Cheung, T., Mak, W.M.: Property-Preserving Petri Net Process Algebra. 1st edn. World Scientific Publishing, Singapore (2012)

6. Lin, Ch-P., Dai, H.-L.: Applying petri nets on project management. Universal J. Mech. Eng. 2(8), 249–255 (2014)

7. Martiník, I.: Workflow petri nets with time stamps and their using in project management. In: Saeed, K., Homenda, W. (eds.) CISIM 2018. LNCS, vol. 11127, pp. 193–206. Springer, Cham (2018). https://doi.org/10.1007/978-3-319-99954-8_17

8. Martos-Salgado, M., Rosa-Velardo, F.: Dynamic networks of timed petri nets. In: Ciardo, G., Kindler, E. (eds.) PETRI NETS 2014. LNCS, vol. 8489, pp. 294–313. Springer, Cham (2014). https://doi.org/10.1007/978-3-319-07734-5_16

9. Nassar, A.H.: Introduction to Project Management Using Critical Path Method, 1st edn. LAP LAMBERT Academic Publishing, New York (2018)

10. O'Brien, J.J., Plotnick, F.L.: CPM in Construction Management. 8th edn. McGraw-Hill, New York (2016)

11. Popova-Zeugmann, L.: Time and Petri Nets. 1st edn. Springer-Verlag, Heidelberg (2013)

Digital Device Design by ASMD-FSMD Technique

Valery Salauyou[✉] ⓘ and Adam Klimowicz ⓘ

Bialystok University of Technology, Wiejska 45A, 15-351 Bialystok, Poland

Abstract. Recently, there has been an increase in the complexity of digital device designs and an increase in the requirements for the development time and the reliability of the products. The developing new techniques for designing digital devices is one of the directions to solve this problem. This paper proposes the technique for designing digital devices based on finite state machines with datapath (FSMD), when the device functioning is described by an algorithm state machine with datapath (ASMD). Different techniques for designing digital devices are compared when implementing a synchronous multiplier on a field programmable gate array (FPGA). The effectiveness of the ASMD-FSMD methodology is compared to the traditional approach in terms of cost (area) and performance. The ASMD-FSMD technique, compared to the traditional approach, reduces the area from 28.6% to 39.7% and increases the speed for some designs to 17.6%. In addition, using ASMD-FSMD technique reduces design time and increases design reliability at least by a factor 2.5.

Keywords: Digital device design · Finite state machines with datapath (FSMD) · Algorithm state machine with datapath (AFSMD) · Field programmable gate array (FPGA) · Design technique · Design time · Reliability · Area · Performance

1 Introduction

Traditionally, the designed digital device is usually represented in the form of a datapath and a control unit (controller), which are designed separately. The datapath is usually implemented as a set of standard function blocks (registers, buses, multiplexers, etc.), and the control unit is implemented as a finite state machine (FSM).

In [1], the control unit and the datapath are proposed to be combined together and presented as a finite state machine with datapath (FSMD). The FSMD model has quickly become popular. In [2], the FSMDs for synchronous and asynchronous designs are presented. The FSMD model proved to be very convenient for testing the equivalence of the two designs obtained from synthesis or various design transformations [3, 4]. In [5], the digital system is proposed to be presented as an FSMD network, which leads to the implementation of racing-free hardware. The overall FSMD model is not always convenient when designing specific applications. In [6], formal FSMD models are presented for both the processor architecture and the ASIC (application-specific integrated circuit) architecture. In [7], the FSMD model with synchronous memory accesses is offered. In

© Springer Nature Switzerland AG 2021
K. Saeed and J. Dvorský (Eds.): CISIM 2021, LNCS 12883, pp. 431–441, 2021.
https://doi.org/10.1007/978-3-030-84340-3_35

[8], the FSMD model for array-handling is discussed. The decomposition of FSMD to reduce the power of digital systems is presented in [9, 10]. A comparison of the efficiency of FSMs and FSMDs is considered in [11].

Due to its visualization, the algorithm state machine (ASM) charts have become widespread to represent an FSM behavior. The ASMs were first proposed in [12] as an alternative to state diagrams. In [13], PROM-, FPLA-, and multiplexer-based implementations of the ASMs is considered. The minimization method of the number of ASM vertices is presented in [14]. In [15], the ABELITE tool for ASM-based controller synthesis is described.

Traditionally, the ASM charts were used to represent an operation algorithm of the control unit, i.e. FSM. In [16], it was proposed to use the ASM to describe both the behavior of the control unit and the register operations that are performed in the datapath. Such an ASM is called an algorithmic state machine with datapath (ASMD). Recently, ASMD charts have been increasingly used in FPGA designs: when implementing industrial control systems [17]; to implement the asin function using the CORDIC algorithm [18]; during hardware implementation of cryptographic algorithm AES [19]; when designing a universal asynchronous receiver transmitter (UART) [20], etc.

This paper proposes a digital device design technique called ASMD-FSMD, which is based on the Verilog hardware description language. The ASMD-FSMD technique is illustrated by an example of the synchronous multiplier when it is implemented on an FPGA.

The ASMD-FSMD technique allows to describe the design code in the Verilog HDL directly according to the ASMD chart without any intermediate descriptions. Using the ASMD-FSMD technique significantly reduces the design time compared to the traditional approach, since there is no need to design the datapath and all its components, as well as the control unit and the top-level module. The ASMD-FSMD technique also improves the reliability of the designs as many stages of traditional design are performed by the developer manually and are the source of difficult to detect errors.

2 Traditional Approach for Synchronous Multiplier Implementation

A simple school multiplication algorithm performs an arithmetic operation of multiplying two binary unsigned numbers $P = A*B$, where A is a multiplicand, B is a multiplier, and P is a product. Let the width of the binary words A and B be the same and equal to N bits, then the product P will have a width of 2N bits. At the beginning of algorithm execution, P is zeroed out. In each multiplication cycle, the least significant bit of the multiplier B is checked. If $B[0] = 1$, then the multiplicand A is added to the product P. If $B[0] = 0$, then zero or nothing is added to the product P. Then the value of the multiplier B is shifted one bit to the right and the value of the product P is shifted one bit to the left. The multiplication algorithm ends after considering all bits of the multiplier B.

In the case of the traditional approach, the hardware implementation of the synchronous multiplier is a sequential circuit, the inputs of which are the words A and B, and a value of the product P is generated at output. The circuit is controlled by the *clk* and *reset* signals. After setting the values at inputs A and B, the multiplication process is started by asserting the *run* signal. The termination of the multiplication process is indicated by asserting the *done* signal, after which the product value can be read from the output P.

Figure 1 shows a block diagram of the synchronous multiplier in the form of the datapath and the control unit, which is implemented as the FSM. The values of the multiplied words A and B are the inputs to the datapath. The P product and the *done* signal are generated at the outputs of the datapath. In addition, the datapath generates the *roll* signal, which is the output of the modulo counter and indicates the termination of the multiplication process.

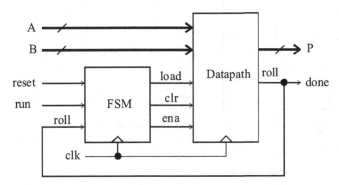

Fig. 1. Block diagram of synchronous multiplier in the form of the datapath and the FSM.

The external *reset* and *run* signals, as well as the internal *roll* signal, are inputs of the FSM. The FSM generates the following control signals: *clr* - to reset the registers of the datapath; *load* - to load values of the multiplied words *A* and *B* into the datapath registers; *ena* - to allow shift operations. The *clk* clock synchronizes both the datapath and the FSM.

A diagram of the datapath that implements the multiplication algorithm is shown in Fig. 2.

The datapath includes the shift register ra to the left by 2N bits for storing the multiplicand A, the shift register rb to the right by N bits for storing the multiplier B, the register rp by 2N bits for storing the product P, the bus multiplexer 2–1 by 2N bits, the adder by 2N bits, and the modulo counter that generates the *roll* signal indicating the termination of the multiplication process. The *roll* signal is the same as the external *done* signal.

The control unit is an FSM. As the FSM, both a Mealy type machine (Fig. 3,a) and a Moore type machine (Fig. 3,b) can be used.

To implement the multiplier in FPGA, all components of the multiplier are described in Verilog HDL. The detailed description of the datapath components (Fig. 2) and the FSMs (Fig. 3) for the implementation of a synchronous multiplier in the case of the traditional approach is given in [21].

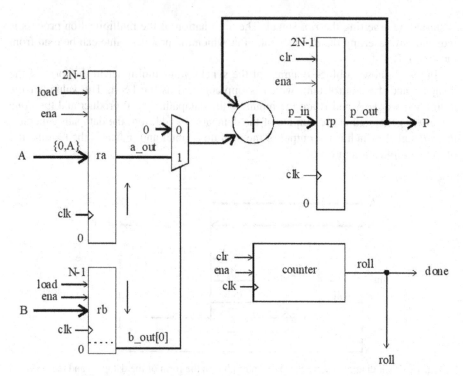

Fig. 2. Diagram of the datapath for the multiplication algorithm.

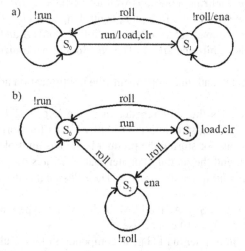

Fig. 3. Control unit representation of the synchronous multiplier as a state diagram: Mealy FSM (a), Moore FSM (b).

3   ASMD-FSMD Technique of the Digital Device Design

Let the ASM chart with datapath (ASMD) is an ASM chart in which any register operations that are valid in Verilog can be written in rectangles and ovals and any Verilog logical expressions can be checked in the decision box. The ASMD chart, as well as the ASM chart, consists of ASMD blocks. The actions described within the ASMD block are performed during one clock cycle. A FSM whose behavior is described by ASMD is *a state machine with datapath* (*FSMD*), and the FSMD design technique based on ASMD is *an ASMD-FSMD technique*.

The formal description of the considered ASMD-FSMD technique can be presented as follows.

Algorithm. The ASMD-FSMD technique of the digital device design.
1.   The FSMD states are determined.
2.   The ASMD block is constructed for each FSMD state.
     2.1. In the ASMD decision boxes, the logical functions are written, the values of which are checked in this state.
     2.2. For the Moore FSMD, the operations are written in the state box that are performed on the content of the registers in this state.
     2.3. For the Mealy FSMD, the operations are written in the conditional output boxes that are performed on the content of the registers on these transitions.
3.   The ASMD blocks are connected to each other in accordance with the algorithm of the device operation. Each output of the ASMD block can be connected to only one input of this or other ASMD block.
4.   If necessary, the ASMD is modified according to [22] for increase the performance or the area of the designed device. For example, the algorithm loops are analyzed and the ASMD is changed in such a way as to minimize the number of states in the loop.
5.   The Verilog-code of the FSMD is built directly by ASMD. In Verilog code, the variables correspond to the device registers. The logical expressions in the **if** statements correspond to the logical functions checked in the ASMD decision boxes. The actions performed in ASMD blocks are described as procedural blocks **begin...end**. For the Moore FSMD, the operations, which are performed in the corresponding ASMD block, are described in state box, and the next states are determined in according to the ASMD transitions. For the Mealy FSMD, all the actions, which are performed in the corresponding ASMD block, are described in the style of the algorithmic description.
6.   The FSMD is implemented using the appropriate design tool.
7.   End.

Note that, unlike [1], our FSMD is not separated into the control unit (FSM) and the datapath, but more closely resembles a behavioral (algorithmic) description of device functioning. However, in contrast to the algorithmic description on Verilog [3], the FSMD states are explicitly defined in ASMD.

Our approach to building the ASMD chart is also different from the ASMD chart defined in [3]. Our ASMD chart can describe any FSM type, both Mealy and Moore (in [3] Moore only), and operations performed in a datapath can be written in both ovals and rectangles (in [3] ovals only).

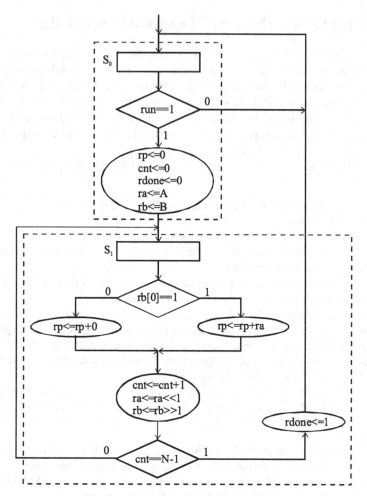

Fig. 4. ASMD chart for the Mealy FSMD.

Note that all methods for optimizing behavioral synthesis [22] can be applied to ASMD: dead code elimination, constant propagation, code motion, in-line expansion, loop unrolling, and tree height reduction. In addition, other ASMD-specific optimization techniques can be applied to ASMD, for example, to reduce the number of the states in a loop.

Figure 4 shows the ASMD that corresponds to the Mealy FSMD to implement multiplication algorithm for our example.

Note some of the features of the ASMD-FSMD technique. The main design stage is building an ASMD chart based on the behavior (the operating algorithm) of a digital device. There is no strict separation of the digital device into the datapath and the control unit (FSM). At the same time, the ASMD chart determines the FSM states that correspond to the states of the control unit. This allows to bind the algorithm of the functioning of the designed device to synchronization clocks. Therefore, according to the ASMD chart, the developer can track how many clock cycles each branch of the algorithm performs. In addition, the ASMD chart does not explicitly define the structure of the datapath.

The ASMD-FSMD technique differs from those known in that the ASMD chart can describe both the Moore FSM and the Mealy FSM. The actions performed in the datapath can be written in both rectangles and ovals.

4 Experimental Research

Using the example of the simple synchronous multiplier, two techniques for designing digital devices were considered: a traditional technique (in the form of a composition of the datapath and the control unit), and a technique using an FSMD (the ASMD-FSMD technique). To check the effectiveness of these techniques, the following designs of synchronous multipliers were studied:

- mult_FSM_Moore – the multiplier built in the form of the datapath and the control unit when a Moore FSM is used as the control unit;
- mult_FSM_Mealy – the multiplier built in the form of the datapath and the control unit when a Mealy FSM is used as the control unit;
- mult_FSMD_Mealy – the multiplier built according to ASMD for Mealy FSMD in Fig. 4.

Experimental studies were performed by the Quartus Prime tool version 18.1 with default synthesis parameters for the FPGA Cyclone IV E family. Tables 1 and 2 show the implementation cost L and the time t of performing the multiplication operation in different designs for different values of N.

Table 1. Implementation cost L of the multipliers (the number of FPGA logical elements).

Designs	$N = 4$	$N = 8$	$N = 16$	$N = 32$	$N = 64$	$N = 128$
mult_FSM_Moore	35	64	124	237	462	916
mult_FSM_Mealy	36	66	123	236	464	919
mult_FSMD_Mealy	28	49	90	172	335	657

Table 2. Multiplication time t (in nanoseconds).

Designs	$N = 4$	$N = 8$	$N = 16$	$N = 32$	$N = 64$	$N = 128$
mult_FSM_Moore	21	63	102	217	599	4118
mult_FSM_Mealy	20	42	76	213	589	4104
mult_FSMD_Mealy	17	39	84	192	582	3969

From Tables 1 and 2, it can be seen that when using the traditional design technique of digital devices (designs mult_FSM_Moore and mult_FSM_Mealy), the type of FSM

(Mealy or Moore) does not play a special role, since the implementation cost and the speed for designs mult_FSM_Moore and mult_FSM_Mealy are approximately the same.

A comparison of the ASMD-FSMD technique (mult_FSMD_Mealy) with the traditional technique (mult_FSM_Mealy) is given in Table 3, where N is the width of input words of multipliers in bits; L_T and L_A are the number of FPGA logical elements used (the implementation cost or the area); t_T and t_A are the time of multiplication operation in nanoseconds; L_T/L_A and t_T/t_A are relations of the corresponding parameters, *mid* is the arithmetic mean.

Table 3. ASMD-FSMD technique results compared to the traditional approach in design of multipliers.

N	LT	L_A	L_T/L_A	tT	t_A	t_T/t_A
4	36	28	1.286	20	17	1.176
8	66	49	1.347	42	39	1.077
16	123	90	1.367	76	84	0.905
32	236	172	1.372	213	192	1.109
64	464	335	1.385	589	582	1.012
128	919	657	1.397	4104	3962	1.036
mid			1.359			1.053

Table 3 shows that the ASMD-FSMD technique exceeds the traditional technique both in area (from 28.6% to 39.7%) and speed (maximum 17.6% for N = 4). Figure 5 shows the area advantage of the ASMD-FSMD technology over the traditional technology.

Note that the ASMD-FSMD technique allows to describe the design code in the Verilog HDL directly according to the ASMD chart. Therefore, using the ASMD-FSMD technique allows you to significantly reduce the design time compared to the traditional approach, since there is no need to design the datapath and all its components, as well as the control unit and the top-level module.

The ASMD-FSMD technique also improves the reliability of the designs. The fact is that many stages of traditional design are performed by the developer manually and are the source of difficult to detect errors. In the ASMD-FSMD technique, after the ASMD chart is built, the Verilog description of the design is performed directly by the ASMD chart without any intermediate descriptions.

In order to quantify the design time and reliability of the synchronous multiplier designs in the case of using the traditional approach and the ASMD-FSMD technique, we compare the code length (the number of lines) of the mult_FSM_Mealy design (the traditional approach) and the mult_FSMD_Mealy design (the ASMD-FSMD technique). The mult_FSM_Mealy design consists of the top-level module (mult_a_Mealy), the control device (fsm_Mealy) and the datapath (datapath_mult). In turn, the datapath contains the following components: the adder, the modulo counter (counter_modulo_M), the bus multiplexer (mux_2), the left shift register (shl_load), and the right shift register (shr_load), as well as the regular register (register) [22]. The number of the code lines for each module is shown in Table 4.

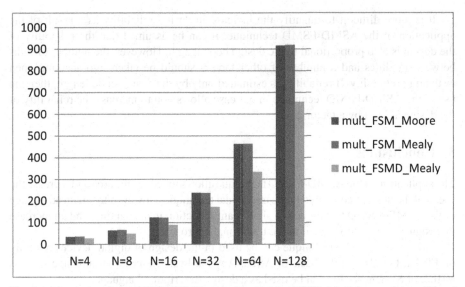

Fig. 5. Advantage of the ASMD-FSMD technique (mult_FSMD_Mealy) over the traditional technique (mult_FSM_Mealy and mult_FSM_Mealy) in the implementation cost.

Table 4 shows that using the ASMD-FSMD technique, compared to the traditional approach, reduces the design code length by a factor $144/58 = 2.483$, i.e. about by a factor 2.5. Let the design development time be directly proportional to the design code length. It can be assumed that for our example of the synchronous multiplier, using the ASMD-FSMD technique reduces the design time by a factor 2.5.

Table 4. Number of code lines for elements of the mult_FSM_Mealy design and for the mult_FSMD_Mealy design.

Module name	Number of code lines
mult_a_Mealy	17
fsm_Mealy	28
datapath_mult	26
Adder	8
counter_modulo_M	23
mux_2	9
shl_load	11
shr_load	11
register	11
$\sum$ (mult_FSM_Mealy)	144
mult_FSMD_Mealy	58

It is more difficult to quantify the increase in design reliability as a result of the application of the ASMD-FSMD technique. It can be assumed that the reliability of the design is also proportional to the design code length. However, the number of links between modules and a number of other factors should be taken into account when evaluating reliability. If reliability is estimated only by the design code length, then the use of the ASMD-FSMD technique in our case allows you to increase the reliability of the design at least by a factor 2.5.

5   Conclusions

The application of the ASMD-FSMD technique allows to reduce the area and increase the speed of the designs compared to the traditional technique. However, the main advantage of the ASMD-FSMD technique is a significant reduction in design time and an increase in design reliability compared to the traditional approach.

The ASMD-FSMD technique can be used in the design of digital devices not only on FPGA, but also on the basis of ASIC. Any hardware description language such as VHDL or SystemVerilog can be used as a design description language.

Acknowledgements. The present study was supported by a grant WZ/WI-IIT/4/2020 from Bialystok University of Technology and founded from the resources for research by Ministry of Science and Higher Education.

References

1. Gajski, D.D., Dutt, N.D., Wu, A.C., Lin, S.Y.: High-Level Synthesis: Introduction to Chip and System Design. Kluwer, Boston, USA (1992)
2. Auletta, R., Reese, B., Traver, C.: A comparison of synchronous and asynchronous FSMD designs. In: Proceedings of the IEEE International Conference on Computer Design (ICCD'93), pp. 178–182. IEEE: Cambridge, USA (1993)
3. Karfa, C., Sarkar, D., Mandal, C.: Verification of datapath and controller generation phase in high-level synthesis of digital circuits. IEEE Trans. CAD **29**(3), 479–492 (2010)
4. Hu, J., Wang, G., Chen, G., Wei, X.: Equivalence checking of scheduling in high-level synthesis using deep state sequences. IEEE Access **7**, 183435–183443 (2019)
5. Schaumont, P., Shukla, S., Verbauwhede, I.: Design with race-free hardware semantics. In: Proceedings of the Design Automation and Test in Europe Conference, pp. 6–12, IEEE, Munich, Germany (2007)
6. Zhu, J., Gajski, D.D.: A unified formal model of ISA and FSMD. In: Proceedings of the Seventh International Workshop on Hardware/Software Codesign (CODES'99), pp. 121–125. IEEE, Rome, Italy (1999)
7. Kavvadias, N., Masselos, K.: Automated synthesis of FSMD-based accelerators for hardware compilation. In: Proceedings of the 23rd International Conference on Application-Specific Systems, Architectures and Processors, pp. 157–160. IEEE, Delft, Netherlands (2012)
8. Banerjee, K., Sarkar, D., Mandal, C.: Extending the FSMD framework for validating code motions of array-handling programs. IEEE Trans. on CAD **33**(12), 2015–2019 (2014)
9. Hwang, E., Vahid, F., Hsu, Y.C.: FSMD functional partitioning for low power. In: Proceedings of the Conference on Design, automation and test in Europe, pp. 7-es. IEEE, Munich, Germany (1999)

10. Abdullah, A.C., Ooi, C.Y., Ismail, N.B., Mohammad, N.B.: Power-aware through-silicon-via minimization by partitioning finite state machine with datapath. In: Proceedings of the IEEE International Symposium on Circuits and Systems (ISCAS), pp. 1942–1945. IEEE, Montreal, Canada (2016)

11. Babakov, R., Barkalov, A., Titarenko, L.: Research of efficiency of microprogram final-state machine with datapath of transitions. In: Proceedings of the 14th International Conference The Experience of Designing and Application of CAD Systems in Microelectronics (CADSM), pp. 203–206. IEEE, Lviv, Ukraine (2017)

12. Clare, C.R.: Designing logic systems using state machines. McGraw-Hill Book Company, New York, USA (1973)

13. Green, D.H., Chughtai, M.A.: Use of multiplexers in direct synthesis of ASM-based designs. IEE Proc. E-Comput. Digital Tech. 133(4), 194–200 (1986)

14. Baranov, S.: Minimization of algorithmic state machines. In: Proceedings of the 24th EUROMICRO Conference, pp. 176–179. IEEE, Vasteras, Sweden (1998)

15. Jenihhin, M., Baranov, S., Raik, J., Tihhomirov, V.: PSL assertion checkers synthesis with ASM based HLS tool ABELITE. In: Proceedings of the 13th Latin American Test Workshop (LATW), pp. 1–6. IEEE, Quito, Ecuador (2012)

16. Ciletti, M.D.: Advanced digital design with the Verilog HDL. Prentice Hall of India, New Delhi (2005)

17. Martin, P., Bueno, E., Rodriguez, F.J., Saez, V.: A methodology for optimizing the FPGA implementation of industrial control systems. In: Proceedings of the 35th Annual Conference of IEEE Industrial Electronics, pp. 2811–2816. IEEE, Porto, Portugal (2009)

18. Saha, A., Ghosh, A., Kumar, K.G.: FPGA implementation of arcsine function using CORDIC algorithm. AMSE JOURNALS-AMSE IIETA publication-2017-Series: Advances A, 54(2), 197–202 (2017)

19. Burciu, P.: An Efficient (Low Resources) Modular Hardware Implementation of the AES Algorithm. J. Electr. Eng. Electron. Control Comput. Sci. 5(3), 1–10 (2019)

20. Sowmya, K.B., Shreyans, G., Vishnusai, R.T.: Design of UART module using ASMD technique. In: Proceedings of the Fifth International Conference on Communication and Electronics Systems (ICCES 2020), pp. 176–181. IEEE, Coimbatore, India (2020)

21. Salauyou, V.V.: Verilog language in embedded systems design on FPGA. Hotline – Telecom, Moscow, Russia (2020). (in Russian)

22. Bergamaschi, R.A.: Behavioral synthesis: An Overview. In: Reis, R., Lubaszewski, M., Jess, J.A. (eds.) Design of Systems on a Chip: Design and Test, pp. 103–131. Springer, Boston, USA (2006)

Bus Demand Forecasting for Rural Areas Using XGBoost and Random Forest Algorithm

Timo Stadler[1]([envelope]), Amitrajit Sarkar[2], and Jan Dünnweber[1]

[1] OTH Regensburg, 93049 Regensburg, Bavaria, Germany
timo.stadler@oth-regensburg.de
[2] Ara Institute of Canterbury, Christchurch 8011, New Zealand

Abstract. In recent years, mobility solutions have experienced a significant upswing. Consequently, it has increased the importance of forecasting the number of passengers and determining the associated demand for vehicles. We analyze all bus routes in a rural area in contrast to other work that predicts just a single bus route. Some differences in bus routes in rural areas compared to cities are highlighted and substantiated by a case study data using Roding, a town in the rural district of Cham in northern Bavaria, as an example. Data collected and we selected a random forest model that lets us determine the passenger demand, bus line effectiveness, or general user behavior. The prediction accuracy of the selected model is currently 87%. The collected data helps to build new mobility-as-a-service solutions, such as on-call buses or dynamic route optimizations, as we show with our simulation.

Keywords: Transportation · Rural mobility · Prediction

1 Introduction

Forecasting demand for buses is an increasingly important factor in public transit planning. Using predictions, an efficient way can be achieved to optimize the utilization of buses and save costs at the same time.

Until now, time-consuming surveys have been conducted in most cases to determine passenger requirements and collect data [8]. Based on these surveys, traffic planners and engineers were able to draw empirical conclusions and thus plan the various bus routes, the number of buses to be provided, and departure times. This type of data collection does not allow for dynamic adjustment of routes and it can quickly happen that the required capacities are wrongly estimated.

This means that if there are changes in customers' driving habits at short notice, it will not be possible to respond to them quickly enough. Besides, a large proportion of customers is not captured by a survey in rural areas because they live too far away from the villages. Our novel, prediction-based method for

© Springer Nature Switzerland AG 2021
K. Saeed and J. Dvorský (Eds.): CISIM 2021, LNCS 12883, pp. 442–453, 2021.
https://doi.org/10.1007/978-3-030-84340-3_36

demand estimation can speed up the analysis of the data. Conclusions about the use of public transport to be drawn immediately from the data provided.

For drawing such conclusions, we take parameters into account which are recorded with every ticket purchase or which emerge from the data. These include, for example, the price of the ticket, the length of the journey, the distance from the starting stop to the center, and the date on which the ticket was purchased.

Previously, this information was transferred from the ticket system to an Excel spreadsheet by an employee of the bus company to provide an overview of all tickets sold. This table was previously only used for accounting and not for statistical evaluations. Through the methods in this paper, automatic analysis of these data will be performed, and predictions will be made based on a machine-learning model.

The idea of using data from ticket sales is not completely new. However, we can evaluate the total amount of sold tickets in the countryside, while in big cities, where at least 100,000 or more tickets are sold for one bus line per evaluation period, the amount of data for all bus lines is too high for a complete evaluation [5]. In our case, a data set of only approximately 5000 entries represents the total amount of sold tickets.

Based on this, the demand for buses at all bus stops in the observed area is analyzed. The biggest problem with the locations is the large distribution over many stops and the small number of customers. Sometimes there are very few or no passengers at a stop, while at the main interchanges the capacity of a single bus is often insufficient. This problem is solved in this paper using a machine-learning model.

By using a machine-learning model, it is possible to generalize the individual smaller bus stops and thus circumvent the problem of insufficient data through combination and generalization.

The methodology presented was applied to a real case study. Roding is a small town with an area of $113 \, km^2$ and about 11,500 inhabitants (as of 2008) in Bavaria, Germany. The results show that the parameters time of day and distance to travel have a significant influence on ticket sales.

For the prediction of passenger demand, some of the best-known machine learning methods, such as XGBoost [7] and Random Forest [1], were tested experimentally by us.

To also cover the smaller towns and thus bus stops where only very few people board the bus in rural areas, we developed an algorithm with the help of which synthetic data is generated. To achieve this, an empirical distribution based on the input data is used. This synthetic data is created based on the real data and supplements the data set so that a set of people who, depending on the parameters, either buy a ticket or choose an alternative method of transport.

Thus, a machine learning model can be used to estimate how likely it is that a user will buy a ticket for a particular journey. Thus, the number of tickets purchased can be predicted for the whole catchment area for each day.

2   Related Work

This section discusses the previous studies that are closely related to this work, divided into Demand forecasting and Rural Transportation.

2.1   Demand Forecasting

A lot of work in recent years has focused on demand forecasting for public transport. However, most researchers work with a large dataset at their disposal or there are ways to automate the demand measurement through electronic support. For example, Bie et al. presented a method to divide a bus schedule into a different time of day intervals using GPS-data [2].

Burger et al. made it possible to identify the filling level of waste bins for a waste management system and were able to determine the demand for garbage trucks. Through transmission using LoRA-WAN [6]. Bie et al. also presented an approach that focuses on high-traffic routes with shared stops and combines an all-stop service with a stop-skipping service [3].

Cyril et al. were able to significantly improve the collection of data by integrating an electronic ticketing machine in Kerala, India. However, they also found those important personal aspects, such as the reason for the journey, transfers, or passenger perception, are still not captured by the system [9].

Ferguson et al. surveyed the travel characteristics of low-income and disabled people and developed a nonlinear model for optimizing departure frequency with the considerations of fairness and demand uncertainty [11].

Kong et al. investigated how a dynamic pricing model can also be implemented by predicting ticket purchases for long-distance buses and thus sell more tickets [13]. Other systems, so-called automated data collectors, are gradually coming onto the market. These systems include, among others, possibilities for automatic passenger counting, automatic vehicle location, and automatic fare collection [8,15,17].

However, these devices are too expensive for rural areas and are not compatible with German data protection conditions.

Unlike these approaches, our functional prediction model requires a comparatively small data set with which to make an accurate prediction. Moreover, only the purchase data of each passenger needs to be collected for an evaluation.

Our presented approach is particularly relevant in the field of this research, as it makes a good prediction even with a small data set and can thus also be used for rural areas.

2.2   Rural Transportation

In addition to predicting demand, another focus of the work in rural mobility. Work has already been done on this topic and important findings have been collected.

The SMARTA (smart rural transportation areas) project, for example, has collected so-called good practice cases that represent successful approaches in which a smart mobility scheme has been implemented and, for each of these programs, also addresses the innovation aspects in addition to the implementation [16]. In addition to describing numerous projects already underway in the field of rural mobility, SMARTA also produces insight papers on various countries (28 EU countries, Canada, and Australia).

Interesting for the implementation of this project are the reports on the countries Germany and Austria. Each of these reports indicates what proportion of the population lives in rural areas and also depicts this graphically using a map. In Germany, this proportion is 23% [19] and in Austria 39.1% [12].

Thus, a relatively large proportion of populations are affected by the problems of lack of mobility in rural areas. In addition to the data on the population and its distribution, the Insight Papers also provide information on the financing of mobility enhancement and regulatory restrictions.

Dickerson et al. address the increasing age of the population in rural areas. They find that the older population is often unable to drive themselves or unwilling to drive due to a lack of confidence, and thus relies on public transport. For older people, the development of mobility is therefore particularly important [10].

To improve mobility in rural areas, Bosworth et al. rely on a so-called place-based approach [4]. Through surveys, they identified the individual needs of different population groups, such as healthcare, housing, and connectivity. Thus, they found that mobility in rural areas also has a high social value and can thus promote personal well-being. Furthermore, three recommendations are made by this work, one of which is better planning through data science and analytics [4].

In addition to the general development of mobility, the rapid availability of transport options is also an important issue, which is addressed by Lakatos et al. They point out that the demand for transport in rural areas is very high, while the number of actual passengers is comparatively low. By expanding traditional public transport with a so-called demand responsive service, operating costs could be reduced and at the same time the saved costs could be invested in a better connection of individual villages [14].

All this work shows that it is not only in larger cities that the promotion and improvement of mobility make sense, but those rural areas can also benefit from the optimization of public transport with the help of data science and comparable methods.

3   Problem of Passenger Prediction in Rural Areas

An alternative approach that is often used to calculate the demand for buses over a short period is the time series model. With this model, however, the percentage of error was too high for some routes, which can be attributed to external factors that were not recorded [18].

As already announced, this work will not examine the determination of the journey time or the arrival time of a bus, but rather the utilization of all buses in the observed area of the city of Roding. The determination of the demand should help the bus company providing the right number of buses. This means neither too many nor too few, and an overcrowded bus is much more critical than an almost empty one. Therefore, noindividual bus routes are examined, but the entirety of bus traffic.

Due to the recently established collection of all sales, a very large amount of up-to-date test data is available. The 1-month tickets are recorded only when they are purchased and further journeys with such passes are not recorded.

For these tickets, it is not possible to say exactly how often they are used. However, as they are mostly used by students or employees, we assumed that they are used for a return journey every working day of the month.

Data collection bias is eliminated as all purchases are recorded. Due to the complete recording, an assessment of the demand is available at any time with comparably low computational effort. Besides, the data set can be used to predict demand at any time. Thus, a forecast daily can be used for short-term planning and a longer forecast over the whole year can be used for traffic planning.

However, the data set does not show why a person buys a bus ticket and how the customer perceives the fill level of the bus, but for many individual cases, such as the journey to work or school, which always happen at the same time, we can appropriately interpret the ticket sales.

It is not possible to make the dataset available to the public right now. For this, the data protection regulations must first be clarified, permission must be obtained from the provider, and the data must be anonymized.

4   Method for Predicting the Trend of Ticket Sales

As already mentioned, the main objective of this work is to identify trends and patterns in user behaviour when buying tickets. The method consists of a total of 4 steps:

- *Data collection*: The data must be extracted from the ticket sales system. Recorded by the ticket system are: Type of ticket, zone, departure time, date, start stop and end stop.
- *Discovery*: Discover patterns in user behaviour. The aim of this step is to identify a correlation between the parameters of ticket purchase. In this way, patterns, i.e. connections between the individual parameters that are not recognisable at first glance, are to be made recognisable later. An obvious example of such a pattern is the daily commute to work, which is obviously linked to the day of the week and the time of day. With the help of these patterns, the decisions of the machine learning models can later be better understood.
- *Setting up the prediction mode*: The main factors identified in 2.) for a ticket purchase are used to train different machine-learning that predict the demand. Machine learning frameworks used are for example XGBoost or Random Forest. They were chosen because they had already performed well in other similar tasks.

– *Synthetic data generation*: With the help of the machine learning model, synthetic data to supplement the original data will be generated with which realistic scenarios can be created in route planning.

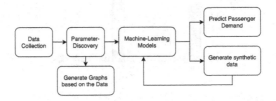

Fig. 1. Flow graph with the individual steps of the methodology

Each of these steps is described in a more formally way in the following sections and is shown in the diagram Fig. 1.

4.1 Data Collection and Analysis

The data must be extracted from the ticketing system. Recorded from the ticketing system are -types of tickets, zone, departure time, date, start-stop, and end stop. In the first step, the data is extracted from the ticketing system and transformed so that it can be processed by our model. The following data is collected from the ticket sales system: The exact time of sale with date and time, the start-stop and zone, the end stops and zone, the price level, the type of ticket the tariff community.

Thus, there are a total of 6 different types of tickets. These are "single adult ticket", "single child ticket", "10-trip ticket", "weekly student ticket", "monthly student ticket" and "day ticket". For the day ticket, only the first journey can be recorded.

The cost of a ticket is measured according to the price zone. Thus, a higher fare must be paid per crossed zone. For use in the prediction model, the price levels 1–7 and City of a ticket were converted directly into the price of a ticket. The length of the route in kilometres was calculated from the start and end stops.

Besides, the distance of the start and end stops to the city centre of Roding is recorded. Furthermore, an origin-destination matrix is generated for each route, which shows how many people travel a certain start/end stop combination. Thus, the most frequented stops, the average demand, and important start/end combinations can be determined later.

On the higher level of the entire bus network, these matrices can be reused. Based on this data, an initial analysis of the data is now carried out and various models are then trained with it.

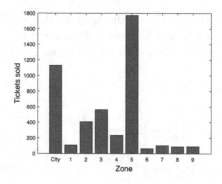

Fig. 2. Tickets bought per price-zone

Since it was found that many tickets were purchased at a central location, the city centre, an analysis of the travel distance of each user, as well as counting the distance of the final stops to the city centre, was also performed. Figure 2 shows the number of tickets sold in each zone. From this, it can be concluded that most tickets are sold at the "Zone 5" level, which roughly corresponds to 15 km. The second most tickets were sold in the City zone, which describes short trips within the city centre up to 3 km.

4.2   Correlation Discovery

An important measure for the evaluation of public transport is the recording of people getting on and off the bus. Usually, a so-called origin-destination matrix is set up for each route. However, this is not practical in our case because too many routes and stops are considered.

Since each bus stop has a different number of stops, a route with 10 bus stops was assumed for the calculation of the load rate based on the mean value. Entrances and exits were divided or combined accordingly.

The load rate is shown in Fig. 3. From this it can be concluded that most people travel the complete route from the start stop to the end stop.

Fig. 3. Load rate of bus stops

A possible reason for this is that these stops are usually located in city centres and therefore many people gather there. The smaller peaks in the middle of the route could be explained by the fact that there are often industrial areas in these areas and people use the bus as a means of transport to work. (In addition, the load rate could also be recalculated for each hour. However, this is not necessary in the case of Roding, as a bus travels a route a maximum of 2 times per day).

4.3   Prediction Model

A time-series analysis is used to model the demand. The programming language R was used for this purpose. R was used as a programming language because it offers many advantages in static data analysis. Data can be evaluated very flexibly with R and also visualised. This programming language is therefore ideally suited for the foreseen task and therefore many functions for implementing the time series analysis are already integrated.

The written programme code is thus mainly concerned with the integration of the data, while the model is implemented by prefabricated functions and only a tuning of individual parameters takes place.

When analysing the data of the Roding transport authority, it was found that the data is non-stationary in mean and variance. In order to detect Auto Regressive (AR) and Moving Average (MA) components in the data set, the Auto Correlation Function (ACF) and Partial Auto Corelation Function (PACF) are plotted. Spikes in the plot indicate that the points are not randomly distributed and thus contain information that can be extracted by ACF and PACF. The function *auto.arima()* was used to fit the best model to the data.

Based on the Bayesian Information Criterion, the best model was selected. Table 1 shows the validation of the selected time-series model for 3 different routes by plotting the predicted number of sales, the actual number, and the percentage error.

For both routes 200 and 282, the error is too high, suggesting that there are many other factors, especially on these routes, that have not been taken into account so far. One of these factors could be, for example, the weather, the temperature or other events not taken into account (e.g. school holidays).

In R, many different packages are available for interpolating missing data. *na.interp()* was particularly suitable for creating further synthetic data because of the consideration of the seasonality of data.

Table 1. Evaluation of the time-series model for three exemplary bus lines

Route	Predicted trips per year	Observed trips	Percentage error
200	307	218	29
230	943	837	11
282	326	173	47

Table 2. Performance evaluation of different machine-learning approaches

Algorithms	Accuracy	Precision	Recall	F1-score
Naive Bayes	0.61	0.64	0.61	0.59
Random Forest	0.84	0.84	0.84	0.84
XGBoost	0.87	0.87	0.87	0.87

4.4 Generation of Synthetic Data and Demand Prediction with Machine Learning

In addition to the comparatively simple prediction of people who buy a ticket on a route, another approach was used. Here, each ticket purchase is assigned to the group "ticket purchased". In addition, further randomised data was generated for which the purchase of a ticket is rather unlikely, whereby a total of two classes "purchase" and "no purchase" are available for classification.

For each new point, it can now be decided to which class the new point belongs, i.e. whether a ticket will be purchased or not. For this purpose, 3 different models were tested experimentally, Naive Bayes, Random Forrest and XGBoost. Each of the 3 models was trained with a learning rate of 0.001 in a total of 100,000 iterations. The test and training data set here consists of the newly generated data. Table 2 shows the accuracy of each model. This shows that XGBoost clearly performs best with an accuracy of 87%.

The main features of this library are model performance and execution speed. XGBoost thus outperforms several other well-known implementations of gradient tree boosting. The library is thus used because it does not sacrifice speed for accuracy or vice versa. It is a semi-perfect balance of both performance and time efficiency. The Naive Bayes classifier performs significantly worse than the other two because it assumes that all features are independent of each other.

However, it is clear from Fig. 4 that all 3 models estimate the same curve for ticket sales across the stations. Naive Bayes, however, estimates the number of tickets purchased much more cautiously and therefore achieves a lower accuracy.

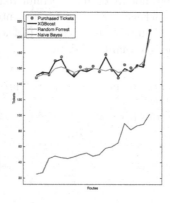

Fig. 4. Prediction of possible ticket purchases with Naive Bayes, Random Forrest and XGBoost

5   Case Study of Roding (Simulation and Results)

The presented method is now applied to the transport system of the transport companies. The problem in the city of Roding is that it is very rural, and the population lives very far apart. Nevertheless, every inhabitant should be able to use the possibility of a bus connection.

Before other possibilities can be explored, the current status and the demand for buses need to be determined first. Based on this, algorithms can later be used, for example, to decide whether a bus stop should be skipped completely or whether the routers should be re-scheduled. In Roding, there is also a very infrequent bus service that is stopped between 18:00 and 05:00. As mentioned above, passenger data was manually transferred to an Excel spreadsheet. Since this was done only recently, the existing data set so far consists of only 4928 tickets sold in the period April to October. In the future, it will no longer be necessary to query the sales database, as Verkehrsbetriebe Roding has switched to a new system that performs this task automatically and reliably.

In the first step, the data is extracted from the database. Here, each sale was combined into a single data point. From the database, the following values can be assigned to each sale: Type of ticket, start and end stops, date, and time. Besides, other parameters were derived based on these values by us. These are: the price of the ticket, current filling level of the bus and distance to the city centre.

With this data, we have performed an initial analysis across all bus stops. The first graph in Fig. 5 shows the distribution of ticket sales across all months covered. From this, it is evident that the number of passengers had a dip in midsummer and increased significantly from fall onward.

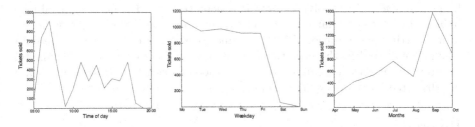

Fig. 5. 1) Number of tickets sold per time of day 2) Number of tickets sold broken down by days of the week 3) Number of tickets sold in each month

The second graph shows a distribution over the individual days of the week and the third graph in Fig. 5 the time of day at which a ticket was purchased. From these two figures, it can be concluded that bus transport is mainly used by students and employees. This becomes even clearer through further analysis, such as the type of tickets sold.

There are very few bus stops, they are spread over a large area and condense towards the town center. This network of bus routes will be analyzed in the following research and the need for buses will be determined.

6 Conclusion

The two main research areas of this thesis are Demand Forecasting and Rural Mobility. However the research and application in this paper is not limited to bus transport, but also includes These findings can also be applied to other areas of smart city planning such as waste management, cab services or other areas of public transport. By identifying and estimating ticket sales, for example, an overview of the population in a given area can be given.

This paper shows that the automated recording of ticket sales can have many advantages over traditional recording. The metrics identified provide an important foundation for further analysis of public transport.

However, a first application of a time series model showed that in some cases the estimation of demand is still too inaccurate and some important parameters are not yet captured. Therefore, in the further course, the data will be supplemented with further parameters such as weather, temperature and special events (public holidays, school holidays, etc.).

In contrast, great success has already been achieved in the use of XGBoost and Random Forrest for classification. Here, however, it is also interesting to see which means of transport people use when they are not travelling in a bus.

In order to find even better coherences between the parameters or impulsive events that would otherwise remain hidden, a continuous wavelet transformation was considered for the future.

This makes it possible to represent an event simultaneously in time and in frequency space. By applying wavelet coherence, new dependencies could be indicated that have so far been lost in the temporal space alone, such as delays or a recurring periodisation. Moreover, due to the progress of time, more data could be collected in the meantime. We expect to yield even more meaningful interpretations once we can apply our methods to ticket sales data which are not distorted by the Corona pandemic.

References

1. Biau, G., Scornet, E.: A random forest guided tour, November 2015
2. Bie, Y., Gong, X., Liu, Z.: Time of day intervals partition for bus schedule using GPS data. Transp. Res. Part C Emerg. Technol. **60**, 443–456 (2015). https://doi.org/10.1016/j.trc.2015.09.016
3. Bie, Y., Tang, R., Liu, Z., Ma, D.: Mixed scheduling strategy for high frequency bus routes with common stops. IEEE Access **8**, 34442–34454 (2020). https://doi.org/10.1109/access.2020.2974740
4. Bosworth, G., Price, L., Collison, M., Fox, C.: Unequal futures of rural mobility: challenges for a "smart countryside". Local Econ. J. Local Econ. Policy Unit **35**(6), 586–608 (2020). https://doi.org/10.1177/0269094220968231

5. Branda, F., Marozzo, F., Talia, D.: Ticket sales prediction and dynamic pricing strategies in public transport. Big Data Cogn. Comput. **4**(4), 36 (2020). https://doi.org/10.3390/bdcc4040036
6. Burger, D., Sarkar, A., Kirsch, K.: Combining fill-level sensing with route optimization for a more efficient waste collection. In: European Conference on Digital Government (2018)
7. Chen, T., Guestrin, C.: XGBoost. In: Proceedings of the 22nd ACM SIGKDD International Conference on Knowledge Discovery and Data Mining. ACM, August 2016. https://doi.org/10.1145/2939672.2939785
8. Cui, A.: Bus passenger origin-destination matrix estimation using automated data collection systems, July 2007
9. Cyril, A., George, V., Mulangi, R.H.: Electronic ticket machine data analytics for public bus transport planning. In: 2017 International Conference on Energy, Communication, Data Analytics and Soft Computing (ICECDS). IEEE, August 2017. https://doi.org/10.1109/icecds.2017.8390198
10. Dickerson, A.E., et al.: Transportation and aging: an updated research agenda to advance safe mobility among older adults transitioning from driving to non-driving. The Gerontologist **59**(2), 215–221 (2017). https://doi.org/10.1093/geront/gnx120
11. Ferguson, E.M., Duthie, J., Unnikrishnan, A., Waller, S.T.: Incorporating equity into the transit frequency-setting problem. Transp. Res. Part A Policy Pract. **46**(1), 190–199 (2012). https://doi.org/10.1016/j.tra.2011.06.002
12. Harris, S.G.: Austria Insight Paper (2019). https://ruralsharedmobility.eu/insight-papers/germany/
13. Kong, X., Li, M., Tang, T., Tian, K., Moreira-Matias, L., Xia, F.: Shared subway shuttle bus route planning based on transport data analytics. IEEE Trans. Autom. Sci. Eng. **15**(4), 1507–1520 (2018). https://doi.org/10.1109/TASE.2018.2865494
14. Lakatos, A., Tóth, J., Mándoki, P.: Demand responsive transport service of 'dead-end villages' in interurban traffic. Sustainability **12**(9), 3820 (2020). https://doi.org/10.3390/su12093820
15. Muller, P.F.B.H.T., Strathman, J.: Using Archived AVL-APC Data to Improve Transit Performance and Management. Transportation Research Board, September 2006. https://doi.org/10.17226/13907
16. SMARTA: Good practice study cases (2020). https://ruralsharedmobility.eu/good-practices/. https://ruralsharedmobility.eu/good-practices/
17. Wang, W., Attanucci, J., Wilson, N.: Bus passenger origin-destination estimation and related analyses using automated data collection systems. J. Public Transp. **14**(4), 131–150 (2011). https://doi.org/10.5038/2375-0901.14.4.7
18. Xue, R., Sun, D.J., Chen, S.: Short-term bus passenger demand prediction based on time series model and interactive multiple model approach. Discrete Dyn. Nat. Soc. **2015**, 1–11 (2015). https://doi.org/10.1155/2015/682390
19. Zeebroeck, B.V., Florizoone, W.: Germany insight paper (2019). https://ruralsharedmobility.eu/insight-papers/austria/

Core Computation and Artificial Fish Swarm Algorithm in Rough Set Data Reduction

Jaroslaw Stepaniuk[(✉)]

Faculty of Computer Science, Bialystok University of Technology,
Wiejska 45A, 15-351 Bialystok, Poland
j.stepaniuk@pb.edu.pl

Abstract. Reducing the redundant attributes is an important preprocessing step in data mining. In the paper, a novel search algorithm COREplusAFSA for minimal attribute set reduction based on rough set theory and artificial fish swarm algorithm is proposed. First, the algorithm identifies the attributes from the core. Second, the artificial fish swarm algorithm is applied. Some well-known data sets from UC Irvine Machine Learning Repository were selected to verify the proposed algorithm. The results of experiments show that the investigated method COREplusAFSA is a better solution to the attribute set reduction problem than the application of only artificial fish swarm algorithm.

Keywords: Artificial intelligence · Rough sets · Data reduction · Artificial fish swarm algorithm

1 Introduction

Reduction of condition attribute set is a quite useful data preprocessing technique, aiming to obtain a minimal attribute subset from a set of condition attributes while maintaining the same classification accuracy by deleting the noisy, irrelevant or misleading attributes. The step of condition attribute set reduction usually includes searching procedure, evaluation function, stopping criterion and validation procedure. From the point of view of evaluation function, it can be divided into two categories: filter method and wrapper method. The filter method constructs a function to evaluate the significance of condition attribute subset, while the wrapper method employs a learning algorithm to evaluate the quality of selected condition attribute subset based on the classification accuracy. Filter methods are usually less computationally intensive than wrapper methods, but filter methods produce a condition attribute subset which is not tuned to a specific type of classification method. This lack of tuning means a condition attribute subset from a filter method is more general than the subset of condition attributes from a wrapper method. Rough set theory has been used successfully as a condition attribute set reduction tool to discover data

© Springer Nature Switzerland AG 2021
K. Saeed and J. Dvorský (Eds.): CISIM 2021, LNCS 12883, pp. 454–461, 2021.
https://doi.org/10.1007/978-3-030-84340-3_37

dependencies and to reduce the number of condition attributes (see e.g. [7,8]). From the point of view of search strategies, there are three search methods for condition attribute set reduction including exhaustive, heuristic and random. Examining exhaustively all subsets of condition attribute set for selecting the optimal subset is impractical for large sets of condition attributes. Usually attribute set reduction algorithms involve heuristic or random search strategies in an attempt to avoid this prohibitive computational complexity. The artificial fish swarm algorithm (AFSA) is a swarm intelligent technique inspired by the natural schooling behavior of fish. AFSA presents a strong ability to avoid local minimums in order to achieve global optimization.

The purpose of this paper is to investigate new algorithm based on core computation and artificial fish swarm algorithm for rough set attribute reduction problem.

The paper is organized as follows. Section 2 provides basic information about rough set data reduction. In Sect. 3 new algorithm COREplusAFSA is proposed. Results of experiments on publicly available data sets are presented in Sect. 4 and compared with the results obtained in [1].

2   Rough Set Data Reduction

In this section we formulate the attribute set reduction problem.

Let $DT = (U, A \cup \{d\})$ be a decision table, where U is a set of objects, A is a set of condition attributes and d is a decision attribute.

Let R be a subset of A. We define fitness of R as follows:

$$Fitness(R) = weight_{POS} \times \frac{card(POS_R(\{d\}))}{card(U)} + weight_{AT} \times \frac{card(A - R)}{card(A)} \quad (1)$$

where $weight_{POS}, weight_{AT} \geq 0$ and $weight_{POS} + weight_{AT} = 1$.

The formula 1 presents that the number of objects in positive region and attribute subset length can have different significance for attribute set reduction task. The optimal solution is the subset R that yields the highest number of objects in positive region with the smallest possible number of attributes in R.

For example, if $R = A$ and $weight_{POS} = 1$ then $Fitness(A) = \frac{card(POS_A(\{d\}))}{card(U)}$ is the dependency of attribute set $\{d\}$ on attribute set A (see e.g. [8]).

The attribute set reduction problem is defined as follows:

Input: Data table $DT = (U, A \cup \{d\})$;

Output: Attribute subset $R \subseteq A$ with maximal value of $Fitness(R)$.

3 Finding Approximate Reducts with Core Computation and Artificial Fish Swarm Algorithm

In this section we sketch the proposed algorithm COREplusAFSA. The algorithm combines two methods and there is an interaction between the methods. Namely, if the core is nonempty set then the search space for AFSA is reduced.

> **Input**: Data table $DT = (U, A \cup \{d\})$;
> Initial parameters: $n, \ldots$;
> **Output**: Optimal attribute subset.
> $Compute(CORE(DT))$; /* (Core computation methods, see [3,5]) */
> **if** $Fitness(CORE(DT)) \geq Fitness(A))$ **then**
> | **return** $(CORE(DT), Fitness(CORE(DT)))$
> **else**
> | Generate n random artificial fish within the search space
> | $SS(DT) = \{R \subseteq A : R \neq \emptyset \ \& \ CORE(DT) \subseteq R\}$.
> | **while** *the stop condition is not met* **do**
> | | **for** *each artificial fish R* **do**
> | | | Compute the fitness value $Fitness(R)$;
> | | | Execute the $Preying(R)$ behavior;
> | | | Execute the $Swarming(R)$ behavior;
> | | | Execute the $Following(R)$ behavior;
> | | **end**
> | | Update the bulletin board; ;   /* to record the best global optimum (i.e., the best fitness function score achieved by the best artificial fish) that has been identified so far */
> | **end**
> | **return** *from the bulletin board* $(R, Fitness(R))$
> **end**

Algorithm 1: Sketch of the algorithm COREplusAFSA

In the consecutive subsections we discuss two main parts of the algorithm COREplusAFSA.

3.1 Core Computation

In decision table $DT = (U, A \cup \{d\})$ some of the condition attributes from A may be superfluous (redundant in other words). This means that their removal cannot worsen the classification. The set $CORE(DT) \subseteq A$ of all indispensable condition attributes is called the core. None of its elements can be removed without affecting the classification power of all condition attributes from A.

Conflict measure $conflict(X)$ of $X \subseteq U$ is the number of pairs $(x, y) \in X \times X$ of objects from different decision classes, it means $conflict(X) = card(\{(x, y) \in X \times X : d(x) \neq d(y)\})$.

For any $B \subseteq A$ there exists an indiscernibility relation $IND(B) = \{(x,y) \in U \times U : \forall_{b \in B} b(x) = b(y)\}$ By $[x]_{IND(B)} = \{y \in U : (x,y) \in IND(B)\}$, we denote the equivalence class of indiscernibility relation $IND(B)$ defined by x. Discernibility measure $disc_d(B)$, can be understood as a number of unresolved conflicts in accordance to the subset $B \subseteq A$ of condition attributes. It can be calculated using the following equation:

$$disc_d(B) = conflict(U) - \sum_{[x]_{IND(B)} \in U/IND(B)} conflict([x]_{IND(B)}) \qquad (2)$$

It was shown in [6] that attribute $a \in A$ is a core attribute if and only if the following inequality is present:

$$disc_d(A \setminus \{a\}) < disc_d(A) \qquad (3)$$

In order to compute the core we can use ideas presented in [3–5].

Example 1. In this didactic example, we illustrate the definitions and formulas presented previously in our algorithm description. Let $DT = (U, A \cup \{d\})$ be a decision table, where the set of objects $U = \{x_1, \ldots, x_{12}\}$ and the set of condition attributes $A = \{a, b, c\}$ (see Table 1).

Table 1. Sample decision table and indiscernibility classes for attribute sets $A, \{b,c\}$, $\{a,b\}, \{a\}$, respectively

	a	b	c	d	$[x]_{IND(A)}$	$[x]_{IND(\{b,c\})}$	$[x]_{IND(\{a,b\})}$	$[x]_{IND(\{a\})}$
x_1	0	0	2	yes	$\{x_1\}$	$\{x_1, x_5\}$	$\{x_1\}$	$\{x_1, x_2, x_3, x_4\}$
x_2	0	1	2	yes	$\{x_2\}$	$\{x_2\}$	$\{x_2\}$	$\{x_1, x_2, x_3, x_4\}$
x_3	0	2	1	yes	$\{x_3, x_4\}$	$\{x_3, x_4, x_8\}$	$\{x_3, x_4\}$	$\{x_1, x_2, x_3, x_4\}$
x_4	0	2	1	no	$\{x_3, x_4\}$	$\{x_3, x_4, x_8\}$	$\{x_3, x_4\}$	$\{x_1, x_2, x_3, x_4\}$
x_5	1	0	2	yes	$\{x_5\}$	$\{x_1, x_5\}$	$\{x_5\}$	$\{x_5, x_6, x_7, x_8\}$
x_6	1	1	0	yes	$\{x_6, x_7\}$	$\{x_6, x_7, x_{10}, x_{11}\}$	$\{x_6, x_7\}$	$\{x_5, x_6, x_7, x_8\}$
x_7	1	1	0	no	$\{x_6, x_7\}$	$\{x_6, x_7, x_{10}, x_{11}\}$	$\{x_6, x_7\}$	$\{x_5, x_6, x_7, x_8\}$
x_8	1	2	1	no	$\{x_8\}$	$\{x_3, x_4, x_8\}$	$\{x_8\}$	$\{x_5, x_6, x_7, x_8\}$
x_9	2	0	1	yes	$\{x_9\}$	$\{x_9\}$	$\{x_9\}$	$\{x_9, x_{10}, x_{11}, x_{12}\}$
x_{10}	2	1	0	yes	$\{x_{10}, x_{11}\}$	$\{x_6, x_7, x_{10}, x_{11}\}$	$\{x_{10}, x_{11}\}$	$\{x_9, x_{10}, x_{11}, x_{12}\}$
x_{11}	2	1	0	no	$\{x_{10}, x_{11}\}$	$\{x_6, x_7, x_{10}, x_{11}\}$	$\{x_{10}, x_{11}\}$	$\{x_9, x_{10}, x_{11}, x_{12}\}$
x_{12}	2	2	2	no	$\{x_{12}\}$	$\{x_{12}\}$	$\{x_{12}\}$	$\{x_9, x_{10}, x_{11}, x_{12}\}$

$conflict(U) = card(\{(x,y) \in U \times U : d(x) \neq d(y)\}) = 70$.
Based on the column $[x]_{IND(A)}$ from Table 1 we have

$$\sum_{[x]_{IND(A)} \in U/IND(A)} conflict([x]_{IND(A)}) = 12.$$

Hence, we obtain $disc_d(A) = 70 - 12 = 58$.

Based on the column $[x]_{IND(\{b,c\})}$ from Table 1 we have

$$\sum_{[x]_{IND(\{b,c\})}\in U/IND(\{b,c\})} conflict([x]_{IND(\{b,c\})}) = 44.$$

Therefore, using the Eq. 2 we obtain $disc_d(\{b,c\}) = 26 < disc_d(A)$. Consequently $a \in CORE(DT)$.

Based on the column $[x]_{IND(\{a,b\})}$ from Table 1 we have

$$\sum_{[x]_{IND(\{a,b\})}\in U/IND(\{a,b\})} conflict([x]_{IND(\{a,b\})}) = 12.$$

Hence, we obtain $disc_d(A \setminus \{c\}) = disc_d(\{a,b\}) = 58 = disc_d(A)$. As a result $c \notin CORE(DT)$. Similarly one can check that $b \notin CORE(DT)$. Based on presented computation we conclude that $CORE(DT) = \{a\}$.

3.2   Artificial Fish Swarm Algorithm for Attribute Set Reduction

Artificial fish swarm algorithm (AFSA, in short) is a population-based optimization technique inspired by the natural feeding behavior of fish (see e.g. [1,9]). Artificial fish systems consist of a population of simple agents interacting locally with one another and with their environment. The agents follow simple rules, and there is no centralized control structure dictating how individual agents should behave. Interactions between such agents lead to the emergence of intelligent global behavior.

We represent the artificial fish position by a binary bit string of length $card(A)$, where $card(A)$ is the number of condition attributes. In a binary bit string the value one means that the corresponding attribute is selected while zero means that the corresponding attribute is not selected. The fitness of artificial fish R is represented as $Fitness(R)$.

Preying behavior of artificial fish

Preying is the basic behavior for a fish R to move to a location with the highest concentration of food. This behavior can be modeled within a radius of neighborhood of a fish. Namely, we can add one random attribute $\{rand(A-R)\}$ to R using the following rule

If $Fitness(R \cup \{rand(A-R)\}) > Fitness(R)$ then $R_{next} = R \cup \{rand(A-R)\}$.

Swarming behavior of artificial fish

The swarming behavior is modeled using a center of sets. We define the center set R_{center} of a family of sets $\{R_1, \ldots, R_m\}$, where $m > 1$ is a natural number, if the following condition is met:

$a \in R_{center}$ if and only if a belongs to at least $\frac{m}{2}$ sets from $\{R_1, \ldots, R_m\}$.

For example, for m equals 3 and three sets $R_1 = \{b\}, R_2 = \{a,b\}, R_3 = \{a,b,c\}$ we obtain $R_{center} = \{a,b\}$.

We use the following rule:

If $Fitness(R_{center}) > Fitness(R)$ and $n_f < \delta \times n$ then $R_{next} = R_{center}$.

Otherwise, the algorithm executes a preying behavior for R.

The condition $n_f < \delta \times n$ means that the swarm is not overly crowded (for more details see [1]).

Following behavior of artificial fish

When a fish finds a location with a better concentration of food, other fish follow it.

If $Fitness(R_{max}) > Fitness(R)$ and $n_f < \delta \times n$ then $R_{next} = R_{max}$.

Otherwise, the algorithm executes a preying behavior for R (for more details see [1]).

Example 2. In this example, we use the data from Example 1. The search space $SS(DT)$ in the artificial fish swarm algorithm is defined by $SS(DT) = \{R \subseteq A : CORE(DT) \subset R\}$. Hence, for data table presented in Table 1, we obtain $SS(DT) = \{\{a\}, \{a, b\}, \{a, c\}, \{a, b, c\}\}$. The search space is significantly smaller than in the case of searching the space of all subsets of the condition attribute set.

Let us compute the value of fitness function for $\{a, b\}$. In our example, we assume that the cardinality of positive region is more important ($weight_{POS} = 0.9$) than the cardinality of attribute subset ($weight_{AT} = 0.1$). The positive region is the union of lower approximations of decision classes i.e. $POS_{\{a,b\}}(\{d\}) = \{x_1, x_2, x_5, x_9\} \cup \{x_8, x_{12}\} = \{x_1, x_2, x_5, x_8, x_9, x_{12}\}$. Hence, we obtain

$$Fitness(\{a, b\}) = weight_{POS} \times \frac{card(POS_{\{a,b\}}(\{d\}))}{card(U)} + weight_{AT} \times \frac{card(\{c\})}{card(A)} =$$

$$0.9 \times \frac{card(\{x_1, x_2, x_5, x_8, x_9, x_{12}\})}{12} + 0.1 \times \frac{1}{3} = 0.9 \times 0.5 + 0.1 \times \frac{1}{3} = 0.483$$

Similarly, one can compute the value of fitness function for sets of condition attributes $\{a\}, \{b\}$ and A. We obtain the following values: $Fitness(\{a\}) = 0.067$, $Fitness(\{b\}) = 0.292$ and $Fitness(A) = 0.45$.

4 Results of Experiments

The results of experiments were compared with other method and summarized in Table 2. The first column from the left contains the names of the data sets selected for experiments from the UC Irvine Machine Learning Repository [2]. The number of objects and the number of condition attributes in each data set are presented in the second and third columns. The fourth column shows the number of core attributes. The fifth column presents the number of attributes in the minimum reduction obtained with the FSARSR (**F**ish **S**earch **A**lgorithm **R**ough **S**et **R**eduction) proposed in [1]. The sixth column shows the number of attributes in the minimum reduction achieved with the COREplusAFSA algorithm proposed in this paper.

In order to make a fair comparison, both algorithms FSARSR and COREplusAFSA were independently run twenty times on each of the data set with the same settings of the parameters involved (number of fish, $Fitness$ function, ...).

Table 2. Average number of attributes (the best solution, in parentheses) for two algorithms FSARSR and COREplusAFSA

Data set	$card(U)$	$card(A)$	$card(CORE(DT))$	FSARSR	COREplusAFSA
Audiology	200	70	3	13.1 (13)	13 (12)
Balance	625	4	4	4 (4)	4 (4)
Chess-king	3196	37	27	30.4 (30)	29 (29)
Lung	32	56	0	4 (4)	4 (4)
Mushroom	8124	23	0	4.3 (4)	4.3 (4)
Soylarge	307	35	2	10.3 (10)	10.1 (9)
Soysmall	47	35	0	2 (2)	2 (2)
Vote	435	17	7	9.2 (9)	9 (9)

The number of fish is half the number of condition attributes and the maximum number of iterations equals one hundred. The stop condition is met after the specified number of iterations or getting the same attribute subset under three consecutive iterations.

In our experiments, we suppose that cardinality $card(POS_R(\{d\}))$ of positive region is more important than the length $card(R)$ of attribute subset $R \subseteq A$ and we set the corresponding weights: $weight_{POS} = 0.9$ and $weight_{AT} = 0.1$. For each run the length of the output is recorded. Thus in Table 2 average number of attributes is based on twenty attempts. Since the Balance data set core is equal to the set of all condition attributes, the algorithm COREplusAFSA finished after core computation. Because core is equal to empty set for Lung and Mushroom data sets the results are similar for both algorithms. FSARSR and COREplusAFSA sometimes find different reducts and sometimes different lengths of reducts.

The results of experiments indicate that a moderate improvement in the reduction of attributes can be obtained.

Conclusions

In this paper, we proposed a new method for minimum attribute reduction based on rough set theory and artificial fish swarm algorithm. On the basis of the conducted experiments, certain conclusions can be drawn. The obtained results allow to determine that the computation of the core and next application of the idea of AFSA is a better solution to the attribute set reduction problem than the application of AFSA algorithm alone. Presented swarm intelligence-based techniques can be successfully combined with rough set methods.

Acknowledgments. The work was supported by the grant WZ/WI-IIT/2/2020 from Bialystok University of Technology and funded with resources for research by the Ministry of Science and Higher Education in Poland. I would like to thank Mr. Mateusz Walendziuk for the implementation of the algorithm.

References

1. Chen, Y., Zhu, Q., Xu, H.: Finding rough set reducts with fish swarm algorithm. Knowl.-Based Syst. **81**, 22–29 (2015)
2. Dua, D., Graff, C.: UCI Machine Learning Repository http://archive.ics.uci.edu/ml. Irvine, CA: University of California, School of Information and Computer Science (2021)
3. Grześ, T., Kopczyński, M., Stepaniuk, J.: FPGA in rough set based core and reduct computation. In: Lingras, P., Wolski, M., Cornelis, C., Mitra, S., Wasilewski, P. (eds.) RSKT 2013. LNCS (LNAI), vol. 8171, pp. 263–270. Springer, Heidelberg (2013). https://doi.org/10.1007/978-3-642-41299-8_25
4. Kopczynski, M., Grzes, T., Stepaniuk, J.: Computation of cores in big datasets: an FPGA approach. In: Ciucci, D., Wang, G., Mitra, S., Wu, W.-Z. (eds.) RSKT 2015. LNCS (LNAI), vol. 9436, pp. 153–163. Springer, Cham (2015). https://doi.org/10.1007/978-3-319-25754-9_14
5. Kopczynski, M., Grzes, T., Stepaniuk, J.: Core for large datasets: rough sets on FPGA. Fundam. Informaticae **147**(2–3), 241–259 (2016)
6. Nguyen, H.S.: Approximate boolean reasoning: foundations and applications in data mining. In: Peters, J.F., Skowron, A. (eds.) Transactions on Rough Sets V. LNCS, vol. 4100, pp. 334–506. Springer, Heidelberg (2006). https://doi.org/10.1007/11847465_16
7. Pawlak, Z., Skowron, A.: Rudiments of rough sets. Inf. Sci. **177**(1), 3–27 (2007)
8. Stepaniuk, J.: Rough-Granular Computing in Knowledge Discovery and Data Mining. Springer, New York (2008)
9. Su, Y., Guo, J.: A novel strategy for minimum attribute reduction based on rough set theory and fish swarm algorithm. Comput. Intell. Neurosci. **2017**, Article ID 6573623, 7 pages (2017) https://doi.org/10.1155/2017/6573623

Performance Analysis of a QoS System with WFQ Queuing Using Temporal Petri Nets

Dariusz Strzęciwilk[1]([✉]), Rafik Nafkha[1], and Rafał Zawiślak[2]

[1] Institute of Information Technology, University of Life Sciences, Nowoursynowska Street 159, 02-787 Warsaw, Poland
{dariusz_strzeciwilk,rafik_nafkha}@sggw.pl
[2] Faculty of Electrical, Electronic, Computer and Control Engineering, Lodz University of Technology, Stefanowskiego 18/22, Łódź, Poland
rafal.zawislak@p.lodz.pl

Abstract. The paper presents the results of analysis and modelling of differentiated services using Petri nets. Mechanisms and methods of implementation of QoS (*Quality of Service*) services in packet networks are discussed. A network model supporting data transfers related to different traffic classes was designed and studied. Traffic shaping mechanisms based on WFQ (*Weighted Fair Queuing*) system used in QoS were studied. The impact of the traffic shaping mechanism was studied and the performance of the modelled systems was evaluated. The application of simulation tools in the form of TPN (*Temporal Petri Nets*) was aimed at verifying the traffic shaping mechanisms and evaluating the performance of the studied WFQ system. Our simulation results show that the number of high-priority flows have a critical impact on average waiting times and queue length.

Keywords: WFQ · Weighted Fair Queuing System · Petri nets · Performance analysis · Modeling · QoS data

1 Introduction

Today's Internet has become an integrated platform for a wide range of applications with different quality of service requirements. Packetized data transmission provides us with increasingly diverse multimedia communication services such as Telepresence, VoIP (*Voice over IP*), VoD (*Video-on-Demand*), IPTV, P2P files containing multimedia content, real-time applications or critical applications. Next generation networks are evolving into very complex systems due to very different service requirements, heterogeneity of applications, devices and networks. Multimedia services are thus becoming one of the main types of streams in NGNs (*Next Generation Network*) [1, 2]. QoS design is the fundamental functionality of the next generation IP router. Determination of QoS parameters such as packet loss probability, end-to-end delays, transmission delay fluctuations for each of such services will allow to determine the limiting values of parameters beyond which the service ceases to fulfill its role [3]. The existing approach to QoS is to estimate traffic characteristics and assign appropriate QoS parameters

© Springer Nature Switzerland AG 2021
K. Saeed and J. Dvorský (Eds.): CISIM 2021, LNCS 12883, pp. 462–476, 2021.
https://doi.org/10.1007/978-3-030-84340-3_38

to them. However, inaccuracy of prediction or estimation in traffic characteristics may result in incorrect QoS parameter settings, congestion and consequent degradation or loss of access to resources. The basic mechanism that supports packet transfer in packet networks is FIFO (*First In First Out*) scheduling. However, FIFO queueing does not perform well in terms of providing good QoS. This is because when packets from different traffic streams are transmitted, we can easily disrupt the flow of the other streams. FIFO processing can lead to a situation where an aggressive stream can hijack more of the router's queue capacity. This can result in a deterioration of transmission quality causing a spike in latency or even loss of transmitted packets. Many packet scheduling algorithms have been developed showing better memory isolation between flows [4–6]. In contrast to best-effort applications, real-time applications require QoS guarantees. Multimedia services are particularly delay-sensitive and require guaranteed bandwidth [7]. The provision of desirable packet QoS along the entire path from sender to receiver has been the subject of research for many years [8–10]. Implementation of QoS mechanisms in packet networks is done using packet queuing mechanisms. A queueing system is understood as a system where, on the one hand, requests requiring service arrive and, on the other hand, there are so-called service apparatuses used to meet the needs of these requests. The core routers classify incoming packets into predefined traffic classes and then handle packets belonging to aggregate streams. The packets are handled according to the implemented queuing mechanism and the defined handling and traffic shaping policy to provide services with the established QoS [11]. If the process of incoming requests exceeds the capacity to handle them immediately, a queue is formed. A queueing system can be characterized by queueing rules, i.e., the way in which the order in which requests in the system are handled is determined. In a priority queueing system, some requests may be handled before others, regardless of when they arrived in the system. Priority queueing systems form a large class of queueing systems where the incoming requests are to be distinguished by their importance [12]. Ensuring the desired quality of service for packets along the entire route from sender to receiver has been the subject of research work for many years [13–15]. The analysis and results of works in this area show that this is not a simple task. The aim of this paper was to analyse and study the performance of the WFQ queueing system with respect to the number of high-priority flows. An attempt was made to apply temporal Petri net models to evaluate the performance and efficiency of QoS models, in particular WFQ in relation to high priority flows. The obtained research results may be useful in the design and analysis of data transport in packet networks, distributed systems, or multiprocessor systems. The study of the WFQ model allowed the estimation of significant features and parameters of the studied system.

2   The DiffServ Architecture Concept

QoS is usually defined as a set of service requirements that needs to be met by the network while transporting a packet stream from a source to its destination [16]. It is a mechanism that allows the use of guaranteed bandwidth and different priorities for given traffic classes. The QoS guarantee mechanism is implemented so that the data flow does not cause links to become so busy that other streams are prevented from using the same link. The QoS issue comprises a set of requirements imposed on a communication link. To ensure QoS, the following mechanisms are used, among others:

• shaping and limiting bandwidth,
• ensuring fair access to resources,
• assigning appropriate priorities to individual packets transmitted over the network.

In addition, for the purpose of QoS implementation in IP packet networks, three models of network traffic are distinguished:

• **BE (Best Effort)** - is by far the simplest model, as it does not require any special techniques, does not guarantee any quality of service in the network, and packets are handled in the order they are sent
• **Int-Serv (Integrated Services)** - this model provides the highest possible level of service but requires that all network elements including user applications can use the special RSVP signalling protocol [17]. This significantly limits the flexibility of the network and its scalability,
• **Diff-Serv (Differentiated Services)** - this model enables high scalability and flexibility of the network for QoS purposes, it assumes that network devices will be able to recognise the type of traffic and group it into traffic classes that can be handled according to different priorities assigned to a given traffic class.

The dominant model in packet networks including the Internet is the BE model. This model assumes that all packets are treated the same. This means that packets such as VoIP or VoD are not distinguished from packets carrying files or e-mail messages. Network behaviour in the BE model is difficult to predict, especially the determination of bandwidth usage, latency or packet loss. The Int-Serv (Hard QoS) model is designed for very demanding applications such as high-definition video transmission. Such streams require constant, dedicated bandwidth to ensure adequate quality of service for the recipients. However, the Hard QoS model requires the entire network to reserve bandwidth, and in addition, no other traffic can use the reserved bandwidth regardless of whether the bandwidth is currently in use or not. The advantage of this model is that the parameters of delay, packet loss or bandwidth size are guaranteed across the entire reserved network. This model treats all data types the same. As a result, all data transfer parameters are preserved and guaranteed. Architectures and models for data traffic in networks are described in RFC 2205[18], RFC 2475[19], RFC 2386 [20]. The disadvantages and limitations of the BE and Int-Serv models discussed above are eliminated in the third model, the Diff-Serv model. This model provides "almost guaranteed" QoS services while being a scalable and flexible solution. It is also called the "soft QoS" model because it does not require a special signalling protocol, all parameters such as bandwidth, delay, packet loss, are checked individually on each network node. In this model, the network traffic is divided into classes according to business assumptions. Each class is assigned to a different level of service [21]. The concept of the DiffServ architecture is based on the definition and implementation of several network services that are designed to transmit traffic streams with similar characteristics and similar QoS requirements. This includes parameters such as the probability of packet loss, the value of delay and the variation in the delay of packets passing through the network. Packets belonging to different services are handled differently by the backbone routers to guarantee the appropriate quality for a given transmission, e.g. for a VoIP stream, which is transmitted by devices in a priority manner. The DiffServ architecture requires that individual traffic streams are identified at the edge routers (*Edge Router*), while the backbone routers (*Core Router*) recognize only aggregate streams, defined by traffic affiliation to a given network service. Thus, the task of the Edge Router is to identify individual traffic streams, monitor their compliance with traffic contracts and assign an appropriate value to the DSCP field in the packet header, according to the desired type of service. The DiffServ architecture specification defines a set of QoS mechanisms that can be applied depending on the location of a given router in the network and the adopted rules for handling traffic classes. Since the DSCP field overlaps with the previously defined IPP field within the ToS byte, RFC 2475 [21] defines a set of DSCP values and PHBs called Class Selector (CS). Table 1 shows the implementation details of the DSCP field handling concept. The priority values shown in the table are based on the so-called MLPP (*MultiLevel Precedence and Preemption*) expropriation scheme.

Table 1. Designation of subfield type of service/class of traffic.

DSCP Class Selector Name	Binary DSCP Value	IPP Binary Value	IPP Name
Default/CS0	000000	000	Routine
CS1	001000	001	Priority
CS2	010000	010	Immediate
CS3	011000	011	Flash
CS4	100000	100	Flash Override
CS5	101000	101	Critical
CS6	110000	110	Internetwork Control
CS7	111000	111	Network Control

The location of the DSPC field in the IP packet header is illustrated in Fig. 1. The Differentiated Services Field (DSCP) occupies 6 bits, the next two bits form a subfield called ECN (*Explicit Congestion Notification*). Differentiated Services and ECN are related to mechanisms that modify standard datagram forwards. The concept of differentiated services should be understood as providing them in standards deviating from the routine non-guaranteed traffic (best-effort delivery). When a datagram passes through a router with many packets queued for processing, the pair of bits forming the ECN field is used to mark such a datagram with a so-called congestion indicator. Routers implementing congestion set both bits to 1. Each DSCP value is associated with a specific packet forwarding strategy of the router, the so-called PHB (*Per-Hop Behavior*) strategy. By defining PHBs for individual DSCPs, we can define different types of service. For example, a DSCP equal to 22 (binary 010110) is mapped to 010 with Delay and Throughput bits set, so the PHB resulting from such a DSCP should be characterized by priority at the "immediate" level (Table 1) and by ensuring the lowest possible delay and the highest possible throughput. In the mapping, the three most significant bits of the DSCP identify the so-called PHB class, while the other two reflect the packet's rejection resistance. This means that the higher the value of this resistance, the lower the probability that in a congested situation the router will discard that packet. This mapping is shown schematically in Fig. 2. The mechanism of differentiated services undoubtedly provides a number of benefits and privileges for their recipients. However, there remains the open question of a fair charging scheme for the services provided, which is still the subject of complex discussions [23]. Many details and explanations on this topic of the mechanisms of implanting differentiated services are provided in the paper [24].

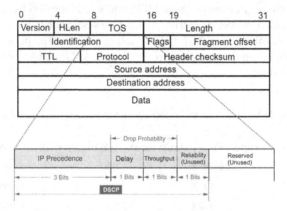

Fig. 1. IP header with marked DSCP field.

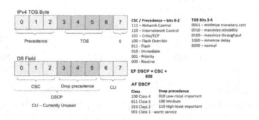

Fig. 2. Marking of DSCP bit groups.

3   Queuing Systems in QoS Service Assurance

A queuing system is understood as a system in which, on the one hand, there are requests that need to be serviced and, on the other hand, there are so-called service apparatuses that serve to fulfil the needs of these requests. If the inflow of requests exceeds the capacity to handle them immediately, a queue is formed (Fig. 3). To analyse any queuing system, it is necessary to determine:

- the arrival/entry process of requests to the system, i.e. the probability distribution of the intervals between successive requests to the system,
- the probability distribution of query service times, the queue rules, i.e., how successive queries are selected for service,
- the possibility of staying in a queue, i.e. whether incoming queries are allowed to wait in a queue, or the way they are rejected when all handlers are busy - the determination of the maximum length of the queue.

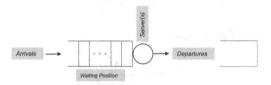

Fig. 3. Model of simple queue

The systematization of queueing systems was done by D. Kendall, who proposed a simple symbolism [25]. The shortcoming of Kendall's notation is that it refers only to single-phase service systems and does not show the accepted queue rules. The classification according to A.M. Lee is devoid of these shortcomings:

$$X/Y/m/d/l, \tag{1}$$

where:

X - is the distribution of time between the arrival of consecutive requests,

Y - is the distribution of service time of a task,

m - number of service channels,

d - queue discipline.

l - length of the queue.

One of the most well-known classical queuing models is the *M/M/1* model. Such a system has one service desk, which handles the stream of requests according to the following assumptions:

- the desk is available for any request as long as it is not busy,
- incoming requests to the system form a straight stream with intensity λ,
- the distribution of handling time is exponential with a parameter μ,
- requests not accepted for service wait in a queue,
- the queue is unlimited,
- the intensity of the inflow of requests is less than their handling time ($\lambda/\mu < 1$).

The basic parameters of the *M/M/1* model are:

- the average number of requests in the system,

$$L = \frac{A}{1 - A} \tag{2}$$

where

A- average traffic,

- the average time a request stays in the system,

$$W = \frac{A}{\lambda(1 - A)} \tag{3}$$

- the average number of requests in the queue,

$$Q = \frac{A^2}{1 - A} \tag{4}$$

- average queue time of the request,

$$T = \frac{A^2}{\lambda(1 - A)} \tag{5}$$

- probability of a vacant service position,

$$p_0 = 1 - A \tag{6}$$

The model in which the handling time is a constant value (t_0) identical for all requests is denoted as *M/D/1*. The variance of handling time is equal to $\sigma_\tau^2 = 0$. The average time a request stays in the system is given by the relation

$$W = \frac{1}{\mu(1 - A)}\left(1 - \frac{A}{2}\right) \tag{7}$$

where:

$$1/\mu = t_0 = const,$$

$$A = \lambda t_0$$

Other characteristics of the *M/D/1* model can be determined using Little's formulas:

- average time a request stays in the queue

$$T = W - \frac{1}{\mu} \tag{8}$$

- average number of requests in the system

$$L = W\lambda \tag{9}$$

- average number of requests in a queue

$$Q = T\lambda \tag{10}$$

- probability of a vacant service position

$$p_0 = 1 - A \qquad (11)$$

The $M/M/1$ and $M/D/1$ queueing models assume that requests arriving at the system are processed according to a FIFO discipline. Queueing is a mechanism used by edge routers that identifies individual traffic streams and routes them to the appropriate queue according to the QoS contract. Of course, queueing disciplines implemented for QoS purposes can be more complex than a simple FIFO queue (Fig. 4). The number of queues is related to the number of PHB forwarding rules implemented at a network node. Queueing can be handled by priority systems such as WFQ.

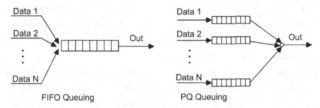

Fig. 4. FIFO and PQ model

This type of queueing is obviously better at providing different levels of service for different types of traffic than simple FIFO queues. In priority weighted queues separate queues are used for packets of different traffic classes (different priorities). Packets to be transmitted over a shared communication channel are always selected starting from the (non-empty) queue with the highest priority. Therefore, packets from lower priority queues are only selected if all higher priority queues are empty. This can cause lower priority traffic to be blocked for an extended period of time. This can result in a degradation of transmission quality causing, for example, a sudden increase in the delay of transmitted packets. In this paper we attempt to apply temporal Petri net models to evaluate the performance and efficiency of PQ (*Priority Queueing*) systems using a WPQ queue supporting 4 classes of traffic with different priorities.

4 Petri Nets and Model

Petri nets are a graphical and mathematical tool used in many fields. In classical terms, a Petri net is defined as an ordered four:

$$\sum = (P, T, F_0, m_0) \qquad (12)$$

where:

P - a non-empty, finite set of places (e.g.: $P = \{p_1, p_2,...,p_n\}$),
T - a non-empty, finite set of transitions (e.g.: $T = \{t_1,t_2,...,t_m\}$), and $P \cap T = \phi$,
F_o - a non-empty, finite set of directed arcs such that: $F_o \subset (P \times T) \cup (T \times P)$,
m_o - initial marking function $m_0: P \rightarrow N \cup \{0\}$.

A Petri net with permitting and forbidding arcs is defined as:

$$\sum\nolimits_{A} = (P, T, F_0, m_0) \tag{13}$$

where:

F - is the set of arcs such that:

$$F = F_o \cup F_e \cup F_i, \cdot F_o : F_o \subset (P \times T) \cup (T \times P), \cdot F_e : F_e \subset (P \times T), \cdot F_i : F_i \subset (P \times T),$$

other symbols as in (12).

Event behaviour is represented by so-called tags (tokens) assigned to p-elements of the network, usually a p-element with at least one tag associated with it means that the condition represented by that element is satisfied. The distribution of tags in p-elements can beescribed by the tagging function $m : P \rightarrow \{0, 1, 2 \ldots\}$ or represented as a vector describing the number of tags assigned to consecutive p-elements of the network $m = [m(p_1), m(p_2), \ldots]$. The network N including the (initial) tagging function m_0 is called a tagged network $M = (N, m_0) = (P, T, A, m_0)$.

To evaluate the performance and speed of certain consecutive events, the duration of the modelled events in Petri nets should be additionally considered [26]. This will allow the model to be used in the analysis of real-time systems. Formally, temporal models are an extension of sign models, with additional description elements defining the times of occurrence of events and the probabilities or frequency of occurrence of random events. A temporal network T is thus defined as a system $T = (M, c, f)$ where: M is a labeled network, $M = (P, T, A, m_0)$, c- is a conflict resolution function$c : T \rightarrow [0, 1]$, which for each decision class gives the probabilities of the individual events belonging to that class, and for the remaining conflict events gives their relative frequencies used for random conflict resolution, and f- defines the event occurrence times$f : T \rightarrow R_+$, where R_+. - denotes the set of non-negative real numbers. The evaluation of model performance using temporal networks is well described in the literature [27].

4.1   The model

In the models studied, it is assumed that the WFQ model will consist of four priority queues. It is assumed that all queues have infinite capacities. This will allow traffic to be visualised for high, medium, low and very low priority data. In the models studied, the data is labelled class-1 (platinum), class-2 (gold), class-3 (silver), class-4 (bronze) respectively. A schematic model of the investigated system is shown in Fig. 5. Timed transitions T_1, T_2, T_3 and T_4 represent the transmission channels for data class-1 (T_1), data class-2 packets (T_2), data class-3 packets (T_3) and data class-4 packets (T_4). In the model studied, for simplicity, it is assumed that the transmission time is deterministic and is 1 token per unit time for all 4 classes. In the model, place P_8, is shared by transits T_4, T_5, T_6 and T_7. To ensure that only one packet is transmitted at a time, place P_8 is marked with a single token (i.e., $m_0(P_8) = 1$). Moreover, inhibitors arc (P_4, T_5) do not allow the transmission of data through T_5 transit in the case when there is a class-1 packet waiting for transmission. Similarly, inhibitors arc (P_4, T_5, P_5, T_6 and P_6, T_7) allow the transmission only in the case when there is no class-1, class-2 or class-2 data waiting for transmission.

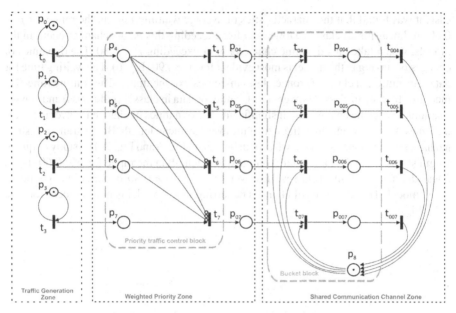

Fig. 5. Petri net model of priority queueing system

A characteristic of the queue under study is that as long as packets are in a higher priority queue, packets waiting in lower priority queues cannot be transmitted. Transmitting data only from higher priority queues can lead to "data starvation" of data that is classified in lower priority queues. The starvation problem in the model was eliminated by introducing CQ (*Custom Queueing*). This mechanism allows queues to be processed on a round-robin basis, retrieving first 8 packets from queue one, then 4 from queue two, then 2 from queue three, and finally 1 from the last queue. This design prevents the less favoured pipelines from dying out. Thus, in the models studied, it was assumed that the model would handle successively 8 packets of class platinum (class-1), 4 packets of class gold (class-2), then 2 packets of class silver (class-3), and finally 1 packet of class bronze (class-4). Based on such models, traffic shaping mechanisms were studied in systems based on WFQ priority queues with priorities of 8–4–2–1. M-timed nets (Markovian nets) were used as a source of data generation in the models.

5   The Results of Research and Discussion

In order to compare the performance of the system, parameters such as average wating time, average queue length, throughput and utilisation were benchmarked. Based on the simulations carried out, graphs were drawn up showing the behaviour of the system at the limits of its stability. The study showed that for the same number of generated data and channel usage, the average waiting times are different for different classes . In this case, it was found that the characteristics of average waiting times in the range for $\rho <$ 0.60 are linear for all classes. However, after exceeding this value, changes occur in the models, which take on a dynamic character after exceeding $\rho < 0.80$. The dynamics of changes occurring in the model is most evident for $\rho < 0.90$ (Fig. 6). The waiting time for data transmitted in class-4 (bronze class) increases exponentially. The waiting time also increases for data in class-3 (sliver class), while for data in class-2 (gold class) and class-1 (platinum class) the changes are insignificant. The dynamics of change for average waiting times is directly related to the size of the average queue length. Both parameters studied have similar characteristics, which can be seen in Fig. 6 and Fig. 7. The study of queue length showed that the parameter Average queue length in the range for $\rho < 0.60$ shows linear characteristics in all classes. However, for values $\rho < 0.80$, dynamic changes occur in the model. The dynamics of changes occurring in the model is most evident for $\rho <$ 0.90 (Fig. 7).

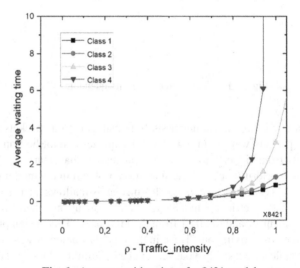

Fig. 6. Average waiting times for 8421 model

Here it is also found that the substitutions of the characteristics for class-4 have an exponential character. The queue increases also for data of class-3 (sliver class), while for class-2 (gold class) and class-1 (platinum class) the changes have insignificant character. This is since the queue for class bronze is only served after data from higher priority classes has been transmitted. When the value $\rho < 0.90$ the amount of transmitted data increases significantly and the system is at the limit of stability, for $\rho < 1.0$ the system already goes into the non-stationary range. In the next stage, the parameters and Utilisation (Fig. 8) Throughput (Fig. 9) were examined. The tests showed that in model

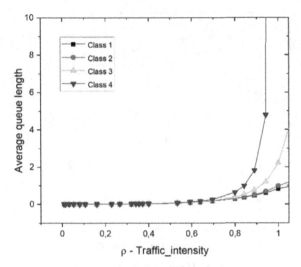

Fig. 7. Average queue length for 8421 model

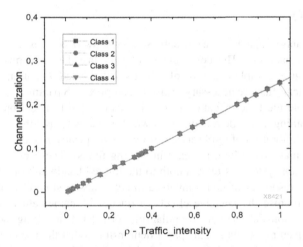

Fig. 8. Utilization for 8421 model

8421 both parameters have linear characteristics. All classes have the same courses of the Utilization characteristic. This is because the value for all classes increased in the same way. As expected, the maximum value of Throughput occurs for value $\rho = 1.0$.

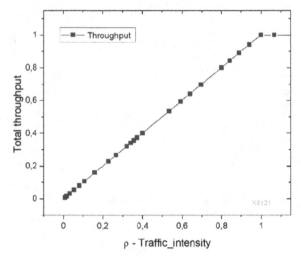

Fig. 9. Throughput for 8421 model

6 Summary

The huge amounts of data that are currently sent by network devices require appropriate quality of data handling. The development of very fast data transmission standards forces the design and implementation of systems with the determination of the capacity of system elements that are necessary to ensure complex QoS parameters. It is relatively easy to calculate the time of data transmission from node to node, but the time and character of waiting in a node remain unknown. Too intensive use of network resources may lead to deterioration of QoS services (increase in queues in nodes, increase in the probability of their overfilling, increase in waiting times). The occurrence of queues in communication systems is related both to the limited bandwidth of links and to the finite hardware resources of nodes involved in data transmission. One of the methods allowing to minimise the negative effects of queues is mathematical modelling and computer simulation. Petri nets are a popular solution used in modelling and performance evaluation of queuing systems. This paper demonstrates that the use of temporal Petri net models can be used to evaluate the performance and efficiency of WFQ queueing-based priority systems. Furthermore, it was found that the advantage of modelling is that complex models can be evaluated at different levels of detail. The model or parts of it under study can be easily subjected to further and detailed analysis. Temporal Petri net models can be used to evaluate a range of performance measures of the system under study.

References

1. Singh, S., Jha, R.K.: A survey on software defined networking: Architecture for next generation network. J. Netw. Syst. Manage. 25(2), 321–374 (2017)
2. Kibria, M.G., et al.: Big data analytics, machine learning, and artificial intelligence in next-generation wireless networks. IEEE Accessed 6, 32328–32338 (2018)

3. Strzęciwilk, D.: Examination of transmission quality in the IP multi-protocol label switching corporate networks. Int. J. Electron. Telecommun. **58**(3), 267–272 (2012)

4. Stephens, B., Akella, A., Swift, M.: Loom: flexible and efficient {NIC} packet scheduling. In: 16th {USENIX} Symposium on Networked Systems Design and Implementation ({NSDI} 19) (2019)

5. Tsai, T.Y., Chung, Y.L., Tsai, Z.:Introduction to packet scheduling algorithms for communication networks. Commun. Netw. **434** (2010)

6. Annadurai, C.: Review of packet scheduling algorithms in mobile ad hoc networks. Int. J. Comput. Appl. **15**(1), 7–10 (2011)

7. Li, M.: Queueing Analysis of Unicast IPTV with User Mobility and Adaptive Modulation and Coding in Wireless Cellular Networks. arXiv preprint arXiv:1511.01794 (2015)

8. Zuberek, W., Strzeciwilk, D.: Modeling quality of service techniques for packet–switche networks. Dependability Engineering (2018). ISBN 978-953-51-5592-8

9. Singh, D., et al.: Modelling software-defined networking: switch design with finite buffer and priority queueing. In: 2017 IEEE 42nd Conference On Local Computer Networks (LCN). IEEE (2017)

10. Bhatti, S.N., Crowcroft, J.: QoS-sensitive flows: issues in IP packet handling. IEEE Internet Comput. **4**(4), 48–57 (2000)

11. Aurrecoechea, C., Campbell, A.T., Hauw, L.: A survey of QoS architectures. MultimediaSyst. **6**(3), 138–151 (1998)

12. Strzeciwilk, D.: Performance analysis of weighted priority queuing systems. In: Silhavy, R. (ed.) CSOC 2019. AISC, vol. 984, pp. 283–292. Springer, Cham (2019). https://doi.org/10.1007/978-3-030-19807-7_28

13. Radivilova, T., Kirichenko, L., Ageiev, D., Bulakh, V.: The methods to improve quality of service by accounting secure parameters. In: Hu, Z., Petoukhov, S., Dychka, I., He, M. (eds.) ICCSEEA 2019. AISC, vol. 938, pp. 346–355. Springer, Cham (2020). https://doi.org/10.1007/978-3-030-16621-2_32

14. Ghorbanzadeh, M., Abdelhadi, A., Clancy, C.: Quality of service in communication systems. In: Cellular Communications Systems in Congested Environments, pp. 1–20. Springer, Cham (2017). https://doi.org/10.1007/978-3-319-46267-7_1

15. Budiman, E., Wicaksono, O.: Measuring quality of service for mobile internet services. In: 2016 2nd International Conference on Science in Information Technology (ICSITech). IEEE, 2016

16. Mohapatra, P., Li, J., Gui, C.: QoS in mobile ad hoc networks. IEEE Wirel. Commun. **10**(3), 44–53 (2003)

17. Braden, R., et al.: Resource ReSerVation Protocol:(RSVP); Version 1 Functional Specification. (1997)

18. Zhang, L., et al.: RFC2205: Resource ReSerVation Protocol (RSVP)--Version 1 Functional Specification. (1997)

19. Blake, S., et al.: Rfc2475: An architecture for differentiated service (1998)

20. Crawley, E., et al. RFC2386: A Framework for QoS-based Routing in the Internet. (1998)

21. Babiarz, J., Chan, K., Baker, F.: Configuration guidelines for DiffServ service classes. Netw. Working Group (2006)

22. Grossman, D.: New terminology and clarifications for diffserv. RFC 3260 (2002)

23. Wu, T., Yoo, C.S.: Keeping the internet neutral?: Tim Wu and Christopher Yoo debate. Fed. Commun. Law J. **59**(3), 06–27 (2007)

24. Wu, Tim.: Network neutrality, broadband discrimination. J. Telecomm. High Tech. L. 2, 141 (2003)

25. Kendall, David, G.: Some problems in the theory of queues. J. Royal Stat. Soc. Series B Methodol. 13(2), 151–173 (1951)

26. Coolahan, J.E., Roussopoulos, N.: Timing requirements for time-driven systems using augmented Petri nets. IEEE Trans. Softw. Eng. **5**, 603–616 (1983)
27. Zuberek, W.: Timed Petri nets definitions, properties, and applications. Microelectron. Reliab. **31**(4), 627–644 (1991)

Runtime Sensor Network Schedule Adaptation to Varying Temperature Conditions

Krzysztof Trojanowski⬤, Artur Mikitiuk⬤, and Jakub A. Grzeszczak$^{(\boxtimes)}$⬤

Cardinal Stefan Wyszyński University, Wóycickiego 1/3, 01-938 Warsaw, Poland
jakub.grzeszczak@uksw.edu.pl

Abstract. We study runtime adaptation methods of sensor activity schedules for wireless sensor networks. Adaptation is necessary when the network operating conditions differ from the ones assumed in the scheduling phase. Usually, the ideal temperature conditions are assumed. When the system has to operate at a lower temperature, sensor batteries discharge faster, resulting in an inability to complete the schedule created with that assumption. We deal with this problem by careful selection of a slot to be executed next from the very beginning of the network activity. We test several slot selection strategies based on battery load levels for all the sensors active exclusively in a given slot. Our experiments showed that in the majority of cases, a tournament–based approach gave the best results. Moreover, we propose and verify experimentally a new selection strategy, which uses the standard deviation of the whole network's battery levels as a decision attribute.

Keywords: Coverage problems in sensor networks · Maximum lifetime optimization · Adaptation to varying temperature

1 Introduction

Wireless sensor networks can be applied in a wide range of real–world tasks, including those where individual sensor placement is infeasible, for example, battlefield or disaster areas. In such a remote or dangerous field, the sensors are usually randomly scattered over the monitored field. These are usually miniaturized sensors having nonchargeable batteries with a limited energy supply. So, they should consume energy wisely and efficiently for the aim of the network operational time maximization.

Our model assumes that the sensors have uniform limited battery capacity and sensing range, and the area contains a set of points of interest (POIs) to cover. The minimum level of coverage, that is, the percentage of POIs, located in the range of at least one working sensor, represents a necessary condition of feasible monitoring. In our earlier research, we developed methods optimizing wireless sensor networks' activity for their most extended lifetime under the conditions mentioned above. These methods assumed fixed temperature conditions.

© Springer Nature Switzerland AG 2021
K. Saeed and J. Dvorský (Eds.): CISIM 2021, LNCS 12883, pp. 477–488, 2021.
https://doi.org/10.1007/978-3-030-84340-3_39

However, in real circumstances, weather conditions, especially the temperature, impact the battery capacity of devices working outdoors. In the low temperature, battery performance drops significantly, and the lifetime of devices shrinks. Thus, the network functionality's makespan may shorten when the actual temperature is lower than the network creators assumed in the design phase.

In this research, we assume that the amount of battery consumption depends on the ambient temperature varying over time. Therefore, the adaptation of the network activity schedule during its runtime is necessary. The sensors' activity control update is computed outside the network. A central computational unit has contact with all the sensors, for example, through mobile sinks moving around in the sensor field to collect data via short–distance radio communication. The sinks get the information about the current temperature from sensors and send them activity configurations in return.

In the proposed adaptation method, we use already found schedules maximizing the lifetime of a network for fixed temperature conditions. These schedules divide operational time into short periods of the same length called slots and define sensors' activity configurations for each slot to guarantee satisfying coverage of the monitored area. Thus, we can regard the already found schedules as collections of coverage sets. The coverage sets serve as building blocks and input data for the proposed adaptation methods.

We do not modify the sensors' configurations in the slots. However, we can change the slots' order, selecting the current slot for implementation according to present weather conditions. The periods are short enough for the assigned temperature to be considered constant over the period. Since battery discharge levels depend on previously executed slots and their execution temperature, we need to update the current battery levels and revalidate all available slots first. We can then find the most appropriate slot among the available ones and implement it in the network. This simple idea is a basis for the proposed sensor network adaptation procedure. We verify experimentally seven strategies of the current best slot selection.

We compare the efficiency of the proposed adaptation method with the one presented earlier in [8]. In the earlier approach, the network executes the schedule obtained for fixed temperature conditions as long as possible. Once it encounters a slot that could not be completed due to a faster discharge rate of sensor batteries under low temperatures, the central computational unit takes control of the slots sequence adaptation by starting the slot selection procedure. This paper presents a different approach where the central unit computes sensors control activity from the very beginning. We also propose and verify experimentally yet another method of the current slot selection. The method aims to minimize the standard deviation value of all the sensors' battery loads.

The paper consists of six sections. Section 2 briefly describes the related work. The model of sensor network control is presented in Sect. 3. Section 4 discusses methods of schedule adaptation to the varying temperature conditions based on seven different strategies of the current best slot selection. Section 5 describes the experimental part of the research. Section 6 concludes the paper.

2   Related Work

In the POIs coverage problem, a limited number of POIs need to be monitored by randomly dispersed sensors, in a way sufficient enough to cover most POIs more than once. Methods for extending such a sensor network lifetime through efficient energy management have been developed and presented in many publications (see, for example, monographs and surveys [2,4,9,11]). These methods divide sensors into subsets, which can be disjoint (e.g., [3]) or non–disjoint (e.g., [1]), and every set guarantees a sufficient level of POIs coverage. In the former case, the goal is to determine a maximum number of disjoint sets. Simply, the larger number of sets, the longer lifetime of the network. When the sets are non–disjoint, we want to determine the operational time for each set such that the sum of all time intervals is maximized. In the presented research, we develop the latter case but extend the model by yet another condition impacting the sensor lifetime, the ambient temperature [6,8].

3   The Model of a Network and a Sensor Battery Discharge

In our simplified network model, we have a set of immobile sensors randomly deployed over an area to monitor a number of points of interest (POI). All sensors have the same sensing range and the same limited battery capacity. We assume that time is discrete and consists of periods of the same length. During every period, a sensor can be active or sleep. At a constant temperature 25°C, an active sensor consumes precisely one unit of energy per time unit. In the sleeping state, the energy consumption is negligible.

3.1   A Battery Discharge Model

For the simulation of the network operating under varying temperature conditions, we model a battery discharge process using rate discharge curves of Li–ion battery given in [10]. In our model, sensor batteries discharge linearly from their initial voltage to a threshold value. For different temperatures, we can estimate respective battery lifetimes in operating time units. Thus, the capacity is measured in time units rather than in milliamps × hours. The maximum capacity T_{batt} is the number of time units when the device can work in the ideal temperature 25 °C. Dividing 100% by the battery life for a given temperature, one can get a percentage amount of discharge in a unit of operating time.

This is a significantly simplified model that does not represent all the physical processes occurring in the battery. This model does not refer to any particular battery or the sensor device's proper discharge curves. In real life, battery capacity depends on various factors. For example, regular turnings on and off shorten the battery's lifetime because of the costs of a transition from low power mode to high power mode and the side effects of drawing current at a rate higher or lower than the discharge rate. Thus, it does matter whether the sensor activity is set over consecutive slots or spread across the whole schedule. Communication between sensors also requires additional power consumption. Depending on the network topology, the batteries of some sensors may discharge faster than the others.

Additionally, even when not in use, a battery loses its capacity over time due to internal leakage. We omit these issues except one, that is, the working temperature of sensors. Due to its simplicity, the model allows a fast approximation of the battery discharge process based on actual temperature conditions. For more details, the reader is referred to [6].

3.2   Sensor Activity Schedule Representation

We represent a schedule as a matrix H of 0s and 1s. Its rows define the activity of the corresponding sensors over time. The columns define the state of all sensors during the corresponding time units (called slots). For every column, all its active sensors cover the appropriate percentage of POIs, called the required level of coverage. Since every slot takes one unit of time, the number of slots is equal to the network's lifetime. Each row represents the working time of a single sensor. Thus the sum of all 1s (active states) should not be higher than T_{batt}.

Schedules that are the subject of our experiments are suboptimal. We assume that turning off any sensor in a slot will make this slot incorrect. The schedules were obtained under the assumption that the network works at a constant temperature 25 °C all the time. It means that the amount of sensor battery discharge in every slot is the same and equals one operating time unit. All schedules used in experiments described in this paper were generated using the algorithm based on the hypergraph model approach. For more details, see [5,7].

3.3   Influence of the Temperature on the Schedule Execution

Let us assume that the temperature can change during the network lifetime. For a single slot, its temperature is constant. However, it can be different from the temperature in the neighboring slots. Moreover, in the real world, the temperature may differ slightly depending on the sensor location because some sensors may be exposed to sunshine while the other ones are in shadow. However, we omit this problem—in our model, the temperature is the same for all sensors.

We also assume that we know neither the sensors nor POIs localization. Thus, we cannot try to fix the coverage by changing the set of active sensors within a slot. If a slot becomes invalid, the only option is to find its new position in the schedule or remove it altogether.

4   Adaptation to Varying Weather Conditions—Slot Selection Strategies

Input schedules consist of slots that are executed successively such that at any time, only one slot is active. We can freely rearrange them in the schedule without any additional adjustments because all slots are context–free; that is, they remain correct regardless of the number and order of already executed slots as far as they all originate from the same schedule. This feature is met when the working temperature is constant and ideal. In the case of a temperature lower than ideal, the battery capacity shrinks, and there is no guarantee that the schedule shall be executed successfully until the last slot. However, the slots' order may influence the makespan of the sequence of slots fully executed.

Due to the lack of reliable, precise forecasts, it is impossible to generate new schedules already adjusted to coming weather conditions. However, even in far from ideal temperature conditions, we can utilize slots from the schedule to create new schedules. We can treat the input schedule as a box of building blocks and schedule slots online, that is, at every time step, execute a slot from the box that is best suited to the current temperature.

There is one catch in this simple solution: what are the criteria for selecting the best–suited slot when the aim is to choose slots in a way that maximizes the lifetime of the network? In [8], we proposed a set of schedule fixing strategies for selecting the best alternative slot when the first non–executable slot is encountered. Here, we apply these strategies for selecting a current slot concerning the given temperature measured by the thermometer. One can divide these strategies into two groups. In the first group, we search for the first slot, which defines the network's feasible activity control for the current temperature. In the second group, for all the remaining slots deemed feasible, we calculate some slot parameters and then select the best one respectively to the calculated values. These groups of strategies are briefly described below.

1. Feasible Slot Selection
   – First–Fit (FF) verifies slots from the queue containing slots ordered from H^{k+1} to H^n, where k is the number of slots executed so far and n is the length of the input schedule.
   – Biased First–Fit (BFF) also verifies slots from the queue just like FF but moves every negatively verified slot to the end of the queue.
2. Slots Ranking
   – MinMax (MIMA) among the active sensors calculates the mean for the two battery load levels: the highest and the lowest. The slot with a higher mean value wins the comparisons.
   – Mean (MEAN) works the same way as MIMA except that we calculate the mean battery load level for all sensors which are active in the slot.
   – STDMean (STDM) for each of the slots, calculates the mean μ and standard deviation σ values of the battery load level for all active sensors. Then, we compare slots to each other. When two slots H^i and H^j have disjoint intervals $[\mu - \sigma, \mu + \sigma]$, the winner is the one with the higher values in its interval, that is, $\mu - \sigma$ of the winner is greater than $\mu + \sigma$ of the loser. When the intervals overlap, we have to make some additional comparisons. Let us assume that H^i has a lesser μ than H^j. In spite of this, H^i may win when: (1) $\sigma^i < \sigma^j$, (2) $\mu^i - \sigma^i$ is greater than $\mu^j - \sigma^j$, and (3) $\mu^i + \sigma^i$ is greater than μ^j. Otherwise, H^j wins.

- Tournament (TOUR), in the beginning, makes sequences of active sensors for both compared slots. Each sequence consists of sensors active exclusively in its slot, sorted in ascending order regarding their battery charge levels. Finally, we compare battery charge levels in sensors occupying the same positions in sequences, pair by pair. If one sequence is longer than the other one, we ignore the sensors with the highest battery levels without a pair. The better slot is the one having higher battery levels in the majority of the comparisons.

In this research, we propose another strategy of the current slot selection, which belongs to the slots ranking group. We calculate the standard deviation value σ of all the sensors' battery loads, which would be obtained by executing each of the available slots. The best slot is the one, which execution returns the smallest σ. This strategy, called MINσ, is more computationally expensive than any of the six mentioned above.

Just like in the sampling without replacement, each slot has only one chance to become selected for execution.

5   Experiments

Experiments are divided into two parts. In the first part, sensor network activity is controlled according to the current ambient temperature. We get six output schedules for every test case due to six versions of the slot selection strategy. Then, in the second part, we analyze sensors' battery levels over time, when the output schedules are executed. The aim is to find the rules of such a slot selection that give the most extended schedules. We anticipated that the most effective strategy balances a load of batteries over time. Therefore, we decided to monitor and compare the standard deviation of battery levels after executing subsequent slots in the best and the worst schedules obtained for each of the problem instances. Moreover, we perform a set of experiments with the strategy MINσ based on minimizing the standard deviation of battery levels.

5.1   Plan of Experiments

Part I. In the first part, we control the sensor network in varying temperature conditions. The six strategies from [8] select and apply slots from the ones given in the input schedules. Every strategy aims at selecting slots best fitted for current weather conditions. The benchmark set of input schedules represents the best–found solutions for the SCP1 benchmark [5,7].

In all SCP1's test cases, 2000 sensors with a sensing range of one unit are dispersed using either a random or Halton generator over the square with a side length of 13, 16, 19, 22, 25, or 28. POIs can be distributed in two ways: in nodes of a triangular grid or a rectangular grid. The number of POIs is the same for different area sizes. Thus, the distances between the POIs stretch as the area grows. To avoid full regularity in the POIs distribution, 20% of nodes in the grid have no POIs. These nodes are selected randomly for every instance of the test case. Then sensors covering no POIs are discarded. There are eight classes of test cases: 1—side length: 13, square grid, and Halton distribution, 2—side length: 19, square grid, and random distribution, 3–5—side length: 16, 22, 28, triangle grid, and Halton distribution, and 6–8—side length: 13, 19, 25, triangle grid, and random distribution.

SCP1 consists of 320 instances of problems (eight classes, 40 instances each), and for each of the instances, we have schedules created for five values of maximum battery capacity T_{batt}: 10, 15, 20, 25, and 30. Eventually, we have 1600 schedules in total.

For every slot selection strategy, we conduct two series of 1600 experiments for the two outdoor temperature conditions: colder weather, called Series A, and warmer one, called Series B. The experiment's outcome is the percentage number of slots in output schedules concerning the numbers of input slots. The percentage numbers of slots are averaged over 40 instances. The approaches returning the most significant mean percentage number of slots in output schedules, or in other words, the smallest mean decrease in the maximum lifetime of the network due to weather conditions, are the best.

Part II. In the second group of experiments, we analyze the network properties during the execution of the schedules returned by the six methods. Notably, we observe the standard deviation of battery levels in all sensors just after the subsequent slots' execution, intending to provide slot selection rules to get the most extended schedule.

In the beginning, when the batteries are fully loaded, the standard deviation equals zero. Typically, just a subset of sensors has to be activated in a single slot. The sets of activated sensors differ in each slot, so battery charge levels' differences appear over time. For each of the problem instances, we compare graphs of the standard deviation for two schedules: the best and the worst one, and compare the standard deviation values in respective time steps pair by pair. Then, we classify the results of comparisons as *straight, reversed,* or *mixed* (Fig. 1).

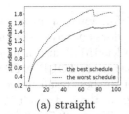
(a) straight

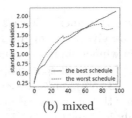
(b) mixed

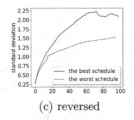
(c) reversed

Fig. 1. Examples of graphs of the mean discharge of sensors batteries and the standard deviation of sensors battery levels after the execution of subsequent slots for two schedules: the best and the worst one

The result is straight when the standard deviation value for the more extended schedule is lower in more than 70% of time steps (see Fig. 1(a)). The result is reversed when the standard deviation value for the more extended schedule is higher in more than 70% of time steps (see Fig. 1(c)). In all other cases, the result is regarded as mixed (see Fig. 1(b)).

Finally, we did additional experiments where we control the sensors network in varying temperature conditions with the slot selection strategy MINσ. Two series of experiments are performed: one for the colder weather and one for the warmer one. This time, like in the first group of experiments, we measure the percentage decrease of the network's maximum lifetime.

5.2 Results for Part I

We computed the mean percentage number of slots in output schedules concerning the numbers of input slots for the six methods from [8]. With the results combined into 80 groups (For each of the eight SCP1 classes, five T_{batt} values and two temperature measurements' series), we measured the number of times each of the tested methods returned the highest mean percentage completion. Figure 2 shows histograms with the numbers of methods wins for eight classes of problems in SCP1.

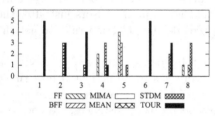
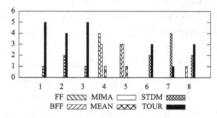

(a) Number of method's wins for Series A   (b) Number of method's wins for Series B

Fig. 2. Numbers of cases when the methods implementing FF, BFF, MIMA, MEAN, STDM, and TOUR returned the highest mean percentage number of slots in output schedules for eight classes of problems in SCP1

The TOUR strategy is the sole winner in 36 cases (45%). Moreover, in 6 cases (7.5%), both TOUR and STDM give a winning result (it does not have to be the same resulting schedule—two winners must be equal in length). Thus, in more than 50% of all the cases, the best result can be obtained using TOUR. STDM is the sole winner in 19 cases (23.75%). Thus, we can get the best result in more than 30% of all the cases using this strategy. FF alone gives the best result in 7 cases (8.75%), BFF alone only in three cases (3.75%). In 7 cases (8.75%), both FF and BFF give a winning result. The MEAN strategy alone gives the best result in two cases (2.5%). In one case (1.25%), three strategies—FF, BFF, and MEAN—give a winning schedule. The MIMA strategy never produces the best result.

The observations about the winning methods may not be correct for all possible test cases. One can see in Fig. 2 that, for example, the most effective method based on TOUR is never the winner for class 5 of SCP1. However, we assume no knowledge about both the sensor network and the set of POIs.

Moreover, analysis of the raw results shows that in all cases, the difference between the best and the second–best mean value does not exceed one percentage point (pp), while the difference between the best and the worst result in no case exceeds 7 pp. In some cases, it is below 1 pp.

We compared the efficiency of the presented approach with the one from [8]. Table 1 represents a change in the completion rate of schedules returned by the two strategies averaged over problem instances and battery sizes for each class.

Table 1. Mean schedule completion rate differences between the approach presented in this paper and the one from [8] for temperature from Series A—left half, and Series B—right half; headings: [1]:FF, [2]:BFF, [3]:MIMA; [4]:MEAN; [5]:STDM; [6]:TOUR

No.	Series A—colder weather						Series B—warmer weather					
	[1]	[2]	[3]	[4]	[5]	[6]	[1]	[2]	[3]	[4]	[5]	[6]
1	0	0	1.667	1.885	1.286	2.597	0	0	1.406	1.706	1.072	2.305
2	0	0	0.566	0.628	0.720	1.104	0	0	0.164	0.230	0.235	0.706
3	0	0	1.177	1.612	1.379	2.340	0	0	1.060	1.263	1.007	2.127
4	0	0	−0.246	−0.309	−0.219	−0.076	0	0	−0.878	−0.880	−1.191	−0.738
5	0	0	−0.809	−1.200	−1.596	−1.880	0	0	−0.919	−1.276	−1.589	−2.107
6	0	0	1.686	2.133	1.515	2.901	0	0	1.313	1.538	1.047	2.205
7	0	0	0.579	0.813	0.784	1.283	0	0	0.170	0.372	0.279	0.888
8	0	0	0.218	0.054	0.542	0.249	0	0	0.013	-0.115	0.272	0.075

Both FF and BFF always give the same results because they follow their definitions that they produce the same schedule. Briefly speaking, they select the current slot as long as it is feasible. The change can be seen in the case of the slot ranking methods. However, it never exceeds 3 pp. In most cases, schedule lengths are longer when we use the approach presented in this paper. However, the opposite is true for classes 4 and 5 of SCP1. In general, in all our experiments, these two classes give results different from those obtained for the remaining classes of the benchmark.

5.3   Results for Part II

Table 2 shows the mean percentage number of slots in output schedules concerning the number of input slots for the method based on $MIN\sigma$. The left half of the table shows the colder weather results, and the right half—results for warmer weather. The rows represent eight classes of problems in SCP1. The columns represent battery capacities T_{batt}. There is just one number printed in bold, meaning this method outperformed the remaining six only once.

Table 2. Mean percentage numbers of slots in output schedules returned by the method based on MINσ concerning the number of input slots for eight classes of SCP1 and for $T_{batt} \in \{10, 15, 20, 25, 30\}$; temperature from Series A—left half, Series B—right half

No.	Series A—colder weather					Series B—warmer weather				
	10	15	20	25	30	10	15	20	25	30
1	59.2%	66.5%	68.3%	70.9%	71.8%	62.0%	66.7%	69.4%	71.5%	73.2%
2	60.2%	64.3%	66.7%	67.4%	69.5%	61.2%	65.0%	67.6%	69.3%	72.8%
3	59.9%	63.2%	64.9%	69.4%	70.5%	60.0%	64.8%	67.7%	71.1%	72.6%
4	59.5%	64.0%	66.7%	68.2%	68.6%	59.6%	65.4%	68.0%	69.6%	**70.9%**
5	59.5%	63.6%	66.2%	68.0%	69.5%	59.1%	70.1%	71.5%	72.2%	72.9%
6	59.7%	65.9%	68.3%	70.4%	71.8%	61.8%	66.4%	69.1%	71.3%	73.2%
7	59.8%	64.3%	66.3%	66.9%	70.0%	60.4%	64.8%	67.3%	69.2%	73.2%
8	59.5%	64.0%	66.6%	68.1%	69.3%	59.7%	69.2%	70.4%	71.6%	72.7%

Table 3. Results of comparisons of graphs with the standard deviation of sensors battery levels after the execution of subsequent slots for two schedules: the best and the worst one for eight classes of SCP1 and $T_{batt} \in \{10, 15, 20, 25, 30\}$; temperature from Series A—top part, Series B—bottom part

No.	$T_{batt} = 10$			$T_{batt} = 15$			$T_{batt} = 20$			$T_{batt} = 25$			$T_{batt} = 30$		
	S	M	R	S	M	R	S	M	R	S	M	R	S	M	R
1	100.0	0.0	0.0	100.0	0.0	0.0	100.0	0.0	0.0	100.0	0.0	0.0	100.0	0.0	0.0
2	75.0	7.5	17.5	72.5	20.0	7.5	87.5	12.5	0.0	85.0	15.0	0.0	85.0	15.0	0.0
3	100.0	0.0	0.0	100.0	0.0	0.0	100.0	0.0	0.0	100.0	0.0	0.0	100.0	0.0	0.0
4	7.5	7.5	85.0	27.5	10.0	62.5	65.0	5.0	30.0	97.5	0.0	2.5	97.5	0.0	2.5
5	100.0	0.0	0.0	7.5	0.0	92.5	5.0	0.0	95.0	0.0	0.0	100.0	0.0	0.0	100.0
6	100.0	0.0	0.0	100.0	0.0	0.0	100.0	0.0	0.0	100.0	0.0	0.0	100.0	0.0	0.0
7	80.0	2.5	17.5	90.0	7.5	2.5	90.0	7.5	2.5	92.5	7.5	0.0	95.0	5.0	0.0
8	97.5	0.0	2.5	45.0	5.0	50.0	42.5	15.0	42.5	52.5	12.5	35.0	67.5	25.0	7.5
1	100.0	0.0	0.0	100.0	0.0	0.0	100.0	0.0	0.0	100.0	0.0	0.0	100.0	0.0	0.0
2	70.0	2.5	27.5	47.5	22.5	30.0	70	22.5	7.5	50.0	50.0	0.0	90.0	10.0	0.0
3	95.0	2.5	2.5	100.0	0.0	0.0	100.0	00	0.0	100.0	0.0	0.0	100.0	0.0	0.0
4	10.0	2.5	87.5	17.5	2.5	80.0	15.0	0.0	85.0	22.5	7.5	70.0	50.0	10.0	40.0
5	12.5	0.0	87.5	65.0	12.5	22.5	17.5	5.0	77.5	2.5	2.5	95.0	2.5	0.0	97.5
6	100.0	0.0	0.0	100.0	0.0	0.0	100.0	0.0	0.0	100.0	0.0	0.0	100.0	0.0	0.0
7	87.5	0.0	12.5	70.0	12.5	17.5	70.0	22.5	7.5	87.5	12.5	0.0	100.0	0.0	0.0
8	15.0	7.5	77.5	85.0	10.0	5.0	32.5	30.0	37.5	40.0	25.0	35.0	35.0	42.5	22.5

Table 3 shows the results of comparisons of graphs with the standard deviation of sensors battery levels after the execution of subsequent slots for two schedules: the best and the worst one. The results are classified as *straight*, *reversed*, or *mixed*. Therefore, the table has five sections of columns—for $T_{batt} \in$

$\{10, 15, 20, 25, 30\}$, each containing columns with the numbers of cases when the result is straight (S), mixed (M), and reversed (R). The top part of the table shows the results for colder weather and the bottom part—for warmer weather. The rows represent eight classes of problems in SCP1. The comparison results are normalized as a percentage of all class instances, i.e., when the comparison is regarded as straight for all the 40 instances from the given class of problems, the table shows three values: S:100.0, M:0.0, and R:0.0.

One can see that in most cases (almost 72%), the result is straight. We got a reversed result in more than 22% of the cases. A mixed result appeared in more than 6% of the cases. However, there are significant differences between different classes of SCP1. For classes 1 and 6, we always have a straight result. For class 3, the result is straight in 99.5% of the cases. On the other hand, for class 5, we have a reversed result in 76.75% of the cases, and for class 4—in 54.5%. A mixed result appears most often for class 2 and 8—in 17.75% and 17.25%, respectively.

Our intuition that the standard deviation of the sensors' battery levels after a slot's execution should be a basis for a slot selection strategy turned out to be inaccurate. For some test cases, this strategy gives good results, but let us stress one more time that we assume no knowledge about the sensor network and the set of POIs in consideration. TOUR usually gives better results and requires fewer computations.

6   Conclusions

This paper discusses runtime adjustment methods for sensor activity schedules in a network working in varying temperature conditions. We consider several strategies on how to find the current most appropriate slot. As input data for our experiments, we used 40 sets of schedules generated earlier (eight classes of SCP1 times five values of initial battery capacity) and two series of temperature measurements. We propose two novelties in this paper. The first is a runtime schedule adaptation scheme implementing slot selection procedures from the beginning of the network activity, which is opposed to our earlier research where selection strategies started working only after encountering the first infeasible slot in the input schedule. The second is a new selection strategy of the current best–adapted slot, which applies the standard deviation of the current moment's battery levels as a decision attribute.

The experiments demonstrated that for the runtime schedule adaptation scheme, the most effective method of generating the most extended schedule is based on tournament selection. In this strategy, when we compare two slots, we sort active sensors in every slot in ascending order of battery charge levels. Next, compare pairwise battery charge levels in sensors occupying the same positions in the sequences. This method produced the most extended schedule in more than one–half of our test cases.

In another set of experiments, we studied graphs representing the mean and the standard deviation of sensors battery levels after executing subsequent slots for the best and the worst schedule obtained for the same initial set of data. These experiments show that in more than 70% of the cases, the result is classified as straight; that is, the standard deviation value for the more extended schedule is lower in more than 70% of time steps. However, this result depends on a specific class of test cases. For some SCP1 classes, the result is always or almost always straight. In contrast, for another class in more than 3/4 of the cases, the result is reversed, i.e., the standard deviation value for the more extended schedule is higher in more than 70% of time steps. Therefore, we reject the hypothesis that the standard deviation of the battery levels in all network sensors should be a universal basis having the most significant impact on a slot selection strategy.

References

1. Cardei, M., Thai, M., Li, Y., Wu, W.: Energy-efficient target coverage in wireless sensor networks. In: Proceedings of the IEEE 24th Annual Joint Conference of the IEEE Computer and Communications Societies. IEEE (2005). https://doi.org/10.1109/infcom.2005.1498475
2. Cardei, M.: Coverage problems in sensor networks. In: Pardalos, P.M., Du, D.-Z., Graham, R.L. (eds.) Handbook of Combinatorial Optimization, pp. 899–927. Springer, New York (2013). https://doi.org/10.1007/978-1-4419-7997-1_72
3. Cardei, M., Du, D.Z.: Improving wireless sensor network lifetime through power aware organization. Wireless Networks 11(3), 333–340 (2005). https://doi.org/10.1007/s11276-005-6615-6
4. Dargie, W., Poellabauer, C.: Fundamentals of Wireless Sensor Networks: Theory and Practice. Wiley Series on Wireless Communications and Mobile Computing, Wiley (2010). https://doi.org/10.1002/9780470666388
5. Mikitiuk, A., Trojanowski, K.: Maximization of the sensor network lifetime by activity schedule heuristic optimization. Ad Hoc Networks 96, 101994 (2020). https://doi.org/10.1016/j.adhoc.2019.101994
6. Trojanowski, K., Mikitiuk, A.: Sensor network schedule adaptation for varying operating temperature. In: Palattella, M.R., Scanzio, S., Coleri Ergen, S. (eds.) ADHOC-NOW 2019. LNCS, vol. 11803, pp. 633–642. Springer, Cham (2019). https://doi.org/10.1007/978-3-030-31831-4_47
7. Trojanowski, K., Mikitiuk, A.: Local search approaches with different problem-specific steps for sensor network coverage optimization. In: Le Thi, H.A., Le, H.M., Pham Dinh, T. (eds.) WCGO 2019. AISC, vol. 991, pp. 407–416. Springer, Cham (2020). https://doi.org/10.1007/978-3-030-21803-4_41
8. Trojanowski, K., Mikitiuk, A., Grzeszczak, J.A.: Run-time schedule adaptation methods for sensor networks coverage problem. In: Saeed, K., Dvorský, J. (eds.) CISIM 2020. LNCS, vol. 12133, pp. 461–471. Springer, Cham (2020). https://doi.org/10.1007/978-3-030-47679-3_39
9. Wang, B.: Coverage Control in Sensor Networks. Computer Communications and Networks, Springer (2010). https://doi.org/10.1007/978-1-84800-328-6
10. Wang, K.: Study on low temperature performance of Li ion battery. Open Access Library J. 4(11) (2017). https://doi.org/10.4236/oalib.1104036
11. Yetgin, H., Cheung, K.T.K., El-Hajjar, M., Hanzo, L.H.: A survey of network lifetime maximization techniques in wireless sensor networks. IEEE Commun. Surv. Tutorials 19(2), 828–854 (2017). https://doi.org/10.1109/COMST.2017.2650979

Author Index

Printed in the United States
by Baker & Taylor Publisher Services